METHOD IN TEACHING INDUCTIVE BIBLE STUDY— A PRACTITIONER'S HANDBOOK:

ESSAYS IN HONOR OF ROBERT A. TRAINA

METHOD IN TEACHING INDUCTIVE BIBLE STUDY— A PRACTITIONER'S HANDBOOK:

ESSAYS IN HONOR OF ROBERT A. TRAINA

EDITORS

FREDRICK J. LONG ◆ DAVID R. BAUER

GlossaHouse
Wilmore, KY
www.glossahouse.com

METHOD IN TEACHING INDUCTIVE BIBLE STUDY—
A PRACTITIONER'S HANDBOOK: ESSAYS IN HONOR OF ROBERT A. TRAINA

© 2019 by GlossaHouse

All rights reserved. No part of this work may be reproduced or transmitted in any form or by any means, electronic or mechanical, including photocopying and recording, or by means of any information storage or retrieval system, except as may be expressly permitted by the 1976 Copyright Act or in writing from the publisher. Requests for permission should be addressed in writing to:

GlossaHouse, LLC
110 Callis Circle
Wilmore, KY 40390

Publisher's Cataloging-in-Publication Data

Method in teaching inductive Bible study.

Method in teaching inductive Bible study : a practitioner's handbook : essays in honor of Robert A. Traina / editors, Fredrick J. Long, David R. Bauer – Wilmore, KY : GlossaHouse, ©2019.

xvii, 419 pages : subject index ; 25 cm. – (GlossaHouse Festschrift Series; volume 2); (The Journal of Inductive Biblical Studies Monograph Series; volume 1)

ISBN: 978-1942697848 and 978-1942697657 (paperback)
ISBN: 978-1942697855 (hardback)
OCLC: 1089134225

1. Bible--Study and teaching. 2. Bible--Hermeneutics. 3. Teaching--Methodology. I. Long, Fredrick J., 1966- II. Bauer, David R. III. Series.

Library of Congress Control Number: 2019902441

BS476 .M47 2019   220.601

Scripture quotations identified by NASB95 are from the NEW AMERICAN STANDARD Bible, © Copyright The Lockman Foundation 1960, 1962, 1963, 1968, 1971, 1972, 1973, 1975, 1977, 1995. Used by permission. Quotations identified by NIV are from THE HOLY Bible: NEW INTERNATIONAL VERSION. Copyright © 1973, 1978, 1984 by International Bible Society. Used by permission of Zondervan Publishing House. All rights reserved. Scripture quotations identified as RSV and NRSV are from the Revised Standard Version and the New Revised Standard Version Bible, copyright © 1971 and 1989, respectively, Division of Christian Education of the National Council of the Churches of Christ in the U.S.A., and are used by permission. All rights reserved.

The fonts used to create this work are available from www.linguistsoftware.com/lgku.htm.

Book Design and Typesetting by Fredrick J. Long
Cover Design by Fredrick J. Long
Indexing by Benjamin J. Snyder and Fredrick J. Long

This book is dedicated to the memory of Prof. Robert A. Traina and to every student of God's Word who has found an apt instructor like Prof. Traina and to those students still looking—may the former increase and the latter decrease.

GLOSSAHOUSE FESTSCHRIFT SERIES

The purpose of the GLOSSAHOUSE FESTSCHRIFT SERIES is to honor mentors, colleagues, friends, and leading experts in the scholarly community while advancing research in the areas of ancient and modern languages, contexts, texts, and hermeneutics.

SERIES EDITORS

T. MICHAEL W. HALCOMB ♦ FREDRICK J. LONG ♦ CARL S. SWEATMAN

GLOSSAHOUSE
WILMORE, KY
www.glossahouse.com

GLOSSAHOUSE FESTSCHRIFT SERIES

VOLUME 2

GLOSSAHOUSE
WILMORE, KY
www.glossahouse.com

THE JOURNAL OF INDUCTIVE BIBLICAL STUDIES MONOGRAPH SERIES

THE JOURNAL OF INDUCTIVE BIBLICAL STUDIES MONOGRAPH SERIES publishes creative, interpretive, hermeneutically informed, and exploratory research from the perspective of Inductive Biblical Study applied to Scripture and other discourse.

SERIES EDITORS

DAVID R. BAUER ♦ FREDRICK J. LONG

GLOSSAHOUSE
WILMORE, KY
www.glossahouse.com

THE JOURNAL OF INDUCTIVE BIBLICAL STUDIES MONOGRAPH SERIES

VOLUME 1

GLOSSAHOUSE
WILMORE, KY
www.glossahouse.com

TABLE OF CONTENTS

Foreword on Robert A. Traina and Overview of Contents — xiii
—David R. Bauer and Fredrick J. Long

PART I: ROBERT A. TRAINA'S PEDAGOGY IN INDUCTIVE BIBLE STUDY (IBS)

Ch. 1 *Method in Bible Teaching* — 3
—Robert A. Traina

Ch. 2 *Traina as Teacher: His Contribution to the Teaching of IBS* — 57
—David R. Bauer

Ch. 3 *The Pedagogy of Robert A. Traina in Educational Theory and Practice* — 67
—Chris A. Kiesling

PART II: IBS AND THE ACADEMY

Ch. 4 *Why Inductive Bible Study? A Defense of Inductive Method in Research and Teaching* — 77
—Kenneth L. Schenck

Ch. 5 *An "Inductive" Friendly Academy and the Need for Explicit IBS in Scholarship* — 89
—Fredrick J. Long

Ch. 6 *Christology & Ethics—Cosmic (Colossians) & Kenotic (Philippians): Practicing New Testament Theology in the Context of Canon and Church* — 101
—Eugene E. Lemcio

PART III: IBS IMPACTING THE CURRICULUM

Ch. 7 *Sequencing Undergraduate Classes in a Curriculum Featuring Inductive Bible Study* — 115
—Fredrick J. Long

Ch. 8 *Inductive Bible Study Principles in General Education Bible Classes at a Christian College* — 131
—John Dendiu

Ch. 9 *Method Follows Content: Interpreting the Bible as the Bible* — 147
—Gareth Lee Cockerill

Ch. 10 *Competent in the Basic Skills of Inductive Bible Study: A Case Study on the Use of Inductive Biblical Studies at Eastern Mennonite Seminary* — 159
—Dorothy Jean Weaver

Ch. 11 *The Use of the Inductive Bible Method in the Teaching of the Book of Isaiah* — 171
—John N. Oswalt

Ch. 12 *Inductive Bible Study and Teaching Social Sciences* — 181
—Lindy D. Backues

PART IV: IBS PEDAGOGY, ASSESSMENTS, AND TECHNOLOGY

Ch. 13 *Teaching IBS in an Age of Immediately Gratifying Technologies* — Michael D. Matlock ... 233

Ch. 14 *Reflections on the Role of Student Assignments in the Instruction of Inductive Bible Study* — David R. Bauer ... 241

Ch. 15 *The Benefits of a General-Analytic Grading Rubric for Book Surveys and Other IBS Assignments* — Fredrick J. Long ... 255

Ch. 16 *Teaching Inductive Bible Study Online* — Rick Boyd ... 275

Ch. 17 *The Use of BibleWorks Software to Perform Inductive Bible Study Tasks* — Mark T. Cannon ... 287

PART V: DEVELOPING DISCIPLES WITH IBS IN THE CHURCH

Ch. 18 *Inductive Bible Study and the Local Church: Creating an Appetite for Bible Study* — Alan J. Meenan ... 315

Ch. 19 *Reflections on Teaching Inductive Bible Study in the Local Church* — Eugene Wen Zhi Quek ... 321

Ch. 20 *Teaching IBS at First UMC Lexington, KY* — Chad M. Foster ... 331

Ch. 21 *The Whole Inductive Bible Study Process for Discipleship Purposes* — Matt Friedeman ... 339

SYLLABUS APPENDICES ... 349

"The Gospel of Matthew" NT(IBS510) ... 351
"Hebrews" NT(IBS)646 ... 359
 —*David R. Bauer*
"Biblical Interpretation" BIBL 201 ... 367
"New Testament I—The Four Gospels: The Life & Teachings of Christ" BIBL 221 ... 373
"New Testament II—Acts and Paul" BIBL 222 ... 379
"New Testament III—The General Epistles and Revelation" BIBL 223 ... 385
"Contemporary Critical Issues in Biblical Studies" BIBL 470 ... 395
 —*Fredrick J. Long*
"New Testament: Text in Context" BVNT 512 ... 399
"Gospel of Matthew" BVNT 631 ... 403
 —*Dorothy Jean Weaver*

SUBJECT INDEX ... 411

ROBERT A. TRAINA: A BIOGRAPHICAL SKETCH

Robert A. Traina was born on August 27, 1921 in Chicago, the son of Italian immigrants. Though a member of the Methodist Episcopal Church, his father served as lay pastor to the Italian Mission Free Methodist Church in Melrose Park, Illinois. In this church Professor Traina was nurtured in the Christian faith and first sensed the call to parish ministry at the age of 16.

After graduating from high school Professor Traina spent a year attempting in vain to find work in depression-era Chicago in order to fund his college education. He was accepted into Spring Arbor Junior College (now Spring Arbor University) with virtually nothing; he worked his way through his first two years of college by employment in the kitchen there: peeling potatoes and waiting tables. At Spring Arbor, he majored in Religious Studies, with a minor in Greek (Biblical and Classical). It was there that he began to develop a serious interest in biblical studies. He graduated with an A.A. degree in 1941, and was valedictorian of his class. Professor Traina completed his undergraduate education at Seattle Pacific College (now Seattle Pacific University), graduating with a B.A. in 1943. Approximately a week after his college commencement he married Jane Odell.

While a student at Seattle Pacific, Professor Traina became aware of the program at The Biblical Seminary in New York. And in the fall of 1943, he and Jane arrived in midtown Manhattan where he began his seminary education. The Biblical Seminary in New York, founded in 1900 by the Yale-educated Semitist Wilbert Webster White, had gained a world-wide reputation for the "inductive method" of the study of the English Bible. Courses in inductive biblical study (called "English Bible" classes) formed the center of the curriculum. The emphasis was upon the direct study of the Bible; and the goal was to allow the text to speak on its own terms, challenging all presuppositions and conforming the person to its message. Professor Traina found this approach to the study of the Bible to be liberating. He had come to seminary, according to his own account, with a deductive personality, and the inductive approach changed his orientation to life and to the Bible.

The Biblical Seminary emphasized effective and creative teaching, and Professor Traina there encountered masters of the classroom, including Caroline Palmer, Dean Greer McKee, Donald G. Miller, Howard Tillman Kuist, and Edwin Lewis. Professor Traina earned both the Bachelor of Sacred Theology (comparable to the current Master of Divinity) and the Master of Sacred Theology (comparable to the Master of Theology) at The Biblical Seminary. He so excelled as a student that upon his graduation with the Bachelor of Sacred Theology in 1945 he joined the faculty at The Biblical Seminary in New York, where he taught for twenty years. During this period, he took graduate courses at New York University, pursued his Ph.D. in Biblical Studies at Drew University, and was ordained in the United Methodist Church. Throughout this time, too, Professor Traina developed a reputation as a stellar biblical scholar and teacher, lecturing at such varied venues as Marble Collegiate Church, Calvary Baptist Church, Fifth Avenue Presbyterian Church, and Jewish Theological Seminary; indeed, he was even a guest on *The Today Show*.

During his early years of teaching at The Biblical Seminary Professor Traina became troubled at the lack of integration between English Bible and traditional exegesis. He judged that English Bible, or inductive biblical studies, as it was taught at The Biblical Seminary, was not as comprehensive and specific as was needed to teach students effectively. Out of this concern Professor Traina expanded and sharpened the method of inductive biblical study. He developed it into an organized and comprehensive approach, combining the unique features of the inductive method as it had been taught over the years with the insights and tools of traditional exegesis. Professor Traina set forth his approach to inductive Bible study in his book, *Methodical Bible Study: A New Approach to Hermeneutics*, published in 1952.[1] This book, translated into several languages, has been used in scores of colleges and seminaries around the world.

In the early 1960s The Biblical Seminary in New York experienced a significant transition, which resulted in a radical change in the nature of the seminary itself. At this time Professor Traina concluded that he could best minister elsewhere; and in 1966, having just earned his Ph.D. from Drew University, he accepted an invitation to join the faculty of Asbury Theological Seminary as a professor of English Bible (later known as "Inductive Biblical Studies"). After serving as Academic Dean and Vice President for Academic Administration from 1967 to 1975 (while he also taught part-time), he resumed full-time teaching in English Bible, from which role he retired at the end of the academic year 1987-1988. Upon his retirement he was awarded the Doctor of Divinity degree from Asbury Theological Seminary.

In addition to *Methodical Bible Study*, Professor Traina also co-authored, with David R. Bauer, *Inductive Bible Study: A Comprehensive Guide to the Practice of Hermeneutics*,[2] which appeared in 2011. He also published two chapters in *God's Word for Today: An Inquiry into Hermeneutics from a Biblical Theological Perspective*,[3] and several articles. But Professor Traina was above all else a teacher; and his most enduring influence is found in the lives and ministries of his students.

Professor Traina died on November 9, 2010, surrounded by his family.

—David R. Bauer, February 2019

---

[1] Robert A. Traina, *Methodical Bible Study: A New Approach to Hermeneutics* (New York: Ganis & Harris, 1952).

[2] David R. Bauer and Robert A. Traina, *Inductive Bible Study: A Comprehensive Guide to the Practice of Hermeneutics* (Grand Rapids: Baker Academic, 2011).

[3] Wayne McCown and James Earl Massey, *Interpreting God's Word for Today: An Inquiry into Hermeneutics from a Biblical Theological Perspective*, Wesleyan Theological Perspectives 2 (Anderson, IN: Warner, 1982).

Overview of Contents

When I discovered from David R. Bauer that Prof. Traina left behind a manuscript unpublished, my first thought was that we needed to make this available in print in some form. After looking at the material, I realized that it was a (revised?) draft of his *Methodical Bible Study* with sixty additional pages of unpublished material on "Method in Bible Teaching," the outline of which alone was three pages detailing its contents. At first, we considered whether we might publish this in *The Journal of Inductive Biblical Studies*. Then, it occurred to me that the best way to honor this material and Prof. Traina's memory was to publish this material in a book dedicated to the pedagogy of *Inductive Bible Study* (IBS) in honor of Prof. Traina. After making this proposal to Prof. Traina's surviving family and kindly receiving their permission to publish this material, David and I began to reach out to prospective contributors. We proposed to them various educational arenas where IBS was taught to help organize the volume. Taking all the contributions together, we settled on five parts with the three or more essays in each. Let me explain briefly.

In **Part I: Robert A. Traina's Pedagogy in Inductive Bible Study (IBS)**, we begin with Prof. Traina's seminal material "Method in Bible Teaching." This rich and superbly insightful material, as one would expect, is carefully and logically presented; its content has not been changed or edited except to update some wording, to correct a handful of typos, and to use gender inclusive language when Prof. Traina addressed teachers with the generic "he" of the 1950s. In testimony to Prof. Traina's legacy, in the next essay "Traina as Teacher: His Contribution to the Teaching of Inductive Bible Study" David R. Bauer reflects on his firsthand experience with Prof. Traina as his student in not one, not three, not five, but seven classes! If anyone can help us understand the formative nature of Prof. Traina, no one is more equipped than David. Finally, rounding out Part I is Chris A. Kiesling's "The Pedagogy of Robert A. Traina in Educational Theory and Practice." As it turns out, Prof. Traina was ahead of the curve and anticipated sound pedagogical practices. Kiesling responds to and reflects specifically on Prof. Traina's "Method in Bible teaching" both bringing illumination to Prof. Traina's approach to instruction and recommending best pedagogical practices today for teachers of IBS.

In **Part II: IBS and the Academy**, the first essay "Why Inductive Bible Study? A Defense of Inductive Method in Research and Teaching" by Kenneth L. Schenck makes a strong appeal for the place of IBS in the academy with its concern for ascertaining "original meaning," especially, among other things, in order to critically evaluate the assumptions of recent trends, for example, as expressed in the movement called "the theological interpretation of Scripture." In the next essay by Fredrick J. Long, "An 'Inductive' Friendly Academy and the Need for Explicit Inductive Biblical Study in Scholarship," readers will discover a dearth of references to IBS or its founding implementers (such as William Rainey Harper, Wilbert W. White, Howard T. Kuist, Robert A. Traina, David R. Bauer) in recent scholarship and a call to engage the academy. Such is warranted, since the academy welcomes inductive/evidential approaches and IBS now has a theoretical grounding in the seminal book by Bauer and Traina, *Inductive Bible Study: A Comprehensive Guide to the Practice of*

Hermeneutics (Grand Rapids: Baker, 2011). The last essay of Part II, "Christology & Ethics—Cosmic (Colossians) & Kenotic (Philippians): Practicing New Testament Theology in the Context of Canon and Church," is by Eugene E. Lemcio, who models the kind of academically rigorous application of IBS methodology that will most certainly be appreciated by the scholarly guild. His lifetime of IBS pedagogy and research has provided him the tools and rationale to correlate seemingly disparate Christologies and Ethics in Colossians and in Philippians through IBS. In so doing, Lemcio is careful to avoid harmonization, preferential treatment of one book over the other, and reductionism to overgeneralized overarching principles.

In **PART III: IBS IMPACTING THE CURRICULUM**, we have collected six essays unified around matters of course content and curriculum. In the first essay, "Sequencing Undergraduate Classes in a Curriculum Featuring Inductive Bible Study," Fredrick J. Long reflects on his attempts to create an optimal sequencing of courses built upon the foundation of IBS in an undergraduate institution. Such a sequence begins with original languages, a prerequisite hermeneutics class, survey classes across the NT, and capstone courses on evaluation and biblical theology. Select syllabi of some of these courses are provided in the SYLLABUS APPENDICES of this volume. Next, in "Inductive Bible Study Principles in General Education Bible Classes at a Christian College" John Dendiu explains his decision in view of IBS to retool his teaching of Bible survey classes to prioritize the students' firsthand exposure to and focus on biblical materials. Then, Gareth Lee Cockerill in "Method Follows Content: Interpreting the Bible as the Bible" reflects on the need for Bible pedagogy to help students reach the practice of obedience and assimilation. In view of this conviction, Cockerill has replaced the traditional IBS steps of *Observation, Interpretation, Evaluation/Application,* and *Correlation* with *Listening, Understanding, Obedience,* and *Assimilation.* Next, Dorothy Jean Weaver offers "Competent in the Basic Skills of Inductive Bible Study: A Case Study on the Use of Inductive Biblical Studies at Eastern Mennonite Seminary." She reflects on the influence of IBS on the design of several of her courses and discusses the "inductive exercises" she created for them. Weaver has provided select syllabi for inclusion in the SYLLABUS APPENDICES. In "The Use of the Inductive Bible Method in the Teaching of the Book of Isaiah," John N. Oswalt discusses how he has taught through the book of Isaiah utilizing the IBS steps of observation, interpretation (analysis), correlation, and evaluation (synthesis). Oswalt shares his approach to lesson creation and the lessons themselves. Finally, Lindy D. Backues offers "Inductive Bible Study and Teaching Social Sciences." Backues importantly demonstrates his thoughtful integration and incorporation of IBS practices to another academic discipline, that of the social sciences. Included here are hermeneutical reflections on observation and the generalization of themes in human discourse and social data. Importantly, Backues's three-part article "Construing Culture as Composition" *is* being published in *The Journal of Inductive Biblical Studies* beginning with Part 1 in the Winter 2019 volume (6.1).

In **PART IV: IBS PEDAGOGY, ASSESSMENTS, AND TECHNOLOGY**, Michael D. Matlock begins with "Teaching Inductive Bible Study in an Age of Immediately Gratifying Technologies." Matlock adeptly reflects on the current trend of "technological instantly gratifying distraction" (TIGD) and how IBS faces this challenge and inherently offers important benefits for the formation of students in their relationship with Christ through vital scriptural study. David R. Bauer next offers "Reflections on the Role of Student Assignments in the Instruction of Inductive Bible Study." Bauer discusses the vital aspect of creating "lessons" for IBS instruction and provides commonly employed comments for the major types of IBS assignments (e.g., surveys, detailed observation, interpretation). Bauer has also provided select syllabi for inclusion in the SYLLABUS APPENDICES. Following Bauer, Fredrick J. Long discusses "The Benefits of a General-Analytic Grading Rubric for Book Surveys and Other IBS Assignments." By means of recent principles of rubric creation, Long describes his development and use of rubrics to help teach students how best to accomplish central IBS observational tasks of book/segment surveys as well as detailed analysis (which he calls semantic diagramming and analysis, SD/SA). Next, based on his many years of teaching IBS online, Rick Boyd discusses "Teaching Inductive Bible Study Online." Since online delivery of course content is an ever-growing trend, educators need to capitalize on the opportunities and challenges of teaching IBS asynchronously and synchronously in this medium. Rounding out Part IV, Mark T. Cannon proposes best ways for "The Use of BibleWorks Software to Perform Inductive Bible Study Tasks." Even though BibleWorks has stopped as a business, resources and a strong community of users still exist around this powerful software platform. Moreover, the areas for software research that Cannon describes (e.g., becoming oriented to general materials, types of observation, major structural relationships, note taking, word studies) are broadly applicable to other platforms.

In the last section, **PART V: DEVELOPING DISCIPLES WITH IBS IN THE CHURCH**, Alan J. Meenan begins by describing his experiences pertaining to "Inductive Bible Study and the Local Church: Creating an Appetite for Bible Study." Churchgoers can get fired up about learning how to study the Scriptures; Meenan details the studies that he implemented for his churches that encouraged them to delve more deeply into God's Word. Next, Eugene Wen Zhi Quek offers "Reflections on Teaching Inductive Bible Study in the Local Church." Quek discusses and includes the study of Jonah that he prepared for the church. In "Teaching Inductive Bible Study at First UMC Lexington, KY" Chad M. Foster describes a two-year discipleship program for lay leadership development and what the leadership team learned in the process. Fittingly, this Part V and the entire volume ends with Matt Friedeman making appeal for "The Whole Inductive Bible Study Process for Discipleship Purposes." Here Friedeman notes that the last two traditional steps of IBS—correlation and application—are too often neglected and explores why it is important that students embrace them.

Finally, I should point out that this volume has been three years in the making. And I am deeply grateful for all who have made it possible, especially the contributors who responded in timely fashion to my emails and have waited patiently to see this volume come to light and David R. Bauer who continues to inspire me with his insight and generous spirit. It is fitting, too, that the cover showcases a blackboard—Prof. Traina filled such up with his observations, charts, and interpretive correlations. In fact, due to his chalk allergy, the first white board on Asbury Seminary's campus was specifically added for his classes. Compiling this volume has been a labor of love inspired by the ongoing influence of Prof. Robert A. Traina. May his legacy continue to God's glory!

—Fredrick J. Long, Epiphany 2019

Part I

Robert A. Traina's Pedagogy in Inductive Bible Study (IBS)

METHOD IN BIBLE TEACHING

Robert A. Traina

Outline of *METHOD IN BIBLE TEACHING*

I. INTRODUCTION TO METHOD IN BIBLE TEACHING—SUPPOSITIONS AND GUIDING PRINCIPLES

II. AIMS IN BIBLE TEACHING
    A. General Aims
        1. In the Realm of Mental Activity
            a. Concerning Content
            b. Concerning Method
        2. In the Realm of Spiritual Activity
            a. Personal Improvement
            b. Social Improvement
    B. Specific Aims
        1. The Basis for Specific Aims
        2. The Main Characteristics of Specific Aims
            a. Relevant
            b. Concrete
            c. Primary and Secondary
        3. The Function of Specific Aims
    C. Exercise on Aims

III. LESSON STRUCTURE AND DEVELOPMENT IN BIBLE TEACHING
    A. General Determinants of Lesson Structure and Development
        1. Nature and Structure of the Passage
        2. Principles of Bound Pedagogy
    B. Specific Kinds of Lesson Structure end Development
        1. Logical or Topical
        2. Interpretative or Structural
    C. Concrete Bases for Deciding the Types of Lesson Structure and Development
    D. Means of Previewing the Composition of a Passage in Lesson Structure and Development
    E. Some Common Errors in Lesson Structure and Development
        1. The Backtrack Approach
        2. The Detour Approach
        3. The Unfinished Approach
        4. The Buckshot Approach
        5. The Deviating Approach

      6. The Swerving Approach
      7. The Non-Transitional Approach
      8. The Wandering Approach
  F. Miscellaneous Principles for Proper Lesson Structure and Development
  G. Exercise on Lesson Structure and Development

IV. FORMULATION AND USE OF QUESTIONS AND ANSWERS IN BIBLE TEACHING
  A. Sources of Questions
    1. General Source
    2. Specific Sources
      a. Objective Sources
        (1) The Nature of the passage
        (2) The Nature of the Class
      b. Subjective Source—The Nature of the Mind
  B. General Purposes of Questions
    1. In Regard to the Student
    2. In Regard to the Teacher
    3. In Regard to the Passage
    4. In Regard to Lesson Development
  C. Kinds of Questions
    1. In Terms of Their Importance—Key and Subsidiary
    2. In Terms of Their Scope and Concreteness—General and Specific
    3. In Terms of Their Effectiveness and Order—Primary and Secondary or Auxiliary
    4. In Terms of Their Precise Aims
      a. The Factual Question
      b. The Elucidative Question
      c. The Analytical Question
      d. The Heuristic Question
      e. The Rhetorical Question
      f. The Choice Question
      g. The Summary Question
      h. The Review Question
      i. The Examinational Question
      j. The Value Question
      k. The Applicatory Question
      l. The Correlative Question
      m. The Adjustment Question
  D. Content and Form of Questions
    1. Practicality
    2. Clarity
    3. Brevity, Directness
    4. Definiteness
    5. Variety
    6. Suitableness
    7. Adaptability
    8. Stimulation
    9. Sincerity
    10. Inductivity

Chapter 1—Method in Bible Teaching 5

        11. Forcefulness
        12. Imaginativeness
        13. Singleness
        14. Relevancy
        15. Suggestiveness
    E. Order of Questions
    F. Manner of Asking Questions
    G. Answers to Questions and Their Use
    H. Some "Do's" and "Don't's" Regarding Questions and Answers
        1. Do:
        2. Don't:
    I. Exercise on Questions and Answers

V. ILLUSTRATIONS IN BIBLE TEACHING
    A. The General and Specific Functions of Illustrations
        1. General Function
        2. Specific Functions
            a. To Interpret or Clarify
            b. To Substantiate
            c. To Arouse and Hold Attention
            d. To Provide Relaxation for the Mind
            e. To Stir the Emotions and Will
            f. To Apply Truth
            g. To Aid the Memory
    B. The Sources of Illustrations
        1. Observation of Life
        2. Imagination
        3. Science
        4. Great Teachers, Preachers, Thinkers, and Expositors
        5. Anecdotes, Proverbs, Fables, Stories, etc.
        6. History
        7. Great Literature and Other Great Art
        8. Scriptures
        9. Current Events and Publications
        10. Anywhere
    C. Principles and Practices in the Formulation and Use of Illustrations
    D. Exercise on Illustrations

VI. SUMMARY IN BIBLE TEACHING

VII. EVALUATION AND APPLICATION IN BIBLE TEACHING
    A. Importance of Evaluation and Application
    B. Place of Evaluation and Application
    C. Purposes of Evaluation and Application
    D. Kinds of Evaluation and Application
        1. The Direct Kind
        2. The Indirect Kind

E. Characteristics of Good Evaluation and Application
   1. Justifiable
   2. Personal
   3. Realistic, Practical
   4. Natural, Easy
   5. Compelling
   6. Constructive
   7. Specific, Definite
   8. Up-to-date, Relevant
   9. Suggestive
   10. Varied
   11. Integrated
   12. Inclusive
F. Exercise on Evaluation and Application

VIII. INTRODUCTIONS IN BIBLE TEACHING
A. Functions and Kinds of Introductions
   1. General Function
   2. Specific Functions and Kinds
      a. Atmospheric Introduction
      b. Problematical or Applicatory Introduction
      c. Historical Introduction
      d. Contextual Introduction
      e. Explanatory or Procedural Introduction
      f. Thematic Introduction
      g. Review or Re-examinational Introduction
B. Qualities of Effective Introductions
C. Exercise on Introductions

IX. BLACKBOARD WORK IN BIBLE TEACHING
A. General and Specific Functions of Blackboard Work
B. Some Types of Blackboard Work
C. Principles and Suggestions for Blackboard Work
D. Exercise on Blackboard Work

X. EXERCISES IN BIBLE TEACHING
A. Definition of "Exercises"
B. Purpose of Exercises
C. Structure of Exercises
D. Miscellaneous Principles and Suggestions for the Formulation and Use of Exercises
E. Exercise on Exercises

XI. (ILLUSTRATIONS OF METHOD IN BIBLE TEACHING) [Note: This section was not completed.]

Chapter 1—Method in Bible Teaching 7

SECTION THREE: METHOD IN BIBLE TEACHING

I. INTRODUCTION TO METHOD IN BIBLE TEACHING—SUPPOSITIONS AND GUIDING PRINCIPLES

II. AIMS IN BIBLE TEACHING

A. General Aims
    1. In the Realm of Mental Activity
        a. Concerning Content
        b. Concerning Method
    2. In the Realm of Spiritual Activity
        a. Personal Improvement
        b. Social Improvement

B. Specific Aims
    1. The Basis for Specific Aims
    2. The Main Characteristics of Specific Aims
        a. Relevant
        b. Concrete
        c. Primary and Secondary
    3. The Function of Specific Aims

C. Exercise on Aims

Footnotes [Note: These "endnotes" have been added as true footnotes in the material below.]

I. INTRODUCTION TO METHOD IN BIBLE TEACHING—SUPPOSITIONS AND GUIDING PRINCIPLES

In Section One, which formed the introduction to the entire manual, there were presented certain general premises which were to undergird both the discussions of methodical study and teaching. It would be well for the reader, therefore, to review that material in preparation for a better understanding of the forthcoming discussion. As a further means of preparing the reader for comprehending what follows, there will be stated additional suppositions and guiding principles which are more specifically concerned with the matter or teaching the English Bible.[1] These will now be set forth in summary fashion.

A. Methodical Bible teaching assumes methodical Bible study. In fact, teaching a passage is essentially the re-creation on behalf of the listeners of the steps followed in one's study, Therefore, the <u>first</u> and <u>major</u> step in the orderly, logical, effective procedure which has as its goal the teaching of the English Bible is the inductive study of the English Bible. The consideration of methodical teaching properly follows the consideration of methodical study.

B. Generally speaking, the teaching of the Scriptures as well as their study should be inductive. This implies that the teaching procedure should be experimental and should therefore utilize primarily the question and answer or the discussion approach.

It should not be inferred, however, that the inductive lesson must always involve active participation on the part of the student. Such participation is certainly salutary, but sometimes it is virtually impossible. For example, the writer has been asked to teach a class of nearly two hundred men who were gathered in an auditorium whose platform was elevated. In such circumstances it is impractical to use the question and answer or discussion method. However, it is possible to proceed inductively, that is, to examine with the group the particulars of a passage and to draw generalizations on the basis of such a study.

Furthermore, these statements do not imply that the formal lecture or other similar approaches have no proper place in the teaching of English Bible. On the contrary, there are certain aspects of Scriptural study which are most adequately and efficiently presented through the use of the formal lecture. However, even the formal lecturer may at times employ induction in his or her presentation, that is, one may begin with particulars and indicate how the conclusions are founded on those particulars.

It should be remembered that, in the last analysis, there is no such thing as pure induction either in study or teaching, but especially in teaching. Therefore, when the term "inductive" is

---

[1] Note that the following discussion is primarily concerned with the teaching of the Scriptures in the vernacular. Its statements, however, should not be construed as a negation of the necessity and value of teaching the Bible in the original languages, just as the section on Bible study does not imply that the Scriptures should never be examined except in the vernacular. There is a definite and indispensable place for both the study and teaching of the Bible in the original. And, in fact, the general inductive principles discussed in this manual may well be utilized in such study and teaching to make them more effective.

Chapter 1—Method in Bible Teaching 9

employed, it really means "relatively inductive." In fact, even if pure induction were possible, it would still be unwise to use it as the sole basis for teaching, since the most <u>proficient</u> pedagogy involves discreet combination of induction and deduction. For it is impractical to proceed as if there had never been any valid generalizations. There are some generalizations that should be presented without tracing exhaustively the precise way in which they were deduced from a study of the particulars. If this is not done, much time is wasted of the already too brief periods which can be devoted to teaching the Scriptures.

C. We are not here concerned with the general problem of Christian education, namely, the adaptation of Bible teaching to all the various age groups. The suggestions, which will be made will be applicable primarily to the teaching of those with more mature minds, who are capable of reasoning, engaging in discussion, and responding to questions. There is, of course, the possibility of adjusting the questions to make them suitable to the intellectual capacity of particular groups. Utilizing this principle of adaptation, many have found the question and answer and discussion methods beneficial even with younger minds.

D. There will be no attempt to exhaust the subject being considered. In fact, this section must of necessity be much briefer than the preceding one on Bible study, not because of the paucity of material, but because of the limitations of space. In view of this, we will concentrate on those facts which are not usually discussed in books on pedagogy and which, at the same time, are peculiarly relevant to the experimental approach to Bible teaching. Even these cannot be fully treated, so that only some of the main factors will be presented, and those very briefly. The bibliography will suggest certain books dealing with the more general phases of teaching procedure as well as others which will discuss further some of the elements presented briefly in this manual.

E. We will be guided by <u>practical</u> considerations in the following presentation. There will be no attempt to engage in academic or theoretical discussions of the problem at hand.

F. The pattern employed in the investigation of the several aspects of Scriptural teaching is not a rigid formula. It will entail a <u>general</u> order within which there is room for the variations and adaptations which arise due to individual differences or the necessities of the situation. However, broadly speaking, it will reflect the logical procedure to be followed in achieving the goal of effective Bible teaching.

G. Some of the factors discussed in this section will inevitably overlap those presented in the section on Bible study. For example, the material on the formulation and use of questions and answers in teaching procedure will be concerned with similar concepts and practices as the material on interpretative questions and answers in Bible study. In fact, the former is and must be an outgrowth of the latter. However, we will attempt to avoid too much duplication by assuming a knowledge and understanding of the subject matter already presented.

II. AIMS IN BIBLE TEACHING

A. General Aims

There are certain common aims which characterize and guide every lesson on a Biblical passage. These objectives concern two main spheres of activity: 1. the realm of mental activity; and 2. the realm of spiritual activity.

1. In the Realm of Mental Activity

   a. Concerning <u>content</u>—It should be the aim of every Bible lesson, insofar as is possible, to enable the student to master the content of the particular Scriptural unit. This involves more than being able to repeat verbatim Biblical language, or to analyze the form of Biblical portions. It ultimately includes a knowledge of the profound meaning and significance and the widespread implications of Scriptural statements. The student should be taken behind the veil of form and language into the sanctuary itself, where he or she will meet face to face the ideas and thoughts of Biblical writers and characters. For only then will she or he truly master the contents of the English Bible.

   b. Concerning <u>method</u>—Edward Thring, Headmaster of the Uppingham School from 1853–1889, once remarked in an address to teachers: "The swallowing system is all wrong…. However good the food, the full belly is not good if the exercise and the strength and the skillful use of the strength is not to be the outcome of feeding. Your business is to train athletes, not to fatten geese." These incisive statements suggest that the teacher should aim at more than conveying to the listener the content of the Scriptures. He or she has the solemn obligation and duty to instruct students concerning the ways which they themselves may utilize the knowledge gained through study, as well as the means by which they may secure more knowledge. In other words, he or she should train students to be <u>methodical</u> in order that they may know how to employ and obtain knowledge for themselves. In fact, it may be added that students should also be trained to train others to acquire and use knowledge for themselves. To summarize, the teacher of English Bible should not only lead those instructed to a mastery of the content of Scriptures, but he or she should also develop in them methodicalness in Bible study and teaching if he or she is to realize his or her ultimate objective.

   There are <u>two excellent ways</u> of accomplishing this final and most important goal. <u>First</u>, the teacher may reveal <u>how</u> he or she arrived at certain conclusions by indicating the <u>exact procedure</u> followed, as well as the discoveries made in following that procedure. When the teacher, who is also methodical, retraces the steps which guided him or her in their study, he or she thereby instructs students in methodical Bible study. <u>Second</u>, he or she can make the students conscious of the techniques being utilized, both in regard to study and teaching. He or she can disclose the "why" of the course being followed in order that, understanding the reasons and purposes for it, the students may more intelligently be able to follow it themselves and instruct others to follow it. Edward Thring closes the address mentioned above with these remarks: "A man is not made a fisherman by buying fish at a fishmonger's, neither is the fishmonger a dealer in the art of catching fish. Fish ready caught and bought, do not make a fisherman…. Take the bandage off the eyes. Never fly hooded hawks."

2. In the Realm of Spiritual Activity

   a. Personal Improvement

   One of the main aims of Bible teaching should be the enhancement of the spiritual life of the listener. Unless the individual emerges from the study of the Scriptures spiritually a better person than when he or she began the study, the Bible lesson has not accomplished one of its most crucial objectives.

   b. Social Improvement

   The further aim of Bible study is to motivate hearers to become effective witnesses to that which they have discovered. In order to accomplish this, the present-day relevance of the material being studied should be made clear and forceful by the teacher. Further, the lesson should be conducted in such a spirit and manner that students will be anxious to teach it to others. Someone has described the aim of teachers in these words: "To interest and instruct is not enough; we must thrill." When this objective is realized, students will go forth to sow the seed and, thus, become instrumental in the betterment of their fellow people.

B. Specific Aims

Besides these general goals in Scriptural teaching, there are some concrete factors that must be considered in the formulation and use of specific aims for a particular lesson.

1. The Basis for Specific Aims

   It is axiomatic that the aim of an individual lesson should correspond with the aim or theme of the Biblical portion being considered in it. Unless this holds true, the passage will need to be distorted to fit the lesson, or the lesson will need to be changed to suit the passage. It is only as the objective of the Biblical unit and the lesson coincide that harmonious agreement will result.

   If this principle is valid, then the goal of a lesson should be adapted to the goal of the passage, rather than the passage to the goal of the lesson. This is a legitimate procedure even if one begins with a topic or a problem which one would like to consider. For a particular part of the Scriptures should be chosen for study only if its topic or problem corresponds with that in the mind of the teacher; a particular subject or question should not be forced upon a unit of Biblical material.

   To put it another way, one of the great temptations in Bible teaching is to make a secondary or incidental idea within a portion the major aim of the lesson. When this occurs, an insurmountable discrepancy will appear between the unit of Scriptural material and the lesson itself. This ought carefully to be avoided by making certain that the <u>primary</u> objective or the <u>lesson</u> accords with the <u>primary</u> objective of the <u>passage</u>.

2. The Main Characteristics of Specific Aims

   a. They should be <u>relevant and suited</u> to the needs, problems, capabilities, and interests of the group being taught.

   b. They should be <u>concrete and precise</u>. It is a wise practice to write them out in full.

   c. They may be and probably will be <u>manifold</u>. If so, a certain objective should <u>predominate</u>, and the others be made <u>subservient</u>. A teacher should not accomplish too many things in one lesson.

3. The Function of Specific Aims

   If an aim means anything, it represents the end toward which the lesson should move and for which every individual part of the lesson exists. Thus, the objective becomes the norm, the standard by which the necessity and worth of the particular aspects of the lesson should be judged. The teacher should therefore ask himself regarding each phase of the lesson, "Does this specific part contribute anything to the accomplishment of my goal? If so, what precisely is its contribution and how is it realized?" If the answer to the first question is negative, then the part being considered should be eliminated from the lesson. If the answer is affirmative, it should be conceived of and treated in such a manner that its contribution to the goal of the lesson is actually and effectively accomplished.[2]

C. Exercise on Aims

State fully the aims of lessons based on the following passages: Matthew 10, Mark 1:14–45, Mark 13, John 1:1–18, John 4:1–42, John 9–10, John 11, John 14, Acts 2, and Acts 16. In so doing, utilize the principles set forth in the preceding discussion.

---

[2] What is true of specific aims in regard to their function is also true of general aims.

Chapter 1—Method in Bible Teaching 13

III. LESSON STRUCTURE AND DEVELOPMENT IN BIBLE TEACHING

A. General Determinants of Leeson Structure and Development
   1. Nature and Structure of the Passage
   2. Principles of Bound Pedagogy

B. Specific Kinds of Lesson Structure and Development.
   1. Logical or Topical
   2. Interpretative or Structural

C. Concrete Bases for Deciding the Types of Lesson Structure and Development

D. Means of Previewing the Composition of a Passage in Lesson Structure and Development

E. Some Common Errors in Lesson Structure and Development
   1. The Backtrack Approach
   2. The Detour Approach
   3. The Unfinished Approach
   4. The Buckshot Approach
   5. The Deviating Approach
   6. The Swerving Approach
   7. The Non-Transitional Approach
   8. The Wandering Approach

F. Miscellaneous Principles for Proper Leeson Structure and Development

G. Exercise on Lesson Structure and Development

Footnotes [Note: These "endnotes" have been added as true footnotes in the material below.]

III. LESSON STRUCTURE AND DEVELOPMENT IN BIBLE TEACHING

One of the most crucial steps in lesson preparation and execution involves the decision regarding the general structure and development of the lesson. For if one's judgment in this connection is sound and valid, the remainder of the phases of preparation and execution will be greatly simplified. If, on the other hand, a wrong conclusion is drawn at this point, no matter what else is done, the lesson is liable to fail in its effectiveness.

A. General Determinants of Lesson Structure and Development

There are two primary factors which guide the structure and development of a lesson: 1. the nature and structure of the passage being taught; and 2. principles of sound pedagogy. These two general elements will be described briefly at this point.

1. Nature and Structure of the Passage

The structure of the lesson plan should correspond in a general way with the arrangement of the passage being examined. If, for example, a unit of Biblical material is "so constructed that an understanding of the first part of the unit is essential for a comprehension of the later points, then it is imperative that the lesson plan be so conceived as to allow for a study of the first part preceding a study of the other parts. Romans 1:18–32 is an example of such a passage. If, on the other hand, the converse is true, then the lesson plan should take this fact into account and begin by an examination of the later parts of the unit. The book of Joshua or the Gospel by John affords an illustration of a passage which may be considered as belonging to this latter category. In these and other ways the composition of a portion of Scripture will be an important factor in determining the structure and development of the lesson based upon it.

2. Principles of Sound Pedagogy

The teacher must not only be guided by the arrangement of the unit being examined, but also by sound pedagogical principles if his or her lesson is to be planned properly. That is, he or she should also be concerned with how best to convey to the class or enable the class to discover what a Biblical writer is saying if his or her teaching is to be effective. Although this factor is closely related to the preceding one, it contains a different element. For because of it, a teacher may sometimes, for example, begin in the middle of a book instead of at its beginning, in spite of the fact that its composition does not demand it. In order better to teach Genesis, for instance, one may commence with a study of the Abraham narrative instead of the creation account. This he or she may do not because the structure of the book makes it necessary, but because of sound pedagogical principles, since Genesis 1 raises so many problems in the mind of the modern student that it is difficult to examine it objectively as an integral part of the book of Genesis without first investigating other units of the book. In this and other ways, considering effective teaching procedure determines lesson structure, as well as the arrangement of the passage.[3]

---

[3] Note that the principles of structure and development may involve a series of lessons as well as an individual lesson.

We shall now see how these two general factors operate more specifically, in connection with decisions concerning the framework and development of a lesson.

B. Specific Kinds of Lesson Structure and Development

There are two <u>primary</u> ways of classifying the particular types of lesson structure and development: 1. logical or topical, which is the basic category; 2. structural or interpretative, which is more secondary in nature.

1. Logical or Topical Development

The <u>logical</u> type at structure involves the steady progression of the teaching procedure from beginning to end, with each part successively building upon that which precedes until the goal is finally reached. It may be diagrammed thus:

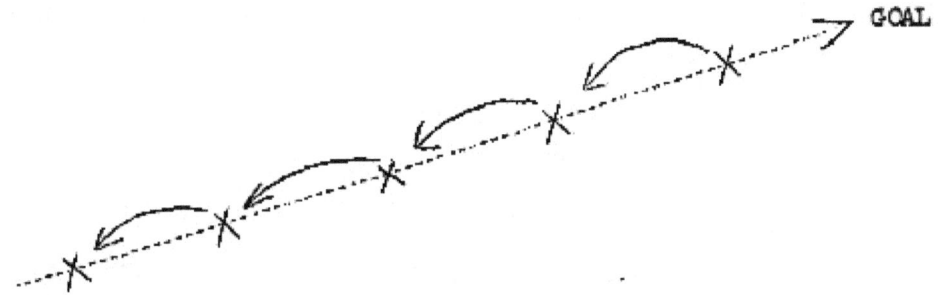

The <u>topical</u> kind of composition entails the consideration of <u>parallel</u> aspects or phases of one idea, the accumulation of which constitutes the realization of the aim of the lesson. It thus involves the approaching of one thing from various directions. It may be pictorialized in this manner:

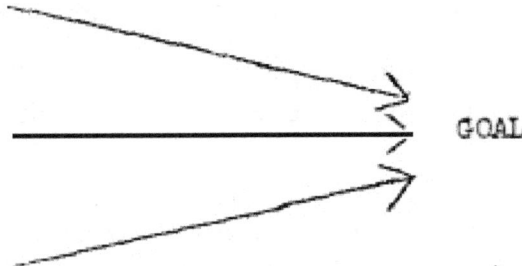

Which of these types of development is employed depends upon the nature of the passage being taught. If the Scriptural unit is logical in character, such as Romans 6:1–7:6 or Romans 8, then the logical kind of lesson arrangement is most valid, A topical treatment of such a passage would probably be misleading as an initial approach. If, on the other hand, the portion is topical in nature, such as John 3:1–21 or Mark 4:35–5:43, then the topical type of development is more legitimate.[4]

---

[4] As a matter of fact, it should be noted that no passage is purely topical, because the various aspects are always logically interrelated to some extent. However, some units of Scripture are more topical than logical. It is these which we are classifying as topical. Incidentally, these facts apply to the structure of lessons as well.

2. Interpretative or Structural Development[5]

There is a further and secondary qualification as to the method of developing a Bible lesson. A logical or a topical lesson may be arranged either interpretatively or structurally, although frequently the logical passage lends itself to interpretative development, whereas a topical unit is often conducive to the structural kind of lesson arrangement.

a. Interpretative or Synthetical Development (parts-whole)

This type of lesson organization involves beginning at the beginning or the passage, and moving consecutively from part to part until the whole has been studied. If the passage as-a-whole is conceived as a circle, and each part of the passage as a segment of the circle, this kind of lesson structure may be diagrammed thus:[6]

EXAMINATION AND RELATION OF INDIVIDUAL PARTS   EXAMINATION OF WHOLE

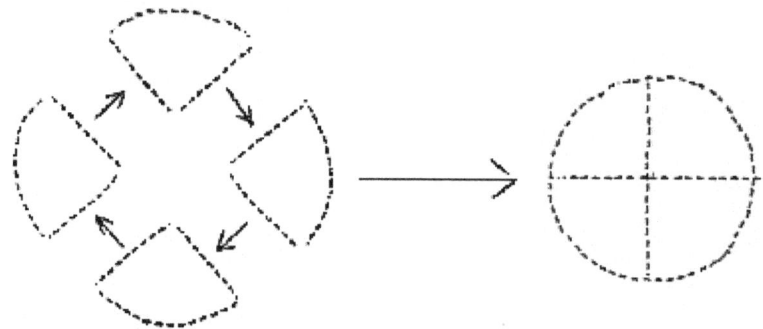

b. Structural or Analytical Development (whole-parts-whole)

The structural approach, on the contrary, commences with a survey or preview of the whole, proceeds to an analysis of the parts, and concludes with an examination of the

---

A third type of structure was not mentioned in this material because it is actually a variation of the other two and therefore subordinate to them. It may be called the circular kind of arrangement. This arrangement is a cross between topical and logical framework, although it is usually utilized in conjunction with the logical approach. It involves beginning with the theme or thesis, then following with a substantiation of it, and finally concluding at the same place at which the teaching procedure commenced. The lesson thus returns to the point of its beginning. This type of development is frequently valid in connection with those passages whose composition is based primarily on the law of particularization, such as Psalm 23 and Romans 1:18–32. However, the circular approach must not be used in such a way as to make the lesson deductive by dogmatically stating at the outset that which ought to await the conclusion of the lesson.

[5] These terms are borrowed from M. J. Adler's *How to Read a Book,* although they are used in a different connection in his discussion. Furthermore, the term "interpretative" is used differently here from the way in which it was employed in the section on Bible study in this manual.

[6] The image of the circle is not a perfect one, since it does not adequately indicate progression. However, it is utilized because it does represent the idea of wholeness, which is primary in the present discussion. The circle is not employed here to represent solely the circular approach, although it does reflect to some extent such an approach.

whole.[7] It may be pictured thus:

PREVIEW OF WHOLE   ANALYSIS AND RELATION   RE-VIEW OF WHOLE
                    OF INDIVIDUAL PARTS

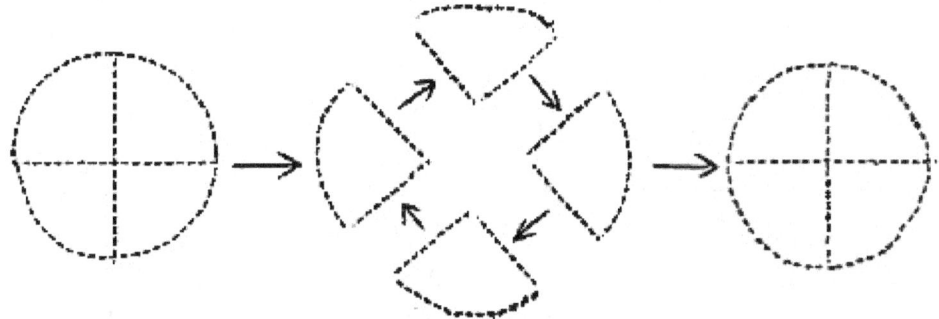

In view of these two means of classifying lesson construction, namely, logical or topical and interpretative or structural, there are four major types of organization: the <u>logical interpretative</u> and the <u>logical structural</u> arrangements, and the <u>topical interpretative</u> and the <u>topical structural</u> kinds of composition. To put it another way, a lesson which is so constructed that there is a progressive study of dependent parts until the goal is finally achieved (logical approach) may be conducted by beginning with the first step and moving a step at a" time until the whole has been studied (interpretative approach), or it may commence with a preview of the whole, proceed to an analysis of the consecutive parts, and culminate with a re-view of the whole (structural approach). The same two alternatives are possible in connection with the topical lesson. It may start with a detailed examination of each unit or topic or, on the other hand, with a preview of the whole.[8]

c. Concrete Bases for Deciding the Type of Lesson Structure and Development

As was suggested, whether a lesson is arranged topically or logically depends primarily on whether the passage itself is topical or logical in nature. However, the decision as to whether the lesson should be structural or interpretative depends on a number of factors which concern both the nature of the unit and principles of sound pedagogy. They may be summarized in terms of the following three questions: <u>first</u>, "Is a preview of the passage necessary for the understanding or interpretation of its individual parts?"; <u>second</u>, "Is a preview of the Biblical unit essential for purposes of orientation or in order to make the lesson intelligible?"; and <u>third</u>, "Is a preview of the passage possible without detracting substantially from the body of the lesson?" Let us consider each of these questions separately.

---

[7] The implication of this analysis of lesson arrangement is that every teaching approach should conclude with a view of the whole, whether the lesson be interpretative or structural.

[8] The kind of preview of which we have been speaking is limited to the particular unit which is being studied. However, it is sometimes essential to preview the structure of the larger context in which such a unit is found in order to obtain the proper background for its study. For example, the effective teaching of John 13:1–35 may well necessitate a preview of the arrangement of the entire book of John.

The first question involves exegetical factors which in turn are dependent upon the character of the Scriptural unit being examined. Certain passages are so constructed, that is, their elements are so interrelated, that a preview of the whole is virtually indispensable for the exposition of' their individual parts. James 1 may well be classified in this category, for the interpretation of the paragraphs in verses 2–15 is contingent upon noting the fact that the term "trials" appears both in verse 2 and in verse 12. In order to observe the recurrence of this term, one needs to preview the whole. Simply to begin at the beginning might not provide the basis for expounding the individual statements and paragraphs.[9]7

The second question, namely, "Is a preview essential for purposes of orientation or so as to make the lesson intelligible?" involves principles of sound pedagogy. At times a preview of the passage as-a-whole will make a substantial contribution toward orienting the class to the lesson or clarifying the arrangement or the lesson, thus making its structure understandable to the students. Such a procedure may supply, for example, an insight into the reason why the lesson is constructed as it is, an insight which might otherwise be absent, thus resulting in a failure to comprehend its development. For instance, John 3:1–21 may be taught from the standpoint of the various characteristics set forth there regarding the new birth. But unless there is a preview of the whole which establishes the fact that the new birth is the Principle theme of that unit, students may not discern why such an idea was chosen as the organizing center of the lesson. Students may well conclude that the choice was an arbitrary one on the part of the teacher, and thus miss in a sense the main point of the lesson. A preview of the whole may therefore afford the listener with the necessary data in order to grasp the grounds for the particular teaching procedure which is being followed.

If the answer to both of these questions is "no," then the approach to the lesson should be interpretative. If, on the other hand, the answer to either of these two queries is "yes," then the third question should be seriously considered, namely, "Is a preview possible without detracting appreciably from the body of the lesson?"[10] If the answer to this question is "yes," then the structural arrangement should be employed. This may occur in relation to a passage which has only surface structure or which has surface structure ae well as underlying structure. However, it may be that a particular passage has only an underlying structure, which is so complex that to preview it would necessitate the minute examination of one or more of its parts, thus detracting from the core of the lesson. What may happen in the treatment of such a unit is that by the time its composition is discovered, a substantial part of it will have been studied, thus leaving little to be done in the rest of the lesson. In such an

---

[9] In a real sense the explanation of every part of a passage depends upon that of every other part of the passage. This is especially true in terms of full interpretation. It is for this reason, for example, that the suggestion is made to close each Bible lesson with a review of the whole. However, in certain instances it is possible to engage in the basic exposition of a part of a Biblical unit without first exegeting the other parts, whereas in other cases this is not possible. It is such a distinction which forms one of the grounds for determining whether a lesson should be interpretative or structural.

[10] Incidentally, if the answer to the first question is "yes," the answer to the second question will also usually be "yes."

Chapter 1—*Method in Bible Teaching* 19

instance one must decide which is the lesser of two evils, that is, whether it is least detrimental to survey the whole in order to make possible the interpretation of individual parts or the better understanding of the lesson development, or to forego these in order to avoid teaching the lesson proper, so to speak, before it begins. This decision must be determined on the basis of the character of the particular passage being studied and the nature of the group being taught.[11] No general principle may determine the answer, unless it be that it is usually disastrous to a lesson to detract <u>too much</u> from its body in order to introduce it.

It should be noted that it is especially helpful to preview the composition of the passage as-a-whole when a large body of material is being studied. And fortunately, few problems arise in surveying the arrangement of a long passage if it is done properly, Therefore, it is usually safe to assume that if a lengthy unit is being taught, the lesson should have a structural development.

All of this discussion emphasizes one outstanding idea: The teacher should not use a certain kind of structure in a particular lesson simply because he or she has seen others use that type of arrangement or because he or she has used it in other connections. Such a decision should not be made cursorily or out of habit, but rather on the basis of careful thought and evaluation in connection with each individual lesson. Even if the aforementioned criteria are not used by teachers, they should develop their own standards and employ them diligently. At times the teacher will unquestionably find it difficult to choose between the logical and topical or the structural and interpretive approaches because of the lack of decisive evidence; however, this should not deter him or her from the obligation and task to pass judgment regarding these matters.

D. Means of Previewing the Composition of a Passage in Lesson Structure and Development

If one decides that the lesson should be arranged structurally, there are two basic means which one may employ in order to preview a passage. <u>First</u>, the teacher himself may point out the structural elements of the unit and suggest how these elements indicate its composition. <u>Second</u>, the instructor may ask the students certain structural questions whose answers will result in the discovery of the arrangement of the passage. Both of these approaches are legitimate and which of them is employed depends on such factors as the time element, since the first is usually the shorter procedure. In no case, however, should the teacher dogmatically and arbitrarily disclose the composition of a Scriptural unit without substantiating his or her statements by reference to the particulars of the passage.[12]

---

[11] It has been previously stated that there are two kinds of structure, namely, <u>surface</u> structure and <u>underlying</u> structure. The first is readily observed because it lies near the surface, and it therefore lends itself to the preview or survey approach. On the other hand, underlying structure lies beneath the surface and is not so readily detected. It therefore is not too susceptible to a preview or survey.

[12] In certain instances the teacher will find it necessary to preview the structure of certain <u>parts</u> of a passage. Such a preview does not come under the category of structural development. Furthermore, a preview of a passage is not

E. Some Common Errors in Lesson Structure and Development

In order to indicate clearly some of the frequent fallacies which occur in the arrangement of Bible lessons, diagrams will be used to pictorialize them. In these diagrams the ideal lesson structure will be represented by the logical type of approach and will be indicated by a broken line. However, those same errors are relevant to the topical kind of arrangement. The reader may draw comparable diagrams showing how these fallacies are applicable to topical lesson structure.

1. <u>The Backtrack Approach</u>—the repetition of that which has already been treated.

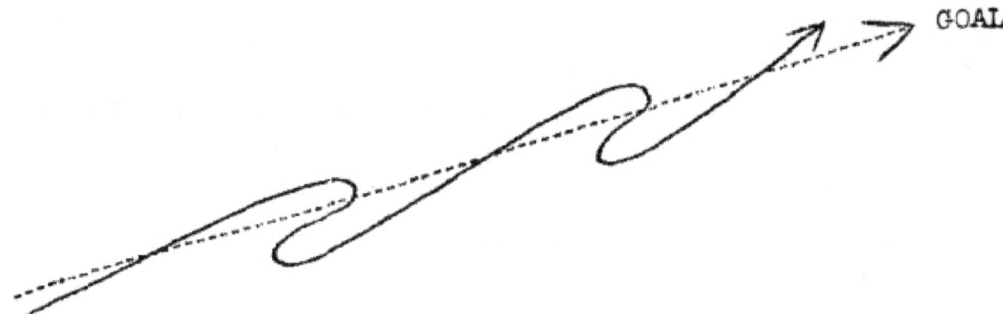

2. <u>The Detour Approach</u>—the taking of periodic excursions from the main road of the lesson.

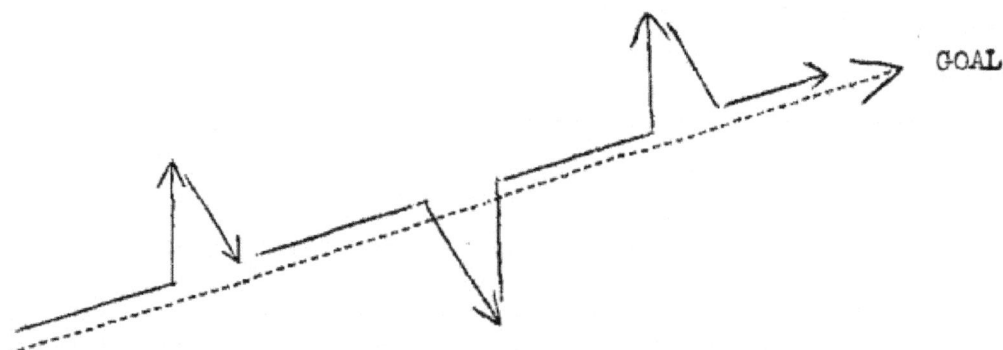

3. <u>The Unfinished Approach</u>—the failure to bring the lesson to its proper and natural conclusion.

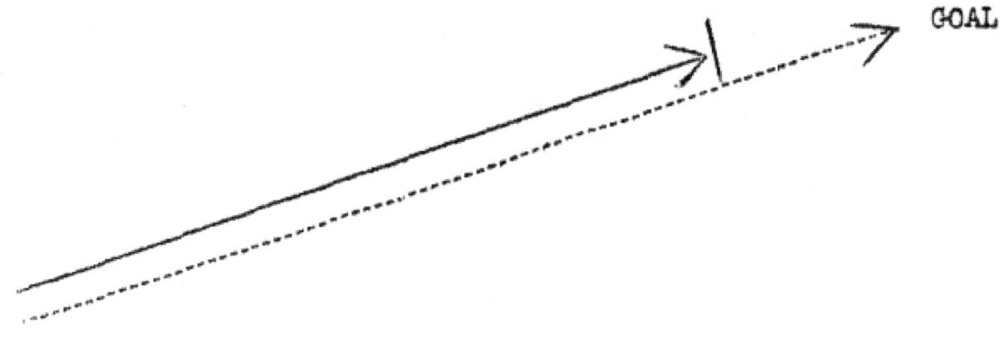

---

to be considered as an introduction, at least generally speaking. The preview, when it is done, is therefore an integral part of the body of the lesson.

4. <u>The Buckshot Approach</u>—the approach to a passage which is not guided by one unifying idea but rather takes various courses in various directions.

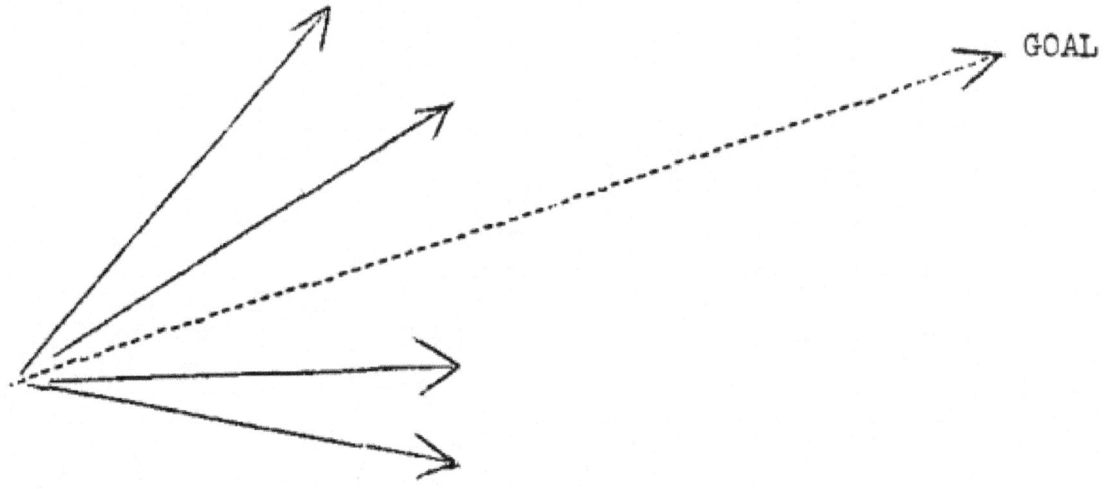

5. <u>The Deviating Approach</u>—the sudden and permanent digression from the course of the lesson.

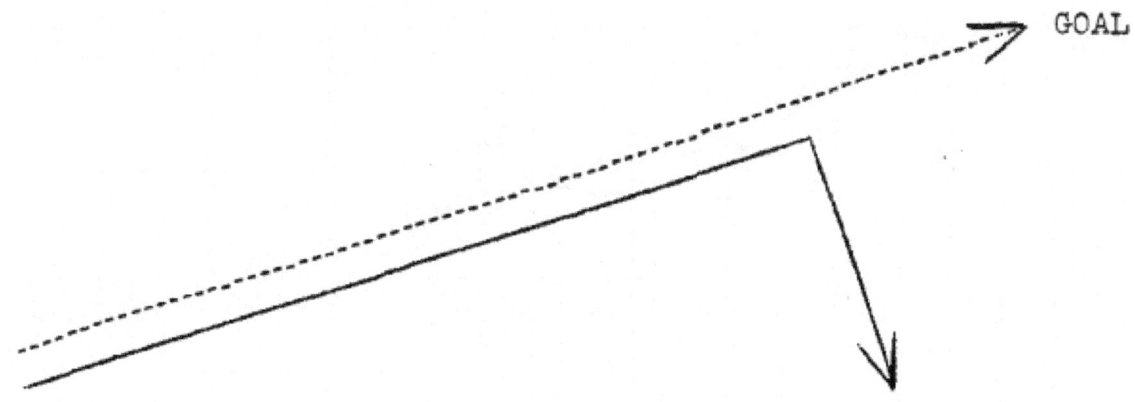

6. <u>The Swerving Approach</u>—the sort of development which is near the main path of the lesson without quite being on it.

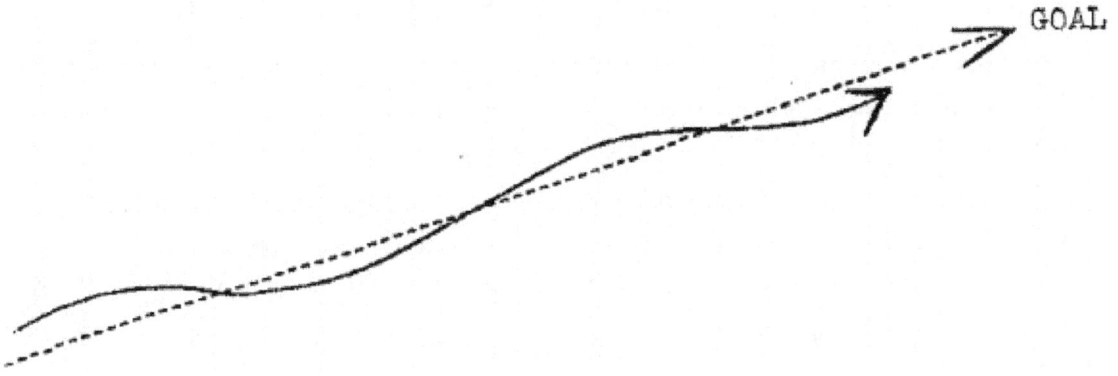

7. <u>The Non-Transitional Approach</u>—the failure to connect or relate the various parts of the lesson.

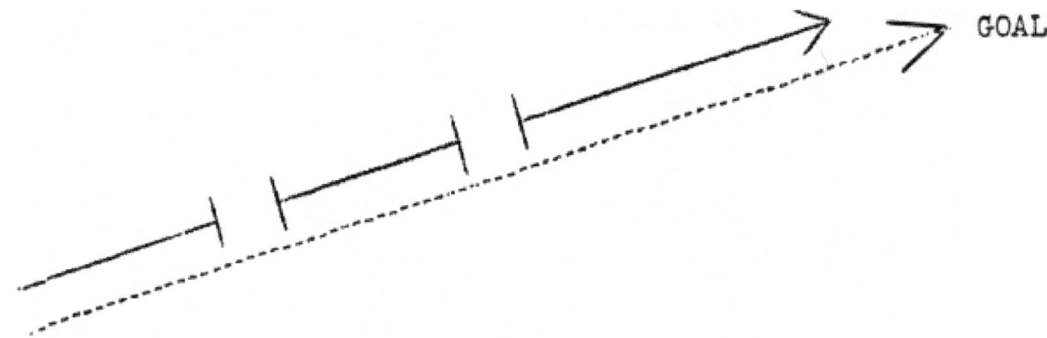

8. <u>The Wandering Approach</u>—the aimless rambling from place to place.

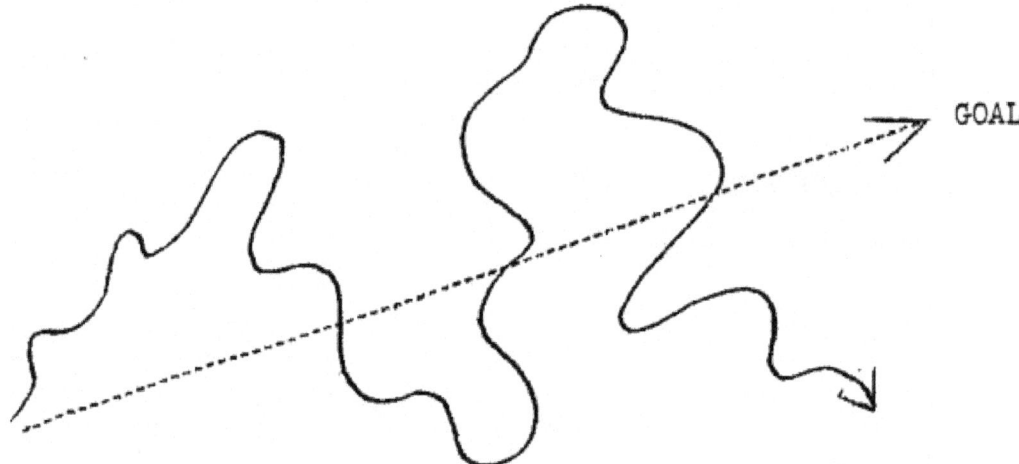

These are merely some of the common errors in lesson development. Readers may be able to add to this list others which they may have observed.

F. Miscellaneous Principles for Proper Lesson Structure and Development

From these fallacious kinds of lesson arrangement, we may learn certain principles which one should follow in order to achieve the proper arrangement of Biblical lessons. To these we shall add other principles which come to mind and which have not yet been stated.

1. The lesson should move steadily toward its objective. Once a certain phase of the lesson has been completed, it should not be repeated. The only exceptions to this principle are those factors which demand repetition for the sake of emphasis.

2. Only that which will contribute to the <u>progress</u> of the lesson should be included in it. All irrelevant parts should be excluded from the teaching procedure. Further, the students should be made conscious of the exact means in which each part or the lesson contributes to its development.

3. The lesson should not be left in mid-air, but should be carried to its logical culmination.

4. If at all possible, the teaching plan should be organized and unified around <u>one</u> main idea, and

nothing should be allowed to cause one to veer away from that one idea. This does not imply that there will be no elasticity or flexibility to the lesson, for if it were rigid it would be deductive rather than experimental. However, the character of that which is elastic is that it returns to its initial shape. This should be true of the teaching procedure. The lesson should give the impression of wholeness, oneness, integrality.

5. The teacher should be certain that he or she is squarely on the main road of the lesson and not just missing it. There is the constant danger of being so near and yet so far in relation to the main course of the lesson.

6. It is of supreme importance to develop adequate, clear, and smooth transitions between the different parts of the lesson. Transitions often make or break a lesson. It is therefore wise to prepare them carefully beforehand.

7. The lesson should move steadily toward a climax, a high point which stands out above all others. If the passage being studied is climactic, the climax of the lesson ought to coincide with the climax or the unit.

8. The plan for developing the lesson together with its basis and significance should be made clear to the class wherever possible and necessary.

9. The latter part of a lesson should be in harmony with the former part, and their agreement should be made clear to the class. For example, if the teaching plan begins with the statement of a problem, it should close with reference to the solution of that problem. In a word, a lesson should have unity in its development.

10. The conclusion should be the natural and logical outgrowth of the rest of the lesson and not something which is an afterthought and superimposed on the rest of the material.

11. Avoid being anti-climactic in the development of a lesson.

12. A teaching plan should have a definite terminus, which is approached gradually but when reached brings the lesson to a precise and prompt close. Rambling on when the lesson should have ended may be disastrous to its overall impression.

13. The progress of a lesson should be as steady as possible. It should not be extremely slow at certain times and extremely rapid at others.

G. Exercise on Lesson Structure and Development

Study the following passages: Mark 2:1–3:6, Mark 4:35–5:43, John 6, John 13:1–35, John 15, Romans 3:21–31, Romans 5, Romans 9–11, 1 Corinthians 12:31–14:1, Hebrews 11, James 1, James 3:1–4:12, 1 John 1:5–26. Would you develop a lesson on each of these particular passages topically or logically, structurally or interpretatively? In answering this question, consider the principles and suggestions found in the preceding pages. Give the exact reasons for your answers. If there is doubt in any case, state the pros and cons for the various possibilities, weigh the evidence, and make your decision.

IV. FORMULATION AND USE OF QUESTIONS AND ANSWERS IN BIBLE TEACHING

    A. Sources of Questions
        1. General Source
        2. Specific Sources
            a. Objective sources
                (1) The Nature of the passage
                (2) The Nature of the Class
            b. Subjective Source—The Nature of the Mind

    B. General Purpose of Questions
        1. In Regard to the Student
        2. In Regard to the Teacher
        3. In Regard to the Passage
        4. In Regard to Lesson Development

    C. Kinds of Questions
        1. In Terms of Their Importance—Key and Subsidiary
        2. In Terms of Their Scope and Concreteness—General and Specific
        3. In Terms of Their Effectiveness and Order—Primary and Secondary or Auxiliary
        4. In Terms of Their Precise Aims
            a. The Factual Question
            b. The Elucidative Question
            c. The Analytical Question
            d. The Heuristic question
            e. The Rhetorical Question
            f. The Choice Question
            g. The Summary Question
            h. The Review Question
            i. The Examinational Question
            j. The Value Question
            k. The Applicatory Question
            l. The Correlative Question
            m. The Adjustment Question

    D. Content and Form of Questions
        1. Practicality
        2. Clarity
        3. Brevity, Directness
        4. Definiteness
        5. Variety

Chapter 1—Method in Bible Teaching 25

      6. Stimulation
      7. Adaptability
      8. Stimulation
      9. Sincerity
      10. Inductivity
      11. Forcefulness
      12. Imaginativeness
      13. Singleness
      14. Relevancy
      15. Suggestiveness

E. Order of Questions

F. Manner of Asking Questions

G. Answers to Questions und Their Use

H. Some "Dos" and "Don'ts" Regarding Questions and Answers
    1. Do:
    2. Don't:

I. Exercise on Questions and Answers

Footnotes [Note: These "endnotes" have been added as true footnotes in the material below.]

IV. FORMULATION AND USE OF QUESTIONS AND ANSWERS IN BIBLE TEACHING

A. Sources of Questions

1. General Source

   Broadly speaking, the source of the questions used in Scriptural teaching is the group of questions which are raised in connection with the study of a Biblical unit and which have already been discussed. This fact is of supreme importance and indicates the great dependence of effective teaching upon thorough and efficient study. For unless one is able in the first place to suggest those questions whose answers result in valid and adequate interpretation, evaluation, application, and correlation, one will not be capable of asking those questions in the teaching process whose replies will enable the class to receive an insight into the meaning, significance, and value of a portion of Scripture.

2. Specific Sources

   Having said this, it may be helpful to examine more particularly the sources of questions to be used in Bible teaching. The questions employed in a lesson originate from two primary areas.

   a. Objective Sources

   <u>Objectively</u>, the questions used in Bible teaching are based on two main factors, namely, the character of the unit being taught and the character of the group being taught.

   (1) The Nature of the Passage

   The questions to be utilized in the lesson derive from the nature and content of the passage itself, that is, its terms, structure, literary form, and atmosphere. This fact has been stressed in other connections. What is even more important to note in this regard is that the questions for teaching must originate from those aspects or a particular unit which are the <u>most</u> <u>significant</u> for its proper understanding. For it is obvious, for example, that the teacher cannot employ in toto the list of interpretive questions which were framed during the process of study. He or she must therefore select those questions which are most <u>crucial</u> and <u>strategic</u> to use in the <u>teaching procedure</u>. And what these questions will be is dependent upon that which is <u>central</u> and <u>determinative</u> in the <u>passage</u>. Thus, in more ways than one the character of the portion being taught dictates the questions which should be asked in its teaching.

   (2) The Nature of the Class

   There is, however, another objective factor which forms the basis for the questions used in the Bible lesson, namely, the needs, problems, interests, and capabilities of the group being taught. There should be no doubt as to the importance of this factor. It not only determines the phrasing of particular questions, but it also accounts in a real way for the kind and content of the questions employed. The teacher should, therefore, be alert to the nature of the group being led if the questions he or she utilizes are to be as effective as possible.

b. Subjective Source—The Nature of the Mind

<u>Subjectively</u>, the questions employed in the teaching procedure spring from the inquisitive, curious, wondering mind. Although this fact has already been stated in the discussion of interpretative questions in methodical study, it is well worth iterating. The prerequisite of teaching others is the kind of mentality which is not satisfied with words or appearances or mechanics or commonplace explanations or trite clichés, but which, on the contrary, pries under the surface of things and raises insistent queries regarding their profound and underlying meaning and significance. This type of mind is in the first place essential for incisive Bible study; it is even more indispensable for Bible teaching, since the teacher takes upon himself the responsibility of leading others to an understanding of the Scriptures. Not only must the mind be inquisitive regarding the passage being studied, but also, in a legitimate way, regarding the nature of the class being taught. Teachers should be concerned with discovering the needs, problems, interests, and abilities of their classes; and they should be concerned as to the bearing of those discoveries upon the construction of their lessons and especially the questions employed. For unless there exists such an interest on the part of teachers, their lessons and questions may have serious deficiencies.

B. General Purpose of Questions

1. In Regard to the Students

a. To enable students to learn how much or how little they have discovered concerning passages of Scripture.

b. To show students the great potentialities inherent in Bible study.

c. To improve the students' knowledge of the content, meaning, and implications of Scriptural units, which may sometimes entail the correction of misconceptions or the emphasizing of certain essentials.

d. To develop initiative in students by enabling them to discover the latent capacities which reside in their own minds and indicating the ways in which they may employ them.

e. To foster in students the power of clear thinking and self-expression.

f. To aid students in seeing the interrelatedness of truth.

g. To give students the opportunity to contribute to the lesson.

h. All of this to enable each student to develop into an <u>independent</u> and <u>effective</u> Bible scholar and teacher, with all the implications attached to these activities.

2. In Regard to the Teacher

a. To make possible vital contact between teacher and student.

b. To show the teacher how much students have learned and how far they have developed, that he or she may begin where the students are and lead them to where they ought to be.

3. In Regard to the Passage—to bring the mind into contact with the thought and aim of the biblical author(s) and the meaning and contemporary significance of their words.

4. In Regard to Lesson Development—to make a substantial contribution to the on-going movement of the lesson so that it may attain its goal.

C. Kinds of Questions

There are several ways of classifying the various types of questions. We shall organize them in four categories: 1. in terms of their importance; 2. in terms of their scope and concreteness; 3. in terms of the effectiveness and order; and 4. in terms of their precise aims.[13]

1. In Terms of Their Importance—Key and Subsidiary

The questions of any one lesson are not all of equal significance. Some will be more important and others will be less important. The questioner should make it a point to determine in connection with the whole lesson what the key question or questions should be, and what supporting or subsidiary questions should be employed in order to realize the answers to the key questions. If at all possible, the lesson should be organized around one or a few crucial questions whose replies constitute the substance of the lesson. All other queries should serve to uphold and fulfil those strategic questions.

The key question or questions should be based upon the principle elements of the passage being studied. For example, Hebrews 11 consists primarily of an opening description of faith followed by the particular outworkings and results of such faith in the lives of specific persons, together with the reasons for the organic relation between faith and its effects. In view of this, a lesson built on Hebrews 11 might embody these <u>key</u> questions: "What is meant by faith, what were its results in each instance, and wherein or why did such faith have such results?" Similarly, Isaiah 55 is essentially a description of God's merciful offer of pardon to Israel. The strategic question may therefore be stated thus: "What are the major characteristics of God's mercy, and what are their meaning and implications?" All other questions employed in the lessons on those passages may well have as their function the answering of those crucial questions.

It is not to be inferred, however, that the key question or questions are to be stated explicitly at the outset of every lesson, for this is not the case. In some instances, it will undoubtedly be helpful to express the central problem at the beginning, but in others it would be impractical to do so. When a lesson is developed structurally, the former approach will probably be valid; if it is arranged interpretatively, the latter procedure will probably be suitable. However, the main point is that the <u>teacher</u> should have <u>in his or her own mind</u> a certain crucial question or questions which will form the core of the lesson and serve to make it a unified whole.

---

[13] To be sure, these classifications are interrelated.

2. In Terms of Their Scope and Concreteness—General and Specific

The distinction between general and specific questions may involve either of the two following factors: a. <u>scope</u>, and b. <u>concreteness</u>. In the <u>first</u> instance, a question may be general because it is <u>broad</u>, or it may be specific because it is narrow and deals with one or more particulars. For example, the question "What attributes of God are set forth in the Abraham narrative?" is general because of its breadth, whereas the question "What Divine attributes are set forth in Genesis 12:1–3" is specific because it narrows the area to a certain few verses. <u>On the other hand</u>, a question may be general because it <u>lacks concreteness</u>. For instance, the general question "What is the atmosphere of Romans 9–11?" may be made specific by asking, "What is the controlling attitude of Paul as found in Romans 9:1–5?"

It should be remembered that "general" and "specific" are often relative terms, and that therefore there are degrees of generality and specification. Some questions may be more specific than others on the one hand, and more general than others on the other hand.

The teacher should make it a point to ask both general and specific questions; for the more general questions develop initiative on the part of the student, whereas the more specific questions enable the teacher to provide direction to the student and to the lesson, as well as help to conserve time.[14]

3. In Terms of Their Effectiveness and Order—Primary and Secondary or Auxiliary

It is difficult to find a descriptive title suitable for this category because it involves an admixture of several factors. However, it is an essential classification, since it is made necessary by important practical considerations. For every teacher who has employed questions knows that many questions are never answered in their initial or primary form. This may be due to one or more of several reasons: a. students may lack insight into the meaning or significance of the question; b. they may have failed to follow the necessary steps of logic leading to the question; and c. they may have neglected to study the lesson. Other reasons may make certain questions ineffective; but, whatever the cause, the teacher finds it necessary to use auxiliary or secondary questions in order to lead the student to discover the answer to the first or primary questions.

Secondary questions may often involve framing the primary questions in different words. However, at times it is necessary to make the secondary or auxiliary question more concrete. For example, one may ask, "What is the structure of Romans 1:18–32?" If the student fails to answer this primary question, which is general in nature, one may inquire, "What is the significance of the 'therefore' of verse 24 for discovering the arrangement of this segment?" In other instances, when the primary question assumes several logical deductions, it is necessary to formulate a series of secondary questions whose intent is to trace those steps in order that the student may understand the initial question. It is difficult to overemphasize the importance of secondary questions in inductive Bible teaching. More often than not the effectiveness of a

---

[14] Key questions are usually the most general, whereas subsidiary questions frequently move toward specification.

lesson will depend upon them. It is therefore helpful for the teacher to prepare himself for secondary questions by practicing formulating them, as well as by having such a thorough knowledge of the subject matter that he or she can approach it from various directions.[15]

4. In Terms of Their Precise Aims

The key and subsidiary, general and specific, as well as primary and secondary questions used in the teaching procedure may be profitably classified in terms of their <u>specific</u> purposes. The various types of questions in this regard will now be enumerated, described, and illustrated. The close relationship between questions in study and teaching will be noted.[16]

a. The Factual Question

This kind of question is sometimes called "informational." It corresponds to the observational question utilized in methodical study, namely, "What is here?" This, of course, is a general question which may and should be adapted in view of the specific portion being taught. For example, in connection with the study of John 17, the factual question may be expressed thus: "What are the petitions made by Jesus and what bases does He give for them? "The answers to such questions frequently stop short of profound interpretation. Factual questions thus have the function of laying the foundation for succeeding and more significant questions by calling attention to the actual facts or statements of the passage.

b. The Elucidative Question

After a fact has been noted, one may ask the type of question which attempts to render intelligible its meaning. This question therefore corresponds to the definitive or explanatory question in study. For example, when the aforementioned factual question is answered by noting Jesus's petition that His disciples be consecrated in the truth (John 17:17), the following question may be asked: "What exactly is meant by this petition?"

c. The Analytical Question

Webster defines analysis in this way: "To decompose or resolve into elements or constituent parts; to separate mentally the parts of a whole so as to reveal their relation to it and to one another."[17] In view of this definition, it is apparent that the analytical question is a structural question and, in a real sense, an observational question. However, it is the type of inquiry which usually presupposes a certain amount of interpretation. This fact was called to the reader's attention in the section on interpretative questions, where the analytical question

---

[15] It may be helpful to note that both key and subsidiary questions are primary in the sense in which we are using the term here, since they may be planned beforehand.

[16] Although some of the questions listed in this connection are identical to those found in the section on study, different names will frequently be used for them, not only for the sake of variety, but also because of a slightly different emphasis due to their relation to teaching procedure.

[17] Webster's Collegiate Dictionary, Fifth Edition.

was previously mentioned. This kind of query has as its intent the discovery as to whether a particular part involves basis, motivation, reason, purpose, etc.

d. The Heuristic Question

This type of inquiry follows logically on the heels of the elucidative and analytical questions. The term "heuristic" is derived from the Greek word εὑρίσκω, which means "to search or to find by careful scrutiny." The heuristic question is therefore a search question and is commonly called a "thought question." Its purpose is to transcend and penetrate literal statement in order to find the purpose of statements as well as their signification and implications. In fact, it includes the rational and implicational types of inquiry, as well as identifying, methodical, temporal, and local questions when they cannot be answered by simply noting the factual statements of a portion.

e. The Rhetorical Question

The rhetorical question demands no explicit reply by the members of the class either because its answer is obvious or because it is answered by the questioner himself. In the first instance, its function is to focus attention on a particular point by engaging the mind and interest of the listener through the medium of inquiry. Jesus's questions recorded in Mark 8:36–37 are of this type. When a rhetorical question is employed in this way, it should not be used in connection with a controversial subject. Its reply should be self-evident. In the second case, it involves the questioner's bringing to the listener's attention a certain subject which he or she wishes to discuss. He or she therefore states the topic in question form, and the ensuing presentation becomes an answer to the question. The function of this kind of rhetorical question is to make possible literary or oral composition. Paul, for example, frequently uses this literary means in Romans.

f. The Choice Question

Such a question gives its recipient two or more alternatives from which to select an answer. It thus may be in the form of a "yes" or "no" question. It serves to delimit the field being examined by calling special attention to certain possibilities. However, it is not self-sufficient, since in order to be beneficial it must be followed by the supporting question, namely, "What are the reasons for your choice?"

g. The Summary Question

The summary question corresponds to integrative questions presented previously in the section on "Integration and Summarization." Therefore, its aim is to lead the student to state in succinct form the essence of the thought and purpose of a passage. For example, one might summarize the idea of John 17 in terms of this general question, "What is the unifying thought or John 17?" Incidentally, every lesson should be summarized and focalized at its conclusion, whether a summary question is used in doing so or not.

h. The Review Question

The review question may be used in two ways.

(1) It may be employed to impress something upon the mind by repetition or to re-learn something which may have been forgotten. Someone has said that we do not really learn a thing until we have learned it, partially forgotten it, and learned it again.

(2) It may be utilized to re-view the material already covered, to approach it from another standpoint in order to gain further perspective and insight or to organize what has already been noted. After studying John 17 in terms of Jesus's prayer, it may be re-viewed by the use of either of the following questions: "What characteristics of effective prayer are exemplified in this segment?" or "What concept did Jesus have of His own nature, life, and mission according to this segment?"

i. The Examinational Question

This kind of inquiry attempts to test how much the student has learned as well as how much he or she has developed. Its answer frequently forms the background for further questioning.

j. The Value Question

Such a question corresponds to those previously presented in the section on evaluation. Its purpose is to lead the student to appraise Scriptural statements from the standpoint of their validity or their exact worth and relevance in a given situation. Often this kind of inquiry will result in a deeper insight into the meaning and signification of a Biblical truth as well as in a value-judgment regarding it.[18]

k. The Applicatory Question

It is sometimes advisable to ask the members of a class questions which will enable them to apply for themselves the passage being studied. However, teachers should be careful to avoid monotony in this regard. They should seldom ask the general question, "How does this apply to you or to us?" They should attempt to use variety and to adapt this general question to the specific unit being taught. For example, in connection with a study of John 17, one may inquire, "What can we do to help answer Jesus's prayer?"[19]

l. The Correlative Question

Just as the preceding inquiry parallels that of application in methodical study, so this one coincides with correlation in methodical study. Its concern is to integrate the truths of various parts of the Scripture so that the outcome of inductive study is a Biblical theology which forms a basis for a Christian philosophy of life. For example, after the members of a group

---

[18] Illustrations of questions of evaluation were given in the section on "Evaluation and Application in Bible Study."

[19] A further discussion on application will follow later.

have studied the decalogue as it is set forth in Exodus 19–20, they may profitably be asked to consider the function and place of the law in the life of the believer in view of the statements of Jesus and Paul.

m. The Adjustment Question

This type of question is important because it helps to ensure that the leader of a group is teaching rather than merely speaking. It makes possible the interplay between the minds of the group and that of the teacher which is so indispensable to effective pedagogy. The question of adjustment may be asked in various ways. Here are two examples: "Do you have any questions on anything that has been said thus far? Is what I've said clear to you?" It is important to remember that it is possible so to employ such inquiries that the student does not feel free to take advantage of them. If they are to be beneficial, the teacher must give the members of the class enough time to reply and must also be willing to consider the questions which are raised. Hurriedly to ask a question of adjustment simply as a matter of form is more detrimental than beneficial.

D. Content and Form of Questions

The following should characterize the content and form of questions.

1. <u>Practicality</u>—They should make a real difference and should serve some useful purpose.

2. <u>Clarity</u>—They should be lucid and cogent.

3. <u>Brevity, Directness</u>—They should state the problem in the fewest possible words.

4. <u>Definiteness</u>—They should have a specific purpose and goal.

5. <u>Variety</u>—They should not always be stated in the same language, nor should they always be factual. There should be variation in both the terms employed and the kind of questions used.

6. <u>Suitableness</u>—They should befit the material being examined and the capacities of the students to whom they are asked.

7. <u>Adaptability</u>—They should be flexible enough so as to be capable of re-statement when the occasion arises.

8. <u>Stimulation</u>—They should not give away the answer but should, on the other hand, quicken thought and concentration on the part of the student.

9. <u>Sincerity</u>—They should not be so phrased as to attempt to fool the student. If they involve a "catch," the class should be warned beforehand.

10. <u>Inductivity</u>—They should be so stated as to direct the student to an examination of the particulars and to prevent him or her from becoming speculative, abstract, and deductive.

11. <u>Forcefulness</u>—They should be compelling and substantial.

12. <u>Imaginativeness</u>—They should capture the imagination of the student whenever possible. Stereotyped, prosaic questions should be avoided.

13. <u>Singleness</u>—They should approach the problem from one angle only.

14. <u>Relevancy</u>—Their content and formulation should be pertinent to the discussion.

15. <u>Suggestiveness</u>—They should indicate a line of thought which the student may profitably follow.

E. Order of Questions

It is of supreme importance that questioning be methodical if it is to be effective. There is a certain orderly arrangement of questions which, if violated, will result in disorder and confusion. Generally speaking, each question should form a link in a chain, attaching itself to what precedes and preparing for what follows. For example, a question of evaluation presupposes one of elucidation and in turn is the basis for a question of application. For to evaluate before one interprets or to apply before one evaluates is disastrous in questioning just as it is in study. It is therefore important to give careful consideration to the precise order of the questions in a particular lesson.

In planning questions, teachers should therefore think in terms of a series or sequence of queries rather than a list of questions. They should be certain that their questions are interrelated and that their interrelatedness is made real and clear by their order, contents, and form. It is often helpful to utilize transitions between questions to indicate their connections.

F. Manner of Asking Questions

Dr. H. H. Horne described the general attitude of the teacher toward the student when asking questions in the following words: "With great sympathy, with confidence in his ability to answer, with expectation that he will answer, with surprise when he does not answer, with interest in his answer, and with particular attention to his answer."[20]

Other principles and suggestions should be kept in mind by teachers as they ask questions. These will now be enumerated.

1. A question should initially be asked of the whole class instead of an individual member of the group. After the question has been stated, the teacher should then call upon the particular person whom he wants to answer. If the name of the individual is called first, the remainder of the class is invited to inattention and the person himself may be so frightened that he or she will not be able to concentrate on the question. For these same reasons, the leader should avoid following a predictable order.

---

[20] This statement, which is loaded with significance, may be found in the section on questioning in Dr. Horne's book entitled "Story-telling, Questioning, and Studying." The writer of this manual has found this section very helpful, as well as the material on pages 42–44 of another of Dr. Horne's books, "The Leadership of Bible Study Groups."

Chapter 1—*Method in Bible Teaching* 35

2. The teacher should sometimes ask for volunteers, and especially in connection with those questions which the members of the class were not asked to consider beforehand. The general suggestion is made because at times those who might otherwise be reluctant to speak will respond in regard to questions in which they are particularly interested. The main danger in this procedure is that certain students will tend to dominate the class. The more specific aspect of the suggestion is made in order to promote fairness, since it is hardly right to expect a particular person to answer a question for which he or she was not expected to prepare.

3. The leader should not ask thought questions and expect a reply before the students have time to think. Members of a group need time to reflect on questions, especially if the questions are profound or if there was no prior preparation for them. It is a fallacy for the teacher to consider a lull after the stating of an inquiry as something to be avoided at all costs. In fact, unless there is a legitimate period of silence after questions, the replies to them will probably be superficial. It is a good practice for the leader to think of the correct answer himself while the members of the group are formulating their replies.

4. Similarly, a person should not ask a number of inquiries because there is no immediate response to the first question or because he or she anticipates that there will be none. One question should be asked of the class. If after a reasonable pause there is no answer, then the teacher may employ one or more auxiliary or secondary questions whose purpose it is to lead the students to discover the meaning and intent of the original or primary question.

5. One should not habitually repeat questions, for to do so encourages inattention.

6. The leader should not give the impression that he or she is "fishing for an answer," but rather is encouraging students to think for themselves on the basis of the data which accessible to them. A question should not be asked in such a manner as to make the class member feel that he or she must be a mind-reader in order to answer it properly.

7. The teacher should not reveal anxiety in his or her questioning. They should be relaxed at all times if they expect the class to be at ease and do its best. Questioning should be, as much as possible, an enjoyable experience for all concerned.

8. If a question requires introductory remarks for its understanding, such remarks should generally precede rather than follow it. If lengthy explanatory statements are made after the question is stated, chances are that it will be forgotten. If in a particular case remarks are needed after a question is expressed, it is well to repeat the question.

G. Answers to Questions and Their Use

This aspect is closely related to the preceding one and involves both the preparation of the answers on the part of the leader as well as the use of the replies given by the class. We shall now set forth certain principles and recommendations which are concerned with both of these phases.

1. One should have a specific and correct reply to a question before one asks the question. In fact,

it is well to write out the answers beforehand and test their accuracy. It is profitable to write more than just a statement or two. One should elaborate the answer and try to make it <u>vivid</u>, <u>compelling</u>, and sometimes even <u>dramatic</u>. One may use imagery and illustrations when possible and necessary. Teachers should try writing answers of a page or two on each question, using as <u>forceful</u> and <u>clear</u> and <u>fresh</u> terminology as possible. They should attempt to make their replies so lucid that they will stimulate the mind and open up new vistas of thought and experience. One should by all means avoid prosaic, dry, stereotyped, matter-of-fact answers. In a word, teachers ought to discipline themselves to answer their own questions <u>fully</u> and <u>well</u>.

2. One should not insist on a certain formula in an answer and disregard those replies which do not employ a particular terminology. If teachers desire to use certain terms as a basis for organizing the lesson, let them contribute those terms themselves rather than expecting the answers of the students to embody them.

3. Find various ways and means of acknowledging answers courteously yet sincerely. Avoid employing repeatedly a certain expression after the answer to each question, such as "yes" or "all right."

4. One should not repeat verbatim the correct replies of members of the class. If necessary they may be re-phrased so as to contribute to their forcefulness and clarity, or they may be acknowledged and related to some other aspect of the lesson. In any case, if the reply is correct, it should be recognized as such.

5. Use as much as possible of the answer of the student. Do not ask a question and fail in some way to use the answer given by the individual.

6. In fact, if the reply is not all that it should be, or even if it is totally in error, the teacher should tactfully lead the person by further questions to explore more deeply or to find the correct answer. For the purpose of questions is not merely to elicit the proper reply, but to enable the individual to grow mentally and spiritually.

7. It follows that the leader should not be satisfied with trite, superficial, or insincere answers. One should by further inquiry lead students to elaborate, clarify, and illustrate their replies.

8. Answers to questions should be kept inductive at all times. They should be grounded on the particulars of the text. The teacher will find that students often need to be reminded of this fact. It is wise frequently to ask the individual for the concrete bases for his or her answer. For it is important not only that the correct reply be made, but also that the one answering and the entire class as well be aware of the specific foundation for his or her reply.

9. One should generally avoid answering one's own questions, since the class will soon learn that it pays not to respond. The teacher should be courteously persistent in his or her inquiry.

10. Once a question is asked, it is generally true that it should be pursued to its conclusion. Its answer should not be left indefinite or forgotten altogether.

H. Some "Do's" and "Don'ts" Regarding Questions and Answers

1. Do:

   a. be self-critical in the examination of your questioning procedure.

   b. develop your ability to ask questions by scrutinizing Jesus's use of questions in the Gospels as well as other Biblical questions, the Socratic questions in the Platonic dialogues, and the questions of outstanding Bible teachers.

   c. make your questions clear and understandable without making them leading.

   d. ask elucidative, heuristic, and value questions as well as the more objective factual ones in order to foster the student's ability to think deeply and evaluate properly; employ questions which will result in vertical knowledge as well as horizontal knowledge.

   e. use questions which will enable the student to see the unity of the Scriptures and of truth.

   f. be selective in your questions, filling in yourself where questions are not profitable, necessary, or efficient.

   g. be informal and spontaneous in your questioning, although you have planned carefully beforehand.

   h. practice stating questions in various ways in order to avoid monotony in the framing of questions.

   i. begin with the concrete and progress to the abstract in your questioning.

   j. conceive of yourself as Socrates conceived of himself, that is, as a mental obstetrician whose incessant questions and proddings delivered human minds and enabled them to give birth to valid ideas.[21]

   k. let your questions and answers penetrate words and symbols to the ideas and realities which they represent.

   l. ask the same questions which the author or character of the passage would ask if they were present.

   m. employ summary and synthetical questions as well as analytical ones.

   n. use questions which will develop an independence of the teacher's questions by training the student to ask himself questions.

---

[21] This image is found in Plato's dialogue entitled "The Theaetetus."

2. Don't:

   a. ask too many questions and thus inject confusion and monotony into the situation.

   b. let your questions be repetitious; give due regard to continuity.

   c. fail to utilize previous preparation when it has occurred, or plan on it when it is absent.

   d. assume too much in your questions or in the answers given.

   e. spend too great a period of time on one question.

   f. give the impression that you are the grand inquisitor or an official of the law putting the class through the third degree.

   g. lead the members of the group to think that they must please you rather than find the truth.

   h. let the students feel that their answers are always inaccurate or incomplete.

   i. be unfair in your questioning, expecting more than you have a right to expect.

   j. pretend you know the full answers to every question.

   k. use other people's questions unless they have become your own.

   l. ask questions which are not essential to the lesson.

   m. be doing something which makes impossible your being attentive when a student is answering a question.

   n. encourage hasty, vague, unanalytical answers.

   o. ask questions without being ready also to answer them.

   p. confuse saying a thing with conveying it.

   q. forget that true and profound Biblical knowledge is caught and self-taught rather than transmitted.[22]

I. Exercise on Questions and Answers

Consult the exercise on interpretation given in the section on methodical study. Consider the passages in connection with which you raised interpretative questions and framed interpretative answers. Select among those questions the ones which are strategic and which may be used to touch the units on which they are based. Analyze each question as to its source, general development, purpose, and specific kind. Re-phrase the questions and elaborate and clarify the answers if necessary. Plan lessons around these questions, keeping before you the principles and suggestions found in the preceding pages.

---

[22] Editors' Note: Prof. Traina had an endnote marker "10" here but there was no corresponding endnote 10.

Chapter 1—Method in Bible Teaching 39

V. ILLUSTRATIONS IN BIBLE TEACHING

A. The General and Specific Functions of Illustration
    1. General Function
    2. Specific Functions
        a. To Interpret or Clarify
        b. To Substantiate
        c. To Arouse and Hold Attention
        d. To Provide Relaxation for the Mind
        e. To Stir the Emotions and Will
        f. To Apply Truth
        g. To Aid the Memory

B. The Sources of Illustrations
    1. Observation of Life
    2. Imagination
    3. Science
    4. Great Teachers, Preachers, Thinkers, and Expositors
    5. Anecdotes, Proverbs, Fables, Stories, etc.
    6. History
    7. Great Literature and other Great Art
    8. Scriptures
    9. Current Events and Publications
    10. Anywhere

C. Principles and Practices in the Formulation and Use of Illustrations

D. Exercise on Illustrations

Footnotes [Note: These "endnotes" have been added as true footnotes in the material below.]

V. ILLUSTRATIONS IN BIBLE TEACHING[23]

A. The General and Specific Functions of Illustrations

1. General Function

Etymologically and broadly speaking, to "illustrate" means to cast light or luster upon a particular subject.

2. Specific Functions

In view of this general definition, the illustration in Scriptural teaching will have one or more of the following concrete purposes.

a. To Interpret or Clarify

This function may be accomplished in several ways. An example from experience may be given of the case in point, that is, a truth may be illustrated by exemplification. Paul's reference to Abraham in Romans 4 involves this type of illustration. Or, on the other hand, a truth may be explained by the use of <u>analogy</u>, whether based on real life or on something from the world of imagination. Jesus's parables are excellent samples of illustration by analogy.

b. To Substantiate

Both of the aforementioned means of explaining truth may also serve to support it. In fact, Paul's use of the example of Abraham to clarify the meaning of justification by faith also functions to uphold his thesis that justification is by faith alone. Analogy may also be employed to substantiate a Biblical statement, although one must be careful not to misuse it in this regard. This is especially true in connection with analogies of the nature of parables, fables, and allegories, since physical truth is never identical with spiritual truth. However, even this type of illustration has corroborative value, as Jesus Himself so forcefully demonstrated.[24]

c. To Arouse and Hold Attention

Every speaker or teacher has experienced how an audience or a class will sit up and take notice when an illustration begins. This is especially true when the discussion has been rather profound and there has been the tendency to lose interest. Thus, one of the primary and important functions of the illustration is to excite and maintain attention.

d. To Provide Relaxation for the Mind

Closely related to the preceding purpose is that of giving rest to the mind when it has been engaging in arduous thought. An illustration will often relax a class and thus prepare it for more work. This function might be conceived as including that of ornamentation as well, that is, the adding of a certain texture or color to the discussion.

---

[23] The writer is greatly indebted to Broadus's book "The Preparation and Delivery of Sermons" for the material in this section. This serves to emphasize the fact that the illustration of truth in Bible teaching is essentially the same as in other types of presentation. And what is true of illustrations is likewise true of some other aspects of teaching.

[24] See Luke 10 for a striking example of this.

Chapter 1—Method in Bible Teaching

e. To Stir the Emotions and Will

Jesus's parables afford an excellent demonstration of this particular aim of illustrations. There is no illustration which rouses the emotions as does the parable of the prodigal son, or none which excites the will as that of the good Samaritan. Illustrations may thus function very effectively to move people to action.

f. To Apply Truth

This goal may almost be combined with the preceding, except for the fact that it emphasizes the intellectual rather than the emotional or volitional. One of the best ways to demonstrate the precise ways in which a truth may be applied is to give an illustration of how others employed it. In this regard a good illustration becomes a good application and likewise, we may note that a good application may serve as a good illustration.

g. To Aid the Memory

Truths are often remembered by their illustrations. A good illustration is therefore a valuable help to the memory.

B. The Sources of Illustrations

1. Observation of life—nature, human experience, including that of children and especially religious experience, and one's own personal life.
2. Imagination—Plato's myths are striking examples of this source of illustrations. Such illustrations should be presented and utilized as imaginary and not as real occurrences.
3. Science—astronomy, geology, physics, zoology, etc.
4. Great teachers, preachers, thinkers, and expositors—In using these as sources, one should not only note the content of the illustration, but the precise way in which it was used.
5. Anecdotes, proverbs, parables, fables, stories, etc.
6. History, both religious and so-called secular.
7. Great literature and other great art, such as music and painting—poetry, novels, drama, biography, hymns, hymn stories, oratorios, pictures, etc.
8. Scriptures—They provide a good source for illustrations, although they are usually overworked in this regard.
9. Current events and publications.
10. Anywhere—wherever they appear or can be found, since the source of a good illustration is where you find it.

C. Principles and Practices in the Formulation and Use of Illustrations

1. The <u>main</u> point of the illustration should coincide with the essence of the truth being clarified. One should not depend on the incidentals of an illustration to provide the elucidation of the truth under consideration.

2. An illustration needs to be <u>adapted</u> to the particular situation in which it is being used. Frequently the same illustration cannot be expressed in identical words to explain different truths.

3. Seek for variety in illustrations both from the standpoint of their sources and their formulation.

4. Avoid controversial illustrations which will divert the interest of the hearers rather than direct it.

5. Avoid utilizing the fantastic to any great degree. Generally speaking, it is best to make illustrations practical and realistic, so as to give the impression that you are dealing with the hard realities of life and not with purely abstract concepts.

6. Illustrations should clarify rather than confuse a point. They should therefore not be used if the illustrations themselves need illustration or explanation.

7. Try testing your illustrations. Practice stating them to someone and then asking him or her to summarize their primary ideas in a sentence.

8. Use enough illustrations on the one hand, and yet be careful not to employ too many on the other. Avoid using no illustrations or making your lesson merely a series of illustrations. Remember that although illustrations are important, yet they are subordinate. They should therefore be included only when they make a specific and significant contribution to the ongoing development of the lesson. A story should never be told for its own sake.

9. Use the kind of illustration and the terminology which befit the group being taught. Appropriate your illustrations to the needs, interests, capacity, and experience of your class.

10. Let your illustrations be brief enough so that the attention of the class is not turned from the truth illustrated to the illustrations themselves. However, do not make them so concise that they do not serve their purpose or leave serious questions in the minds of the listeners.

11. Use illustrations which are relevant and, whenever necessary, make their relevancy abundantly clear. Watch closely the transition between the subject and the illustration and back to the subject again. It is often helpful to insert a summary sentence either before or after an illustration.

12. Let each illustration clarify only <u>one</u> point.

13. State the illustrations as clearly and pointedly as possible, eliminating all excess verbiage.

14. One's illustrations should engage the emotions, imagination, and will as well as the intellect. In a word, they should appeal to the whole person.

15. Keep human interest in illustrations. Avoid too much of the purely conceptual and the technical.

16. Change your tone of voice in illustrating truth. This will serve to relax the group and break the monotony of tone which frequently develops.

17. Be on the lookout for illustrations, and devise some means of filing them for future use.

D. Exercise on Illustrations

Formulate in full some illustrations on the passages utilized in the exercise on questions and answers in Bible teaching, keeping before you the principles and suggestions heretofore made. Analyze them as to their source and precise function.

Chapter 1—Method in Bible Teaching 43

VI. SUMMARY IN BIBLE TEACHING

VII. EVALUATION AND APPLICATION IN BIBLE TEACHING

A. Importance of Evaluation and Application

B. Place of Evaluation and Application

C. Purposes of Evaluation and Application

D. Kinds of Evaluation and Application
   1. The Direct Kind
   2. The Indirect Kind

E. Characteristics of Good Evaluation and Application
   1. Justifiable
   2. Personal
   3. Realistic, Practical
   4. Natural, Easy
   5. Compelling
   6. Constructive
   7. Specific, Definite
   8. Up-to-date, Relevant
   9. Suggestive
   10. Varied
   11. Integrated
   12. Inclusive

F. Exercise on Evaluation and Application

Footnotes [Note: These "endnotes" have been added as true footnotes in the material below.]

VI. SUMMARY IN BIBLE TEACHING

Each Bible lesson should move to a view of the whole, which should occur prior to the final evaluation and application. In fact, at times such an integration and summarization of the individual parts of the passage and lesson will constitute the conclusion or climax of the lesson, especially if such a procedure implicitly or explicitly includes the aspects of evaluation and application. At any rate, each teaching procedure should have near or as its conclusion a unification of the whole. This may be accomplished through the use of the summary question or by other means.

Such a summary should involve a clear and forceful integration of the lesson as-a-whole. The teacher should be careful to indicate lucidly how the various parts of the Biblical unit are gathered up in the summary. The summary should also be phrased cogently so as to provide either the preparation for the climactic application or the climax itself. Every lesson should progress to a peak or climax, and the final summarization serves an important function in regard to it.

Exercise: Prepare a lesson summary of one or more of the passages you have been utilizing.

VII. EVALUATION AND APPLICATION IN BIBLE TEACHING

A. The Importance of Evaluation and Application

The application of Biblical truth is that for which all else exists, whether it be in study or in teaching. Spurgeon once said, "Where application begins, there the sermon begins." This may be said also of Scriptural teaching. If this is true, then evaluation is important as well, since it is that which prepares for and makes possible valid application.

B. The Place of Evaluation and Application

There are two primary views as to the place of these aspects in the lesson proper. The <u>first</u> is that evaluation and application should occur only at the culmination of the lesson and thus form its climax and conclusion. Various reasons are given in support of this standpoint. It is said that only after thorough observation and interpretation are the clues prepared for the appraisal and application of a Biblical unit. And this is equivalent to saying that application must await the completion of the bulk of the lesson. Further, it is suggested that one main evaluation and application at the end of the lesson leaves one major impression on the mind of the listeners, which is pedagogically sound. The <u>second</u> view is that evaluation and application <u>may</u> occur during the process of the lesson as well as form the conclusion of the lesson. Those who share this opinion maintain that though it is true that judicial criticism and application must follow observation and interpretation, it should be remembered that the leader has already studied the whole, so that whatever he or she does in the way of evaluation and application may take that fact into account. Further, there may be a final integrating evaluation and application at the conclusion which summarizes all the others and thus leaves the listeners with one primary idea. In addition, there is the fact that value-judgments and applications cannot always be avoided during the lesson. As we have already noted, a good illustration will frequently involve the employment of Biblical truth, and applications are sometimes needed to clarify the statements of a passage. Students will in certain cases suggest appraisals and applications. Moreover, it is best to assess the worth of certain parts and apply them while they are fresh in mind rather than wait until the conclusion of the lesson. In view of these arguments, it seems to the writer that the second view is more valid and practical than the first, although it is true that evaluation and application should <u>primarily</u> occur at the end of the teaching procedure and that, when it does, it should function as the climax of the lesson. The remainder of the discussion is therefore founded on this particular view.

C. The Purposes of Evaluation and Application

1. To discover the validity and relevance of Scriptural statements and subsequently to discover how they may be employed in life. This involves the <u>theoretical</u> application of truth.

2. To provide <u>practical</u> and <u>concrete</u> suggestions which will enable the class to put into action that which it has learned.

3. To <u>motivate</u> and <u>persuade</u> the listeners to action. Thus, application should appeal to the emotions and the will as well as to the intellect. This function may be realized in several ways, one of which is the hortatory approach, used so effectively by Paul in his epistles.

4. To comfort as well as to instruct and stimulate. Applications should not always "harp" on weaknesses; they should, when legitimate, indicate to the listener the great value of that which he or she possesses.

D. Kinds of Evaluation and Application

1. The Direct Kind

This type appraises and applies Scriptural statements in a straightforward manner. It involves saying, in effect, "This is how this passage is relevant to your experience and may be employed in it. "The book of Jude is a forceful example of such a procedure.

2. The Indirect Kind

This involves evaluation and application by example or by analogy. It is, in fact, appraisal and application by illustration. Nathan's approach to David (2 Samuel 12) was primarily of this type, although he made it direct by the statement "Thou art the man."

E. Characteristics of Good Evaluation and Application

1. <u>Justifiable</u>—This needs no further explanation, since it was discussed in the section on "Evaluation and Application" in methodical Bible study.

2. <u>Personal</u>—They should make a concrete difference to each individual, even if they be concerned with the truths which have national and universal significance. Each person should leave the lesson with something specific which he or she can and should do as a result of it. The common practice of evaluating and applying Biblical statements for the absent party, such as the so-called "Modernist," should be diligently avoided.

3. <u>Realistic, Practical</u>—They should be grounded on the hard facts of existence, and not consist of the stuff dreams are made of. For those who in appraising and applying Scriptural truth overlook actual problems and difficulties and pretend that the whole matter is very simple will not be effective in their teaching.

4. <u>Natural, Easy</u>—They should not be forced, extraneous or superimposed on the passage. They should be the logical outgrowth of the statements themselves. It is helpful to make a smooth and clear transition between interpretation and evaluation and application.

5. <u>Compelling</u>—Evaluation and application should be of such a nature and so expressed as to move people to action.

6. <u>Constructive</u>—The aim should be the upbuilding of the listeners rather than their tearing down.

7. <u>Specific, Definite</u>—The members of the group should know exactly where they stand in relation to the truths of a Biblical unit.

8. <u>Up-to-date, Relevant</u>—They should be pertinent to the very day on which the lesson is being taught.

9. <u>Suggestive</u>—Certain concrete lines of action should be indicated which may be followed by the listeners.

10. <u>Varied</u>—Both direct and indirect approaches should be used. Further, there should be variety as to the spheres with which the evaluations and applications are concerned, that is, they should be addressed not only to one's personal life, but to the individual as a member of a local church and community, or a nation and a denomination, and of the universal Church and the world.

11. <u>Integrated</u>—If evaluations and applications are made during the process of the lesson, they should all have a common goal and purpose; they should contribute to the main stream of the lesson.

12. <u>Inclusive</u>—Leaders should include themselves in their evaluations and applications. Further, he or she should direct remarks to the entire class and not to a few individuals in it.[25]

Exercise on Evaluation and Application: Consider the passages which were evaluated and applied in the section on study. Think in terms of appraising and applying these units in and for a <u>concrete</u> class situation. What determinant factors must be given careful thought? Formulate fully your applications. Analyze them from the standpoint of their place in the lesson, their purposes, and their kinds. Attempt to determine whether they exemplify the characteristics of good evaluation and application set forth in the preceding discussion.

---

[25] It may be noted that this section is primarily concerned with application rather than evaluation, since evaluation exists for the purpose of application.

VIII. INTRODUCTIONS IN BIBLE TEACHING

A. Functions and Kinds of Introductions
    1. General Function
    2. Specific Functions and Kinds
        a. Atmospheric Introduction
        b. Problematical or Applicatory Introduction
        c. Historical Introduction
        d. Contextual Introduction
        e. Explanatory or Procedural Introduction
        f. Thematic Introduction
        g. Review or Re-examinational Introduction

B. Qualities of Effective Introductions

C. Exercise on Introductions

VIII. INTRODUCTIONS IN BIBLE TEACHING

The reader may wonder why the matter of introductions is treated in this place rather than at the outset of the section on teaching. The reason is that the introduction should be one of the last phases of the lesson to be prepared if the procedure is to be methodical; for a good introduction presupposes a knowledge of the contents and direction of the lesson as-a-whole, just as building a good porch on a house presupposes a knowledge of the nature of the building proper.

A. Functions and Kinds of Introductions

1. General Function

   All introductions, no matter what their particular purposes may be, should serve to interest the hearers in that which will follow. This fact should be uppermost in the mind of the teacher as he or she prepares the introduction. For, if the attention of the group is not engaged at the very outset of the lesson, it may be permanently lost. It is therefore of supreme importance that the introduction be so designed as to capture the interest of the class.

2. Specific Functions and Kinds

   Besides this general function, an introduction may involve one or more particular purposes. As a means of indicating what these may be, we shall now list the main types of introductions. It should be noted that these types of introductions are not mutually exclusive; therefore, two or more of them may actually be combined at times. However, since it is usually true that one particular function dominates over the others, the following names may be validly employed to classify introductions.

   a. <u>Atmospheric Introduction</u>—This type has as its function the creating of the atmosphere of the lesson by re-creating the spirit and mood of the passage.

   b. <u>Problematical or Applicatory Introduction</u>—The problematical or applicatory introduction attempts to set forth the problem with which the lesson and unit of Scripture will be concerned and to which they will apply. It therefore not only focusses the attention of the group upon a particular issue, but it also serves to indicate the relevance of the lesson.

   At times the problematical introduction may be expanded in order to utilize the <u>problem approach</u> to a Scriptural unit. In such instances, a <u>substantial</u> part of the class period is used to discuss the exact nature and ramifications of a particular problem in order to whet the appetite and provide insight into the solution which is found in the passage being studied.

   c. <u>Historical Introduction</u>—It is often needful and helpful to depict the historical background of a portion of Scripture in order to make its study more meaningful. The source for such a background may either be Biblical or extra-Biblical.

   d. <u>Contextual Introduction</u>—The purpose of this kind of introduction is to set forth the context of the passage being studied in such cases where an awareness of the context is essential to the understanding of the passage.

e. <u>Explanatory or Procedural Introduction</u>—This serves to elucidate the main steps of the lesson by suggesting what they will be, together with their grounds and purposes. It thus interprets the procedure which is to be followed in order to enhance the comprehension of its aim and integrality.

f. <u>Thematic Introduction</u>—It is sometimes beneficial to begin a lesson by presenting its major theme. One should be cautious, however, not to make habitual use of this type of introduction, since it tends to make the lesson deductive rather than inductive.

g. <u>Review or Re-examinational Introduction</u>—The review or re- examinational introduction is used in connection with a lesson in a series of lessons. Its purpose is either to go back over what has been done in order to re-learn it and to prepare for what follows, or to reconsider from a different point of view that which has already been treated us a means of introducing a particular lesson.

There are other kinds of introductions, but these are the major types. The teacher should attempt to classify his or her introductions in terms of these and related categories in order to be aware of their specific function or functions. For it is important that the teacher know the precise purpose of the introductions he or she employs.

B. Qualities of Effective Introductions
   1. They are <u>preparatory</u> in regard to the lesson and do not detract substantially from it.
   2. They are simple, involving one idea preferably. It is best, generally speaking, not to use heavy or involved introductions.
   3. They are concise and yet not too concise, since too abrupt an introduction fails to prepare the class psychologically for the lesson.
   4. They are connected with the body of the lesson by a clear, smooth, and legitimate transition, since the transition often makes or breaks the introduction.
   5. They are relevant to the lesson and their relevancy is apparent to the class.
   6. They do not raise any serious barriers which may hinder the progress of the lesson.
   7. They contain nothing which is foreign to the body of the lesson.
   8. They establish a point of contact between teacher and listeners.
   9. They are specific rather than vaguely general.
   10. They introduce the whole lesson instead of the first part of it, and thus may be utilized and capitalized upon throughout the procedure.
   11. They have variety as to type and phraseology.
   12. They are suited to the nature of the passage and the nature of the class. They are accommodated to the lesson, just as a porch is accommodated to the house, and not vice versa.

C. Exercise on Introductions: Prepare introductions to several of the passages which you have been using in the preceding exercises on methodical teaching. Attempt to formulate two or three kinds of introductions to each Biblical unit, employing the principles heretofore set forth. Write them out in full. Analyze each as to its specific function and type.

IX. BLACKBOARD WORK IN BIBLE TEACHING
    A. General and Specific Functions of Blackboard Work
    B. Some Types of Blackboard Work
    C. Principles and Suggestions for Blackboard Work
    D. Exercise on Blackboard Work

X. EXERCISES IN BIBLE TEACHING
    A. Definition of "Exercises"
    B. Purposes of Exercises
    C. Structure of Exercises
    D. Miscellaneous Principles and Suggestions for the Formulation and Use of Exercises
    E. Exercise on Exercises

XI. (ILLUSTRATIONS OF METHOD IN BIBLE TEACHING)

Chapter 1—Method in Bible Teaching 51

IX. BLACKBOARD WORK IN BIBLE TEACHING

A. General and Specific Functions of Blackboard Work

    1. Utilizes the eye-gate in teaching.

    2. Helps to provide a unified, overall impression of the whole.

    3. Gives students time to take notes.

    4. Indicates what the teacher deems to be most important.

    5. Provides the basis for talking about the various parts of a passage, especially from the standpoint of their relations to one another, since connections are very often seen with a force that cannot be duplicated by the mere use of words.

    6. Demonstrates the way in which visual aids may be used in study.

    7. Facilitates the student's ability to follow the progress of the lesson.

B. Some Types of Blackboard Work

    1. Charts or diagrams.

    2. Outlines.

    3. Listings.

    4. Pictures and object lessons.

    5. Informational notes, such as the spelling of words, references, etc.

    6. Maps.

C. Principles and Suggestions for Blackboard Work

    1. What is written on the board should be legible from any part of the room. This is a difficult suggestion to carry out and yet it should be followed as closely as possible.

    2. Blackboard work should leave an integrated, overall impression. It should clarify rather than confuse the structure of the lesson.

    3. It should represent and reflect the lesson by stressing the same idea or ideas as the lesson as-a-whole.

    4. It should be planned beforehand, but should be flexible and adaptable as the need arises. There is little chance that blackboard work which results from an experimental or laboratory approach will be neat, precise, and completely in accordance with a predetermined plan.

    5. It should show the major relationships between parts and provide the student with perspective.

    6. It should reveal definite organization.

7. It should neither include too much nor too little.

8. It should be self-explanatory as much as possible.

9. Generally speaking, blackboard work should not be placed on the board before the class begins, since it distracts the attention of the group. Members of the class will often read or copy what is there while the teacher is presenting his or her introduction. Further, to write things on the board beforehand tends to make the procedure deductive rather than inductive, formal rather than informal.

10. It should represent a combination of the work and thought of the teacher and the members of the study group.

D. Exercise on Blackboard Work

Plan the blackboard work on some of the units you have been treating, utilizing the principles and suggestions in the preceding pages.

X. EXERCISES IN BIBLE TEACHING

A. Definition of "Exercise"

This phase of Bible teaching has commonly been called "assignments." However, such a name does not accurately describe their underlying purpose and most significant function. For an "assignment," according to Webster, is "a duty or piece of work allotted as the responsibility of a particular person or group." The emphasis is therefore on the obligation laid upon the student because the leader has authoritatively commanded that the work be done. On the other hand, Webster defines "exercise" as "exertion for the sake of training and improvement, whether physical, intellectual, or moral." This comes much closer to the outstanding intent of the phase being discussed, since the stress is upon the benefits and values which may derive from it rather than the responsibility which is attached to it because of external authority. In a word, its compulsion is inward rather than outward; it is not of the law, but of grace. In view of these facts, then, we shall utilize the term "exercise" rather than "assignment."

B. Purposes of Exercises

The outstanding aim of exercises has already been discussed in a measure in the preceding paragraph. However, it will be beneficial both to elaborate this function and to suggest another. Exercises have two primary purposes.

1. They are the means of training and developing the student in regard to knowledge, skills, insight, and independence.

2. They prepare the student for more effective participation in the class procedure and for a greater understanding of what occurs therein.

The <u>first</u> of these is undoubtedly the most significant of the functions of exercises. In fact, so important is it that the writer has made this startling statement to his classes, namely, that if he were forced to choose between their attending the formal session or doing the exercises outside of class, he would without hesitation choose the latter.

The key term in the description of this purpose is "<u>independence</u>." Exercises should intend to train the student to swim for himself or herself so that, when the life belt is removed, he or she will not drown. This implies that exercises should not be so formulated that students are told everything that they must do, but should rather be framed so as to provide them with an opportunity to utilize their own initiative. To change the image, exercises should not serve as crutches, but rather as guides within which there is room for personal expression.

In order to realize this purpose, exercises should involve primarily and first of all the first-hand study of the vernacular. This does not mean that there will be no place for the examination of secondary sources. But the initial approach should involve the first-hand examination of the Scriptures if an independent Bible student is to be developed.

The <u>second</u> and secondary function of exercises is to prepare the member of the class for intelligent participation in and an understanding appreciation of that which is done in the formal session. In regard to this purpose, there are two kinds or exercises: a. the supplementary exercise, and b. the parallel or identical exercise. The <u>former</u> serves to supplement that which is to occur in the class period. It takes a different approach from that to be followed in the formal session, and yet it complements that which occurs there. The <u>latter</u> type involves the exercise which contains the exact questions which will be used in class, the assumption being that because of the aggregate mind of the students and the contribution of the teacher the formal session will not be a mere repetition of individual study but will rather transcend it. Both of these types are valid and which of them is used in a particular instance will depend on the nature of the class and the subject matter being discussed.

C. Structure of Exercises

Exercises may be classified into two main categories in terms or their structure. The <u>first</u> is the purely progressive type, each question or suggestion involving a distinct and further step in the process. All of the individual questions are progressively numbered and none of them is grouped together. The <u>second</u> kind, though progressive, is concentric and topical as well. It includes both general and subordinate specific questions, as well as questions which are repetitious in that they express the same thing in different words or approach the same problem from various angles. In this instance certain suggestions are grouped together, such as those which are virtually synonymous.

The first of these is simpler to follow, but the second utilizes certain pedagogical principles which may enable the exercise better to accomplish its purpose. For as we have already stated, truth has so many phases and the finite mind is so limited in its ability to grasp and penetrate them that whatever can be used to assist it should by all means be employed. One inevitably finds that others seldom catch the full significance and force of the suggestions one makes. It therefore seems salutary to approach the subject from various standpoints and to state things in different ways so us to goad and stimulate the mind in order that it may function incisively.

D. Miscellaneous Principles and Suggestions for the Formulation and Use of Exercises

1. There are two dangers in the formulation of exercises: a. the lack of clarity, and b. the lack of questions which require insight and develop independence. One should attempt to avoid both of these swamps. The suggestions should be expressed as lucidly as possible, and yet they should include both heuristic and value questions whose answers do not depend on merely reading and copying the words of the text.

2. The nature of the passage being studied should determine the general structure of the exercise. If the passage is so constructed that it should be approached interpretatively, the exercise should be interpretative; if the passage is so arranged that it should be approached structurally, the exercise should be structural. For the specific factors involved here, consult the section on "Lesson Structure and Development."

3. Exercises should be suited to the capacities of their participants. A six-year-old child is not given a two-hundred-pound weight in order to develop his or her physic.

4. Exercises should always include summary questions.

5. They should be characterized by definite development and progress, and the connections between the successive suggestions should be made as clear as possible. their major units should stand out, if such there be.

6. General questions should be utilized in order to train the student to become independent.

7. The exercise should be prepared after the passage has been thoroughly studied and after the lesson has been planned, and both of these factors should be taken into account in its formulation.

8. Self-reflection is helpful in the framing of exercises. It is often beneficial to retrospect regarding the particular steps one followed in study and to pattern the exercise after those procedures. Of course, such a practice is not always wise and should be followed with discretion. However, it is based on a valid principle, namely, that minds are basically similar and that they function in much the same way.

9. All unnecessary questions should be deleted from the exercise in order to conserve time and avoid confusion.

10. Let your exercises be varied and imaginative.

11. Exercises should at one time or another include all four aspects of methodical study, namely, observation, interpretation, evaluation and application, and correlation. Of course, all of these do not need to be injected into every exercise.

Chapter 1—Method in Bible Teaching 55

12. It is often helpful to accompany the giving of exercises with explanatory remarks and suggestions as to which questions are most significant, how much time should be spent on each, and the reasons and purposes of the questions. The last of these is especially important, since to know the "why" of things enhances an intelligent doing of them.

13. Exercises should be used whenever possible, even in lay situations. Laymen need to be developed and trained as well as professional workers, and one is surprised how much they too are willing to "exercise" if they are motivated in the proper way.

14. Exercises may be of two types as to the completeness with which they should be done. The first may be called the <u>exhaustive</u> kind, which is meant to be carried out fully. The second is the <u>suggestive</u> type, which indicates lines of study which may be partially completed for a particular class period, but whose possibilities may be altogether beyond realization. Most exercises are of the latter kind, and students ought to be made aware of that fact.

15. In the class period the teacher should capitalize as much as possible on the exercise given to the students. It is well frequently to call attention to the meaning and signification of its suggestions.

16. The superficial and hasty doing of exercises should be discouraged. The essential need for concentration and meditation should be stressed. Students should be urged to put Biblical statements into their own words and elaborate them. In fact, it would be helpful for the teacher to demonstrate the potentialities of certain suggestions as well as the concrete means of following them.

    It should be noted that many of the suggestions made in the discussion on "The Formulation and Use of Questions and Answers," although applicable in this connection were not repeated. The reader is urged to discover wherein this holds true.

E. Exercise on Exercises

Formulate exercises in connection with the Scriptural units you have been utilizing in the preceding projects. Be guided both in your formulation and in your analysis by the principles and suggestions given in the discussion.

XI. (ILLUSTRATIONS ON METHOD IN BIBLE TEACHING)

Again, the parentheses indicate a vision rather than an actuality. The writer anticipates that at some future time he will be able to take the same passages employed in the proposed illustrations at the close of the section on methodical study and demonstrate how lesson plans may be prepared for teaching them.

CONCLUSION

The reader has probably deduced by this time that one cannot learn methodicalness in Bible study and teaching by merely reading the preceding discussion on the subject. This is true not only because of the limitations of this treatment, among them that of brevity, but primarily because of the nature of the subject itself. Methodicalness cannot be taught like geometric theorems or algebraic formulas. The purpose of this manual has therefore been to indicate certain basic principles and concrete procedures whose personal evaluation and adaptation and thoughtful and persistent application will enable the reader to develop methodicalness in study and teaching. This presentation, then, has been merely <u>suggestive</u>. It has set forth <u>some means</u> by which one may teach oneself to become orderly and logical, <u>For, in the last analysis, methodicalness must be self-taught if it is to be realized</u>. If, then, the preceding pages have motivated the reader to think seriously about methodicalness in Bible study and teaching, they have accomplished their purpose.

The writer is acutely aware of the inadequacy of this manual in view of the subjects it purports to treat. Further, he knows that it will need constant revision. However, in spite of its limitations, it is hoped that it will contribute to the accomplishment of the worthwhile goals of effective Bible study and teaching.

Robert A. Traina as a Teacher:
His Contribution to the Teaching of Inductive Bible Study

David R. Bauer
Dean of the School of Biblical Interpretation, Asbury Theological Seminary
Ralph Waldo Beeson Professor of Inductive Biblical Studies

1. Introduction

It is an immense privilege to offer these reflections on the teaching of Dr. Robert A. Traina as part of his memorial *Festschrift*. But it was an even greater privilege to sit under this masterful teacher in seven courses at Asbury Theological Seminary. And I am not alone in my appreciation for this remarkable opportunity. Eugene H. Peterson, one of Dr. Traina's students at The Biblical Seminary in New York, has written:

> A few days after arriving at the Seminary, I found myself sitting in a classroom led by a professor, Robert Traina, who over the next three years would profoundly change the Bible for me, and me along with it, in ways that gave shape to everything I have been doing for the rest of my life. This is not an exaggeration.... It took only three or four weeks in Professor Traina's classroom to become aware of the seismic change beginning to take place in me regarding the Bible.... The experience was not merely academic. The passion and patience that permeated that classroom instilled in me an inductive imagination: fiercely attentive to everything that is there and only what is there, alert to relationships both literary and personal, habitually aware of context—the entire world of creation and salvation that is being revealed in the Bible. And always accompanied by the insistence that I do it firsthand, not first filtered through the hearsay of others or the findings of experts.[1]

Yet my purpose is not to praise Dr. Traina or bestow adulation on him as a teacher, but rather to identify and analyze some of the chief aspects of his teaching, with a view toward our learning from his prowess. In this way he will continue in some sense to teach; and that opportunity for ongoing instruction would please him greatly.

---

[1] Eugene H. Peterson, *The Pastor: A Memoir* (New York: HarperCollins, 2011), 84–85.

2. The Human Factor

The instructional performance of all teachers is in large measure a reflection of the persons themselves. Their teaching is an expression of their deepest selves. Great teachers are great souls who think deeply. And I can testify that this principle certainly applied in the case of Dr. Traina. I am humbled to say that I knew Dr. Traina extremely well, having studied under him both inside and outside the classroom, having worked for him as his student assistant, having served with him as a colleague on the faculty of Asbury Theological Seminary, having traveled with him, and having co-authored with him an extensive book on inductive hermeneutics.

At the center of Dr. Traina's life was a vibrant and thoughtful relationship with the God and Father of Jesus Christ. And Dr. Traina considered God to be above all else both loving and truthful. Because his God was loving, Dr. Traina related to all persons, and especially his students, with respect and care. He had an authentic regard (albeit a realistic one) for the abilities and perspectives of his students, and consequently believed that they had insights to offer that were beneficial not only to fellow students but also to him; he was truly interested in hearing what students had to say. And he always made time for his students. For him teaching was not confined to the periods when the class was scheduled. Indeed, he always made himself available after class and would often remain in the classroom for long periods discussing various matters with students. I will cite one incident that illustrates this point. I remember that during my first year of teaching at the seminary I was working in my office late one Friday afternoon when Dr. Traina's wife, Jane, called me, asking if I know where Bob was. He had not returned home, and because it was after 6:00 she was concerned, especially since his class had ended at 3:00. When I went to the classroom I found him energetically discussing exegetical and theological issues with a student, which he had been doing for three hours. Indeed, he would often schedule extra discussion sessions, inviting students to bring any questions or issues they wanted to explore. Although usually no more than four or five students would attend, he would make himself thus available.

In spite of his great and inquiring intellect, he would always deal with the most elementary student comments or questions with consummate patience. In fact, he would treat students with the same respect he showed the President of the Seminary. This attitude of love was not only a spiritual quality, it was also a powerful mode of teaching; for he was incarnating relationally the chief attribute of the God of the Bible. He was teaching the Scriptures through his life in a most profoundly formative way.

But for Dr. Traina, God was also the Lord of truth. And consequently, Dr. Traina deeply valued truth. In fact, his entire professional life was the pursuit and promotion of truth. It was this passion for truth that led him to embrace enthusiastically the inductive approach, which he considered to be the courageous and honest pursuit of what is true. For Dr. Traina, induction was not essentially a method for studying the Bible, it was an epistemology that guided his whole life. He was basically an evidentialist; he had a commitment to examine the evidence and to follow that evidence to whatever conclusion it led, and then to embrace that conclusion, no matter how uncomfortable or risky it might be.

Accordingly, in terms of religious epistemology, Dr. Traina appreciated the role of reason and was adamantly opposed to all forms of fideism, i.e., the notion that knowledge depends on faith. He thus took exception to Anselm's dictum, "faith seeking understanding." To be clear, Dr. Traina was equally opposed to rationalism, i.e., the notion that reason is the ultimate reality and is sufficient for all knowledge. It was for him not a matter of faith being irrelevant for understanding; rather, he adopted Calvin's notion of religious truth as supra-rational. According to this view, the truth of God accords with the legitimate and best operations of reason, yet one cannot reach the truth of God by reason alone, for reason can take one only so far. Reason points to faith, but faith must take over where reason leaves off. In short, Dr. Traina adopted the path of a "reasonable faith." As far as Dr. Traina was concerned, the Holy Spirit is involved in this entire process; for the operation of the Spirit is necessary for reason, which is marred by sin, to function well, and this is especially true in terms of understanding the revelation of God. And, of course, the ability to believe comes ultimately from the Holy Spirit.

These basic philosophical convictions were the foundation for Dr. Traina's commitment to the teaching of inductive Bible study. For him, inductive Bible study was not primarily a method for reading and understanding the Bible; rather, it was basically an attitude towards the Bible that involved a radical openness to the evidence in and surrounding the biblical text, and a willingness to allow that evidence to determine our conclusions. For those persons who, like Dr. Traina, accepted the supreme authority of the Bible (and he readily acknowledged that by no means did everyone fall within this camp), this meant a theology, and indeed an entire world-view, that was deeply and broadly shaped by the Scriptures.

Yet Dr. Traina was a pragmatist and a realist. He knew that an "inductive attitude," though necessary and foundational, was in itself insufficient, and that it must lead to an inductive practice, or method. In other words, a commitment to ascertaining the true meaning of the Scriptures must be expressed in a process of scriptural study that is intentional in allowing the Bible to speak on its own terms. Some practices, or sets of practices, obstruct the hearing of the text on its own terms, while others make possible and promote such a hearing. And if this process is to be inductive, it must accord with the very character of the object of study, the Bible itself. But it must also attend to the realities of the other major factor in Bible study, viz., the student. And if these two realities—the biblical text and the student who reads it—determine the shape of inductive Bible study they must also determine the character of the teaching of inductive Bible study. I shall return to this point shortly.

3. The Practice of Teaching

This description of the personal and intellectual framework of Dr. Traina's life leads to the discussion of his performance of teaching. But I must mention here at the outset that Dr. Traina's ultimate concern was not with his own teaching, but rather with the students' learning. For him, teaching was not the end, but rather the means to facilitate learning on the part of his students. This model of education implies that the students are active participants, not passive hearers, in the instructional process, and that the classroom experience is characterized by significant interaction.

Dr. Traina's concern for the educational process, with an emphasis upon student learning, is actually a legacy of the inductive Bible study movement and The Biblical Seminary in New York. From the very beginning, the advocates of inductive Bible study were deeply interested in pedagogy. Indeed, the original name of The Biblical Seminary was "The Bible Teachers College;" and throughout the years the school had a close relationship with the College of Education at New York University, and particularly with Herman Harrell Horne, who was the Distinguished Professor of Education at that university. Inductive Bible study necessarily involves inductive Bible learning.

Dr. Traina embraced the emphasis on instruction that was so much a part of the ethos of The Biblical Seminary. Yet, true to his nature, he was not content simply to continue the kind of teaching to which he had been exposed, but instead engaged in his own serious reflection on both the theory and practice of the teaching of the Bible. In the process, he perceived that such teaching revolves around the subject of instruction, i.e., the Bible, and the student, and that effective teaching must take the character of each of these realities seriously into account.

As he considered these two realities at the center of the learning process Dr. Traina came to appreciate, above all, the comprehensiveness of the subject (the Bible) and the complexity of the student learner. These considerations led to a teaching practice that was holistic and balanced.

I begin with the complexity of student learning. Dr. Traina's teachers at The Biblical Seminary had insisted that learning required that students bring their own abilities, knowledge, and powers of observation to the table and that the role of the teacher was to encourage and celebrate student insights into the Scriptures. Dr. Traina affirmed this perspective, but realized that students were characterized not only by insight but also by a measure of ignorance, not only by understanding but also by some confusion; otherwise, they would have no need of the course at all. Thus, Dr. Traina fostered a blended class experience, which involved both the professor's presentation in which he discussed and modeled competent treatment of the text, and student participation. I use the term "blended" deliberately, for Dr. Traina seamlessly wove together these two aspects of instruction.

Similarly, Dr. Traina insisted that students engage in their own independent study of the text through assignments, or (as he preferred to call them) exercises, with the view toward bringing their insights and findings to class where they could share their work and also compare what they had found with what the professor and other students had to say regarding the passage. This dynamic combination of individual study and corporate conversation and exposure proved to be extremely effective.

Furthermore, Dr. Traina realized that various students had different learning styles, or learning preferences, and therefore effective teaching must take a multiplicity of forms. I mentioned immediately above a combination of independent study outside of class and class debriefing and conversation. But, in addition, Dr. Traina recognized that the class should not be an exclusively auditory experience, characterized only by speech, whether from the professor or among the students, but that it should include also the visual aspect; Dr. Traina referred to this variety as "ear-gate" and "eye-gate." And he was a master of diagramming or charting on the blackboard (and later the whiteboard). In fact, his work on the blackboard was artistically similar to a charcoal artist. At the beginning of the class he would write at the edge or bottom of the board, and I would wonder why he

Chapter 2—Robert A. Traina as Teacher

didn't place it right in the center; but as the class proceeded he would progressively add to the blackboard, so that by the end of the class he had produced a beautiful and (even more importantly) illuminating mosaic.[2] Diagram 2.1 below is one simple example of Dr. Traina's "blackboard art."

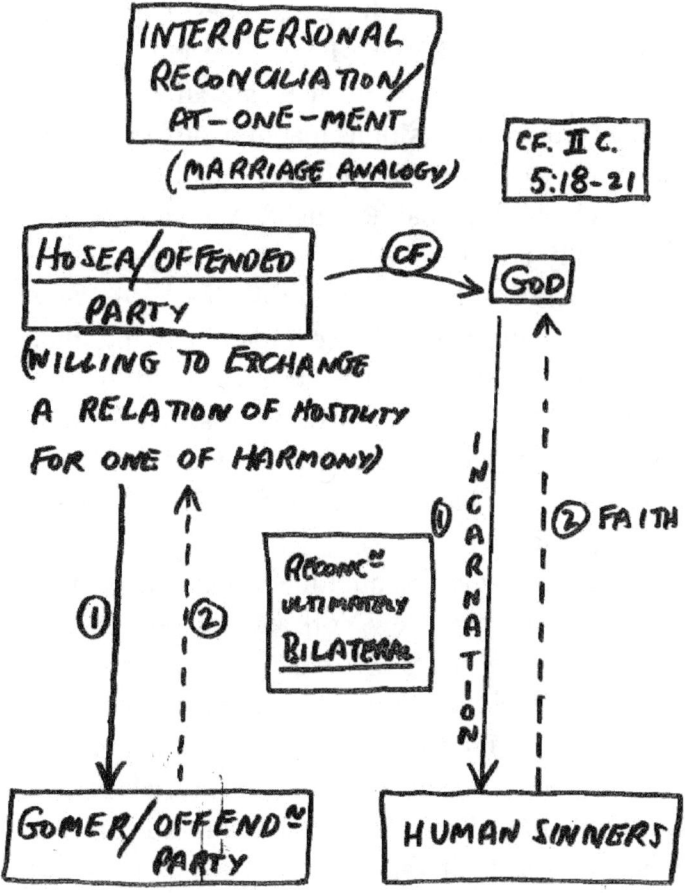

Diagram 2.1—Dr. Traina's "Blackboard Art"

Moreover, Dr. Traina realized that insofar as an inductive approach necessarily involves the movement from evidence to (interpretive) inferences, or conclusions, students must become skilled both in the observation of the text, since such observations constitute evidence,[3] and in the process of inferential reasoning, which is the logical process of drawing conclusions from evidence. Practically his entire instructional project focused on the development of these two skills. He would often invest class time in interacting with students over their observations and over their lines of reasoning from evidence to inferences, being careful to provide both encouragement and correction.

---

[2] It is telling that his book, *Methodical Bible Study*, contains an appendix on "Charts." See Traina, *Methodical Bible Study: A New Approach to Hermeneutics* (New York: Ganis & Harris, 1952), 235–43.

[3] I shall point out below that evidence is not limited to what is found within the text but includes also such matters as historical background that the student typically encounters in secondary literature. Nevertheless, observations from the text itself form the primary source of evidence, and indeed, the data from the text determine the significance of historical considerations.

In addition, Dr. Traina pressed the point (which I mentioned above) that the learning of inductive Bible study requires that students both adopt a commitment to allow the evidence in and surrounding the biblical text to determine conclusions and become skilled in a method that operationalizes such a fair interpretation of the text. Student learning thus involved both attitude and process. A general impression exists that Dr. Traina's teaching was all about process, or method. But, in fact, he was at least as concerned to inculcate an inductive attitude according to which students identified and shelved presuppositions that may distort interpretation. Indeed, he was quite concerned that students might carelessly or unknowingly allow presuppositions to creep in and thus undermine the purpose of the process that he taught. And consequently, he would frequently have students interpret theologically controversial or difficult passages and would help them to see how their theological prejudices, and not the evidence of the text, often determined their interpretation.

But Dr. Traina was not only aware of the complexity of the student learner, and of the student learning process, but he grasped also the comprehensiveness of biblical study. Specifically, he was convinced that the Bible is literary in terms of its essence, historical in terms of its context, theological in terms of its purpose, and Christological in terms of its focus; and he believed that all four of these aspects are profoundly interconnected. Therefore, he was careful to address all of these components in the learning process.

Dr. Traina's affirmation of the essential literary character of the Bible was in line with the perspective of The Biblical Seminary in New York and the inductive Bible study movement, and led to his emphasis upon *the literary study of the Bible by books*, since the book is the basic literary unit of the Bible. He insisted that the student must be intentional and specific in interpreting every passage in light of its function within the book of which it is a part. The Bible's literary character led him also to focus upon the *literary form* of the text, which of course involves both genre and literary and grammatical structure. Dr. Traina attended to all three of these matters,[4] although he gave much more attention in class to literary structure than to genre or to grammatical structure, out of the conviction that, in most cases, literary structure was relatively more significant for interpretation.[5] I should mention that he always related structure to content and attempted to draw

---

[4] Dr. Traina's attention to grammatical issues was something of an innovation in the teaching of inductive Bible study at The Biblical Seminary, where grammatical analysis was not typically part of the instruction in inductive Bible study but was relegated to courses in Greek and Hebrew exegesis. Dr. Traina reported that when he first attempted to publish *Methodical Bible Study* one of his former teachers at The Biblical Seminary complained that there was too much grammar in it.

[5] From almost the very beginning the practitioners of inductive Bible study emphasized literary structure, which involved especially "structural relationships," e.g., contrast, comparison, and climax. They originally derived these relationships from John Ruskin's "Essay on Composition," which is reproduced in Howard Tillman Kuist, *These Words Upon Thy Heart: Scripture and the Christian Response* (Richmond: John Knox, 1947), 161–81. But Dr. Traina developed and expanded these structural relationships far beyond his predecessors in the inductive Bible study movement. See Traina, *Methodical Bible Study*, 49–59; David R. Bauer and Robert A. Traina, *Inductive Bible Study: A Comprehensive Guide to the Practice of Hermeneutics* (Grand Rapids: Baker Academic, 2011), 94–122; Fredrick J. Long, "Major Structural Relationships: A Survey of Origins, Development, Classifications, and Assessment," *Journal of Inductive Biblical Studies* 1 (2014): 22–59.

out the significance of structure for the meaning of the text, over against identifying literary structure for its own sake, or leaving in doubt how structure contributed to meaning.

When Dr. Traina insisted that the Bible is historical in its context he had three things in mind. First, the Bible is historical in the context of its origins: It was written by certain historical persons of the past and directed to other historical persons in the past, and referenced past historical events. Thus, the student must become acquainted with matters of critical introduction (e.g., the author, audience, provenance, occasion for writing of the book) as well as historical background relevant to references and allusions within the text, and be intentional in making use of this information in the interpretation of passages. Dr. Traina was himself immersed in these critical matters and in historical background, and repeatedly drew attention to these issues in his class presentations and modelled the way in which they could be incorporated into an inductive process.

Second, the Bible is historical in the context of its reception: It has been the object of study and thought, which have led to personal and corporate formation, especially within the community of faith, throughout its existence. The student was therefore obliged to become exposed to the history of interpretation and to engage in critical conversation with this history in light of the data of the text so as to arrive at a full and robust interpretation.

The attention both to the history of origins and the history of reception required that students consult secondary sources, especially commentaries. The early proponents of inductive Bible study, including most of Dr. Traina's own teachers at The Biblical Seminary, believed that students engaged in inductive study only when they were dealing directly with the biblical text, and that they moved into deductive study whenever they consulted secondary sources, and particularly the interpretation of others.[6] Here is a major point where Dr. Traina parted company with the early practitioners of inductive Bible study. For Dr. Traina insisted that induction has to do not with the object of study, but rather with the manner of study. Inductive Bible study involves an attitude of radical openness to all evidence pertaining to the meaning of the Bible, whether students find that evidence within the Bible itself or encounter it in the secondary literature; though he insisted that students must give priority to the direct study of the text in terms both of sequence (i.e., students should begin with the study of the text) and emphasis.

Third, the Bible is historical in the context of its contemporary application in that the Bible speaks into the present historical situation. Dr. Traina believed that the observation and interpretation of the text existed finally for the sake of its contemporary appropriation, that is, putting the message of the text into practice, so that it becomes incarnate in the life of the student. The student's very existence, which includes the complex of behaviors, emotions, will, and thinking, is to become the text in life-form. Dr. Traina insisted on the necessity of the intersection of the historical message of the biblical text with the contemporary historical situation of the student, so that the student's history is transformed by the text's message. Dr. Traina challenged students to consider all the dynamics

---

[6] This understanding led some of them to suggest that Bible study should be both inductive and deductive. See, e.g., Charles R. Eberhardt, *The Bible in the Making of Ministers, The Scriptural Basis of Theological Education: The Lifework of Wilbert Webster White* (New York: Association, 1940), 130–31.

that are involved in this task of appropriation and to creatively and profoundly reflect upon how the specific meaning of biblical passages and books informs the particular situations in which students and their communities find themselves today.

If Dr. Traina was convinced that the Bible was literary in its essence and historical in its context, he also believed it was theological in its purpose. He considered it a basic observation that, from beginning to end, the concern of the Bible is upon God, and God's dealings with his (especially human) creation. Dr. Traina brought his broad and deep understanding of historical and systematic theology into conversation with the message of individual biblical passages and books, and, while being careful never to read later theological formulations into the Bible, he demonstrated how a theologically trained mind could draw from the Scriptures profound theological truth. And his theological insights were compelling and often breathtaking. Students frequently remarked that they learned as much theology in Dr. Traina's inductive Bible study classes as they did in courses taught within the Theology Department. Although foundationalism is out of favor in many academic circles today, Dr. Traina was a foundationalist in that he believed that the theology of the Bible should form the grist, or basis, for the student's systematic theology. And he constantly urged students, through a process he called "correlation," to consider how the message of individual passages contributes to the theology of the Bible as a whole and ultimately to the student's own broad theological vision.

But I would be remiss if I did not mention also that for Dr. Traina the Bible was Christological in its focus. Part of Dr. Traina's sense of the theological character of the Bible was the conviction that the Bible manifested a theological structure, and that structure pointed to the centrality of Jesus Christ. Thus Dr. Traina was Christocentric. But he was not Christonomistic;[7] for he rejected the crude tendency on the part of some to find a reference to Jesus in practically every passage. The view of biblical theology and hermeneutics that he taught was much subtler and more nuanced. For Dr. Traina, every passage bears witness to Jesus Christ in the sense that we can finally understand its function within the Bible and its continuing relevance only if we consider it in relation to God's ultimate revelation in Christ. But not every passage is *directly* about Christ. Thus, the student must attend to the content and immediate communicative purpose of each passage, whether that passage has to do with treatment of the poor, or relations with the state, or idolatry, or the consequences of sin, or any of hundreds of other matters. But the student must also ask: How does this passage contribute to our understanding of Christ, and how does God's revelation in Christ clarify the precise meaning, canonical function, and applicatory value of this passage?

---

[7]The term "Christonomistic" means Christ-exclusive. I am using "Christonomistic" here in a hermeneutic rather than a soteriological sense. Dr. Traina was soteriologically Christonomistic insofar as he taught that Jesus Christ is exclusively necessary for salvation. But he was not hermeneutically Christonomistic, since he believed that although the Bible centered on Christ it was not exclusively concerned with Christ, but dealt with a multiplicity of theological and ethical issues, all of which were finally related to Christ and found their ultimate meaning in Christ, but were not all directly and exclusively about Christ.

4. THE GOAL OF TEACHING

As we have just seen, Dr. Traina recognized the many dynamics involved in the task of instructing students to learn and understand the Bible well. But he was confident that his students could become competent and confident interpreters of the Scriptures for themselves. For Dr. Traina the goal of his teaching was to produce genuine, independent, life-long learners. Dr. Traina realized that this goal has an affective element, i.e., students must feel enthusiastic about the study of the Bible. Students emerged from Dr. Traina's classes with a sense of amazement and wonder about what they were able to find within the text. Dr. Traina did not consider it necessary—or helpful—to attempt to generate excitement; he believed that the clear, articulate, relevant exposition of the Bible as the Word of God was more than enough to motivate students to energetic, life-long study. And the biblically centered ministry of thousands of his students bears witness to the validity of that conviction.

But Dr. Traina realized, too, that eagerness is not sufficient to produce life-long learners. Students must also encounter and then internalize a workable, effective process, or method, for their ongoing study. Dr. Traina understood that unless students were taught *what* to do in Bible study they would not be able to engage in effective Bible study for themselves.

This concern to focus his teaching on the inculcation of method within his students is perhaps the greatest contribution Dr. Traina made to inductive Bible study. For never before in the history of the inductive Bible study movement was there an emphasis upon methodology. His professors and colleagues at The Biblical Seminary in New York did not explicitly teach students a method to study the Bible for themselves. These professors typically produced questions directed to the text that the student was expected to answer; but they did not provide their students with any instruction regarding how they were to answer these questions, nor did they develop within their students the ability to raise their own questions.[8]

Dr. Traina came early to see that such an approach ill-equipped students to study the Bible once they left the classroom or graduated from the seminary. Dr. Traina used to tell of an incident that occurred during his first year of seminary teaching that brought this reality crashing in upon him. When he asked the class to make observations about the text, a student asked, "What is an observation?" At that moment, Dr. Traina realized that he was wrongly assuming that his students knew what to do, and he recognized that his instruction was not providing students with the resources to study the Bible for themselves. Immediately he went to work developing a syllabus in which he laid out a method for independent Bible study. That syllabus became the primary textbook of inductive Bible study for generations of students and thousands of pastors and Christian educators. It was called *Methodical Bible Study*.

---

[8] According to Dr. Traina, insofar as these earlier practitioners of inductive Bible study reflected upon methodology in the study and teaching of the Bible at all, they assumed that students would "catch" the intellectual process that was implicit in their instruction, with the hope that the students would progressively be shaped in their thinking so as to study the Scriptures in the same fashion as the professors did.

FOR FURTHER READING AND INFORMATION

Readers who are interested in learning more about Dr. Traina as a teacher are encouraged to visit **https://www.seedbed.com/inductive-bible-study/** where they can view an eighteen-hour video presentation by Dr. Traina on inductive Bible study method as well as two interviews with Dr. Traina conducted by David Bauer and David Thompson. The website also contains the syllabi, audio-recordings, and overheads of all the courses Dr. Traina taught at Asbury Theological Seminary.

THE PEDAGOGY OF ROBERT A. TRAINA IN EDUCATIONAL THEORY AND PRACTICE

Chris A. Kiesling
Professor of Christian Discipleship and Human Development
Asbury Theological Seminary

ABSTRACT: This essay offers comparison and contrast between Robert A. Traina's pedagogy and some contemporary theories of teaching and learning. It aims to highlight the layered depth and formative value embedded in Dr. Traina's thoughtful notes to teachers while also offering recommendations for extending his legacy through future generations of IBS teachers.

1. INTRODUCTION

Giving myself a break while writing on sabbatical I sat munching on a bag of Cousin Willie's white cheddar mauve popcorn. On the back of the bag I read the bold claim that after 75 years this family-owned company believed that they now have created the "perfect" popcorn. With virtually no hulls and endowed with anti-oxidants, Cousin Willie and his family confidently claim that their popcorn is "Simply Better." I wondered if this was just a marketing scheme or if there was grounding for such a claim and so I conducted some elemental research.

I soon discovered that Cousin Willie's popcorn begins with careful selection of seed to insure the proper size hull. Consideration is then given before planting to forecast the most favorable weather conditions because too much rain or too many 100-degree days can alter the amount of moisture retained in the kernel. When harvest time arrives, the settings on the combine are adjusted to avoid scuffing the hulls which might result in a leakage of moisture. The kernels come from the fields retaining somewhere between 16–20% moisture, but are dried in silos until approximating an ideal 14% retention. Among other processes, this dehydration avoids having too many "spinsters"—the name the popcorn industry apparently gives to those stubborn kernels that never pop. A National Public Radio segment I came across elaborated on the physics of popcorn. Using animal metaphors, they explained that the liquid starch inside the popcorn hull can burst the kernel in several different ways: a) unilaterally—like the tentacles of an Octopus that point in one direction, b) bilaterally—like a butterfly with appendages in two direction, or c) multilaterally—in which case the tasty starch bubbles poof out in every direction like a turtle extending head and legs from its shell. Cousin

Willie's claim of virtually no hulls, I thought, must be indicative that that their popcorn is scientifically engineered to provide the finest, tortoise-like form, minimizing the size of the hull relative to the edible part that was now sumptuously enhancing my pastime. So, I concluded, my research unequivocally convinced me that because Cousin Willie had adopted a comprehensive and careful application of method to his production of virtually hull-free kernels, that I was indeed ingesting white cheddar popcorn that was "simply better."

If you can pardon the inanity of the analogy, what Cousin Willie claims to have done with popcorn, Dr. Robert A. Traina brought to five generations of Bible students providing them a methodology that insures an interpretation and appropriation of Scripture that said in folksy colloquialism is "simply better." I had the privilege of being a student in the last class on the Pentateuch that Dr. Traina taught at Asbury Seminary, and count it a high privilege to contribute to a festschrift in his honor. The measure of who he was and the impact of what he taught is captured well by David R. Bauer's preceding essay. My task here is to elaborate on how his unpublished notes on "Method in Bible Teaching" resonate with contemporary understandings of pedagogy. Hence, the bulk of this essay provides anchor points that substantiate the value of Dr. Traina's "Method in Bible Teaching" by linking it to contemporary theory about teaching and learning. In a concluding section I offer a few recommendations to future teachers of IBS who carry a passion to see this important work extended to new generations.

2. Linking IBS Study to Contemporary Educational Theory and Practice

Parker Palmer contends that the best classroom is neither teacher-centered nor student-centered, but rather subject-centered. He conceptualizes the classroom as a community of truth that gathers around a "great thing" that both teacher and student reverence and regard together.[1] Though the logistics in a Traina classroom resembled the traditional positioning of teacher-in-front-of-students, it was Dr. Traina's own disposition toward the revealed word of God that brought students to sense the "great thing" that they were not only apprehending, but which was also apprehending them and laying claim on their lives. In his instruction to teachers, leaders are directed to include themselves in evaluation of application, and offer self-reflections in framing exercises for students, hence locating themselves as also standing under the truth being realized. I find it intriguing that Palmer recognizes that in order to grasp the significance of great things, it behooves one to teach from the microcosm, that is, to present "less truth" but to do so at a deeper level, diving deeply into particularity.[2] IBS mirrors this pedagogical directive. How is the student to possibly ascertain the whole truth of a biblical book, much less the grand narrative of Scripture? Dr. Traina's method evinces the prescriptions given by Palmer: survey the whole, but then focus on the observation of particulars allowing the microcosm of smaller units to build to the general.

There are essentially five aspects to the methodical study of the Scriptures taught by Dr. Traina, as the chapter titles of his landmark book make apparent—observation, interpretation,

---

[1] Parker J. Palmer, *The Courage to Teach* (San Francisco: Jossey-Bass, 1998), 115–41.
[2] Ibid., 120–32.

evaluation and application, and correlation.³ Anyone acquainted with the field of education will quickly recognize how these movements link with educational theory, what we now know about how students learn, and what makes for effective teaching. Halfway through the twentieth century, educators began synthesizing findings from psychology, neuroscience, and classroom observations that convinced them that humans differ in their preferred means of perceiving reality (e.g. feeling or thinking) and their preferred ways of processing the reality they encounter (e.g., reflecting or acting).⁴ To honor these different preferences, numerous modes of learning were needed. Furthermore, for educators to optimize various patterns of learning for every student, a learning cycle that moved through each mode of perceiving and processing was deemed essential. The correlation between the educational models built on this premise and the IBS method is perhaps best illustrated via a brief comparison with two diverse but representative pedagogical models—Kolb's learning style theory and Thomas Groome's praxis method.

Dr. Traina's inductive method begins with an evidential reading of a text. Students are led to "see" or perceive the biblical passage; to feel what the author felt and to think as the author thought. Curiosity and inquisitiveness are encouraged as the student infers the meaning of what is perceived. With careful observation of authorial intent, interpretation minimizes subjective bias or prejudicial interpretation.⁵ Particular observations are then summarized, reflected upon and evaluated, sharpening and deepening their benefit to the student and relating these particulars to more general understandings. Lest fruit be "picked and not eaten,"⁶ Dr. Traina's method then sets the student to carefully discern those situations to which the interpretation of the text might apply, prompting attunement to associated correlations. Although Kolb focuses first on honoring the *concrete experience* of the learner, his learning cycle similarly begins by attuning the student to their own observations— i.e., engaging learning by pressing students to regard their own examinations.⁷

In Groome's praxis model the first movement is posed via the question, "What is present reality?"⁸ Groome delays introducing textual analysis until his third movement, but the posturing of the student to become inquisitive and attentive, whether to the biblical world or to the world they inhabit is intriguing. This awareness in turn leads to *reflective observation,* drawing inferences and becoming inquisitive about the meaning behind things, but suspending judgment until various perspectives are considered. Groome captures this movement by posing the question, "Why is this reality the way it is?"⁹ As IBS moves from the particular to the general, so Kolb observes that the

---

³ Robert A. Traina, *Methodical Bible Study: A New Approach to Hermeneutics* (Wilmore, KY: Robert A. Traina, 1952; repr., Grand Rapids: Zondervan, 1980/2002).

⁴ Bernice McCarthy, *The 4Mat System: Teaching to Learning Styles with Right/Left Mode Techniques* (Manchester, UK: About Learning, 1955).

⁵ Traina, *Methodical Bible Study,* 152.

⁶ Robert A. Traina, "Method in Bible Teaching," Section Three.

⁷ Alice Y. Kolb and David A. Kolb, *A Comprehensive Guide to the Theory, Psychometrics, Research on Validity and Educational Application,* 2013. A PDF of this resources may be found at http://learningfromexperience.com/.

⁸ Groome, *Christian Religious Education: Sharing Our Story and Vision* (San Francisco: Jossey-Bass, 1980).

⁹ Ibid.

natural progression of learning takes what is perceived in specific experience and processes it by naming and relating the experience to other understandings. Real learning is thought to occur through adaptation to a new understanding typically forged through logical analysis. Kolb called this *abstract conceptualization*.[10] In Groome's model, transformative possibilities emerge as the dialectic between what *is* perceived and the norm of what *should be* creates the prerequisite tension for change.[11] Learning however can only be regarded as complete as it moves through the final aspect, *active experimentation* in Kolb's theory, application and correlation in Traina, decision and response for lived Christian Faith in Groome—i.e., action that is now taken through risk-taking to influence people or events with the truth one has now ascertained. By comparing these models, it can be concluded that Dr. Traina's methodical approach to the study of the Bible provides a comprehensive and sound cycle of learning, engaging the student in important modes of perception and processing. These theories can also be contrasted to one another surfacing differences that will be commented on later in this essay.

A related emphasis that emerged in education philosophy created a shift in assessing learning rather than, or in addition to, assessing teaching. Professors for example were driven to name and evaluate student learning outcomes rather than only state course objectives. Attention became focused on whether students could demonstrate understanding and competencies gained from the educational experience. In this regard, Dr. Traina was ahead of his time. The very nature of methodical Bible study implies experimental procedures that move away from banking models of education where the professor is "to tell" the student what to know, to a mode of guided discovery. Dr. Traina wanted his students to arrive at a mastery of biblical content not through memorization, but through an internalization of method that would fortify pathways for them to become masters of exposition. In numerous places his guidelines to instructors reflect this conviction. He writes, "saying a thing is not the same as conveying it."[12] The task he notes is to "train athletes, not fatten geese" quoting Edward Thring, Headmaster of the Uppingham School, in an address to teachers.[13] He advocates creating a *sequence* of questions to guide the student toward deeper understanding, not simply a list to cover content. He prompts instructors to ask questions in such a way not to please the professor, but to lead the student to find truth; and when insight is not apparent, he would have instructors prepared with a secondary line of questioning. Robert Pazmino's theologically grounded book for Christian educators, *God Our Teacher,* captures the significant role of the teacher in these processes by noting that as God the Creator brings forth order out of chaos, so does our teaching need form to build discipline and control.[14]

Dr. Traina's approach was to create independence of learning, not reliance on external authority. His profound insights into a passage of Scripture would often have students copiously taking

---

[10] Kolb and Kolb, *Comprehensive Guide*.
[11] Groome, *Christian Religious Education*.
[12] Traina, "Method in Bible Teaching," 205.
[13] *Ibid.,* 173.
[14] Robert Pazmino, *God Our Teacher: Theological Basics in Christian Education* (Grand Rapids: Baker, 2001).

notes, trying to capture his thought. Yet, Dr. Traina demonstrated his skillfulness not so students would rehearse his expert knowledge, but to inspire them to engage the discipline of study themselves. To borrow a phrase from Steve Garber, Dr. Traina invited an "over the shoulder and through the heart" approach to teaching his methodology.[15] He instructs teachers to reveal to the student the procedure that is being used, and then inform them of "why" so that they grow in discernment and efficacy. As such his instructional methods reflect characteristics of adult learners identified in Malcolm Knowle's androgogy: self-directed learning, honoring one's own experience as a resource for learning, and encouraging internal motivation.[16] Dr. Traina's handbook concludes each section not with *assignments* suggestive of a task imposed by a superior, but with *exercises* enticing students to come and explore.

It should not surprise us that the largest section of Dr. Traina's "Method in Bible Teaching" focuses on the formulation and use of questions and answers in Bible teaching. Given that a fundamental task is to help student "see" a passage within its context and in the depth of its layered meaning, posing questions to progressively stimulate deeper observation and advance more adequate interpretation and application makes logical sense. Educators have long recognized that the way a student progresses toward higher forms of knowledge largely depends upon the way a teacher scaffolds the learning experience.[17] A key component of building a scaffold for effective learning is choosing the questions asked when crafting a learning task. Benjamin Bloom, for example, posited that attaining higher level skills and attitudes were preconditioned by attaining a particular form of knowledge. Recalling facts and basic concepts required a different skill set than applying information to a new context which, in turn, differs from producing an original work. Bloom's taxonomy moves a student from simple to complex forms of understanding—knowledge, comprehension, application, analysis, synthesis and evaluation. More complex learning tasks are often distinguished by the kinds of questions posed and the associated learning tasks enjoined at that level—recall, explain, apply, analyze, evaluate, create.[18] Jane Vella crafted her whole educational philosophy premised on this basis. As she defines it "a learning task is an open question put to learners who have all the resources needed to respond."[19] Vella recognized that the key to crafting effective learning tasks—i.e., the key to asking good open question is found in the verb that is chosen.[20] Dr. Traina's

---

[15] I first encountered Garber using this phrase in leadership clips available through The Murdock Foundation. The concept is developed in Steve Garber, *Visions of Vocation: Common Grace for the Common Good* (Downers Grove, IL: InterVarsity Press, 2014).

[16] Malcolm Knowles, *Andragogy in Action* (San Francisco: Jossey-Bass, 1984).

[17] Scaffolding has been attributed to the contributions of Lev Vygotsky; see his 1987 essay, *Thinking and Speech* in R. Rieber and A. Carton, eds., *The Collected Works of Lev Vygotsky, Vol. 1*, trans. N. Minick (New York: Plenum, 1960).

[18] This summation of Bloom's taxonomy is taken from https://cft.vanderbilt.edu/guides-sub-pages/blooms-taxonomy/ accessed 7/17/2017.

[19] Jane Vella, *Taking Learning to Task: Creative Strategies for Teaching Adults* (San Francisco: Jossey-Bass, 2000), xiii.

[20] Ibid., 49–58.

taxonomy of questions is built on different dimensions than Bloom's or Vella's, but it reflects some of the same intentions. Questions are chosen in terms of their importance, their fit with the principle elements of a passage, the scope being explored, and such practicalities as the student's exhibited understanding. Dr. Traina foresaw that a whole Bible lesson could be structured around one or a few crucial questions. His chronicling of the general purpose of questions with infinitives exemplify a similar valuing of the verbs that direct Vella's learning tasks: "to enable, to show, to improve, to develop initiative, to foster, to aid, to give, and to make possible."

Perry Shaw provides a good illustration of the importance of structured questioning following Bloom's taxonomy of learning from the parable of the Good Samaritan in Luke 15.[21]

> Knowledge: "Who left the man lying half-dead on the edge of the street?" The answer is found in the text and only requires a person to know the text to know the answer.
>
> Comprehension: "Why did the priest and the Levi pass by on the other side?" The answer is not given directly in the text but pushes the student to consider historical and cultural background to the text.
>
> Application: "Who are your enemies ...What could you do to be like the Good Samaritan with these people?" This question causes the student to apply the teaching of the parable to a specific situation.
>
> Analysis: "What is the connection between the actions of the Good Samaritan and the ethos of Jesus's own life and ministry?" Now the student is required to sift through both the elements of the parable and the life and ministry of Jesus to make comparisons.
>
> Synthesis: "What is the relationship between word and deed in Christian witness?" Here an apparent contradiction is raised whose resolution forces consideration of the broader issues at stake and brings them together in comprehensive understanding.
>
> Evaluation: "What are the main things which prevent us from doing good to our enemies? ... Do you really think that the Tamils should forgive and show active love towards the Sinhalese?" Judgments are solicited based on relevance to real life situations.

Germane to the task of asking and ordering good questions is the consideration of how the teacher views themselves as teacher. Parker Palmer's watershed work, *The Courage to Teach,* focused educators beyond the *what* of teaching (content) and the *how* of teaching (methods), to a penetrating look into the *who* of teaching. Palmer recognized that the crux of good teaching was an offering of one's selfhood, because knowing is inherently relational and communal, constituted by the identity and integrity of the teacher.[22] Teachers inevitably project the condition of their own souls onto their students. One of the more intriguing exercises that Palmer advocates is to have teachers identify

---

[21] Perry Shaw, *Transforming Theological Education: A Practical Handbook for Integrative Learning* (Cumbria, UK: Langham Global Library, 2014), 74–75.

[22] Palmer, *Courage to Teach,* 9–34.

metaphors that capture the way teachers see themselves in the act of teaching: "When I am at my best teaching, I am most like a _____"—e.g., a choreographer orchestrating a dance, a sheepdog herding sheep, a swordsman in desperate battle. Quite enthralling are the metaphors Dr. Traina evokes for his teachers: "conceive of yourself as Socrates conceived of himself, that is, as a mental obstetrician whose incessant questions and proddings delivered men's minds and enabled them to give birth to valid ideas."[23] "Don't give the impression that you are the grand inquisitor or an official of the law putting the class through the third degree."[24] Lest the metaphor of a mental obstetrician is perceived as too clinical or impersonal, or the conjuring of Socrates too intimidating for some students, I hasten to set these images in the context of additional imperatives that Dr. Traina advances for teachers. He quotes H. H. Horne in describing the general attitude of the teacher toward the student when asking questions: "With great sympathy, with great confidence in his ability to answer, with expectation that he will answer, with surprise when he does not answer, with interest in his answer, and with particular attention to his answer."[25] Consider likewise the relational dynamics of Dr. Traina's injunction to carefully prepare an introduction after mastering the content of a lesson to "establish a point of contact between teacher and listeners,"[26] or the sensitivity of occasionally using an illustration for the purpose of providing relaxation for the mind.[27]

Educators who work in settings of higher education soon discover that the salience of most any teaching event is predicated on the preparation of the teacher. Numerous decisions are made by an instructor before entering the classroom that determine the effectiveness of one's teaching. Chief among these judgments, as Dr. Traina duly notes, is choosing the structure for the lesson. His depiction of possible lesson structures and the common errors that can derail a class is material that I plan to use in teaching doctoral students. In developing teachers as in spiritual formation, it is essential to anticipate and name possible impediments before they are encountered. Not only is this naming beforehand important, it can also be highly formative for students to be given the chance to correct a misjudgment when it is made. Thomas Guskey distinguishes summative from formative evaluations.[28] Summative evaluations are administered at the conclusion of a lesson to test a students' comprehensive knowledge, but they give no chance for the student to demonstrate corrective judgment or behavior. Formative evaluations occur midstream in one's teaching and allow the teacher to customize a response and provide resources and guidance germane to each student's particular need. The student then has another chance to demonstrate correct judgment and behavior. Guskey discovered that a high percentage of students could be brought to mastery of a subject if careful attention is given to formative evaluations along the way. My experience, and the experience of my peers, leads me to believe that few students perform well on their first survey of a whole book of the Bible

---

[23] Traina, "Method in Bible Teaching," 204.
[24] Ibid.
[25] Ibid., 201.
[26] Ibid., 220.
[27] Ibid., 208.
[28] Thomas R. Guskey and Jane. M. Bailey, *Developing Grading and Reporting Systems for Student Learning* (Thousand Oaks, CA: Corwin, 2001).

or on their first observation of a particular passage. Critical in mastering hermeneutical skills are formative evaluations that come through repeated practice with corrective input and guidance. Though Dr. Traina does not use the language of summative versus formative, it is clear in his comments on evaluation and application that he advocates for formative evaluations while not abandoning the importance of summative evaluation as well.

Numerous other mechanics of effective pedagogy are made readily available in Dr. Traina's handbook. The brevity of this essay prevents broader elucidation, but I would be remiss to not at least give mention to the following:

- Illustrations lead to illumination and internalization
- Problematizing provides a useful strategy for introductions
- Summarizing a lesson increases comprehension and application
- Insuring that each person has something they can and should do at the end of a lesson promotes transformation
- Exercises must be fitted to the capacities of the students
- Stirring the emotions as well as the will is the aim of truth and formative for the whole person

These are rich gleanings that can only come from years of practice and reflection. How grateful we should be that this master teacher would have on his heart future Bible teachers and set to pen such rich reflections.

3. EXTENDING THE TEACHING OF IBS TO FUTURE GENERATIONS

My contribution to this Festschrift is foremost to honor the life and work of Dr. Traina, and secondarily to provide commentary on how his handbook resonates with contemporary educational theory and practice. Perhaps one of the best ways to honor one's legacy is to build on the seminal work laid in previous generations. In this concluding section then I want to offer a few challenges and elaborations from the perspective of education that might guide future Bible teachers.

First, in his book on transforming theological education, Perry Shaw argues that students in contemporary society need to develop the capacity for not only moving from text to context, but also moving from context to text. Practical theologians contend that there are numerous issues that emerge in modern society and ministry practice that were not the direct focus of biblical authors— e.g., transgender sexual identity, addiction, cohabitation, navigating dysfunctional and blended family systems. Further, education specialists contend that the best learning is problem-based, involving critical reflection on real-life situations, and valuing one's own experience as a source of knowledge. The biblical text can certainly speak to all the issues named above, but how does the Bible instructor, utilizing the inductive method, explore such issues while at the same time avoiding eisegesis? One possible solution is to address these kinds of issues in the remainder of a student's curriculum, integrating methodical Bible study with other courses in the degree program.

Second, a number of educational theories are premised on the view that transformative change occurs as a student encounters or contemplates disequilibrating experiences that typically occur outside the classroom, bringing them into a process of theological reflection. Groome, for example, begins with the student's own history or current experience and brings this into a dialectic with His-story—e.g., the biblical text. Jack Mezirow et al. describe a disorienting dilemma typically brought about by a life crisis or life transition as the catalyst for real change.[29] As younger generations are especially eager to recruit into their lives compatriots who can help make meaning of their own personal experiences, how can the Bible instructor honor these experiences or even misadventures, while still maintaining the biblical text as "norming" these experiences? When a student is in a period of disorientation or in the delicate place of exploring where they belong or what to believe, support and a listening ear is often more predictive of where they will land ideologically and communally than corrective comments. What disposition can a Bible teacher hold toward those who are in a life crisis, skeptical of authority, and/or disillusioned toward anything "religious?" This may be especially crucial in the development of what Friere termed the development of "critical consciousness" among the oppressed.[30]

Third, Dr. Traina's instructions assume real time conversation primarily in a classroom setting. With the increasing demand for on-line learning where interaction typically occurs in asynchronous time limiting immediate feedback, "classroom" dynamics change. Those who teach Methodical Bible Study in these delivery systems will likely encounter additional considerations in preparation, evaluation, and the presumed context for application.

Fourth, the primary technology reflected in Dr. Traina's handbook is the use of the blackboard. Newer technologies open unfathomable opportunities for students of the Bible—e.g., virtual reality that allows a student to walk through the Old Testament tabernacle or an avatar that walks down the *via delorosa* giving the student multiple choices of perspective. Discriminant use of such technology in addressing these challenges and all the interpretive questions that emerge with it will likely constitute the challenges of the next generations of Bible teachers who stand as "dwarfs on the shoulders of giants"[31] such as Dr. Robert A. Traina.

---

[29] Jack Mezirow, Edward W. Taylor, and Associates, *Transformative Learning in Practice: Insights from Community, Workplace and Higher Education* (San Francisco: Jossey-Bass, 2009), 18–32.

[30] Paulo Freire, *Pedagogy of the Oppressed* (New York: Bloomsbury Academic, 2000).

[31] This phrase is usually attributed to Bernard of Chartres; cf. the website at www.dictionary.sensagent.com.

FOR FURTHER READING

Groome, Thomas. *Christian Religious Education: Sharing Our Story and Vision.* San Francisco: Jossey-Bass, 1980.

Merriam, Sharan B. and Laura L. Bierema, *Adult Learning: Linking Theory and Practice.* San Francisco: Jossey-Bass, 2014.

Mezirow, Jack, Edward W. Taylor, and Associates. *Transformative Learning in Practice: Insights from Community, Workplace and Higher Education.* San Francisco: Jossey-Bass, 2009.

Palmer, Parker J. *The Courage to Teach.* San Francisco: Jossey-Bass, 1998.

Pazmino, Robert. *God Our Teacher: Theological Basics in Christian Education* (Grand Rapids: Baker, 2001).

Perry Shaw, *Transforming Theological Education: A Practical Handbook for Integrative Learning* (Cumbria, UK: Langham Global Library, 2014),

Vella, Jane. *Taking Learning to Task: Creative Strategies for Teaching Adults.* San Francisco: Jossey-Bass, 2000.

Why Inductive Bible Study?
A Defense of Inductive Method in Research and Teaching

Kenneth L. Schenck
Dean of the School of Theology & Ministry, Indiana Wesleyan University
Professor of New Testament & Ancient Languages

ABSTRACT: In the wake of post-modernism, it is no surprise that IBS has faced its share of critique. IBS assumes that we can approximate the original meaning of texts using an inductive reasoning and logic that is available to all regardless of one's faith commitments. It assumes that logical relationships are omni-cultural and that an interpreter can be sufficiently objective to make the quest feasible. By contrast, the voices of presuppositionalism, post-liberalism, and theological interpretation call these working assumptions into question. This chapter argues that the goal of the original meaning remains intact and a valuable pursuit despite the obstacles of subjectivity and under-determinism. The original meanings were the first moments of inspiration for these texts and they related to the foundational events of Christian faith. While the chapter values the insights that these critiques bring for the appropriation of the text, it questions some of the assumptions of IBS's detractors. Finally, from a pragmatic standpoint, the practice of IBS is worthwhile for the very effect it has on the interpreter.

1. Challenges to IBS

In many circles, IBS has fallen on hard times. The reason seems easy to discern. It is ostensibly a modernist method, and we have entered postmodern times. For example, IBS as Robert A. Traina developed it makes a distinction between observation and interpretation, a distinction that seems impossible to make fully in practice. To observe is to interpret. Traina's English Bible method supposed that the number of logical ways in which two thoughts can relate to each other is finite and universal, unaffected by culture or context. Such an omni-cultural suggestion understandably meets with suspicion in our multicultural environment. Traina speaks of textual structures in a poststructuralist age. Perhaps most to the point, IBS seems to operate on the basis of a subject-object distinction that the postmodern critique would say does not exist. We cannot be objective. For good or ill, all our interpretations take place in the world in front of the text, and we as subject are inseparable from the world as object.

The pages that follow address some of the concerns that have been raised about IBS. While acknowledging the force of these concerns, I would argue that IBS remains the best option for approximating the first meanings of the biblical texts and that those meanings remain important. We should wrestle with considerations that some have raised, like the role that faith should play in interpretation as well as the problems of objectivity, under-determinism, and relevance. Nevertheless, the goal of inductive interpretation is real. It is valuable for Christian interpreters and it is attainable enough for us to strive after it.

The goal of IBS is legitimate in the sense that these words had a meaning to their original authors and audiences. If God had other meanings in mind for these words beyond the original contexts, those are then by definition *different* meanings than the original ones, ones that must be read against some other context. For those who consider the Bible Scripture, the Word of God, the original meanings are valuable not least because they give us a witness to God's action in history. Furthermore, for those who are broadly evangelical, the original meaning was the first inspiration. Even if God continues to speak through these same words in new ways, surely the first speaking is valuable and much to be desired because it was in fact the voice of God. It was the voice of God in relation to the very foundational events of the Christian faith, not least, the incarnation, atonement, and enthronement of the Son of God.

Finally, we would argue that the goal of the original meanings is sufficiently attainable to be pursued. The quest for the first meaning can be elusive, in part because of a lack of evidence and in part because of the lack of human objectivity. Nevertheless, the cumulative journey of inductive biblical scholars has yielded some consensus and has eliminated vast numbers of proposed interpretations from the past. Indeed, we are arguably in a better position to speak to the original meanings of the Bible than ever before. We have more evidence at hand than ever in the past. We have the accumulated wisdom of millennia of interpretation. IBS is arguably the most likely method to approximate these first meanings.

The process of IBS itself is enlightening to the user, regardless of his or her specific conclusions. The distinctions between observation, interpretation, integration, and appropriation are useful, even if impossible to distinguish fully in practice. The very act of asking questions—even when you think you already know the answers—helps you see your own assumptions. IBS makes one a better and more critical thinker without any contradiction to the principle of faith seeking understanding. In what follows, I will particularize these general statements.

2. Faith Seeking Understanding

Christians have long debated the proper relationship between faith and human reasoning. On one end of the spectrum are the likes of Tertullian and Søren Kierkegaard. "What does Athens have to do with Jerusalem, the Academy with the Church?"[1] "I believe because it is absurd."[2] Interestingly, Tertullian himself still paid significant attention to grammatical and historical details in his

---

[1] *De praescriptione* 7.

[2] A paraphrase of Tertullian's statement in *De carne Christi*: the resurrection "is certain, because it is impossible."

interpretation. However, he did not believe that non-believers should be allowed to discuss the meaning of Scripture.³ Scripture must be read through the eyes of the rule of faith. In this regard, he would have rejected any sense that IBS (e.g., Traina's method) might provide an objective approach to the original meaning of Scripture apart from the eyes of faith.

In the late nineteenth-century and the twentieth-century, a strand of Calvinism developed that emphasized the exclusivity of Christian presuppositions and rationality. Its origins trace especially to Abraham Kuyper, who developed a form of presuppositionalism that denied to non-believers the ability to reason properly.⁴ Within his framework, only a person with the proper Christian worldview could come to correct conclusions about the Bible and its meaning. Kuyper's most important heir, Cornelius Van Til, did temper his approach slightly, synthesizing it with earlier Calvinist thinkers like B. B. Warfield and A. A. Hodge.⁵ These earlier Calvinists believed Christianity was rationally defensible and saw reason as common ground between believer and non-believer. Non-believers could partially reason, although they were doomed to be inconsistent and self-contradictory because their presuppositions were wrong. In the mid-twentieth century, R. J. Rushdoony took this line of thinking even further, asserting that the only valid knowledge non-Christians can have is stolen, and that all other non-Christian thinking is rebellion against God, an attempt to assert intellectual autonomy from God.⁶ Suffice it to say, all of these approaches would reject any attempt to establish an interpretive method that is not heavily determined by uniquely Christian paradigms and faith commitments—and Calvinist ones at that.

A much subtler and yet currently dominating influence is that of post-liberalism. Following the lead of individuals like George Lindbeck and Hans Frei, post-liberalism rejects the location of Scripture's meaning within a predominantly historical framework.⁷ Whereas IBS assumes a universal framework of evidence and reason through which the meaning of the biblical texts can be processed, postliberal approaches to Scripture seek a vantage point from within the Scriptural narratives, one that processes all reality from within the story itself. While IBS implicitly locates the meaning of Scripture within broader truth in general, postliberalism locates truth from within the narrative of Scripture.⁸ We might note the affinity of this approach to the hermeneutic of Karl Barth, which has

---

³ *De praescriptione* 15–19.

⁴ He especially developed this perspective in six lectures he delivered at Princeton Theological Seminary in 1898, "The Stone Lectures on Calvinism."

⁵ Cornelius Van Til, *The Defense of the Faith* (Phillipsburg, NJ: P & R Publishing, 1955).

⁶ Rushdoony, *By What Standard? An Analysis of the Philosophy of Cornelius Van Til* (Vallecito, CA: Ross House, 1995), 24–30.

⁷ The key works here are George Lindbeck, *The Nature of Doctrine: Religion and Theology in a Postliberal Age* (Louisville: Westminster John Knox, 1984) and Hans Frei, *The Eclipse of Biblical Narrative: A Study in Eighteenth and Nineteenth Century Hermeneutics* (New Haven: Yale University, 1980).

⁸ Ironically, while I will invoke Wittgenstein below in appeal to the use of everyday language, Lindbeck appealed to Wittgenstein for the notion that religious language constitutes its own language game. See Michael W. Nicholson, "Abusing Wittgenstein: The Misuse of the Concept of Language Games in Contemporary Theology," *JETS* 39 (1996): 617–29.

also dominated the recent theological landscape.[9]

In a similar vein is the rise of theological interpretation.[10] Daniel J. Treier provides a starting point for understanding such approaches: "Whatever else it means, theological exegesis deals with the Bible as a word about God and from God."[11] In my opinion, the difficulty of identifying a precise definition of theological interpretation or its practice reflects a certain hermeneutical ambiguity intrinsic to its nature. If we were to analyze theological interpretation from the standpoint of Traina's method, we might say that theological interpreters tend to blur interpretation with evaluation and application.[12] The theological interpreter would no doubt respond that one cannot actually distinguish these moves from each other in practice, and they are correct. However, the abandonment of these categories implies that theological interpretation becomes at its very starting point an intrinsically eisegetical enterprise *by design*. All interpretation is inevitably eisegetical to some extent, but theological interpretation implicitly makes such eisegesis normative.

Looming in the theoretical background of theological interpretation is of course Hans-Georg Gadamer.[13] With Gadamer we have a recognition of the dialogical nature of interpretation, as we attempt to fuse our "horizon" with the horizon of the text.[14] On the one hand, Gadamer is often quoted for his advocacy of an openness to the text, a posture of absolute necessity in Traina's IBS method. Joel B. Green quotes with affirmation Gadamer's insistence that "a person trying to understand a text is prepared for it to tell him something."[15] In that same passage, Gadamer indicates, "a person trying to understand something will not resign himself from the start to relying on his own accidental fore-meanings."[16] However, Gadamer is also invoked to diminish the value of the quest for the original meaning in light of the fact that we do not have direct access to it. I as subject am always part of my interpretation of the text as object. The text does not come to me directly but through layers of interpretive tradition. Often, the baby is thrown out with the bath water. Why then even pursue this supposed "original meaning" if it is ultimately unattainable?

In the next section, I will argue that the notion of a first or original meaning to a text is compelling and that it is beneficial and appropriate to keep it as an exegetical goal. At its worst,

---

[9] Cf. George Lindbeck, "Barth and Textuality," *ThTo* 43 (1986): 361–76.

[10] Both Daniel J. Treier and Steven Joe Koskie see Barth as a forerunner to theological interpretation; see Daniel J. Treier, *Introducing Theological Interpretation of Scripture: Recovering a Christian Practice* (Grand Rapids: Baker, 2008), 14–21 and Steven Joe Koskie, Jr., *Reading the Way to Heaven: A Wesleyan Theological Hermeneutic of Scripture*, JTIS 8 (Winona Lake, IN: Eisenbrauns, 2014), 14–17.

[11] Treier, *Introducing Theological Interpretation*, 36.

[12] In my own practice, I refer to evaluation as "integration" and prefer the term "appropriation" to application. Traina and Bauer have also shifted to "appropriation" in David R. Bauer and Robert A. Traina, *Inductive Bible Study: A Comprehensive Guide to the Practice of Hermeneutics* (Grand Rapids: Baker Academic, 2011). See also my forthcoming book, *How to Read the Bible: Scripture as History and Sacrament* (Eugene, OR: Pickwick, 2019).

[13] Hans-Georg Gadamer, *Truth and Method*, 2nd ed. (New York: Crossroad, 1990).

[14] An early exploration of how Gadamer might be appropriated for NT hermeneutics was Anthony C. Thiselton, *The Two Horizons: New Testament Hermeneutics and Philosophical Description* (Grand Rapids: Eerdmans, 1980).

[15] Joel B. Green, *Seized by Truth: Reading the Bible as Scripture* (Nashville: Abingdon, 2007), 90–91.

[16] Gadamer, *Truth and Method*, 269.

theological interpretation simply provides a justification for reading the text however we wish as a mirror of our own theological sensibilities, a form of reader-response. As Francis Watson once warned about Lindbeck and Frei, a purely intratextual approach can degenerate into a self-referential theology.[17] Perhaps Gadamer has "dethroned" the historical-cultural method as primary;[18] but, to the extent that he has done so, he has dethroned the original meaning of the biblical texts. IBS remains the method most likely to lead us to these meanings. By contrast, the hermeneutical concerns raised by Gadamer and recent theological "interpreters" have recovered important elements in the *appropriation* of these texts.

In terms of the first meaning of the text, Gordon D. Fee and Douglas Stuart are no doubt correct, "A text cannot mean what it never meant."[19] However, texts do take on meanings unintended by their original authors, and the NT use of the OT suggests that God can speak well beyond the original intention. Theological interpreters are quite right to recover the figural dimensions of appropriation.[20] Nevertheless, the categories remain intact. It meant what it meant, even if we do not have certain access to that meaning. Then we integrate and appropriate the texts as believers with a view to the rule of faith and the law of love. The latter is a spiritual task, an art. The former is a quasi-scientific task. IBS is most appropriate for interpretation, theological "interpretation" for appropriation.

It is no surprise that those in the Wesleyan tradition most influenced by post-liberalism and theological interpretation would resist the notion of the Wesleyan Quadrilateral, the sense that tradition, reason, and experience play significant roles in the formulation of Christian faith and practice. Its most notorious detractor is of course William J. Abraham, who considers the Quadrilateral more a product of Albert Outler's own hermeneutic than an accurate reflection of Wesley himself.[21] Nevertheless, Wesley had an openness to natural revelation and used reason at times in modernist ways.[22] Abraham arguably re-appropriates Wesley's pre-critical dimension from within a postliberal framework and thereby attempts to eliminate the independent force that reason and experience had in his thinking.[23]

---

[17] Francis Watson, *Text, Church and World: Biblical Interpretation in Theological Perspective* (Grand Rapids: Eerdmans, 1994), 152.

[18] Cf. Green, *Seized by Truth*, 24–25.

[19] Gordon D. Fee and Douglas Stuart, *How to Read the Bible for All Its Worth*, 3rd ed. (Grand Rapids: Zondervan, 2003), 30.

[20] Although I thus find their enterprise hermeneutically imprecise, I applaud the general broadening of biblical appropriation in a work such as Ellen F. Davis and Richard B. Hays, *The Art of Reading Scripture* (Grand Rapids: Eerdmans, 2003).

[21] William J. Abraham, *Waking from Doctrinal Amnesia: The Healing of Doctrine in the United Methodist Church* (Nashville: Abingdon, 1995); also, idem, "The End of Wesleyan Theology," *WTJ* 40 (2005): 7–25. For Albert C. Outler's seminal essay, see "The Wesleyan Quadrilateral—in John Wesley," in *The Wesleyan Theological Heritage: Essays of Albert C. Outler*, eds. Thomas C. Oden and Leicester R. Logden (Grand Rapids: Eerdmans, 1991), 21–37.

[22] See Donald A. D. Thorsen, *The Wesleyan Quadrilateral: Scripture, Tradition, Reason and Experience as a Model of Evangelical Theology* (Grand Rapids: Zondervan, 1990).

[23] A kind of postliberal Jumanji that sucks reason and experience into Scripture.

So, we return to the question of how faith and reason relate to each other. There is a middle way between the extreme that sees Christian faith as irrational or entirely presuppositional and the opposite extreme that sees faith as almost entirely a matter of reason available to all. The philosophical approach known as "critical realism" is a case in point.[24] Truth is both revealed and discovered. There is both natural and special revelation. Our minds are finite. Our minds are doomed to blur subject with object. Presuppositionless exegesis is impossible.[25] Nevertheless, there are better and worse hypotheses. There are interpretations that account better for existing information in the simplest fashion without being too simple. In short, reason can work, and there is no discussion to be had by anyone if it cannot.

IBS is not hostile to faith. Practically speaking, it is the appropriation of Scripture that is most impactful. Spiritually speaking, it is the appropriation of Scripture that most requires the community of faith and the inspiration of the Spirit. Nevertheless, the use of reason is also inevitable no matter what one's hermeneutic is. Faith can seek understanding by way of the logic intrinsic to the universe as well as by way of the direct inspiration of the Holy Spirit. As far as the original meaning goes, it is IBS that is most likely to reach the target, as we argue in the next section.

3. The Relevance of the Original Meaning

The human mind has a capacity to convince itself of the most implausible things. Jonathan Haidt has argued in *The Righteous Mind* that our thinking processes are like a rider on an elephant.[26] The rider can steer the elephant a little, but ultimately the elephant is going to go where it wants to go. He thus argues that our subconscious intuitions play a greater role in the use to which we put our reason than anything like a truly objective quest for truth. Thomas Kuhn argued for analogous conclusions in his well known, *The Structure of Scientific Revolutions*.[27] There is a gravity to prevailing paradigms that is difficult to overcome. To a significant extent, even scientists find what they are looking for.

James K. A. Smith has argued a similar case in works like *Desiring the Kingdom* and *You Are What You Love*.[28] He argues the Cartesian model of human beings as "thinking things" does not capture the nature of human choice and action nearly as well as a sense that we operate in terms of more "gut-level" compasses—our loves. "We are primarily desiring animals rather than merely

---

[24] N. T. Wright attempts to develop a model of critical realism in his work, *The New Testament and the People of God* (Minneapolis: Fortress, 1992), 32–37. His goal is to avoid the "optimism" of the positivist position and the "pessimism" of the phenomenologists.

[25] As Rudolf Bultmann indicated so long ago: "Is Exegesis without Presuppositions Possible," in *Existence and Faith: Shorter Writings of Rudolf Bultmann* (Cleveland: The Word Publishing Company, 1965), 289–96.

[26] Jonathan Haidt, *The Righteous Mind: Why Good People Are Divided by Politics and Religion* (New York: Vintage Books, 2012), 52–56.

[27] Thomas S. Kuhn, *The Structure of Scientific Revolutions* (Chicago: The University of Chicago Press, 1962).

[28] James K. A. Smith, *Desiring the Kingdom: Worship, Worldview, and Cultural Formation* (Grand Rapids: Baker Academic, 2009) and *You Are What You Love: The Spiritual Power of Habit* (Grand Rapids: Brazos, 2016).

thinking things."²⁹ He draws on Charles Taylor's sense that we operate with "social imaginaries" by which we imagine our world in ways like images, stories, and legends (more than theories).[30]

These are important correctives to the impulse to view human beings predominantly as creatures of logic and reason. Nevertheless, there *are* circumstances where the world stops our elephants in their tracks and insists they move in a different direction. There is also everyday reason that is compelling to those with an open mind. Take the following statement: "The books of the Bible had a meaning to those who first heard/read them." This proposition has a ring of truth to it. It would boggle everyday reason to suggest that God inspired Paul to write the Corinthians and yet that neither party understood the letter or believed the meaning was for them to any great extent. Surely, they thought the letter was for them rather than for some generation thousands of years later.

It is true that some NT passages did *not* see certain OT texts as written primarily for their first audiences. Paul seems to imply as much in 1 Cor 9:9–10: "Oxen are not a concern to God, are they? Or is it not entirely because of us?" First Peter 1:12 expresses a similar sentiment when it says of the prophets, "to them is was revealed that they were not serving themselves but you." Upon reflection, however, it is difficult not see in such statements an implication that God meant *more* for the meaning of the OT texts than *merely* the original sense. Inductive readings of the OT texts in question, using everyday reason, compel us to recognize that these texts likely had meanings for their first audiences as well, in addition to the extended meanings or "fuller senses" that the Spirit often led the NT authors to see in those texts.

The books of the Bible thus had meanings to those who first heard/read them, the "first meanings" of these texts. To be sure, there are complicating factors. No doubt authors encoded potential meanings into their texts unintentionally, some of which they might have agreed with, others of which they would not have. Once written, the texts took on an autonomy independent of their authors.[31] To the extent that an "intentional fallacy" exists, it is the presumption that an author can perfectly encode his or her intended meaning or that a reader is bound to decode a text according to the intentions of an author.[32] Nevertheless, using everyday reason, it makes sense to say that authors do manage to communicate through texts, despite the inevitable entropy of meaning loss.

How do the decoders of texts decode them? Here the work of Ludwig Wittgenstein and speech-act theorists like J. L. Austin and John Searle is quite helpful.[33] The meaning of words is in how they are used, and we decode them on the bases of the "language games" we know in various "forms of life." In short, at the time when Amos prophesied to the northern kingdom, Israelites were using Hebrew words in certain ways in that context. The original meaning of Amos was a function

---

[29] Smith, *Desiring the Kingdom*, 26.

[30] Charles Taylor, *A Secular Age* (Cambridge, MA: Belknap Press of Harvard University, 2007), 171–76

[31] Paul Ricoeur, *Interpretation Theory: Discourse and the Surplus of Meaning* (Fort Worth: Texas Christian University, 1976), 29–30.

[32] W. K. Wimsatt, Jr. and M. C. Beardsley, "The Intentional Fallacy," *Sewanee Review* 54 (1946): 468–88.

[33] See especially his *Philosophical Investigations*, G. E. M. Anscombe, trans. (Englewood Cliffs, NJ: Prentice Hall, 1958). See also J. L. Austin, *How to Do Things with Words* (Oxford: Oxford University Press, 1962) and John R. Searle, *Speech Acts: An Essay in the Philosophy of Language* (Cambridge: Cambridge University Press, 1969).

of those uses. No meaning in human minds exists outside of such language games. In the oft repeated words of Bob Lyon, NT professor and one of Bob Traina's long time colleagues at Asbury Theological Seminary, "Context is everything." Context determines meaning. The only way for a text to have universal meaning is for it to be *omni*-contextual. For humans, there is no such thing as "timeless" meaning removed from context or culture.

So, the books of the Bible had a first meaning to those who first wrote/spoke them and that meaning was a function of the way words were being used at that time. Next comes the sobering point. The way that they used words in that eighth-century BC context was different than the way we use words in English today because our language games and forms of life are different. Even if we can find an approximate word in English that corresponds to a Hebrew word, there are likely to be socio-cultural differences in the connotations of the word between the two worlds. We can infer this fact from our own experiences of different contexts and languages in our own world.

Everyday reasoning thus leads us to some simple yet compelling conclusions. There is likely a distance between us and the original meaning. These texts were not written to us in the first instance. We are reading someone else's mail. The Scriptures may be for us, but they were not written to us. Our default ways of defining the words are likely to vary—at times subtly, at times not so subtly—from the original connotations. From this is born a hermeneutic that questions my assumptions about the meanings of texts.

At the same time, it is at this point that our faith presuppositions do come into play. First, they come into play with regard to the events and persons to which these words referred. Might the text actually refer to a miracle? Might the text actually refer to a spiritual being? Our faith expands the possibilities of what these texts might actually have meant in relation to the world. Second, they come into play in our belief that God inspired these words in some way for their original audiences. Assuming that he did, he must have inspired the words within their language games and forms of life. Otherwise, they would have misunderstood them.

When the NT authors heard new meanings in the OT words, these were meanings that were a function of *their* language games and forms of life—of their contexts. As omniscient, God of course knew those potentialities to the words when inspiring the first meaning. They were not likely in the "bubble" above the human mind of the OT at that time. Nevertheless, we can suggest that God not only inspired a first meaning, but other possible meanings the words might have even down to today when a verse jumps out at you or me in a new way. All these meanings are context-dependent, and the only way to determine the first meaning is to delve into the original context. Any other inspired meaning is a *sensus plenior*, a fuller sense dependent on a different context.

IBS is thus a method that is perfectly suited to this situation. We make observations and raise questions. The questions are intended to suspect ourselves and our assumptions about what these words mean. We try to make only the most obvious of observations, and we might question even those. When we try to answer those questions, we painstakingly gather literary evidence and draw possible inferences. When we finally engage historical sources, we do so after letting the text speak as much as possible on its own. We suspend our use of commentaries until late in the enterprise, so that we do not bias ourselves further. Such a method is painstakingly designed to hear the text on its own terms rather than on ours.

Again, as a faith presupposition, we believe that these first meanings were the meanings that related to the foundational events of the Christian faith. These are central events like the incarnation, atonement, and resurrection/enthronement of Jesus Christ. The books of the NT gave witness to these central events of salvation history, and the books of the OT provide us with God's doings in the time leading up to them. How could the first meanings of these books not be relevant to Christian faith when they give witness to these foundational events?

4. THE PRAGMATISM OF THE ATTEMPT

A critical realist approach believes that the "other" is real and that it is possible to "represent" that other in our own conceptual frameworks in a way that at least approximates the other. Alternatively, perhaps we could say that we can express the other in our minds in ways that lead to thought patterns and behaviors that are consistent with the intentions of the other. IBS seems the most likely method to recreate the original meanings in our world in front of the text. Further, even for the most pessimistic of epistemologists, there is a pragmatism to the quest that potentially dissolves the problem of meaning. That is to say, IBS is a useful quest.

First, with regard to the approximation of the original meanings, IBS helps eliminate interpretive options that are anachronistic or extremely unlikely. When I am forced to produce evidence from the literary context to defend my sense of the words, then instances where I am blatantly reading my definitions into the words are exposed. When I belong to a faith tribe with a peculiar interpretation, the inductive process holds those interpretations up to the scrutiny of literary and historical evidence. I am required to ask questions of the meaning that do not assume what I have assumed.

Perhaps I am doing a detailed observation of Gen 1:27 and I raise the question, "Who is the *we* of this verse?" Theological interpretation might push me to suggest the Trinity, but what evidence can I adduce for that from the text of Gen 1 or its likely historical context? The Spirit of God is present in Gen 1:2, but I must ask of that verse also whether it is referring to the breath of God or a wind from God. When I dig into historical context, I encounter texts like Ps 82 that picture a plurality of heavenly beings (cf. also Deut 32:8 in the Septuagint and Dead Sea Scrolls), and these texts are much closer historically to Gen 1 than the Council of Nicaea. The point is that IBS, if done properly, forces me to raise these questions where I might otherwise have made unexamined assumptions. One might argue that a theological interpretation is a more Christian reading of the verse, but it is not likely to result in as accurate a sense of what the verse originally meant to author and audience.

As far as historical background information is concerned, we arguably have more evidence at our disposal today than any of the interpreters of the last two millennia. More artifacts may have existed at the time of Augustine, but he did not have access to them. More significantly, he did not operate with an inductive paradigm, which means he was not as likely to interpret the texts in context as someone practicing IBS today. He was a theological interpreter, which means he can help us with the appropriation of Scripture but is less likely to help us determine the original meaning of the biblical texts.

Furthermore, while it would be easy to mock the guild of Biblical Studies for its wandering path on various subjects, there are consensuses that reflect the cumulative wisdom of inductive study. For example, it is the current consensus of Pauline scholarship that Rom 7 does not refer to some ongoing struggle with sin for those in Christ. The inductive study of Rom 6–8 convincingly leads the interpreter to see Paul in 7:14–25 dramatizing the plight of a person who knows the Law and wants to keep it but is unable because he or she is still a slave to Sin and not in the Spirit. This consensus was not always a consensus, but the ongoing dialog between inductive interpreters eventually led to this understanding.

A theological interpreter might not reach this conclusion. With nothing to tether the theological interpreter down, the texts are free to mean whatever the theology of the interpreter wants them to mean. Even if such a meaning is the consensus of the church, it is still more a form of reader-response than interpretation proper. For those of us who are Protestants, how likely is there to be reformation unless the text is truly an "other" with which to dialog rather than a mere mirror of the church's theology? The church is still free to speak, but it is a voice in the appropriation of these texts, not its interpretation. The Spirit can help illuminate our minds to see the original meaning in interpretation, yet when the Spirit speaks freshly through a text, that is a voice of appropriation rather than interpretation.

From a pragmatist point of view, the inductive process is valuable if for no other reason than that it shapes the interpreter in a positive way. To listen to the text is to submit to the possibility of meanings that are not the ones you expected or desired. You begin to see yourself and your assumptions as you are forced to raise questions whose answers seemed obvious to you before. You are required to provide literary evidence for your conclusions and are asked not to engage the thinking of others until you have formed your own provisional thoughts. Your critical thinking muscles are improved in the process. An awareness of a multiplicity of options makes you a freer person in the option you choose, even if it is the one with which you started. Now, however, you choose it freely rather than because you did not recognize any other possibilities.

Accordingly, even if the text is underdetermined at many points, the process of IBS is beneficial in itself, and the distinction between interpretation and appropriation is important heuristically and theoretically. Stephen E. Fowl is particularly known for developing a model of biblical texts as underdetermined.[34] While he refers to texts apart from contexts, he is known for advocating a determination of meaning that focuses on communities of faith and the Holy Spirit. In doing so, he collapses interpretation into appropriation, as is typical of theological interpreters. I hope it is clear by now that I do not disagree with the moves he makes as *appropriation* strategies. However, if as we have argued there is likely to be some distance between us and the original meaning of these texts, then Fowl's strategy moves us in the opposite direction of that which is more likely to help us hear what they actually meant.

---

[34] Stephen E. Fowl, *Engaging Scripture: A Model for Theological Interpretation* (Hoboken, NJ: Wiley, 1998), 56–61.

From an inductive standpoint, we will often have to accept the fact that we cannot be certain of the first meaning of the text. We responsibly set out possible options, aided by centuries of exegetical investigation. We may suggest some ranking of the likely options. We can then fill the gaps at the stage of appropriation. In the end, it is more helpful to maintain these distinctions than to blur them together in a way that opens wide the door for mirror readings to become the word of God.

5. Conclusion

Although the bulk of this chapter has addressed the benefits of IBS, we should make it clear that the postmodern critique is valuable. In his book *Seized by Truth*, Green alludes to the possibility that one might be able to dissect the biblical text like a frog and label all the parts yet only have a dead frog on your hands.[35] It is not Scripture if it is not in some way a living word. Similarly, an inductive reading of the OT is not yet fully Christian. The difference between the Jewish Bible and the OT is a sense that the original meaning of these books is on its way to the Jesus of the NT. Without Christ, the Jewish Bible only gives us a partial sense of who God is. It is not yet Christian Scripture.

IBS gives us the most likely sense of what these individual texts meant originally, of God's first revelation. However, for the most part these books do not tell us how to connect their teaching together. A biblical theology of necessity requires us to bring at least some organizing principles from outside these texts into the process of connecting them to each other even as we try to be faithful to the inductive meanings of the individual texts. Similarly, these books do not tell us how to re-contextualize them in our contemporary contexts. So, while interpretation can be an individual task, the appropriation of the Bible as Christian Scripture also requires the community of faith, the church, under the inspiration of the Holy Spirit. Ideally, our inductive conclusions fit hand in glove with the direction that appropriation takes providing a kind of tether that keeps the church grounded. Nevertheless, the most crucial step—where the text impacts us—involves factors that move us beyond the merely inductive. Appropriation is also a spiritual task and a community task.

I am incredibly grateful to have learned Robert A. Traina's English Bible method in my days at Asbury Theological Seminary, then extended into the original languages. My first year was Dr. Traina's final year; unfortunately for me, his final Pentateuch class immediately filled with third-year students. Alas, I was nevertheless privileged to take a number of classes with Dr. David R. Bauer and Dr. David L. Thompson, worthy heirs of the master. In my days in Biblical Studies ever since, I have often noted how the discipline of induction has helped me see points where world-class scholars have "cooked the books." Such scholars, often consummately aware of historical background and the history of interpretation, have seemed to stumble because they lacked when it came to the evidence of the text itself. In such moments, I pause to remember those who gave me this gift of IBS!

---

[35] Green, *Seized by Truth*, 12. I have extended his metaphor.

FOR FURTHER READING

Davis, Ellen F. and Hays, Richard B. *The Art of Reading Scripture*. Grand Rapids: Eerdmans, 2003.

Gadamer, Hans-Georg. *Truth and Method*, 2nd ed. New York: Crossroad, 1990.

Green, Joel B. *Seized by Truth: Reading the Bible as Scripture*. Nashville: Abingdon, 2007.

Haidt, Jonathan. *The Righteous Mind: Why Good People Are Divided by Politics and Religion*. New York: Vintage Books, 2012.

Koskie, Jr., Steven Joe. *Reading the Way to Heaven: A Wesleyan Theological Hermeneutic of Scripture*. JTIS 8. Winona Lake, IN: Eisenbrauns, 2014.

Ricoeur, Paul. *Interpretation Theory: Discourse and the Surplus of Meaning*. Fort Worth: Texas Christian University, 1976.

Smith, James K. A. *Desiring the Kingdom: Worship, Worldview, and Cultural Formation*. Grand Rapids: Baker Academics, 2009.

Thorsen, Donald A. D. *The Wesleyan Quadrilateral: Scripture, Tradition, Reason and Experience as a Model of Evangelical Theology*. Grand Rapids: Zondervan, 1990.

Traina, Robert A. and Bauer, David R. *Inductive Bible Study: A Comprehensive Guide to the Practice of Hermeneutics*. Grand Rapids: Baker Academic, 2011.

Treier, Daniel J. *Introducing Theological Interpretation of Scripture: Recovering a Christian Practice*. Grand Rapids: Baker, 2008.

Watson, Francis. *Text, Church and World: Biblical Interpretation in Theological Perspective*. Grand Rapids: Eerdmans, 1994.

Wright, N. T. *The New Testament and the People of God*. Minneapolis: Fortress, 1992.

AN "INDUCTIVE" FRIENDLY ACADEMY AND THE NEED FOR EXPLICIT INDUCTIVE BIBLE STUDY IN SCHOLARSHIP

Fredrick J. Long
Professor of New Testament and Director of Greek Instruction
Asbury Theological Seminary

ABSTRACT: The term "inductive" is used commonly and broadly in scholarship to refer to "evidential" research. Inductive Bible Study (IBS) embraces this evidential orientation towards Scripture, but represents, beyond that basic hermeneutical commitment, a particular tradition of Bible study, associated originally with William Rainey Harper and Wilbert W. White, and The Biblical Seminary in New York. This specific process of biblical study possesses its own emphases and structure. Moreover, the approach has been taught in many leading educational institutions around the world and has influenced several globally recognized scholars. Yet IBS is rarely mentioned in the scholarship of the academy even though the academy generally appeals to "inductive" research in many sub-disciplines. Since many active scholars have been formally trained in IBS and have expressed deep appreciation for it, IBS belongs in the academy and deserves more explicit representation in scholarly presentation and academic publications.

1. INTRODUCTION

1.1 Venues of IBS

Many venues exist for using IBS or formally teaching the Bible inductively as IBS—classrooms, sermons, Sunday School classes, discipleship groups—but neglected venues include scholarly presentations and academic collaborations. Although there are numerous scholars trained in Inductive Bible Study (IBS) who have been "active in the guild," nevertheless IBS as a hermeneutical approach to scriptural interpretation has very rarely been presented academically in scholarship. The basic premise of this essay is that IBS is not just for students or laity, but also for our scholarly peers in the academy.

1.2 "Inductive" Defined and IBS Practitioners

David R. Bauer and Robert A. Traina begin their book on *Inductive Bible Study* by distinguishing the broader and narrower sense of the word "inductive." More broadly, the term refers to "evidential" and is contrasted with deductive: "one examines the evidence in order to determine what may properly be inferred from the evidence for the meaning of passages."[1] More narrowly, inductive in terms of Bible study (IBS) refers to the hermeneutical approach to Bible study espoused by William Rainey Harper, his student and colleague Wilber Webster White, and developed subsequently by such persons as Howard T. Kuist, Robert A. Traina, David R. Bauer, and others. Currently, numerous scholars have been formally trained in IBS including the following: Bill T. Arnold, Rick Boyd, Gareth Lee Cockerill, Joseph R. Dongell, Gabriella Gelardini, Thomas W. Gillespie, Kyle Greenwood, T. Michael W. Halcomb, Victor P. Hamilton, John E. Hartley, L. Daniel Hawk, Ryan P. Juza, Eugene E. Lemcio, Fredrick J. Long, Michael D. Matlock, James C. Miller, Patrick D. Miller, Jr., Suzanne Nicholson, John N. Oswalt, Kenneth L. Schenck, Eric A. Seibert, Frank Anthony Spina, Lawson G. Stone, John T. Strong, Stanley D. Walters, Dorothy Jean Weaver. This does not include those who have now passed away, e.g., Brevard S. Childs, James Luther Mays, Edward P. Blair, Donald G. Miller, and Eugene H. Peterson. Nor does this list include those doctoral students at Asbury Theological Seminary and elsewhere who have been formally trained in IBS, some of whom are dissertating explicitly utilizing IBS in their scriptural interpretation of passages and whole books.

2. "Inductive" and IBS in the Academic Papers of the last Fifteen Years

2.1 Is IBS for the Academy?

Yes. Is IBS *in* the Academy? No, since there is a notable paucity of explicit use of IBS as a hermeneutical approach in scholarly presentations. This claim is supported by reviewing thousands academic paper titles and their abstracts in the program books for the Annual Society of Biblical Literature (SBL) meetings (in November each year) and the International SBL meetings (in July) since 2004; also, a search of Asbury Scholar provided very limited results. While other databases could have been included, the SBL Meetings reflect a breadth of current global scholarly research in the areas of Bible and Religion with many thousand attendees each year.[2] Moreover, academic papers reflect ongoing and emergent research that often results in printed articles, essays, and even monographs. Thus, they are a fairly accurate barometer of scholarly interest and research trends.

2.2 "Inductive" and IBS in SBL Meetings

Searching through the titles and abstracts resulted in dozens of references to "inductive"[3]

---

[1] Bauer and Traina, *Inductive Bible Study: A Comprehensive Guide to the Practice of Hermeneutics* (Grand Rapids: Baker Academic, 2011), 1.

[2] These abstracts and programs were found and searched individually here: https://www.sbl-site.org/meetings/congresses_pastmeetings.aspx. It is difficult to determine how many papers searched, but it is in the thousands.

[3] I exclude here a reference to "inductive divination" as described by David A. Skelton in the abstract of his paper "Implicit Exegesis as a Mean of Transmitting Divine Knowledge in the Thanksgiving Psalms" 2018 (International SBL meeting in Helsinki) and "inductive argument" (occurring one time), "inductive case" in developing an argument (also occurring only once), or "inductive instruction" as found in Scripture (once). Also, one paper in in the annual SBL

(summarized below) and only a few interactions with the main practitioners of IBS. In addition to the word "inductive," searches were made for "methodical"[4] as well as the last names "White", "Harper", "Kuist", "Traina", and "Bauer" to find relevant papers. I will discussion papers chronologically year-by-year and place the relevant phrases that contain the word "inductive" in bold.

In the 2006 International Meeting of SBL in Edinburgh, David R. Bauer's *The Structure of Matthew* was reviewed and critiqued by Paul Landgraf at the Synoptic Gospels Section. Then, in the 2006 Annual SBL Meeting in Washington, DC, Gabriella Gelardini in her paper "*Anadiplosis Iterata* or Literary-Rhetorical Criticism and Concentric Structure Revisited" advocates for "a modified literary-rhetorical criticism given that it excellently servers the goal to gain an exegetical pre-comprehension of a text." She continues, "While addressing structural "problem zones" and discussing obvious literary structural markers, I want to demonstrate that the argumentation on the macro structural level is arranged in a concentric catena (or *anadiplosis iterata*). In correspondence to that the text on the micro structural level is arranged in concentric thought circles (Gedankenkreise) throughout the entire book as well. **This inductive approach** allows not only an interpretative comparison of sister paragraphs it also generates a hermeneutical key that is able to put all parts of the book into a logical and coherent whole." The recognition that her approach is "inductive" is quite notable. At this same meeting, Charles A. Anderson in the Biblical Greek Language and Linguistics section utilizes "**an inductive examination**" of all instances of an aorist circumstantial participle in relation to an aorist main verb in his "Time, Time, Time. See What's Become of It': Factors on the Temporal Relation of Aorist Participles and Verbs in the New Testament."

In the 2007 Annual SBL Meeting in San Diego, David S. E. Stein applies an inductive philological approach in his research on "The Grammar of Social Gender in Biblical Hebrew."

In the 2009 Annual SBL meeting in New Orleans, Humphrey H. Hardy II "examines this claim of dialectic divergence in the Aramaic of the Tell Fekheriyeh stele by providing **an inductive analysis** of Old Aramaic verbal clause word order and comparing it to the constructions found in the Tell Fekheriyeh inscriptions" in his paper "The Tell Fekheriyeh Stele: Dialect, Word Order, and Scribal Symbiosis." In the same conference, Philip Alexander warns against substituting ancient rhetorical theory as a mode of genre analysis "to short-circuit inductive analysis of the texts

---

meeting in 2015 by Josh Westbury described a computational approach to linguistically tagging phonology in morphology using a deductive and inductive approach. At the 2010 International meeting in Tartu, Estonia, Richard K. Min presenting "Biblical Paradox and Coinductive Reasoning" in the "Biblical Studies and Technology" program unit proposed "**coinductive reasoning**" to study circularity and paradoxical reasoning in Scripture (e.g., Exod 3:14; John 14:10; 1 Tim 1:12) focusing on Matt 22 and its linguistic construct, "its literary genre and analysis, and its logic and reasoning including modal and nonmonotonic logic." In the next International SBL meeting 2011 in London, Min explored **coinductive reasoning** again in Jesus's self-referential arguments in John 8:12–18. Finally, excluded too is the paper of the 2015 Annual SBL meeting in which, while discussing hermeneutics and preaching in her paper entitled, "Preaching Paul's Letters as Narrative: Philippians and Empathetic Imagination," Jennifer Garcia Bashaw affirms "Fred Craddock's inductive approach, which uses the exegetical process of interpretation as a schematic for sermon preparation" that reflects "the importance of preaching the form of the text."

[4] The word "methodical" and its derivatives are sometimes used, often less than four times to none at all; however, the forty-eight instances at the 2013 Annual SBL Meeting and the sixty-nine in 2017 are truly quite remarkable.

themselves" in his paper, "On the Value or Lack of It of Ancient Genre Labels." At the 2009 International SBL meeting in Rome, Peter M. Head when considering "The Identification of Letter-carriers in Subscriptions to the Pauline Letters: Manuscripts, Sources and the Development of a Tradition" asks whether traditional or "**inductive study**" can determine whether letter-carrier identification found in the letter manuscripts were made from tradition or inductive study of the letters.

At the 2010 Annual SBL Meeting in Atlanta, Jonathan M. Watt affirmed scholarly "**inductive conclusions** about Greek diminutives" in his paper, "A Short Study of Greek Diminutives."

At the 2012 Annual SBL Meeting in Chicago, in an important paper "Critical Engagement with the Biblical Text: Classroom and Online" Paul Borgman advocates "to help students become more biblical literate" by proposing three repeatable steps throughout the course (quoted from the abstract, bold added):

(1) With a specific biblical text in view, though not yet assigned, students are assigned appropriate secondary reading that sufficiently establishes the important cultural and literary contexts (ancient rhetorical practices, primarily, the dominant techniques of repetition). Written questions or insights—two or three—would be required to be posted online, or brought to class in hard copy.

(2) An **inductive reading** of a limited biblical text (e.g., poetry; Esther, Jonah, or Ruth the most obvious beginning entry points into the repetitive patterns shaping biblical narrative; a short epistle, like Galatians or 1 Thessalonians). The assignment would involve online posting of the professor's prompt questions, necessitating student responses either online or handed in at the beginning of class. Class time could break into smaller groups, with designated presenters from each group offering group findings to the larger class Throughout, or toward the end, the professor would interact with the student findings.

(3) A reassessment of **inductive findings** in light of further and specific secondary sources on the particular text or portion of text chosen. Such secondary material could be the professor's own lectures, posted online, or published essays and/or books (put on library reserve?), or possibly an assigned text addition to the introductory text (depending on how sophisticated this text is regarding the rhetorical shaping of ancient literary texts). Students write short paragraphs summarizing in what way the secondary reading has challenged or broadened or brought questions regarding their initial close readings. Again, the class time could have a breaking into groups, with presenters' offering major insights and/or questions. The professor then guides a "circle" of critical conversation and engagement.

Borgman, an emeritus faculty of literature of Gordon College, proposes pedagogy amenable to IBS.

At the same meeting, directly appealing to Bauer and Traina's book *Inductive Biblical Study*, Matthew Hamilton of Southwest Virginia Community College presented in the Academic Teaching and Biblical Studies program unit, "Overcoming the Challenge of Under Prepared Students: Teaching Biblical Studies in a Community College Setting." Due to the relevance of Hamilton's paper to

IBS pedagogy, its abstract is given here in full:

> Freshmen and Sophomore college students taking introductory biblical studies courses are usually in the process of adjusting to the rigors of college work, and are therefore unprepared to read, write, or think critically. This problem is particularly prevalent in the community college setting, where religious studies courses usually have no prerequisites. In order to overcome this difficulty, I have modified the Inductive Bible Study methodology, which was published by Dr. David R. Bauer and the late Dr. Robert A. Traina, in an effort to increase the students' ability to read, write, and think critically while also becoming very familiar with the material presented in New Testament and Old Testament Survey courses without being restricted by secondary sources and textbooks.

Readers should refer also to John Dendiu's essay in this volume "Inductive Bible Study Principles in General Education Bible Classes at a Christian College" (Chapter 8).

Also at this meeting, Andrew Knapp in his paper "Apologetic in Biblical and Ancient Near Eastern Literature" argues against the assumption that "apologetic" is a "literary genre with a particular form"; rather, "Literary genres are historical categories which **can be used inductively to draw conclusions** about any example of the genre." Then, too, addressing the problems of generalized conclusion in historiographical research, "[b]ased on his studies on Rome and on Phrygia, combining archaeological, epigraphic and literary sources, Peter Lampe looks at chances and drawbacks of an **inductive approach**" in his paper "**Induction** as Historiograhical Tool: Methodological Reflections on Locally and Regionally Focused Studies." Also at this conference, Fredrick J. Long presented "Emphasis and Prominence Markers in Greek: A Proposal and Case Study within 2 Corinthians" affirming "the theory and explanations of discourse theory and semantics from **Robert Traina, David Bauer**, Robert Longacre, Eugene Nida, Johannes Louw, George Guthrie, Stanley Porter, Runge, and others."

In the same year (2012) International SBL meeting in Amsterdam, Rebecca Raphael in the Apocrypha and Pseudepigraph program unit presented "Proposing the Anomalous Body: Disability, Monstrosity, and Metamorphosis in Second Temple Apocalypses" in which she "combines an **inductive assessment of body imagery** in the primary texts (1 Enoch, Daniel, 4 Ezra, Qumran, and others) with the contemporary confluence of disability studies, monster theory, and critiques of body-focused ideology, as these have developed in literary criticism (L. Davis; Garland-Thomson; Gilmore; Mitchell & Snyder; and others) and in biblical studies" (abstract).

In the 2013 Annual SBL Meetings in Baltimore, Ingrid Faro presented two papers investigating "evil" in Genesis. In one paper, "Lexical Semantics of Evil in Genesis," she explains: "**This inductive study** moves from word to syntactical units, through exegetical context and intertextual linkages toward building a conceptual understanding of evil from the text." In a second paper, "A Contextual Approach to the Lexical Semantic Use of Evil in Genesis," Faro describes her rationale and approach:

> Recognizing the importance of context to the meaning and use of a word, **an inductive study** was conducted to map every occurrence of this through the Hebrew text of Genesis. Paradigmatic and syntagmatic collocations were analyzed from the immediate clause level, to near contextual occurrences of the lexeme, and traced through widening circles of interlinking linguistic and literary units in narrative and direct discourse. The most frequent paradigmatic collocation is, not surprisingly, good. The most frequent syntagmatic collocations center upon words related to internal and external senses, such as to know, to eat, food, with the most frequent collocations pertaining to the word grouping related to sight. Evil was found to be a hypernym with a broad semantic range referring to anything bad: from lacking, deficient, and displeasing; to harmful, sinful and wicked. A taxonomy of evil was developed for comparative and contrasting domains of meaning. This lexeme contributes to the literary framework of the plot conflict between good and evil. Application of cognitive linguistics provides additional insights contributing to the concept and theology of evil that weave throughout the structure of Genesis.

The thoroughness of Faro's inductive contextual research is notable.

At the 2014 Annual SBL Meeting in San Diego, Naphtali Meshel in "Bellowing Buffalo and Other Grammars" espouses developing "operative categories … **abstracted inductively** from the ritual texts" for their study such as zoemics, jugation, hierarchics, and praxemics. Here inductive research leads to more accurate and native description of primary materials.

At the 2015 Annual SBL Meeting in Atlanta, Fredrick J. Long presented "Vital Relations and Major Structural Relationships: A Heuristic Approach to Observe and Explore Biblical and Other Discourse" in the Cognitive Linguistics in Biblical Interpretation program unit. The abstract mentions This research has been subsequently published and is available online.[5] Then, too, at this conference Melinda Cousins considers "Re-Structuring for Engagement: An Experiment in Changing How Class Time Is Allocated in Old Testament Survey." In her presentation abstract, Cousins describes moving from a lecture model to "discussion groups based on students' pre-reading of significant sections of the OT text, critical reflection on contemporary interpretations of the text, **inductive learning through Q & A**, and the teaching of interpretive and study skills." Cousin's pedagogical concerns mirror several included above that work with an "inductive" approach to learning.

At the 2016 Annual SBL meeting in San Antonio, Kenneth Schenck in a paper "'Through His Own Blood' (Heb 9:12): Did Jesus Offer His Blood in Heaven?" investigates the role that bodily or spiritual resurrection plays in Hebrews. He "concludes that a 'spiritual' resurrection still best fits the **inductive evidence** of Hebrews, referencing Jubilees and 1 Enoch as providing precedents." Similarly, at the 2017 Blake Wassell argues his "case **inductively** first, pointing to the broader **evidence** … and deductively second, presenting new readings…" in his paper "The Beloved Disciple

---

[5] Fredrick J. Long, "Vital Relations and Major Structural Relationships: Heuristic Approaches to Observe and Explore Biblical and Other Discourse," *The Journal of Inductive Biblical Studies* 4.2 (2017): 92–128 available online at http://place.asburyseminary.edu/jibs/vol4/iss2/3.

Reads Jesus into Deuteronomy: Concluding Torah with the Second Prophet." At the 2016 International SBL meeting in Seoul, Scott N. Callaham in his paper "Biblical Hebrew in Chinese: Fostering the Rethinking of Teaching Method through Language Defamiliarization" espouses "defamiliarization" when teaching/learning Hebrew which aligns with "more **inductive and communicative approaches** that exploit the findings of second language acquisition research."[6]

Finally, at the 2018 Annual SBL Meeting in Denver, Shane Patrick Gormley interacts with J. D. Kingsbury and Bauer's work on the structure of Matthew. He argues that the threefold division of the genealogy corresponds to the three-fold division proposed by Kingsbury and Bauer (1:2-6a // 1:18-4:16; 1:6b-11 // 4:17-16:20; 1:12-16 // 16:21-28:20). At the same conference, Gary P. Klump in "Cognitive Linguistics and Intertextuality: A Methodological Proposal" posits "a methodology that employs the insights of the cognitive linguistic notion (per Halliday) of "register," which will allow for a **more inductive approach** to form criticism, while freeing source criticism from what can often be simple verbal comparison." In the same program unit, Cooper Smith shows the failure deductive models to intertextual "which demonstrates the need for this **inductive approach**" which he advances in his paper, "Intertextuality and the Direction of Dependence: Toward a Comprehensive List of Criteria."

2.2. "Inductive Bible Study" in Asbury Scholar

Searching within the Asbury Scholar in the library portal for "Inductive Bible Study" shows eighty-six results, but actually there are seventy-five with some duplicates. The first listed, not surprisingly, is Bauer and Traina's *Inductive Bible Study*; the second were video cassettes by the same title by Prof. Traina. The following thirty-one results contained a number of book reviews of Bauer and Traina, many articles from *The Journal of Inductive Biblical Studies*, and several from the 2013 volume of the *The Asbury Journal* 68.1 which published the papers presented in the Asbury postgraduate internal conference featuring responses to Bauer and Traina's book. Search result thirty-four was an 1894 article by Edwin M. Poteat "The Spiritual Value of Inductive Bible Study," *The Biblical Word* 3 (1894): 454–55 and then Traina's essay in two parts, "Inductive Bible Study Reexamined in the Light of Contemporary Hermeneutics" pages 53–83 and 85–109 in *Interpreting God's Word for Today: An Inquiry into Hermeneutics from a Biblical Theological Perspective*, ed. Wayne McCown and James E. Massey (Anderson, IN: Warner, 1982). The remaining search results generally fall within the following three categories.

<u>Magazine Articles, Journal Articles, and Essays</u>
    Arthur, Kay. "Steps to Powerful Teaching: An Introduction to Inductive Bible Study." *Evangelizing Todays Child* (January 1985): 8–12.

---

[6] In 2005 Annual SBL Meeting in Philadelphia, Helen Dallaire urged moving past "the traditional 'inductive/deductive' methods to explore the field of Second Language Acquisition, and apply its techniques to the learning of biblical Hebrew" in her paper "From Modern Hebrew Immersion to Classical Hebrew Proficiency." In the 2013 Annual SBL Meeting in Baltimore, Elizabeth Hayes describes an approach to teaching Greek informed by cognitive stylistics in "an inductive, introductory Greek class."

De Lacy, Pete. "Discovering Truth for Yourself: The Inductive Bible Study Method." *Bible Study Magazine* 1.2 (2009): 41.

Graham, Mary L., ed., *Inductive Bible Study Network Newsletter*, no. 1-30 (1991-2001); Pasadena, CA: Inductive Bible Study Network.

Inock, Joo Kim. "Post-Critical Interpretation and Application with Inductive Bible Study Method for Transformation." *Journal of Christian Education in Korea* (2008): 259–82.

Lea, Thomas D. "Inductive Bible Study Methods." *Biblical Hermeneutics: A Comprehensive Introduction to Interpreting Scripture*. Edited by Bruce Corley, Steve Lemke, and Grant Lovejoy. Nashville: Broadman & Holman, 2002.

Seon Young Lee. "Planning of Creative Teaching-Learning Model for Effective Bible Teaching—Focused on the HBLT Approach by Lawrence O. Richards." *Journal of Christian Education in Korea* 38 (2014): 255–80.

Tennant, Christy. "Kay Arthur on Inductive Bible Study." *Bible Study Magazine* 1.1 (2009): 11–15.

Un Chu Kim. "Understanding of Elizabeth J. Shepping's Educational Mission and Its Challenge to Christian Education." *Theology and Society* 29.2 (2015): 45–46.

Th.M. and D.Min Theses

Castillo, Metosalem Quillupras. "Inductive Bible Study and Its Place in the Curriculum of Ebenezer Bible College." Th.M., Asbury Theological Seminary, 1972.

Lovejoy, Owen Bryant. "The Word of God is not Imprisoned: An Inductive Bible Study with Prison Inmates." D.Min., Erskine Theological Seminary, 2002.

Mackey, Burl E. "Teaching Men at First Baptist Church Stroud, Oklahoma Inductive Bible Study as a Spiritual Discipline." D.Min., Midwestern Baptist Theological Seminary, 2002.

Taylor, James Edward. "A General Consideration of Inductive Bible Study." Th.M., Asbury Theological Seminary, 1961.

Zebulske, Terry E. "Manual for Training in Inductive Bible Study Methodology." D.Min., Westminster Theological Seminary, 1988.

Discipleship and Lay-level Books

Barber, Cyril J. *Unlocking the Scriptures: The Key to Inductive Bible Study*. Eugene, OR: Wipf & Stock, 2004.

Friedeman, Matt, and Lisa Friedeman Ausley. *Life Changing Bible Study*. Wilmore, KY: Francis Asbury Press, 2009.

Graham, Mary Creswell. *Inductive Bible Study Explained*. Pasadena, CA: M. L. Graham, 1990.

Joy, Donald M. *Concepts in Inductive Bible Study: Three Programmed Sequences*. Wilmore, KY: Asbury Theological Seminary, 1975.

Van Dolson, Leo R. *Hidden No Longer: A Guide to Inductive Bible Study*. Mountain View, CA: Pacific Press Publishing Association, 1968.

Williams, Don. *Celebrate Your Freedom: An Inductive Bible Study on Galatians*. Waco, TX: Word, 1975.

———. *An Introduction to Inductive Bible Study: Using Paul's Letter to Philemon.* Van Nuys, CA: BIM Publishing, 1977.

Surveying the abstracts and contents of these works, one might conclude that IBS is geared *only* towards Christian education and lay-discipleship.

2.3 Amazon Top 15 Hits on "Inductive Bible Study"

In addition to Bauer and Traina's book and Cyril J. Barber's (above) and a few Inductive Study Bibles, the following works appeared that attests both to the diversity of IBS and to the popularization and lay-appeal of Kay Arthur's IBS approach.[7]

Arthur, Kay. *Lord, Teach Me to Study the Bible in 28 Days.* Eugene, OR: Harvest House Publishers, 2008.
Arthur, Kay, and Janna Arndt. *How to Study Your Bible for Kids.* Eugene, OR: Harvest House Publishers, 2001.
Arthur, Kay, David Arthur, and Pete De Lacy. *How to Study Your Bible: Discover the Life-Changing Approach to God's Word.* Reprint edition. Eugene, OR: Harvest House Publishers, 2014.
Fuhr, Richard Alan, and Andreas J. Köstenberger, *Inductive Bible Study: Observation, Interpretation, and Application through the Lenses of History, Literature, and Theology.* Nashville: B&H Academic, 2016.
Hendricks, Howard G., William D. Hendricks, and Charles Swindoll. *Living by the Book: The Art and Science of Reading the Bible.* New edition. Chicago: Moody, 2007.
Henry Jackson III. *Stop Reading, Start Studying: Inductive Bible Study Method Explained.* Self-published: Inductive Bible Study LLC, 2015.

2.4 Additional Significant Books Treating Inductive Bible Study

The following books also reflect a lay-focused or ministerial orientation to IBS:

Halcomb, T. Michael W. *People of the Book: Inviting Communities into Biblical Interpretation.* Eugene, OR: Wipf & Stock, 2012.
Jensen, Irving Lester. *Independent Bible Study.* Rev. ed. Chicago: Moody, 1992.
Long, Fredrick J. *In Step with God's Word: Interpreting the New Testament with God's People.* GlossaHouse Hermeneutics & Translation 1. Wilmore, KY: GlossaHouse, 2017.
Thompson, David L. *Bible Study That Works.* Rev. ed. Nappanee, IN: Evangel, 1994.
Wald, Oletta. *The New Joy of Discovery in Bible Study.* Rev. ed. Minneapolis: Augsburg Fortress, 2002.

---

[7] For a genealogical presentation of the various strands of IBS, see Long, Fredrick J. Long, "Major Structural Relationships: A Survey of Origins, Development, Classifications, and Assessment," *The Journal of Inductive Biblical Studies* 1.1 (2014): 22–58 at 27–28 available at http://place.asburyseminary.edu/jibs/vol1/iss1/3.

3. Considerations Why IBS has Not Been Explicitly Represented Academically

Before proposing avenues for contributing to the scholarly discussion, it may be helpful first to diagnose the "problems" of why IBS has not been more academically represented.

1. IBS is associated with "lay study" of the Bible and a bias exists that IBS is not scholarly or related to the proper academic study of the Bible. Yet, Bauer maintains, "It is a sophisticated, hermeneutical approach—there is nothing to be ashamed of in terms of participation within the Academy."[8]
2. Prior to Bauer and Traina's *Inductive Bible Study*, IBS had no sufficient, thoroughgoing scholarly theoretical or hermeneutical grounding. However, this deficiency has now been met.
3. IBS may encourage a hermeneutical stance of suspended, tentatively held truth that may discourage scholarly presentation and writing since one remains "open" to the evidence in the text. However, while this may be true of committing words to print (article, essay, or book), the same does not apply to scholarly presentations where tentative and unfolding research is valued and regularly presented.
4. IBS's central focus on the Bible as the Church's Scripture may (rightly) produce a "ministry-mindedness" that is "more practical" and ministerial and consequentially perceived as less "academic."
5. IBS places great value on individual study rather than relying on the research and engagement of others; this self-imposed "restriction" may inadvertently discourage practitioners from engaging in scholarly discourse, resulting in less interest in presenting and/or publishing.
6. IBS may have missed pivotal opportunities for scholarly recognition and engagement. For example, Bauer has also related, "I was told that Norman Gottwald, who held the W. W. White Chair at New York Theological Seminary but had himself embraced a Marxist hermeneutic, was interested in starting an Inductive Biblical Study section at SBL. Nothing came of it...."[9] Also, Brevard Childs thought that IBS (then English Bible) would become an alternative to the Biblical Theology Movement built upon the English Bible approach of Harper at The University of Chicago and Kuist at Princeton, both "championing an inductive, compositionally oriented approach to interpretation."[10] One wonders, What if IBS had been able to gain scholarly acceptance and engagement in the early twentieth-century?

4. Considerations for IBS being more Explicitly Represented Academically

It occurs to me that the following are current and important considerations that would warrant and foster bringing IBS more and more into conversation with the Academy:

1. IBS has been hermeneutically grounded with Bauer and Traina's *Inductive Bible Study*.

---

[8] Quotation from David R. Bauer recorded from a conversation.
[9] Email correspondence July 20, 2018.
[10] Lawson Stone, email correspondence Jan 14, 2019, who indicated Childs said this to him more than once.

2. *The Journal of Inductive Biblical Studies* (*JIBS*) has begun (since 2014), of which this volume is a part (vol. 5.1–2). As rightly discerned by Fred Sanders, "What's unusual about this journal is that 'inductive Bible study' seems more like a technique or style of popular-level, that is to say non-academic, interaction with Scripture. But by using the phrase 'Biblical Studies' in the journal title, the editors are signaling that this is a Bible study movement that has come of age and is ready for more critical reflection, methodological self-awareness, and—who knows—intellectual respectability."[11]
3. More and more IBS-based dissertations will be forthcoming in the coming years.
4. Collaborative Projects, such as an IBS Commentary Series, have been discussed as well as the new JIBS Monograph Series with GlossaHouse that begins with this present volume.
5. Finally, IBS's hermeneutical distinctives such as Major Structural Relationships and its graphical depiction of biblical materials has connections with various fields of human knowledge[12] and NT methodologies.[13]

Thus, what makes IBS vital for the academy are its call for attentive observation of biblical and other materials, its "re-creative" endeavor to understand the texts on their own terms in relation to God's self-revelation and the complete human experience, and its concern to convey concepts integratively and graphically. In this regard, intriguingly a core feature of IBS—major structural relationships—finds seminal connection points with very important and increasingly prominent disciplines: ancient rhetorical theory, conceptual blending theory, cognitive linguistics, and metaphor theory.

5. Conclusion

My essay is in part a call to more explicit reference to IBS as a matter of stewardship of the approach by which we have been (in)formed. Since the Academy is responsible for shaping the thinking and approaches to interpretation for the next generations of pastors and educators, practitioners of IBS have a responsibility to draw hermeneutically and self-consciously upon IBS. Fortunately, as indicated by a review of many thousands of papers presented from 2004 to 2018, the Academy as reflected in the Annual and International SBL meetings generally accepts evidential, inductive approaches to researching biblical and other materials; thus, our more explicit use of IBS as a hermeneutical foundation should only encourage fruitful dialogue and further refinement of our perspectives. As aptly noted by Sanders, "Inductive Bible Study has been vastly influential, but has occupied a strange twilight region so far, not well enough recognized in academia to present itself as a self-conscious force; and not clearly branded enough to be called the same thing from place to place at the popular level."[14] It's time to move boldly onward in our IBS based research and scholarship.

---

[11] From http://scriptoriumdaily.com/journal-inductive-biblical-studies/

[12] See especially my two articles, "Major Structural Relationships" and "Vital Relations" cited above.

[13] For example, Mark Allan Powell describes the fifteen "compositional relationships" in his book, *What Is Narrative Criticism?* GBS (Minneapolis: Augsburg Fortress, 1990), 32–33.

[14] From http://scriptoriumdaily.com/journal-inductive-biblical-studies/

Christology & Ethics—Cosmic (Colossians) & Kenotic (Philippians):
Practicing New Testament Theology in the Context of Canon and Church

Eugene E. Lemcio
Emeritus Professor of New Testament, Seattle Pacific University

ABSTRACT: The critical movement from interpretation to developing a biblical theology within IBS method is rewarding, but not always straightforward. This study proposes a dialogical method of relating the diversity of Colossians (an exalted Christology should lead to exalted ethics) and Philippians (a self-emptying Christology should lead to self-emptying ethics) in a manner that avoids harmonization, preferential treatment, and reduction to an essence or principle. Examples of moving from canonical dynamics to ecclesial conversations are provided.

1. Introduction

I have been blessed with many fine teachers; but it was Robert Traina who influenced me most—both with regard to my own inductive study of the text and also as a model of classroom instruction in that approach. Although I did not become a formal practitioner of IBS in the sense that he promoted and that the eponymous journal (*The Journal of Inductive Biblical Studies*) seeks to foster, I did retain certain sensibilities and ways of proceeding that bear witness to my three years at ATS under his tutelage.

As an illustration, I conduct this exercise in particularization, the opposite of generalization (his students will recall).[1] One would have thought that noting frequency of terminology as a first step would be a no-brainer: "It's just the application of common sense [as many also say about psychology] and is a technique that 'born teachers' instinctively use." True, most keep track of repeated words and, at some point, make use of a concordance. But doing so systematically and joining it to distribution and to what I would call the "clustering" of synonyms takes repetition to another level. For example, if one reads quickly through the books of Daniel and Revelation (perhaps the most prior step of all), s/he is almost forced to notice how often the language of "kingdom" and

---

[1] Robert A. Traina, *Methodical Bible Study: A New Approach to Hermeneutics* (New York: Ganis & Harris, 1952).

"rule" occurs. Furthermore, associated with these terms are "power," "might," "authority," and "glory." They thus quadruple the vocabulary of politics—human and divine.[2]

Moreover, in Daniel, this cluster belongs to a pattern of another set of stock terms that recount 1) a powerful figure's 2) granting 3) a subordinate one 4) various political endowments. Specifically, the set of categories is consistent within each chapter—as they are among chs. 1–6 and between them and ch. 7, which is of a different genre altogether. This application of IBS made it possible for me to demonstrate an integrated, literary-theological whole throughout the first half of this allegedly disintegrated but impactful book of Scripture[3]—recapitulation organizing much of chs. 8–12.

Examples of such procedures appear in the essay that follows. However, my question is, having performed IBS on each of the passages in question, what then? How does an interpreter (scholar, student, clergy, layperson) make "hermeneutical hay" of them without exercising preferential treatment, harmonization, or reduction of both to some essence—each operation of which denies their diversity of content and rhetorical approach? Of course, the complementary challenge lies in exploiting the canonical testimony that neither is fundamentally contrary to the other.[4] The dialectical/contrapuntal method proposed makes use of these diverse documents as canonically legitimated "adversaries."[5] This then provides an example of how diverse scriptural resources that do not "militate" against each other in such a manner may also be used in theological reflection.

It is important to underscore that I do not mean to presume that this is the only use to which these two or any other letters can be put. It is simply one among several ways to exploit the diversity in a constructive way. Furthermore, in making the point, it would be possible to select themes other

---

[2] Eugene E. Lemcio, *Navigating Revelation: Charts for the Voyage. A Pedagogical Aid* (Eugene, OR: Wipf and Stock, 2011), 1–4.

[3] Eugene E. Lemcio, "Daniel and the Three (Principally in the Old Greek): 'Historical' Signs of the Apocalyptic Son of Man and Saints of the Most High?—A Paradigm for Christology and Discipleship," in *A Man of Many Parts: Essays in Honor of John Westerdale Bowker on his Eightieth Birthday*, ed. Eugene E. Lemcio (Eugene, OR: Wipf & Stock, 2015), 43–61.

[4] At the very least, they share a six-member kerygmatic recital that I detected in 19 of the 27 books of the NT. See the appendix "The Unifying Kerygma of the New Testament" in my *The Past of Jesus in the Gospels*, SNTSMS 68 (Cambridge: Cambridge University Press, 1991), 115–[122–23]–131, 158–62. This combines and expands two earlier articles of the same title in *JSNT* 33 (1988): 3–17 and *JSNT* 38 (1990): 3–11. A chart on pages 130–31 displays the data. For an eight-member recital, see "*Kerygmatic* Centrality and Unity in the First Testament?" *The Quest for Context & Meaning:* STUDIES IN INTERTEXTUALITY IN HONOR OF JAMES A. SANDERS, ed. C. Evans and S. Talmon (Leiden: Brill, 1997), 357–73.

[5] Robert W. Wall and Eugene E. Lemcio, *The New Testament as Canon: Readings in Canonical Criticism* (Sheffield: Sheffield Academic Press, 1992). Pages 28–77 reproduce essays of mine published elsewhere covering the period of 1981–1986; a fresh contribution appears on pages 78–108. Since then, see my "Images of the Church in 1 Corinthians and 1 Timothy: An Exercise in Canonical Hermeneutics," in *Essays in Honor of Professor Robert Lyon,* ed. Laurence W. Wood, *Asbury Theological Journal* 56.1 (Spring 2001): 45–59 and "The Synoptics and John: The Two So Long Divided. Hearing Canonical Voices for Ecclesial Conversations," *HBT* 26.1 (2004): 50–96. Because publication of the latter journal transferred hands, and because sufficient care was not taken to ensure electronic correspondence with the Greek program used originally, the text omits footnote 3 and contains a jumble of accents and breathings, for which the editor apologized in the next number.

than the ones that I have chosen. Since the secondary literature is abundant regarding the Christology and ethics of Colossians and Philippians, I shall not be conducting a review of nor adding anything new to the discussion. Rather, I should like to take fairly standard conclusions about such matters and use them in a unique inter-epistolary way. In other words, given what many have claimed about *each* of them, what can be said about them *both* in their capacity as canonical witnesses to God's deed in Christ and the life that should be lived as a result? As is the case with all NT documents, the conversation between Philippians and Colossians will not occur apart from the role of a moderator (the interpreter), both in the act of initiating the dialog and also in sustaining the discussion.[6]

Among the reasons for interrogating Colossians and Philippians in the first place is that they bear witness to the most developed Christologies in literature attributed to Paul. Nowhere is the "person and work of Christ," to use older doctrinal categories, as explicit, developed, and focused as here.[7] Where are they more diverse? Also distinct in each document is the way by which the listener/reader is to appropriate the Christ so portrayed. Furthermore, one finds in these letters opposite ethical problems, which in turn originate from different quarters. How the author moves from Christology to ethics differs, too, i.e., the rhetorical strategy in making the case. About all that these letters have in common is the clear grounding of ethics in Christology.

Finally, as an exercise in canonical hermeneutics, this study need not deal with questions of authorship since it is not primarily an historical exercise. *Canonical* authority does not lie in an historian's reconstruction of Paul's life or literary legacy.[8] Instead, it resides in the literature attributed to him that has served the Church across the centuries, in diverse places, and among various cultures. My treatment will proceed according to the following divisions: 2. Colossians: Cosmic Christology for Cosmic Ethics, 3. Philippians: Kenotic Christology for Kenotic Ethics, 4. Canonical Paradigms, 5. Ecclesial Conversations before offering some concluding remarks.[9]

2. COLOSSIANS: COSMIC CHRISTOLOGY FOR COSMIC ETHICS

2.1 Introduction

Because the form and content of epistolary literature are so determined by the problem(s) addressed, it is necessary to review the situation as described in Col 2–3. In the former, the presumed author Paul attacks conformity to certain liturgical and cultic practices that have been foisted upon the readers by outsiders. In the latter, Paul attempts to address the awful behavior of their pre-Christian life that still exercises such a hold on them. In both cases, his approach is governed by 2:6: "as you

---

[6] Scripture, as literature, cannot interpret itself. Thus, the NT does not *per se* interpret the OT. Such personification of ink on a page claims too much. Human agents are always needed.

[7] Perhaps some might find a rival in Ephesians.

[8] I affirm that the determination of authorship as an *historical* exercise—rather than a dogmatic one—must be guided by argument and evidence, not by a particular view about the nature of Scripture. For myself, the data and rationales offered for Pauline authorship are at least as strong as those for non-Pauline authorship.

[9] I shall be using the UBS text: http://www.academic-bible.com/en/online-bibles/novum-testamentum-graece-na-28/read-the-bible-text/bibel/text/lesen/stelle/53/10001/19999/ch/8d500f4cad20274481fa01feb4c75ae7/

have received Christ Jesus as Lord, so live in him." The change in behavior is grounded in two matters: (1) the manner by which they had received Jesus and (2) his identity as their Lord. The "as ... so" adverbs signal comparison (a relationship of similar elements), which contains a causative element. The resultant argument will amount to "comparative causation."

2.2 Cosmic Christology (the Lord whom they had received)

Paul proceeds with the latter first. Very early on in ch. 1, he portrays Jesus as the "Cosmic" (or now, "Intergalactic") Christ, the image of God through whom and for whom all has been made, by whom everything now holds together, and in whom God's fullness was pleased to dwell (1:15–20a). It was in his death at the cross that peace throughout the universe is to be achieved (ἐν τῷ σώματι τῆς σαρκὸς αὐτοῦ), the overloaded physical language militating against any suggestion of dualism (1:22).

2.3 Appropriation (the Manner of his Reception)

As in Rom 6:1–10 and Eph 2:1–10, the author testifies to their union with Christ: They had shared in his entombment, resurrection, and enlivening: συνταφέντες ... συνηγέρθητε ... συνεζωοποίησεν (Col 2:12–13).[10] That experience is even more comprehensively stated in 3:1–4. They had been raised with Christ (συνηγέρθητε); their life now stands hidden with Christ in God (ἡ ζωὴ ὑμῶν κέκρυπται σὺν τῷ Χριστῷ ἐν τῷ θεῷ); and they will be manifested with him in glory (ὑμεῖς σὺν αὐτῷ φανερωθήσεσθε ἐν δόξῃ). Thus, their entire history (past, present, and future) is bound up with Christ's. Of the twenty-one instances of independent and compound uses of σύν, eight of them stress this matter of their incorporation into or association with the experience of Jesus.

2.4 Cosmic Ethics (so living "in him" whom they had received)

Given this intimate connection with the cosmic Christ, they ought to be expressing "cosmic ethics." In other words, how can they be engaged in such "low-life" behavior when they are so closely linked to such a "high and mighty" Christ? Therefore, the practices described require drastic action: killing them off (νεκρώσατε 3:5), putting them away (ἀπόθεσθε 3:8). Of course, positive action is required as well (3:12–17).

But the troubling question remains, how is it that such activity persisted beyond the point of their becoming Christians? Does not this kind of behavior automatically cease upon conversion? This document and all of Paul's letters and our common experience tell us that it does not, at least not in every instance. Why? Might one reason be that they had originally been presented with a low

---

[10] Moule, Wall, and others locate the receiving language with their reception of the tradition about Jesus' life, death, and resurrection. However, this interpretation does not do justice to the parallel and to the way in which the dynamics are expressed: "As you have received" is parallel to "so now live." Thus, they had earlier become united with the one about whom the tradition had told; their subsequent life was to be lived in union with him as well. See C. F. D. Moule, *The Epistles of Paul to the Colossians and Philemon* (Cambridge: Cambridge University Press, 1957), 89 and Robert W. Wall, *Colossians & Philemon* (Downers Grove, IL: InterVarsity Press, 1993), 103.

Christology tolerant of this sort of behavior? This would square with the need to have full knowledge (ἐπίγνωσις) of the truth (1:9, 10; 2:2; 3:10), a term used here more than any other Pauline letter.

3. PHILIPPIANS: KENOTIC CHRISTOLOGY FOR KENOTIC ETHICS

3.1 Kenotic Ethics

A reader looking for low-life ethics in this letter will be severely disappointed. Nothing of what we saw in Colossians (and could also find in 1 Corinthians) can be identified here. At this level, the readers are exemplary. More specifically, nowhere else is there a portrait of a church so thoroughly-engaged in Paul's mission at so many points. The language of partnership and joint-effort, obvious enough in translation, is even more explicit in the Greek (and even more numerically prominent than in Colossians), with so many expressions with συν- and so many cognates with εργ-. No wonder he experienced such joy.

However, there are problems, in evidence as early as 1:27: "Conduct your life together in community [πολιτεύεσθε] in a manner worthy of [ἀξίως] the gospel." (The "law" of comparison is at work here.) One is made to wonder why Paul needed to address the readers along these lines. The answer comes by implication in 2:1–4. We have only to hold a literary mirror against the text to see what is reflected. What condition or behavior called forth the string of exhortations? The imperatives reveal that the readers had not been like-minded (otherwise, why command them to change?). There had not been accord, single-mindedness, or a sharing of the same love. Rather, they had engaged in strife and empty glorying. Not lowly in mind, they were esteeming themselves better than others. Each had been concerned with his/her own matters and ignored others' concerns. Although the Philippians had demonstrated commendable solidarity with Paul, they had failed to do so among themselves.[11]

3.2 Kenotic Christology

The problem dictates the solution: Christ-mindedness. In Colossians, the Christ is regarded as "the image [εἰκών] of the invisible God" (1:15). Here, he had existed in the μορφή, the form of God. Equality with God, though within his reach (or in his possession), was not something to be grasped after (or jealously guarded).[12] Emptying of self, embracing the μορφή of a slave, was his *modus operandi*. Exaltation and Lordship came only after (and because of) obedience that led directly to death by crucifixion. Although Jesus gets universal acclaim, the glory goes to the Father (2:11). This

---

[11] See Peter Oakes, *Philippians: From People to Letter*, SNTSMS 110 (Cambridge: Cambridge University Press, 2001), 179. He has attempted to argue that the disunity which Paul attempts to prevent results from external pressure, as implied by 1:27–30. However, he ignores the probability, based on the contextual evidence of 2:1–4, that there were sufficient internal causes for disunity. In other words, he fails to consider that threats to unity can come from various quarters.

[12] See C. F. D. Moule, "Further Reflections on Philippians 2:5–11," in *Apostolic History and the Gospel: Biblical and Historical Essays Presented to F. F. Bruce on his 60th Birthday*, ed. W. W. Gasque and R. P. Martin (Exeter: Paternoster, 1970), 264–76.

is the Christology of the Significant Other. It is the foundation of all servanthood: from self to others. It also defines the character of God: to be his equal, to share his nature, is to empty self and to take on the nature of humanity.

3.3 Appropriation

The connection between Christology and ethics is differently forged than in Col 2:6 ("As you have received Christ Jesus as Lord, so live in him"), although the matter of lordship is common to both (see Phil 2:11). Despite the occurrences of twenty free-standing or compounded forms with σύν, there are only two which involve connection with Christ; and these refer to the future: Paul's preference to be "with him" (σὺν αὐτῷ 1:23) and of one day sharing the form (σύμμορφον) of his body (3:21).

Between now and then, instead of participating in Christ's death and resurrection, believers are urged to "mind" (φρονῶμεν ... φρονεῖτε 3:15) and imitate his entire life "cycle" as they see Paul imitating it (Συμμιμηταί μου γίνεσθε, ἀδελφοί 3:17). In a sense, Paul is developing the prior Christological question not dealt with in Colossians: before his death and resurrection, what was on Jesus' mind? What was it that led him to die such a death? Thus, by its sheer numbers, the language of "minding" attracts one's attention, not the readers' union with Christ or their sharing of his history, as in Colossians. Φρονοῦν occurs ten times in this letter, more than in any other book of the NT. This number represents almost half of the twenty-three instances in the Pauline corpus.[13] Colossians has just one (3:2). The only example which comes close to the more typically Pauline view (seen so often in Colossians) is found at 3:9: gaining Christ and being found in him and at 3:10, where Paul speaks of his desire to know Christ and the power of his resurrection and the fellowship of his suffering (τὴν κοινωνίαν τῶν παθημάτων αὐτοῦ), which involves being made conformable to his death (συμμορφιζόμενος τῷ θανάτῳ αὐτοῦ).[14] Paul's own resurrection from the dead is viewed as an eschatological event (3:11), something which he has not yet received (3:12). He then calls those who are mature (τέλειοι) to be "of similar mind" (3:15).

4. CANONICAL PARADIGMS

Too summarize, Paul, in seeing that the Colossians' manner of life was too low, portrayed the exalted Christ. A higher ethic would require them to lift their vision of him and of their identity in union with him. In order to keep the Philippians from being too high and mighty towards one another, he portrayed the lowly, self-emptying Christ. Through this single strategy in both instances, Paul illustrated more vividly than anything else that Christology was developed (or at least was applied) to

---

[13] Romans comes second with eight instances. If one includes φρόνημα and φρόνησις in the count, then Romans takes the lead with five additional occurrences of the stem. But then the latter is four times longer than either Philippians or Colossians. Plato said, know thyself; Paul says, empty thyself in order to know Christ. On the basis of this teaching, one could say that con*firm*ation in the faith is to be the start of a life-long process of con*form*ation or, better Christ*form*ation.

[14] Twelve of the twenty instances of "with" language refer to relationships within the community.

meet the needs of particular circumstances.[15] The two letters contain distinctive "high" and "low" Christologies. Of course, each contains elements of the other. Though cosmic, the Christ (through whom the universe was created and is now sustained) reconciled it in his "body of flesh" at the cross. The one who took on the form of a slave and lived a life of obedience to the point of death on the cross shared the form of God and its commensurate status.

Unique to each is the manner by which one relates to the Christ: the more characteristic union with his death and resurrection (Colossians) and the less usual minding or imitating of his example (Philippians). Again, this is a matter of degree. Each of these in turn determines the means by which Paul uses the Christology to address the special ethical problems in each congregation. If one has been united with Christ, how can s/he on the one hand submit to mere human tradition (however conducive to visible religiosity) and on the other hand continue to live in the old pagan ways? If one has the (selfless) mind of Christ, how can one live for self alone? Then there are the origins of the problems themselves: in Colossae, they had stemmed from external sources (but with obvious internal ramifications); those in Philippi had arisen primarily from internal ones (but with the obvious external threat alluded to in 3:2).[16] Another difference lies in the rhetorical strategy by which they are put to use: in Colossians, the Christology precedes the problem which it is to solve. The move is from cause to effect. In Philippians, the opposite is the case: the ethical problem posed first dictates the Christological solution that follows—a movement from effect to cause (or, in Trainerian terms, "substantiation"). However, both testify to the fact that, whatever the ethical problem, Christology is the solution. Here is yet another evidence that NT Christology is more functional than speculative (although this should not prevent appropriate doctrinal reflection on the implications of the functional Christology).

---

[15] Long ago, C. F. D. Moule argued that various Christological terms arose to meet the needs of particular circumstances: "The Influences of Circumstances on the Use of Christological Terms," *JTS* 10 (1959): 247–63. Recognizing Christian teaching as need-based in nature is as old as Papias' defense of the order and content of Mark's gospel, which had come under attack. Eusebius reports in his *Ecclesiastical History* that an Elder, whom Papias cited, took the matter back to apostolic practice: no less a personage than Peter himself related the Lord's teachings, not according to chronological order, but "as necessity demanded." For the text of this statement, see K. Aland (ed.), *Synopsis Quattuor Evangeliorum*, 11th ed. (Stuttgart: Deutsche Bibelstiftung, 1976), 531. Of course, the same principle can be found throughout Pauline literature; but it is most evident here. See for instance the Apostle's argument in 2 Corinthians when, in soliciting the church's generous support for the saints in Jerusalem, he appeals to the example of Christ: "For you know the grace of our Lord Jesus Christ that, though he was rich, yet for your sake he became poor, so that by his poverty you might become rich" (8:9).

[16] The point here is that in Philippians, though there is an external threat, it has to be inferred in 1:27–30. At 3:2, the external opposition is explicit, but not expanded beyond this verse. However, the outside influence upon the Colossians is both explicit and extensive.

5. Ecclesial Conversations

5.1 Introduction

As in the case of the gospels and with the epistolary corpora, the canonically-approved diversity prevents us from harmonizing the themes of these letters, preferring one, or collapsing the teaching of both to a common denominator (reductionism). This point is particularly important for what may be termed an "arithmetic" approach to doctrinal or even biblical theology: one simply "adds up" the features of both Christologies to gain a fuller view of Jesus and how one ought to live. But this is an exceedingly wooden view, assuming that Christian theology is mainly the "sum" of the Bible's various parts. I have proposed a more dynamic, dialectic, contrapuntal approach.

My alternative canonical approach also prevents one from insisting upon exclusive views of Jesus, singular ways of relating to him, a uniform method for grounding one's ethics, and a univocal dialect for expressing these realities. Sloganeering then becomes forbidden, as do language litmus tests for community inclusion. The tendency to use the heresy label becomes minimized as do charges of schism. Ecumenism finds a Scriptural foundation. At the same time, the variety is bounded by the available models; deviations are "standard deviations." Diversity and pluralism are of the kind that neither dilute truth nor destroy community.

5.2 Colossians: Challenging Mis-readings of Philippians

So far as Christology is concerned, a misreading/misappropriation of Philippians might construe its portrait of Jesus as being too low. In the 1960s, an author who had been known chiefly as the translator of a widely-used Bible in modern idiom departed from that role with a provocatively titled book, *Your God is Too Small*.[17] It could be said that the message of Colossians for some readers needs to be, "Your Christ is Too Small." And because your Christology is so feeble, your understanding of what took place at the cross is constricted, which leads to a minimizing of the change of behavior that is both possible and necessary. Unless Jesus was God's agent of creation, unless he currently sustains it, then there is no way that he can reconcile everything and everyone in it.[18] In other words, a robust doctrine of creation is the indispensable condition for a comprehensive understanding of Christology and soteriology.

Since there is little about Jesus's pre-incarnate status and nothing about his current exalted status and role in this letter, a series of questions might be raised. Why put so much emphasis on self-emptying, humility and obedience? Where is the fullness? Is not the self a creation of God pronounced "good" at the beginning? Would not so much humility deprive Christ and us of sufficient "muscle"? Besides, where is any mention of *pro nobis* (benefits accruing to humankind) in the report of kenosis, death, and exaltation? And what of relating to this Jesus? Is there not a danger of emphasizing the mind so much? Imitation can go only so far. It can become so superficial and mechanical,

---

[17] J. B. Phillips, *Your God is Too Small* (New York: Macmillan, 1953).
[18] One is reminded of Isaianic theology, whereby a defeated Israel is encouraged by this word from God: "Because I made you, I can rescue you" (43:1; 44:2–3).

so reliant on one's own effort, so lacking in the intimacy of being *in* Christ and experiencing death and resurrection *with* him. Where is the subjective / experiential / interpersonal dimension?

5.3 Philippians: Challenging Mis-readings of Colossians

So far as the Christology of Colossians is concerned, its misreading/misappropriation might feed a view of Jesus that is too "muscular." The potential for triumphalism (a *Christologia gloriae*) is great. In an extreme form, the Christology of Colossians could be appropriated by a triumphalist. So high and mighty a Christ, so exalted a Son might be regarded as unreachable. Such loftiness could lead to a view of Jesus detached from the world or from embodied life, although it is clear that attention to significant details in the context would prevent one from justifying such a position. Did his feet ever really touch the ground—except at the end, at the cross? Is he really flesh of our flesh and bone of our bone? Such detachment from the "real" world makes him an unlikely model. What did he actually accomplish during his life? What did he do besides die? Was there anything "behind" the cross? What during his life led to it? Did not the original sacrifice occur at the beginning—when the self was initially given up, not just at the end? Furthermore, relating to such a Christ could get too subjective / emotional / touchy-feely. More objectivity is needed.

Here is where Philippians provides the major Pauline antidote to removing Jesus from the realm of history and human experience. The heights of equality with God and sharing the divine form did not impede the movement upwards via kenosis. The Apostle in 2:5–11 calls a halt to all egoism, for here the Self by whom the Father created selfhood and from whom all selves originate emptied himself. Of what did the pre-incarnate Son empty himself? Interpreters have attempted to plumb the depths of this claim from the beginning. In more recent centuries, Charles Wesley sang, "Emptied himself of all but Love." But this much can be said from the way by which St. Paul employs the Christology to address the problems in 2:1–4: he who shared God's status and nature emptied himself of that which would resist such self-emptying. He dismantled that self which might ignore or exploit other selves. His understanding of selfhood enabled him to embrace the μορφή of both God and humans.[19] In imitation of Christ (and of Paul), the mind must be engaged, the intellect involved. One needs to know how to behave—which acts to do. Here is where the life of Jesus, even as related in a compressed narrative, is vital. The self, while good and a creation of God, can become self-absorbed, turned in on itself and away from God and others. Only self-emptying can counter self-aggrandizement and the manipulation of other selves that it brings.

---

[19] This heavy dose of Christology causes one to examine certain approaches to evangelism where the appeal is to "receive/accept" Jesus as one's "Lord and Savior." On the authority of these texts, does the latter role include Christ as the Reconciler of the universe? If one has died and risen with him, ought not the experience set the agenda for one's life, not only as one who has been reconciled to God but also as one who is also engaged in the process of cosmic reconciliation? If one "owns" Jesus as Lord, and is constantly being conformed to him, does this not oblige one to be like-minded about the nature of power, status, and service?

6. Concluding Caveats

Obviously, one can derive benefits from texts whose original situation does not match his contemporary one. For example, the cosmic Christology that Paul used to combat gutter ethics in Colossae need not presuppose that only those readers in such a condition will find it applicable. Being engaged in promiscuity is not a qualification for benefiting from the teaching that one's life is joined with Christ's in every respect, thereby over-ruling certain kinds of behavior and promoting others. Furthermore, the modern reader who is a cosmological dualist can find her worldview challenged in Col 1, which provides ingredients for both a theology of creation and a Christology of the natural order.

This sort of sensitivity is required when applying the Philippian paradigm of servanthood to people whose history has included long periods of oppression. Perhaps only Black Americans, especially those in positions of power as well as empowered women can speak authentically of the need for the kind of "downward mobility" exemplified by the Christ of Philippians: "If you want to get UP in this world, you have to get DOWN on your knees." Perhaps, only they can make the point that to be master means to serve, that divinity and servanthood are two aspects of the single Reality, which is God.

6.1 Theology, Per Se

Central to the "Unifying Kerygma of the New Testament" that I identified twenty-five years ago[20] (a sort of proto-*regula fidei*) is a theocentric Christology: The recital narrates the salvific acts of God that Jesus mediates. The Father is also the recipient of both Jesus's and Christians' response. He is the beginning and end of the story. Of course, the recital is cast in the language and idiom particular to each letter. In Colossians, Paul renders thanks to the *Father*, who has qualified us to share in the inheritance of the saints in light. *He* has delivered us from the dominion of darkness and transferred us to the kingdom of *his* beloved Son (1:12–13). He is the image *of God* (1:15). In him the fullness *of God* was pleased to dwell (1:19; see 2:9). In keeping with the rest of the NT, it is *God who raised* both Jesus and those joined with him. The author makes this point both actively and with the ("divine") passive voice (2:12–13; 3:1–3). Furthermore, one's faith is in *the working of God* who raised him from the dead (2:12).

Likewise, Phil 2:5–13 contains a version of these dynamics.[21] Although the point is often missed, God is the reference at both the start and the finish of this super-Christological passage as well. Jesus existed in the μορφή *of God*. The equality that he refused to grasp at or jealously guard was equality *with God* (2:6). *God* highly exalted Jesus (as is the universal pattern of the NT); it was *he* who bestowed upon him the name of "Lord," whom the universe is to confess *to the glory of God the Father* (2:9–11). The readers are to work out their own salvation with fear and trembling "for *God* is at work in you, both to will and to work for *his* good pleasure" (2:13).

---

[20] See note 4.

[21] The letter opens with Paul's assurance that the *God* who began a good work among the letter's recipients will perform it on the Day of Jesus Christ (Phil 1:6).

6.2 Teaching an Inductively-Derived Hermeneutic

It would be a fair criticism to say that, by leaving the text *qua text* (and I have done so twice!), one is no longer doing Inductive Bible Study. Furthermore, it might be argued that my particular approach to hermeneutics is sufficiently idiosyncratic that it could not (and should not?) be standardized. My only defense lies in that the approach illustrated above depends upon the demonstration of diversity among NT documents, even within a corpus by the same author. I contend that the most reliable (because systematic and disciplined) way of doing so is by IBS.

Early in this essay, I raised the question, "having performed IBS on each of the passages in question, what then? How does an interpreter (scholar, student, clergy, layperson) exercise responsible hermeneutics with them without exercising preferential treatment, harmonization, or reduction of both to some essence—each operation of which denies their preserved (and therefore validated) diversity of content and rhetorical approach?" Furthermore, how can one avoid a "flat" reading of a text's literary terrain—not only within a single book of the Bible but across the entire gamut of biblical literature? How can one eschew a blended or summative or arithmetic way of doing Biblical Theology: simply adding up everything that the inspired authors say about God, creation, humankind, Christ, sin, redemption, consummation, etc.? Conventional studies of "themes" across the canon risk falling into such mechanistic and wooden methods.

Furthermore, simply *describing* the theology of various books in a more sophisticated manner does not get us much farther. Instead, a more *dynamic* or functional approach ought to be taken up, as I have tried to demonstrate above and in the literature cited in footnote 5. This is a more situational or circumstantial way of treating texts. One could begin by asking of the two passages (to use an analogy from photography), "What sort of negative produced this positive image?" Or, putting it another way, to whom would Philippians provide consolation—both then and now? Who would be critiqued? The same queries would be put to Colossians as well. So far as teaching-learning the method is concerned, students might be assigned practice exercises after watching the instructor present multiple case studies.

Conducting such a dialectic with diverse texts would free one from being locked into a particular dialect in expressing convictions about Jesus and about the life in Christ that should follow. Using various images could help one to transcend parochial paradigms that exclude believers from other faith/denominational traditions. Of course, one would risk facing accusations of "sermonizing" or of providing pastoral counseling ("meddling," in each instance) rather than adopting a more detached, classically academic manner. However, would not this be entirely in keeping with the canon's being a collection of need-based literature—whether that need be for a particular theology (broadly understood) or a corresponding ethic?

FOR FURTHER READING

Castello, Daniel, Sara M. Koenig, and David R. Nienhuis, eds. *The Usefulness of Scripture. Essays in Honor of Robert W. Wall*. University Park, PA: Eisenbrauns, 2018.

Edwards, Aaron. "Preacher as Balanced Extremist: Biblical Dialectics and Sermonic Certainty." *Expository Times*. 126.9 (June 2015): 424–35.

Lemcio (Лемцьо), Eugene E. "The Woman & Her Children in 4 Maccabees 16–18 and Revelation 12: An Experiment in Theological Reflection Upon the Witness of the Bible in Greek," in *Наукові Записки: Серія Богослов'я* [*Academic Texts. Series Theology*]. Lviv: Ukrainian Catholic University, forthcoming 2019.

Sanders, James A. *From Sacred Story to Sacred Text*. Philadelphia: Fortress, 1987.

Wall, Robert W. and Eugene E. Lemcio. *The New Testament as Canon. A Reader in Canonical Criticism*. Sheffield: Sheffield Academic Press, 1992.

PART III

IBS IMPACTING THE CURRICULUM

Sequencing Undergraduate Classes in a Curriculum Featuring Inductive Bible Study

Fredrick J. Long
Professor of New Testament, Director of Greek Instruction
Asbury Theological Seminary

ABSTRACT: Within higher-education, a well-designed curriculum provides an optimal opportunity for students to be formed within a discipline. This essay explores the development of an undergraduate program in biblical studies with particular focus on Inductive Bible Study (IBS). By offering strategically sequenced classes moving from IBS hermeneutical foundations, to survey classes in the NT, to focused Book Studies, to capstone courses featuring evaluation-application and biblical theology, students were afforded repeated and progressive opportunities to practice, develop, and synthesize IBS for application and theology over a four-year curriculum.

1. INTRODUCTION

1.1 The Need for the Church to be Taught IBS

One of the highlights of teaching IBS in my "Biblical Interpretation" class for undergraduate students was when a young woman after three weeks approached me after class and said, "This class makes me mad!" "Oh," I said taken aback, "How come?" She continued, "In these few weeks I've learned more about how to study the Bible than nineteen years growing up in the church!" The problem is that this sentiment was expressed again and again to me in different ways as students learned first-hand how to read Scripture attentively and inductively. Most of these undergraduate students would graduate and immediately enter into ministry; there was no requirement from their denomination that they receive an M. Div. degree. It was at this point that I began thinking more deeply about how best to help these young ministers of the gospel learn how to study and teach the Scriptures to their congregations and youth groups through IBS.[1]

---

[1] The sentiments expressed by this comment and my involvement in discipleship within the church were the beginning of my development of an interpretive manual for laity now published as *In Step with God's Word: Interpreting the New Testament as God's People*, GlossaHouse Hermeneutics & Translation 1 (Wilmore, KY: GlossaHouse, 2017).

1.2 Teaching Various Types of Courses

The collective wisdom about "teaching" passed on to me was that the first year would be the hardest since it entailed new course preparations. However, I discovered it was the first two years. As the first NT professor with PhD hired at Bethel College, Mishawaka, Indiana, I had to teach a great number of classes in general education but especially for our Bible and Ministry majors. In my tenure there from 1999 to 2007, I averaged teaching five courses per semester and taught twenty-one different courses within traditional undergraduate, non-traditional adult evening, and graduate intensive venues. My courses included Greek (I, II, Readings, Exegesis), Hebrew (I and II), Biblical Interpretation, NT Literature, Gospels, Acts and Paul, the Latter NT, Book Studies (Luke, Romans, 1 Corinthians, Ephesians), Biblical Theology, and Contemporary Critical Issues in Biblical Studies. I would not wish anyone to have such an intensive teaching load, yet this demand is not all that uncommon for new professors. Needless to say, during the first two years, I was simply trying to stay afloat. In hindsight, I am grateful for teaching broadly across the biblical Canon and the NT in particular; however, I began to notice a problem.

1.3 The Problem of Class Sequencing

The courses listed above that I taught span the more foundational (biblical languages) to the two most advanced "capstone" courses that were eventually developed for our Biblical Studies majors. However, when I first arrived on the scene, students could take all of these courses in basically any sequence. In other words, few prerequisites for courses existed except for the biblical languages (e.g., Greek I was a prerequisite for Greek II). Thus, not uncommonly fourth-year seniors often enrolled in the hermeneutical class "Biblical Interpretation." From my vantage point, this needed to stop for at least two reasons. First, fourth-year students who delayed taking that course too often were not well-matched with first-year students; these fourth-year students came with biblical studies skills developed from other courses, a heightened maturity level, and too often a condescending attitude towards the class which sometimes resulted in their not taking the class seriously. Second, students in general were not enjoying a more thoughtful progression of courses that should begin with biblical languages and hermeneutics as foundational and that then could be reinforced in subsequent classes. This problem needed to be nipped in the bud.

2. SEQUENCING CLASSES WITHIN THE UNDERGRADUATE CURRICULUM

2.1 The Proposed Sequencing

In view of this problem, I developed the following depiction of course sequencing for our Biblical Studies, Christian Ministry, and Youth Ministry majors (Figure 7.1). This planning chart was then presented to my colleagues and subsequently voted into action.

Figure 7.1—*Proposed Class Sequences for Biblical Classes at Bethel College, IN*

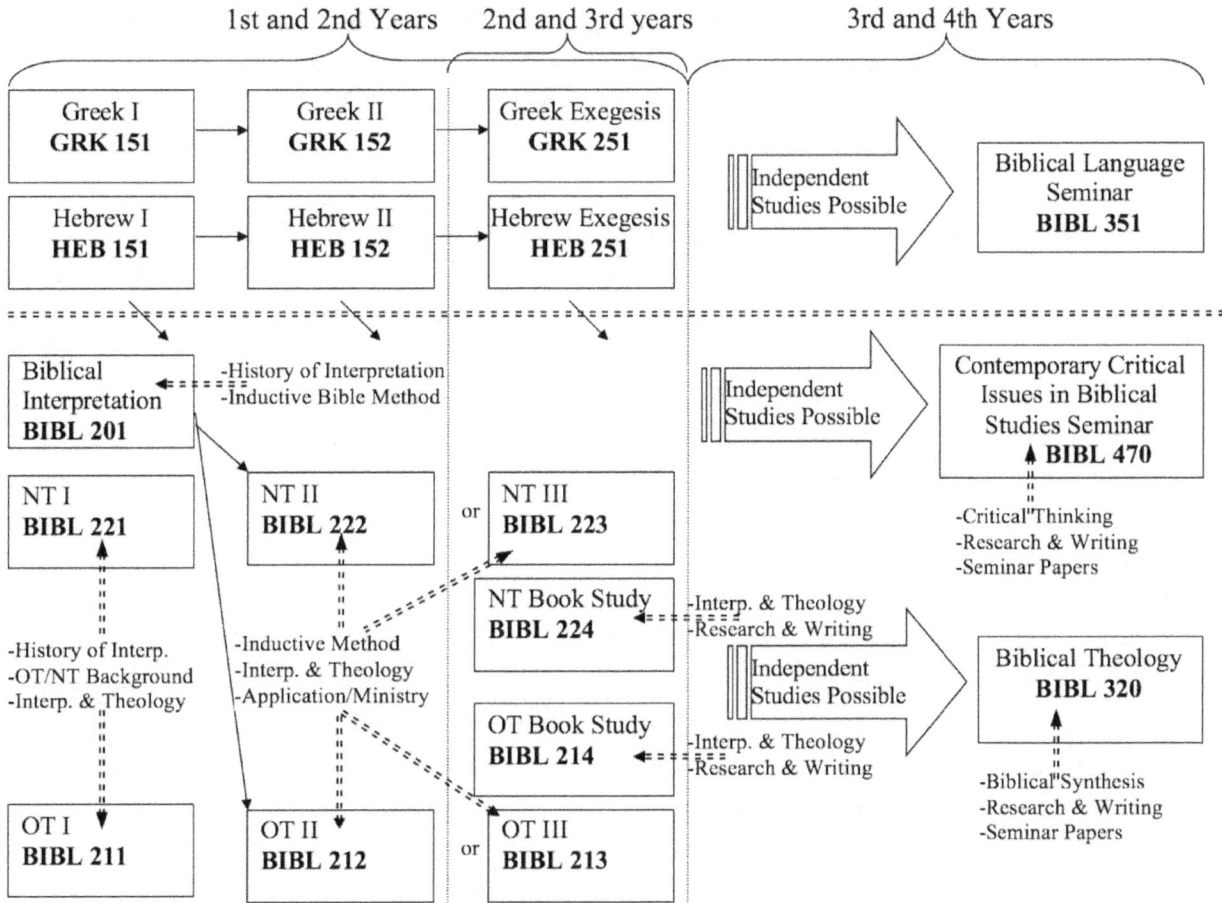

As one can see, the map has the undergraduate year of study indicated across the top (some of which overlap) and at various points includes short lists with dashed arrows indicating the basic goals and areas covered in the class. The biblical languages are in the first row of classes and feed into the other courses (hence, the short solid slanted arrows). Students were encouraged quickly to begin and finish a sequence of Greek or Hebrew by their third year all the way through Greek or Hebrew Exegesis. Significantly, students in Greek I and II began to explore Major Structural Relationships and make other types of observations. They also learned semantic diagraming and semantic analysis (SD and SA), which is a kind of detailed analysis that fosters careful observation and interrogation of biblical materials.[2] In the center, immediately below Greek and Hebrew, is "Biblical

---

[2] For step-by-step descriptions and examples in English and Greek, see Fredrick J. Long, *Koine Greek Grammar: A Beginning-Intermediate Exegetical and Pragmatic Handbook*, Accessible Greek Resources and Online Studies (Wilmore, KY: GlossaHouse, 2015), 296–313; idem, *In Step with God's Word*, ch. 4. SD and SA are comparable to David Bauer's lecture material in which he "maps out" the narrative thought flow with embedded MSRs; see ch. 13 "Focused Observation" in David R. Bauer and Robert A. Traina, *Inductive Bible Study: A Comprehensive Guide to the Practice of Hermeneutics* (Grand Rapids: Baker Academic, 2011).

Interpretation" (BIBL 201) which in turn leads into the NT and OT sequenced rows of classes; the solid arrows from BIBL 201 indicate that it is a prerequisite for NT II/III and OT II/III courses. At the far right are capstone courses on "Contemporary Critical Issues in Biblical Studies" and "Biblical Theology." I also prepared the description in 2.2 immediately below (that reads like an advertisement) to explain for students the sequence of these courses within the Biblical Studies Major.

2.2 Courses with the Biblical Studies Major

For those interested in learning God's Word for teaching and preaching, Bethel College has a program to match: The Biblical Studies Major. The Biblical Studies Major offers the student an intensive and rigorous program to foster a love of the Scriptures and a competence for interpretation and application in the life of the church. God's Word has been given to us through multiple authors, languages, literary forms, cultures and across diverse historical circumstances and geographical settings. Furthermore, there are many methods and approaches by which the Scriptures may be interpreted. Therefore, the Biblical Studies Major has been carefully designed to develop a fundamental competency in biblical history, literature, interpretive methods and theology. Contemporary critical methodology is taught, engaged and evaluated. A number of Biblical Hebrew and Greek courses have been designed to facilitate the careful exegesis of Scripture. Opportunities abound for grasping biblical history, geography, and archeology through annual trips to the Oriental Museum at the University of Chicago and possible trips to and study in Israel. Furthermore, the inspiration, authority and unity of God's Revelation is affirmed with the aim of articulating a vital biblical theology. Finally, the Biblical Studies Major offers tremendous cross-curricular flexibility with many elective hours and thus welcomes students who want to pursue the benefits of a double major with Philosophy, Literature, or any other compatible field of study. The professors in the Biblical Studies Division at Bethel College are committed to the integration of intensive study of the Bible and personal devotional study in the context of ministry within Christ's church body.

	FALL SEMESTER	SPRING SEMESTER
years 1-2	-**Greek I** or **Hebrew I** -**NT I (Gospels)** or **OT I (Pentateuch)**–focus on the revelation and mighty acts of God; history of interpretation, critical methodology, historical background, interpretation of texts with special attention to biblical themes and theology.	-**Greek II** or **Hebrew II** -**Biblical Interpretation**—in order to mine the great riches of God's word, students learn the inductive method, principles of interpretation, literary genres, historical background, and how to apply biblical truth to our modern world.
years 2-3	-**Greek** or **Hebrew Exegesis**—teach students how to use the biblical languages and exegetical tools for interpretation for use in one's life and ministry.	-**NT II (Paul)** and **NT III (Later NT)** and **OT II (Wisdom)** and **OT III (Prophets)**—continues to build interpretive skills and a foundation for biblical thinking, theology, and ministry, through a thorough

	-OT Book Study—an in-depth study of the major theme(s) of an OT book, with additional exposure to secondary literature and study resources, especially commentaries, while working closely with the biblical text.	investigation of the major themes, historical background, and critical issues surrounding the particular biblical books. **-NT Book Study**— an in-depth study of the major theme(s) of a NT book, with additional exposure to secondary literature and study resources, especially commentaries, while working closely with the biblical text.
years 3-4	**-Seminar on Contemporary Critical Issues of Biblical Interpretation**—a capstone course that focuses upon selected contemporary critical issues in Bible, biblical theology, and hermeneutics thus enabling the student to effectively engage contemporary critical challenges with integrity.	**-Seminar in Biblical Languages** –a continuing study of the biblical languages and related tools to develop the student's ability to use Scripture effectively to build a biblical worldview that will serve as a basis for sound Christian ministry and scholarship. **-Biblical Theology**—a capstone course that helps the student to develop a biblical theology through an examination of major biblical texts and themes while honing biblical and theological skills through use of a proper methodology for doing biblical theology.

Other courses that my colleagues later developed that are not included above were "Biblical Archaeology," "Israel Among the Nations," and "Intertestamental History & Literature" (this latter being taught by an OT professor Dr. Tony Tomasino, another Asbury Theological Seminary graduate and IBS trained). Altogether, these Biblical Studies courses were designed and offered in sequence across multiple semesters.

2.3 Schedule for Mapping the Biblical Studies Courses Each Semester

Below in CHART 7.1 is a very slightly edited "Course Scheduling Plan" created by Gene Carpenter, at that time Chair of the Religion and Philosophy Department and an excellent OT scholar who was very beloved by students and peers and sadly is now deceased. Gene had formerly taught at Asbury Theological Seminary as an OT professor and appreciated IBS fundamentally. He created this schedule for our departmental course planning for the Fall 2004 through Spring 2008. With all the Religion and Philosophy courses, this three-page chart was a massive enterprise; a printout was made available to students to help them plan their coursework with the caveat that sometimes a course would not be offered for various reasons. I have edited out all the other Religion and Philosophy classes.

CHART 7.1—COURSE SCHEDULING PLAN OF BIBLICAL STUDIES COURSES (FALL 2004 TO SPRING 2008)
E = Every Semester; EF = Every Fall; ES = Every Spring; AF = Alternate Fall Semesters; and AS = Alternate Spring Semester

FALL 04		SPRING 05		FALL 05		SPRING 06	
Bibl 201 E	Biblical Interpretation	Bibl 201 E	Biblical Interpretation	Bibl 201 E	Biblical Interpretation	Bibl 201 E	Biblical Interpretation
Bibl 211 EF	OT I	Bibl 212 AS	OT II	Bibl 211 EF	OT I	Bibl 213 AS	OT III
Bibl 221 EF	NT I	Bibl 222	NT II	Bibl 221 EF	NT I	Bibl 223	NT III
Bibl 330 AFE	Intertestamental History & Lit	Bibl 320 ES	Biblical Theology	Bibl 250 AFO	Biblical Archaeology	Bibl 320 ES	Biblical Theology
Bibl 470 EF	Contemp. Issues in Bibl. Studies	Bibl 350 ES	Israel Among the Nations	Bibl 470 EF	Contemp. Issues in Bibl. Studies	Bibl 350 ES	Israel Among the Nations
Bibl 214 EF	OT Book Study	Bibl 224 ES	NT Book Study	Bibl 214 EF	OT Book Study	Bibl 224 ES	NT Book Study
Grk 151 EF	Elementary Greek I	Grk 152 ES	Elementary Greek II	Grk 151 EF	Elementary Greek I	Grk 152 ES	Elementary Greek II
Grk 251 EF	Greek Exegesis	Grk 351 AS	Seminar: Greek Readings	Grk 251 EF	Greek Exegesis		
Heb 151 EF	Elementary Hebrew I	Heb 152 ES	Elementary Hebrew II	Heb 151 EF	Elementary Hebrew I	Heb 152 ES	Elementary Hebrew II
Heb 251 EF	Hebrew Exegesis	Heb 351 AS	Seminar: Hebrew Readings	Heb 251 EF	Hebrew Exegesis		

FALL 06		SPRING 07		FALL 07		SPRING 08	
Bibl 201 E	Biblical Interpretation	Bibl 201 E	Biblical Interpretation	Bibl 201 E	Biblical Interpretation	Bibl 201 E	Biblical Interpretation
Bibl 211 EF	OT I	Bibl 212 AS	OT II	Bibl 211 EF	OT I	Bibl 213 AS	OT III
Bibl 221 EF	NT I	Bibl 222	NT II	Bibl 221 EF	NT I	Bibl 223	NT III
Bibl 330 AFE	Intertestamental History & Lit	Bibl 320 ES	Biblical Theology	Bibl 250 AFO	Biblical Archaeology	Bibl 320 ES	Biblical Theology
Bibl 470 EF	Contemp. Issues in Bibl. Studies	Bibl 350 ES	Israel Among the Nations	Bibl 470 EF	Contemp. Issues in Bibl. Studies	Bibl 350 ES	Israel Among the Nations
Bibl 214 EF	OT Book Study	Bibl 224 ES	NT Book Study	Bibl 214 EF	OT Book Study	Bibl 224 ES	NT Book Study
Grk 151 EF	Elementary Greek I	Grk 152 ES	Elementary Greek II	Grk 151 EF	Elementary Greek I	Grk 152 ES	Elementary Greek II
Grk 251 EF	Greek Exegesis	Grk 351 AS	Seminar: Greek Readings	Grk 251 EF	Greek Exegesis		
Heb 151 EF	Elementary Hebrew I	Heb 152 ES	Elementary Hebrew II	Heb 151 EF	Elementary Hebrew I	Heb 152 ES	Elementary Hebrew II
Heb 251 EF	Hebrew Exegesis	Heb 351 AS	Seminar: Hebrew Readings	Heb 251 EF	Hebrew Exegesis		

Omitted in these charts, too, was the general education course "NT Literature" (BIBL 216) that I would teach on occasion, but also taught by Prof. John Dendiu who specialized in Christian Ministry, another Asbury Theological Seminary alumnus. John has graciously contributed the next chapter in honor of Prof. Traina in which he describes how he came to incorporate IBS while teaching this "NT Literature" course. In the next section, I'll discuss the development of "Biblical Interpretation" course that increasingly featured IBS methodology and assignments. Then in the following section, I'll discuss how the other basic courses (NT I, II, III, Book Studies) and the capstone course "Contemporary Critical Issues in Biblical Studies" built upon the IBS methodology taught in "Biblical Interpretation" before concluding with some reflections on the effectiveness of the curriculum.

3. DEVELOPING THE FOUNDATIONAL IBS "BIBLICAL INTERPRETATION" CLASS

3.1 Textbooks and IBS

Shortly after arriving at Bethel College, I inherited the "Biblical Interpretation" BIBL 201 course from Dr. LaVerne Blowers, another Asbury Theological Seminary alumnus, who taught Missiology and NT courses. I taught the course ten different times with no single syllabus ever being considerably the same.[3] I tried different textbooks in different years; this actually tells part of my story of trying how best to teach biblical hermeneutics, especially IBS, to undergraduate students.

2001: 1. Virkler, Henry A. *Hermeneutics: Principles and Processes of Biblical Interpretation.* Grand Rapids: Baker, 1981.
      2. Bray, Gerald. *Biblical Interpretation: Past and Present.* Downers Grove, IL: InterVarsity Press, 1996.
      3. Arthur, Kay. *How to Study Your Bible.* Eugene, OR: Harvest House, 1994.

2002: 1. Duvall, J. Scott and J. Daniel Hays. *Grasping God's Word: A Hand's On Approach to Reading, Interpreting, and Applying the Bible.* Grand Rapids: Zondervan, 2001.
      2. Duvall, J. Scott and J. Daniel Hays. *Grasping God's Word: A Hand's On Approach to Reading, Interpreting, and Applying the Bible Workbook.* Grand Rapids: Zondervan, 2001.

2003: 1. Duvall, J. Scott and J. Daniel Hays. *Grasping God's Word: A Hand's On Approach to Reading, Interpreting, and Applying the Bible.* Grand Rapids: Zondervan, 2001.
      2. Wald, Oletta. *The New Joy of Discovery in Bible Study.* Minneapolis: Augsburg, 2002.

---

[3] When a former student, Cami Brubaker, requested syllabi samples of my Biblical Interpretation class, I sent ten iterations of it from 2001 through 2006. She commented in response, "Thank you so much for sending all those syllabi! ... I LOVE that the syllabi are so different. It is awesome to see how you put so much time, effort and consideration into each class you taught. It is no wonder that this class was the catalyst for altering the course of my life (changed my major from music education to Bible, discovered I loved teaching Bible when you asked me to tutor a few of the kids in the class who were struggling, decided to pursue masters/potential doctorate)!"

2004: 1. A Bible with Old and New Testaments (preferably **NASB**; but NIV is acceptable).
2. *Logos Scholar's Library Series X* from Logos Software.
3. Morris Proctor's Video Reference Guide on CD-ROM for Logos Series X.

2005 Spring:
1. A Bible with Old and New Testaments (preferably **NASB**; but NIV is acceptable).
2. *Logos Scholar's Library Series X* from Logos Software.
3. Fee, Gordon and Douglas Stuart. *How to Read the Bible for All Its Worth.* 3rd ed. Grand Rapids: Zondervan, 2003.

2005 Fall through 2006:
1. Duvall, J. Scott and J. Daniel Hays. *Grasping God's Word: A Hand's On Approach to Reading, Interpreting, and Applying the Bible.* Grand Rapids: Zondervan, 2001.
2. *Logos Scholar's Library Series X* from Logos Software.

Let me explain my thinking when selecting which textbooks to use. In my estimation, Robert A. Traina's seminal *Methodical Bible Study* (1952; repr. Grand Rapids: Zondervan, 2002) would be too detailed and "dry" for undergraduate students; also, I was familiar with David L. Thompson's clear and simply presented *Bible Study that Works*, rev. ed. (Nappanee, IN: Evangel, 1994) but I feared it did not go far enough with examples and exercises. I eventually learned about Oletta Wald's revised *The New Joy of Discovery in Bible Study* (2002) with its workbook/exercise approach, and so I used it in 2003. One year earlier, my attempt to incorporate IBS began in earnest in 2002 when I used J. Scott Duvall and J. Daniel Hays's first edition of *Grasping God's Word* and its *Workbook* which is now in its 3rd edition. It had the benefit of teaching observational skills right from the start, which are very similar to IBS's major structural relationships (MSRs) as well as addressed issues of the Holy Spirit and various genres and literary forms in the Bible. I would also supplement this textbook with IBS notes and examples of my own drawn from Matthew, thanks to having taken David R. Bauer's seminal class. Also helpful about Duvall and Hays's approach is that they featured examples and assignments in a workbook from pericopes across the Bible; in my estimation, working with small chunks of texts rather than a full book gave undergraduate students a better chance to learn MSRs. After two years of using Duvall and Hays, while supplying my own notes and examples, then I adopted a "Scripture only approach" using Bible Software (2004). I then moved briefly in the spring of 2005 to Gordon Fee and Douglas Stuart's fine book, *How to Read the Bible for All Its Worth* only to return in the fall of 2005 to Duvall and Hays (but without their *Workbook*) still requiring a Bible software.

3.2 Incorporating Inductive Assignments

In my various iterations of "Biblical Interpretation" (BIBL 201), I developed many different types of assessments in different configurations. These included memorizing Scripture, tests, premade textbook assignments, workbook observations, a synthetic exegetical paper, a notebook portfolio, collaborative group assignments, in-class group work, reading interaction worksheets, the development of a church devotional (for which I provided a template), planning workshops for an "Church Retreat Seminar on Biblical Interpretation," and various IBS assignments such as Book and Segment surveys, detailed analyses, interpretation, and reflections on evaluation and application. Below are some of the more explicit IBS assignments that began to use from different years. A slightly edited syllabus for BIBL 201 Fall 2005 is in included in the SYLLABUS APPENDICES in this volume.

2002: Relied on Workbook Assignments from Duvall and Hays.

2003: Supplemented Workbook Assignments from Duvall and Hays with these IBS assignments:

1. Matthew 5–7 Segment Survey
2. Book Survey of Ephesians
3. Semantic Diagramming and an Analysis of Matt 5:13–20
4. Semantic Analysis of Matthew 7:13–20

2004: For this syllabus, my only required textbooks were a Bible and Logos Bible Software. I required among other assessments, these twelve IBS assignments:

IBS Assignment #1: Perform a Detailed Observation of Matt 5:9–12 (2-3 hours)

IBS Assignment #2: Perform a Detailed Observation of Psalm 1 (2-3 hours)

IBS Assignment #3: Perform a Detailed Analysis of Matt 5:43–48. As a way to summarize your findings, briefly develop an expository Sermon Outline from your study. (3 hours)

IBS Assignment #4: Perform a Detailed Analysis of Deut 6:1–12. As a way to summarize your findings, briefly develop an expository Sermon Outline from your study. (4 hours)

IBS Assignment #5: Perform a Segment Survey of Nehemiah 1 (3 hours)

IBS Assignment #6: Perform a Segment Survey of Acts 20:17–38 (Paul's Farewell Address) (3 hours)

IBS Assignment #7: Perform a Book Survey of Ephesians (5 hours)

IBS Assignment #8: Find the Hebrew word behind "fear" in Deut 6:2, its occurrences in the OT, and its range of meanings. Find the Greek word behind "perfect" in Matt 5:48, its occurrences in the NT, and its range of meanings. (2 hours)

IBS Assignment #9: Interpretation: What is the meaning of the statement to "fear the LORD" in Deut 6:2? Be sure to begin considering this more broadly: What is the Old Testament conception of "to fear the Lord"? (6 hours)

IBS Assignment #10: Interpretation: What is the meaning of the Jesus' statement in Matt 5:48a, "you must be perfect"? (6 hours)

IBS Assignment #11: Choose either Matt 5:27–30, Matt 5:38–42, or a passage of your choice and do any necessary interpretation in order to Evaluate what are the underlying truths in the passage and then distinguishing between the transcultural and the cultural ones.

IBS Assignment #12: Take the passage from IBS Assignment 11 and the transcultural truths determined therein, and develop various suitable application points.

2005: I returned to Duvall and Hays's textbook while still requiring Logos Bible Software. In addition to select assignments from Duvall and Hays, I incorporated these eight IBS assignments:

1. Segment Survey of Psalm 1
2. Segment Survey of Nehemiah 1
3. Book Survey of Ephesians
4. Detailed Analysis of Matt 5:13–16 or Matt 5:17–20
5. Perform a detailed analysis of your exegetical paper passage. Be sure also to identify interpretive issues or questions.
6. Choose a hard to understand or morally significant word in your exegetical passage, and do an inductive study following the guidelines in Duvall-Hays ch. 8 (This counts as an "Inductive Assignment").
7. Perform an Interpretation using Inductive Method on this question: What is the meaning of the statement to "fear the LORD" in Deut 6:2? or Perform an Interpretation using Inductive Method on this question: What is the meaning of the Jesus's statement in Matt 5:48a, "you must be perfect"? Be sure to focus not merely on whether it is possible to be perfect, but especially on specifically what it means to be perfect (6 hours).
8. Correlate Deut 6:4–6 with Matt 5:48

Sometime while teaching these courses, I developed a book and segment survey grading rubric and semantic diagramming grading rubric that I describe in Chapter 15 of this present volume ("The Benefits of a General-Analytic Grading Rubric for Book Surveys and Other IBS Assignments").

4. Subsequent Courses to Continue learning IBS

4.1 New Testament I: The Four Gospels

While taking or after taking "Biblical Interpretation" (BIBL 201), students had repeated opportunities to practice and (re)learn IBS. This began typically with "NT I: The Four Gospels—The Life and Teaching of Jesus" (BIBL 221) which could be taken during "Biblical Interpretation." Because some students had already taken "Biblical Interpretation" and others not, I often offered two types of "Inductive Assignments" (IAs). For example, early in the semester I assigned these:

IA 1= Perform an Inductive Book Survey of Mark's Gospel (4 hours)
IA 1= For Non-Inductive People—Create a graphical chart of Mark's Gospel. Consider where the introductory material ends, note any repeated themes or events, and identify where you think the Climax is (4 hours).

For this class, students did twelve types of Inductive Assignments, mainly segment surveys, but also detailed observation, detailed analyses, and semantic analyses. To see these assignments in the context of the whole class, see the slightly edited syllabus for BIBL 221 Fall 2005 included in the Syllabus Appendices in this book.

4.2 New Testament II: Acts and Paul

Sometimes students could immediately follow up "Biblical Interpretation" in the next semester with "NT II: Acts and Paul" (BIBL 222). Since "Biblical Interpretation" was a prerequisite, I could really help the students continue to develop and improve their IBS skills. I offered various types of assignments including developing a preaching and teaching notebook, group interpretive work, and reading reflections from the textbook. But I also included fourteen inductive assignments of which students needed to do twelve: Book surveys of Galatians, 1 Thessalonians, 1 Corinthians, Romans, Ephesians, and 2 Timothy, as well as segment surveys of 1 Cor 5–6, Rom 9–11, and Eph 2 and detailed analyses of 1 Cor 13, Rom 1:18–32, Rom 3:21–26, Eph 5:15–6:9, and 2 Tim 3:14–4:5. To see these assignments in the context of the whole class, see the slightly edited syllabus for BIBL 222 Spring 2005 included in the SYLLABUS APPENDICES at the end of this book.

4.3 New Testament III: The General Epistles and Revelation

Since "Biblical Interpretation BIBL 201" was a prerequisite for NT III (BIBL 223), I offered students nineteen inductive assignments from which they were required to do seventeen. These assignments drew upon those exercises developed by David R. Bauer in his IBS Asbury syllabus on the General Epistles.[4] Since by this point Bethel students had taken two or more IBS focused classes, in addition to book surveys, segment surveys, and detailed analyses, it was important to incorporate interpretation assignments and synthetic assignments. For example, two of these are provided here:

Assignment #2: Perform an interpretation of James 2:14–26 following these steps (2 hrs):
1. State in your own words the main principle set forth in 2:14–26.
2. Trace the lines of reasoning James employs to substantiate this main principle.
3. Answer these questions: In what sense were Abraham and Rahab justified by their works? What is the complete and precise relationship between faith and works?
4. Be prepared to discuss your work and questions in class.
5. Indicate on the top of the first page how much time you spent on this assignment.

Assignment #3: Book Synthesis of James based upon the Person of God (4 hrs).
1. There is something interesting about James: throughout the letter God is multifariously portrayed: Master (1:1; 4:7); Benefactor (1:5, 18, 21; 2:5; 4:6); the "Father of Lights" (1:17, 27); as righteous and the one who sets standards of righteousness (1:20, 27; 2:5, 23; 4:4); Friend (2:23); as good (1:13) and as one (2:19); and Lord (1:1; 2:1; 3:9; 4:10; 5:4, 7-8, 10, 11, 14, 15); Judge (1:12; 4:8, 8; 5:9), etc.
2. As you synthesize the message of the Book of James consider what these various portraits of God contribute to understanding **how we ought to live**.
3. Do you notice any patterns or general ideas in the order or emphasis of how God is portrayed?
4. Indicate on the top of the first page how much time you spent on this assignment.

---

[4] Bauer's influence is seen directly and indirectly in many other assignments in my various syllabi.

To see the NT III assignments in the context of the whole class, see the slightly edited syllabus for BIBL 223 Spring 2004 included in the SYLLABUS APPENDICES at the end of this book.

4.4 Book Study Courses

In addition to broad NT survey courses, students could also take focused classes on particular biblical books. I taught three such courses on 1 and 2 Corinthians (2000), Luke (2001), and Ephesians (2002). Below is the stated course description, objectives, and format for the 1 and 2 Corinthians course:

> **COURSE DESCRIPTION:** The textual examination and application of inductive principles of Bible study are applied to 1 and 2 Corinthians.
>
> **OBJECTIVES:** Upon completion of this course, students will have a greater understanding of
>
> 1) the application of the inductive Bible study method on Paul's letters;
> 2) the driving force of Paul's calling and his missionary/ministry practice;
> 3) the issues facing emerging Christianity, e.g., authority/leadership, Jew/gentile relations;
> 4) the socio-rhetorical culture of which Paul and Corinth was apart;
> 5) other methods appropriate to interpret Paul's letters such rhetoric and intertextuality;
> 6) how one can appropriate and apply the message of Paul today.
>
> **CLASS FORMAT:** I will teach this course using lecture, discussion, and guided group assignments. If possible, we will also adopt a seminar format when student assignments are due by assigning a respondent for each individual assignment when presented.

Although I stressed "inductive principles" and "the application of inductive Bible study method," these were not strictly seen in the types of assignments students were expected to do, but more in the evidential manner of exegetical investigation and exploration. I set these courses up more like seminars and taught students how to write book reviews and exegetical papers. In hindsight, I think these courses were missed opportunities; however, I taught them before I really introduced IBS foundationally into the overall curriculum, which occurred in 2002.

4.5 Capstone Course: Contemporary Critical Issues in Biblical Studies

One of the most interesting classes that I taught was the capstone course, "Contemporary Critical Issues in Biblical Studies" (BIBL470) which I subtitled, "Slaves, Women, and Homosexuals" based upon our core textbook with that name by William J. Webb.[5] Essentially, I designed the course as a seminar on biblical evaluation. Here is my course description, objectives, and class format:

> **COURSE DESCRIPTION:** A capstone course that draws contemporary critical issues in Bible, Biblical Theology, and hermeneutics together. This year our focus is on "exploring the hermeneutics of cultural analysis" based upon William Webb's book. As such, this course will

---

[5] William J. Webb, *Slaves, Women & Homosexuals: Exploring the Hermeneutics of Cultural Analysis* (Downers Grove, IL: IVP Academic, 2001).

supplement the Inductive Bible Study method by filling out our understanding of and practice of the steps of evaluation, application, and correlation.

OBJECTIVES: Upon this course's completion, students should have a greater understanding of

1. the critical place within biblical interpretation, and specifically Inductive Bible Study Method, that evaluation, application, and correlation occupy;
2. the exegetical, theological, and hermeneutical issues that exist when attempting to faithfully apply Scripture to one's own contemporary setting;
3. a hierarchy of principles to assist one in this attempt to faithfully apply Scripture;
4. and, lastly, to better understand the biblical topics of slavery, women, and homosexuality in light of this task of attempting to faithfully apply Scripture to one's own contemporary setting.

CLASS FORMAT: Since this is a capstone course for biblical studies, we will be adopting a seminar format that assumes that students will openly participate and discuss course content with the professor; there will be some lecture material presented. **Note:** Due to the nature of the course content, and the need for us all to speak frankly and openly, I will ask that the comments, questions, and propositions discussed in our class not be repeated outside of class with indiscretion, but rather with the utmost respect for the persons involved.

After walking through Webb's book carefully and critically, I wanted students to perform this assignment (half of their grade):

(50%) **Preparation for and Final Paper on a topic of your choice:** Essentially, select from one of these topics (check with professor) and go through the procedure that Webb follows for the determination of what is transcultural in Scriptures on this topic and the relevance this has in today's life and thought.
1. Sabbath Observance
2. War/Killing
3. Fornication
4. Tithing (10% required still, or something else)
5. Divorce and Remarriage
6. Creationism (What are believers expected to believe)
7. Historicism of Gen 1–11 (Historicity of Adam and Eve, or Flood, etc.)
8. OT Land and Temple Fulfillment (Should we expect a temple in God's future plan?)
9. Church Organization (elder board, or Overseer, or Charismatic)
10. Spiritual Gifts Today (which ones, and when used)
11. Another topic in consultation with the professor.

To see a slightly edited syllabus for "Contemporary Critical Issues in Biblical Studies" BIBL 470 taught in the Fall 2005, see the SYLLABUS APPENDICES at the end of this present volume.

5. Conclusion

As a new "green" NT professor in 1999, my course load required me to teach across the biblical canon and eventually through every NT book; this was strenuous but provided a great foundation to engage students from whom I expected so much effort to excel as we studied Scripture together. I constantly had in mind that such learning was to prepare them to serve the church. Fairly early on, I realized the need to integrate the Biblical Studies curriculum around the foundations of biblical languages and IBS. Once the curriculum was established, it required me to prepare book surveys for most NT books as well as numerous other segment surveys, semantic analyses, several interpretations, and special inductive studies.

By the end of my tenure at Bethel College in 2007, I was quite astounded at the performance of undergraduate and graduate students engaging the Scriptures earnestly. They learned how to perform surveys and semantic analyses of the NT extremely well in large part because after learning how to do them, they performed them again and again for three to four years in multiple class settings. Moreover, those students who took my Elementary Greek I and II classes were also taught my semantic analysis approach that incorporated MSRs and urged students to make all types of observation.

Some work of these students was particularly memorable to me since their observations led to quite fascinating structural observations with important ideological significance.[6] One female student observed a chiasm across the whole of 2 Timothy; the hinge is 1:17 and Paul's desire for companionship in view of those rejecting him. Another graduate student observed a chiasm across John 17; the center is "Protect them from the evil one" in 17:15b; one may correlate this observation with the climax of the Lord's Prayer, "Deliver us from the Evil One" (Matt 6:13b). Another undergraduate student performed a word study on "temple" (ναός) and insightfully described a movement across the NT from the geo-physical temple in Jerusalem, to Jesus being temple-like, to believers being the temple, and finally to the New Jerusalem not having a temple "because almighty God the Lord and the Lamb are its temple" (Rev 21:22). In my "Biblical Interpretation" class Spring 2006, this same student also observed a basic chiastic structure in Eph 2:14–16 centering on Christ's annulment of the Law. I extended the detail and length of the chiasm in conversation with other Bethel students and have described and reflected on the oral nature of this structure in various places.[7]

---

[6] For my discussion of the oral-nature and ideological importance of chiasms, see Fredrick J. Long, "The Oral, the Textual, and the Visual (or, The Good, the Bad, and the Ugly) in Jesus's and Paul's Chiastic Performance of Scripture in 2 Corinthians, Ephesians, and Mark," in *Orality and Theological Training in the 21st Century*, ed. Jay W. Moon and Joshua Moon (Wilmore, KY: Digibooks, 2017), n.p.

[7] For a structural presentation of the seven-tiered chiasm of Eph 2:11–22, see Fredrick J. Long, "Ephesians: Paul's Political Theology in Greco-Roman Political Context," in *Christian Origins and Classical Culture: Social and Literary Contexts for the New Testament*, ed. S. E. Porter and A. W. Pitts; The New Testament in its Hellenistic Context (Leiden: Brill, 2012), 255–309 at 308–9. It was not until after further reflection that I realized where this basic structural observation originated and how it developed subsequently; I have since credited these students in Long, "Learning Christ: The Dynamics of Moral Formation in Ephesians," *Reflections* 16/17 (2014): 73–91 at 90n27. For a discussion of the literary forms and their significance in Eph 2:11–22, including the chiastic structure, see Long, "The Oral, the Textual, and the Visual" and *In Step with God's Word*, 247–50.

Thus, teaching IBS has enriched not only students but my own teaching and learning in innumerable ways through my extensive course preparations, classroom discussions, and the questions raised about God and Scripture in and outside of class sessions. The most significant result of teaching IBS across the curriculum most likely is the continued impact that these students, their students, and their congregations make as they live as Christ's disciples because they have earnestly and directly encountered the Word of God and deeply pondered its implications for human life and God's mission in the world.

FOR FURTHER READING

Backues, Lindy D. "Inductive Bible Study and Teaching Social Sciences." Chapter 12 of the present book.

Castillo, Metosalem Quillupras. "Inductive Bible Study and Its Place in the Curriculum of Ebenezer Bible College." Th.M., Asbury Theological Seminary, 1972.

Cockerill, Gareth Lee. "Method follows Content: Interpreting the Bible as the Bible." Chapter 9 of the present book.

Dendiu, John. "Inductive Bible Study Principles in General Education Bible Classes at a Christian College," Chapter 8 of the present book.

Oswalt, John N. "The Use of the Inductive Bible Method in the Teaching of the Book of Isaiah." Chapter 11 of the present book.

Weaver, Dorothy Jean. "Competent in the Basic Skills of Inductive Bible Study: A Case Study on the Use of Inductive Biblical Studies at Eastern Mennonite Seminary." Chapter 10 of the present book.

INDUCTIVE BIBLE STUDY PRINCIPLES
IN GENERAL EDUCATION BIBLE CLASSES AT A CHRISTIAN COLLEGE

Dr. John Dendiu, Retired Associate Professor of Bible and Religion (May 2016)
Bethel College, Mishawaka, IN

ABSTRACT: This essay explores the rationale and methods used in applying IBS principles in teaching general education Old and New Testament classes in a liberal arts Christian college setting. The author explored several approaches in teaching these classes before deciding to use IBS principles as the basis of his instruction. This paper outlines the author's philosophy and methodology, as well as giving several examples of materials used and types of assessments given.

1. INTRODUCTION

I met Dr. Traina in the fall of 1984 during my first semester as an M. Div. student at Asbury Seminary. Prior to coming to seminary, I taught public school music for four years, spent two years in a parachurch ministry, and then three and half years on staff at a church in youth and music ministry. I came to seminary eager to prepare for a lifetime of Christian service. I enrolled in his class on the gospel of Mark. Little did I know what a new world would open to me. I was drawn immediately into the methodology that Dr. Traina taught and modeled during that class. I quickly realized that IBS would be crucial in laying a foundation for a lifetime of teaching and ministry. Consequently, I took three more classes from him (including an independent study) and four classes from Dr. David Bauer.

After graduating in 1987 and spending two years serving overseas, I became a senior pastor in 1990 and served as senior pastor in two churches over the next seven years. I used my IBS training heavily in preparing sermons each week as well as in leading church-wide Bible studies. I found that people responded very well to studying the Bible in this way. In the Bible studies, I would hand out a survey chart of the book we were studying, explain the overview of the book, and then walk through the book in modified IBS fashion. The people loved it! The Bible opened up to them in new and transforming ways and it was gratifying to see the text come alive for these people.

2. Early Teaching Experience

In 1997, I had the opportunity to join the faculty of Bethel College in the department of religion and philosophy. Bethel College is the liberal arts school affiliated with the Missionary Church, Inc. I taught there for 19 years, retiring in May of 2016. During my first several years, I taught some of the upper level New Testament classes in the adult college Bible and ministry major. I structured these classes similar to the IBS classes I had in seminary. I had students do their own book surveys, segment surveys, and some interpretive/application/correlation assignments. These classes were well received by the students; they had never studied the Bible in this way. This experience further reinforced my conviction that IBS was absolutely critical for training the next generation of Christian workers.

The bulk of my Bible teaching at Bethel involved the introductory survey courses in both New Testament and Old Testament in the undergraduate college. These courses were part of the general education curriculum; all students were required to take both of these classes. For the goals and objectives of these courses, see SUPPLEMENT 8.1. For the last 15 years before retirement, my teaching load was generally divided between the introductory general education Bible classes and upper level ministry classes (such as worship, evangelism and discipleship, and pastoral care). Every semester I taught either one or two Bible classes; by the end of my time at Bethel I estimate that I taught about fifty of these classes.

During the first several years of teaching I experimented with a number of different formats. I started by using an introductory textbook on either Old or New Testament geared for college survey classes. I found benefit in using these texts, as they provided wonderful background materials to the Scriptures. But after a few semesters, I realized that having students read a 400-page textbook and then engage in any meaningful way in the actual text of the Bible was challenging. Only so much reading material could be assigned in any one semester. The textbooks were becoming a hindrance to getting into the biblical text itself, which was what I really wanted to do.

3. Transition in Teaching Philosophy

One day I was talking with my colleague Dr. Fred Long about this. He suggested trying something that he was doing. He had prepared a number of inductive worksheets that he used with his upper level students. He was willing to share these with me; this began a significant change in the way I taught. Building upon the worksheet concept, I decided to develop a complete workbook for each of the classes—one for Old Testament and one for New Testament. The first part of the workbook contained basic material on the Bible itself (historical information, issues of original languages, translations, an overview of the inductive method, etc.). Then I transitioned into a discussion of each book. I included a survey chart as well as some basic introductory information about the book (that I would expand on in class). The rest of the material on any given book consisted of a series of inductive questions that the students would work through in preparation for class (as well as other pertinent information specific to the book). Before students came to class, the assignment was to read through the introductory materials and the assigned portions of the biblical text and answer the questions in the workbook. The goal of the pre-class work was to be prepared to engage in discussion in class. The bulk of each class was spent in encountering the text via the inductive questions. See SUPPLEMENT 8.2 for a sample portion of the workbook.

My philosophy in approaching each class was simple: I did not want to be a dispenser of information. I wanted to facilitate discussion, interaction, and application of the biblical text. Ultimately, I was teaching with the spiritual formation of my students in mind. Because of this, I wanted students to read parts of the Bible, reflect upon them, write their own thoughts down, and discuss their findings with peers. Some days, the class would take the form of a discussion with the whole class—with me moderating, directing, and encouraging dialogue. Some days I put students in groups to discuss the questions and then share insights with the rest of the class. Above all, I wanted the students to be talking about the text, gaining insight and making application.

The students would read the entire New Testament during the course of the semester. As for the Old Testament, I had students read what I felt were the most important parts and skim the rest (they read about half of the Old Testament). We worked through each biblical book during the semester, spending more time on the more significant ones. I ended up teaching the Old Testament class about twice as often as the New Testament class. As a result, I became even more convinced of this methodology, as many students had never read much of the Old Testament at all. Students were grateful for exposure to the riches of the Old Testament text of which they were unaware. In addition, they preferred to read the Bible as their textbook and not a large book about the Bible. They were also glad to save the money that a textbook would cost. I would simply post the entire workbook (about a 90-page Word document) on our campus learning management system and students would print it off, put it in a three-ring binder, and bring it to class every day. I encouraged them to do this rather than recording their answers directly into the workbook on their computers. Perhaps I was old-fashioned, but I did not allow computers in class. I wanted students to hand-write responses and take notes. I also required the use of a physical Bible in class; they were not to use a digital one on their phone or other device.

4. GRADING AND ASSESSMENT

My grading/assessment was fairly simple. Since these were relatively large classes—ranging in size from 35–70 students—I settled on giving four objective exams each semester as well as grading completion of the workbook questions. I felt that the exams were comprehensive but fair—nothing was on the exams that had not been discussed in class. I did not collect the student workbooks to evaluate—I had students record on a reading form the amount of work they completed before each class. They turned in this form at the time of each exam. Grading the workbook was on an honor system; I explained my expectations for the type of reading and written responses I wanted from them. I allowed them to determine how faithful they were each day in completing the work before class started. They did not receive any credit for work they did after the class period in which it was assigned, as we would have already talked through the material. In essence, the workbook was a completion grade. If students read the assigned portions of the text and recorded their own insights, they received full credit. I was not as concerned with the content of their answers as in their own independent thinking and wrestling with the questions. The four exams together totaled 80% of the semester grade and the reading/workbook completion was 20%. See SUPPLEMENT 8.3 for a reading report form and SUPPLEMENT 8.4 for a sample exam.

In addition to the exams and workbook, I allowed the students write a paper for extra credit (the paper could add up to 5% to the final grade). The following is a description of the paper:

> A 4-5 page paper (double-spaced, one-inch margins, 12 pt. font) on a character of the Old Testament. This is not a research paper; it is your own first-hand study of the biblical material about this person (do not consult other sources except the Bible). Include character qualities, analysis of their life, what they did that was significant, why they are important to the story of God's working in the Old Testament, and personal applications and lessons for your own life. Be sure to include biblical references (book, chapter, verses) to support your writing.

I designed this assignment as a way to give students further application of IBS principles.

During my years teaching these introductory Bible courses, I made small adjustments to both the introductory content of the books as well as minor changes to the inductive questions. Every year I discovered things that worked better than others, and my own continuing study of the text yielded new insights that I included as well.

Teaching general education Bible classes brings with it a certain set of challenges and frustrations (not enough time to go in depth, the varying levels of interest of the students, etc.). But as a way to expose students to both the broad story line and important themes of both testaments, I believe that using IBS principles and getting students to read and interact with as much of the biblical text as possible is the best way to keep the students' interest as well as allow them to encounter the God of the Bible.

5. Conclusion

My introduction to and work with inductive Bible methodology as taught by Dr. Traina served me in invaluable ways as I had the privilege of teaching the Bible in a Christian college setting. I am forever grateful for Dr. Traina, his life, and his opening the Bible to me in ways that have transformed my life and ministry.

SUPPLEMENT 8.1
COURSE DESCRIPTIONS FOR NT AND OT INTRODUCTION COURSES

COURSE DESCRIPTION: New Testament Literature—This course is a study of the literature, historical background, geography, and significance of the books of the New Testament.

OBJECTIVES:

1. To understand the central message, themes, and characters of each New Testament book.
2. To have a basic understanding of the historical, geographical, and cultural setting of the New Testament books.
3. To be able to articulate the significance of Jesus' life, death, and resurrection.
4. To be able to describe the basic chronology and interrelation of the New Testament books.
5. To understand basic important issues in New Testament studies.
6. To have read through and interacted with each New Testament book.
7. To create a desire to know and study the New Testament in greater depth as a means of getting to know the Lord Jesus Christ in a fuller and more intimate way.

COURSE DESCRIPTION: Old Testament Literature—An introduction to the literature, theological themes, historical background, geography, and significance of the Old Testament.

OBJECTIVES

1. To enable the student to read and interact with significant parts of the Old Testament.
2. To help the student to put the Old Testament in its historical, cultural, social, and religious context.
3. To give the student a broad understanding of the content of the Old Testament, with the ability to recall major themes and emphases of each book.
4. To introduce the student to various higher critical issues in the study of the Old Testament.
5. To create in the student a desire to know and study the Old Testament in greater depth as a means of getting to know the God and Father of our Lord Jesus Christ in a fuller and more intimate way.

SUPPLEMENT 8.2
THE STRUCTURE OF EXODUS FROM DR. TRAINA[1]

Need for, Accomplishment of, Process of Redemption *Deliverance*	Responsibilities of Redemption *Covenant*
1-12 – in Egypt 13-18 – Travelling in the desert	19-24 – Legislation at Mt. Sinai 25-40 – Building the Tabernacle (32-34 – Golden Calf incident)
1 18	19 40

Introduction

"Exodus" is from a Latin word meaning exit or departure and describes the "going out" of the nation of Israel from slavery in Egypt. This book is the early history of God's chosen people. Exodus lays the foundation for understanding about God's attributes, redemption, law, and proper worship. The Mosaic Covenant is central to the relationship between God and His people.

Time Frame of Exodus
- Chapters 1–18—approx. 430 years (12:40) – from the 1800s–1400s BC. During this time period the Egyptian empire was at the height of its power and influence.
- Chapters 19–40—approximately 10 months

Historical Problems with the Exodus event:
- Historicity – did the Exodus actually happen? The Exodus is the central event of Israel's history. No direct historical evidence exists for the event, but there is much indirect evidence to support its historicity. Joseph's life accurately reflects Egyptian life of the time

---

[1] The survey chart of Exodus as well as the various comments on the text have been adapted from syllabus and notes from Dr. Traina's class on the Pentateuch, Fall 1985.

period, Egypt employed several neighboring peoples as slaves for their building projects, and several Israelite names (especially those of Moses' family) are known to be Egyptian names. It seems reasonable to conclude that God's people were indeed slaves in Egypt and that God miraculously intervened to deliver them.
- Date—1446 BC (1 Kings 6:1 states that the Exodus was 480 years before Solomon built the Temple in 966 BC) or about 1275 BC (some archaeological evidence points to this date). If the later date is preferred, it is possible to see the number 480 as more symbolic – perhaps 12 generations of 40 years each.
- Route—Sea of Reeds (Red Sea). Scholars have suggested several possible routes. See map below.[2]

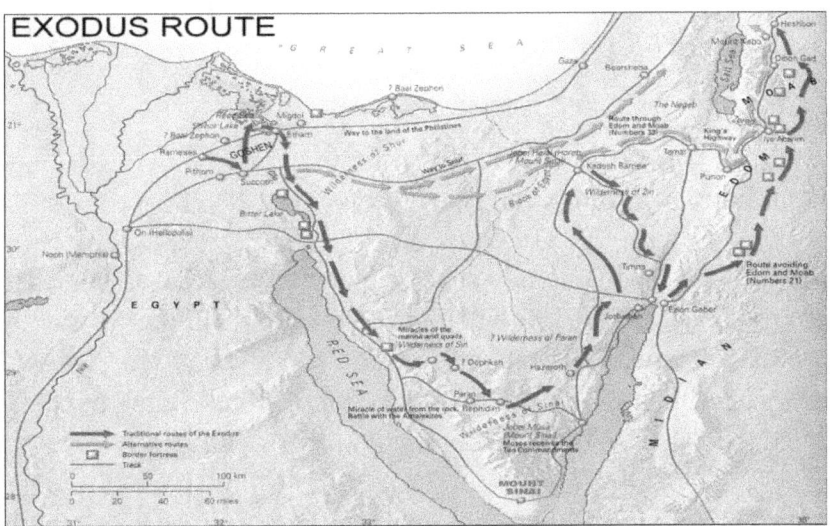

Reading Through Exodus.

Read Exodus 1–12. This section describes God's choice and preparation of Moses as the human deliverer for His people as well as the process of deliverance.
What problems surface in ch. 1? Do you see any ethical dilemmas? If so, what are they?

Chapters 3–4 describe Moses's call from God. How does Moses respond? How does God respond to Moses?

Chapters 5–12 describe the process of deliverance in Egypt. What challenges did Moses face in these chapters?

---

[2] Map of Exodus route is found on Wikipedia. deb-network.com

What reason(s) do these chapters give for God sending the Ten Plagues?

How do you understand the "hardening" of Pharaoh's heart that is described in chs. 5–12? See 7:3, 13, 22; 8:15, 32; 9:7, 34; 10:1, 20, 27; 11:10.

Skim Exod 13–18. Especially note the crossing of the Red Sea in ch. 14, the provision of manna in ch. 16, and the grumbling of the people all throughout.

Read Exodus 19–24. The Israelites have traveled to the foot of Mt. Sinai and are ready to receive the covenant from God to be His people (often call the Mosaic or Sinai covenant). Notice the initial statement of the covenant (in general terms) in 19:4–6. How do you react to all the laws and regulations in chs. 21–23? Which of these stand out to you and why? What relationship do they have to the Ten Commandments of ch. 20?

It is important to note that the Mosaic covenant builds upon the covenant God made with Abraham. The people would need to know what God expected of them and how they were to live as His people. All the laws and regulations that made up this covenant were not designed to be works that the people could do to earn God's favor; these laws were about maintaining a relationship with God. Furthermore, the Abrahamic covenant was **unconditional**; God's choice of Abraham was not dependent on his actions. But the Mosaic covenant was **conditional**. The people would be blessed in their land and be a blessing to all the nations IF they upheld their end of the bargain. Failure to do so would result in curses and eventual exile from the land. Unfortunately, the rest of the Old Testament is mostly the story of Israel's inability to be faithful to their part of the covenant. But this did not change God's heart toward His people. He was still faithful to them despite their unfaithfulness.

Place of the Law—Exodus 19–24 (and through the end of Deuteronomy)
- Exodus does not begin with Law (legalism = trying to earn God's favor by law obedience).
- Exodus does not end with chapter 18 (antinomianism = no need of law because God has saved by grace).

- Redemption involves responsibilities, i.e., to live as God's people and to be a blessing to all the nations.
- Grace (deliverance) comes before the Law.
- The New Covenant in Christ is the fulfillment of this Law, i.e., a love ethic.
- The whole law code involves morality.

How to Best Interpret the Old Testament Law: Some "Dos" and "Don'ts"[3]
1. Do see the OT law as God's fully inspired Word *for* you. Don't see the OT law as God's direct command *to* you.
2. Do see the OT law as the basis for the Old Covenant, and therefore for Israel's history. Don't see the OT law as binding on Christians in the New Covenant except where specifically renewed.
3. Do see God's justice, love, and high standards revealed in the OT law. Don't forget to see that God's mercy is made equal to the severity of the standards.
4. Don't see the OT law as complete. It is not technically comprehensive. Do see the OT law as a paradigm – providing examples for the full range of expected behavior.
5. Don't expect the OT law to be cited frequently by the prophets or the NT. Do remember that the *essence* of the Law (10 Commandments and the 2 chief laws – love God and love your neighbor) is repeated in the prophets and renewed in the NT.
6. Do see the OT law as a generous gift to Israel, bringing much blessing when obeyed. Don't see the OT law as a grouping of arbitrary, annoying regulations limiting people's freedom.

Skim Exod 25–31. These chapters describe the design of the tabernacle that God wanted the people to build.

Read Exodus 32–34. This is the incident of the Golden Calf. What catches your attention in this section? Note especially the reason the people built the idol, Moses' responses and actions as leader of the people, the tent of meeting in 33:7-011, and the description of God in 34:6–7.

Skim Exod 35–40. These chapters describe the actual construction of the tabernacle. Notice the climax in ch. 40—God descending upon the Tabernacle; His presence with His people.

---

[3] From Gorden D. Fee and Douglas Stuart, *How to Read the Bible for All Its Worth*, 2nd ed. (Grand Rapids: Zondervan, 1993), ch.9.

The Tabernacle[4]

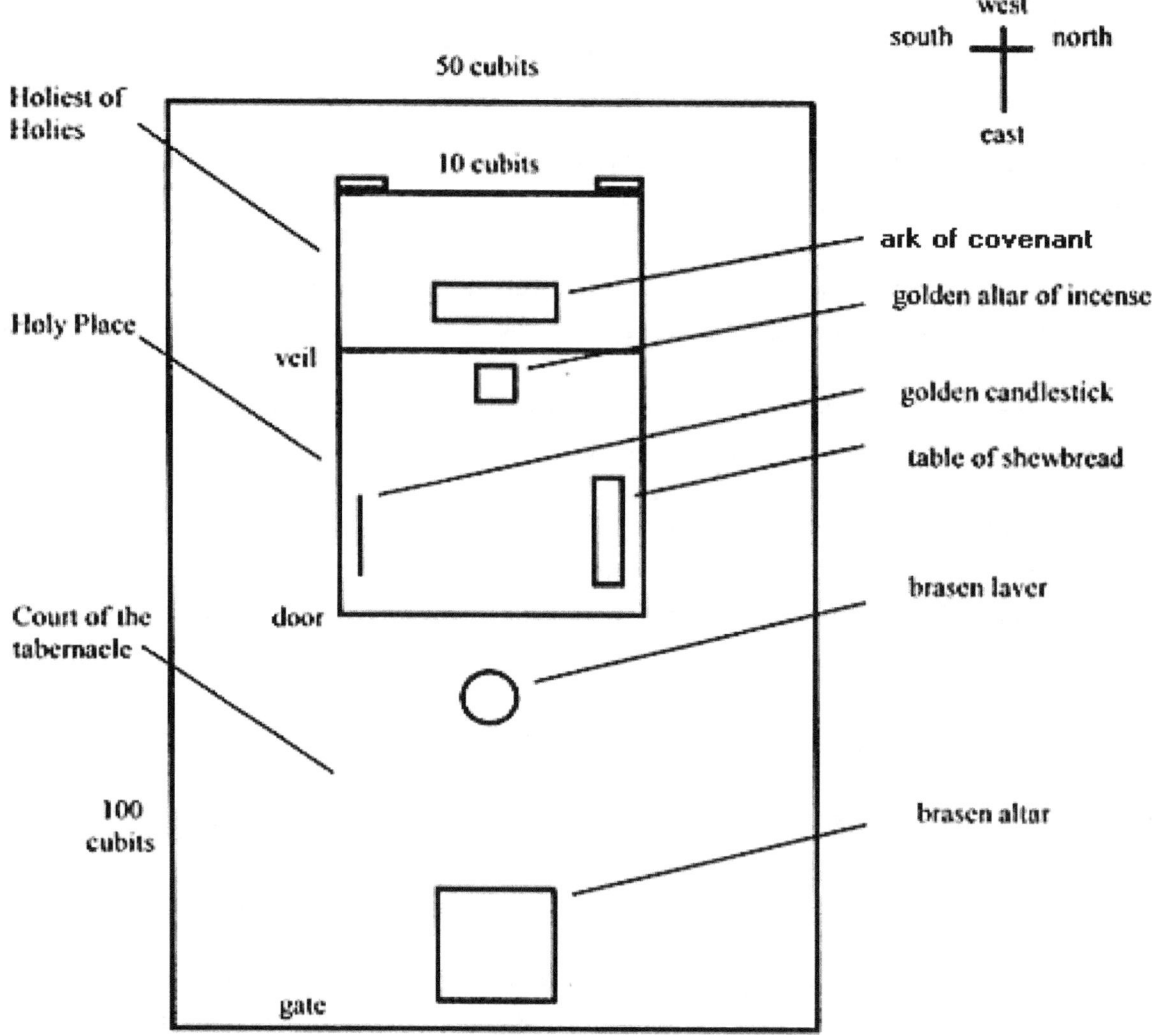

Significance of the Furnishings of the Tabernacle[5]
- Ark of the covenant and the mercy seat – the presence of God
- Table of bread – the provision of God
- Lampstand – the guidance of God
- Veil between the Holy Place and the Holy of Holies – the barrier between a Holy God and sinful humans
- Bronze altar (place of sacrifice) – a great divide between God and man, bridged by the atoning work of a sacrifice rather than human works

---

[4] Chart of overhead view of tabernacle is found on Wikipedia tabernacleofmoses.org.
[5] Side picture of tabernacle that shows its tent-like structure is found on Wikipedia. try-god.com

- Single doorway – only one way into God's presence
- Laver (for cleansing) – a person must be cleansed physically and spritually before approaching God
- Altar of incense – represents the importance of worship and prayer.

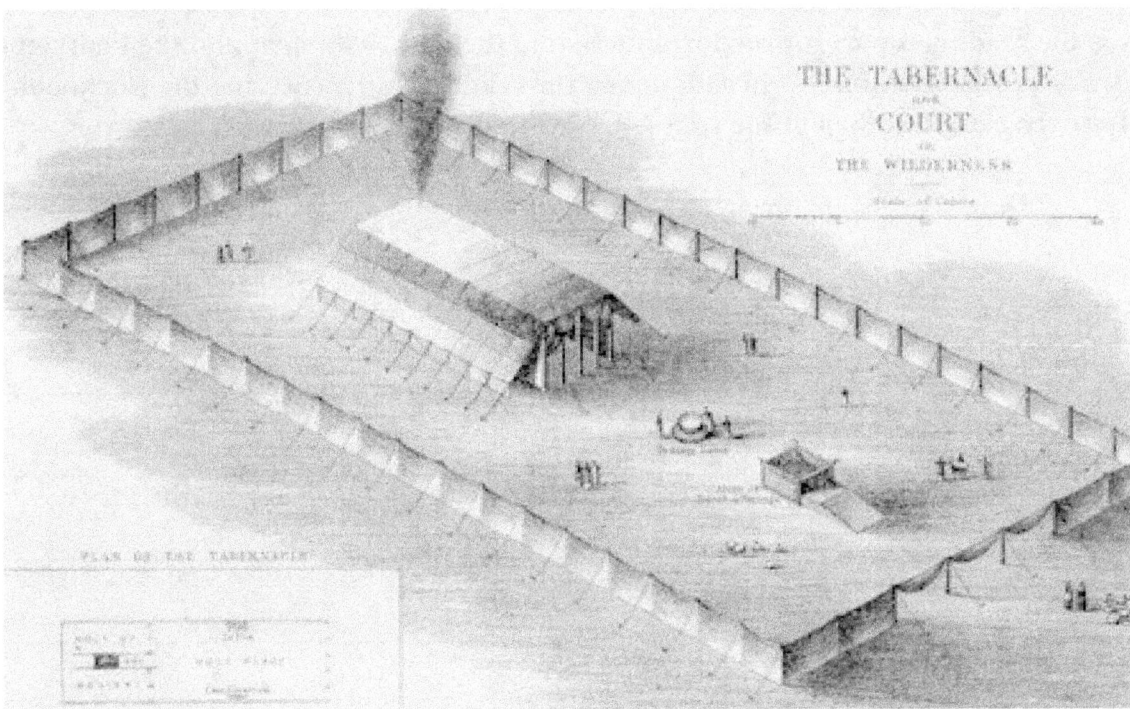

Theological Significance of the Exodus

- **Deliverance** (chs. 1–18) – The great act is parallel to Christ. The people were delivered out of bondage into covenant relationship.
- **Covenant** (chs. 19–40) – The Torah was at the center of Israel's relationship with God.
- **Presence of God** – God in their midst is the distinguishing feature of Israel. This climaxes in ch. 40.
- **Sea of Reeds** – A key symbol of salvation in the Old Testament.
- **Mosaic (Sinai) Covenant** – The symbol of an enduring relationship with God.

SUPPLEMENT 8.3
OT LITERATURE – READING REPORT – SPRING 2016

Name_____

Below is the reading report for the Introduction to the Old Testament and the Pentateuch. Keep track of your faithfulness in completing the reading and answering the workbook questions for each class and then grade yourself as to your readiness for each class.

Date	Assignment	% of reading and questions completed by class time
M 1/11	Intro. to Old Testament	No score here
W 1/13	Introduction to the Pentateuch Genesis 1-11	
F 1/15	Genesis 12-26	
M 1/18	Genesis 27-50	
M 1/20	Exodus 1-18	
F 1/22	Exodus 19-40	
M 1/25	Leviticus	
W 1/27	Numbers	
F 1/29	Deuteronomy	
M 2/1	Catch-up and Review Reading Report Due	No score here
W 2/3	Exam #1 Pentateuch	No score here

Add your percentages, divide by 8, and enter the total here _____
I certify that the above report accurately reflects my level of completion of the work assigned for each class.

                    Signed_____

Supplement 8.4
Exam #1 – Pentateuch   Old Testament Literature

I. Multiple choice. Put the letter of the best answer in the blank.

1. _____ Which man and his family is the focus of Genesis 12–50?
   a) Isaac b) Abraham c) Moses d) Noah
2. _____ In Exodus, what is the best way to understand the hardening of Pharaoh's heart?
   a) God hardened Pharaoh's heart b) Pharaoh's heart was hardened c) Pharaoh hardened his own heart d) all of the above
3. _____ The theme of Genesis 3–11 is
   a) perfection of God's creation b) power of Satan c) moral failure of humankind and the spread of sin d) universality of humankind's dominion
4. _____ The two main things that God promised Abraham were land and a) cattle b) gold c) descendants d) wives
5. _____ Who was Hagar? a) a distant cousin of Abram b) the slave of Sarah and mother of Ishmael c) the sister of Sarah d) the teacher of Sarah
6. _____ Who tricked his brother out of both his birthright and his blessing? a) Esau b) Ephraim c) Jacob d) Manasseh
7. _____ What are the three steps in inductive Bible study? a) observation, interpretation, application b) reading, thinking, praying c) context, genre, observation d) hear, read, study
8. _____ God changed Jacob's name to a) Ishmael b) Jacobi c) Israel d) Haran
9. _____ What was the main purpose of the desert tabernacle?
   a) to provide a place for worship, sacrifice, and God's presence to dwell b) to allow the Hebrews a place to gather c) as a center of civic life
10. _____ The central event of the Old Testament parallel to the cross in the New Testament is
    a) life of Moses b) the exodus from Egypt c) giving of Ten Commandments d) consecration of priests
11. _____ The last half of Leviticus ("staying holy") speaks primarily about
    a) right living outside the tabernacle b) issues of right sacrifices c) guidelines for lives of the priests d) the order of tabernacle worship
12. _____ The best way to understand the laws of the Mosaic covenant (as found in Exodus and Leviticus) are a) as ways to limit the freedom of the Israelites b) as gracious gifts to help God's people live in the fullest way that would honor God c) as laws that are all binding on us as New Testament Christians
13. _____ If taken numerically (and literally), each of the 2 census lists in Numbers would indicate a population of a) 2 million b) 4 million c) 6 million d) 8 million
14. _____ How did God punish the Israelites because they did not enter the Promised Land at the time planned? a) a plague of grasshoppers b) wandering in the desert without any guidance c) wandering in the desert for 40 years and no one over age 20 would be allowed to see the Promised Land d) they would have to fight many battles

15. _____ Numbers is primarily intended to be a) a census registration b) an essay about the consequences of sin c) a historical document d) an account of the journey of the Israelites

16. _____ The four main people of Genesis 12–50 are a) Noah, Joshua, Abraham, Joseph b) Abraham, Isaac, Jacob, Joseph c) Isaac, Adam, Jacob, Eve d) Abraham, Sarah, Jacob, Rachel

17. _____ The four main events of Genesis 1–11 are a) Creation, Fall, Flood, Exodus b) Exodus, Tower of Babel, birth of Isaac, Fall c) Fall, Flood, Tower of Babel, Entering the Promised Land d) Creation, Fall, Flood, Tower of Babel

18. _____ The two major covenants of the Pentateuch (the first one is associated with the story that first begins in Genesis 12). a) Mosaic and Abrahamic b) Noahic and Israelite c) Adamic and Egyptian d) Isaac and Joseph

19. _____ The three major festivals that the Israelites celebrated.
a) Lent, Easter, Christmas b) Passover, Pentecost, Tabernacles c) Mt. Sinai, Exodus, Purim d) New Year, Passover, Building of the Tabernacle

20. _____ The bread-like food that God provided the Israelites as they wandered in the desert.
a) matzah b) gluten c) manna d) unleavened bread

II. True or false.

1. _____ There is disagreement among scholars as to the exact date and route of the Exodus.

2. _____ Conservative scholars generally believe that Jeremiah is the author of the Pentateuch.

3. _____ In Genesis 15, Abraham was declared righteous before God because of his faith and trust in God's promises.

4. _____ A correct interpretation of the Old Testament does not need to take into account the difference between types of literary writing (poetry, narrative, etc.).

5. _____ Moses received the Ten commandments at the top of Mt. Sinai when he met with God.

6. _____ Circumcision was the sign of the covenant given to Moses at Mt. Sinai.

7. _____ The sacrificial system of the Old Testament found its ultimate fulfillment in the death of Christ.

8. _____ According to Deut 5–11, the fear of God and the love of God are the two major motivations for obedience to the covenant.

9. _____ Balaam and Balak were the only two Israelites from the original people that came out of Egypt who were allowed to enter the Promised Land.

10. _____ The providence and sovereignty of God are major themes in the life of Joseph.

III. Fill in the blank with the correct term. Use each term only once.

Canon
Apocrypha
Dead Sea Scrolls
Fall of Humankind
Fertile Crescent
Torah
Pentateuch
Promise
Election
Holiness
Patriarch, Genealogy Tabernacle
Golden Calf
Day of Atonement
Suzerainty Treaty
Shema
Theories of inspiration (i.e., dictation theory, neo-orthodox theory, verbal-plenary theory)

1. _____ Hebrew word meaning "law" or "instruction."
2. _____ Term for the first Five books of the Old Testament.
3. _____ Men who are the pioneers or stand at the fountainhead of the faith – refers to Abraham, Isaac, and Jacob.
4. _____ Declaration of monotheism and summary of faith found in Deut 6:4–5.
5. _____ Authoritative body of documents. Literally means "measuring rod" or "standard."
6. _____ The idol that the Israelites built at Mt. Sinai after growing impatient waiting for Moses.
7. _____ The extra books included in the Roman Catholic Bible but not accepted as Scripture by evangelical Protestants.
8. _____ Sin of Adam and Eve in Genesis 3.
9. _____ Area of the world in which the events of the Old Testament occurred (especially the events of Genesis through Deuteronomy).
10. _____ The theory of inspiration that states that God spoke the Bible word-for-word to the human authors.
11. _____ The theory of inspiration that states that God worked in cooperation with the human authors of the Bible so that all the words are inspired.

12. _____ Moveable tent that the Israelites constructed and used for worship.
13. _____ The theory of inspiration that states that the Bible contains the Word of God, but is not the Word of God per se. It becomes the word as someone reads it and encounters God.
14. _____ Manuscripts found in 1947 that verify the accuracy of the Old Testament text.
15. _____ The national day of repentance for the nation of Israel; a goat was sacrificed by the high priest and another goat (the scapegoat) was set free.

IV. Write the name of the biblical book (Genesis, Exodus, Leviticus, Numbers, Deuteronomy) that corresponds to each of the following statements.

1. _____ The sacrificial system is explained in detail.
2. _____ The theme is the wandering of the Israelites in the wilderness as a consequence of their sin of rebelling against God and not being willing to enter the Promised Land.
3. _____ The plagues against the Egyptians and Pharaoh are described.
4. _____ This book is structured like an ancient Suzerainty treaty.
5. _____ The story of Jacob found here.
6. _____ The sin of the Golden Calf is described.
7. _____ Describes two censuses taken of the Israelites.
8. _____ This book recounts Moses's three sermons given to the people as they were ready to enter the Promised Land.
9. _____ The Abrahamic covenant first given in this book.
10. _____ This book describes the instructions for and the building of the tabernacle.
11. _____ The Day of Atonement is described in detail.
12. _____ The incident of the twelve spies is recorded here.
13. _____ Story of Abram's call is found here.
14. _____ The story of the Israelites delivered from slavery in Egypt is described.
15. _____ This book is concerned with "becoming holy" and "staying holy."
16. _____ This book describes the renewal of the covenant ("second law").
17. _____ The story of Joseph is found here.
18. _____ The Ten Commandments were first given at Mt. Sinai in this book.
19. _____ The call of Moses by God at the burning bush is found here.
20. _____ This book climaxes with the glory of God descending on the tabernacle in the form of a cloud.

METHOD FOLLOWS CONTENT:
INTERPRETING THE BIBLE AS THE BIBLE

Gareth Lee Cockerill
Biblical Scholar
NT Editor, Evangelical Theological Society (ETS) Dissertation Series
Co-Chair, Institute for Biblical Research (IBR), OT in NT Study Group

ABSTRACT: A clearer understanding of the interpersonal nature of Scripture and a desire for a sustainable approach to IBS have led to significant modifications in philosophy and practice. Realization that one should listen to Scripture humbly as one person to another has resulted in replacing *Observation, Interpretation, Evaluation/Application,* and *Correlation* with *Listening, Understanding, Obedience,* and *Assimilation*. Concern for sustainability has birthed an approach that begins by establishing the "place" of a passage within the whole as interpretive context. Next one analyzes the "plan" (structure), which becomes the context for the "particulars" (terms). One concludes with the "point" as a basis for preaching.

1. INTRODUCTION

I owe a great debt to the inductive method that I was taught at Asbury Theological Seminary as outlined in Robert A. Traina's *Methodical Bible Study*.[1] The first assignment returned to me as a first-quarter seminary junior was a review of this book. I came to seminary as one who read and loved the Bible, ready for the inductive approach. Furthermore, the inductive method prepared me for doctoral work in biblical interpretation at Union Theological Seminary in Richmond, Virginia. I came to realize that exegesis using Greek, Hebrew, and Aramaic was IBS with the added benefit of the original languages.

2. THE PROBLEM

As I have taught IBS over the past thirty-five years, I have developed and changed in both my understanding of the philosophy behind this method and its practice. Two factors have been primarily

---

[1] (Wilmore, KY: Robert A. Traina, 1952, 1980; reprinted Francis Asbury Press, 1985).

responsible for these developments. First, I have diligently pursued introducing students to a sustainable method, one that they could effectively continue to use in their ministries. Second, I have become more aware of the unity of the Bible, the "I-Thou" nature of God's communication in Scripture, and of what actually happens when we read.

The students I have taught often faced four significant hurdles in their attempt to master a sustainable approach to IBS. First, they had difficulty relating book survey to the interpretation of a passage. They lacked a sense of a particular passage's place in the whole.[2] Second, they often found it difficult to distinguish the more important structural relationships of a passage from the less important. Third, they sometimes failed to locate the passage within the broader context of divine revelation. Fourth, students often found it difficult to move from their IBS to a sermon.

As the Bible lies before us, it purports to be the story of God's self-revelation through which he would bring human beings into fellowship with himself as a new people of God, a renewed humanity. The history of Israel culminating in Christ and his church is the backbone of this story. Such things as canonical criticism, literary criticism, and intertextuality have helped us see the manifold, interlocking relationships between the books of the canon and the distinct roles of each part within the whole.[3] The inductive method as traditionally practiced does not deny the fact that the Bible addresses its readers and calls them to account. Nevertheless, I've striven to formulate an approach to IBS that clearly incorporates the humility of the reader before a holistic understanding of Scripture as divine revelation.[4] Contemporary analyses of the reading process have also been helpful. I turn now first to this new paradigm that emphasizes humility before the Word of God and then present modifications in method to address student needs.

3. A New Paradigm

My concern for the interpersonal "I-Thou" nature of Scripture, i.e., God's addressing His people in the Word of God, has produced discomfort with the traditional categories of IBS method. *Observation, Interpretation, Evaluation/Application,* and *Correlation* no longer seemed to fit the material that we were studying. I began to feel like I was entering a laboratory wearing a white apron when I approached Scripture. I was the master, the scientist, and the Bible was the object of my study to be dissected and then put back together. Too often, passages were interpreted with little sensitivity

---

[2] Advances in the study of ancient rhetoric and in the structural analysis of various Biblical books have sensitized us to the role individual passages play within the larger whole; e.g., on the rhetorical structure of Hebrews, see Gareth Lee Cockerill, *Hebrews,* NICNT (Grand Rapids: Eerdmans, 2012), 60–77.

[3] On the different functions of the various sections of the canon, see Cockerill, *Christian Faith in the Old Testament: The Bible of the Apostles* (Nashville: Thomas Nelson, 2014). It is a mistake to assume that the unity of Scripture is simply imposed from without. Almost all of the biblical books anticipate the continuation of the biblical story and/or assume its past.

[4] Postmodernity has helped us to see the hypocritical futility of professed neutrality. To approach the Bible without the assumption that it is the Word of God is, in fact, to assume reductionistically that it is not God's Word; and such an approach is no more objective than beginning with the assumption that the Bible is what it claims to be. Neither starting position need be blind to counter-evidence.

to the broader role they played in the rhetorical structure of the book or with insufficient attention to their intertextual connections or place in the canon. I found myself relating individual bits to one another. I was treating the Bible as so many chemical or biological specimens to be examined rather than *Listening* for the author's (human and divine) voice. To use Martin Buber's terms, I felt that I was approaching the Bible as "I-it" when I should have been approaching it as "I-thou."[5] I wanted to know how knowledge of God and spiritual growth related to IBS.

I began to search for a set of categories that preserved IBS method but recognized the complexity and interrelatedness of the Bible, its claim to address us with the Word of God, and what actually happens in the reading process. I wanted to approach Scripture not as a master scientist but as a "servant" before his master ready to hear and obey. These are the categories that emerged: *Listening, Understanding, Obedience,* and *Assimilation.*[6]

In *Listening* and *Understanding* we do many of the things formerly covered under observation and interpretation. Most of the modifications in these two steps were a response to the needs of students. I will review those changes below. These new categories, however, help us to approach the Bible more humbly and interpersonally. We are no longer scientists manipulating the data before us. We are now listening for the message of the God who speaks through the human author.[7]

Replacing *Evaluation/Application* with *Obedience* is significant. Of course, one must wrestle with how a passage relates to oneself and to the people of God in the present. For me this process always began in the interpretation step with Traina's implicational questions. Furthermore, it extends into *Correlation*, or into what I now more appropriately call *Assimilation*. For instance, I can hardly

---

[5] Martin Buber, *I and Thou*, trans. Walter Kauffman (New York: Touchstone, 1971).

[6] Others have found the term "assimilation" useful because it "more accurately describes the broadly formational character of the process of relating a text's values to contemporary existence" that the term "application" (David R. Bauer and Robert A. Traina, *Inductive Bible Study A Comprehensive Guide to the Practice of Hermeneutics* [Grand Rapids: Baker Academic, 2011] 279 n. 2). Bauer and Traina have a good discussion of "appropriation" as the process of determining the relationship between the Biblical text and contemporary situations. Their discussion includes both personal and corporate aspects of appropriation, describes pitfalls to be avoided in appropriation, and gives a comprehensive example of appropriation (319–35). See also Fredrick J. Long, *In Step with God's Word: Interpreting the New Testament as God's People* (GlossaHouse Hermeneutics & Translation 1, Wilmore, KY: GlossaHouse, 2017) 397–430. He uses the term "assimilation" in a somewhat more restricted sense.

[7] Some may think this a horribly naïve return to authorial intent. It is true that we may not be able to recapture "the attitudes, motives, thoughts, and emotions of its [the Bible's] writers and of those concerning whom they wrote" as completely as Traina described (*Methodical Bible Study*, 94); he followed Friedrich Schleiermacher, who urged us to do so. Yet, Speech-Act theory has convinced me that we can understand the author's interpretive intent. We can grasp the subject at hand, the position the author takes toward that subject, and the corresponding intended response sought from the hearers. See, e.g., Kevin J. Vanhoozer, *God, Scripture & Hermeneutics: First Theology* (Downers Grove, IL: InterVarsity Press, 2002), 127–58. If the Bible is merely a text without personal intention, we can have no divine revelation in the way in which the church has understood such revelation throughout history. The words of the Bible have always been important to Christians, but they have been important because of the reality to which they point. See David Lyle Jeffrey, *People of the Book: Christian Identity and Literary Culture* (Grand Rapids: Eerdmans, 1996), 1–18. Traina's familiar image of a young man interpreting a love-letter fits well with those who listen carefully to Scripture because they have a passion to understand its author (see *Methodical Bible Study*, 97–98).

know how a passage from Deuteronomy impacts us today without wrestling with the role of Deuteronomy in the canon and its relationship to the fulfillment in Christ revealed in the NT.

Obedience, however, is a hermeneutical and spiritual necessity.[8] Correct interpretation of a document does not require agreement with or obedience to an author, but it does require a type of submission. When I read, I try not to impose my own meaning on the text but to submit to its constraints in order to hear the author's point of view. When approaching Scripture as the Word of God, this submission becomes *Obedience*. Remember Jesus's words, "anyone who chooses to do the will of God will find out whether my teaching comes from God" (John 16:7 NIV). When we obey what we do understand from Scripture, our presuppositions are brought closer to Scripture's presuppositions and thus we are able to understand Scripture more deeply. We become what Lyle Geoffrey calls the "willing reader."[9] Some have called this cycling from understanding to obedience to deeper understanding and further obedience the "hermeneutical spiral."[10]

Many, today, who practice pragmatic criticism, deconstruction, or ideological criticism, intentionally impose their own presuppositions upon the text. They are rebellious or "willful" readers. It is possible, of course, for unbelievers to gain a certain accurate understanding of the biblical text if they will, as noted above, submit to the constraints of the text. Without obedience, however, that understanding provides little help to the pastor or nurture for the believer. The person who does not obey will never understand Scripture from the "inside."

Under *Assimilation* one can do what one once did under the rubric of *Correlation*. That is, one can pick a topic and bring together what different passages and parts of Scripture teach about that topic. In this process, one needs to pay particular attention to the way selected passages function in their respective books and to the parts of the canon from which they come. But *Assimilation* goes beyond such study. It refers to the reader's or interpreter's personal assimilation of scriptural truth. New insight that I gain from Scripture is then assimilated with, modifies, and enriches the scriptural understanding that I already have. I may gain insight, say, into how OT Wisdom relates to the Mosaic Law, how Hebrews' Christology enriches the portrait of Christ in John's Gospel, or how the NT relates to the OT. In the process, I develop what I once heard John Stott refer to as "bibline blood"—I myself am molded by this depth of insight and I acquire a better framework for biblical interpretation.

Traina acknowledged that while the steps of IBS were distinct and should be pursued sequentially, one could not avoid overlap.[11] I have found such overlap a necessity. Of course, one cannot begin to *listen* (or *observe*) without some *Understanding* (or *Interpretation*). The data would make no sense. Most of us begin to think of the relevance of a passage even as we interpret it or come to understand it. Obedience sends us back better equipped for more listening and

---

[8] See Long, *In Step with God's Word*, 406. He says, "The most important attribute that interpreters of God's Word have is their willingness to obey."

[9] Jeffery, *People of the Book,* passim.

[10] See Grant R. Osborne, *The Hermeneutical Spiral: A Comprehensive Introduction to Biblical Interpretation* (Downers Grove, IL: IVP Academic, 2006), 30–33.

[11] Traina, *Methodical Bible Study,* 20.

understanding. Assimilation provides a richer context for further study. The important thing is that we not cut our listening or understanding short because we think we already know what the passage means. When we unduly curtail these first two steps, we are like people who interrupt a person who has not finished speaking because they think they already know what the person is going to say.

4. MODIFIED METHODS: *LISTENING* AND *UNDERSTANDING*

Now let's look at modifications in the practice of the inductive method. These changes were largely developed in response to student need, but they also reflect the paradigm change described above. I instruct students to approach a text using these four phases: *Place, Pattern, Particulars,* and *Point*. These phases correspond to the different elements of the text: *Place* to the relationship of the passage to the larger whole; *Pattern* to the passage's structure; *Particulars* to its important terms and expressions; and *Point* to its interpretation. This approach highlights the importance of context since each phase establishes the biblical context for the following phase. Each phase involves *Listening* and *Understanding* that leads to *Obedience* and *Assimilation*. These four phases have been crafted to address the four student problems noted above. *Place* addresses the need to meaningfully relate book survey to the interpretation of a passage. *Pattern* addresses the distinguishing of more important structural relationships from less important. Noting inter-biblical connections under *Particulars* facilitates locating the passage being studied within the broader context of divine revelation. The brief interpretation developed in the *Point* phase serves as a bridge from interpretation to sermon.

4.1 Phase One: Place

Instead of beginning with book survey, I identify for the students the major section of Mark that contains 2:1–12, in this case, 1:14–3:12.[12] They will learn the basis for my structural analysis of Mark by the end of the course. Our purpose is to determine the *Place* of 2:1–12 within this section. Students have been introduced to the structural relationships and shown how such things as introductory and concluding phrases and attention to changes in persons, places, time, events, and ideas help to determine structure. The assignment, then, has three steps.

First, they analyze the location and wording of each section heading in the ESV of 1:14–3:12 by answering two questions about each:

1. Is the section heading in the right place (does it need to be moved, does the section need to be divided or combined with another)?

2. Does the title adequately cover the content of the section?

Here is the analysis of one section heading from 1:14–3:12 as an example:

---

[12] Cockerill, "The Invitation-Structure and Discipleship in the Gospel of Mark," *The Journal of Inductive Biblical Studies* 3.1 (Winter, 2016): 28–43 at 32–35.

Part 1: The Location and Wording of Each Section Heading

Jesus Heals Many. Mark 1:29–34

Location: This section opens with a change of time designated by the term "immediately." It has a new setting—the house of Simon and Andrew. The event, though a healing like the event in the previous section, is still a new event in this new location. In vv. 29–31, Jesus heals Simon's mother-in-law. In vv. 32–34, Jesus heals many people with physical and spiritual ailments. Although this could be seen as two separate events designating two sections, the period of time and the setting have not changed, thus supporting ESV's decision to make this one section. Furthermore, vv. 29–31 and 32–34 are much closer to each other than they are to what goes before or comes after.[13]

Wording: As noted above, this section covers both Jesus's healing many and the specific incident of Jesus's healing Peter's mother-in-law. These healings demonstrate Jesus's authority emphasized in the previous section. Thus, one might expand the title as follows: **Jesus Heals Peter's Mother-in-Law and Many More** or **Jesus Demonstrates His Authority by Healing Peter's Mother-in-Law and Many More.**[14]

Second, students are to group the sections of 1:14–3:12 into larger units describing why they have grouped them in this way. Here is an example:

Part 2. Sections Grouped into Larger Units

The announcement of Jesus's Galilean preaching in 1:14–15 introduces this major division about Jesus's public ministry in Galilee. The summary of Jesus's Galilean ministry in 3:7–12 parallels this opening announcement and signifies the end of this major division. There are two large sections between this introduction and concluding summary.

The first of these two sections, 1:16–45, is united by Jesus's demonstrations of his authority and by the resulting growth of his popularity among the people. He demonstrates his authority by preaching (1:14–15), by calling disciples (1:16–20); by teaching and casting out the unclean spirit (1:21–28); by healing Peter's mother-in-law and many others (1:29–34); by his commitment to preach throughout Galilee (1:35–39); and, finally, by cleansing the leper (1:40–45). In each of these events his popularity grows, climaxing in 1:40–45 where he is no longer able to enter a town because of the crowds.

In the second section, 2:1–3:6, Jesus begins to make his claim to authority in ways that anger the religious leaders. Thus, the opposition of these leaders grows to a climax in 3:1–6. The scribes murmur to themselves (2:1–12), then they accost the disciples

---

[13] The principle stated in this sentence is often important in analyzing divisions.

[14] Section headings in the various English translations often highlight some particular aspect or striking event in the passage. When practicing IBS, we want each heading to be as comprehensive a description of the content of the passage as possible. The NASB often locates section headings in places that differ from other versions. Thus, it is often profitable to compare the headings in the ESV, NIV, or NRSV with those in the NASB and to ask what features of the text caused the NASB to choose a different location.

(2:13–17); then the "people" question Jesus (2:18–22); next the Pharisees directly challenging Jesus (2:23–28); and, finally, the Pharisees make common cause with their mortal enemies the Herodians to do away with Jesus (3:1–6).

Third, students are to identify the relationship between these larger sections. This stage begins *Understanding* (*Interpretation*) because it asks what light the relationship between these larger sections throws on the text to be interpreted, in this instance, 2:1–12. Here is an example:

> **Part 3: The Relationships Between These Larger Units**
> We have already noted the introductory and concluding function of 1:14–15 and 3:7–12, respectively. Jesus's demonstration of his unique authority joins the two major sections, 1:16–45 and 2:1–3:6. The turning point of this passage comes between these two sections where popular approval becomes official hostility. Thus, these two sections contrast with each other. In 1:15–45 Jesus's ever-increasing popularity among the people climaxes in 1:40–45. In 2:1–3:6 the ever-increasing opposition of the leaders climaxes in the plot to murder Jesus in 3:1–6. The reader/hearer is invited to join the disciples and those who affirm Jesus in 1:16–45 and to disassociate from those who oppose him in 2:1–3:6.
>
> Note the "place" of our passage 2:1–12. It comes at the point where public approval becomes official opposition. Thus, the larger context invites us to approach this passage with a question: Why does public approval give way to official opposition? Put more specifically, why does Jesus's demonstration of his authority in this passage, which up till now has brought him popularity, turn the rulers against him? In this way the larger context sets the agenda for our interpretation of 2:1–12.

4.2 Phase Two: Plan

Plan refers to the structure of the passage itself, in this instance, Mark 2:1–12. This phase addresses the second problem mentioned above—students' propensity to observe, but not prioritize, structural relationships. Students are asked to carefully read the passage several times and identify its main sections. They are to write a paragraph identifying these main sections and the way these sections relate to each other. Here is an example of this paragraph based on 2:1–12:

> Verses 1–4 **prepare** for Jesus's **turning-point** statement to the paralytic in v. 5, which is **questioned** or **challenged** by the scribes in vv. 6–7 and **substantiated** by Jesus in vv. 8–12. Verse 12 is the **climax** of Jesus's substantiation and the conclusion of the passage.

Then students are to write paragraphs on each of the sections they have identified in this first paragraph. They identify the structural relationships within each of these sections. Here is an example of these paragraphs based on 2:1–12:

> The scene of the crowded house in vv. 1–2 **prepares** for vv. 3–4 by showing why the four men had to un-roof the house and lower the man. Verses 3–4, then, **prepare**

specifically for Jesus's action in v. 5.

As noted above, v. 5 is the **turning point** of the passage because Jesus forgives the paralytic instead healing him as anticipated. It appears that Jesus's seeing "their faith" (v. 5a) is the occasion, if not the **cause**, of his forgiving the man's sin (v. 5b).

The scribes' challenge to Jesus's forgiving sin in vv. 6–7 can be divided into several parts. Verse 6 **prepares** for their challenge in v. 7a: "'Why does this man speak like that? He is blaspheming!'" Verse 7b **explains** this questioning of Jesus's authority by affirming that only God has authority to forgive sin. Thus, their challenge serves also as an **explanation** of the significance of Jesus's action.

Jesus brings their objection into the open with his **question** in v. 8 and then counters it with a **question** of his own in v. 9. With this second question he **substantiates** his authority to forgive. He implies that it is just as easy for him to forgive as it is for him to heal. In vv. 10–11 he then demonstrates how easy it is for him to heal—the paralytic is healed instantly by his mere word. We are left with the question as to how his authority to heal demonstrates his authority to forgive.

In v. 12 the tension reaches its resolution by the healing of the paralytic in **substantiation** of Jesus's authority. The **contrast** between the way the paralytic entered and the way he left emphasizes the effectiveness of Jesus's authority. There is **comparison** and **contrast** between the crowd's glorifying God at this healing, the scribes' rejection of Jesus (vv. 6–7), and the faith of the four and the paralytic (vv. 3–4, 12).

4.3 Phase Three: Particulars

Next students turn to key terms (words and phrases) that constitute this passage. This phase involves both careful *Listening* and *Understanding* (*Observation* and *Interpretation*). The study of *Place* provided the context for the structural analysis of the *Plan* phase. Now the structural analysis from the *Plan* phase provides the context for interpreting the *Particulars*.

Note how this works. We have identified Mark 2:1–4 as **preparation** for the **turning-point** of v. 5. Thus, when looking at terms in vv. 1–4 students will pay particular attention to how they prepare for v. 5. They will pay attention to how the key terms in vv. 5 make this v. the turning point. In order to do this, they will draw on the **explanation** element provided by the scribes' challenge in vv. 6–7. When they turn their attention to vv. 8–11 they will focus on how key terms contribute to Jesus's **substantiation** of his authority. We have space for two examples. First, from the **turning-point** in v. 5:

> **Son, your sins are forgiven:** Jesus is the one who forgives the helpless paralytic's sin. The paralytic came for healing. Thus, by claiming to forgive his sin Jesus turns the passage in a new and surprising direction. The challenge of the scribes (vv. 6–7) shows the significance of this action. Jesus is claiming a prerogative that belongs only to God. Thus, the claims of the prologue (1:1–13), and the nature of Jesus authority that has been demonstrated by his healing and casting out demons by a word of command, become

clear in this claim to do what only God can do. The divine compassion indicated by the way in which Jesus addresses this man as "son" (see "daughter" in 5:33) is reinforced by Jesus's identification with and declaration that he came to save "sinners" in 2:13–17. Jesus's forgiving sin invites us to see Jesus in the larger Scriptural context as the promised solution to the perennial and seeming intractable problem of human sin. We are also invited to acknowledge Jesus's claim and accept his forgiveness.

Second, an example from the **substantiation** of vv. 8–11:

> **Which is easier? ... Authority:** How does Jesus's healing the paralytic demonstrate his divine authority to forgive sin? We begin with Jesus's question: "which is easier" for him to say "your sins are forgiven" or to say "take up your bed and walk"? The obvious implication is that both are equally "easy" for Jesus. The scribes must accept Jesus's claim, or insist that the one who could restore this paraplegic was a blasphemer. This argument extends into the scribes' official response in 3:20-27. The scribes must accept Jesus's claim or assert that the one who was sovereignly delivering people from evil spirits was none other than the prince of those spirits. Their determination to pronounce his claim to forgive as blasphemous led them to blaspheme by absurdly attributing his power over evil to the devil himself. Thus, the consequences of their (our) response to Jesus's claim become clear.

4.4 Phase Four: Point

Students are now ready to write a concise interpretation of the passage within half a page (single spaced 12 point font). They must state the main point of the passage in the first sentence of this concise interpretation. We talk about how to use structural relationships as a guide to the main point. In this instance, one looks first at the **turning-point** in v. 5 that is explained in vv. 6–7 and substantiated in vv. 8–11(12). In the rest of this exercise, they use the structural relationships of the passage as a guide to flesh out what it says about this main point. Here is an example from Mark 2:1–12:

> *Jesus claims to have divine authority by forgiving sins here and now* (turning-point in v. 5). The magnitude of this claim as a claim to divine authority is shown by the scribes accusing Jesus of blasphemy (explanation/challenge, vv. 6–7). He proves his authority to forgive by healing the lame man and implying that it is all one to him—by merely speaking a word he can heal and by merely speaking a word he can forgive. Jesus's ability to heal with such authority and his claim to forgive with such authority forced the scribes to choose—either he was of God or of the devil (substantiation, vv. 8–12). People reacted to this claim in different ways (contrast). The scribes rejected Jesus and used their correct theology to rationalize their rejection. The crowds were amazed, but their involvement seems superficial. The four men who brought the paralytic had faith and were rewarded for it. The paralytic, who came in complete helplessness, received from Jesus not only healing but forgiveness.

Students are now ready to write a sermon based on this concise interpretation. Most sermons I have heard on this passage use the four men as examples of evangelism. Our interpretation shows that the person and authority of Jesus are central to the passage. It leaves us with the question of whether our response to Jesus will emulate the scribes, the four men and/or the paralytic, or the crowds. Space prevents further development of these ideas.

5. Further Considerations: *Obedience* and *Assimilation*

It has been my experience that *Evaluation/Application* and especially *Correlation* receive less attention in teaching the inductive method. This situation is no surprise, especially in relation to *Correlation*, since *Correlation* assumes an extensive, broadly based amount of IBS. My comments about *Obedience* and *Assimilation* will be brief but important.

One might say that *Obedience* is a presupposition of this new paradigm. One begins to listen for the purpose of obedience. In regard to the text we have studied above *Obedience* would mean acknowledging Jesus as the one with divine authority to forgive and humbly receiving that forgiveness as one who follows him. Such initial *Obedience* prepares us to mature in *Obedience* as we walk with the disciples through the rest of Mark's Gospel. It enables us to return to this passage with presuppositions more in tune to the account so that we can enter it more fully and understand it more deeply. The interpretation given above is the result of many returns to 2:1–12. One should also note that the response of the scribes warns those of us who are theologians not to use correct theology as an excuse for disobedience.

Assimilation actually begins when we study a passage within its context. Thus, we have already related Jesus's authority to forgive to his authority to heal and to cast out evil spirits. When we looked at the "particulars" above, we began to see that Jesus's authority to forgive sins must be seen within the context of the promises of God and the history of sin found in the OT.

Further study of Mark's Gospel provides opportunity to expand this assimilation. By the time we come to the end of the course in Mark, students are able to see that Jesus's public ministry in Galilee recorded in 1:14–3:12 climaxes in and is paralleled by his public ministry in Jerusalem recorded in 11:1–13:36 (or 16:8).[15] In the first, he presents his claim in faraway Galilee inviting people to follow him. In the second, he fulfills that claim in Jerusalem. We can then see that there is a certain correspondence between Jesus's claim in 2:1–12 and the claim of the parable of the vineyard in 12:1–12. These connections give further impetus to seeing Jesus's claim to forgive within the history of salvation. They also make it clear that the claim to forgive in 2:1–12 cannot be divorced from the fact that he came "to give his life a ransom for many" (10:45).

Moreover, as one meditates on these things with an attitude of willing *Obedience*, these truths are *assimilated* into one's life. We might also say that one is *assimilated* into the Scripture. The Scriptural narrative and world mold and shape our person and worldview. We are back to John Stott's "bibline blood."

---

[15] Gareth Lee Cockerill, "Invitation-Structure and Discipleship," 35, 40.

6. Concluding Postscript

Finally, I would like to comment on a related and important issue. Proponents of IBS have always emphasized the tentativeness of finite human interpretation. Thus, students often ask how, even after all their study, they can proclaim the Word of God with confidence? Yes, we should pursue our study with diligence, check our interpretations with the work of others throughout church history, and remember that an incomplete interpretation is not the same as an inaccurate or false interpretation. In addition, however, St. Augustine, in his long-influential work *On Christian Doctrine* (I.35–40 [39–44]; III.2 [2–5]), provides a helpful answer. He offers the "rule of faith" and the "rule of love," not as a substitute for rigorous biblical interpretation, but as a safety net for human limitation. The "rule of faith" contained the fundamental tenants of the Christian faith roughly equivalent to our Apostles Creed. The "rule of love" affirmed that all biblical exposition should lead to the edification of the church. Thus, if ambiguity remains when one has done one's best one should not interpret a passage contrary to fundamental Christian teaching as expressed in the ecumenical creeds or in a way that does not foster love of God and neighbor. According to Augustine, fostering such love is the goal of all ethical biblical interpretation.[16]

For Further Reading

Augustine, *On Christian Doctrine,* I–III.

Bauer, David R., and Robert A. Traina. *Inductive Bible Study: A Comprehensive Guide to the Practice of Hermeneutics*. Grand Rapids: Baker Academic, 2011. Ch. 11 "Appropriation."

Cockerill, Gareth Lee. *Christian Faith in the Old Testament: The Bible of the Apostles*. Nashville: Thomas Nelson, 2014.

David Lyle Jeffrey, *People of the Book: Christian Identity and Literary Culture*. Grand Rapids: Eerdmans, 1996.

Long, Fredrick J. *In Step with God's Word: Interpreting the New Testament as God's People*. GlossaHouse Hermeneutics & Translation 1. Wilmore, KY: GlossaHouse, 2017. Ch. 11 "Evaluated Applications."

McCartney, Dan, and Charles Clayton. *Let the Reader Understand: A Guide to Interpreting and Applying the Bible*. 2nd Edition. Phillipsburg: Puritan and Reformed Publishing, 2002.

---

[16] See ***Remember the principle of love*** in Long, *In Step with God's Word,* 417 (bold and italics original).

COMPETENT IN THE BASIC SKILLS OF INDUCTIVE BIBLE STUDY:
A CASE STUDY ON THE USE OF INDUCTIVE BIBLICAL STUDIES
AT EASTERN MENNONITE SEMINARY

Dorothy Jean Weaver
Professor Emerita of New Testament, Eastern Mennonite Seminary

ABSTRACT: This essay offers a pedagogical case study of a wide range of inductively-based NT and/or thematically-focused biblical studies courses which I have taught at Eastern Mennonite Seminary throughout my tenure here: (1) "New Testament: Text in Context," the EMS NT introduction course; (2) NT book studies on Matthew, Luke/Acts, John, Romans, Corinthians, and Revelation; and (3) thematic biblical studies (OT/NT) on "Women and Men in Scripture and Church" and "Creation Care in Scripture and Church." The essay opens with discussion of the inductively-oriented pedagogical philosophy which undergirds these courses collectively. It then presents specific illustrative examples of the "inductive exercises" which constitute the central and daily class assignments or in-class activities within these courses and reflects on their pedagogical intentions. And it concludes with overarching reflections on questions of classroom effectiveness, best pedagogical practices, and the challenges/rewards of such inductively-based biblical studies courses.

1. INTRODUCTION: INDUCTIVE METHOD, PEDAGOGICAL INTENTION, AND BASIC COURSE DESIGN

1.1 Introduction

It was bound to happen, my career-long engagement with Inductive Biblical Studies.[1] I had cut my own biblical studies "eye teeth" on inductive methodology in NT classes at Associated Mennonite Biblical Seminaries (now Anabaptist Mennonite Biblical Seminary), Elkhart, IN, in the mid-1970's. Dr. Howard Charles, clearly a student of Traina methodology (and very likely of Dr. Robert Traina himself), taught us well. Day by day Howard put us through our "inductive" paces, as he assigned us inductive questions which required us to scour the relevant NT texts in order to find the answers. It was a skill that I would

---

[1] The phrase "competent in the basic skills of inductive Bible study" shows up on each of my course syllabi as I reflect on the first of our fourfold set of common instructional rubrics at Eastern Mennonite Seminary, namely the goal of enabling students to become "Wise Interpreters."

never lose and a methodology that I would never abandon. And even as I gained significant narrative critical "lenses" throughout my doctoral studies (1979–1987) at Union Theological Seminary (now Union Presbyterian Seminary), Richmond, VA, it was always and above all those same "inductive" skills which provided me with the basic tool for engaging in narrative criticism.

So, when I began my own NT teaching career at Eastern Mennonite Seminary, Harrisonburg, VA, in 1984, it was inductive methodology that I employed—both instinctively and intentionally—as the primary *modus* for my classroom instruction. The practical reason for this was obvious. This was how I had learned to engage the biblical texts. This was the skill I brought with me into the biblical studies classroom. And this was, accordingly, my immediate and instinctive approach to classroom teaching.

But there was much more to this classroom *modus* than simple habit and sheer instinct. There was deep pedagogical intention as well. I realized from the beginning that what I wanted to do most of all within my NT courses was to equip my students for their own first-hand work *in* and *with* the NT texts. Far more than I wanted them *to read about* the NT writings, I wanted them above all *to dig into* these texts and *to make their own exegetical and theological discoveries*. And the best way I knew to accomplish this was to engage my students in their own hands-on inductive work with the NT text(s). So began my inductively-focused NT pedagogy. And some 33 years down the road I have never once looked back.

My standard course load throughout my tenure at EMS has included both the NT introduction course ("New Testament: Text in Context") and two cycles of NT book studies (Matthew, Luke/Acts, John; and Romans, Corinthians, Apocalyptic). In addition, I have co-taught or anchored several thematically-focused courses which range across the biblical canon ("Women and Men in Scripture and Church" and "Creation Care in Scripture and Church"). These are, collectively, the courses in which my use of inductive methodology comes into greatest prominence. And these are the courses on which I will reflect within the present essay.

1.2 Book Studies

My first experience with designing inductively-focused courses was with NT book studies. And my standard *modus operandi* for these book studies has been to structure them predominantly around written study guides based on one or multiple inductive study questions focused on the text(s) at hand for any given session. The students, for their part, have the task of searching the text(s), identifying the relevant substance with which to respond to the inductive question(s), writing up their responses, and bringing their written work back to class. My role as classroom instructor, in turn, is to engage the inductive question(s), to invite the students' responses in oral fashion within the class discussion, to collect these responses visually on the chalkboard (sic!) at the front of the room, and to lead the students in corporate classroom reflection on the broader significance—historical, sociological, literary, theological, ethical, etc.—of the discoveries that we have made collectively.[2]

---

[2] This generic *modus operandi* does not fully represent the course design created for "Epistle to the Romans" and "Corinthian Epistles," both of which I structure partially as biblical simulations and for which I draw on the

1.3 New Testament Introduction

"New Testament: Text in Context," the NT introduction course, grew out of my prior teaching experiences on two fronts, (1) my book study courses and (2) my initial flagship course, "Reading the Biblical Text." In the book studies I worked, as noted above, with written study guides. In "Reading the Biblical Text" I first offered the students several weeks of introductory lectures on "Gospel as Story." Then I set the students loose on the Gospel of Matthew, segment by segment, from beginning to end. Their first task for any given class session was to read a segment of the Gospel and identify one narrative-critical question from that Matthean text. Their follow-up task was to go back to this Matthean text once again and to answer their own question on the basis of the evidence at hand. Accordingly, this entry-level course, similar to my book studies, was inductively focused.

So, when I designed "New Testament: Text in Context," I intentionally co-opted the inductive component from "Reading the Biblical Text" (which was then disappearing from the curriculum) for the newly-emerging NT introduction course.[3] And from my book study courses I co-opted the use of regular inductive study guides as a means to engage the NT texts one by one. By design "New Testament: Text in Context" is a course which begins with a shorter lecture unit on "context" and a lengthier and inductively-focused unit on "text." Within this major "text" unit the students and I engage the books of the NT in sequence, not only by way of assigned readings from the NT and the required NT introduction text, but most prominently by way of inductive exercises focused on the NT texts under discussion. Our class sessions, which inevitably begin with a lecture component on significant features of the NT writing in focus, always move on crucially to the specific inductive exercise drawn from that text, an exercise which the students have prepared in advance as their class assignment.

1.4 Thematic Biblical Studies.

The third classroom format which I engage for biblical studies courses, language classes aside, is one that I have developed for such courses as "Women and Men in Scripture and Church" and "Creation Care in Scripture and Church." These thematic courses range broadly over the biblical canon, Old and New Testament alike, and engage a wide selection of individual texts as these are relevant to the topic of a given class session.[4] These courses, structured around a sequence of specific topics, involve the students in what I designate as "in-class inductives." Here I hand out either (1) a sheet

---

methodological resources of Reta Halteman Finger, *Roman House Churches for Today: A Practical Guide for Small Groups* (Grand Rapids: Eerdmans, 2007) and Reta Halteman Finger and George D. McClain (*Creating a Scene in Corinth: A Simulation* (Harrisonburg, VA: Herald, 2013). These courses likewise include an inductive study component as well, however. For an illustrative example of a book study syllabus, see the "Gospel of Matthew" syllabus for Fall 2014 included in the SYLLABUS APPENDICES at the end of this book.

[3] This course and its Old Testament counterpart, "Old Testament: Text in Context," were brought into our curriculum as 3-hour courses to replace their 2-hour predecessors, "Old Testament Survey" and "New Testament Survey." For an illustrative example of the syllabus for "New Testament: Text in Context," see the Spring 2017 syllabus included in the SYLLABUS APPENDICES at the end of this book.

[4] For an illustrative example of such a syllabus, see the Fall 2017 syllabus for "Creation Care in Scripture and Church" included in the SYLLABUS APPENDICES at the end of this book.

listing chapter/verse (ch/v) references for a category of texts (stories of women in the NT, for example) and framing an inductive study question(s) by which to engage these texts or (2) a sheet or sheets on which I have printed out one or several biblical texts themselves, for which I then frame an inductive question verbally and/or on the chalkboard. With such "in-class inductives" I normally divide the class into groups of twos or threes, each of which works together on one portion of the collective task at hand before I call the class back together for group discussion.

But regardless of the course or the questions at hand, the chalkboard is, by the end of the class session, inevitably filled to overflowing with lists of this or that and often rendered virtually illegible by the addition of countless lines and circles that connect various bits and pieces of information to each other. Not infrequently students have stopped me at the end of the class period and before I take eraser in hand to erase the day's collection of inductively-gathered material, so that they can take a photo of the chalkboard on their cell phone. What ultimately happens with these photos I will never know. But, bottom line, I have long since concluded that NT students will carry far more with them from the classroom, if it is based on their own "case in point" inductive work within the NT than if it is based on lengthy and encyclopedic lectures from the front of the classroom, no matter how erudite. And based on the number of times former students have commented with appreciation on the "inductives" they have done for my classes, I am willing to trust my instinct on that question.

2. Chapter and Verse: "Case in Point" Examples of Inductive Methodology in My Classroom

2.1 Introduction

If there is one instructor-comment that students in my classes see more frequently than any other on their written work, it is surely the penciled question in the margin, "ch/v?" meaning "chapter/verse?" My inductive approach to biblical studies is one in which the only way to "build the argument" or "make the case" is to provide chapter/verse references for the reader, so that they can see that I have a solid basis for my conclusions. So now, I also need to offer my own metaphorical "chapter and verse" to "make [my own] case." Here are illustrative examples of my inductive assignments along with brief pointers to their pedagogical goals.

2.2 Concerning Historical and/or Sociological Questions

As I begin the semester in Pauline book studies, I regularly assign an overall search of Romans or 1 Corinthians for the "Paul's-Eye View of Jewish History." My goal with this type of assignment is to provide the students with an overall perspective on the letter in focus and to invite them to reflect both historically on the Jewish history which undergirds Paul's letter and also theologically on the manner in which Paul makes use of Jewish history as he proclaims the gospel. The "Paul's-Eye" exercise for "Epistle to the Romans" reads as follows:

Step One: Skim Romans 1:1–11:36 very carefully and make note of the world of Jewish history (names of people, special events, etc.) and Jewish faith and practices (Jewish beliefs and/or religious practices) to which Paul makes reference. (There is very little "evidence" in 12:1-16:27 except for 15:8, "the promises given to the patriarchs.") You may want to take notes on what you are finding as you go along. And as you do, cite chapter/verse references along with the items you are finding.

Step Two: Now gather your findings into a (vertical) "time line" of Jewish faith and history. Where possible, connect Old Testament chapter/verse references to your Romans chapter/verse references, so that you can link Paul's references to the Old Testament accounts in which these stories are found. A Study Bible will give you significant assistance with this task.

Step Three: Now step back and reflect briefly (several paragraphs or a page) in a written essay on what you have encountered. This is the Jewish background that Paul brings to his letter to the Roman house churches. How does Paul's Jewish background and history shape Paul's message to the Roman believers, Jewish and Gentile alike? You might ask yourself the following sorts of questions:

> What kind of significance do the historical figures and religious practices in Jewish history have for Paul?
>
> How (or why) does Paul use these historical figures and religious practices to communicate the "gospel"?
>
> What appear to be the key issues that Paul is dealing with in his letter to the Roman believers?

The inductive exercise for the Philemon/Philippians/Galatians session in "New Testament: Text in Context" focuses on the biography and personal characteristics of the Apostle Paul as reflected in these three undisputed Pauline letters. The goal here is to engage students not only with the historical/sociological/religious background of the Apostle Paul but also with the multiple and varied "faces" of Paul as he presents himself in life and via letter to the churches he has founded. My favorite question for classroom reflection following our inductive work is essentially the following: "How much has Paul changed in character from "before Damascus" to "after Damascus" and how much has he stayed the same? What does this suggest to us about the ways and purposes of God?" The inductive exercise itself reads as follows:

> On the basis of the texts of Philemon, Philippians, and Galatians draw up a biographical/character sketch of the Apostle Paul. Who is he and what has made him this way? You may write your inductive up as an essay; or you may write it up in the form of lists of characteristics grouped under major headings. (NOTE: Some of this evidence will be "what Paul says" in so many words; some of it will be "what you think about

Paul" on the basis of the letters he writes.) The following sorts of questions may help you to focus on your task:

> What do we learn from these texts about Paul's family, social, and religious background?
>
> What do we learn from these texts about Paul's personal characteristics?
>
> What do we learn from these texts about Paul's gifts/skills as a church leader?
>
> What do we learn from these texts about Paul's challenges as a church leader?

Make your lists or your discussion as specific as you can; use specific language from the text and cite chapter/verse references where possible.

2.3 Concerning Questions Concerning Rhetoric

On occasion I engage students with inductive exercises focused on rhetorical features and/or the rhetorical force of the text in question. One such assignment concerns the rhetorical questions which provide the diatribe format of Paul's Epistle to the Romans. The goal of this inductive exercise for "New Testament: Text in Context" is first to identify this prominent rhetorical feature of Paul's letter to the Roman house churches and then to use the findings as a tool for assessing Paul's overall message to the Roman believers. The inductive exercise reads as follows:

> Walk through the text of Romans and make a list of the rhetorical questions that Paul addresses to his listeners/readers. (Cite the questions verbatim or summarize their substance, using as much of the specific language of the text as feasible. Indicate chapter/verse. If certain questions come in a cluster, keep them together.) These questions create the "diatribe" format of Paul's letter to the Romans; and they should give you a good idea what this letter is about. DO NOT list the answers to these questions—if you do, you will end up reproducing the bulk of the text of Romans!
>
> Now reflect on the overall impact of these rhetorical questions:
>
> > What do they tell you about the "argument" of the letter to the Romans?
> >
> > Which of the two major interpretations represented in [the NT intro text] does this "evidence" best support?
> >
> > Why do you think so?

I pose a very different rhetorically-focused question as we study Ephesians in "New Testament: Text in Context." Here the assignment is to create a "visual layout" of Ephesians 5:21–6:9, the so-called "household code," and then to reflect on the message which it conveys through its form with its specific content and within its context. My goal with this inductive exercise is first to engage the students with the actual substance and the evident structure of this "household code" and then to invite them to reflect on the communication of this text within its historical/social/religious context. The inductive exercise reads as follows:

> Create a visual layout for the household code found in Ephesians 5:21–6:9. A visual layout is a method of putting all the words of a passage into a visual (poetic) format which highlights/uncovers the structure of the passage. Basic rules for a visual layout are the following:
>
> 1) All the words of the text have to appear in the same order on the page as they do in the biblical text. In other words, the idea is NOT to "rearrange" the words of the text in any way.
> 2) The visual layout needs to indicate where a sense unit begins and ends. One of the most important things about a visual layout is having a strong reason for where (with which words) each line begins and where (with which words) each line ends. As much as possible, work with entire phrases or clauses rather than smaller groupings of words. Do not break up phrases (for example: in the house).
> 3) What you are looking for in a visual layout is the element of sequence and/or parallelism. Use indentation to indicate parallel elements of a text; and move the indentations from left to right to indicate subsections or dependent sections that fit under a heading of some type. In order to identify structural elements of the text, look for similar sentence structures, repeated vocabulary, repeated ideas of one sort or another, lists of any kind, contrasts between two things, etc. Be on the lookout for clauses which serve as headings to what follows or conclusions to what has gone before.
>
> With your visual layout in hand, now consider and respond to the following in essay format:
>
> > What does this household code communicate in its present shape, with its present content, and in its present context?
> >
> > Is this reflective of the status quo, or is it a radical directive?
> >
> > Why do you think so?

2.4 Concerning Comparison/Contrast Questions

One obvious and frequently fruitful way to engage students inductively lies in the task of comparing and/or contrasting literary texts with each other and reflecting on the findings. An inductive exercise for "Gospel of John" focuses on the similarities and differences between the Johannine call accounts and their Synoptic counterparts and invites the students to reflect on the literary/theological significance of these call accounts within their respective Gospel narratives. The goal of this exercise is to highlight the striking differences and yet the visible correspondences between these call accounts and to reflect on the historical origins of these texts and their literary and/or theological function within their respective Gospels. The inductive exercise reads as follows:

> Compare/contrast the call accounts of John 1:19–51 with the Synoptic call accounts as found in Mark 1:16–20 and Matt 4:18–22. Cite ch/v references as appropriate.

a) What are the primary similarities in these accounts?
b) What are the primary differences?
c) What do you see as the primary thrust or focus of the Synoptic call accounts?
- Reflect on the key details, the shape and length of the story, etc.
- What function do these accounts serve in their respective stories?

d) What do you see as the primary thrust of the Johannine call account(s)?
- Reflect on the common roles played by John the Baptist, Andrew, and Philip and the complementary roles played by Simon and Nathaniel.
- What significance does this account/do these accounts have in terms of John's own message to his readers?

In "New Testament: Text in Context Online" I raise a "comparison/contrast" question concerning the divergences between the ecclesiology portrayed within the Pastorals and that portrayed within 1 Cor 12 and 14. The goal of this exercise is to identify the significantly differing visions of "church" reflected within these two texts, to reflect on these visions theologically, and to consider the history and development of the Jesus movement which leads from the 1 Corinthians' ecclesiology to the Pastorals' ecclesiology. The inductive exercise reads as follows:

Read (1) 1 Corinthians 12:1–31 / 14:1–40 and (2) 1 Timothy 1:1–6:21. Then reflect on their respective "ecclesiologies," or in other words, their respective understandings of the church, its structure, and how it functions. Cite the language of the text where helpful and identify ch/v references where possible. You might use the first two broad questions as guidelines for your reflections and the following narrower questions as means to answer the broad ones:

What is the theological vision of the church in this writing?

What *is* it? What is its *purpose*? What does it *do*?

How is the church structured in order to be who it is and do what it does?

How does the worship and/or the work of the church get done and by whom?

How are the tasks of the church assigned and by whom?

What "structure" or "organization" is visible in these churches?

What differences and/or similarities are visible between these two "ecclesiologies"?

How do you compare or contrast what you have found in 1 Corinthians and in 1 Timothy?

What are the differences and/or the similarities between these two visions of church?

Reflect on the movement of the early church from the ecclesiology visible in 1 Corinthians to that visible in 1 Timothy and on what we can learn from their experience. The following questions might give you help in focusing your reflections:

How and/or why has the early church "progressed" from the ecclesiology of 1 Corinthians to that of 1 Timothy?

How do you evaluate this "progression"?

What, if anything, might be helpful or unhelpful in this "progression"?

What, if anything, might be inevitable about this shift?

2.5 Concerning Narrative Critical Questions

Since three of my six book studies are Gospels courses and since the Gospels are a significant component of "New Testament: Text in Context," many of my inductive exercises are narrative-critical in character. These questions typically focus on such narrative elements as character, plot, and theme. The goal of these questions is to assist students in understanding the overall character and communication of the narrative in question. Illustrative examples include the following:

Character Study from "Gospel of John"

Read John 12:1–8, John 12:20–50, and John 13:1–38 and respond to the following. Cite chapter/verse references as appropriate.

Who is the Mary whom we encounter here (12:1–8)?

What sort of character does she appear to be, judging from the details that John offers?

What does she appear to intend with her action in anointing the feet of Jesus?

What do Jesus's words add to the portrait of Mary?

How does John's juxtaposition of Mary and Judas add to her portrait?

How does John invite us (as the readers of the Gospel) to respond to Mary?

[NOTE: Similar questions on Peter, Judas, and Jesus follow this one on the study guide.]

Thematic Study from "Gospel of Matthew"

Read Matthew 2:1–23, focusing on the major characters (the magi, Herod, Joseph, the child), and write an essay on the theme of "Power" as viewed from Matthew's perspective. Make your reflections as specific as you can. Cite the language of the text and/or ch/v references where appropriate. You may use the following questions to assist you in your reflections:

Who has "power" in this story? Think broadly and inclusively.

What kind of "power" do they have? Where does it come from?

What do people do with this "power"?

Who is "powerless" in this story? Think broadly and inclusively.

In what ways are they "powerless"?

What can they not achieve because of their "powerlessness"?

What are the surprises in the way this story unfolds?

Who ultimately "wins" in this story? Who ultimately "loses" in this story?

What do you think Matthew wants to tell us about "power" by telling this story?

What is the "Good News" of this terrifying story?

Plot Study from "Luke/Acts"

Read Luke 9:51–19:28. With this large text as your backdrop, respond to the following: What is the significance of Jerusalem for Luke's Gospel up to 19:28?

Use the following references to Jerusalem as the basis for your reflections: 2:22, 25, 38, 41, 43, 45; 4:9; 9:31, 51, 53; 13:22, 33, 34; 17:11; 18:31; 19:11, 28.

a) What positive reality does Jerusalem symbolize initially within the Gospel of Luke? Why does Jerusalem occupy such prominence within Luke's overall narrative? *Check the language/structure/communication of the texts from 2:22–4:9 for help here.*

b) What negative significance does Jerusalem acquire as the narrative progresses? Why must Jesus go to Jerusalem and what significance does this journey have within the narrative? What does all this say about Jesus? What does it say about Jesus's opponents? *Check the language/structure/communication of the texts from 9:51–19:28 for help here.*

c) How does Luke correlate the two-handed (positive, negative) symbolism of Jerusalem within his narrative? What significance does the Jerusalem motif have for Luke's overall story?

3. WHAT WORKS AND WHAT DOESN'T: BRIEF REFLECTIONS ON LEARNINGS AND BEST PRACTICES

3.1 Introduction—The Importance of Good Questions

One thing I have learned above all else in the course of working with inductive methodology in my NT classes: Writing good questions is both the single most important and the single most difficult task I face pedagogically. Finding that crucial question which opens up a text or set of texts to the students and provides them with opportunity for genuine and significant discoveries requires from me the very best energies and skills that I have to offer. Not all questions are equally productive or fruitful for classroom discussion. And not all approaches to engaging a specific text work equally well to anchor a class session. I learn day by day, class session at a time, what works and what doesn't. And my learnings shape both my classroom procedures and the inductive exercises that undergird them. Here I offer a few broad and basic reflections on what I find to be "best pedagogical practices" vis-à-vis the creation of fruitful inductive questions as well as the format of fruitful inductively-focused class sessions.

3.2 Number and Scope of Questions.

When I look back at my inductive study sheets from early in my teaching career, I am often chagrined to discover how many small and/or major questions I would include on any given study guide. My instinct now tells me that such a plethora of questions could only have discouraged even the most energetic and committed students. The longer I have worked at the task of inductive-question writing, the more deeply I am committed to the discipline of finding a single, overarching question (or at the most one such "large" question and one additional "smaller" question) with which to engage my students for any given class session. This discipline forces me always to be thinking in terms of the "big picture" and how the text as a whole "functions" within its literary context. And this discipline gives the students, for their part, the freedom to pursue one "central" question per class session, a far more viable strategy than splitting their time and energies over a wide range of separate questions.

3.3 *Single Major Question and Multiple Sub-Questions*

As one can see from the illustrative examples above, my clear instinct for inductive-question writing is to name a major question (the significance of "Jerusalem" for Luke's Gospel, for example) and then to provide a lengthy list of secondary questions by which the students might approach that overarching question in focus. I frequently attach the "caveat" that these sub-questions are not necessarily intended for answering one after the other in mechanical fashion but rather for assisting the students in opening up the large central question and working with it.

3.4 *Engaging the Students in "So What?" Reflection*

As I see it, the single and signal value of drawing students into inductive work with the biblical text(s) is to provide the class collectively with "evidence" that opens out into wider reflection and wider class discussion on any of a range of levels: historical, sociological, literary/narrative, theological, ecclesiological, ethical, etc. I am never finished with an inductive exercise until I have framed those larger "so what?" questions that engage the students in serious reflection both about the text they are studying and about the world in which they themselves live. And I am never happier in the classroom than when I can point to a well-filled chalk board reflecting the fruits of my students' inductive labors and ask them by whatever words, "What do you see here? What is this text about? And what is the overall significance of what we have found?"

3.5 *Inviting Students to Teach Each Other*

It took me years to observe the obvious, but I have long since learned that a crucial pedagogical practice for my inductively-focused classrooms is to engage the students in teaching each other in pairs or threes before we participate in collective class discussion. The reasons for this are basic and truly obvious. Perhaps the single most "obvious" piece of this pedagogical wisdom is that it puts all of the students on notice that they need to be well-prepared for class. It likewise ensures that all students, no matter how introverted or extroverted, have both opportunity and necessity to engage in direct discussion with their peers in a non-threatening context. And in courses or on occasions where I have groups of students working on different questions, it gives the students solid access to discussion on the question that was not their own assignment.

3.6 And One Thing More

Inductive Biblical Studies is undeniably hard work and serious business. It is both exegetically challenging and theologically crucial on all fronts. But it is also the most fascinating task I might ever think to engage and the most fun I could ever imagine having in the classroom. Hands down. Thanks, Howard!

*The Use of the Inductive Bible Method
in the Teaching of the Book of Isaiah*

John N. Oswalt
Asbury Theological Seminary

ABSTRACT: This essay explains the way in which the book of Isaiah may be studied using the methods of Inductive Bible Study. It begins with whole book survey, and then, as it proceeds through the book seeks to move the student progressively through the steps of observation, interpretation (analysis), correlation, and evaluation (synthesis).

1. Introduction

It is a privilege to write this article in memory of Dr. Robert A. Traina. Although I was never registered as a student in one of his classes, he graciously allowed me to sit in on his course on the Pentateuch when I joined the faculty of Asbury Theological Seminary. I had previously read his book on Methodical Bible Study, and it was not only eye-opening to see the method applied by a master teacher, it was also exciting to see the insights that emerged when the method was carefully applied. Later he invited me to teach the Pentateuch course, and encouraged me to use any of the notes I had taken in his class. I eagerly did so and learned even more in that process. Thus, I am thankful to have been one of the thousands of students for whom Bob Traina brought the scriptures to life.

2. The Book of Isaiah and IBS Lessons

One of the problems that has dogged students of the Book of Isaiah across the centuries has been its complexity. The riches that are contained in the book are often overwhelming to the casual reader. This problem has only been increased by the hypothesis of multiple authorship. Now it seems we must read the book as a somewhat random collection of oracles and reflections on oracles that originated over a span of more than 500 years and at least three or four different cultural settings.

Inductive Bible Study brings a different set of assumptions to bear on this study. First of all, its purpose is to study the piece of literature *as it now presents itself to us*. It is assumed that the piece is in its present form because the author(s) or editor(s) intended it to have this form and that he/she/they intended to communicate something by putting the material into this form. Even if they did not have a completely coherent understanding of purpose in doing so, by putting the literature into this particular form they *are* communicating thoughts whether they intend to or not, and it is the legitimate task of the interpreter to seek to ferret out what this form of the literature is indeed saying. Thus, the task is not to recover a hypothetical original (however plausible that hypothetical original might be in certain cases), but to interpret the text as it stands. For the Christian believer who sees the Bible as the word of God, an additional factor enters in. It is not only the author(s) and/or editor(s) who gave the book this form, it was also the inspiring Holy Spirit.

Closely connected with this insistence on interpreting the book in its present form is the attention this method puts on the "wholeness" of the book, division, sub-division, etc. This differentiates Inductive Bible Study, as practiced and taught by Traina, from the usual "exegesis" course. Exegesis, as it is commonly taught, tends to focus on the grammatical and linguistic details of limited passages. For this reason, students often see the two as different and even contradictory approaches, with inductive study the tool for "ordinary" people, and exegesis the tool for those "linguistic geniuses." This is unfortunate, because they are really complementary, and both are necessary tools for the fullest understanding of the text. Inductive Bible Study utilizes the vernacular of the student in order to facilitate the grasping of "wholes," something that even the most proficient student can hardly do when working with original languages. However, having recognized the shape and direction of the whole, detailed exegesis of what Traina called "strategic areas" is vitally important for grasping the fullest implications of what the author/editor is seeking to convey. Because of the size of the book of Isaiah, I was not able to include much exegetical work in the course. However, the ideal "exegesis" course, working with a smaller book, would in my mind incorporate both methods.

One of the great strengths of the Harper/White/Kuist/Traina method of Bible study is its insistence on the importance of context. Words have meaning in the context of a sentence, sentences in the context of a paragraph, paragraphs in the context of a section, sections in the context of a sub-division; sub-divisions in the context of the division; divisions in the context of the book, and if the book is in a collection, as the Biblical books are, in the context of that collection. Thus, if we are to correctly understand and interpret any particular statement, it must be not only in its immediate context, but also in its larger and largest ones, as well. In the case of a smaller book like Jonah, that is not so difficult. In the case of Isaiah, it is mind-boggling. Nevertheless, it is important that students beginning their study of Isaiah have some sense of the book in its wholeness. Thus, the first assignment is to scan the book, and record what they see as their most important observations especially as regards relationships among ideas.

One feature of Dr. Traina's assignments was the inclusion of the number of hours in which he believed the assignment could be completed. These suggestions were often a source of amusement both for his students and mine since they thought the numbers were unrealistic. In this case, my suggestion is for eight hours. Often, as I meet with graduates and they are talking about my course with others in the group, they will say something like, "This man expected me to read the *whole* book of Isaiah in eight hours!" Usually they say it with a smile, although sometimes the smile is strained. Then, it is my turn to say, "You didn't read the assignment; I didn't say 'read,' I said 'scan.'" That is a vitally important distinction that I try to emphasize when making the assignment.

If they try to read the whole book, they will frustrate the purpose of the assignment. It is only in scanning the book, hopefully two or three or more times, that they will begin to get a feel for the book's layout and contours. They will become more conscious than before of its diversities, but they will also begin, almost unconsciously at first, to sense that it holds together, in some deep thematic ways. One of the things I hope to hear when we come to discuss their findings is the interplay between judgment and hope that runs throughout the book and provides a theological framework. I am also eager to hear their ideas on the relationship between Isaiah 1–39 and Isaiah 40–55. Is it continuity or discontinuity and why either one.

In the four class days when the students are working on that first assignment, I lecture on the prophets and on my interpretation of the inductive method. I usually elect not to have them read a book on the prophets for fear that it will undercut induction. The great value of induction is that it seeks for what the piece *does* say, and not for what it *should* say. At the same time, the student does need to have some sense of how the book of Isaiah sits in the context of the Hebrew prophetic literature. But I seek to present this information in as broad and general a way as possible.

In my lectures on the method, I present it much as Traina formulated it: observation (especially of structural relations, although not limited to those); interpretation of what was observed through the use of interpretive questions; synthesis through correlation and evaluation; and application. In the assignments following the first dealing with the book as a whole, and identifying the basic grouping of materials, I seek to introduce students to these steps in a methodical way. Thus, in the early Lessons a primary emphasis is upon developing skills of observation. I try to strike a balance between giving too little guidance and too much. On the one hand, in the Lesson on Isaiah 1–5 it might be possible to say simply, "Observe these chapters and record your observations." For an accomplished student this might be enough, but most students are not that accomplished. On the other hand, it might be possible to say, "Study the ways in which contrast functions in these chapters." This is already to have made the observation for them. So, the first question I have developed for this assignment is this: "Observe the content of these chapters. Identify the main blocks of material. What structural laws unite and separate these blocks? Observe carefully judgment and promise. What is Israel/Judah judged for? What is promised? How are these ideas related to each other?"[1] As is evident, I believe that the striking contrast between judgment and promise that characterizes Isaiah 1 on a more detailed level and then Isaiah 2–5 on a broader level is the dominant and uniting feature of this segment. I am seeking to guide the student toward that discovery without actually making it for them.

One of the most helpful contributions that Traina made, in my judgment, is his elucidation of the laws of literary relationship. Obviously, none of these are original to him, but his collection of them and his explanation of them is extremely helpful. If a student can get a firm grasp of these relationships and how they function, it will go far toward enabling him or her to understand what the Scriptures are saying and to assist others to a better understanding. For this reason, in the early Lessons I put a premium on the observation of these relationships. So, one of the questions in Lesson 3 (on Isaiah 6) is: "Identify each of the components of this experience. How do they relate to each

---

[1] For the remainder of this assignment as well as the rest of the study guide, see SUPPLEMENT 11.1.

other (what law of relationship)?" A second question moves beyond the chapter itself to its relation with Isaiah 1–5: "Defend or refute the suggestion that chapter 6 offers a solution to a problem raised in chapters 1–5 (Law of interrogation). In any case propose alternate structural relationships between these two segments." Again, I am aware that these questions might be more directive than some would be comfortable with, but I think both the mass and complexity of the materials in the book requires a bit more direction than study of some other books might.

I should say that my method in class is a combination of discussion and lecture. Most of the sections in the book can be covered in either two or three class periods. The assignment for a given section is due at the beginning of the first class period devoted to the section. Typically, the first part of that period, and sometimes all of it, will be given over to a discussion of the assignment. I try not to pit students against each other, but do try to encourage differing points of view where they arise. While I have well-developed conclusions, and present them and the reasons for them in the lecture portion, I do not want to suggest that there is only one possible way to understand the riches of the book, and continually emphasize that it is not necessary to reach the same conclusions I have in order to receive a good grade for the assignment and ultimately for the course. Rather, the question is concerning the accuracy of the observations and the way in which interpretive questions have been applied to those observations.

As the study reaches deeper into the book I seek to become less directive and at the same time to begin to expect more use of the interpretive questions. So, in the study of Isaiah 7–12 one of the questions is: "What are the interrelationships among these chapters? What laws of relationship are operable? Particularly note repeated words and phrases." The next is "What is the significance of children as prophetic symbols here? How does Immanuel fit in? Is this material primarily prophecy of Christ? Why or why not? Consider the relationship between the "shoot" (branch) and "the child." Here I am assuming that they will have observed the recurrence of the various words connoting children and I am now wanting them to employ the three interpretive questions (what is recurring? why is it recurring? what are the implications of such a recurrence?) to determine the meaning of the recurrence. Although the assignment itself does not specify the application of the questions, I would have emphasized this aspect in the discussion of the assignment. The process becomes both more explicit and more general by Lesson 6 where one of the questions is: "Identify a few key observations, especially those related to section structure, and utilize interpretive questions for the purpose of finding the meaning and significance of your observations."

By Lesson 5 (on Isaiah 13–23) I am beginning to look for some correlation and evaluation. So, one of the questions is: "Observe the type of language used in chapters 13 and 14. What are the implications of this type of language concerning the meaning and usage of Babylon in these chapters. Cf. Rev. 18." Sometimes, simply for the sake of time and space, such questions are located in the section labeled "For further study." That is the case with Lesson 9 where "Compare and contrast such a (representative?) passage as 43:10–13 with John 15:12–27." I should say a word about this part of each Lesson: I want to stretch the best students if I can and so for this reason have included this section. I specify as carefully as I can how this will be evaluated (see footnote 3 in the

SUPPLEMENT 11.1—IBS LESSONS THROUGH THE BOOK OF ISAIAH below) so as to avoid someone's rushing through the main Lesson to get to this for extra credit. I have not always felt that the work I have received on this section was of the highest quality, but in some cases, it was very good indeed.

Progressing in the Lessons, students are directed to summarize the content of sections. Such a request appears in Lesson 9: "Summarize the content of the segment in no more than one page." This is an attempt to move the student toward theological synthesis. Another is the final question on Lesson 11: "In the basis of the implications discovered in C. above, summarize the main teachings of this unit in a synthetic paragraph. As I review the study guide, I see it as a weakness that I do not do more of this. However, in my defense, I have to say that it is partly the huge size of the book, as well as its complexity, that demands more of the time of the course be given to the basic discoveries.

There is also a paucity of attention given to matters of application. My colleague Dr. Michael Matlock has made some helpful suggestions of ways in which this deficiency might be corrected. One possibility is to have the students listen to or view examples of what I consider good and bad interpretations of various passages from Isaiah and to write evaluations of them. Another is to add some questions throughout later Lessons in which students are asked how a given passage might relate to a current question. An example might be: "How does Isaiah 58 view fasting? How does this teaching relate to the practice of fasting today?" In my lectures I do address these kinds of topics regularly, but more could be done to give the students experience in performing this process.

The final Lesson 12 seeks to engage the students in synthesis of the message of the book and its relationship to the rest of Scripture. Some students do exceptionally well on this assignment while others struggle with it. In my observation over the years this has a great deal to do with temperament. Those who are able to think globally do well, whereas those who are more detail-oriented are often somewhat overwhelmed. In grading this assignment, I try to take these issues into account.

One final matter has to do with charts. Dr. Traina's charts were magnificent; they managed to incorporate so much of the structure and content of the material being covered in creative and imaginative ways that succeeded in making it memorable to the students. I became a devotee of charting in his course and have continued to use them ever since. I must confess that mine are a great deal more prosaic than his, but I still think they are helpful in my attempts to help the students grasp what I think is going on in the book. So, I have developed several charts for every section and use them extensively in the lecture portions of the course. Two examples are included below in SUPPLEMENT 11.2. In an earlier assignment, Lesson 7 E., students are asked to represent their findings from the Lesson in chart form. Then the final synthesis Lesson includes a major chart.

3. CONCLUSION

Overall, the teaching of this course on Isaiah using inductive Bible methodology has been one of the more rewarding experiences of my career. It has been exciting to see students developing skills in interpretation that I know are going to serve them in good stead throughout their lives. Then it has been equally exciting to see them coming to understand more deeply what is without question one of the richest books in the Biblical canon: Isaiah.

SUPPLEMENT 11.1
IBS LESSONS THROUGH THE BOOK OF ISAIAH

LESSON 1: Survey (8 hours)
- A. Scan the book rapidly and record a few major observations. (If you need guidance on the process of observation, consult *Inductive Bible Study*[2] [hereafter IBS], pp. 79–142).
- B. Identify one or two structural relationships that unite the book. Explain your answer.
- C. Identify the main divisions. What is the main relationship uniting each of these divisions?
- D. Record the findings of B. and C. in chart form (cf. IBS, pp. 90–94, 137 for examples).

For further study:[3]
- A. Give titles to the chapters.
- B. List a few interpretive questions that arise from your observation of the structural laws in B. and C. above.
- C. Indicate the strategic areas of the book and explain why you chose each in a few sentences. If you complete this further study, be sure to include the results on your chart.

LESSON 2: Chapters 1–5 (6 hours)
- A. Observe the content of these chapters. Identify the main blocks of material.[4] What structural laws unite and separate these blocks? Observe carefully judgment and promise: What is Israel/Judah judged for? What is promised? How are these ideas related to each other?
- B. List the figures of speech used in this section and identify what each conveys (e.g., People compared to great trees—beauty, power, self-sufficiency, etc.). Summarize your findings and observations in paragraph form.
- C. What is the concept of God in this section? Be specific in your discussion, citing specific passages.
- D. Could these chapters be seen as an introduction to the book as a whole? Cite reasons for and against this hypothesis. (For instance, are all or most of the significant themes of the book introduced here, or not?). Summarize your conclusions.

For further study:
- A. Observe the person (1st, 2nd, or 3rd) in which God's addresses are put. What are the implications of this phenomenon?
- B. Compare 2:2–4 with Micah 4:1–3. How would you explain this phenomenon?
- C. Compare the use of the vineyard motif in chapter 5 with that in Mark 12.

---

[2] David R. Bauer and Robert A. Traina, *Inductive Bible Study: A Comprehensive Guide to the Practice of Hermeneutics* (Grand Rapids: Baker Academic, 2011).

[3] Some students will have the time and inclination to dig deeper into the book. This section is included for such persons. It is not necessary to complete this section to receive an A on the assignment. Complete all sections of the main assignment before going on to the "For further study" section. If the work on this material is of equal or better quality to that on the main assignment the overall grade on the assignment will be raised by 1/3 of a letter grade (e.g. B>B+)

[4] Note that while chapter divisions often coincide with content divisions, this is not always the case. It is not infrequent that content units cross chapter lines.

LESSON 3: Chapter 6 (6 hours)
- A. Observe and record the imagery in this chapter. What do the various images convey?
- B. Identify each of the components of the experience. How do they relate to each other (what law of relationship)?
- C. Defend or refute the suggestion that chapter 6 offers a solution to a problem raised in chapters 1–5 (law of interrogation). In any case propose alternative structural relationships between these two sections.
- D. What is the concept of sin here?

For further study:
- A. Consider possible reasons for Isaiah's dating this experience as he does.
- B. Why the negative tone (no gospel) of the message Isaiah is given?
- C. If you have Hebrew, study the word *sur* 6:7 "turned aside, removed." (Others may consult Young's Analytical Concordance, p. 48, column 1, [Hebrew Index] for a listing of the English translations of the word.) What insights emerge from your study?

LESSON 4: Chapters 7–12 (6 hours)
- A. Read II Kings 16:5–20.
- B. What is the relationship between chapters 7–12 and chapter 6?
- C. What are the interrelationships among these chapters? What laws of relationship are operable? Particularly note repeated words and phrases.
- D. What is the significance of children as prophetic symbols here? How does Immanuel fit in? Is this material primarily prophecy of Christ? Why or why not? Consider the relationship between the "shoot" (branch) and the child.
- E. Study the theme of trust in God vs. arrogance. Summarize your findings in a synthetic paragraph.

For further study: Study the forestry imagery. Summarize your findings in a synthetic paragraph.

LESSON 5: Chapters 13–23 (6 hours)
- A. What are the major emphases of the section? Support and explain your conclusions in the light of this study. Summarize the message of the segment.
- B. How is this section related to the preceding and the following? What is its function at this point in the book? Cf. 11:10–16.
- C. Observe the type of language used in chapters 13–14. What are the implications of this type of language concerning the meaning and usage of Babylon in these chapters? Cf. Rev 18.
- D. Upon what principle are these chapters organized, if any? Climax? Cruciality? Chronology? Geography? Etc.?

For further study:
- A. Look at 13; 14; 21:9 and 23:13. What does the presence of this Babylon material suggest about the unity and/or organization of the book? Chapter 39?

B. Compare 13:2 and 5:26. Implications?

C. Check commentaries for the interpretations of chapter 14 (King of Babylon). What are your reactions?

D. Compare chapters 15–16 to Jeremiah 48, especially with 48:29 and following. What are your conclusions?

LESSON 6: Chapters 24–27 (4 hours)

A. Read the section slowly, giving titles to paragraphs and recording observations. (Reread relevant portions of IBS, if necessary.)

B. Identify a few key observations, especially those related to section structure, and utilize interpretive questions for the purpose of finding the meaning and significance of your observations. (Consult IBS, pp. 126–34, 179–238 for guidance.)

C. In what ways does chapter 26 grow out of the preceding chapters? How is it the effect of a prior cause? (Notice that this is an interpretive question.)

D. Compare and contrast this section with the previous one. In the light of these findings, what is the relationship between the two? Note the similarities between 11:10–11 and 27:12. What does this bracketing effect suggest about the relationship?

For further study: Interpret John 15:1–5 in the light of 27:2–6.

LESSON 7: Chapters 28–35 (8 hours)

A. Read the material quickly to determine content and structure. Is it one unit or more? What laws of relationship support your conclusions?

B. List the sins for which the prophet pronounces judgment. How does Egypt figure in this? Consider the theme of trust (cf. chs. 7–12).

C. Study the references to leaders and leadership in these chapters. List what is being said about each group. Summarize your conclusions.

D. Compare and contrast chs. 34 and 35.

E. Present key findings of A. through C. in chart form.

For further study:

A. List the references to God and His nature. What elements are stressed? Are there unique elements as compared to previous chapters? Summarize.

B. Consider the possibility that chs. 13–35 form a unit. What are the arguments pro and con?

LESSON 8: Chapters 36–39 (4 hours)

A. Observe the structure and content of these chapters. Record your observations.

B. Formulate key interpretive questions concerning your observations.

C. Answer these questions. (IBS, 239–77).

D. Compare the content and structure of this section with that of chs. 7–12. Conclusions?

LESSON 9: Chapters 40–48 (8 hours)

A. Identify the recurring themes in the segment. How are they related? Show these relations

in chart form. What is the main point being made? Justify your answer.
- B. Examine all references to servant and servanthood. Determine the identity of the servant wherever possible. Attempt to define the nature, role, character, function and benefits of servanthood in each of these occurrences.
- C. Note the recurrence of contrast between God and idols. Through the use of interpretive questions attempt to discover the meaning of these recurrences in this passage.
- D. Choose a key verse and indicate your reasons.
- E. Summarize the content of the segment in no more than one page.

For further study: Compare and contrast such a (representative?) passage as 43:10–13 with John 15:12–27.

LESSON 10: Chapters 49–55 (8 hours)
- A. What is the structure of this section? Is it a unit? Why?
- B. What is the relation of 52:13–53:12 to the other sub-units in this section? What structural laws are operable?
- C. Examine all references to servant or servanthood in the manner of 9B above. (Pay special attention to the 1st person pronouns in this regard.)
- D. Contrast your findings in C. with those made in the study of servanthood in chs. 40–49. What are your conclusions?
- E. Following the pattern established in IBS, observe 52:13–53:12 and raise interpretive questions on the basis of your observations.

LESSON 11: Chapters 56–66 (8 hours)
- A. List the major themes of chapters 56–66 in the order mentioned. What relationships do you see in the segment? What is the overall point being made? Support your answer.
- B. How is the point being made in these chapters different from that in chapters 40–55? What is the relationship between the two units?
- C. Formulate and answer interpretive questions on the two or three main relationships you see in this unit.
- D. On the basis of the implications discovered in C. above, summarize the main teachings of this unit in a synthetic paragraph

For further study: Make a study of "highway" (including such related terms as "road," "path," "way," etc.) as used thus far in the book. Summarize your findings and conclusions.

LESSON 12: Synthesis (6 hours)
- A. Create a chart showing the major units and their relationships.
- B. Identify the main themes of the book and explain how these relate to one another (for instance, consider how the book as a whole might be a reduplication of chapter 6 on a national scale).
- C. Briefly discuss how the message of Isaiah relates to the rest of Scripture.

Supplement 11.2
Chart of Isaiah 1–39

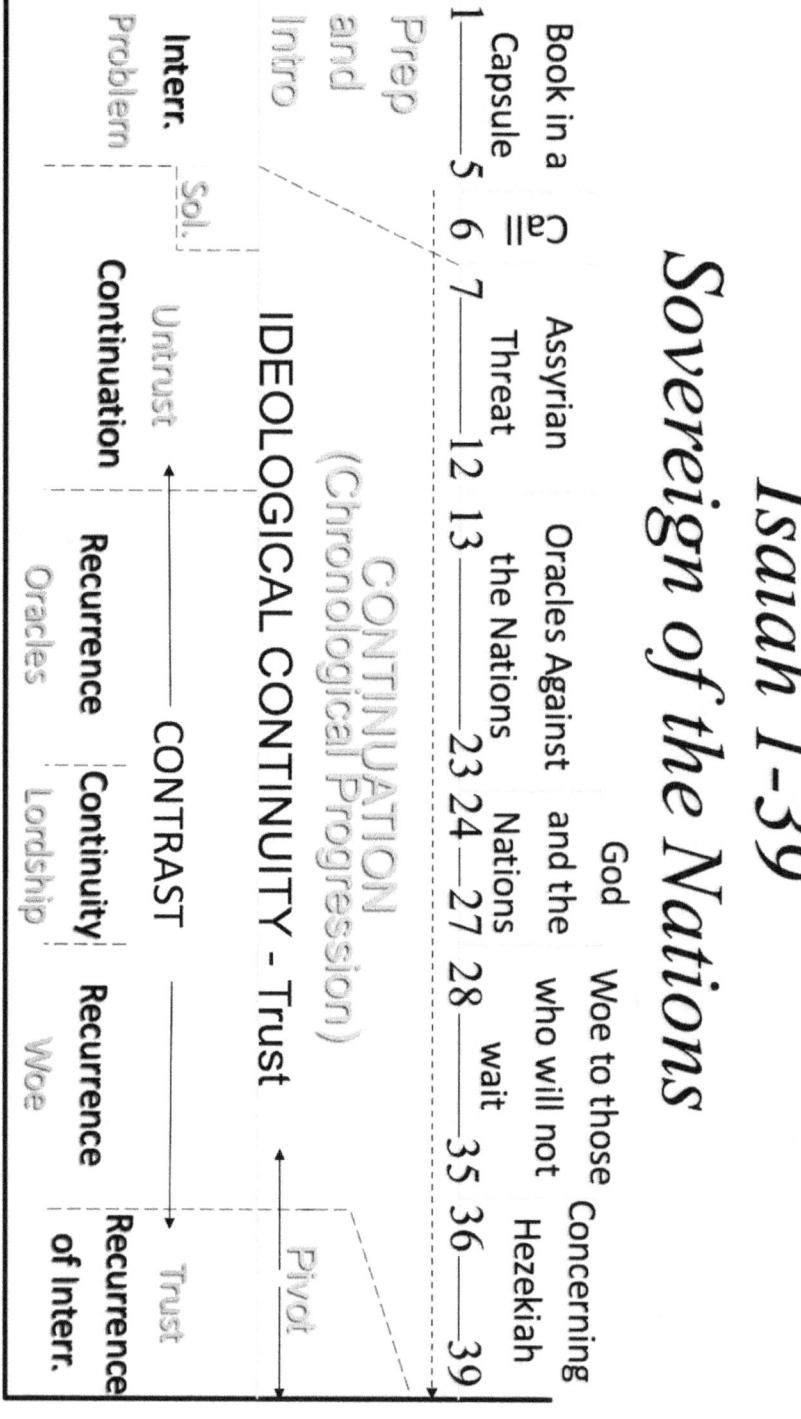

INDUCTIVE BIBLE STUDY AND TEACHING THE SOCIAL SCIENCES

Lindy D. Backues
Associate Professor of Economic Development at Eastern University

ABSTRACT: This chapter explores the application of Robert A. Traina's Inductive Bible Study methodology when employed in the social sciences. After examining the narrative nature of human understanding, five academic disciplines are surveyed in order to test the fit of Traina's narrative approach in each field, after which examples of social science application of Traina's method are then provided with illustrations drawn from the author's close to thirty years of social science research and teaching.

> Analysis, then, is sorting out the structures of signification—what Ryle called established codes, a somewhat misleading expression, for it makes the enterprise sound too much like that of the cipher clerk when it is much more like that of the literary critic—and determining their social ground and import.[1]

> A theme takes shape in the mind of a writer who sees the world in his own way. To Brecht man is a political animal, to Eliot a spirit capable of salvation, to Beckett a useless passion. Theme, at its very roots, is fed by a personal vision of this kind—which is not just a way of looking but a way of thinking and feeling. And from this it follows that the form of a play (structure, character, speech, etc.) does more than explore and clarify a particular theme. It also expresses and defines a distinctive vision of human life.[2]

1. INTRODUCTION

I am so very pleased to be able to write a personal tribute to my former professor and mentor, the late Dr. Robert A. Traina. I do not exaggerate when I say that this gentleman completely reconfigured how I go about understanding and making sense of things—not simply in relation to the biblical text, but also in relation to wider components linked to all of human life and existence. I resonate

---

[1] Clifford Geertz, *The Interpretation of Cultures* (New York: Basic Books, 1973), 9.
[2] Ronald Gaskell, *Drama and Reality: the European Theatre Since Ibsen* (London: Routledge and Kegan Paul, 1972), 60-61.

deeply with Mary Creswell Graham when she describes her experience as a student at The Biblical Seminary in New York.[3]

> I enrolled in [founder] Dr. White's seminary, called The Biblical Seminary in New York, with no idea that I would receive a skill that would make life long learning so stimulating and inspirational. For over forty years I have used the method in Bible study and in many other areas of learning—English literature, history, visual analysis of art works, psychology, and education.[4]

I simply cannot say it better. As will be obvious soon enough, that sentiment gets at the heart of what I hope to explore below.

I was a Master of Divinity student at Asbury Theological Seminary (ATS) between the years 1984 and 1988. Dr. Traina retired from Asbury the same year I graduated, so I had the pleasure of sitting under his teaching and tutelage his last years at the place.[5] In the process, I became fascinated by his Methodical Bible Study approach and, consequently, I chose to make the field of biblical studies my primary scholastic emphasis while in seminary (I even had the good fortune of being chosen as a Robert A. Traina English Bible Scholarship recipient in 1986-87 and 1987-88). At the same time, I also became deeply involved in Asbury Seminary's School of World Mission and Evangelism, exploring with absorbed interest the fields of cultural anthropology and missiology. I have described elsewhere how these separate experiences at different ends of ATS's campus surprised me by oddly mirroring each other.[6] Essentially, I discovered then that my two chosen disciplines– biblical exegesis and cultural anthropology—are concerned with the same process: the interpretation of meaning, whether that be in the presence of a text or a context.

Arising from that realization, the thesis for this chapter is simple: since the quest for meaning in all of life seems related to discovering and understanding a theme (a "leitmotif"[7] or a controlling idea that, in Gaskell's words "expresses and defines a distinctive vision of human life"[8]), and since Traina's method of biblical exegesis has proved so very powerful in fleshing out "the structures of

---

[3] The Biblical Seminary in New York was Traina's alma mater and employer prior to his arrival at Asbury Seminary in 1966. For more on The Biblical Seminary, see Fredrick J. Long, "Major Structural Relationships: A Survey of Origins, Development, Classifications, and Assessment," *The Journal of Inductive Biblical Studies* 1.1 (2014): 22–58 at 27, 31, 32, and 33, as well as David R. Bauer and Robert A. Traina, *Inductive Bible Study: A Comprehensive Guide to the Practice of Hermeneutics* (Grand Rapids: Baker Academic, 2014), 1–2 and 383n48. For the standard work on W. W. White and the Biblical Seminary in New York, see Charles Richard Eberhardt, *The Bible in the Making of Ministers; the Scriptural Basis of Theological Education: The Lifework of Wilbert Webster White* (New York: Association Press, 1949).

[4] Cited in Long, "Major Structural Relationships," 31.

[5] I was also very impacted by the ideas and guidance of his colleague and former student, David R. Bauer, co-author of *Inductive Bible Study*.

[6] See Lindy D. Backues, "Construing Culture as Composition—Part 1: The Narrative Nature of Truth," *The Journal of Inductive Biblical Studies* 6.1 (2019): 7–54.

[7] "A recurrent theme throughout a musical or literary composition, associated with a particular person, idea, or situation" (http://en.oxforddictionaries.com/definition/leitmotif accessed March 9, 2018).

[8] See above.

signification"⁹ in terms of themes in biblical literature,¹⁰ I maintain that Traina's approach can also be a powerful model in quests to understand human endeavors not textual or biblical. I write this chapter because I have gladly experimented with this idea in much of my teaching of the social sciences at the university level. In the limited space below, I will attempt to describe some of the results of this experimentation. But, I have a bit of spade work to do. I must first show how such a thematic emphasis has richly taken hold—not just in biblical studies, not just in the humanities, but also in the social sciences. It is toward this claim that I now turn.

2. THE STRUCTURED, METAPHORICAL NATURE OF HUMAN THINKING

I begin with an observation: many philosophers, social scientists, and neuroscientists believe there are key overarching structures and configurations in the human mind that serve to order thought and aid humans in making sense of existence. This is not a new observation; it goes back millennia, though—as we will see in a moment—research on the human brain and cognition seems now to verify the proposition, giving it even greater empirical validity.¹¹

As a notable historical example, the eminent thinker Immanuel Kant—positioning himself squarely in the tradition of Aristotle¹²—took

> elementary concepts of the pure understanding—such as quantity (unity, plurality, and totality); quality (reality, negation, and limitation); relation (substance and accident, cause-and-effect, and reciprocity); modality (possibility, existence, and necessity)—[to] constitute the mental equipment, the pure synthesizing concepts with which human understanding is endowed. These alone allow the individual to make sense of his [sic] experiences.¹³

Likewise, many Gestalt psychologists, after examining "a whole raft of 'form qualities,' whose ... appearance could be explained in terms of analogous brain processes" thereafter

> put forth laws purporting to explain how perception is organized. For instance, they showed that objects that are close together tend to be grouped together (*the law of proximity*); the more symmetrical a closed region, the more it tends to be seen as a figure (*the*

---

⁹ Geertz's statement above.

¹⁰ Traina's method does that by being structurally tied to and specifically arising from the materials it attends.

¹¹ Bauer and Traina emphasize the non-parochial nature of their proposed set of cognitive structures—or something quite like them—in the following: "[The structural] relationships [we describe] ... are found in all cultures, all genres, all time periods, and all forms of art, not simply in literature. They are pervasive and foundational for communication. Communication seems to be impossible without these structural features; therefore a recognition of their presence and an analysis of their use is extremely helpful in accurate, specific, and penetrating interpretation" (*Inductive Bible Study*, 94). We will look very briefly at their list of structural relationships below.

¹² Calling to mind Aristotle's famous tenfold "doctrine of categories" of the natural world: (1) Substance, (2) Quantity, (3) Quality, (4) Relation, (5) Place, (6) Time, (7) Position, (8) State, (9) Action, and (10) Affection.

¹³ Howard Gardner, *The Mind's New Science: A History of the Cognitive Revolution* (New York: Basic Books, 1985), 58.

law of symmetry); and the arrangement of figure and ground seen is the one featuring the fewest changes or interruption in straight or smoothly curved lines (*the law of good continuation*).... Though usually referring initially to visual demonstrations, versions of these laws also applied to auditory sequences—for example, rhythmic patterns.[14]

It soon will be clear that the categories above bear a striking resemblance to the groupings Traina and others have employed in their methodology; in fact, I will underscore this suggestive similarity as I develop my argument below.[15] But, before going on, I would like to make an accompanying observation. Recent research on cognition underscores the role that metaphor plays holding together these sorts of conceptual arrangements. Cognitive linguist George Lakoff represents an increasing number of scholars who assert that *all* thinking is systematically founded upon the structure of metaphor.[16] Lakoff himself maintains, "ordinary everyday English is largely metaphorical, dispelling once and for all the traditional view that metaphor is primarily in the realm of poetic or figurative language."[17]

---

[14] Gardner, *The Mind's New Science*, 112, emphasis added.

[15] It is not important for my argument that a settled number or listing of relationships be established. The point I am making here is simply that some sort of list can serve as the framework for exploring the mental structures apparent in all human cognition. Much of the focus of Long's article, *Major Structural Relationships*, centers on the fact that a variety of practitioners of Inductive Bible Study enumerate differing collections (and thus put forward varying number) of structural or compositional configurations. For a clear explanation of the nature and function of structural relationships as envisioned here, see Bauer and Traina, *Inductive Bible Study*, 94–122.

[16] See George Lakoff and Mark Johnson, *Metaphors We Live By* (Chicago: The University of Chicago Press, 1980) and *Philosophy in the Flesh: The Embodied Mind and Its Challenge to Western Thought* (New York: Basic Books, 1999), Paul Ricoeur, *The Rule of Metaphor: Multi-disciplinary Studies of the Creation of Meaning in Language* (London: Routledge, 2003), Matthew Stephen Wood, "Aristotle and the Question of Metaphor" (PhD Dissertation; Ottawa: University of Ottawa, 2015), and Kuang-ming Wu, *On Metaphoring: A Cultural Hermeneutic* (Leiden: Brill, 2001)as representative of this growing band of thinkers. Psychologist David Leary asserts that "...all knowledge is ultimately rooted in metaphorical (or analogical) modes of perception and thought" (David E. Leary, "Psyche's Muse: The Role of Metaphor in the History of Psychology," in *Metaphors in the History of Psychology*, ed. David E. Leary [Cambridge: Cambridge University Press, 1990], 1–78 at 3).

Note what I am *not* saying here, though: Lakoff does not believe—*nor* does Leary assert—that *all* thinking is metaphorical. Instead, the thesis before us is a bit softer, namely, that all thinking is *rooted in* and *funded by* metaphor, even that which is not metaphorical. There is an on-going and unsettled debate revolving around the stronger assertion, the one not being defended here. For a summary of the issues related to this debate, see Bipin Indurkhya, "The Thesis that All Knowledge is Metaphorical and Meanings of Metaphor," *Metaphor and Symbolic Activity* 9.1 (1994): 61–73. For a look at experimental test results on the influence of metaphors on thinking, see Paul H. Thibodeau and Lera Boroditsky, "Metaphors We Think With: The Role of Metaphor in Reasoning," *PLoS ONE* 6.2 (2011): 1–11.

[17] George Lakoff, "The Contemporary Theory of Metaphor," in *Metaphor and Thought*, 2nd. ed.; ed. Andrew Ortony (Cambridge: Cambridge University Press, 1993), 202–51 at 204. Note Lakoff's two additional clarifying statements: "[A] huge system of everyday, conventional, conceptual metaphors has been discovered. It is a system of metaphor that structures our everyday conceptual system, including most abstract concepts, and that lies behind much of everyday language. The discovery of this enormous metaphor system has destroyed the traditional literal-figurative distinction, since the term 'literal,' as used in defining the traditional distinction, carries with it ... false assumptions" (204); and, "[T]hose concepts that are not comprehended via conceptual metaphor might be called 'literal.' Thus, although I will argue that a great many common concepts like causation and purpose are metaphorical, there is

This realization is very important, primarily because it frames all knowledge-seeking as endeavors akin to investigating literary and figurative materials. Many theorists now see that truth quests in the social sciences bear more of a family resemblance to poetic analysis than to mathematical calculation.[18] As we will soon see, taking up practices in anthropology, sociology, psychology, and other human sciences is now advanced as a campaign more analogous to hermeneutically investigating texts than to scientific dissection, calculation, or analysis. There is a reason for this. As Thiselton points out, if one truly wishes to understand or interpret that which is human, "only the language of poetry, rather than the language of 'analysis' which takes things apart[,] can engage with anything foundational. (Heidegger call this 'Being' or 'Being-as-Event'.) Instrumental language merely reflects back the concepts which we already use, and which merely reflect 'our' world."[19]

By its very nature, metaphor is anything but instrumental. To the degree we recognize its integral role in all human knowledge-acquisition, we will also recognize the importance of comprehending, not just dissecting or classifying. Such a shift is at the root of the celebrated "interpretive turn" in the social sciences (a development we will look at more closely below).[20]

We need not fear, though, that such a focus on metaphor, thematic discovery, or literary analysis will consign us to a fuzzy, less-then-rigorous process. On the contrary, folding all of this into the categorization and structures of the human mind pointed to above, we now can see that grasping the function of metaphor also contributes to a clearer understanding of the ordered, conceptual framework of all thinking and language: "Because the metaphorical concept is systematic, the language we use to talk about that aspect of the concept is systematic."[21] The goal for us is to find a methodology that accords with the deeper mechanisms of the way metaphorical thinking works in human conception.

---

nonetheless an extensive range of non-metaphorical concepts. A sentence like 'the balloon went up' is not metaphorical, nor is the old philosopher's favorite 'the cat is on the mat.' But as soon as one gets away from concrete physical experience and starts talking about abstractions or emotions, metaphorical understanding is the norm" (205). So, while it important to note that Lakoff (a leading metaphor theorist) does not take all human thinking to be metaphorical in quality, he still recognizes metaphor as the backbone for human conceptualizing.

[18] This accords with Aristotle's famous dictum: "[T]he greatest thing by far is to be a master of metaphor. It is the one thing that cannot be learnt from others; and it is also a sign of genius, since a good metaphor implies an intuitive perception of the similarity in dissimilars" (*On the Art of Poetry*, trans. Ingram Bywater [Oxford: Oxford University Press, 1920], 78).

[19] Anthony C. Thiselton, *New Horizons in Hermeneutics: The Theory and Practice of Transforming Biblical Reading* (Grand Rapids: Zondervan, 1997), 325.

[20] I have addressed elsewhere matters related to the "interpretive turn" in the social sciences; see especially Lindy Backues, "Humility: A Christian Impulse as Fruitful Motif for Anthropological Theory and Practice," in *On Knowing Humanity: Insights from Theology for Anthropology*, ed. Eloise Meneses and David Bronkema (New York: Routledge, 2017), 101–36 at 118 and 120, and Backues, "Part 1: The Narrative Nature of Truth."

[21] Lakoff and Johnson, *Metaphors We Live By*, 7. They go on to say, "since metaphorical expressions in our language are tied to metaphorical concepts in a systematic way, we can use metaphorical linguistic expressions to study the nature of metaphorical concepts and to gain an understanding of the metaphorical nature of our activities" (*Metaphors We Live By*, 7.)

3. A Selective Look at Traina's Method: The Central Role of Recurrence, Contrast, and Questions

Due to space limitations, I will not parse Traina's methodology thoroughly—fortunately, I have tried to do so elsewhere, as have others.[22] I refer interested readers to those sources for a more detailed look at his method. But it is still necessary to get a working list of Traina's structural relationship before us. When I sat under his teaching, he employed the following bundle of primary structural relationships:[23]

1. Preparation/Realization (Introduction)
2. Contrast
3. Comparison
4. Recurrence
5. Causation/Substantiation
6. Generalization/Particularization
7. Climax
8. Pivot[24]
9. Interrogation
10. Summarization
11. Instrumentation[25]

With this list in mind, I would like to take a closer look at two of the relationships, since it seems these two configurations uniquely enable us to recognize and categorize common subject matter. This is a necessary goal as we seek interpretive insight since, in this way, we can begin to isolate interpretive themes that give insight into materials under scrutiny (it will soon be clear that unearthing key themes is vital for the interpretive process).

---

[22] For my contribution, see Lindy D. Backues, "Construing Culture as Composition—Part 2: Robert Traina's Methodology," *The Journal of Inductive Biblical Studies* 6.2 (2019): forthcoming. See also Bauer and Traina, *Inductive Bible Study*, 94-116, and Long, "Major Structural Relationships," as well as several chapters in the present volume.

[23] Bauer and Traina settle upon this list as well (though they separate causation from substantiation and generalization from particularization. I do not, since each pairing is but a mirror image of its twin – consequently, they list thirteen relationships [*Inductive Bible* Study, 94–16]). I will not here elaborate upon the three-fold, overarching categories into which they group these eleven relationships more broadly (alongside a few others); those categories are: (1) recurrence structures, (2) semantic structures, and (3) rhetorical structures (*Inductive Bible Study*, 95.) Before this 3-fold terminology was employed, Traina designated the latter grouping (the rhetorical structure category) "secondary relationships", which were constructs (e.g., chiasm, interchange, or intercalation) that simply assisted but that could not stand alone; to his way of thinking, these by necessity can only appear alongside one of the 11 primary relationships listed here.

[24] Bauer and Traina employ the term "cruciality" for this structure; but in the first sentence of their explanation of the relationship they succinctly say this: "Cruciality involves the device of pivot" (*Inductive Bible Study*,108). On his part, Traina also initially used the term "cruciality" (see Robert A. Traina, *Methodical Bible Study: A New Approach to Hermeneutics* [New York: Ganis & Harris, 1952; repr., Grand Rapids: Zondervan, 2002], 51—although, in that place, Traina describes cruciality in a way almost identical to the sentence from Bauer and Traina quoted just above), yet in classes I had with him between 1984 and 1988, he employed the term "pivot" almost exclusively.

[25] See SUPPLEMENT 12.1 for a handout I distribute to my university classes to explain these constructs in my teaching of the social sciences. That three-page sheet offers a more detailed explanation of each relationship than I provide here. I shall return to a brief explanation of this handout below.

The two relationships from above that I would like to examine are Recurrence and Contrast.

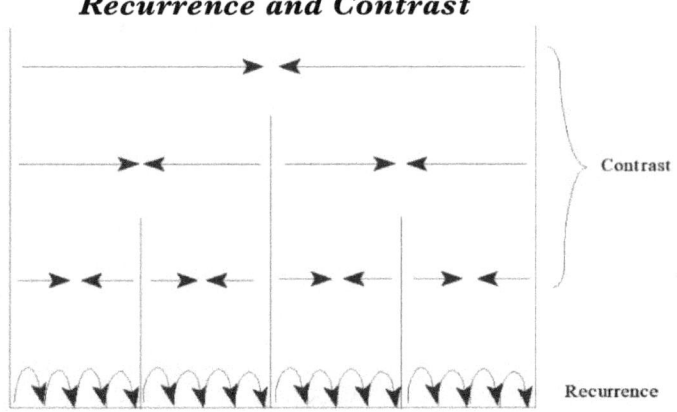

Recurrence and Contrast

These two constructs—operating in conjunction—serve to identify where boundaries are between passages or between units of thought. The diagram below illustrates the point for us. This plays out rather simply: contrasting elements serve to segregate units one from the other (represented in the diagram by in-turned arrows), whereas recurring elements indicate a continuance of the same topic and, therefore, a reappearance of the same idea or a similar idea over and over (this is illustrated by the "bouncing" arrows across the bottom of the diagram). Properties or qualities that extend over a wide range of material signal the presence of the structural relationship of Recurrence (note, too, that certain features recur over larger portions of material than do others). When a recurring item fades away, a contrasting element takes over and, itself, begins to resound. With such a shift, a different unit of thought begins to repeat, in contrast to the one just before it (this highlights the structural relationship of Contrast).

We must not overlook what is happening when the relationship Recurrence emerges. Bauer and Traina point out that this construct denotes

> the repetition of the same or similar terms, phrases, or other elements, which may involve motifs, concepts, persons, literary forms, or other structural relationships…. [Literary critic] William Freedman insists that one of the major emphases of recent literary investigation is the attempt "to discern clusters or families of related words or phrases that, by virtue of their frequency and particular use, tell us something about the author's intentions, conscious or otherwise."[26]

As I stated in the Introduction, the quest for meaning in life revolves around discovering and understanding primary themes, leitmotifs, or controlling ideas, whether these appear in texts or in contexts. It is helpful to realize, then, that this process of discovery is accomplished primarily by way of identifying the relationships of Recurrence and Contrast. Primary themes present themselves by way of recurring terms, phrases, motifs, concepts, persons, literary forms, or, structural relationships. Taking note where these occur again and again—where they recur, or repeat, or reappear in materials

---

[26] *Inductive Bible Study*, 95.

before us—will help us better parse the meaning of what we are trying to understand. Likewise, at those points where repeating features no longer appear, where another theme or leitmotif or controlling idea takes over and begins to redound, we are then presented with a new theme, a new motif. Contrasting elements point out where this happens.[27]

Traina's methodology promises something very valuable then: by strategically identifying what it is that is recurring, and by noticing when those elements cease to recur, we can identify key themes, motifs, or theses in materials we are attempting to understand. As elements reverberate across the horizon of meaning in these materials, and as those elements are replaced by different themes that repeatedly appear as well, those recurring elements "… by virtue of their frequency and particular use, tell us something about the author's intentions, conscious or otherwise."[28]

Let me make one final point before considering the role interpretation plays in disciplines outside of interpreting sacred texts. One primary reason for isolating themes is to know the types of questions we should pose in the interpretive process. In class, Traina frequently cited this statement that he attributed to St. Jerome: "Before one knows the antidote, one must first know the poison."[29] His point was that one can never know what sort of answer or solution is best if one does not first know the problem one is facing or the question one is being asked.[30] As Bauer and Traina underscore, "interpretation that involves the answering of questions extraneous to the text and dissonant with the agenda of the text will likely be skewed."[31] In a word, we dare not scratch where it does not itch.

This is where the value of interpretive questions comes in. Interpretive questions are bridging devices between Traina's observation phase—where structural relationships are identified—and the interpretive phase proper. This is true since questions are intimately connected to structural relationships (they are directed at observations brought to light by these relationships), yet they also serve as instruments from which meaning is directly derived (since they are posed to be answered).

---

[27] Bauer and Traina explain more precisely the nature of recurrence of a theme or topic in the following: "Recurrence has three major functions. First, it is usually *employed to indicate emphasis*. When an implied author makes use of recurrence, he is normally indicating that this term or concept is important and the reader should take pains to ascertain its meaning and significance. Second, recurrence *allows a writer to develop a theme or concept throughout the book*…. Third, recurrence *allows the writer to develop depth and richness of presentation*, for it invites readers to interpret individual occurrences in light of the other occurrences and in light of the recurring pattern as a whole" (*Inductive Bible Study*, 96, emphasis added).

[28] See Bauer and Traina's statement above.

[29] I must admit that, over the years, I have looked for but have not yet located a reliable source for this quote from Jerome. The only thing I have located that bears any resemblance to it is: "[P]oison is the only antidote known for poison; great pain can only be relieved by inflicting greater pain" (Saint Jerome, *The Principal Works of St. Jerome*, trans. W. H. Fremantle with assistance of G. Lewis and W. G. Martley [Oxford, UK: James Parker and Company, 1893], 216). Nevertheless, the statement emphasized by Traina illustrates the point well.

[30] Bauer and Traina helpfully explain that the structural relationship interrogation can appear in an alternate form—as problem-solution, in contrast to the more customary way we envision it: question-answer (cf. *Inductive Bible Study*, 113–14).

[31] *Inductive Bible Study*, 126.

As underscored elsewhere, Traina's method identifies three categories of interpretive questions, and the order in which these questions are to be posed is critically important.[32] Definitive or explanatory questions—"What?" questions—should be posed first, since it is important to know the nature of the material encountered before moving on to other sorts of questions. These "What?" questions are then followed by rational questions—"Why?" questions—so that we might more fully delve into the meaning and rationale of what is there. The posing of implicational questions—the "What is being assumed?" and the "What does all of this lead to?" questions—is a third step, to allow for a deeper probing behind the more obvious surface features of the text or the context. These interpretive questions—put forward in this order—must be targeted at key features of each structural relationship discovered, in order that those structural features identified might be sufficiently interrogated in search of meaning and answers.[33]

It is hard to overstate how such critical questions are tools in the program of understanding in the enterprise of hermeneutics. As philosopher of hermeneutics Hans-Georg Gadamer says,

> [T]he essence of the question is to open up possibilities and keep them open. If a prejudice becomes questionable in view of what another person or a text says to us, this does not mean that it is simply set aside and the text or the other person accepted as valid in its place. Rather, historical objectivism shows its naivete in accepting this disregarding of ourselves as what actually happens. In fact our own prejudice is properly brought into play by being put at risk. Only by being given full play is it able to experience the other's claim to truth and make it possible for him to have full play himself.[34]

In fact, says Thiselton, Gadamer viewed Plato's greatest contribution to be his analysis of the details of "*dialogue* as a process in which truth 'arises' in the to-and-fro of questions and conversation"[35] Such is the importance of well-placed questions.

We will see below that the deft use of questions also plays a fruitful role in social science approaches as well. But, at this juncture, it is most important to remember that questions are of maximum use when connected directly to materials before us (by way of structural relationships) since, in this way, they help us ferret out details related to interpretive themes, leitmotifs, and controlling ideas—seeing as how these are our primary portals for understanding.

4. The Search for Themes: Keys to Understanding in Other Disciplines

I propose now that we widen our quest. When it comes to our search for themes in relation to social science research, Ellen Joanne Millard makes the following observation:

> There are four important criteria for generative themes. The first is that they "exist ...

---

[32] Cf. Bauer and Traina, *Inductive Bible Study*, 126–34, and Backues, "Part 2: Robert Traina's Methodology."

[33] Bauer and Traina, *Inductive Bible Study*, 126.

[34] Hans-Georg Gadamer, *Truth and Method*, trans. revised by Joel Weinsheimer and Donald G. Marshall; 2nd rev. ed. [New York: Continuum, 1998], 299.

[35] *New Horizons in Hermeneutics*, 321, emphasis in the original.

with reference to concrete facts".... These facts of everyday life are usually expressed in "limit situations" which hinder oppressed people from perceiving or exercising their ability to act in order to change their conditions.

[T]he second key characteristic of a generative theme, therefore, is the peoples' "awareness of that situation—the various levels of perception of themselves and of the world in which they exist"....

[T]he third key component of a generative theme is that of an implicit, though perhaps unrecognized, task. The potential for social change is thus present in every theme as "an untested feasibility"....

The fourth essential characteristic of generative themes is that they generate others; that "however they are comprehended and whatever action they may evoke,... they contain the possibility of unfolding into again as many themes, which in their turn call for new tasks to be fulfilled...."[36]

What follows below is a brief survey of five social science disciplines. I seek to illustrate that practitioners in these fields often hunt for motifs or themes as a central feature for exploring their subject matter. As will soon be clear, I see these themes functioning as something akin to conceptual paths along which academic investigation can take place.[37] Personally, I have long associated the act of theme discovery with that stressed by German sociologist and philosopher Jürgen Habermas when he points to "deep grammar" components in any given context. Habermas believes that being able to navigate the controlling motifs—the deep grammar—of a cultural scene necessitates a certain level of "communicative competence" on the part of social actors. Habermas was here inspired by linguist Noam Chomsky's notion of "linguistic competence", i.e., the innate human ability that language users exhibit when they follow a "set of rules ... that allows [them] to learn and use any particular language."[38] As Habermas frames it, "deep grammar" competence empowers the capable social actor to successfully navigate social contexts. As we discover meaning-soaked themes embedded within cultures, contexts, or texts—as we will hear many thinkers below exhort us to do—we end up unearthing the deep grammar of those contexts; it is almost as if we excavate "thesis

---

[36] Ellen Joanne Millard, "The Investigation of Generative Themes in E.S.L. Needs Assessment" (MA Thesis; Vancouver, British Columbia: The University of British Columbia, 1986), 9–10.

[37] Sociologist Robert Merton helped pioneer a recognition of the role of themes in scientific research in general; see Robert K. Merton, "Thematic Analysis in Science: Notes on Holton's Concept," *Science* 188.4186 (1975): 335–38. Given my thesis and my argument here, his definition of what he labels "themata" is quite interesting: "The themata of scientific knowledge are tacit cognitive imageries and preferences for or commitments to certain kinds of concepts, certain kinds of methods, certain kinds of evidence, and certain forms of solutions to deep questions and engaging puzzles" ("Thematic Analysis in Science", 335).

[38] Andrew Edgar, *Habermas: The Key Concepts* (New York: Routledge, 2006), 163. For the place where Chomsky first advanced this notion of "deep grammar" or "deep structure" of a language, see Noam Chomsky, *Current Issues in Linguistic Theory* (Berlin: Walter de Gruyter, 1988).

statements" of purpose nested meaningfully within the many sectors of society. Put another way, we can discover communal rails along which cultural competence can roll forward. And, of course, this is where Traina's methodology might come in quite handy.

5. THE SEARCH FOR THEMES IN THEOLOGY

Theologian Anders Nygren once famously mused,

> When a theologian speaks of what is essentially and distinctively Christian, this does not need to mean that he has arbitrarily picked out of Christianity certain ideas which are of personal importance for him, and is claiming these as "the essence of Christianity." What is uniquely distinctive about Christianity is discovered by going to Christianity itself and observing its history. *There, in the struggle of the Christian fundamental motif, the distinctive character of Christianity is revealed.* In this way systematic theology obtains the firm, objective starting point that it needs.[39]

To begin this survey with theology is to begin with low-hanging fruit. The academic discipline of Christian theology is presumably built, at least in part, upon the study of sacred texts. So, as Nygren argues above, we can discover principal motifs or themes of this faith merely by looking at "Christianity itself and … its history." Such an historical examination, by definition, includes an examination of the Christian story as put forward in the Bible. By examining that story, of course, we are staying close to the path Traina has explored.

A good many persons have sought to identify the central core—the primary theme—of the Christian message in the Bible. Given space limitations here, I am able only to cite the examples of Swedish theologian Anders Nygren, Swiss theologian Karl Barth, and American New Testament scholar Richard B. Hays. Moreover, stress will not be placed on appraising the correctness of the themes they discovered. I will highlight instead a common method employed by all three of these persons: each thinker suggests that isolating controlling themes or motifs is the key to advancing theological understanding.

I begin by quoting Nygren since he overtly championed theme identification and motif recognition as *the* central step in his theological method.

> Proceeding from [an] artistic and literary definition of the term [motif], Nygren particularized it for use in theological study. He especially focused attention on two features of the motif that are relevant here: (1) To qualify as a motif, an idea must be of fundamental or categorical significance. A motif in a body of religious thought is an answer to a basic or recurring question. Hence, there are only a few motifs that characterize a subject. (2) Because of its nature as a theme of fundamental or underlying significance, the motif can

---

[39] Anders Nygren, *Meaning and Method: Prolegomena to a Scientific Philosophy of Religion and a Scientific Theology*, trans. Philip S. Watson (London: Epworth, 1972), 376, emphasis added.

be expressed through a variety of means.[40]

In the process, Nygren settled upon what he called "the agape motif" as the key interpretive code for his understanding of the entire biblical story.

> God is agape. Here is the starting point for the whole of the Christian life, and here is the reason why the entire Christian ethos can be summed up in the one word "love", or in the double commandment of love for God and one's neighbour. The fundamental Christian motif is the Agape motif. Without this, Christian fellowship with God loses its coherence and its distinctively Christian character.[41]

Nygren felt that the discovery of themes should serve as the key to all theological understanding. And, once again, in this he has not been alone—many others have felt likewise.

That being so, let us turn to Karl Barth. Though he did not press the discovery of themes qua method as overtly as did Nygren, Barth nonetheless did see thematic discovery as an indispensable means for making sense of biblical materials.[42] For Barth, "God as One who loves in freedom" serves as the dominant theme running throughout the Bible; in his view, love bound to freedom serves as the scripture's singular refrain, its core message.

> While desiring to hold the proposition as a unified whole, Barth of necessity ... begins to discuss what is the second stage of his formal construction. He accomplishes this by speaking first of "the being of God as the One who loves" and secondly of "the being of God in freedom." Here some consideration must be given to Barth's material understanding of love as God's essence and as God's life, as this relates to how he later formally ties the perfections to either love or freedom respectively.[43]

---

[40] Donald G. Dawe, *The Form of a Servant: A Historical Analysis of the Kenotic Motif* (Eugene, OR: Wipf and Stock, 2011), 19–20.

[41] Nygren, *Meaning and Method*, 374.

[42] See Richard E. Burnett, *Karl Barth's Theological Exegesis: The Hermeneutical Principles of the Römerbrief Period* (Grand Rapids: Eerdmans, 2004), 78–79.

[43] Eric J. Titus, "The Perfections of God in the Theology of Karl Barth: A Consideration of the Formal Structure," *KAIROS-Evangelical Journal of Theology* 4.2 (2010): 203–22 at 206; cf. Dawe, *The Form of a Servant*, 169–70. Barth makes the point directly and explicitly:

> God's being consists in the fact that He is the One who loves in freedom. In this He is the perfect being: the being which is itself perfection and so the standard of all perfection; the being, that is, which is self-sufficient and thus adequate to meet every real need; the being which suffers no lack in itself and by its very essence fills every real lack. Such a being is God. He is this being because He lives as such. It is as we return to life as the fundamental element in the divine being that we also move forward to God's perfections. The one perfection of God, His loving in freedom, is lived out by Him, and therefore identical with a multitude of various and distinct types of perfection. There is no possibility of knowing the perfect God without knowing His perfections. The converse is also true: knowledge of the divine perfections is possible only in knowledge of the perfect God, of His loving in freedom. But because God lives His perfect being the knowledge of His perfections is also a way—the way which in the presence of the living God we must tread. In other words,

As one can see, this thematic core—for Barth—is intimately linked to the nature and character of God.[44] Since God is the central actor in the biblical record, thematically understanding "God's perfections"—God's love and God's freedom—is Barth's first step for gaining insight into the Bible's viewpoint.[45] All theology, he believed, needs to be erected on this two-fold emphasis.

Finally, very briefly, New Testament scholar Richard B. Hays also follows a similar path as Nygren and Barth—though, he arrives at a slightly different destination. Hays realizes that the biblical record is a telling of a particular story as represented by many different perspectives, many different people, at many different times. That being so, he acknowledges that thematic unity in the New Testament story will never appear in the form of "… the unity of a dogmatic system."[46] Instead, he recommends that we look for

> key *images* that all the different canonical tellings share. Why look for images, rather than concepts or doctrines, as a ground of coherence? As David Kelsey has demonstrated, every theological reading of Scripture depends upon "a single synoptic, imaginative judgment" in which the interpreter "tries to catch up what Christianity is basically all about."[47]

Hays essentially recommends a search for themes or controlling metaphors that can serve as guides for sound biblical interpretation, a discovery of "single synoptic imaginative judgments"; elements he labels *focal images*.[48]

After methodically sifting through New Testament materials in his book for nine chapters, Hays offers the reader three focal images he believes serve as "*lenses* to focus our reading of the New Testament: when we reread the canonical documents through these images, our blurry multiple

---

even in the knowledge of the one perfect God we are confronted by His richness. The real God is the one God who loves in freedom, and as such is eternally rich. To know Him means to know Him again and again, in ever new ways—to know only Him, but to know Him as the perfect God, in the abundance, distinctness and variety of His perfections (Karl Barth, *Church Dogmatics* II/1, §29, 322).

[44] "Barth's ethical method ... is to proceed from the Bible through its notion of salvation history to incarnational Christology, out into a systematic trinitarian theology and then on to ethics; and only at this last point does the Bible's specifically ethical material come into play" (Nigel Biggar, "Barth's Trinitarian Ethic," in *The Cambridge Companion to Karl Barth*, ed. John Webster [Cambridge: Cambridge University Press, 2000], 212–27 at 224).

[45] For Barth, theology was all about encountering God as revealed in Christ; cf. Ruth Page, *The Incarnation of Freedom and Love* (London: SCM, 1991), 51–53.

[46] Richard B. Hays, *The Moral Vision of the New Testament: A Contemporary Introduction to New Testament Ethics* (Edinburgh: T&T Clark, 1996), 193.

[47] *Moral Vision of the New Testament*, 194.

[48] It is interesting to note that Hays leans heavily upon finding thematic images in the form of visual metaphors—this, of course, aligns well with my emphasis on metaphor above. Note this from Hays: "[T]his single metaphorical judgment [i.e. identifying focal images] not only shapes 'decisions about how to construe and use particular passages of Scripture' but also governs 'the sort of "wholeness" each [theologian] [sic] concretely ascribes to Scripture.' In other words, the unity and sense of Scripture can be grasped only through an act of metaphorical imagination that focuses the diverse contents of the texts in terms of a particular 'imaginative characterization'" (*The Moral Vision of the New Testament*, 194).

impressions of the texts come more sharply into focus."⁴⁹ The three images Hays settles upon in his survey are (1) community, (2) cross, and (3) new creation.⁵⁰

Once again, I am not seeking to appraise the soundness of Hays's choices here. Instead, my much simpler goal is to show that a quest for themes or theme-like images is at the heart of his interpretive methodology. Thus, it appears that Traina's approach above—a method rich in potential for quarrying meaning from texts and contexts alike—should help us do the very thing that Nygren, Barth, and Hays (with many others besides) encourage us to do: to look for themes in biblical and theological materials in our quest to understand sometimes confusing materials that confront us.

6. THE SEARCH FOR THEMES IN CULTURAL ANTHROPOLOGY

Anthropologist Stephen A. Tyler has aptly surmised,

> [A]nthropology in the postmodern world has taken a "poetic turn," manifest both in the writing of poetry and in an interest in "poetics"—in the form and functions of discourse and rhetoric. This turn to poetics is also a "turning away" from formal linguistics and modern logic as the dominant models of discourse, for it acknowledges figurative synthesis as the previously constituted ground of all analysis and as the enabling discourse that analysis can neither explicate nor transcend.⁵¹

So, coxswained by the illustrious Clifford Geertz, many in cultural anthropology—over the past 50 years or so—have negotiated what is now called "the interpretive turn."⁵² These persons envision culture as a text analogue, a conceptual move that casts events, activities, and artifacts as "readable," a position that reworks "our whole sense of what such interpretation is and shifts it toward modes of thought rather more familiar to the translator, the exegete, or the iconographer than to the test giver, the factor analyst, or the pollster."⁵³ Given this change, Geertz and his backers began exhorting

---

⁴⁹ *Moral Vision of the New Testament*, 195, emphasis in the original.

⁵⁰ *Moral Vision of the New Testament*, 196–98. After isolating these three focal images, Hays goes on in the balance of his book to illustrate how they might be employed to establish Christian positions in the face of various ethical dilemmas. It is interesting that Hays, for reasons I have no space to go into here, rejects "love" as a focal image in the New Testament. In this way, of course, he diverges significantly from Nygren's opinion.

⁵¹ Stephen A. Tyler, "The Poetic Turn in Postmodern Anthropology: The Poetry of Paul Friedrich," *American Anthropologist* 86.2 (1984): 328–36 at 328.

⁵² This is virtually identical to what we have just heard Tyler call the "poetic turn." For two representative social theorists who have applied hermeneutical approaches to the social sciences more generally, in ways consonant with the "interpretive turn", see Zygmunt Bauman, *Hermeneutics and Social Science: Approaches to Understanding* (London: Routledge, 2010) and Paul Ricoeur, *Hermeneutics and the Human Sciences: Essays on Language, Action and Interpretation* (Cambridge: Cambridge University Press, 2016). Ricoeur's ideas, especially, had significant influence on Geertz's thinking. For application of hermeneutics and hermeneutical ideas and the interpretive turn to the field of economics, see Deirdre N. McCloskey, *The Rhetoric of Economics*, 2nd ed. (Madison: University of Wisconsin Press, 1999) and Don Lavoie, ed., *Economics and Hermeneutics*, 1st ed. (New York: Routledge, 2014).

⁵³ Clifford Geertz, *Local Knowledge: Further Essays in Interpretive Anthropology* (New York: Basic Books, 1983), 31.

colleagues to employ "thick description" in their field work—a phrase he borrowed from philosopher Gilbert Ryle.[54] Such a call amounted to an appeal for a more literary, exegetical, and hermeneutical approach to anthropology—an emphasis, not just on description, but on the interpretation of cultures as if they were texts (in fact, as we have seen, *The Interpretation of Cultures* is the title of one of Geertz's most celebrated publications).[55] To me, this is quite similar to Habermas's emphasis on "deep grammar" and "communicative competence", not to mention his assertion that an actor competent in deep-grammar understanding of situations will have an enhanced ability to "successfully navigate social contexts."[56]

So, with ethnography and field work now seen as deep grammar activities "thick" or primarily interpretative in nature, quests for constructs comparable to leitmotifs or controlling ideas in the field should not be surprising. But, what is surprising is that Geertz and his colleagues were not the initiators of such a search in anthropology; rather, it has enjoyed quite a long history in the discipline.

For instance, several illustrious pioneers of cultural anthropology highlighted cultural themes early on as being integral to anthropological analysis. For instance, one need only recall Ruth Benedict and her influential *Patterns of Culture*,[57] or the effect linguist Edward Sapir's youthful aesthetic sense, musical ability, and poetry writing apparently had upon his subsequent innovative insights concerning culture and personality,[58] or Margaret Mead's concern for the role patient pattern discovery must play in all authentic ethnographic methodology,[59] to recognize that an interpretive approach to culture and the unearthing of cultural themes in anthropology did not begin with Geertz.

In fact, anthropologist Morris Opler—another of Ruth Benedict's students at Columbia University—a bit later explicitly championed the following:

---

[54] Clifford Geertz, *The Interpretation of Cultures* (New York: Basic Books, 1973), 6–10; cf. "A thick description has the following features: (a) It gives the context of an action, (b) it states the intentions and meanings that organize the action, (c) it traces the evolution and development of the action, and (d) it presents the action as a text that can then be interpreted. A thin description simply reports facts, independent of intentions or the circumstances that surround the action" (Norman K. Denzin, *Interpretive Interactionism [Applied Social Research Methods]* 2nd ed. [Thousand Oaks, CA: Sage, 2001], 53–54).

[55] Also called "interpretive anthropology," this type of cultural study is also known as "symbolic anthropology."

[56] See my comments on Habermas (and Chomsky) above.

[57] See Ruth Benedict, *Patterns of Culture* (New York: Mariner Books, 2005). For instance, "... *with their comparative isolation, many primitive regions have had centuries in which to elaborate the cultural themes they have made their own.* They provide ready to our hand the necessary information concerning the possible great variations in human adjustments, and a critical examination of them is essential for any understanding of cultural processes. It is the only laboratory of social forms that we have or shall have" (*Patterns of Culture*, 17, emphasis added; see also 46).

[58] Richard Handler, "Sapir's Poetic Experience," *American Anthropologist* 86.2 (1984): 416–17.

[59] Mead states that a successful ethnographer must attend to "the problem of how unformalized aspects of culture are to be studied" ("More Comprehensive Field Methods," *American Anthropologist* 35.1 [1933]: 1–15 at 1); she suggests this be accomplished by making "a great number of minute and consecutive observations ..." ("More Comprehensive Field Methods," 13), since "only by carefully recording a series of them may *the cultural pattern* ... be derived" ("More Comprehensive Field Methods," 3, emphasis added). Mead was a student of Benedict's at Columbia University, and she was Sapir's romantic partner for a time.

> [A] limited number of dynamic affirmations ... can be identified in every culture and ... the key to the character, structure, and direction of the specific culture is to be sought in the nature, expression, and interrelationship of these themes.... The term "theme" I use here in a technical sense to denote a postulate or position, declared or implied, and usually controlling behaviour or stimulating activity, which is tacitly approved or openly promoted in a society.[60]

Illustrating this claim—in a way remarkably reminiscent of Traina's methodology—is ethnographer James Spradley, by way of his "Developmental Research Sequence Method."[61] This approach breaks down into two somewhat overlapping steps:

1. The identification and analysis of cultural domains, which then serve as conceptual containers for
2. The identification and analysis of cultural themes.[62]

As tools for accomplishing this task, Spradley (and McCurdy) put(s) forward a collection of "universal semantic relationships" that assist in isolating cultural domains.[63] As I have emphasized elsewhere, Spradley's collection bears a striking resemblance to Traina's list of structural relationships.[64] Also of note is the emphasis that Spradley places upon theme identification as the essential goal of good ethnography.[65]

---

[60] Morris E. Opler, "Themes as Dynamic Forces in Culture," *American Journal of Sociology* 51 (1945): 198–206 at 198. For a tribute to Opler and his notion of cultural themes, see Mario D. Zamora, J. Michael Mahar, and Henry Orenstein, ed., *Themes in Culture: Essays in Honor of Morris E. Opler* (Quezon City, Philippines: Kayumanggi, 1971).

[61] James P. Spradley, *The Ethnographic Interview* (New York: Holt, Rinehart and Winston, 1979), 41–204, esp. 227–35; cf. James P. Spradley and David W. McCurdy, *Anthropology: The Cultural Perspective* (second ed.; New York: John Wiley & Sons, 1980), 355–69. Whitehead provides a helpful summary of much of Spradley's ideas concerning ethnography (*Basic Classical Ethnographic Research Methods: Secondary Data Analysis, Fieldwork, Observation/Participation Observation, and Informal and Semi-structured Interviewing* [College Park, MD: University of Maryland, 2005]). I take a more comprehensive look at Spradley's approach in comparison to Traina's methodology in Backues "Part 1: The Narrative Nature of Truth" and "Part 2: Robert Traina's Methodology."

[62] Spradley, *The Ethnographic Interview*, 94. These two steps resemble the way the structural relationships Contrast and Recurrence help identify boundaries between units of thought. In a word, Spradley's first step is like how Contrast segregates units of thought, one from the other (in this case, into distinct domains); the second step is aligned with the way Recurrence points to a continuance of the same topic or theme over a collection of material.

[63] Spradley, *Ethnographic Interview*, 111; Spradley and McCurdy, *Anthropology*, 361.

[64] "Part 1: The Narrative Nature of Truth."

[65] Based upon his field research in Java, Geertz identified three themes—he calls them "doctrines"—that serve as "implicit principles in terms of which religious life was conducted ...": (1) the doctrine of the exemplary center; (2) the doctrine of graded spirituality, and (3) the doctrine of the theater state (*Islam Observed: Religious Developments in Morocco and Indonesia* [Chicago: The University of Chicago Press, 1968], 36). He claims that, in Java in the 60s, these three doctrines "make up a world view and an ethos which is elitist, esoteric, and aesthetic, and which remains, even after the adaptations and reformulations forced upon it by four hundred years of Islamization, three hundred of colonial domination, and twenty of independence, *a powerful theme* in the contemporary Indonesian consciousness" (*Islam Observed*, 36, emphasis added).

Moreover, Spradley bolsters the interpretive potential of locating semantic relationships and theme detection by pairing the process with three distinct types of questions: the descriptive question, the structural question, and the contrast question.[66] He does this since "…the task of the ethnographer is to discover questions that seek the relationship among entities that are conceptually meaningful to the people under investigation."[67] Remember, too, that—according to Gadamer—the essence of the question-posing process is so that we might "… open up possibilities and keep them open" and thereby "… experience the other's claim to truth and make it possible for him to have full play himself." This rings true whether "the other" is a person from a culturally distant context, or a sacred text that lays claim upon us. I think that Traina would agree.

7. THE SEARCH FOR THEMES IN SOCIOLOGY

James Thomas and Angela Harden offer a helpful statement on the place of "thematic analysis":

> As [organizational theorist Richard] Boyatzis … has observed, thematic analysis is "not another qualitative method but a process that can be used with most, if not all, qualitative methods.…" Our approach concurs with this conceptualisation of thematic analysis, since the method we employed draws on other established methods but uses techniques commonly described as "thematic analysis" in order to formalise the identification and development of themes.[68]

As has happened in anthropology, so too in sociology: thematic discovery can easily be spotted as a central component to research in the field. While I do not have space to explore this extensively, an example or two should help to establish this fact.

Greg Guest, Kathleen M. MacQueen, and Emily E. Namey situate the sociological practice of "thematic analysis" squarely within the framework of "qualitative research" and "grounded

---

[66] *Ethnographic Interview*, 60; cf. 78–91, 120–31, and 155–72.

[67] Black and Metzger, as cited in Spradley, *Ethnographic Interview*, 84. Says Spradley, "the ethnographer's main tools for discovering another person's cultural knowledge is the ethnographic question" (*Ethnographic Interview*, 60). Note, too, the following from Whitehead: "As Spradley comments, every thing [sic] that the ethnographer observes are actually answers, and the process of observation is actually finding questions to those answers" (*Basic Classical Ethnographic Research Methods*, 11). Spradley's statements here concerning the role of questions agree significantly with views expressed by Bauer and Traina in their book: "Having identified a major structural relationship, readers may raise questions directed toward that relationship. These questions serve as the bridge between observation and interpretation. They arise from observations made…, and they form the basis for interpretation. In fact …, interpretation is the answering of questions raised in the observation stage. This principle of making use of questions raised in observation as the bases for interpretation is extremely critical. Often eisegesis (reading our own ideas into passages) occurs because interpreters (at least implicitly) direct improper questions to the text, questions that the text does not invite the reader to pursue and that the text is not prepared to answer. In other words, interpretation that involves the answering of questions extraneous to the text and dissonant with the agenda of the text will likely be skewed" (*Inductive Bible Study*, 126).

[68] James Thomas and Angela Harden, "Methods for the Thematic Synthesis of Qualitative Research in Systematic Reviews," *BMC Medical Research Methodology* 8.45 (2008): 1–18 at 5.

theory."[69] As qualitative research, thematic analysis frames sociological research as more than simply counting words, coding, or numerical-validation and statistical relevance. By way of thematic analysis, research interests instead

> *focus on identifying and describing both implicit and explicit ideas within the data, that is, themes.* Codes are then typically developed to represent the identified themes and applied or linked to raw data as summary markers for later analysis. Such analyses may or may not include the following: comparing code frequencies, identifying code co-occurrence, and graphically displaying relationships between codes within the data set.[70]

Hence, whatever coding thereafter undertaken is provoked, not so much by a blunt documenting of the frequency of certain words or phrases, but by the detection of fertile themes and the appearance of motifs of significance. This, of course, is quite like what we have seen occurring in other disciplines.

It is interesting to note, too, that renowned sociologist Peter Berger would prefer it if his discipline's intellectual home were repositioned, with sociology seen more as part of the humanities and less of a "social science" (this, of course, mirrors Geertz's sentiments for anthropology). He apparently has long held this view, though he now feels uncomfortable with the way he once expressed that position (at the time he called his position "humanistic").[71]

> I would now question whether [humanistic] was a felicitous adjective, though I would not quarrel with the basic intention. I had intended two meanings: One was to stress the contribution of sociology to a *humane* society, based on its debunking of the myths legitimating cruelty and oppression. I suppose that came out of the Enlightenment roots of the discipline. But more relevant was the second meaning, sociology as one of the "humanities" (or *Geisteswissenschaften*), closely related to history and philosophy but also to the institutions of the literary imagination.[72]

Repositioning sociology in this way makes it more of an interpretive affair (it frames it as one of the *Geisteswissenschaften* = sciences of the spirit), as opposed to an endeavor concerned with conformity to immutable laws and hard-fast principles. And as an interpretive endeavor, thematic analysis can portal research more deeply toward authentic sociological understanding.

---

[69] Greg Guest, Kathleen M. MacQueen, and Emily E. Namey, *Applied Thematic Analysis* (Thousand Oaks, California: Sage Publications, 2012). For a survey of grounded theory (and its application toward concerns of social justice), see Kathy Charmaz, "Grounded Theory in the 21st Century: Applications for Advancing Social Justice Studies," in *The Sage Handbook of Qualitative Research*, 3rd. ed.; ed. Norman K. Denzin and Yvonna S. Lincoln (Los Angeles: Sage, 2005), 507–35.

[70] Guest, MacQueen, and Namey, *Applied Thematic Analysis*, 10.

[71] See Peter L. Berger, *Invitation to Sociology: A Humanistic Perspective*, 1st ed. (New York: Anchor, 1963).

[72] Peter L. Berger, *Adventures of an Accidental Sociologist: How to Explain the World Without Becoming a Bore* (Amherst, NY: Prometheus, 2011), 25.

8. THE SEARCH FOR THEMES IN PSYCHOLOGY

Psychologists Braun and Clarke have aptly said that "thematic analysis should be seen as a foundational method for qualitative analysis. It is the first qualitative method of analysis that researchers should learn, as it provides core skills that will be useful for conducting many other forms of qualitative analysis."[73] We need not dive very deeply into details concerning the possibility for thematic research in psychology, seeing as how much of its history in this regard mirrors what we have witnessed happening in sociology and anthropology. For several decades now, a quest for interpretive themes has been at the heart of much psychology research methodology.[74] Psychologists Braun and Clarke emphasize that what is important in thematic analysis in psychology is for the researcher to identify "… a theme [that] captures something important about the data in relation to the research question, and [that] represents some level of *patterned* response or meaning within the data set."[75] This sort of recommendation sounds quite familiar to us by now.

Of more interest at this juncture are the six stages outlined later in the article, phases Braun and Clarke put forward as constituting steps in thematic analysis.[76] The stages (or phases) they list are the following:

> Phase 1: Familiarize Yourself with the Data
> Phase 2: Generate Initial Codes
> Phase 3: Search for Themes

---

[73] Virginia Braun and Victoria Clarke, "Using Thematic Analysis in Psychology," *Qualitative Research in Psychology* 3 (2006): 77–101 at 78.

[74] Representative of this trend are Jodi Aronson, "A Pragmatic View of Thematic Analysis," *The Qualitative Report* 2.1 (1995): 1–3; Hélène Joffe and Lucy Yardley, "Content and Thematic Analysis," in *Research Methods for Clinical and Health Psychology*, ed. David F. Marks and Lucy Yardley (London: Sage, 2004): 56–68; Braun and Clarke, "Using Thematic Analysis in Psychology"; Thomas and Harden, "Methods for the Thematic Synthesis of Qualitative Research in Systematic Reviews"; Hélène Joffe, "Thematic Analysis," in *Qualitative Methods in Mental Health and Psychotherapy: A Guide for Students and Practitioners*, ed. David Harper and Andrew R. Thompson (Chichester, UK: John Wiley & Sons, 2011): 209–24; and Victoria Clarke and Virginia Braun, "Teaching Thematic Analysis: Overcoming Challenges and Developing Strategies for Effective Learning," *The Psychologist* 26.2 (2013): 120–23. As the latter point out, "…since being named as an approach in the 1970s…, a number of different versions of thematic analysis have been proposed within psychology…." ("Teaching Thematic Analysis," 120). In a different place, Braun and Clarke point to Holloway and Todres as research theorists—one a medical sociologist, the other a clinical psychologist—who "…identify 'thematizing meanings' as one of a few shared generic skills across qualitative analysis" ("Using Thematic Analysis in Psychology," 78; see Immy Holloway and Les Todres, "The Status of Method: Flexibility, Consistency and Coherence," *Qualitative Research* 3.3 [2003]: 345–57).

[75] "Using Thematic Analysis in Psychology," 82, emphasis in the original.

[76] Though Braun and Clarke put forward these six steps in a linear order, they nonetheless make the following qualification cautioning against a too-strict lock-step research program: "These stages … should not be viewed as a linear model, where one cannot proceed to the next phase without completing the prior phase (correctly); rather analysis is a recursive process" ("Using Thematic Analysis in Psychology," 121). It should be noted that these six steps are now frequently cited in the psychology literature when thematic analysis is described.

> Phase 4: Review Themes
> Phase 5: Define and Name Themes
> Phase 6: Produce the Report.[77]

Rather than exploring the details of each of these steps (which will take us far afield), I shall limit myself to a couple of features resonant with Traina's methodology.

Of note in this regard is a point made by Braun and Clarke as they describe Phase 3 listed above. They claim that—after "immers[ing] yourself in the data to the extent that you are familiar with the depth and breadth of the content" in Phase 1,[78] and after "organising your date into meaningful groups" in Phase 2[79]—the researcher must begin "to analyse … codes and consider how different codes may combine to form an overarching theme. It may be helpful at this phase to use visual representations to help you sort the different codes into themes."[80]

Those familiar with Traina's inductive methodology should immediately detect features of correspondence at this point. Their statement seems to mirror a long-standing emphasis in inductive methodology related to the complicated relationship between granular particulars on the one hand, and macro structures that constitute the larger whole on the other. Traina frequently described the tension as a difference between "the bird's-eye view and the worm's-eye view." Put in another way, "… every holistic entity is comprised of material and structure, of stuff and the arrangement of stuff."[81] By immersing oneself in specifics and thereby taking note of details, one may seek unifying themes that provide insight, both to the whole considering specifics, as well to specifics in light of the whole. For Traina's method as well for thematic analysis in psychology, tacking back and forth between details, general materials, and thematic conclusions is encouraged. It is seen as the key for deepening understanding.[82]

An emphasis related to Traina's structural relationships also comes into view by way of Braun and Clarke's statement here, especially in terms of the way he taught his students to present those relationships. Utilizing a children's story (*The Giving Tree* by Shen Silverstein) as raw material for interpretive work (see SUPPLEMENT 12.3), I offer an example of how structural relationships might be visualized and presented. Likewise, in my forthcoming articles focused upon utilizing Traina's methodology for interpreting cultural scenes, I present visual breakdowns of material twice more (once in relation to the book of Nehemiah; the second based upon my field work in Indonesia,

---

[77] "Using Thematic Analysis in Psychology," 87–93.

[78] "Using Thematic Analysis in Psychology," 87.

[79] "Using Thematic Analysis in Psychology," 88.

[80] "Using Thematic Analysis in Psychology," 89.

[81] Bauer and Traina, *Inductive Bible Study*, 87.

[82] Geertz, too, explicitly recommends a type of oscillation between what he calls "experience-near" and "experience-distant" approaches to understanding (*Local Knowledge*, 55–70). The tension between these two points strongly resembles what has long been known as "the hermeneutic circle." For a seminal analysis of the critical role played by the hermeneutic circle in the process of all understanding, see Gadamer, *Truth and Method*. For a brief look at the role the hermeneutic circle plays in the analysis of a cultural scene, see Lindy Backues, "Construing Culture as Composition—Part 3: Traina's Methodology Culturally Applied," *Journal of Inductive Biblical Studies*, forthcoming.

centered on a cultural scene).[83]

In doing this I am simply following in time-honored footsteps. When Bauer and Traina offer detailed explanations of the mechanisms of structural relationships,[84] they do so assisted by a variety of visual images.[85] As professors in the classroom, Traina and Bauer each typically employed visual charts and diagrammatic representations for depicting the results of their own exegesis. Furthermore, in all written work submitted and for most in-class presentations, they also urged students to do likewise. Finally, below I also offer "visual representations" produced by my graduate students to explore the inner workings of human cognition and epistemology; these submitted visualization projects are known as "epistegraphs"—five examples are in SUPPLEMENT 12.4. Each of these visual representations is held together by linkages analogous to Traina's structural relationships—the bits and pieces "hook and eye together", as Traina (quoting W. W. White) used to say. Braun and Clarke are therefore completely justified in their claim that visual representations are helpful for sorting through data (for them, "codes") so that one might recognize themes operative in material explored. We have once again discovered a social science discipline—psychology this time, with emphasis on "thematic analysis"—that seeks to unearth interpretive themes, leitmotifs, and/or controlling ideas as tools for achieving greater insight concerning its research domain. It is my opinion that something like Traina's methodology could also be very helpful in this field if employed toward that end.

9. THE SEARCH FOR THEMES IN PARTICIPATORY DEVELOPMENT PRACTICE

> [L]imit-situations imply the existence of persons who are directly or indirectly served by these situations, and of those who are negated and curbed by them. Once the latter come to perceive these situations as the frontier between being and being more human, rather than the frontier between being and nothingness, they begin to direct their increasingly critical actions towards achieving the untested feasibility implicit in that perception. On the other hand, those who are served by the present limit-situation regard the untested feasibility as a threatening limit-situation which must not be allowed to materialize, and act to maintain the status quo. Consequently, liberating actions upon an historical milieu must correspond not only to the generative themes but to the way in which these themes are perceived. This requirement in turn implies another: the investigation of meaningful thematics.[86]

We now arrive at academic territory where I feel quite comfortable. For close to thirty years, development theory and practice has been my professional home; forays I have made into theology, into anthropology, or into any of the other academic disciplines over the years have always been

---

[83] "Part 2: Robert Traina's Methodology" and "Part 3: Traina's Methodology Culturally Applied."

[84] Beginning on page 90 of *Inductive Bible Study*.

[85] I.e., tables, charts, and graphs; note that their specific use of tabular/graphic illustrations for depicting structural relationships extends to page 93 of *Inductive Bible Study*; visual representations and graphical aids, thereafter, continue to appear throughout the book.

[86] Paolo Freire, *Pedagogy of the Oppressed* (New York: Continuum, 2005), 102.

undertaken to buttress my work in this sphere, whether in terms of activities in the field (mostly in Indonesia), or in relation to teaching and research at the university level. As will soon be seen, emphases related to thematic analysis and motif-discovery in participatory development practice seem to permeate the discipline.

First, there are open-ended hints that point in the direction of theme identification, mostly centered upon language use as played out in given communities. For example, Marxist theorist Raymond Williams pioneered a particular type of analysis that revolves around "keywords"; unique, pivotal terms he claims are embedded in societal discourse.[87] In Williams's view, keywords are "… vocabulary of a crucial area of social and cultural discussion, which has been inherited within precise historical and social conditions and which has to be made at once conscious and critical…."[88] He recommends we attend to these as portals for understanding, in order to more deeply decipher tacit community discourse when power-laden speech reverberates in societies, thereby forming and shaping its hegemonic mechanisms. Inspired by Williams's approach, not a few participatory development theorists have even reflexively doubled back upon the discipline itself, exposing terms that betray conceptual emphases that (often surprisingly, and sometimes destructively) animate the discipline itself.[89]

Next, there are representatives in the field who urge that certain themes be pressed as guides for the implementation of participatory development practice itself. For instance, noted development theorist Robert Chambers—who agrees with Williams that language "…shapes and interacts with the ways we think and behave"[90]—claims that the notion of what he calls "reversals" must be at the heart of all participatory development practice efforts. Tangible proof of these "reversals" will appear, he claims, as development professionals become willing to (1) empty power, (2) sacrifice status, and (3) relinquish privilege.[91] More germane to our current point, though, is when Chambers—after explaining that one of his earlier books[92] is centrally "about rural poverty and the perceptions, attitudes, learning, ways of thinking and behaviour of professionals …"—reveals that "its original title was 'Putting the Last First: Reversals for Rural Development', and *it retains reversals as a*

---

[87] Williams was the founder of that potage of academic disciplines known as "Cultural Studies." His most celebrated book is a collection of words that he felt were overlooked clues for understanding Western society. See Raymond Williams, *Keywords: A Vocabulary of Culture and Society* (revised ed.; New York: Oxford University Press, 1983). For an interesting example of this approach in relation to the keyword "development" as historically employed by those in power in Indonesia, see Ariel Heryanto, "The Development of 'Development'," trans. Nancy Lutz, *Indonesia* 46 (1988): 1–24.

[88] *Keywords*, 24.

[89] See, e.g., Wolfgang Sachs, ed., *The Development Dictionary: A Guide to Knowledge as Power* (New York: Zed Books, 1992) and Andrea Cornwall and Deborah Eade, *Deconstructing Development Discourse: Buzzwords and Fuzzwords* (Warwickshire, UK: Practical Action, 2010).

[90] "Editorial: Responsible Well-Being—A Personal Agenda for Development," *World Development* 25.11 (1997): 1743–54 at 1745.

[91] Robert Chambers, *Rural Development: Putting the Last First* (Essex, UK: Addison Wesley Longman, 1983).

[92] *Rural Development*.

central theme—the need for them, their feasibility, and their personal implications."[93]

Chambers represents many who take thematic emphases in the field to be very important, primarily because these themes can then serve as conduits for authentic grassroots change and community empowerment. For those of us who are Christian, linking these discipline-related thematic emphases to themes discovered in the biblical text can offer robust opportunity for fashioning on-the-ground development programs that are based on biblically funded ethics (i.e., ethics rooted in the themes of the biblical narrative itself). I hope to show below that this has been an emphasis of mine these past few years.

Finally, and possibly most important, many development theorists take a search for themes in local contexts to be the first step in instantiating authentic efforts of demonstrable justice. The reason is, many believe that the poor are marginalized and denigrated because they *simply are not sincerely listened to*! Representative of this position is well-known Brazilian educator Paolo Freire, who defines poverty as when persons are trapped in "a culture of silence."[94] He explains,

> [T]he masses are mute, that is, they are prohibited from creatively taking part in the transformation of their society and therefore prohibited from being. Even if they can occasionally read and write because they were "taught" in humanitarian—but not humanist—literacy campaigns, they are nevertheless alienated from the power responsible for their silence.[95]

Freire claims that the only way to address such "voice-muting" structural oppression is for the poor to regain their voices, principally by discovering what Freire calls their own "generative themes," i.e., issues about which they care deeply and for which they themselves are willing to sacrifice. Such efforts involve an

> investigation of ... the people's "thematic universe"—the complex of their "generative themes"—[which] inaugurates the dialogue of education as the practice of freedom. The methodology of that investigation must likewise be dialogical, affording *the opportunity*

---

[93] *Rural Development*, 1 of the Preface, emphasis added.

[94] Paolo Freire, *The Politics of Education: Culture, Power, and Liberation* (Westport, CT: Bergin & Garvey, 1985). Persons inspired by Freire's ideas are many. Representative here are Dave Beck and Rod Purcell, *Popular Education Practice for Youth and Community Development Work* (Exeter, UK: Learning Matters, 2010), David Cavallo, Paulo Blikstein, Arnan Sipitakiat, Anindita Basu, Alexandra Camargo, Roseli de Deus Lopes, and Alice Cavallo, *The City that We Want: Generative Themes, Constructionist Technologies and School/Social Change* (Joensuu, Finland: Advanced Learning Technologies, IEEE International Conference on [ICALT], 2004), 1034–38; bell hooks, *Teaching to Transgress: Education as the Practice of Freedom* (New York: Routledge, 1994); and Ellen Joanne Millard, "The Investigation of Generative Themes in E.S.L. Needs Assessment" (MA Thesis; Vancouver, British Columbia: The University of British Columbia, 1986). "Participatory Action-Research", or PAR, could also be mentioned as another liberative research methodology (unfortunately, I do not have room to explore PAR, even though it also emphasizes the discovery of indigenous themes and motifs). For a description of the theory behind PAR and its implementation, see Orlando Fals-Borda and Mohammad Anisur Rahman, ed., *Action and Knowledge: Breaking the Monopoly with Participatory Action-Research* (London: Intermediate Technology, 1991).

[95] Freire, *Politics of Education*, 50.

> *both to discover generative themes and to stimulate people's awareness in regard to these themes.* Consistent with the liberating purpose of dialogical education, the object of the investigation is not persons (as if they were anatomical fragments), but rather the thought-language with which men and women refer to reality, the levels at which they perceive that reality, and their view of the world, in which their generative themes are found.[96]

Freire also suggests that a collection of these themes coming together constitutes an "epoch", i.e., "a complex of ideas, concepts, hopes, doubts, values, and challenges in dialectical interaction with their opposites, striving towards plenitude."[97] In sum, generative themes are first unearthed, relationships between these themes are identified, and this results in a larger composite known as an "epoch": one could rebrand it a "cultural domain." I believe this accurately equates to something like the Indonesian cultural scene I label "Clean-up as a Cultural Domain" in one of my other publications.[98] And, to identify such a domain and thereafter appraise it for meaning, the interpretive (ethnographic) methodology I use there is one I adapt from Traina's approach.

We haven't the space here to unpack Freire's specific recommendations on how to identify generative themes or epochs.[99] Nonetheless, as I have shown above, the process of theme identification seems best undertaken by way of something like the structural relationships of contrast and recurrence. Additionally, an approach akin to Spradley's ethnographic method might also assist in isolating generative themes. Nonetheless, the primary point I am making is that unearthing of themes like these is an integral feature of Freire's approach to empowerment of the poor, since he asserts this as the way they best voice their own interests and passions. As the poor begin speaking for themselves—as they discover and utilize their own themes, metaphors, and motifs—they themselves become agents, making choices by putting forward their own perspectives and conclusions.

We need to attend to one last point here. Many a theorist has advocated that participatory, thematic approaches are all about prompting appropriate questioning—what is hoped for is a collective quizzing of problems so that meaning previously overlooked might be uncovered. Clearly, this sort of interrogative probing mirrors steps in Traina's methodology, too. Yet, as we also saw, it is all too easy to get the question-posing process confused: there are risks in posing ill-chosen questions and it is possible to assume too much as questions are selected, allowing bias to slip in by way of

---

[96] *Pedagogy of the Oppressed*, 96–97, emphasis added.

[97] *Pedagogy of the Oppressed*, 101. Freire goes on to describe what he means by "epoch": "The concrete representation of many of these ideas, values, concepts, and hopes, as well as the obstacles which impede the people's full humanization, constitute the themes of that epoch. These themes imply others which are opposing or even antithetical; they also indicate tasks to be carried out and fulfilled. Thus, historical themes are never isolated, independent, disconnected, or static; they are always interacting dialectically with their opposites. Nor can these themes be found anywhere except in the human-world relationship. *The complex of interacting themes of an epoch constitutes its 'thematic universe'*" (*Pedagogy of the Oppressed*, 101, emphasis added).

[98] "Part 3: Traina's Methodology Culturally Applied."

[99] Perhaps Freire's most concise description of the process of eliciting generative themes can be found in his *Education for Critical Consciousness* (New York: Harper & Row, 1973).

artificial imposition of one's private perspective. We must remember, the goal is to scratch where it itches. Not surprisingly, persons like Holstein and Gubrium have noticed this problem, too.

> Traditionally, qualitative inquiry has concerned itself with *what* and *how* questions. *Why* questions have been the hallmark of quantitative sociology, which seeks to explain and ostensibly predict behavior. Qualitative researchers typically approach *why* questions cautiously. Explanation is a tricky business, one that qualitative inquiry embraces discreetly in light of its appreciation for *interpretive elasticity*. It is one thing to describe what is going on and how things or events take shape, but the question of why things happen the way they do can lead to inferential leaps and empirical speculations that propel qualitative analysis far from its stock-in-trade. The challenge is to respond to *why* question [sic] in ways that are empirically and conceptually consonant with qualitative inquiry's traditional concerns.[100]

Indeed, as we have seen, this *is* the challenge. But, it is also quite interesting that these authors put forward a solution very much like that we heard Traina (and Bauer) recommend above.

> One way for qualitative inquiry to approach *why* questions without hazarding its traditional analytic interests is to proceed from the *whats* and *hows* of social life. Provisional explanatory footing can be found at the junction of concerns for what is going on in everyday life in relation to how that is constructed, centered in the space we have located interpretive practice. Bracketing the *whats*, footing for explaining the constructive nuances of social patterns can be found in discursive practice. Bracketing the *hows*, footing for explaining the delimited patterns of meaning consequent to social construction processes can be found in discourses-in-practice.[101]

Thus, they recommend that (1) we keep questions tied to structure (as we wish to do, given our understanding of structural relationships as explored above), and (2) there be a proper sequencing of questions, with "what" and "how" questions being posed before "why" questions (of course, we heard Traina recommend something like this, too; he also recommended that these be followed by posing "implicational" questions, as well). These observations—those related to structure and others linked to how questions should be tendered—represent an interesting convergence of emphasis for us, a similarity to Traina's method that confirms that his interpretive system can happily coexist with those advocated for qualitative, social science research methods. More than that, since Traina's method is so robust, I believe it can strengthen them.

---

[100] "Interpretive Practice and Social Action," in *The Sage Handbook of Qualitative Research*, 3rd ed.; ed. Norman K. Denzin and Yvonna S. Lincoln (Los Angeles: Sage, 2005): 483–505 at 498, emphasis in the original. As I explain more fully in "Part 2: Robert Traina's Methodology," Traina categorized "How" questions (what he called modal questions)—alongside "Where" questions, "When" questions, and "Who" questions—seeing those as a subset of "What" question (variations on the definitive or explanatory question). As he put it, these types of questions function as definitive questions in terms of different aspects: "What?" in terms of *means, geography, time,* and *biography,* respectively.

[101] Holstein and Gubrium, "Interpretive Practice and Social Action," 498, emphasis in the original.

10. STRUCTURAL RELATIONSHIPS AND THE SEARCH FOR THEMES IN MY OWN PRACTICE

Ruth Page offers the following helpful description of the interrelations between different subject matter:

> Some metaphors ... work only as surprising, suggestive figures of speech and cannot take the strain of having their implications teased out in the extension of a model.... But drama, which concerns action and relationship through time, has already proved fruitful enough for social psychologists to use it as a model for all interaction in the serious play which is human life. It is equally serviceable for the action of salvation and the person of the saviour. Both sociological and more strictly dramaturgical aspects will come into play in this model. But it will remain a model: that is to say that sets of relationships in a known sphere (drama, society) will be used to illuminate relationships in another (God, Christ, humanity) to assist comprehension and action. Models are human and finite *ways* of understanding which work when they are appropriate to their subject-matter and fruitful in practice.[102]

So how might all of this play out? If there has indeed been an interpretive turn—a metaphorical turn, if you will—in the social sciences these past decades, how might Traina's model for interpretation be used to advantage in activities involving social science research, teaching, or writing? I wish to suggest some answers to these questions. As I said at the outset, for a good many years I have experimented with these ideas: in my teaching, in my research, and even in my own writings. I therefore now turn in order to briefly explore each of these areas, complete with examples of the role Traina's interpretive method has played in the process.

10.1 Teaching

Due to what we have seen above, if properly adapted, Traina's method is quite useful for students in the social sciences. Much depends, though, on the way it is introduced. I have found it important to begin simply, employing materials easily approached, easily accessed, and easily understood.

When I first introduce Traina's methodology to students, I begin by distributing handouts that summarize the approach. SUPPLEMENT 12.1—STRUCTURAL RELATIONSHIPS HANDOUT represents a list of Traina's structural relationships, complete with (1) an explanation of each relationship, (2) an illustration of each connection within the biblical materials, and (3) an example of an overt "linguistic indicator" that points to the presence of the relationship (if that relationship manifests such an indicator—not all of them do). Next, I hand out what is found in SUPPLEMENT 12.2—SHORT EXPLANATION OF METHODICAL BIBLE STUDY. This is an abbreviated, 2-page unpacking of Traina's methodology, a short introduction to the steps found in the process.[103] These two tools permit me to walk students conceptually through Traina's approach, familiarizing them with its basic components.

---

[102] Page, *Incarnation of Freedom and Love*, 92–93, emphasis in the original.
[103] As can be seen in the document itself, there are several other handouts distributed in support of these two pages. For examples of these additional handouts, see Backues, "Part 2: Robert Traina's Methodology."

For development of skills like this, though, learning is in the doing. To give students opportunity for immediate application of the method, I ask that they try it out on a children's story: I have found Shel Silverstein's *The Giving Tree* works well.[104] A short children's story enables students to quickly read the materials in question in one sitting, with the added benefit of attempting something relatively easy to accomplish (since the story is simple to understand).[105] As we work through the various structural relationships evident in *The Giving Tree*, students become increasingly familiar with the process. Moreover, since meaning previously unrecognized inevitably opens before them, their appreciation of the method increases. Finally, using Traina's inductive Bible study methodology with materials that are not sacred scripture helps students to realize how universal the hermeneutical process is. These materials serve as introductory instruction, giving students opportunity to use and get comfortable with Traina's method.

An additional way I underscore the importance of themes for students (to cultivate their realization that social sciences are built upon motifs) is by assigning reading materials that accentuate themes as central planks in their research programs. I will cite three examples; I assign each of these as readings to students in my undergraduate class *Faith and Economic Justice*.

First there is Richard Hays's *The Moral Vision of the New Testament*, a volume already highlighted above. As I pointed out there, Hays emphasizes three focal images that he claims act like "single synoptic imaginative judgments" in the New Testament materials, "root metaphors embedded in the New Testament texts ... [that] encapsulate the crucial elements of the narrative and serve to focus our attention on the common ground shared by the various [NT] witnesses."[106] Hays argues that the principal focal images in the New Testament materials are (1) community, (2) cross, and (3) new creation. He cites community as a focal image because there is significant emphasis on the church as "a countercultural community of discipleship ... the primary addressee of God's imperatives"[107] Hays takes the Cross to be a focal image since "Jesus' death on a cross is the paradigm for faithfulness to God in this world"[108] And, finally, Hays believes new creation serves as a focal image because "the church embodies the power of the resurrection in the midst of a not-yet-redeemed world."[109]

Hays points to community, cross, and new creation as synoptic imaginative judgments—the controlling root metaphors or themes in the New Testament—because (a) they "find ... textual basis in all of the canonical witnesses", (b) they do not "stand in serious tension with the ethical teaching or major emphases of any of the New Testament witnesses", and (c) they "highlight central and

---

[104] Shel Silverstein, *The Giving Tree* (New York: HarperCollins, 1999). For my own structural breakdown of that story, see SUPPLEMENT 12.3—SURVEY/ANALYSIS OF SHEL SILVERSTEIN'S *THE GIVING TREE*.

[105] I distribute several copies of the book to groups of students in the class—with that, they have the materials in question directly before them.

[106] *Moral Vision of the New Testament*, 194.

[107] *Moral Vision of the New Testament*, 196.

[108] *Moral Vision of the New Testament*, 197.

[109] *Moral Vision of the New Testament*, 198.

substantial ethical concerns of the texts in which [they appear]."[110] That being so, community, cross, and new creation can function as central ballasts for understanding and applying the New Testament, tropes helpful for operationalizing biblical truth in the here and now.[111]

Clearly, Hays is undertaking what social scientists call "thematic analysis." More connected to our purposes is the fact his approach corresponds well with Traina's system as described above—an outcome I point out to students (after I have introduced them to Traina as described above) by comparing Hays's theme-search methodology with Traina's. I underscore to students the way Hays sets the stage for us; if we agree with him about the centrality of these themes (community, cross, and new creation), we then must ensure they play a prominent role in helping us determine which economic configurations and systems we should embrace.

We now turn to another thinker who uses thematic analysis in his research program: Donald Hay,[112] especially as exemplified by his eight *Biblical Principles for Economic Life*.[113] Hay begins by deriving these eight principles from the biblical narrative, standards he thereafter uses to assess the theological legitimacy of capitalism and socialism. Before doing that, though, he sorts these eight principles into three overarching categories:[114]

1. Creation and Humanity's Dominion,[115]
2. Humans and Work,[116] and
3. Distribution of Goods.[117]

Thereafter, he distills these three categories—that encompass the eight principles—into a single, thematic image: *stewardship*, an idea he sees as "the organizing concept for [our] biblical principles...."[118] Stewardship, he explains,

> reminds us that our personal talents and abilities, and the natural resources with which we work, are God's provision for us. They are not our personal possessions but are entrusted to us. We will, therefore, have to give account to God as to the use that we have made of them. We exercise our stewardship particularly in work, which involves an exercise of the will to direct our energies and talents. The fruits of our work are goods and services, the purpose of human dignity as a person created in the image of God, placed in a good creation. But work does not imply the right to consume all the fruits of our

---

[110] *Moral Vision of the New Testament*, 195.

[111] In the remainder of his book, Hays utilizes these three focal images for addressing various contentious issues found in society today.

[112] Students in class frequently confuse these two authors: one is Richard *Hays*, the other Donald *Hay*.

[113] Donald A. Hay, *Economics Today: A Christian Critique* (Vancouver: Regent College, 2004), 72–76.

[114] Hay does not employ gender inclusive language; thus, I have taken liberty to modify his language a bit in what follows.

[115] Hay, *Economics Today*, 72–73.

[116] Hay, *Economics Today*, 73–75.

[117] Hay, *Economics Today*, 75–76.

[118] Hay, *Economics Today*, 71.

labours, since we are stewards working on God's behalf with the talents he has provided. There is therefore an obligation on those who have much to provide for those who have little. There is also an implicit warning that the desire to hold on to what one has produced is a denial of God's ultimate ownership. Materialism is closely related to idolatry in biblical thought.[119]

The rest of Hay's book is somewhat of a primer on how to apply these eight economic principles, these three overarching categories—this one, decisive leitmotif—in theological analysis toward the global economy. It is a case study on how to interpretively sound out a social science by way of biblical, thematic analysis.

Hay's example is very instructive for my students. He represents a social scientist who overtly moves toward biblical materials in search of guiding, interpretive themes—of course, he settles upon the central leitmotif of *stewardship*—and then he theologically appraises contemporary economic systems using those same principles. With Hay as a model—potentially combined with and strengthened by Traina's methodology—students witness the fruit interpretive methods can produce when focused upon social science research. I make sure to point that out, every chance I get. And, once again, they are left with a central theme—this time, stewardship—that can assist them in coming to grips with the economic choices placed before them.

Our third example comes from two prominent Christian ethicists, David Gushee and Glen Stassen, who approach biblical teaching by giving attention to the life and teachings of Jesus, especially as understood through the prism of the Sermon on the Mount.[120] I haven't space here to examine their method in its entirety, but it is important to note their central concern is to explore how scripture should inform ethics. They begin by observing that

> Christians (and, in fact, all people) organize and communicate their moral convictions—technically known as moral norms—at four different levels: the particular judgments/actions level, the rules level, the principles level, and the basic-convictions level. Finding congruence between these levels is vital so that ethics is neither too vague and abstract nor too legalistic and superficial. Scripture offers numerous examples of each level of moral norms.[121]

Gushee and Stassen tease out differences between these four levels. Basic-convictions are those tacitly-embraced beliefs each of us hold concerning the nature of reality; one could say these convictions make up our world view at the most rudimentary level. Far more concrete are rules, since they "… give reasons for particular judgments/actions…." A bit more abstract than rules are principles, which "… give reasons for rules. Rules can also criticize particular judgments/actions;

---

[119] Hay, *Economics Today*, 71.
[120] David P. Gushee and Glen H. Stassen, *Kingdom Ethics: Following Jesus in Contemporary Context*, 2nd ed. (Grand Rapids: Eerdmans, 2016).
[121] *Kingdom Ethics*, 64.

principles can criticize rules. Rules serve principles, not the other way around."[122] In short, we are to establish rules—thereafter living our lives by way of particular judgments/actions—based upon principles. This being so, the authors spend much of the early part of their book trying to understand what principles are, seeing as how "... a principle is more general than a rule; it does not tell us directly and concretely what to do."[123] When viewed in this way, principles are virtually identical to what we have been calling themes.

Later in the book the authors, utilizing these themes/principles as tools for ethicizing, concern themselves specifically with materials presenting implications for economics. After examining these materials, they proffer five major principles/themes they claim derive from Jesus's teaching on money in the gospels.[124]

1. The relative (un)importance of possessions:

    "Possessions are intrinsically insignificant beyond the basic sufficiency provided by our gracious God."[125]

2. The role materialism often plays in inciting greed:

    "Misreading the value of possessions stimulates greed."[126]

3. The pervasive lifestyle implications of greed:

    "Greed encourages a lifestyle of luxury, pride, hoarding, self-indulgence, oppression and lack of generosity."[127]

4. The stunting, strangling effect wealth can have on one's spiritual maturity:

    "The deceptive allure of wealth can choke discipleship and imperil the soul."[128]

5. The profound degree to which Jesus identified with the poor:

    "Jesus identified with the poor and promises abundance and justice in a coming 'great reversal'."[129]

Exploring this further threatens a drift away from our main point. Yet, it is good to note that Gushee and Stassen present us with—as did Hays and Hay—probing scriptural themes and noteworthy governing principles; these can function as ethical scaffolding enabling us to cultivate ethics more biblically faithful in relation to money, to wealth, and to possessions. If we agree with these five

---

[122] *Kingdom Ethics*, 68.
[123] *Kingdom Ethics*, 68.
[124] *Kingdom Ethics*, 365.
[125] *Kingdom Ethics*, 365.
[126] *Kingdom Ethics*, 366.
[127] *Kingdom Ethics*, 367.
[128] *Kingdom Ethics*, 368.
[129] *Kingdom Ethics*, 369.

principles, it might just be possible to establish rules related to economics that are conceptually sponsored by these themes. These will be rules that yield judgments and actions more faithful to the specific generative themes initiating action in the first place (note the similarity here to Freire's language as noted above).

Returning directly to our original aim, it is quite helpful to recognize what Traina's methodology permits students to do. First, it allows them to test the biblical centrality of a set of narrative themes suggested by a given author (for instance, that put forward by Hays, Hay, or Gushee and Stassen). Should the centrality of these themes end up corroborated by the biblical text,[130] they then can be used to establish sound Christian positions on a variety of issues.[131] Traina's methodology affords students opportunity to verify the veracity and accuracy of themes they discover or those put before them.

The second possibility follows from the first. Having established—with a degree of confidence—the scriptural centrality of a given theme, it can then be compared to a social science theme unearthed by way of thematic analysis. In this way, "deep grammar" can be compared with "deep grammar", "thick description" with "thick description", biblical text emphasis can be juxtaposed alongside vital social science postulate. Comparing and contrasting themes in this way frequently offers rich insight. I hope to show briefly below how I have attempted to do this in my own writings in several places.

Returning to my attempts to underscore themes in teaching, I am also drawn to experiences I have had teaching in the field of anthropology—I have lectured on the subject both at the undergraduate and the graduate levels. In introductory courses, I generally endorse the value of Traina's eleven relationships in the doing of ethnography (I highlight the similarity between these relationships and Spradley's steps in his "Developmental Research Sequence Method"). I encourage students to be mindful of where these relationships appear, and I also urge them to make full use of interpretive questions as the relationships come into view (I point to Traina and Spradley's common directives concerning the use of questions).[132] Here, again, in order to offer to them an illustration of how these relationships work, I find it useful to point to my analysis of *The Giving Tree* as parsed in SUPPLEMENT 12.3.

I have also found elements of Traina's method useful for my graduate anthropology students as they complete a collection of assignments for an epistemology class I teach. Three times a

---

[130] For instance, with an adequate grasp of Traina's methodology, it is possible for students to verify or reject the "community, cross, and new creation" idea from Richard Hays; or the idea that "stewardship" is best seen as *the* central notion in the Bible in respect to land, assets, and property holdings; or the centrality of the five themes in Jesus's teaching on the economic life underscored by Gushee and Stassen.

[131] Something like this flow—from biblical material, to themes, to ethical application—is one of the two ways Bruce C. Birch and Larry L. Rasmussen in *Bible and Ethics in the Christian Life* (Minneapolis: Augsburg Fortress, 1988) recommend biblical ethics be done. The other is a flow in the opposite direction, from principle/theme to text. They highlight the methodologies and pitfalls found in each way.

[132] Backues, "Part 3: Traina's Methodology Culturally Applied," gives an example of my use of Traina's methodology as means for doing ethnography.

semester, students submit to me something I call an "epistegraph"—a visual representation depicting how they see belief systems functioning.[133] Alongside a visual component, each epistegraph must also include a narrative portion, a description that gives insight to their drawing. At the end of each semester, they must also present a collective epistegraph: how they, as a group, see it constructed, how it works, how it withstands challenges, how it bends, buckles and perhaps deconstructs. This becomes their final epistegraph, and students consistently find the cooperative process of putting it together enlightening. They have repeatedly told me that Traina's structural relationships are useful for describing linkages between components depicted in their epistegraphs—his description of these (and the questions accompanying them) often play an important role in the narrative descriptions they write. Moreover, his methodology and his description of structural relationships also provides for them a common language useful in their group project.

10.2 Research Supervision

I have also guided graduate research in the use of structural relationships and themes, both in the fields of anthropology as well as in urban studies and development. I will briefly highlight the product of these emphases by pointing to the work of two of my research students.

In a thesis entitled *Liminality and the Chinese Indonesian Experience in South Philadelphia*, one student employed a variation on Traina's method in her research methodology (she gave attention to the appearance of recurrence and contrast in her field materials); in doing so, she helpfully excavated a multi-tiered network of thematic relationships, concepts that later served as the backbone of her analysis. Four themes seemed to arise in her investigation: (1) *quest*, (2) *liminality*, (3) *loss*, and (4) *living under the radar*. These ideas became refrains she was able to further deconstruct, resulting in a final write-up that traced the contours of these keywords and what they suggest. Here is the outline of what she discovered:

Chinese Indonesian Immigrants in South Philadelphia:

> **were on a *quest*, for:**
> *a)* **safety,**
> *b)* **belonging,**
> *c)* **economic stability, and**
> *d)* **providence (implying movement and an ability to imagine the future).**

As immigrants, they also:

> **experienced *liminality*, resulting in:**
> *a)* **fear,**
> *b)* **trauma,**
> *c)* **vulnerability to: scapegoating, attacks, discrimination, exploitation, and**
> *d)* **an arrested journey (not being allowed to arrive).**

---

[133] Examples of individual epistegraphs from my students can be found in SUPPLEMENT 12.4—STUDENT EPISTEGRAPHS FROM *EPISTEMOLOGICAL INSIGHTS FOR ANTHROPOLOGICAL PRACTICE*.

They also:

faced *loss*:
- *a)* of home, and
- *b)* of family.

Finally, they:

ended up *living under the radar*, **resulting in:**
- *a)* avoidance of trouble,
- *b)* a life without documentation, and
- *c)* being trapped in a culture of silence.

By posing questions to this arrangement—in a manner akin to what Traina and Spradley suggest—this student managed to bring to light features that she otherwise would have overlooked. Furthermore, in the process of working with these themes and their questions, she unearthed clues related to more research possibilities, hints that kicked up additional questions upon returning to her informants. This student's thesis ended up a rich example of thick description.

A different research student—this time working in anthropology—walked a similar path. In her thesis, *Folk Art and Fine Art from the Puerto Rican Diaspora: Exploring the Tension between Beauty and Pain,* she, too, gave significant attention to recurring themes, noting in which domains they surfaced, paying attention to when (and in what way) a shift in thematic emphasis took place (thus, looking for contrasts in themes). In this way, she managed to isolate three powerful tropes—1) tension, (2) cultural preservation, and (3) resistance—with the first concept further divided into additional groupings: (a) beauty and (b) pain. This is the outline she produced:

Puerto Rican residents in north Philadelphia employ both folk art and fine art to exploit

tension **between**
- *a)* *beauty*, **and**
- *b)* *pain.*

These residents creatively utilize this tension to fashion their own notions of Puerta Rican

cultural preservation,

ones that offer resources for

resistance

in the face of encroaching North American, Anglo cultural and political forces.

In doing her analysis, this student simply traced the contours of her breakdown, allowing it to guide her as she explored its nuances in context. Perhaps the key coupling she discovered was a creative tension between local emphases on beauty and on pain (at some level, this appears to be a contrast, of course). A whole battery of questions arose from such these configurations:

What is meant by beauty in this context? What is meant by pain? How are they different? How are they alike? Are they opposites or are they mutually supporting emphases? What is meant by tension? What makes it a tension (what cultural components are contrasting)? Why the tension here? What is meant by cultural preservation? Why the need for cultural preservation? Who is doing the preserving (agency)? What is resistance? Who is doing the resisting (agency again)? How does cultural preservation differ from resistance? Are agents of the two processes different people/actors? If so, in what way do they differ? What are the similarities between cultural preservation and resistance? Why the need for resistance? What are the implications (the assumptions and the outgrowths) found embedded in the questions above?

Simply by selecting a few of these questions and exploring answers to them (utilizing data and information derived from the context), this student produced a fine example of field-based research, ushering the reader into a Geertzian interwoven glimpse of the situation obtaining in north Philadelphia Puerto Rican neighborhoods.

10.3 Themes in My Own Research

Since the dawn of my academic career—from my PhD work carrying forward until today—theme discovery has been evident. My practice has been to investigate the biblical text, to examine theological materials, to explore the social sciences, and to engage in a variety of cultural contexts, all by way of something approaching the methodology just described. Surely, one can detect the arc of such a process on display as I have laid things out above. In my writing, I have searched for themes in texts and contexts, and I have tried to bring these together in written results, both in terms of comparisons as well as contrasts. The approach has proved very fruitful for me. And at the heart of it all has been Traina's methodology, a stance that has helpfully colored all my efforts.

In *The Image of the Incarnation as Motif for Development Practice in West Java, Indonesia*—and in its abridged version—I put forward six marks of the Incarnation (as I call them), points that suggest the picture of Jesus may serve as a singular guiding image or paradigm for development practice.[134] For me, these themes aggregate into a defining portrait—a controlling metaphor—for all of Christian ethics: the image of the Incarnation, the theological prospect "God become flesh." I soon discovered that this notion of Incarnation carries with it ethical implications, a point underscored by Bonk when he calls for mission models more faithful to the pattern.

> At the very least, the Incarnation means giving up the power, privilege, and social position which are our natural due. Christ's mission in Christ's way must always begin, proceed, and end with the great renunciation. And this sacrifice is made not merely with reference to "what could have been" back home, but by the standards of the people among whom the missionary is called to incarnate the gospel. This does not leave much room for the power-generating, status-inflating, career-building, self-protecting affluence to

---

[134] Backues, "The Image of the Incarnation as Motif for Development Practice in West Java" (PhD Thesis; Leeds UK: The University of Leeds, 2003) and idem, "The Incarnation as Motif for Development Practice," in *World Mission in a Wesleyan Spirit*, ed. Darrell L. Whiteman and Gerald H. Anderson (Nashville: Providence, 2009): 310–23. The six-marks model that I put forward encourages development practice that is (1) narratively enacted, (2) residentially near, (3) physically encountered, (4) socially embedded, (5) flexibly available, and (6) verifiably emptied.

which emissaries of the Western churches have become accustomed.[135]

Without the notion of the Incarnation as a controlling image—as a living metaphor ethically funding Christian practice—such a call makes little sense.[136]

I also found that this overarching image of the Incarnation suggests an analogous principle: the idea of "kenosis" or self-emptying. In some of my writings I have emphasized this idea as a standard—at times doing so overtly, at other times more tacitly.

I have stressed self-emptying overtly as "a unifying theme in Christian thought, both in terms of how Christians are to understand God as well as how the Christian life should be taken up by adherents of the faith."[137] I found that the reason for this is simple: self-emptying is "a constituting, divine characteristic fundamental to the Christian concept of God—one could say kenosis, Christianly understood, represents a distinctive attribute of God's very being."[138] Thus, what we have in this image is "a word-picture replete with an ethical principle one might emulate, exhorting adherents to exhibit a certain lifestyle and a corporeally-involved manner of behavior in the world."[139] For the Christian, this is *the* primary narrative theme.

More tacitly, I have championed self-emptying as important in all authentic attempts at interfaith dialogue, since this sort of discourse demands that participants listen deeply, be willing to surrender control, and engage interpersonally with "mutual respect, dialogue and humble listening...."[140] In these contexts, "hubristic bravado and a will to win should be given no space...."[141] I have also tacitly underscored kenosis in other ways, by encouraging development professionals to deftly and semiotically subvert hierarchical patron-client relationships in the manner of the self-emptying Christ—by imploding these couplings from the inside-out—thereby embracing "… the symbolic oppositions and contests that the poor and marginalized face."[142]

---

[135] Jonathan J. Bonk, *Missions and Money: Affluence as a Western Missionary Problem* (New York: Orbis, 1991), 117.

[136] As Bonk says, the image of the Incarnation is not just theologically descriptive; it is also strategically prescriptive (*Missions and Money*, 116).

[137] Backues, "Humility," 111.

[138] Backues, "Humility," 112. WH Vanstone claims that the God "revealed is the very God who 'empties Himself'—Whose whole and total activity is the activity of self-emptying, or Kenosis. The Kenosis of the Redeemer, His surrender of that which He might have held, will then be the perfect manifestation of the Kenosis of God. The 'emptiness' of the Redeemer, in the poverty and humility of His historical existence, will point to the 'emptiness' of God in and through His eternal activity: and the Kenosis in Christ, so far from impairing the fullness of His disclosure of God, will in fact contain the very heart and substance of that disclosure" *Love's Endeavour, Love's Expense: The Response of Being to the Love of God* (London: Darton, Longman, and Todd, 1977). 58.

[139] Backues, "Humility," 112.

[140] Lindy Backues, "Interfaith Development Efforts as Means to Peace and Witness," *Transformation* 26.2 (2009): 67–81 at 77.

[141] Backues, "Interfaith Development Efforts," 77.

[142] Lindy Backues, "Symbols of the Weak, Symbols of the Gospel: The Upside-Down Gospel in Relation to Patronage Systems in West Java, Indonesia," in *Christian Mission and Economic Systems: A Critical Survey of the Cultural and Religious Dimensions of Economies*, ed. John Cheong and Eloise Meneses (Pasadena, CA: William Carey

We have seen this posture before. We need only recall Robert Chambers's summons to development professionals to embrace "reversals", i.e., to surrender power, sacrifice status, and relinquish privilege. This, he admonished, is the bedrock of all good development work. It just so happens it is also thematically equivalent to the biblical idea of kenosis and self-emptying. Likewise, it parallels Bonk's exhortation toward "the great renunciation", a move that—as he says—epitomizes "Christ's mission in Christ's way" (cf. his statement above). These thematic parallels are very interesting. I will make something of them in the conclusion.

Finally, in a work concerned mostly with the discipline of anthropology and its vocational tool—ethnography—I have emphasized the importance of humility as a principal theme.[143] My interest was to link humility in theology to epistemological and methodological humility in anthropology, showing how the idea is key for each. In a word, I believe that a sincerely embraced spirituality that is true to the Christian narrative can help produce profound ethnographies—ones that are thick, multi-valent, deep, complex, and faithful in nature. A theological image centered on incarnational humility endorses embodied, personal praxis in concrete, local communities, because humble, reflexive ethnographic research ends up

> sacredly endorsed as a form of religious piety and devotion, a style endorsed and motivated by transcendent purpose that the Christian sees as worshipful faithfulness to a God who did it first. The nature of this endorsement (1) mitigates abstract epistemology detached from actual communities, while it also (2) safeguards against a distorted, reified anthropology. The first pitfall (theoretical abstraction) threatens to replace concrete understanding of the context with theoretical intellectual models that often do not obtain; the second snare (a caricatured image of others) replaces local people's actual beliefs, feelings, and experiences with disembodied notions of who they are (or who we think they should be).[144]

I contend that developing humility allows the social scientist to come alongside—to be "with"—in a way that makes possible authentic understanding and true insight as the payoff.

Library, 2015), 113–47 at 115.

[143] Backues, "Humility."

[144] Backues, "Humility," 128. I believe the statement below by Karl Barth to be very pertinent to my point:

> We may believe that God can and must only be absolute in contrast to all that is relative, exalted in contrast to all that is lowly, active in contrast to all suffering, inviolable in contrast to all temptation, transcendent in contrast to all immanence, and therefore divine in contrast to everything human, in short that He can and must be only the 'Wholly Other.' But such beliefs are shown to be quite untenable, and corrupt and pagan, by the fact that God does in fact be and do this in Jesus Christ. We cannot make them the standard by which to measure what God can or cannot do, or the basis of the judgment that in doing this He brings Himself into self-contradiction. By doing this God proves to us that He can do it, that to do it is within His nature. And He shows Himself to be more great and rich and sovereign than we had ever imagined. And our ideas of His nature must be guided by this, and not *vice versa* (*Church Dogmatics* IV/1, §59, 186).

In this brief survey of my own research and writings, one can clearly see that the identification of themes plays a consequential role in constituting my own ethical horizon. First, by approaching the biblical text by way of Traina's methodology for many years now, three themes—Incarnation, self-emptying, and humility—have arisen as central optics for me, ones that have shaped my personal moral outlook as well as my ethical framework. Secondly, in my evaluation of various social science constructs on offer—after organizing themes in each have been identified (by way of an approach similar to that illustrated above)—I embrace only those approaches whose central theses comport with my three ballasting, central motifs. I feel utterly at liberty to take up those anthropological, sociological, political, and development praxis approaches that mirror at their core the Incarnation, the notion of kenosis, and a posture of humility. Those that do not, I eschew.

Traina's methodology has been central for me in this entire process, from beginning to end. For thirty years.

11. Conclusion

> [T]he omnipresence of God is fundamental, so that God is part of every situation, whether recognized and acknowledged or not. The whole vertical axis of God above and humanity below, although it is so frequent in the tradition, is here replaced by the horizontal axis of God accompanying creation, vividly expressed in the fire and smoke which companioned the Israelites in the wilderness. There are therefore no "sending" motifs in this christology, at least as far as pre-existence and descent are concerned, although Jesus, like the prophets, was called or sent by God. "Sending" as it was developed in christology implies God's distance and absence from the world, whereas God, our companion, is always Immanuel, God with us. This means that instead of Christ mediating between creation and its distant creator, Christ becomes the visibility in human conditions of the here, now, but invisible God through which Christians understand the character of God's constant presence.[145]

I have shown above that life is a journey toward understanding the world around us, one that places us on a quest for illustrative themes— explanatory propositions—so that we might make sense of that world. This is not a controversial statement; in fact, it is rather commonplace in many circles these days. Next, I also pointed out that, over the years, many have found Robert A. Traina's method for biblical exegesis to be an extremely powerful tool for interpreting biblical literature. Once again, not terribly controversial: other chapters in this book substantiate this claim.

But, I wished to push things a bit further in this chapter. I have sought to argue that Traina's approach is a powerful tool for understanding human endeavors in general, not simply those related to biblical exegesis. Specifically, I believe it to be a viable method fruitful for exploring the social sciences. This point I needed to prove. And I set out to do just that.

First, I established that the human brain seems uniformly configured, causing all humans to

---

[145] Page, *Incarnation of Freedom and Love*, 50.

dice and slice reality into common overarching metaphorical configurations. These arrangements are what we use to organize thought and make sense of experience, and we seem to do it in a uniform manner the world over.

Next, I briefly explored Traina's methodology, looking at the eleven structural relationships that he believes make possible all human reasoning, connections that bear a striking resemblance to the universal configurations just examined. Given our aim, two of these relationships proved most important to us, since they assist humans in identifying themes. These two interconnections are recurrence and contrast. In a word, by taking notice of recurring elements, and by noticing when that repetition stops, we can identify key themes. This point would prove especially useful in social sciences terrain later, since we would seek themes there, as well.

I then surveyed five social science disciplines, noting that subject specialists in these fields hunt for motifs or themes to explore their fields, too. We found that, in many of these fields, there is even a specific term that describes this type of research: "thematic analysis." Given this surprising similarity, Traina's methodology need only be modified in order for scholars in these disciplines to more rigorously accomplish what they are already attempting to do—thematic analysis.

Finally, I turned to my own experience, describing how I have fruitfully employed Traina's methodology over the years, in my teaching, in my supervision of students, and in my writing and social science research. I have used what I learned from Traina both to discover research themes as well to assess themes proffered by others. I trust I managed to validate how generative this methodology has been for me over the years.

In summary, I recommend a three-step process for encapsulating and summarizing that laid out above. In order to broaden the applicability of methods like Traina's for materials outside biblical materials, I suggest that we:

1. Utilize Traina's method in its original habitat, identifying themes in scripture to establish, with confidence, the nature of biblical emphases in given passages, in given books, and in given corpuses.
2. With a provisional list of these biblical emphases in hand, we may then test the fidelity of suggested narrative themes put forward by other authors (like we witnessed in the thought of Nygren, Barth, Hays, Hay, and Gushee and Stassen above). If their thematic suggestions end up validated by our biblical exegesis, we may then embrace these as trustworthy representations of thematic Christian positions on a topic.
3. Finally, we then should be poised to compare these corroborated biblical principles (the results of step 1), or these suggested narrative themes (the results of step 2), with themes put forward by those in social science research—whether by others, or by ourselves as we take up social science thematic analysis. In this way, deep grammar can be compared with deep grammar: an established theme from the biblical text may be placed alongside a social science postulate under question, with interaction between these two themes offering us possibilities for deeper study and consequent fruitful future action.

For instance, several additional thematic emphases of my own specialty—development studies—

might be tested by way of this three-step process: James Scott's "Weapons of the Weak" thesis,[146] David Korten's "Blueprint vs. Learning Process" distinction,[147] or Herman Daly and John Cobb's "Fallacy of Misplaced Concreteness" principle.[148] This sort of analysis could either robustly validate these themes, or it could encourage Christians to reject them as not sufficiently valid from a theological vantage point (or, one could also markedly modify the theses, if possible). As a result, the sort of approach described here offers to us rich opportunities for faithful living and faithful witness.

I would like to end this investigation by returning to two ideas previously mentioned: "deep grammar" and "thick description." Once again, the "deep grammar" notion derives from German social theorist Jürgen Habermas,[149] whereas "thick description" is generally attributed to anthropologist Clifford Geertz, as part of his call for robust approaches to ethnography.[150] When a social actor demonstrates communicative competence and deep grammar fluency, considerable facility with the cultural "language" of a society ends up on display; this represents a social actor's ability to navigate controlling themes operative in a context. Linking "deep grammar" to "thick description," a person fluent in the former manifests an ability to comprehend societal themes more deeply and with greater "thickness," an ability to understand in a manner increasingly multi-layered. This ends up being much more than understanding spoken grammar; it also includes a fluency in respect to what one does, regarding the trajectory of one's life and what it means.

If we ask ourselves about the deep grammar/thick description trajectory of the Christian message, one could say—in line with my emphasis on the Incarnation, on self-emptying, and on humility above—that it might be framed by way of this famous passage from Phil 2 (NRSV):

> 5 Let the same mind be in you that was in Christ Jesus,
> 6 who, though he was in the form of God,
>   did not regard equality with God
>   as something to be exploited,
> 7 but emptied himself,
>   taking the form of a slave,
>   being born in human likeness.
>   And being found in human form,
> 8 he humbled himself
>   and became obedient to the point of death—
>   even death on a cross.

---

[146] James C. Scott, *Weapons of the Weak: Everyday Forms of Peasant Resistance* (New Haven, CT: Yale University Press, 1985).

[147] David Korten, "Community Organization and Rural Development: A Learning Process Approach," *Public Administration Review* 40, (1980): 480–511.

[148] Herman E. Daly and John B. Cobb, Jr., *For the Common Good: Redirecting the Economy toward Community, the Environment, and a Sustainable Future*, 2nd ed. (Boston: Beacon, 1994). The notion of the fallacy of misplaced concreteness they borrow from philosopher Alfred North Whitehead.

[149] Habermas borrows the idea from linguist Noam Chomsky, modifying and broadening its application.

[150] Though, Geertz admits he borrowed the phrase from philosopher Gilbert Ryle.

Curiously, the sort of movement and trajectory on display here—the "deep grammar" it carries—parallels what is thematically embraced in much of grassroots development these days: a downward mobility, a positional divestment, the type of style we heard Robert Chambers refer to as "reversals." One could even be forgiven for thinking that Chambers himself (not a Christian) plucked the subtitles of two of his books straight from this Phil 2 passage (the subtitle of one book is "Putting the Last First";[151] the subtitle for the second is "Putting the First Last"[152]). In this trend, Chambers is not alone. Roland Bunch—a theorist and practitioner in agricultural development—offers a poignantly deep grammar recommendation for grassroots development when he admonishes,

> the closer program leaders come to living as the villagers do—the more we can leave behind our cities, towns, embassy crowds, and missionary compounds—the better our work will be. It is only when we have spent all day stooped over while transplanting rice in flooded paddies, when we have raced out into the family courtyard to rescue drying millet from a sudden rain, when we have survived for days on nothing but boiled field corn, and when we have fallen in love with the villagers' enchanting children, that we can come to speak with the villagers' vocabulary, understand their priorities, and fathom their feelings and wants. And it is only then that they will truly come to trust us.[153]

This movement—such a stance—points to a deeply embedded grammar mirroring the Incarnation; a thematic, thick description motif that echoes the trajectory of the Christian picture of God self-emptying in Christ. With a bit of imagination and a smattering of license, the Phil 2 passage ends up sounding strangely familiar when glossed in language similar to Bunch's observation:

> The closer I come to living as my creatures do—the more I leave behind my Father's presence and the comforts I have known there—the better will my work be. It will only be after I spend my childhood struggling toward maturity and purpose, only when I have left my home village and ventured out into the midst of a hostile world, only when I have traveled far and wide to communicate God's love to a sinful race, when I have fasted for days on end in an attempt to intercede for these people, and only when I have fallen in love with their enchanting children—ones springing from the same people who will later hate, vilify, and even crucify me—only then will I come to speak with the world's vocabulary, understand their priorities, and fathom their feelings and wants. And, likewise, it is only then that some will truly come to trust in me.

The parallels are striking. As we notice them, not only do we end up with thematic faithfulness in respect to sources (whether those be textual or contextual), not only are we provisioned with development practice more effective vis-à-vis marginalized communities (as Bunch encourages above), but this style will also offer opportunities for enacted witness by way of development practice, since

---

[151] Chambers, *Rural Development*.

[152] Robert Chambers, *Whose Reality Counts?: Putting the First Last* (London: Intermediate Technology, 1999).

[153] Roland Bunch, *Two Ears of Corn: A Guide to People-centered Agricultural Improvement* (Oklahoma City: World Neighbors, 1982), 54.

the "emptying" trajectory of the work we attempt can serve as thick description examples of the incarnational, kenotic God we serve, the one we are scripturally admonished to honor.[154] Development efforts become occasions for witness by way of the mirroring gift of thematic (re-)enactment.

Such opportunities for deep grammar witness, though, will only be available to us in the event we grasp what common themes can be found in the Christian message and in those social science constructs that we choose to embrace. I believe that Traina's methodology—as I spell it out here—can help us do that when applied in both scriptural and contextual spheres.

FOR FURTHER READING

Bauer, David R. and Robert A. Traina. *Inductive Bible Study: A Comprehensive Guide to the Practice of Hermeneutics*. Grand Rapids: Baker Academic, 2014.

Bauman, Zygmunt. *Hermeneutics and Social Science: Approaches to Understanding*. London: Routledge Revivals, 2010.

Birch, Bruce C. and Larry L. Rasmussen. *Bible and Ethics in the Christian Life*. Revised and expanded edition. Minneapolis: Augsburg Fortress, 1988.

Geertz, Clifford. *The Interpretation of Cultures*. New York: Basic Books, 1973.

Geertz, Clifford. *Local Knowledge Further Essays in Interpretive Anthropology*. New York: Basic Books, 1983.

Hauerwas, Stanley. *The Peaceable Kingdom: A Primer in Christian Ethics*. Notre Dame: University of Notre Dame Press, 1991.

Lakoff, George and Mark Johnson. *Metaphors We Live By*. Chicago: The University of Chicago Press, 1980.

Neyrey, Jerome H., ed. *The Social World of Luke-Acts: Models for Interpretation*. Reprint edition. Grand Rapids: Baker Academic, 1999.

Resseguie, James L. *Narrative Criticism of the New Testament: An Introduction*. Grand Rapids: Baker Academic, 2005.

Ricoeur, Paul. *Hermeneutics and the Human Sciences: Essays on Language, Action and Interpretation*. Cambridge: Cambridge University Press, 1981.

Spradley, James P. *The Ethnographic Interview*. New York: Holt, Rinehart and Winston, 1979.

---

[154] Cf. Backues, "Interfaith Development Efforts," 76.

SUPPLEMENT 12.1
STRUCTURAL RELATIONSHIPS HANDOUT

STRUCTURAL RELATIONSHIP	EXPLANATION	BIBLICAL EXAMPLE	EXPLICIT LINGUISTIC INDICATORS
1. PREPARATION/ REALIZATION (INTRODUCTION)	The setting up of a scene or setting	The book of Job begins with a framing of the scene of events in chapters 1–2	*None*
2. CONTRAST	Association of opposites	Recurring contrast between Jesus and the religious leaders in the Gospel of Mark	but, however, yet, etc.
3. COMPARISON	Association of like things	The book of 2 Kings is structured according to a comparison between the fall of the Northern Kingdom and the fall of the Southern Kingdom	like, as...so, etc.
4. RECURRENCE	Repetition of the same or similar terms, phrases, or elements. Can be in the form of: (a) Repetition (recurrence of the same motifs) (b) Continuity (recurrence of similar motifs)	"Life" in the Gospel of John	*None*
5. CAUSATION	Causation involves the movement from cause to effect	The book of Judges is characterized by recurrence of causal cycles	therefore, so, hence, etc.

Chapter 12—IBS and Teaching Social Sciences

STRUCTURAL RELATIONSHIP	EXPLANATION	BIBLICAL EXAMPLE	EXPLICIT LINGUISTIC INDICATORS
6. SUBSTANTIATION	Substantiation involves the movement from effect to cause	Psalm 1 is structured according to substantiation; v. 6 provides the basis, or the reason, for vv. 1–5	for, since, etc.
7. GENERALIZATION	Generalization involves the movement from the particular to the general	The book of Acts involves a progressive geographical generalization - from Jerusalem (chs. 1–7) to Judea and Samaria (chs. 8–12) to "the uttermost parts of the earth" (chs. 13–28)	*None*
8. PARTICULARIZATION	Particularization is the movement from general to particular	The prologue to John's gospel (1:1-18) is particularized throughout the remainder of the gospel	*None*
9. CLIMAX	Movement from the lesser to greater to greatest (toward culmination)	The book of Revelation reaches its climax in the description of the final judgment in 20:11–22:21	*None*
10. INSTRUMENTATION	A causal movement made possible by an agent of change; a relation of ends and means	The gospel of John contains an explicit statement of the purpose of the gospel as means, John 20:30–31	by, through (often couched in the subjunctive, i.e., "these [words] are written that you *may* believe...")

STRUCTURAL RELATIONSHIP	EXPLANATION	BIBLICAL EXAMPLE	EXPLICIT LINGUISTIC INDICATORS
11. PIVOT	A radical reversal or change of direction	Description of Paul in the book of Acts; Paul is a persecutor of the Church and an enemy of Christ prior to his conversion in 9:1–19, but after this event he becomes a mighty herald of the gospel	*None*
12. INTERROGATION	A question or problem followed by an answer or solution	The book of Genesis is structured around the primordial problem of sin in Genesis 1-11 which is answered/solved by the calling of Abram and his family in Genesis 12–50	*None*
13. SUMMARIZATION	The summation of logic or events in an extended discourse	The book of Joshua ends with Joshua summarizing the events of the children of Israel in Joshua 24	*None*

SUPPLEMENT 12.2
SHORT EXPLANATION OF *INDUCTIVE BIBLE STUDY*

Dr. Robert A. Traina, in his work *Methodical Bible Study*, lists a total of 11 primary structural relationships (interconnections which are the building blocks for all meaningful statements):

1. Preparation/Realization (Introduction)
2. Contrast
3. Comparison
4. Recurrence
5. Causation/Substantiation
6. Generalization/Particularization
7. Climax
8. Pivot
9. Interrogation
10. Summarization
11. Instrumentation

While particulars involving the majority of these relationships seem fairly self-evident once sufficiently attended to,[155] special mention is still in order concerning a couple of the less than perspicuous features concerned. In explaining these features, I will touch upon the charts designated **Simple & Complex Structural Relationships** and **Structural Analysis of Nehemiah** as found in the accompanying handouts.

First, it should be noted that several of the relationships above are mirror images of each other. For example, the configurations known as *Causation* and *Substantiation* both consist of identical components: a cause and an effect. In the former, the cause precedes and brings on the effect, whereas in the latter it is the effect which appears first, validating and corroborating the cause. The same inversion of elements holds true for the *Generalization/Particularization* dyad. The first is a movement from particular to general, whereas the second is from general to particular.

Second, Traina was accustomed to pointing out that the categories of *Contrast* and *Comparison* are altogether relative concepts depending a great deal upon emphasis—what we have here are actually two points appearing at different ends of the same continuum. When comparing two items (say, two apples) there are always differing components, otherwise the two items would not actually be two in number but instead one and the same item—in which case, there would in fact be no comparison at all since only one item would be under consideration. Consequently, within every comparison a contrast is invariably implied (e.g., two apples are always slightly different in size, shape, color, etc.).

A similar clarification should be made in relation to contrasts. If there were absolutely no points of similarity in a given contrast (say, between an apple and an orange), pointing to differences between them would be untenable since the elements under consideration would be extant on two completely separate planes of reality, in which case the two objects could not even be touched upon in the same breath by the same person (after all, when contrasting apples with oranges, we *are* at that time contrasting two pieces of *fruit*!). Hence, within every contrast there always exists a latent comparative relationship.

Third, the structural relationships of *Recurrence* and *Contrast* in tandem serve a singularly vital function, to wit, marking off boundaries between passages or units of thought. This is illustrated in the diagram on the following page. As can be seen, contrasting elements separate units one from another, whereas recurring elements signal a continuance of the same topic and thus a prolongation of the same unit of thought. Since certain properties extend over a wider range of material than do others, the structural relationship of

---

[155] See the handout **Inductive Structural Relationships** for an annotated list of Traina's relationships as well as a biblical example and various explicit linguistic indicators for each construct. While Traina lists a certain collection of relationships in his book *Methodical Bible Study* (:57-59), he later modified it, arriving at what is presented above.

Recurrence asserts itself in these places in relation to whichever element happens to be in question. However, when this recurring element no longer surfaces within a given passage, a contrasting element takes over and itself begins to resound. Thus, a new unit of thought begins, contrasting with that just before.

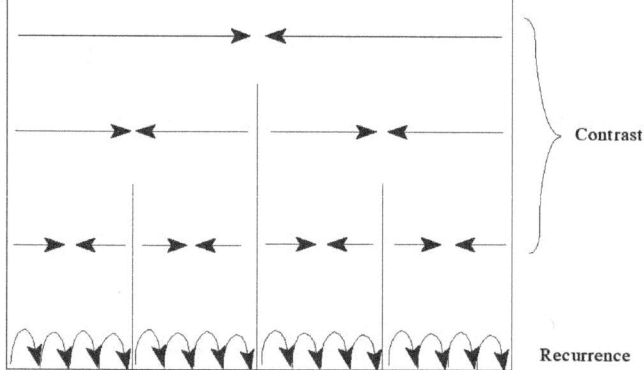

Fourth, structural laws often function jointly as compound relationships. In order to explain this point, it is perhaps best to look at an example of Traina's methodology as found in its original habitat: in application to the biblical text. Found in one of your handouts is what I have chosen to call the **Structural Analysis of Nehemiah**.

One of the primary structural laws operative in this book is a compound relationship known as *Comparative Causation*. The building of the wall in 2:9-6:19 brings about and therefore serves as cause for the building and regathering of the community in 7:1-13:31. However, this causal movement is not the only way in which these two units seem to be linked. In a related fashion there also seems to be an implicit comparative coupling depicted in the text: the manner in which the wall is built is tacitly likened to the manner in which the community is built and reestablished. This is especially obvious as one takes into consideration the recurring appearance of opposition[156] which plays a notable role (or should I say anti-role) in each of the two units compared. Hence, the two relationships—*Comparison* and *Causation*—actually function as one overall configuration, mutually augmenting and highlighting each other.

Finally, this discussion once again leads us to the **Simple and Complex Relationships** handout wherein several structural relationships deemed *Simple* and *Complex* are listed. Complex relationships are those composite structures consisting of a blend of other primary relationships. For instance, each and every one of the complex configurations *Particularization/Generalization, Causation/Substantiation, Instrumentation*, and *Interrogation* have immured within them the simple relationship *Preparation/Realization*. In other words, all of the former contain a preparatory segment which is later realized in ensuing material. And while it certainly would not be wrong to say that each of these are examples of *Preparation/Realization*, it would however be less than precise. As can be seen, the complex structural relationships *Climax, Interrogation*, and *Pivot* all also embrace their own simple relationships.

The *Nehemiah* study offers an illustration of the above. The first structural relationship noted is that of *Interrogation*, i.e., the problem of disarray in Jerusalem in 1:1b-2:8 is solved by means of the community organization process evident in 2:9–13:31. As seen in the **Simple and Complex Relationships** handout, the relationship of interrogation includes within it the couched simple relationships of *Contrast* and *Causation*. Therefore, in the process of analysis it is possible to direct our attention not only to the subtleties of problem-solution inherent within, but also toward the other two included relationships as well. Once again, however, designating this as merely *Contrast* or *Causation* would surely lack the precision of recognizing the fuller relationship at work here, i.e., *Interrogation*.

---

[156] I refer overtly to this recurring opposition by listing it as Structural Relationship III *(Recurrence of Contrast [with Comparison])* in my breakdown. Needless to say, this is another example of a compound structural relationship.

SUPPLEMENT 12.3
SURVEY/ANALYSIS OF SHEL SILVERSTEIN'S *THE GIVING TREE*

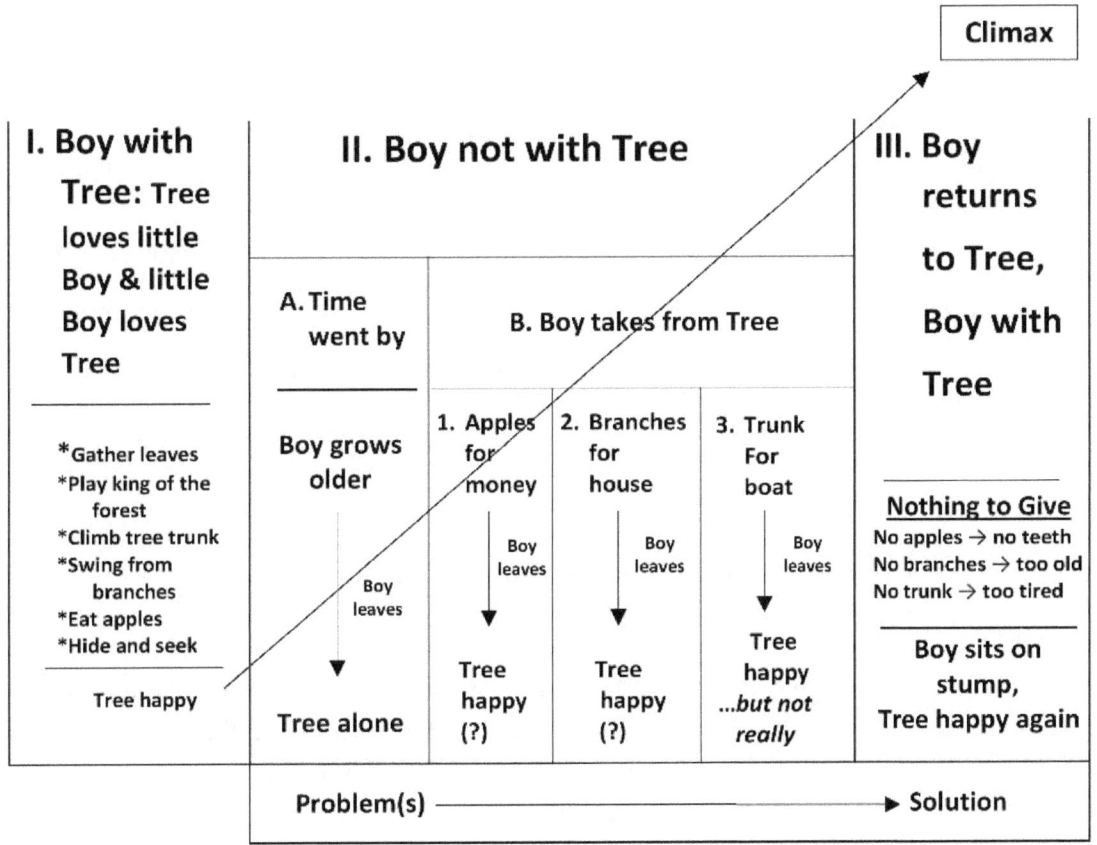

1. **Particularization**

   General: Boy grows older, Tree is alone
   Particulars: 3 ways in which Boy grows older (and leaves, and leaves, and leaves), Tree is alone
           a. Apples for money (Boy leaves)
           b. Branches for house (Boy leaves)
           c. Trunk for boat (Boy leaves)

2. **Contrast**

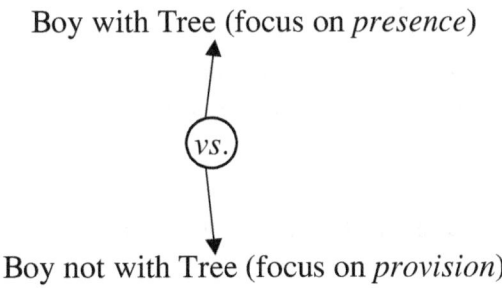

3. **Recurrence of Interrogation (with ineffectual Instrumentation)**

   Boy's Problems: no money, no house, no boat—no happiness

   Tree's Means as Potential Solutions:
   apples (for money),
   branches (for house),
   trunk (for boat)
   —happiness still questionable

4. **Cruciality**

   a. *Boy goes away*: returns only to take from Tree (only Tree gives)

   Pivot: Boy grows old/youth depleted, Tree's resources depleted

   b. *Boy returns*: stays with Tree (each gives and receives)

5. **Climax**

   a. *Boy young*: Tree loves little Boy, Boy loves Tree—Tree happy
   b. *Boy grows older*: Tree gives to Boy, Boy uses Tree—Tree not happy
   c. *Old Boy and Depleted Tree together*: Tree happy
      (nothing left to use on the part of Tree, nothing more needed on the part of Boy)

6. **Recurrence of "Leaving and Returning" Motif**

   Emphasis on "leaving and returning" predominates
   (Boy repeatedly leaves Tree, then returns to Tree)

7. **Recurrence of "Giving" Motif**

   Emphasis on "giving" throughout
   (with an emphasis on the nature of giving)

8. **Recurrence of "Happiness" Motif**

   Emphasis on "happiness" throughout
   (authentic and specious happiness)

Another Major Impression

Boy is called "Boy" throughout even though he obviously grows older and is no longer a boy.

Chapter 12—IBS and Teaching Social Sciences

SUPPLEMENT 12.4
STUDENT EPISTEGRAPHS FROM
EPISTEMOLOGICAL INSIGHTS FOR ANTHROPOLOGICAL PRACTICE

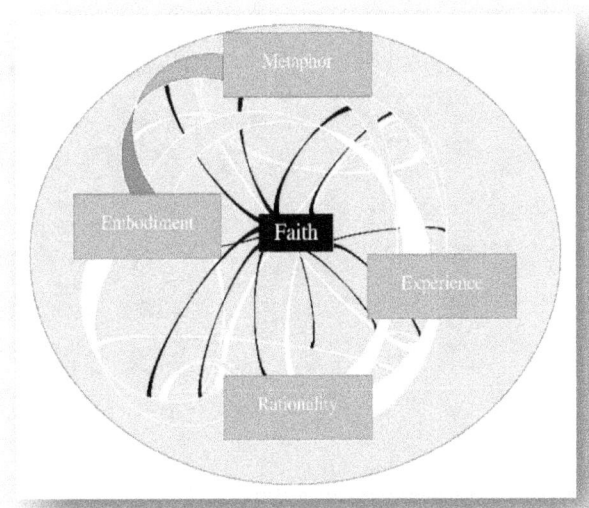
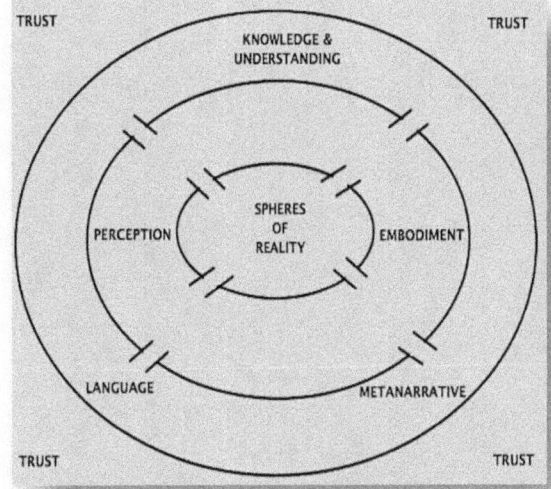
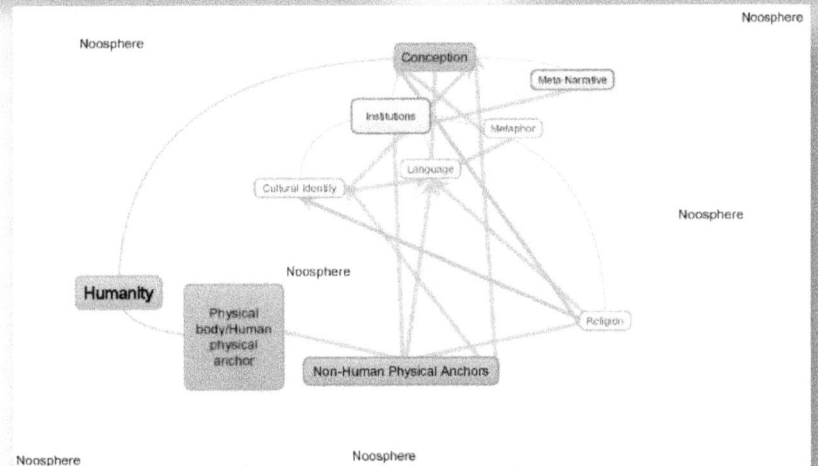
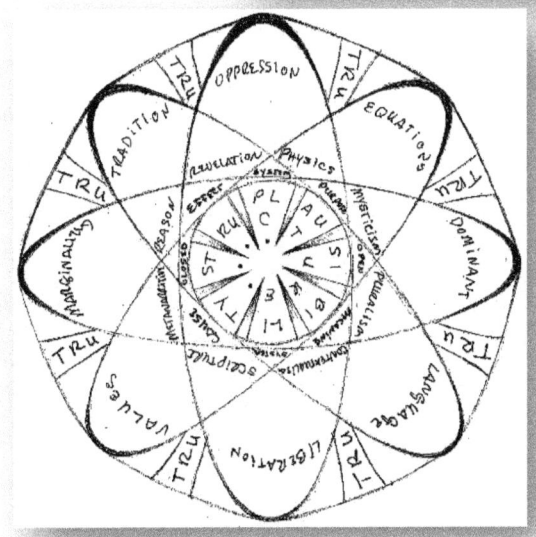
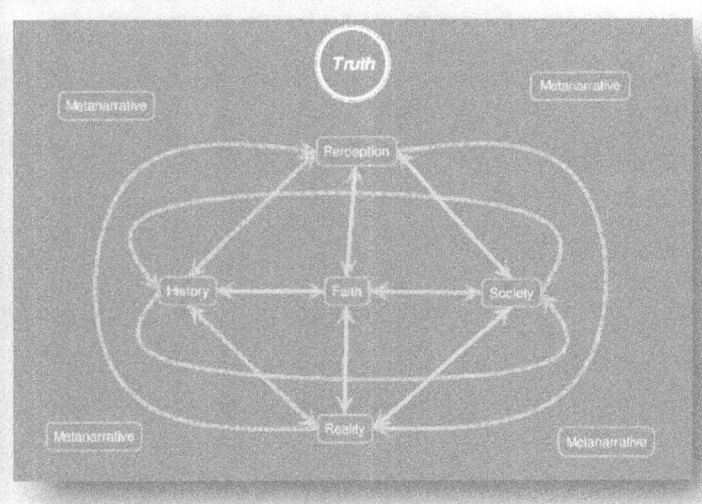

Part IV

IBS Pedagogy, Assessments, and Technology

Teaching Inductive Bible Study in an Age of Immediately Gratifying Technologies

Michael D. Matlock
Professor of Inductive Biblical Studies, Old Testament, and Early Judaism
Asbury Theological Seminary

ABSTRACT: Like all sustained, highly significant habits, the manner in which Christ's followers approach Scripture study is vitally important. Serious interpreters of Scripture tend to analyze biblical texts persistently, consistently, conscientiously, sequentially, and creatively. Unfortunately, there are many impediments to this type of study of God's Word. One of the increasing hindrances to robust and insightful inductive study of the Bible is a technological instantly gratifying distraction (TIGD). With increasing daily functions tied to technology, we should have more and more time available. Yet, the opposite is often true. In this essay, we will consider wise strategies that can assist Christians in the battle against such hindrances. In order to keep our relationship with Christ growing and healthy, it is essential to enhance our communication with God through Scripture study. And, the fewer the distractions, more optimal potential exists for vitality.

1. Introduction

Managing one's time well for the important priorities of life is a pervasive problem in achieving Asbury Theological Seminary's mission to exist as a "community called to prepare theologically educated" students. For well over a decade, at the beginning of a course I have required students to give an inventory of where they are spending their time during a typical week. For many, this is the first time a professor has asked for a report of their time management. For some students this is an "aha" moment that reveals how busy they are before the course begins. This simple assessment gives me an opportunity to counsel the busiest students in regard to educational success in the course. I am able to discuss basic time-management principles, specifically ways to cull back responsibilities in a student's life. However, what I have not often discussed with students is an issue that I would like to reflect upon in this article—how to be successful educationally in the midst of so many instantly gratifying technologies available to us. A large measure of any student's success is dependent upon "resisting temptations that are immediately gratifying in order to increase the likelihood of accomplishing some temporally remote and presumably more important goal."[1]

Many of my millennial students (people in their twenties and early thirties) have struggled to harness the prevalent technological and other cultural immediately gratifying enticements. The seductive entrapments are fairly obvious and ubiquitous: internet usage, social media, Google searching, "smart" and other mobile devices, noncommercial television, on-demand movies, FastPass tickets, gaming, fast-food restaurants, microwaves, credit cards, and the many other instant societal satisfactions. According to a 2011 Pew study, mobile phone owners between the ages of 18 to 24 swap an average of 109.5 text messages a day. From a 2010 Pew review, 90 percent of 18 to 29 year-olds sleep with their phones.[2] I hasten to add that many of my students who are older than millennials also struggle with these same immediately gratifying, culturally made distractions when it comes to sustained focus and important prioritizing of work. Moreover, I know of many non-students over seventy who spend exorbitant amounts of time on social media.

At this initial juncture, I need to make an embarrassing confession. As I sit at my computer writing this article, I too am struggling to resist the temptation to check my email, read the latest news on my favorite sports or political websites, or check for text messages. When the words are not flowing freely, the urge to utilize these instantly gratifying communication vehicles surfaces as an easy escape from my primary task. I, too, desire a gratifying message, the satisfaction of knowing the latest news about my sports team, or whether my political views are being advanced or impeded. Not very long ago, reading an entire journal article was quite easy for me. Now, I tend to read the abstract, conclusion, and respectable peer reviews in an attempt to acquire the essence of the piece before I take the time to read an entire article.[3]

Wanting things faster is by no means a new phenomenon. The Polaroid instant camera was invented in 1948, the same year the first McDonald's fast-food restaurant opened in San Bernardino, California. FedEx created its intoxicating international brand with the 1980s ad slogan, "When it absolutely, positively has to be there overnight." Popular quick and easy weight loss slogans like "lose 7 lbs. in 7 days" have been commonplace for many decades. The list of available immediately gratifying options is seemingly endless. The progression and effects of this cultural reality have certainly given me pause as an educator over the past decade.

In the remainder of the essay, I will take inventory of some of the negative effects of immediate gratification and the ways they affect the spiritual discipline of inductive Bible study (IBS). Strategies for combatting the negative effects and implementing tactics of delayed gratification will

---

[1] Héfer Bembenutty and Stuart A. Karabenick, "Inherent Association Between Academic Delay of Gratification, Future Time Perspective, and Self-Regulated Learning," *Educational Psychology Review* 1 (2004): 35–57 at 36.

[2] Aaron Smith, "Americans and Text Messaging," *Pew Research Center: Internet, Science & Tech*, September 19, 2011, http://www.pewinternet.org/2011/09/19/americans-and-text-messaging/; Amanda Lenhart, "Cell Phones and American Adults," *Pew Research Center: Internet, Science & Tech*, September 2, 2010, http://www.pewinternet.org/2010/09/02/cell-phones-and-american-adults/.

[3] Not all activities of task reduction are necessarily inappropriate. However, too much streamlining of one's primary work does alter the focus and comprehension of sustained discussion and argumentation.

also be discussed. My pedagogical reflections serve as a tribute to Professor Robert A. Traina, whose legacy continues in the curriculum through the manner in which Asbury Theological Seminary students study Scripture. Traina possessed an unflinching desire to teach Scripture study by modeling a careful, patient, wise, skillful, and enduring study of the Bible.

2. THE CHALLENGE FROM TRAINA

Professor Traina sometimes began teaching an introductory inductive Bible study course by noting certain inspiration he himself had acquired to study God's Word from the words of the protracted Psalm 119: "I have laid up thy word in my heart, that I might not sin against thee. I will delight in thy statutes; I will not forget thy word. Give me understanding, that I may keep thy law and observe it with my whole heart. [For] I find my delight in thy commandments, which I love. I revere thy commandments, which I love, and I will meditate on thy statutes. I will never forget thy precepts; for by them thou hast given me life. Oh, how I love thy law! It is my meditation all the day. Thy word is a lamp to my feet and a light to my path" (Ps 119:11, 16, 34, 47–48, 93, 97, 105 RSV).

Traina would continue by saying "what wonderful words those are about a psalmist who is excited about the word of God, who loves the word of God, who mediates on the word of God, [and] who lives by the word of God." Next, he would offer an exhortation to his students as to whether the words and feelings of the psalmist expressed their and his words and feelings toward the Word of God. He would then ask the questions, "or, do we really say when we read God's Word, I will grudgingly do this because God demands this of me. It is very boring. I wish I did not have to do it. I do not need to do it. It does not give me much understanding, and I am not interested in meditating upon it." The point of Traina's devotional exhortation was not to be judgmental, but rather to describe a distressing reality among students of the Bible. Too many students who have come to seminary to grow in Christlikeness are surprisingly not ready to engage at a deeper level the words and teachings of Christ and the larger redemptive narrative found in Holy Scripture. And, it is certainly not surprising, Traina would hasten to add, that parishioners under the care of these same seminary students find their own study of God's Word unnecessary and neglected.

Like Traina, I also teach my students that much of a Christian's success in conducting a consistent, engaged, profound, and fruitful Bible study pertains to attitudinal and affective elements possessed by the student. Thus, I ask myself, how do we change our negative attitudes, reluctant moods, and feelings into positive contributors for flourishing inductive biblical study? Part of the answer stems from practicing habits of uninterrupted reading and critical thinking. We develop routines that either will assist us in thriving Scripture studies or will hinder us and cause our Bible study to be less fruitful. On the negative side, too many of us have developed choppy, inconsistent, dispassionate, and lethargic Bible study habits that are driven by or end in very short-term goals. But, on the positive side of the ledger, some students have developed significantly in this area by displaying great effort in finding out what the words of Scripture mean with precision and perceptiveness. Students who possess long-term goals and know how to practice delayed gratification tend to be better Bible study students in seminary and beyond.

3. Areas of Bible Study Impacted by Instant Gratification and Remedies

3.1 Prayer in Scripture Study

Many features of IBS are affected by succumbing to a steady diet of cultural instant gratification. The first and most pervasive step of Bible study is consistent and effective prayer. Because our God is personal, prayer provides the necessary communication for our relationship to flourish. And yet, the lures of instant gratification have pulled too many of Christ's disciples from constant prayer. We are taught through the Parable of the Persistent Widow (Luke 18:1–8) to offer prayer day and night so that we may be prompted to allow God to work in us. In practice, however, we think we are too busy to pray and thus spend our lives out of rhythm with God's heartbeat. Prayer and study of Scripture are two of the three most fundamental means of grace (the third being the sacrament of Holy Communion) that transform us into Christ's likeness; they are interdependent. The Word of God sustains, encourages, directs, and forms prayer which calls up and receives down illumination and understanding in our study of the Word of God as well as provides inspiration to obey its directives. It is impossible to have a long-term obedience toward God without faithfully asking for the Spirit's clarity and power in our study of God's Word. And, equally important, prayer cannot mature our walk with God without the sustained study of the Bible and ensuing obedience of Christ's followers.

One way that I have tried to counter the assaults of instant gratification upon my own prayer life and that of my students is to introduce the Daily Office from the Book of Common Prayer. I now invite students to pray morning and/or evening prayer during the semester of Scripture study if they are not already practicing daily, regular prayer. Moreover, I allot a few minutes of each class to pray portions of the daily office to give students a flavor of this rich prayer tradition. I am convinced that one of the first things I should teach my students in regard to inductive study of the Bible is the practice of prayer. Many of my students believe that prayer is only genuine if it is extemporaneous and creates a certain feeling inside of them. Common prayer of Christians throughout centuries can build a habit of prayer that is robust theologically and deeply formational in us. Many are surprised to learn that Cranmer designed the Book of Common Prayer almost five hundred years ago to offer Christians words to pray that clearly proclaim the gospel of grace and gratitude for the opening and closing of each day. He simplified the seven times of monastic prayer down to two times, morning and evening, and softened the reading of the entire Psalter to a more manageable thirty-day cycle rather than a one-week period. Another beautiful contribution from Cranmer is that he introduced voluminous readings of Scripture moving book by book into the Daily Office, which became the foundation for our lectionary readings of Scripture today. Certainly, allowing the Holy Spirit to work in me by regularly praying the Daily Office has strengthened my and some of my students' prayer lives.

Students also need copious amounts of wisdom and discernment to engage the Scriptures inductively and consistently. Yet, technological instant gratifying distractions (hereafter TIGD) are contributing to the lack of wisdom and discernment. Harold Schweizer, Professor of English at Bucknell University, reminds us that "the promise of technology was that it would make us masters of time. [But, i]t has ironically made us into time's slaves."[4] He insightfully educates his students regarding the importance of waiting when reading a text or studying other subjects by drawing an analogy to a type of courtship between a woman and man. Objects and experiences (and I would add subjects), he notes, attain value because we have waited for them; on the contrary, without time investment, these things (and people) remain without value.[5]

3.2 Reading and Surveying Scripture

This leads me to consider the next step of inductive Bible study affected by TIGD. Our inductive study of Scripture commences with reading and surveying a biblical book because the Bible came to us in books, not snippets of texts or some other form. So, with the advent and onslaught of TIGD, attention deficit has become an all too common problem. Many students report that they have great difficulty "finding" the time to read a book like Genesis in its entirety, which takes on average three hours and thirty minutes to read. Even if they have the time, some report that they cannot concentrate for this length of time. Even more disturbing is the fact that too many are having little success in reading the biblical text for ten or fifteen minutes before they are distracted by TIGD, and they struggle continuously throughout the assignment to focus and finish. When I tell these same students that they should try to read a book at least twice, three times if possible, I often feel as though I am their archvillain who now stands in the way of completing the Bible study assignment.

Overcoming these kinds of challenges begins with developing what Stanford psychologist Carol Dweck calls a "growth mindset."[6] To possess a solid work effort and stay motivated, one must believe that one's learning ability is not fixed but can change with effort. As students are educated about how our brains change and grow in reaction to challenges, they are more likely to persevere when they fail since they do not believe that failure is a permanent condition. In terms of how practically to read a biblical book several times without distraction, I encourage my students to listen to Scripture as they read the text. Lest the reader feel that I am advocating being a Luddite, using technology for obtaining audio of Scripture is a good endeavor. The pace is set by the reader on the audio, not the student, and this pace can force the student to keep in step with the audio.

Moreover, I encourage students to reduce TIGD and other detrimental distractions to an absolute minimum by putting one's phone on airplane mode, turning off the laptop and other internet accessible options, studying in the quietest place possible like a library carrel, maybe reading with another student taking the course, and clearing the mind for one minute with utter silence and then praying. Finally, I recommend reading in fifty-minute intervals (or less for some students) and then stretch, walk around, and then commence for another reading session. The first reading through the

---

[4] Cited in Ronald Alsop, "Instant Gratification & Its Dark Side," *Bucknell Magazine*, Summer 2014, http://www.bucknell.edu//about-bucknell/communications/bucknell-magazine/recent-issues/summer-2014/instant-gratification-and-its-dark-side.

[5] Ibid. For his larger treatment on the value of waiting, see Harold Schweizer, *On Waiting,* Thinking in Action (London: Routledge, 2008).

[6] See her book *Mindset: The New Psychology of Success* (New York: Random House, 2006).

book should be done without specific goals in mind. During the second time reading the book, students should actively read and have specific goals such as assigning each chapter a short description to allow easy memory of contents, determining the major structural units and relationships that are in force for the majority of the book's contents, noting evidence of authorship, date, audience, genres, and other critical issues that determine how one understands the intent of the book.

After a careful observance of the entire biblical book, the next step of inductive study is to pick a segment of the book (smaller units that were noted during the whole book survey process) and to seek to account for the literary makeup of the unit. Again, students are reading the Scripture and must combat the same TIGD and other distractions with the same solutions and strategies as mentioned above. Many students, whether struggling with TIGD or not, battle the urge to move too quickly into an interpretation mode of Bible study by answering questions that sketch out what the text meant for the original implied readers (or worse yet, for contemporary readers). They are enticed not only to answer their questions with few interpretive resources such as concordances, grammars, and other literary contextual evidence, but some students like to seek out answers from their favorite interpreters.

So, I ask myself, why are my students drawn too quickly into answering interpretive questions? There are many reasons, but for those who love to find informational answers to other questions by "asking Google," TIGD seems to be a major component of the problem. Retraining ourselves to wait through a methodological process has to occur in order for us to receive the greatest benefits from the inductive study of Scripture. To use the analogy I mentioned above, learning to understand the original meanings of the Word of God is like a proper courtship that has to occur before the marriage should be consummated. Waiting for the proper place and time of interpretation allows each interpreter a time for thinking, inspiration, reflection, regeneration, and thus adds the necessary value to our study of God's Word. Proper delay in the hermeneutical process assists us by not viewing our study of the Word as studying an object, but rather as seeking to understand an inspired human author and the triune God who inspired this writer. God, in three persons, is a personal and relational God. If we want to understand the personal Word of the triune God, we must seek ways of study that do not devalue our personal relationship with Jesus Christ.

3.3 Interpreting Scripture

When we reach the actual interpretive step of Bible study, which is normally a very intensive, rigorous step of study involving much critical thinking and responding to numerous research questions, the TIGD issues prevalent in the other steps of Bible study surface as nemeses once again. Make no mistake about it, exegetical steps utilized to interpret a biblical text demand much focus and energy on the part of the student. We are seeking to understand more fully how languages function and work, how and where words and texts are placed, tracking down historical details of the text, understanding the way genre(s) work, and other processes that demand our best critical thinking. It is not surprising that many seminary students want to consult other interpreters' work on a passage before they independently investigate and absorb the meanings. As I said, inductive interpretation work involves a great deal of sustained rigor. If a student has trouble working through the steps of exegesis, can he or she attain higher and more effective proficiency in working with Scripture? I certainly think so. But, has it become more difficult in the age of TIGD? Surely this is the case. More than is the case with almost any other type of course in our current curriculum, our inductive Bible study courses are designed to build lengthy, focused study time on a regular, consistent basis throughout the ten to fifteen lessons in the course. Because these exegetical steps require honing skills, it is essential that students learn to utilize their regular, consistent time wisely. Built into the design of the course, these interpretive skills are to be enhanced bit by bit.

Finally, students must also develop the most effective determinant that is consistently present in countless people who have successfully reached their lofty goals: an increased grit, also known as strength of character or resolve. Becoming competent interpreters of God's Word qualifies as a lofty, worthy, goal. The characteristics of grit are passion, stamina, a sticking with your future plan, day in and day out, for months and years. Grit has been described as working hard as though your life depended on it. Grit views developing skills for Scripture study as a marathon, not a sprint. Unfortunately, I see fewer and fewer students who possess grit and have little desire to attain it. Nevertheless, my goal will always remain to instill as much grit as possible in my students during the course. It is easily verifiable that the best interpreters keep persistently looking at a text for more love to experience, beauty and glory to behold, and power to sustain life. That glory and beauty is God the Father; that love is Christ Jesus himself; and that power is the Holy Spirit. We are beckoned to know and experience this relational God, which involves all that we are in understanding the literary, historical, and theological makeup of the Word of God.

Thus, with the psalmist I urge my students and myself to "teach us to count our days that we may gain a wise heart." (Ps 90.12). Those who are prepared to delay gratification in their inductive Bible studies will put off reward to a future time, enjoying the anticipated reward in the interim. In this way, students maximize their pleasure, combining the anticipation with the pleasure of the event itself in knowing Jesus through the process of exegesis. Thus, the burden and possibilities of pleasure are thrown back on us and how we will respond. The burden to make good choices about how we handle our struggles with TIGD should be guided and informed by the kind of character we want to cultivate.

4. Conclusion

Briefly, I conclude with some surprising characteristics of people who have attained very lofty goals by becoming more productive in what they set out to achieve.[7] Ultra-constructive people increase their attention, focus, decision-making, and overall productivity. According to a survey of such persons, they had learned to master minutes, not days or even hours, because these people understand quite well that there are 1,440 minutes every day. They focus on the most important thing each day for about one or two hours. Ultra-productive people use and live by their calendar schedule. They

---

[7] Kevin Kruse, "15 Surprising Things Productive People Do Differently," *Forbes*, n.d., https://www.forbes.com/sites/kevinkruse/2016/01/20/15-surprising-things-productive-people-do-differently/#be0187544b27. Kruse interviewed over 200 ultra-productive people including seven billionaires, 13 Olympians, 20 straight-A students and over 200 successful entrepreneurs by asking them an open-ended question, "What is your number one secret to productivity?"

eat at least one meal a day with their family or close friends. They almost always carry a notebook for writing down important ideas.[8]

These most productive people work with email only a few times a day by scheduling it; thus, they do not answer every ding or vibration on their phone. Ultra-productive people avoid meetings at all costs and keep short the ones they must hold. They say no to as many things as they can. Ultra-productive people know which activities drive the greatest results and focus on those and ignore the rest. They delegate what responsibilities they can and touch email and mail only once to reduce stress so as not to have the task in the back of their mind to reread or reevaluate in the future.

These productive individuals practice a consistent morning routine and nurture their bodies in the morning with water, a healthy breakfast and light exercise. Ultra-productive people nurture their mind with meditation or prayer, inspirational reading, and journaling. Ultra-productive people do not skip meals, sleep or breaks in the pursuit of more, more, and more. Instead, they view food as fuel, sleep as recovery, and pulse and pause with "work sprints." All of these practices of ultra-productive people contain helpful nuggets of wisdom, and Bible study students could adapt new practices and habits from them that might assist them in harnessing TIGD and other annoying distractions. In order to do so, we must habitually learn to act on the important and enduring and not be so quick to react to the urgent or instant.

FOR FURTHER READING:

Alsop, Ronald. "Gotta Have It Now, Right Now." *Notre Dame Magazine*, Winter 2011. http://magazine.nd.edu/news/gotta-have-it-now-right-now/.

_____. "Instant Gratification & Its Dark Side." *Bucknell Magazine*, Summer 2014. http://www.bucknell.edu//about-bucknell/communications/bucknell-magazine/recent-issues/summer-2014/instant-gratification-and-its-dark-side.

Dweck, Carol S. *Mindset: The New Psychology of Success*. New York: Random House, 2006.

Bembenutty, Héfer and Stuart A. Karabenick. "Inherent Association Between Academic Delay of Gratification, Future Time Perspective, and Self-Regulated Learning." *Educational Psychology Review* 1 (2004): 35–57.

Hummel, Charles E. *Freedom from Tyranny of the Urgent*. Downers Grove, IL: InterVarsity, 1997.

Kruse, Kevin. "15 Surprising Things Productive People Do Differently." *Forbes*, n.d. https://www.forbes.com/sites/kevinkruse/2016/01/20/15-surprising-things-productive-people-do-differently/#be0187544b27.

Lenhart, Amanda. "Cell Phones and American Adults." *Pew Research Center: Internet, Science & Tech*, Sept 2, 2010. http://www.pewinternet.org/2010/09/02/cell-phones-and-american-adults/

Schweizer, Harold. *On Waiting.* Thinking in Action. London: Routledge, 2008.

Smith, Aaron. "Americans and Text Messaging." *Pew Research Center: Internet, Science & Tech*, Sept 19, 2011. http://www.pewinternet.org/2011/09/19/americans-and-text-messaging/.

---

[8] Áine Cain, "Bill Gates, Richard Branson, and Sheryl Sandberg All Use the Same Old-School Organizational Hack," *Business Insider*, n.d., https://www.businessinsider.com/bill-gates-richard-branson-sheryl-sandberg-carry-notebooks-2017-8.

*REFLECTIONS ON THE ROLE OF STUDENT ASSIGNMENTS
IN THE INSTRUCTION OF INDUCTIVE BIBLE STUDY*

David R. Bauer
Dean of the School of Biblical Interpretation, Asbury Theological Seminary
Ralph Waldo Beeson Professor of Inductive Biblical Studies

ABSTRACT: Student assignments are a central component of learning in Inductive Bible Study (IBS) classes. As such, instructors have the responsibility to develop assignments, or lessons, with care, making sure that they are easily understandable, that they represent the primary learning objectives of IBS, and that students recognize them as extensions of IBS classroom work. IBS instructors must also be intentional in the marking of lessons, providing in a timely fashion specific, encouraging comments that are sensitive to the feelings of students. It may be helpful for instructors to develop a list of commonly employed comments; however, it is questionable whether such a list should be used as "rubrics" that carry direct, predetermined implications for grades. Furthermore, the process of grading should be informed by a consideration of what students can reasonably be expected to achieve given where they are in the process of IBS instruction.

1. INTRODUCTION

Many teachers give too little attention to the crafting of student assignments. Moreover, quite often teachers consider the reading and marking of student work to be among their least enjoyable tasks. A majority of instructors consider such tasks to be the necessary dues they must pay for the more pleasing experiences of classroom presentation and dynamic interaction with students. However, such a low opinion of instructional involvement with students' own work may betoken a fundamental confusion regarding education, namely, a failure to recognize that education is not finally about the instructor's teaching, but about the student's learning. Arguably, the most significant opportunity for learning comes at the point where students engage the material of the class through their own work and receive feedback from the instructor on that meaningful work. And, indeed, part of that feedback are the grades, or scores, that the instructor gives.

If student assignments are (at least potentially) a critical means for learning in general, such is the case particularly for IBS. The primary goal of teaching IBS is that students will develop their own competencies to observe, interpret, and appropriate the Bible for themselves. This focus upon students' acquiring skills for the study of the Bible implies the centrality of their sustained, direct engagement with the biblical text and assessment by the instructor on that engagement.

2. Development of Lessons

2.1 Lessons and Student Learning Objectives

Given the importance of assigned lessons for student learning, it follows that the instructor should give careful thought to the development of these lessons. In accordance with Dr. Traina's preference, I will speak not of "assignments," but of "lessons" since, as Dr. Traina mentions, the latter nomenclature expresses the positive learning outcome that is the intended effect of such student work over against the instructor-generated and requirement-oriented connotations of "assignment."[1] The instructor should be sure, first, that each lesson addresses one or more of the student learning objectives (SLO) for the course, and that such connection with the SLOs is made clear to the students. The purposes of a specific lesson may go beyond stated SLOs, but they should center on the SLOs so as to ensure integrity and coherence in the overall learning experience of the class.

2.2 Clear Lessons Connected to Classroom Instruction

The instructor should also make the lessons clear and understandable so that there is no room for misunderstanding on the part of the student nor any sense that the student is left to "figure out" what the instructor intends. Contrary to the opinion of some teachers, this kind of specificity and explicitness does not hinder students' creativity and resourcefulness, but rather provides the means whereby the best thinking of the student can be most efficiently and effectively channeled. Such clarity is achieved both by meticulous crafting of the lesson and by instructions regarding the lesson that the instructor offers in class. Accordingly, the instructor should explicitly connect the tasks contained in the lesson with class presentation and interaction. This means, on the one hand, that the instructor is committed to demonstrating, through the very content and structure of the lesson, that the lesson is an extension of the classroom experience, and on the other hand, that the instructor will typically so arrange the class schedule that the substance of the lesson will be the subject of classroom presentation or interaction in the days immediately following the submission of the lesson.

2.3 The Nature of Lessons for IBS

The suggestions that I have offered thus far pertain to instruction in general and are not specific to IBS. But given the emphasis in IBS upon the development of students' own thinking skills in relation to the biblical text, they are particularly important for the instruction of IBS. This mention of enhancing thinking skills in IBS, however, points to an aspect of the construction of lessons that is especially relevant for IBS, namely, that these lessons should be designed in such a way that they inculcate effective patterns of thinking over against having as their *focus* the acquisition of cognitive information. On the one hand, in IBS students generally use cognitive information as data that they

---

[1] For Traina's own discussion on this point, see his comments above in Ch. 1 "Method in Bible Teaching," 8–10.

process in order to reach valid and helpful conclusions; and, on the other hand, greater cognitive understanding on the part of students is the result of their application of a process that focuses not upon cognitive content itself but upon the development of thinking skills. This means, then, that although in IBS cognitive knowledge has its place and is important, it is not the primary goal. The relative emphasis in IBS instruction is not upon knowing *what* is in the text or lies around or behind the text, but *how* to use this information to construe the text. Lessons, therefore, are carefully and deliberately designed so as to enhance especially the complex thinking skills that are necessary for accurate, faithful, and penetrating construal of the biblical text.

Indeed, students most effectively acquire and implement these complex thinking skills by adopting certain concrete practices, that is, by attending to "best practices" for observation, interpretation, and appropriation. This emphasis upon the instrumental role of concrete practices, incidentally, is one of the chief contributions of Robert A. Traina to the development of instruction in IBS. Consequently, both classroom instruction and the shaping of lessons should attend to what the teacher of IBS believes are the most effective specific ways by which students can reliably derive truth from the biblical text. For example, in the observation of an entire biblical book—what we call the "survey of the book"—the lesson may require the student to perform certain tasks and to do so in specific ways. Thus, the student may be directed to identify the main units and sub-units of the book, to give discrete and descriptive headings to each, to locate dynamic organizational systems operative within the book ("structural relationships") such as contrast or climax, and to make sure that any such relationships identified control the bulk (i.e., more than half) of the material within the book (see Lesson 2 in the NT[IBS]510 syllabus found in SYLLABUS APPENDICES in this volume). As students consider how they might develop their own method for Bible study outside of the class, they may, of course, choose to exchange these specific practices with others that they deem more legitimate or congenial. However, the purpose of the lessons is to provide the student experiential exposure to those practices that have proved useful to many who have utilized IBS over the years so that the student will be in a position to make an informed judgement as to whether, and how, these practices might become part of the student's method for his/her own ongoing practice of Bible study.

This concern for concrete practices is most pronounced in the lessons for the beginning IBS class where students are introduced to IBS methodology. For advanced IBS classes (IBS-2 classes at Asbury Theological Seminary), the lessons allow greater flexibility for the student in terms of specific practices; this is particularly the case in interpretation and appropriation. It is expected that students will keep in mind the principles of IBS learned in the introductory course but will adapt them in accordance with their own thinking processes, judgments, and time constraints. Time constraints are especially important since interpretive lessons in IBS-2 classes cover larger swaths of material (whole segments and sometimes whole books) over against the focus in IBS-1 classes in which students typically interpret an individual verse or at most a paragraph. Additionally, the lessons in IBS-2 attend not only to observation and interpretation, but also to contemporary appropriation and to proclamation, areas that are not so easily reducible to specific tasks as are observation and interpretation (see Lessons 2-13 in the syllabus for NT[IBS]646 in the SYLLABUS APPENDICES).

3. CHARACTERISTICS OF MARKING IBS LESSONS

Substantive feedback is critical for learning and growth in IBS. Such substantive feedback is *specific* in that it indicates precisely what the student has done well and is thus to be commended or identifies omissions or missteps that the student may have committed and therefore offers particular suggestions for improvement. Students should be able to discern clearly from such comments exactly what they can do to improve their work.

This substantive feedback is also *encouraging*. It is important that comments not only flag errors or deficiencies but also lavish praise on students insofar as they have performed well. In my experience, students are very anxious and lacking in self-confidence to master what for most of them is the new and daunting world of IBS; this is especially the case with beginning students. They long to receive commendation and affirmation; when this is legitimately offered, it goes far in addressing the affective domain that is so important for student learning.

Such substantive feedback is also *kind*. I have just mentioned the insecurity many students feel in the face of IBS. Comments that come across as harsh lead students to believe that they are not being valued; instead, in this case they believe that they, or at least their work, are demeaned. Such comments foster discouragement and erode the sense of support and personal approachability that students have a right—and need—to expect from their instructor. On a few occasions in the past, I have employed grading assistants who, as it turned out, seemed to be genuinely angry with students and especially those students they considered were not performing according to their standards. I fear that some instructors also harbor such attitudes. It is absolutely essential that our sense of frustration as instructors never seeps through into our comments on students' work. In this regard, it is important to remember that the issue is not finally what *we intend to communicate*, but rather *how we will be heard* by students. My practice has always been to "go the extra mile" to be sure that any corrective comments are couched in the gentlest language and carry the most inoffensive tone as possible.

Moreover, substantive feedback may be *direct*, by which I mean it may involve face-to-face conversation with the student over against simply written comments on the submitted lesson. The regular submission of lessons that is characteristic of most IBS classes (in contrast to a single term paper submitted at the end of the course) allows the instructor to become aware of problems that students may be experiencing at the beginning or middle of the term—when face-to-face intervention is most effective. I have found that students who are "struggling" benefit greatly from one-on-one discussion and instruction; and in some cases, this is the only effective remediation. Granted, these kinds of interventions may be time-consuming; but teachers have an obligation to *each* student and such investment of time is a critically important part of our work. At the same time, the value of direct feedback obtains also for the exceptional student since face-to-face meetings with superior students afford the opportunity to encourage them to fulfill their outstanding potential and to explore ways in which they can move forward to greater heights.

In addition, substantive feedback should be *timely*. Again, timely feedback is important for all instruction, regardless of the course, since students benefit most when they receive interaction on work that is relatively fresh in their minds; but quick turnaround is especially critical for IBS. The considerations that IBS classes typically require the regular submission of lessons and that these lessons either require the same practices as earlier lessons or build upon earlier lessons underscores the need to deliver feedback to students as soon as possible. Otherwise, students will tend to make the same mistakes that will then become reinforced and may be difficult to correct.

Finally, substantive feedback should be *consistent*. The same problems or issues tend to appear repeatedly in lessons; therefore, it is helpful to develop a list of comments that address each of these recurring issues. Such a list is particularly important if grading assistants are being employed, or if the course is sometimes taught by adjuncts who are expected to provide the same kind of feedback as continuing professors. Included below are my own list of comments that pertain to various kinds of IBS lessons: the survey of the book and the segment, detailed observation, and interpretation generally and of parables. The designation "ST" indicates that the issue involves a standard whose "violation" will result in grade penalty of some sort; "SU" indicates a suggestion that is not an expectation or requirement, but simply something for the student to consider.

4. COMMENTS FOR BOOK AND/OR SEGMENT SURVEYS

4.1 Comments Unique to Book Surveys

B1 Please begin your book survey by noting the General Materials (Biographical, Historical, Chronological, Geographical, or Ideological). (ST)

B2 Note that General Materials is not the same as Literary Form (Prose Narrative, Poetry, Apocalyptic, Discursive, Parable), which is noted in segment survey. There is no need to identify Literary Form in your book survey. (ST)

B3 Difficult though it may be, selected only ONE type of General Material that best represents the material of the book as a whole. It may help to ask yourself, "What is it about the book that most clearly governs its meaning?" (ST)

4.2 Comments Unique to Segment Surveys

S1 Please include in your segment survey the Literary Form (Prose Narrative, Poetry, Apocalyptic, Discursive, Parable). (ST)

S2 Note that Literary Form is not the same as general Materials (Biographical, Historical, Geographical, or Ideological) which is noted in Book Survey. There is no need to identify General Materials in your segment survey. (ST)

S3 Please note the difference between paragraphs and subunits. Although the two are sometimes the same, paragraphs are explicit in how the text has already been divided (you should see the paragraph divisions in the use of indentation in your English Bible). In contrast, subunits are established through your own observations and determination of how the material should be divided. (ST)

4.3 Comments Regarding both Book and Segment Surveys

C1 Please remember to describe the structure of the material in terms of major units and subunits. (ST) It may help you to do this as either a figure or a simple table. (SU)

C2 Be sure to make your units as broad as the material will allow, yet not broader than the material allows. Usually, two to four major units and two to four subunits per major unit will divide the material well. Too few divisions will fail to help you to see the real development of the material, while too many divisions will cause you to fail to see the overall movement of the text. (ST)

C3 When observing structural relationships, please be sure that the structure you have noted governs at least 50% of the text under observation. In completing your survey, it's natural to notice structures that occur in narrow portions of the text. However, such a structure should not be included as a major structure in your survey. (ST)

C4 After each major structure has been identified, please substantiate/explain the structure with a description as well as specific verse citations, indicating exactly what and where this structure is. For example, it is insufficient to note simply that there is a structure of comparison. Instead, please indicate what exactly is compared, specific ways in which the comparisons are made, and specific examples from the text. (ST)

C5 Recurrence is a common structure, so it's always helpful and somewhat easier to begin by looking for recurring terms and themes (especially if you feel "stuck" in observing structures). However, recurring terms are often involved in broader and more specific structures (e.g., recurrence or contrast). Therefore, when you identify recurrence, be sure to ask yourself if the recurrence is pointing to another more specific structure within the text. (ST)

C6 When noting recurrence of structural relationships, be sure that individual instances are directly and materially related by a common theme. For example, the recurrence of contrast most typically involves the same two elements (e.g., freedom and slavery) contrasted throughout. The recurrence of essentially unrelated contrasts (e.g., freedom and slavery, followed by heavenly and earthly) does not constitute recurrence of contrast, but rather two separate instances of contrast. Be sure to ask yourself, "How is each instance related to the other so as to constitute recurrence?" (ST)

C7 Note that some apparent structural relationships are inherent or implicit (naturally occurring) within other structural relationships. For example, particularization naturally involves an element of preparation/realization. It's best to note the most specific and precise relationship. See the handout on major structural relationships for a review of general relationship implicit in more specific ones. (ST)

C8 Narrative material, such as found in the Gospels, contains a natural element of "plot" that is often hard to differentiate from the recurrence of causation. This natural "concatenation" (chain-like causal connection between events) is necessary to keep the story moving forward (e.g., A causes B, B causes C, C caused D); without it, there would be no connection to the elements of the story. Be sure to ask yourself, "Is this apparent causation simply a part of the plot, or is the author specifically emphasizing a causal relationship?" (ST)

C9 Rhetorical relationships (inclusio, interchange, chiasm, intercalation) are most often used to reinforce a semantic structural relationship (especially contrast and comparison). They are not usually employed independently. Therefore, whenever you identify the presence of a rhetorical relationship, be sure to ask yourself, "Is there be a semantic structural relationship that this rhetorical relationship is supporting?" (ST)

C10 The frequent citation of Old Testament verses as evidence of fulfilled prophecy within NT books should not normally be considered preparation/realization, but rather, recurrence of OT citations. Preparation/realization should be identified only when the prediction is made within the material itself and then is later realized within the same material. (ST)

C11 For each major structural relationship noted, be sure to ask all three types of questions: Definitive (what, how, who, when), rational (why), and implicational (what are the implications). (ST)

C12 Please group your structural questions by type (definitive, rational, implicational) and ask the structural questions in the following order: definitive, rational, implicational. (ST)

C13 It's best not to be too specific in asking the implicational question, lest you find yourself wandering into premature interpretation. Simply ask, "What are the implications," or simply, "Implications?" (ST)

C14 Try to avoid asking questions that can simply be answered with a "yes" or "no." (ST)

C15 Please direct your questions specifically to the structure under observation rather than directing questions toward details of specific passages. (ST)

C16 When asking definitive questions, try to avoid asking "What is the significance?" or "What is the importance?" These actually move toward implicational questions. Therefore, it would be better to simply ask, "Implications?" and to ask them last. (SU)

C17 When asking definitive questions, try to avoid asking "What is the Purpose?" or "What is the author's intent?" or "What did the author want to do?" These are actually rational questions. (ST)

C18 Be sure to indicate one or two strategic verses that specifically address each major structural relationship you've observed, and explicitly identify what structural relationship is represented by this verse or these verses (strategic areas). (ST)

C19 These verses are to be strategic, so keep them few in number and narrow in scope. (ST)

C20 Verses that appear to be significant to you but are not specifically related to a major structural relationship should not be included as "Strategic Verses." (ST)

C21 Please include, as your final portion of the survey, a section entitled, "Other Major Impressions." This is a place for you to note observations that don't fit into previous survey categories. (ST) Such impressions may help you in later interpretive work, including observations regarding the tone or mood of the material. You might also note here some unresolved questions you'd like to pursue in more detail later. (SU)

C22 Be sure to explain/substantiate your "Other Major Impressions" with sentences as well as specific exemplary verses. (ST)

5. COMMENTS FOR DETAILED OBSERVATION

O1 When referring to the biblical text, always provide verse numbers for each observation made. (ST)

O2 Neither quoting the text nor paraphrasing the text constitutes a legitimate observation. Rather, make specific and descriptive observations about what is in the text. (ST)

O3 Please be sure to make a variety of types of observations, including Term-al, Grammatical, Structural, Logical, and Contextual observations. See the handout on Detailed Observations for definitions of each type of observation. (ST) You might find it helpful when examining each verse, clause, etc. to step through mentally each of the 5 types of observation, stopping after each type to see if you can make that type of observation for the text being observed. (SU)

O4 Be sure to make "bite-sized" observations, favoring specificity and clarity in several smaller observations rather than trying to observe too much at once. (SU)

O5 For each detailed observation, please substantiate/explain the observation with sentences indicating exactly what and where the term, structure, grammatical construction, etc. is. It is insufficient to simply note that there is a structure of comparison, e.g., in a verse. Instead, please indicate exactly what is compared. (ST)

O6 Rhetorical structures (inclusio, interchange, chiasm, intercalation) are most often used to reinforce a semantic structural relationship. They are not often used independently. Therefore, whenever you identify the presence of a rhetorical structure, be sure to ask yourself, "Where may there be a semantic structural relationship that the rhetorical relationship is supporting?" (ST)

O7 It's best to be methodical in making observations, moving from broad observations (paragraph as a whole) to more specific observations (whole verses and groups of verses, individual clauses within each verse) to the most detailed observations (phrases and terms within each clause). After having made observations of a specific verse as a whole, it usually helps with continuity of thought to move next to individual clauses and words for that verse before moving on to consideration of the next verse as a whole. For example, observe verse 1, 1a, terms within 1a, 1b, terms within 1b, then move on to verse 2. Note that this example simply illustrates the flow of observation, not a rigid procedure. See the handout on Detailed Observations for an illustration of this movement. (SU)

O8 It's common, but erroneous, to engage in premature interpretation during detailed observation. It might help to ask yourself, "Could this observation be once it is pointed out?" If the answer is "yes" you may be moving prematurely into interpretation. (ST)

O9 Giving the definition of a term is actually part of the process of interpretation rather than detailed observation. Consequently, this attempt to define should be excluded from the detailed observation. (ST)

O10 For each observation made, be sure to ask all three types of questions: Definitive (what, how), rational (why), and implicational (what are the implications). (ST)

O11 Please group your questions by type (definitive, rational, implicational) and ask the questions in the following order: definitive, rational, implicational. (ST)

O12 It's best not to be too specific in asking the implicational questions, lest you find yourself wandering into premature interpretation. Simply ask, "What are the implications," or simply, "Implications?" (ST)

O13 Try to avoid asking questions that can simply be answered with a "yes" or "no." (ST)

O14 Please direct your questions to the observation you made regarding the specific term, grammar, structure, etc. under observation. (ST)

O15 When asking definitive questions, try to avoid asking "What is the significance?" or "What is the importance?" These actually move toward implicational questions. Therefore, it would be better to simply ask, "Implications?" and to ask them last. (SU)

O16 When asking definitive questions, try to avoid asking "What is the Purpose?" or "What is the author's intent?" or "What did the author want to do?" These are actually rational questions. (ST)

6. COMMENTS FOR INTERPRETATION

6.1 General Comments Regarding Interpretation

I1 It's helpful to list the interpretive determinants you intend to use, in the order you'll use them at the top of your first page. You can always add or subtract from this list as time allows, but this should help to guide you in how you plan to use your time. (SU)

I2 It's helpful to separate clearly and identify explicitly your use of each interpretive determinant (Preliminary Definition, Context, Historical Background, Scriptural Testimony,

Interpretation of Others, etc.). In other words, label and complete each determinant before moving on to the next one. You can always go back and add to your work if time allows.[2]

I3 It's helpful to summarize periodically your major evidence and conclusions, usually following your treatment of each interpretive determinant. (SU)

I4 Preliminary Definition is often a helpful interpretive determinant. When used, this determinant should normally be the first determinant cited. (SU)

I5 When citing preliminary definitions, try to limit inferences to those taken from the lexical evidence itself, leaving contextual observations until your separate treatment of that interpretive determinant. (ST)

I6 Preliminary Definitions should draw from lexical entries (e.g., Thayer, BDAG, BDB) rather than English dictionaries, concordance entries, theological wordbooks (e.g., Kittel, Colin Brown), or your own experience or reasoning. (ST)

I7 After dealing with Preliminary Definition, move on to other interpretive determinants only after you have given detailed and thorough attention to context, both the immediate context (the text being interpreted and the passages immediately surrounding it) and the broader book context (the passages of the book within which the text being interpreted falls). (ST)

I8 When including the interpretive determinant of Word Usage, be sure to account for every occurrence of the word (regardless of inflections). (ST)

I9 Structural observations (contrast, climax, etc.) belong within the determinant of Context. (ST)

I10 Please substantiate/explain structural evidence with sentences indicating exactly what and where major structural relationships exist. For example, it is insufficient to note simply that there is a structure of climax. Instead, please indicate what exactly is involved in the climax and how and where the climax is reached. (ST)

I11 Be careful to site specific evidence to substantiate any inferences you draw. It might help to ask yourself, "Could this inference be challenged as an opinion, or have I made its factual basis clear with specific evidence?" (ST)

I12 Be careful not to cite evidence without also drawing all relevant inferences from the evidence. It might be helpful to ask yourself, "What are the inferences that can reasonably be drawn from this evidence?" (ST)

---

[2] IBS-1 only, since it is important for beginning students to differentiate among various types of evidence. Once they come to understand what is involved in each type of evidence, they may find it helpful to compose lists of premises that represent different types of evidence. See the distinction between "analytical" and "synthetic" models of interpretation in David R. Bauer and Robert A. Traina, *Inductive Bible Study: A Comprehensive Guide to the Practice of Hermeneutics* (Grand Rapids: Baker Academic, 2011, 239-46).

Chapter 14—Reflections on the Role of Student Assignments in the Instruction of IBS

I13 It's a common mistake to offer inferences as evidence, or evidence as inference. Inferences come from your own careful analysis of the evidence. (ST) One helpful strategy for encouraging this differentiation is to preface evidential statements with "whereas…" and inferential statements with "therefore…" (SU)

I14 It's easy to get sidetracked from the central issue in interpretation. One way to stay focused is to make clear statements of focus in each inferential statement (e.g., "Therefore, the meaning of "loose" in Matt 5:19 is…"). (SU)

I15 Be careful not to infer more nor less than the evidence cited will support, and avoid committing interpretive fallacies (see *Inductive Bible Study*, pp. 249–69). (ST)

I16 Be specific in both citing and describing evidence and in drawing inferences from evidence. (ST)

I17 The terms "infer" and "imply" are commonly confused. As they relate to the task of interpretation, you (the interpreter) are the one who *infers*, or draws inferences from biblical and extra-biblical sources of evidence. The author (or redactor) of the biblical text may make *implications* through their construction of the text. With respect to commentators, they may both draw inferences from the biblical text (and other sources of evidence) as well as imply things through their own written comments. (SU)

I18 Neither quoting the biblical text nor simply paraphrasing the text constitutes sufficient evidence from which to draw inferences. You need briefly and tentatively to say something about what you think the passage you are citing as evidence means (this explanation of the meaning of the cited text should itself be included, with the textual citation, under evidence). Such explanations of the meaning of the text are necessary to make specific, well-grounded inferences. (ST)

I19 Interpretation of Others is a required interpretive determinant. Be sure to engage the work of at least two major commentators when addressing this determinant. (ST)

I20 Interpretation of Others should be the last interpretive determinant you consider (i.e., be sure to make your own judgments prior to assessing those of others). (ST)

I21 Remember that commentators are just that—people offering educated comments on the text. As such, be sure to engage commentators critically. Examine the evidence and arguments offered by a commentator and indicate what it is about their evidence and arguments that you find either persuasive or unconvincing (draw your own inferences based on our interaction with their evidence rather than simply listing inferences supplied by the commentator). (ST)

I22 Always conclude your interpretation with a general summary of your findings and interpretive options – a paraphrase in which you present specifically your answer to the interpretive question raised. (ST)

I23 Please cite specific sources when possible (author, source title) when referring to the work of others for Preliminary Definition, Historical Background, Interpretation of Others, and other relevant interpretive determinants. (ST)

6.2 General Comments Regarding the Interpretation of Parables

C1 You should begin your interpretation of parables by noting the structure of the parable. (ST)

C2 Please substantiate/explain the structure of the parable with one or more sentences indicating exactly what and where major structural relationships exist. It is insufficient to simply note that there is, e.g., a structure of climax in a parable. Instead, please indicate what exactly is involved in the climax and how and where the climax is reached. (ST)

C3 Rhetorical structures (inclusio, interchange, chiasm, intercalation) are most often used to reinforce a semantic structural relationship. They are not often used independently. Therefore, whenever you identify the presence of an auxiliary structure, be sure to ask yourself, "Where may there be a major structural relationship that this auxiliary relationship is supporting?" (ST)

C4 Be careful to cite evidence to substantiate any inferences you draw. It might help to ask yourself, "Could this evidence be challenged as an opinion, or have I made its factual basis clear?" (ST)

C5 Be sure to be clear about what is evidence and what is inference. It's common to mistakenly offer inferences as evidence, or evidence as inference. This may be particularly true for parables where Jesus supplies an interpretation. For example, in the parable of the sower, 13:19–23 constitutes a body of evidence from which to draw, not inferences. Inferences come from your own careful analysis of the evidence. (ST)

C6 Be careful in your interpretation not to extrapolate beyond what is warranted by the evidence. Extrapolation is particularly tempting in the interpretation of parables because we can usually supply details to the metaphor from our own experience that are not directly given in the text itself. Pressing these self-supplied details can lead to erroneous interpretation. (ST)

C7 Neither quoting the text nor paraphrasing the text constitutes legitimate evidence. (ST)

C8 Let the context and the structure of the parable be the primary means for determining the major issues and details you explore in your interpretation. (ST)

C9 Be sure to note the various audiences of the parables. What is the significance of each parable for each audience? For example, how does the significance of the parable of the sower differ or remain the same for disciples versus the crowd? (ST)

C10 Be sure to engage the work of at least two major commentaries in the course of your interpretation. (ST)

C11 Remember that commentators are just that – people offering educated comments on the text. As such, be sure to engage commentators critically. Examine the evidence and arguments offered by a commentator and indicate what about their evidence and arguments that you find either persuasive or unconvincing. (ST)

C12 Conclude your interpretation with a clear summary of your major interpretive option. Which interpretation do you prefer, and why? (ST)

7. The Assessment of Lessons

Everyone recognizes that grades are not a perfect measure of student achievement; but they can, and should, serve as a proximate guide to student performance. Since the list of comments for lessons that I have included above reflect standards of performance, they could, of course, serve as "rubrics" for grading. And for me in some measure they do; but with two significant qualifications.

First, no list of comments, including the ones I have provided, can exhaust the possible issues or problems that might surface in students' work. The IBS process is simply too dynamic to be thus contained. Therefore, for me grades are not totally and exclusively dependent upon matters represented in this list.

Second, the reader will note that the comments I have listed above are not weighted. Some of the issues represented in these comments are more significant than others; deficiencies in more significant matters would have a greater effect on the grade for the lesson than would be the case for comments that pertain to less central concerns. Of course, it would be possible to weight these comments. However, I have personally resisted developing a list of rubrics that are specifically calibrated to grade score, so that, for example, deficiency for C2 would automatically reduce the student's score by five points. In my judgment, the work of IBS is just too dynamic and complex to be reduced to this kind of simple numerical scoring. In the case of C2, for example, the grade consequence would depend upon how egregiously the student failed to see the broad, overarching movement of the material and therefore into how many small, choppy units the student divided the material. And we need to take into account the nature of the biblical material. Continuing the example from C2, we note that the major breaks in some books or passages are more evident than is the case with others. A student who misses an obvious and clear-cut break should be penalized more significantly than one who fails to see one that is more subtle and difficult to detect.

I want to emphasize that what I have said regarding the use of rubrics is simply my own opinion. I do not fault colleagues who employ rubrics that carry specific numerical scoring implications. In fact, I understand the advantage of doing so, especially in the sense that such a practice may assist in offering a level of objectivity to grading. But my own conclusion is that the complex character of the practice of IBS requires a host of individual, and sometimes subtle, judgments on the part of the instructor that together should be considered in the assignment of grades.

8. Conclusion

I wish to mention, in conclusion, a couple principles that I keep in mind in the process of assigning grades in conclusion. The first is the principle of *progress*. By this I mean that my expectations for student work increase throughout the period of the term. I recognize that it is only fair to give students more leniency as they are beginning to master a certain aspect of IBS; but it is reasonable to anticipate that as the semester proceeds, so also their competency should increase. The rise of expectations corresponds to the degree of rigor in grading.

I also attend to the principle of *realism*. I wish to grade students on the basis of what I can reasonably expect them to accomplish. I recognize that students cannot be expected to approximate the quality of work that could be produced by a scholar, or by someone who has significant experience in IBS or in biblical studies in general, or someone who has had an entire semester to work on a passage which I have given them only a week to do. This is one of the reasons I do not grade students on the basis of whether or not they agree with my conclusions.[3] I grade them on the basis of their understanding of IBS method and their ability to apply that method to the biblical text, according to where they are in the process. Fortunately, after having taught IBS for more than 34 years, I think (or perhaps I should say, I hope) that I have acquired some sense of what I can realistically expect of students.

---

[3] Other reasons exist for my not grading students on this basis. For one thing, in the specific interpretation of many passages there is room for at least some differences in conclusions; equally competent scholars do not always agree.

The Benefits of a General-Analytic Grading Rubric for Book Surveys and Other IBS Assignments

Fredrick J. Long
Professor of New Testament and Director of Greek Instruction,
Asbury Theological Seminary

ABSTRACT: Grading rubrics describe levels of performance according to the criteria of an assignment in order to best assess it for optimal student learning. The proper selection of the type of rubric can assist students to learn IBS skills. Among the benefits of using a general-analytical rubric for IBS assignments are the clear partition of the assignment into observable criteria, its learning benefits for students, and the efficiencies for grading/evaluation. This essay summarizes select sound principles of rubric creation while describing the creation of a Book Survey Evaluation Rubric developed for undergraduate and graduate students and showing the design features of a Semantic Diagramming and Analysis Evaluation Rubric.

1. Introduction to Rubrics

1.1 Definition

"What is a rubric?" asks Susan M. Brookhart. "A rubric is a coherent set of criteria for students' work that includes descriptions of levels of performance quality on the criteria…. It should be clear from the definition that rubrics have two major aspects: coherent sets of criteria and descriptions of levels of performance for these criteria"; the simple purpose is "to assess performance."[1] Similarly, Dannelle D. Stevens and Antonia J. Levi proffer the following definition: "At its most basic, a rubric is a scoring tool that lays out the specific expectations for an assignment. Rubrics divide an assignment into its component parts and provide a detailed description of what constitutes acceptable or unacceptable levels of performance for each of those parts."[2] According to Brookhart grading rubrics should be both well-designed and used for learning/grading. Regarding their design, two features must be present: "First, rubrics must have clear and appropriate criteria about the learning students

---

[1] Susan M. Brookhart, *How to Create and Use Rubrics for Formative Assessment and Grading* (Alexandria, VA: ASCD Member Book, 2013), 4. On the difference between rubrics and checklists and rating scales, see ch. 7.

[2] Dannelle D. Stevens and Antonia J. Levi, *Introduction to Rubrics: An Assessment Tool to Save Grading Time, Convey Effective Feedback, and Promote Student Learning* (Sterling, VA: Stylus, 2005), 4.

will be demonstrating (not about the task). Second, rubrics must have clear descriptions of performance over a continuum of quality."[3] In what follows, I will describe how I came to develop an IBS book survey rubric which is also applicable to segment surveys. I did not follow any method at the time in the development of this rubric; however, it just so happens that I incidentally (!) followed fairly sound principles; I will thus present recent perspectives and practical steps for creating a rubric using the rubric I developed as an illustration.

1.2 Types of Rubrics

Brookhart helpfully displays four types of rubrics in two alternative pairings: Analytical or Holistic and General or Task-Specific; each has relative advantages and disadvantages (see Figure 1). In the first pairing, one asks how many assessment judgments are being made: Is it over the whole assignment (holistic) or on different portions of it (analytic). In the second pairing, one considers whether the rubric may be applied to any number of individual assignments (general) or is applicable to one specific assignment (task-specific).

Figure 1—Four Types of Rubrics (from Susan M. Brookhart)[4]

Holistic or Analytic: One or Several Judgments?			
Rubric Type	**Definition**	**Advantages**	**Disadvantages**
Analytic	• Each criterion (dimension, trait) is evaluated separately.	• Gives diagnostic information to teacher. • Gives formative feedback to students. • Easier to link to instruction than holistic rubrics. • Good for formative assessment; adaptable for summative assessment; if you need an overall score for grading, you can combine the scores.	• Takes more time to score than holistic rubrics. • Takes more time to achieve inter-rater reliability than with holistic rubrics.
Holistic	• All criteria (dimensions, traits) are evaluated simultaneously.	• Scoring is faster than with analytic rubrics. • Requires less time to achieve inter-rater reliability. • Good for summative assessment.	• Single overall score does not communicate information about what to do to improve. • Not good for formative assessment.

---

[3] Brookhart, *How to Create and Use Rubrics*, x.
[4] Ibid., 7–8. The chart has been recreated with some adjustment in headings.

\multicolumn{4}{c}{**Description of Performance: General or Task-Specific?**}
Rubric Type	**Definition**	**Advantages**	**Disadvantages**
General	• Description of work gives characteristics that apply to a whole family of tasks (e.g., writing, problem solving).	• Can share with students, explicitly linking assessment and instruction. • Reuse same rubrics with several tasks or assignments. • Supports learning by helping students see "good work" as bigger than one task. • Supports student self-evaluation. • Students can help construct general rubrics.	• Lower reliability at first than with task-specific rubrics. • Requires practice to apply well.
Task-specific	• Description of work refers to the specific content of a particular task (e.g., gives an answer, specifies a conclusion).	• Teachers sometimes say using these makes scoring "easier." • Requires less time to achieve inter-rater reliability.	• Cannot share with students (would give away answers). • Need to write new rubrics for each task. • For open-ended tasks, good answers not listed in rubrics may be evaluated poorly.

Since the book/segment survey rubric that I developed treats different portions of a book survey and may be applicable to different assignments (i.e., different biblical books or segments being survey), it is classified as a General-Analytic rubric. Brookhart argues that "general" rubrics are preferable since they help students "build up general knowledge and skills" as well as "conceptualize their learning targets and to monitor their own progress"; "General rubrics are particularly useful for fundamental skills that develop over time."[5]

2. Rationale for Rubrics in IBS Instruction

Two broad reasons support the use of well-crafted grading rubrics, especially of the general variety (since they are used for different assignments): studies on learning and the grading demands typically associated with the great number of assignments found in an IBS or IBS-related course. First, studies have shown that at all grade levels across different disciplines effectively constructed and implemented rubrics enhance learning.[6] Brookhart further explains:

---

[5] Ibid., 10–11 and 40. Specifically, general-analytic rubrics are promoted in ch. 4.
[6] Ibid., 12–14.

The criteria and performance-level descriptions in rubrics help students understand what the desired performance is and what it looks like. Effective rubrics show students how they will know to what extent their performance passes muster on each criterion of importance, and if used formatively can also show students what their next steps should be to enhance the quality of their performance. This claim is backed by research at all grade levels and in different disciplines. [7]

Moreover, rubrics help distill essential aspects of complex assignments for achieving learning targets when shared with the students ahead of time. Thus, according to Brookhart, "Rubrics make especially good vehicles for sharing learning targets when the target is complex and not just a matter of recall of information. The reason is that rubrics bring together sets of relevant criteria. The nature of a complex understanding or skill is that several qualities must operate at one time."[8] The methodical study of Scripture that involves the development of skill in complex operations seems well-suited for the development of assessment rubrics.

Second, when IBS is taught well, students are allowed many opportunities for practicing the various types of IBS assignments, especially book and segment surveys. I experienced this firsthand in an undergraduate setting. Once establishing IBS as the framework for the first-year Biblical Hermeneutics class at the core of the undergraduate Bible curriculum (which every student majoring in Bible and Ministry had to take), I realized the need to help students improve their survey skills as painlessly as possible, both for them and for me as their instructor/grader. This foundational course was prerequisite for two subsequent courses in which I would have students practice again and again book and segment survey skills—"Acts and Paul" and "The Latter NT"—altogether comprising twenty-three books of the NT. However, the prospect of grading hundreds and hundreds of book and segment surveys was quite daunting.[9] Since "A" papers are much easier to grade than "C" ones and as Brookhart affirms, "over time general rubrics help students build up a concept of what it means to perform a skill well," I was motivated to help students learn well as soon as possible how to perform surveys.[10] Again, "If the rubrics are the same each time a student does the same kind of work, the student will learn general qualities of good essay writing, problem solving, and so on."[11] In one graduate class alone I had seventeen IBS assignments with close to twenty students equating to over 300 assignments to grade. (Incidentally, in the next iteration of the course I required only ten IBS assignments.) Indeed, among the reasons that Stevens and Levi give (somewhat humorously) for creating a grading rubric are the following which applied in my situation:[12]

---

[7] Ibid., 12.

[8] Ibid., 101.

[9] For details of this curricular move and sample syllabi, see my essay above "On the Proper Sequencing of Classes: The Foundation of Inductive Bible Study."

[10] Brookhart, *How to Create and Use Rubrics*, 10.

[11] Ibid.

[12] Stevens and Levi, *Introduction to Rubrics*, 4–5.

- grading fatigue (carpal tunnel syndrome)
- getting behind on one's grading
- students complain about not being able to read your grading comments
- inconsistency in grading and comments (the last ones suffering the most)
- the assignment is complex, involving multiple parts
- the need to explain complex matters in succinct ways to prompt deeper student reflection
- despite your clear statements/explanations, students repeatedly ask the same 2–3 questions
- students regularly perform poorly or inconsistently on certain parts of the assignment.

Additional reasons for creating a rubric for surveys would be to standardize assignment descriptions and evaluations between different classes taught by different faculty. For these sorts of reasons, I set out to create a rubric for grading book/segment surveys.

3. Constructing a Book or Segment Survey Rubric

One principle of rubric creation stated clearly by Stevens and Levi is as follows:

> In general, the degree to which rubrics facilitate grading by avoiding repetition is in direct inverse ratio to how long it took us to create the rubric. Some rubrics take longer to construct precisely because we are adding all of those feedback details ahead of time that is, before the students even start the assignment.
>
> Three-to-five level rubrics with check boxes are the most time consuming to create but the fastest and easiest to use. Three-to-five level rubrics that require us to circle relevant text take a bit more time to use. Scoring guide rubrics designed to give narrative feedback are the easiest and fastest to create, but their grading ease is somewhat limited by the time it takes to write out the feedback.[13]

My development of a book/segment survey rubric evolved over several semesters; one should consider that trial and error is always a healthy way to approach adding new components to a course, whether it be assignments, ordering of lecture, grading implements, and especially rubrics. My rubric requires circling items observed in students' work but also contains room to write in brief comments. Below I will describe a step-by-step approach one can take to develop a rubric, using as an example the one that I have created and still use.

3.1 Basic Parts of a Rubric

Stevens and Levi explain that there are four components to rubric creation:[14]

1. Task Description
2. Componental Parts (and their relative score value)
3. Scales
4. Description of the Componental Parts

---

[13] Stevens and Levi, *Introduction to Rubrics*, 75.

[14] I have reordered these by switching Componental Parts (what they call "Dimensions") with Scales; see Stevens and Levi, *Introduction to Rubrics*, 5–13.

The basic worksheet they provide (slightly modified) is as follows:

	Title:			
Task Description:				
	Scale 1	Scale 2	Scale 3	Scale 4
Componential Part 1				
Componential Part 2				
Componential Part 3				
Componential Part 4				

How to use this worksheet will become more apparent in the following sections.

3.2 Task Description

Below I provide my basic Book Survey description from an undergraduate course (BIBL 223 from Spring 2006) and a graduate class (NT 631 from Fall 2017).[15] I should state here that in my approach, I am Bauerian (i.e., I follow more or less the format and procedure taught by David R. Bauer). I have been able to adapt this rubric for those following a Dongellian approach (Joseph R. Dongell) or a Thompsonian approach (David L. Thompson). Since a segment survey does not require students to collect Historical-Critical information found in the book concerning authorship, audience, and provenance (a component of a book survey), in the book segment rubric I moved the 10% value of this Historical-Critical component to the Structural Presentation component (10% to 20%) (see below).

BIBL 223 "NT III—General Epistles and Revelation" at Bethel College (Spring 2006)	**Book Survey of James (4 hours)** 1. Identify general literary form (poetry, discursive and logical, letter, historical, etc.). 2. Give chapter headings for each chapter (two or three words maximum). 3. <u>Locate</u> the Major divisions and sub-divisions of the book and <u>identify</u> the Major Structural Relationships (MSR) operative in the book (introduction, summarization, causation, etc.). **Be prepared to discuss these in class.** 4. Ask 4 types of interpretive questions for each MSR observed (what? how? why? implications?) 5. Summarize strategic areas from MSRs identified. 6. Identify data that bear on such questions as authorship, audience, provenance, etc.

---

[15] I have used these nearly identical descriptions to explain my "Tertiary Procedures" for the exegetical step of "Contextual Location" in my *In Step with God's Word: Interpreting the New Testament as God's People*, GlossaHouse Hermeneutics & Translation 1 (Wilmore, KY: GlossaHouse, 2017), 71; however, I do not include a grading rubric in that chapter.

Chapter 15—Benefits of a General-Analytic Grading Rubric for Book Surveys and Other IBS Assignments   261

	7. Note other important impressions about the book (tone of author, atmosphere, etc.) 8. Indicate on the top of the first page how much time you spent on this assignment. 9. Be sure to consult the Book or Segment Survey Evaluation Rubric.
NT 631 "Ephesians Exegesis" at Asbury Theological Seminary (Fall 2017)	**100 pts. Book Survey of Ephesians** (7 hours max) 0. Indicate your name and *the amount of time spent* on this assignment in hours; 1. Identify general literary form or genre (e.g. poetry, discursive and logical, letter, historical, parable, miracle, prophetic, legal, proverbial, apocalyptic). 2. Give short (3 words max), unique, accurate, but catchy titles for each chapter. 3. Locate the Major divisions and sub-divisions of the Book and depict them in a clear way; 4. Identify and briefly describe the major structural relationships operative in the book (such as introduction, summarization, causation, etc.). In order for the structural relationship to be major, it must govern a majority of the text (If there are six chapters, then it must span three or more chapters; e.g. three verses at the start of a letter may provide an Introduction to the rest of the letter, and thus govern a majority of the text). 5. Ask the four types of interpretative questions <u>for</u> <u>each</u> structural relationship identified. These summarized are What? How? Why? What are the Implications? <u>BUT</u>, do <u>not</u> answer these questions. 6. Summarize the Strategic Areas for <u>each</u> MSR identified and described in the Survey. Basically, the strategic areas are a <u>restatement</u> of the <u>key</u> verses associated with each Major Structural Relationship. So, for each major structural relationship identified, you should have one strategic area. There is no new information here; just a selective recap of what you observed. In the case of repetition or reoccurrence, select the occurrence that is most representative of the set of occurrences. 7. Note Other Major Impressions, such as tone, atmosphere, figures of speech, or other structurally significant observations *not already accounted for previously in the Book Survey.* 8. Include information found within the book on Authorship, Audience, and Provenance (that is, the dating and historical circumstances surrounding the writing). Consider what evidence exists from within the Book itself; do <u>not</u> use outside sources or secondary works like Bible Dictionaries here! First, be sure to consult the Grading Rubric provided in order to assist in the performance of your Book Survey.

It is perhaps not surprising that my description of the Book Survey has become more robust and specific. My purpose in doing so is to clarify important areas where students may go astray. For example, under 8. above for the Ephesians Class, I clarify that students should not consult outside source like Bible Dictionaries.

3.3 Componental Parts

The purpose of delineating componental parts, or what Stevens and Levi call "dimensions," is to "represent the type of component skills students must combine in a successful scholarly work, such as the need for a firm grasp of content, technique, citation, examples, analysis, and a use of language appropriate to the occasion."[16] Also, these componental parts should not have qualitative descriptors like "*Good* Structural Presentation"; instead, they should simply state the discrete skill/performance feature being assessed. Also, one should consider the relative value of each of the component parts as contributing to the students' final scoring.

With the above Book Survey descriptions in mind, then, I had to decide how best to envision the componental parts and their relative weight/value. I eventually settled on these seven parts upon which to create a rubric. Questions will help define what is being evaluated:

1. <u>Completeness and Time Spent (20%)</u>: Have all the parts of the assignment as described been attempted/completed? Also, has the assignment been done within the parameters of time allotted for the assignment?
2. <u>Chapter or Paragraph Titles (10%)</u>: Has the student given appropriate titles for each chapter in the book survey or paragraphs in the segment survey?
3. <u>Structural Presentation (10%; for segment surveys 20%)</u>: How well has the student accounted (graphically) for the book's or segment's structure?
4. <u>Major Structural Relationships (30%)</u>: How well has the student identified and described the major structural relationships operative in the book or segment?
5. <u>Questions (10%)</u>: Has the student asked appropriate questions for each major structural relationship?
6. <u>Other Major Impressions/Observations (10%)</u>: Has the student made other "major" observations pertaining to tone, atmosphere, figures of speech, etc.?
7. <u>Higher Critical Information (10% for book surveys only)</u>: For book surveys, has the student addressed information in the book that speaks to authorship, audience, and provenance?

One may envision the relative weighting of the component parts differently. Four principles guide my weighting of the value of assignments in this rubric and in my classes: the time spent performing the task, the complexity of the task, the importance of the task for completing the assignment well, and simplicity of round/whole numbers. Since I place a high value on properly identifying and describing the Major Structural Relationships (30%), this receives the highest value in the rubric. Next would be Completeness (20%). Notice, too, that the values are all in increments of 10%.

---

[16] Stevens and Levi, *Introduction to Rubrics*, 10.

Two matters deserve some further comment. First, although it may have been prudent to separate Completeness and Time Spent, in my estimation these are very closely related. My desire to evaluate these together has to do with helping students be mindful of time spent and how to work efficiently so as to complete the entire survey process. Second, since I don't expect students to cull "Higher-critical Information" in a segment survey (which would be redundant with book survey work already completed presumably), the 10% value needs to go elsewhere. In my thinking, the best place was "Structural Presentation." This encouraged students to represent structural relationships creatively within their structural presentation; I would explain to them that more detail was expected to correspond with the increased value (from 10% to 20%). After identifying the component parts of an assignment, the next step is to determine the Scale description and values.

3.3 Scales

Very helpfully, Stevens and Levi summarize some of the most common verbal descriptors of scales as compiled from various sources by M. E. Huba and J. E. Freed:[17]

less competence			————> most competence
Not yet competent	Partly competent	Competent	Sophisticated
Unacceptable	Marginal	Proficient	Exemplary
Novice	Intermediate	Intermediate high	Advanced
Novice	Intermediate	Proficient	Distinguished
Beginning	Developing	Average	Accomplished

The Harriet W. Sheriden Center for Teaching and Learning provides the following scales for different numbers of levels:[18]

Three Levels

Weak	Satisfactory	Strong
Beginning	Intermediate	High
Weak	Average	Excellent
Developing	Competent	Exemplary
Low Mastery	Average Mastery	High Mastery

---

[17] Huba and Freed, *Learner-Centered Assessment on College Campuses: Shifting the Focus from Teaching to Learning* (Boston: Allyn & Bacon, 2000), 180 as cited by Stevens and Levi, *Introduction to Rubrics*, 8. I have reversed the order to have weak competency on the left moving to stronger competency on the right.

[18] https://www.brown.edu/sheridan/teaching-learning-resources/teaching-resources/course-design/classroom-assessment/grading-criteria/rubrics-scales accessed 6-25-2018.

Four Levels

Unacceptable	Marginal	Proficient	Distinguished
Beginning	Developing	Accomplished	Exemplary
Needs Improvement	Satisfactory	Good	Accomplished
Emerging	Progressing	Partial Mastery	Mastery
Not Yet Competent	Partly Competent	Competent	Sophisticated
Inadequate	Needs Improvement	Meets Expectations	Exceeds Expectations
Poor	Fair	Good	Excellent

Five Levels

Poor	Minimal	Sufficient	Above Average	Excellent
Novice	Intermediate	Proficient	Distinguished	Master
Unacceptable	Poor	Satisfactory	Good	Excellent

Six Levels

Unacceptable	Emerging	Minimally Acceptable	Acceptable	Accomplished	Exemplary

Be mindful, however, that the more levels are represented in the rubric, the more rigorous is the teacher's grading.[19]

3.4 Description of the Componential Parts

At this point, we are ready to bring all the component parts together to continue to develop the rubric: the component parts, values, and scale. I decided on a four-level scale: beginning, developing, accomplished, exemplary.[20] On the next page, one can see this next stage of developing the rubric.

---

[19] Stevens and Levi, *Introduction to Rubrics*, 9.

[20] Incidentally, the usefulness and value of these particular descriptors is demonstrated in that, when I introduced them to our curriculum committee at Asbury Theological Seminary, they were adopted for our institutional assessment rubrics.

BASIC BOOK SURVEY RUBRIC

Componential Part and Weight/Value	beginning	developing	accomplished	exemplary
1. Completeness and Time Spent (20%): Have all the parts of the assignment as described been attempted/completed? Has the assignment been done within the time allotted for the assignment?				
2. Chapter or Paragraph Titles (10%): Has the student given appropriate titles for each chapter in the book survey or paragraphs in the segment survey?				
3. Structural Presentation (10%; for segment surveys 20%): How well has the student accounted (graphically) for the book's or segment's structure?				
4. Major Structural Relationships (30%): How well has the student identified and described the major structural relationships operative in the book or segment?				
5. Questions (10%): Has the student asked appropriate questions for each major structural relationship?				
6. Other Major Impressions/Observations (10%): Has the student made other "major" observations pertaining to tone, atmosphere, figures of speech, etc.?				
7. Higher Critical Information (10% for book surveys only): For book surveys, has the student addressed information in the book that speaks to authorship, audience, and provenance?				

One could conclude with this basic chart; this is called a "holistic rubric."[21] Note that if one stopped here, the rubric would be better oriented on a horizontal page to create more room for comments. However, I wanted more detail to explain what students should avoid and how students could improve—an analytic rubric. This required identifying criteria for each componential part (i.e., items 1.–7. listed above) as well as describing these criteria along the four-level scale (beginning,

---

[21] Brookhart, *How to Create and Use Rubrics*, 5–6.

developing, accomplished, exemplary). Crucial here is "**The Performance Description Question**: What does student work look like at each level of quality, from high to low, on this criterion?"[22] In this regard, Brookhart provides two helpful charts; the first, "Desired Characteristics of Criteria" and the second "Desired Characteristics of Descriptions of Levels of Performance" and explanations (recreated here as lists):[23]

DESIRED CHARACTERISTICS OF CRITERIA FOR CLASSROOM RUBRICS

Appropriate—Each criterion represents an aspect of a standard, curricular goal, or instructional goal or objective that students are intended to learn.

Definable—Each criterion has a clear, agreed-upon meaning that both students and teachers understand.

Observable—Each criterion describes a quality in the performance that can be perceived (seen or heard, usually) by someone other than the person performing.

Distinct from one another—Each criterion identifies a separate aspect of the learning outcomes the performance is intended to assess.

Complete—All the criteria together describe the whole of the learning outcomes the performance is intended to assess.

Able to support descriptions along a continuum of quality—Each criterion can be described over a range of performance levels.

DESIRED CHARACTERISTICS OF DESCRIPTIONS OF PERFORMANCE LEVELS FOR CLASSROOM RUBRICS

Descriptive—Performance is described in terms of what is observed in the work.

Clear—Both students and teachers understand what the descriptions mean.

Cover the whole range of performance—Performance is described from one extreme of the continuum of quality to another for each criterion.

Distinguish among levels—Performance descriptions are different enough from level to level that work can be categorized unambiguously. It should be possible to match examples of work to performance descriptions at each level.

Center the target performance ... at the appropriate level [i.e., scale]—The description of performance at the level expected by the standard, curriculum goal, or lesson objective is placed at the intended level on the rubric.

Feature parallel descriptions from level to level—Performance descriptions at each level of the continuum for a given standard describe different quality levels for the same aspects of the work.

Creating the criteria that could be placed along a scale of performance proved challenging. Below is my "general-analytic" Book Survey Evaluation Rubric.

---

[22] This is Figure 3.2 in Brookhart, *How to Create and Use Rubrics*, 27.
[23] Brookhart, *How to Create and Use Rubrics*, 28.

Chapter 15—Benefits of a General-Analytic Grading Rubric for Book Surveys and Other IBS Assignments

BOOK SURVEY EVALUATION RUBRIC (50 PTS. POSSIBLE)

Student's Name: _____   Final Score: _____

	Beginning (2 pts.)	Developing (5 pts.)	Accomplished (8 pts.)	Exemplary (10 pts.)
COMPLETENESS AND TIME SPENT 20% score: ____	1. Missing two or more steps of the Survey; **or** 2. Several steps may be incomplete; **or** 3. Spent significantly less time than required; **or** 4. No "time spent" was indicated.	1. Missing a step of the Survey; **or** 2. Some steps may be incomplete; **or** 3. Spent more than an hour less time than required; **or** 4. Spent *more than one hour <u>over</u>* the time required for the assignment.	Each Step of the Survey is 1. *present*; **and** 2. *complete*; **and** 3. *finished within one hour (plus or minus)* of the time required for the assignment.	In addition to items 1. through 3. from "Accomplished," Each Step of the Book Survey is 4. *clearly demarcated*; **and** 5. *well-formatted*.

	Beginning (2 pts.)	Developing (3 pts.)	Accomplished (4 pts.)	Exemplary (5 pts.)
CHAPTER or PARAGRAPH TITLES 10% score: ____	Titles often 1. are 4 or more words; **or** 2. contain repetitive elements; **or** 3. are *not accurate* of material's content.	Each Title 1. is mostly 2 or 3 words, *with a few more than 3 words*; **or** 2. is catchy, but *not very accurate* of the material's content.	Each Title 1. is *mostly* 2 or 3 words; **and** 2. is catchy; **and** 3. is *fairly* accurate to the material's content	Each Chapter Title 1. is 2 or 3 words; **and** 2. is catchy; **and** 3. is accurate to the material's content.

	Beginning (2 pts.)	Developing (3 pts.)	Accomplished (4 pts.)	Exemplary (5 pts.)
STRUCTURAL PRESENTATION 10% score: ____	1. incomplete; **or** 2. unclear	1. Contains basic outline only; **or** 2. Layout lacks clarity; **or** 3. Contains some typos.	1. complete and balanced in detail; **and** 2. clear and understandable; **and** 3. free of typos.	In addition to items 1. through 3. in "Accomplished," the Structure 4. *embeds some MSRs*; **or** 5. is *presented creatively* or *graphically*.

	Beginning (8 pts.)	Developing (10 pts.)	Accomplished (13 pts.)	Exemplary (15 pts.)
MAJOR STRUCTURAL RELATIONSHIPS 30% score: ____	1. includes *less than four* MSRs; **or** 2. conception of MSRs is very *poor;* **or** 3. description of MSRs is *poor* or *lacking*; **or** 4. contains many typos (more than 3 different kinds).	1. includes *four or five* MSRs; **or** 2. does *not* have a *good* grasp of the meaning of MSRs identified; **or** 3. MSRs are *not* described clearly; **or** 4. MSRs <u>as described</u> *does not govern* a majority of the material; **or** 5. some typos.	1. includes five or more MSRs; **and** 2. has a good grasp of the meaning of the MSRs identified; **and** 3. each MSR <u>as described</u> governs a majority of the material; **and** 4. Each MSR is described clearly; **and** 5. free of typos.	In addition to items 1. through 5. from "Accomplished," 6. *Some MSRs are presented creatively* or *graphically*.

QUESTIONS 10% score: ____	**Beginning** (2 pts.) 1. Often asks less than 4 questions for each MSR; **or** 2. Questions are often unclear; **or** 3. Questions contain several typos (more than 3 different kinds).	**Developing** (3 pts.) 1. Questions are *not* located immediately after MSR; **or** 2. *Does not ask* all 4 types of questions for each MSR; **or** 3. Questions are often *unclear*; **or** 4. Questions are often *not* asked according to the *dynamics* of the MSR identified.	**Accomplished** (4 pts.) 1. Questions are located immediately after MSRs; **and** 2. *Asks* all 4 types of questions for *each* MSR; **and** 3. Questions are *clear* and often asked according to the dynamics of the MSR identified; **and** 4. free of typos.	**Exemplary** (5 pts.) In addition to items 1. through 4. from "Accomplished," 5. *Questions are often asked according to the particulars or specifics of the material.*
OTHER MAJOR IMPRESSIONS 10% score: ____	**Beginning** (2 pts.) 1. Not completed; **or** 2. *inadequately* done with many missing elements; **or** 3. contains many typos (more than 3 different kinds).	**Developing** (3 pts.) 1. Contains discussions on *only two of these*: tone, figures of speech used, and other significant observations; **or** 2. Discussions are not well-supported with Scripture citations; **or** 3. contains some typos (2-3 different kinds).	**Accomplished** (4 pts.) 1. Contains scripturally supported discussions of tone, figures of speech used, and other significant observations; **and** 2. is basically *not redundant* of material previously observed in the Survey; **and** 3. is free from typos.	**Exemplary** (5 pts.) In addition to items 1. through 3. under "Accomplished," 4. this section in the Survey is *done well and thoroughly.*
HIGHER CRITICAL INFORMATION 10% score: ____	**Beginning** (2 pts.) 1. Not completed; **or** 2. *Inadequately* done with many missing elements; **or** 3. Cites secondary sources; **or** 4. Contains many typos (more than 3 different kinds).	**Developing** (3 pts.) 1. Contains discussions on *only two of these*: authorship, audience, or provenance; **or** 2. Discussions are not well-supported with Scripture citations; **or** 3. Contains some typos (2-3 different kinds).	**Accomplished** (4 pts.) 1. Contains scripturally supported discussions of authorship, audience, or provenance; **and** 2. is basically *not redundant* of material previously observed in the Survey; **and** 3. is free from typos.	**Exemplary** (5 pts.) In addition to items 1. through 3. from "Accomplished," 4. This section in the Survey is *done well and thoroughly.*

A number of features of the proficiency scales and their assessment values deserve special comment.

- Each componential part should be given a point value. Brookhart argues, "Whether you summarize the performance for each criterion into a total-performance description or not, students should see how they scored on each criterion. Criterion-level results provide more useful information for students than one amalgamated score."[24]

---

[24] Brookhart, *How to Create and Use Rubrics*, 113.

- Concerning the grade value, one must carefully assess the gradation of point values for different scales of proficiency. For example, if you wanted a Developing level of performance to be equivalent to a "C," then the cumulative total for this scoring should correspond to your grading scale value for such. As the rubric stands, however, a student performing at a Developing level would only receive 30/50 points, or 60%, which is a D- in my grading scale in my syllabus. Thus, based upon my gradation of points, students working at a Developing and Accomplished level would receive a "C"; at an Accomplished level, a low "B" (41/50 points), etc. If you need more gradation, the scale for the rubric could be based upon 100 points possible.
- *Important information* is placed in *italics* in the performance descriptions for stress.
- Some descriptions involve "high-inference" assessments that require more intensive reflection; for example, whether a student has a poor, not good (fair), or good grasp of the meaning of Major Structural Relationships (criterion 2. under that componential part);
- Other descriptions are "low-inference" to assess, that is, low hanging fruit to observe; for example, completeness and time spent (either a student has done all the steps or they have not; either the student has or has not done the assignment within the allotted time frame) or the number and types of questions asked.[25] In this regard, Brookhart recommends, "*Aim for the lowest-inference descriptors that you can use and still accomplish your purpose of assess important qualities.*"[26]
- Across each componential part, I assess "typos" in some way. The reason is that typos can detract from any part of the survey work, even making such work unclear.[27]
- When observing/assessing assignments, I began to observe, if several different types of elements were present, they would detract from the componential part being done well and thus place the students' performance in the "beginning" or "developing" range; so, I listed these elements with "**or**" (**underlined and in bold**) to indicate such possibilities.[28]
- Conversely, several good elements may be present that would qualify the students' performance as an "accomplished" and "exemplary" achievement; and, so, I listed these with "**and**" (**underlined and in bold**) between these elements.
- I urged students to study the rubric before, during, and after performing their Book surveys. I wanted their assessment/grading not to be a mystery.
- Finally, I provided a sample book survey that I created (usually, the Book of Romans).

---

[25] This taxonomy of low or high-inference is from Brookhart, *How to Create and Use Rubrics*, 33.

[26] Ibid. (italics original).

[27] Brookhart provides a generic rubric for written reports which may be adapted to specific situations that assesses Content, Reasoning & Evidence, and Clarity (*How to Create and Use Rubrics*, 49–50, Figure 4.2). Under Clarity are assessed "errors of grammar and usage."

[28] Somehow, I discerned the need to add "or" whether through some example I found online at the time or simply out of necessity. Some justification for this comes from an "or" that Brookhart includes in one of her many example rubrics (*How to Create and Use Rubrics*, 32).

4. Implementation

This Book Survey Evaluation Rubric was and is included in my course syllabi when I require students to create a book survey. I might even print off copies to give to students while teaching through the assignment description; we would walk through the rubric together to clarify expectations.

In the literature on rubric creation, one intriguing exercise is having the students develop the rubric with the instructor after presenting the assignment; this is called a "bottom up approach."[29] Obviously, the instructor would need to guide the rubric creation. But, if an instructor would spend time interacting with students at this level and clarifying optimal features of this or that area of book survey work, I could imagine that students (especially, Bible and Ministry majors) would better retain and be motivated to follow the book survey method. Alternatively, after the explanation of the assignment how to perform a book survey and handing out the rubric, the instructor could ask students in pairs or groups to work through the rubric to clarify anything that was unclear and/or restate each criterion in their own words.[30]

Is such a rubric too restrictive? As is seen in the full Book Survey Evaluation Rubric, I have provided significant details in the multiple elements used to describe each level of scaled proficiency. One potential objection to using such a regimented rubric is that it may not allow for variability as indeed exists from one student's book survey to another student's book survey. However, by being so detailed, this allowed me to circle which elements were present that either detracted from or improved the quality of the area being assessed.[31] (The alternative to this is to create check boxes.[32]) For example, if evaluating "Questions" for a student's Book Survey, the final result might look like this with the items present being circled:

QUESTIONS 10%	Beginning (1 pts.)	Developing (2 pts.)	Accomplished (3 pts.)	Exemplary (4 pts.)
score: 2.5　2? .... 3?　Due to needing to better understand MSRs	1. Often asks less than 4 questions for each MSR; **or** 2. Questions are often unclear; **or** 3. Questions contain several typos (more than 3 different kinds).	1. Questions are *not* located immediately after MSR; **or** 2. *Does not* ask all 4 types of questions for each MSR; **or** 3. Questions are often *unclear*; **or** 4. Questions are often *not* asked according to the *dynamics* of the MSR identified.	1. Questions are located immediately after MSRs; **and** 2. *Asks* all 4 types of questions for *each* MSR; **and** 3. Questions are *clear* and often asked according to the dynamics of the MSR identified; **and** 4. free of typos.	In addition to items 1. through 4. from "Accomplished," 5. *Questions are often asked according to the particulars or specifics of the material.*

---

[29] Brookhart, *How to Create and Use Rubrics*, 30–31.
[30] Ibid., 95.
[31] On the practice of circling performance level, see Brookhart, *How to Create and Use Rubrics*, 103, 113.
[32] Reviewing the relative strengths of check boxes over circling elements in rubrics, see Stevens and Levi, *Introduction to Rubrics*, 74–78.

In this case, descriptors from different performance scales characterized the student's work: he or she showed features of "Accomplished" and "Developing" proficiency. Although all four types of questions were asked and placed immediately after the Major Structural Relationships (MSRs) without typos, the questions were often *unclear*. In this case, the resulting score given might be 2.5; however, depending on other factors, I could score this a 2 or a 3. For example, I would need to consider why the student's questions were unclear; it may be that the student did not properly understand MSRs and will lose points in the MSR evaluation area. In this case, I might decide to award the student's performance on "Questions" 3 points so as not to doubly penalize him or her. In this case, I could write in the space provided, "Due to needing to better understand MSRs."

5. Semantic Diagraming and Analysis Evaluation Rubric

5.1 SD and SA Assignment Description

Before concluding, it may be helpful to show one more rubric used for an IBS assignment that I have developed, viz., Semantic Diagramming and Semantic Analysis (SD and SA).[33] Essentially, SD/SA is a type of detailed observation work particularly helpful with argumentative discourse where the logic is fairly tight.[34] This type of work can be performed in any language; for example, I have presented SD/SA work on 1 Pet 1:22–25 in adult Sunday class settings in English.

Below is the description of an assignment from a NT III class (the Latter NT) from 2006 for which the following rubric was used. I supplied students with an example of SD/SA work from Heb 1:1–4. Notice also that students were expected to consult the rubric as they performed their work. In hindsight, I should have selected a smaller verse range for them to analyze and/or given them more time to complete the assignment.

Perform a Semantic Analysis of Hebrew 2:1–18 (follow my example for Heb 1:1–4) (3 hours)
1. Follow the steps for layering and alignment sentence elements of a passage.
2. Follow the steps for performing an Analysis of Sentence elements.
3. Include a Summary of Key Findings, Key Word(s), and Questions.
4. Be prepared to discuss your work and questions in class.
5. Indicate on the top of the first page how much time you spent on this assignment.
6. Be sure to consult Semantic Diagramming and Analysis Evaluation Rubric.

---

[33] For step-by-step descriptions and examples in English and Greek, see Fredrick J. Long, *Koine Greek Grammar: A Beginning-Intermediate Exegetical and Pragmatic Handbook*, Accessible Greek Resources and Online Studies (Wilmore, KY: GlossaHouse, 2015), 296–313; idem, Fredrick J. Long, *In Step with God's Word: Interpreting the New Testament as God's People*, GlossaHouse Hermeneutics & Translation 1 (Wilmore, KY: GlossaHouse, 2017), ch. 4.

[34] It is comparable to David Bauer's lecture material in which he "maps out" the narrative thought flow with embedded MSRs; see ch. 13 "Focused Observation" in David R. Bauer and Robert A. Traina, *Inductive Bible Study: A Comprehensive Guide to the Practice of Hermeneutics* (Grand Rapids: Baker Academic, 2011).

5.2 Semantic Diagramming and Analysis Evaluation Rubric

When creating the rubric, I decided that the key componental parts of SD/SA work are Layering, Alignment, Analysis, and Summary. Then, under each componental part, I was able to identify three discrete sub-tasks that I placed in bold for emphasis: for Layering, the initial coordinating conjunction, the main sentence, and major modifiers/subordinate clauses; for Alignment, the main clause elements, modifiers, and subordinate clauses; for Analysis, each modifier, other observations, and larger structural patterns; and, lastly, for Summary, key findings, key words identified, and asking interpretive questions. Then, for each sub-task I was able to describe four rating levels of performance that are worded accordingly with some variation. As far as grading, the circled ratings are not "points" per se, but provide some sense of performance relative to the final assessment, which may be assigned as a letter grade, percentage, etc. For this rubric, see SUPPLEMENT 15.1 below.

6. CONCLUSION

In my estimation, undoubtedly my undergraduate students benefited from having a Book Survey Evaluation Rubric; furthermore, they benefitted seeing it and being evaluated by it in more than one class. Such attests to the benefit of using a general rubric. In this case, too, the rubric is adaptable for segment surveys by removing "Higher Critical Information" (10%) and adding the percentage value to "Structural Presentation," thus increasing this area from 10% to 20%. By specifying details of relative performance in each componental part, the rubric becomes a general-analytic type that encouraged enhanced learning while also creating efficiency in my grading. Some students had multiple classes with me and were able to practice their book and segment survey multiple times—first, in the Biblical Hermeneutics course, but then in subsequent required NT classes. For another observational IBS assignment, I also developed a general-analytic rubric for grading Semantic Diagramming and Analysis. The use of these rubrics does not preclude writing out comments, either on the rubric form or the assignment itself. Additionally, I would write out a final word of encouragement on students' assignments. Such encouragement along with identifying specific areas for improvement often spurs students to excel more and more in their efforts to learn IBS.

FOR FURTHER READING

Brookhart, Susan M. *How to Create and Use Rubrics for Formative Assessment and Grading*. Alexandria, VA: ASCD Member Book, 2013.

Huba, M. E., & Freed, J. E. *Learner-Centered Assessment on College Campuses: Shifting the Focus from Teaching to Learning*. Boston: Allyn & Bacon, 2000.

Stevens, Dannelle D., and Antonia J. Levi. *Introduction to Rubrics: An Assessment Tool to Save Grading Time, Convey Effective Feedback, and Promote Student Learning*. Sterling, VA: Stylus, 2013.

SUPPLEMENT 15.1
Semantic Diagramming and Analysis Evaluation Rubric

Student's Name _____ final total (12–48): _____

final assessment: _____

Circle appropriate rating (1, 2, 3, 4) for each category:

LAYERING total=____	**Initial Coordinating Conjunctions** are isolated and placed to the far left	Each **Main Clause** (Subject, Verb, Direct Object) is highlighted	**Major Modifiers** (prep. phrases and some adverbs) and **Subordinate Clauses** are isolated and layered
	1. hardly any 2. some 3. most 4. all	1. hardly any 2. some 3. most 4. all	1. poorly. 2. with some confusion. 3. well; **and** 4. with clarity.
ALIGNMENT total=____	The Order of **Main Clause Elements** (S, V, DO) is	**Modifiers** are aligned 3 spaces (above or below) what they are modifying	**Subordinate Clauses** are aligned 3 spaces (above or below) what they are modifying
	1. not done well. 2. done consistently. 3. done fairly well. 4. done excellently.	1. poorly. 2. with some confusion. 3. well; **and** 4. with clarity.	1. poorly. 2. with some confusion. 3. well; **and** 4. with clarity.
ANALYSIS total=____	**Each Modifier** (prep. phrases, subordinate clauses, adverbs, adjectives, pronouns, etc.) is given analysis	Makes **Other Observations** about grammar, scope, or implicit structural relationships	Makes **Observations of Larger Structural Patterns** across clauses and sentences
	1. none or hardly any 2. some 3. most; **and** 4. done *very* clearly	1. none or hardly any 2. some 3. many; **and** 4. accessed the Greek	1. none or hardly any 2. some 3. many; **and** 4. used arrows or symbols to convey <u>these</u> observations
SUMMARY total=____	Summary of **Key Findings**	Identify **Key Word(s)**	Asks **Interpretive Questions**
	1. none 2. basic 3. detailed; **and** 4. well-organized	1. none 2. yes; **and** 3. well-selected; **and** 4. Accessed the Greek	1. none 2. some 3. many; **and** 4. excellent questions

TEACHING INDUCTIVE BIBLE STUDY ONLINE

Rick Boyd
Associate Professor of Biblical Studies
Wesley Biblical Seminary

ABSTRACT: This essay addresses the matter of teaching the Inductive Bible Study (IBS) method in an online environment. It includes identifying the characteristics of IBS instruction, opportunities available online, challenges to success and potential solutions to those challenges, and personal reflections from someone who has taught IBS online at the seminary level for more than five years. The combination of asynchronous and synchronous elements in online courses appears to provide the greatest efficacy and be the direction IBS distance-learning is headed.

1. INTRODUCTION

I was introduced to the method of Inductive Bible Study (IBS) at Asbury Theological Seminary through Prof. David R. Bauer in the spring of 1995 and, as it is for most students, the inductive approach changed how I read Scripture. The emphasis on the interrelatedness of form and content in the study of the text was revolutionary to me. However, beyond the simple logic of the direct study of the text as primary, the feature of Bauer's course that convinced me of the genius of the method involved the numerous examples he presented in class. His careful inductive study of various passages throughout the canon showed a depth that had heretofore been unimaginable to me, and the soundness of the method satisfied my prior training as a mechanical engineer. I was convinced of this decorous method of studying the Bible, and my conviction was strengthened with each successive course that I took from Professors Bauer, Joe Dongell, and David Thompson.

Now, more than two decades later, I teach IBS to seminary students in both geophysical and online settings, and though I never did get the opportunity to take a course from Prof. Robert A. Traina, I did receive instruction from the aforementioned professors, each of whom were students and/or colleagues of Bob Traina. The method which he was so instrumental in formalizing was further developed through those who directly helped shape me and my ministry, and for that I am truly grateful.

This essay will consider some of the opportunities and struggles specifically associated with teaching IBS in an online environment. This particular delivery system has become more popular as technology has made possible the ability to provide a certain environment for and quality of education previously unavailable. I will first summarize what I think are general characteristics of IBS instruction to provide a framework for what follows. Next, I discuss a few of the opportunities available with online IBS instruction as well as some of the challenges while also proposing possible solutions to these problems. Finally, I will conclude with a few brief reflections based upon my limited yet invaluable experience with IBS.

2. General Characteristics of IBS Instruction

IBS instruction in general, regardless of synchronicity, requires certain qualities in order to be successful. The method and philosophy behind it must be carefully explained, the steps of the method must be delineated, and the nature of the study must be understood. In the words of Traina, "It is an epistemology, a way of knowing truth";[1] and this epistemology demands careful explication. However, the most valuable of the general qualities, as noted above, involves sharing examples of the various steps in the method by using actual studies of the biblical text, and this applies whether teaching classes face-to-face or online.[2] Once a specific step is introduced and explained, the student benefits from multiple examples of the step, preferably using a different book or part of the canon as the illustration. For example, in an introductory IBS course using the Gospel of Matthew to teach method while attempting to teach students how to do a book survey, I have found it effective to step through a book survey of Luke, Genesis, Philippians, 1 John, and Joel (or similar examples). This allows the students to see the method they are learning applied to other books and portions of Scripture and helps them understand the breadth of application of the method. It may also benefit students to work through the process of a book survey with the instructor during a given class period by using a short book (e.g. Philemon). This allows both teacher and student to read the entire text multiple times in class and work through the various elements of the book survey together.

Providing multiple examples also allows students to better grasp the benefits of IBS in general and book surveys in particular (or other parts of the IBS method) by seeing books-as-wholes in a new way. Yet, once a particular assignment is completed by the students (e.g., a detailed observation of Matt 5:17–20), it is also imperative for the teacher to show the students what he or she found in the study of the same passage. This is particularly effective in leading the students forward because the students have just invested their time and effort in studying the same text. Then they can see what the teacher has found beyond what they themselves did, and the students are always amazed at what they missed. This kind of approach —the instructor doing the same assignment as the students and showing his or her work to the students after they have handed in their work—is always

---

[1] Robert A. Traina, "Inductive Bible Study Reexamined in the Light of Contemporary Hermeneutics, Part I: Interpreting the Text," in *Interpreting God's Word for Today: An Inquiry into Hermeneutics from a Biblical Theological Perspective*, ed. Wayne McCown and James Earl Massey (Anderson, IN: Warner, 1982), 53.

[2] When learning method, both examples and practice (assignments) are essential pedagogical tools for training the student. See Tisha Bender, *Discussion-Based Online Teaching to Enhance Student Learning: Theory, Practice, and Assessment*, 2nd ed. (Sterling, VA: Stylus, 2012), 60.

effective. Students can become intimidated by the method, especially when being introduced to it; however, the intimidation is quickly replaced by a desire to 'go and do likewise' as they see the method applied and the fruit they had simply overlooked.

A second general and essential trait of good IBS pedagogy involves providing substantive and timely feedback to each student on each assignment.[3] This is dependent on an axiomatic principle that method is best learned through active repetition, and learning proper method requires corrective and hortatory comments in an expeditious fashion. When this is provided, students can grow more quickly and effectively as they come to understand what to do—and just as importantly, what not to do—as they learn this new approach to studying Scripture. Students need personal, concrete, and expedient feedback to help them learn the method and improve their work, and it is incumbent upon the teacher to provide this to the best of his or her ability.

Providing substantive, timely feedback is the single most demanding aspect of teaching IBS, regardless of the format (face-to-face or online), and it requires the right mindset to remain faithful to this part of the teaching exercise. Effective ministry in teaching IBS simply demands substantive and timely feedback on the student's work. The best way for students to learn IBS, no matter what the platform, is to actively engage in the practice of the method and the only way students can learn and improve their method is by receiving pointedly detailed comments to encourage them and guide them along as they progress. This part of IBS instruction demands a significant investment of time and energy but is absolutely essential and must be maintained throughout the coursework.

3. Opportunities Available in Online IBS Instruction

Teaching IBS online offers a number of advantages to students over the face-to-face environment, the most apparent of which is an increased opportunity to reach and teach students in difficult-to-reach locales.[4] Correspondingly, this also leads to an increase in the number of students for a given course. With online instruction becoming so readily available and with the continual improvement of technology and technique that increasingly allow for more of a geophysical-like shared experience, students from far and wide can take courses with other students while physically being separated by great distances, even on different continents.

While geographical separation has been a challenge to distance learning since its inception, a related 'distance' has been identified and referred to as 'transactional distance.' Tisha Bender, in her book *Discussion-Based Online Teaching to Enhance Student Learning: Theory, Practice, and Assessment*, quotes Michael G. Moore in reference to distance learning: "There is now a distance between learner and teacher which is not merely geographic, but educational and psychological as

---

[3] Substantive and timely feedback is critical regardless of the mode of IBS instruction; see Mark A. Maddix, "Developing Online Learning Communities," in *Best Practices of Online Education: A Guide for Christian Higher Education*, ed. Mark A. Maddix, James R. Estep, and Mary E. Lowe (Charlotte, NC: Information Age Publishing, 2012), 38.

[4] See Mark H. Heinemann and James Riley Estep Jr., "Educational Theory and Online Education," in *Best Practices of Online Education: A Guide for Christian Higher Education*, ed. Mark A. Maddix, James R. Estep, and Mary E. Lowe (Charlotte, NC: Information Age Publishing, 2012), 5.

well. It is a distance in the relationship of the two partners in the educational enterprise. It is a 'transactional distance.'"[5] Bender further states, "[I]f a teacher, whether online or on campus, can establish meaningful educational opportunities, with the right degree of challenge and relevance, and can give students a feeling of responsibility for their own learning and a commitment to this process, then the transactional gap shrinks and no one feels remote from each other or from the source of learning."[6] In essence Bender asserts that an online course, if carefully designed and attentively executed, can overcome the distances that separate students and teachers, which includes the geographical distance to a significant degree.

An added benefit of online discussion forums is the development of techniques and tools students begin to use in working through the IBS method together and ministering to one another as they do so.[7] If students from across the globe are struggling together to learn IBS and one of them posts a question or shares some personal difficulties, the other students can (and do) minister to that student through support, encouragement, counsel, and prayer. Often the more mature students lead the way in reaching out to the one who is struggling, and other students join in to offer their assistance. Every fellow student can see this ministry in action and learn how to reach out to brothers or sisters in need. Students are shaped for ministry through this aspect of online forums which can help provide not just spiritual formation[8] but ministry formation.

Another advantage of the asynchronous format is the convenience of participating in the course as the student's schedule permits. This allows each student to view lectures, work on assignments, and enter into discussion with other students and the professor when time becomes available each week. Deadlines for assignments are still necessary and must be kept, but these can be met with appropriate planning. Online education allows students to maintain existing work and home arrangements while answering the call to ministerial training and to do so with a minimum of disruption to schedules. This is a major appeal for many online students and is probably the most influential factor in the growth of online education. The ability to fit schoolwork around work and home life with a minimum of imposition makes online education alluring. However, the convenience of fitting seminary (and, in particular, online IBS) into an existing schedule can be deceptive to the multi-tasking student. The temptation to fit an asynchronous IBS class into an already full schedule opens up the

---

[5] Bender, *Discussion-Based*, 10. See Michael G. Moore, "The Individual Adult Learner", in *Adult Learning and Education*, ed. M. Tight (London: Croom Helm, 1984), 155.

[6] Bender, *Discussion-Based*, 10.

[7] Discussion forums within an online class encourage interaction and relationships between students, something that tends to grow organically in a face-to-face class but something that requires intentionality in an online setting.

[8] IBS, by its very nature, facilitates a deep study of Scripture which should enhance spiritual formation, and mandatory discussion forums can further that aspect of IBS. See Mary E. Lowe, "Spiritual Formation as Whole-Person Development in Online Education," in *Best Practices of Online Education: A Guide for Christian Higher Education*, ed. Mark A. Maddix, James R. Estep, and Mary E. Lowe (Charlotte, NC: Information Age Publishing, 2012), 55; Mark A. Maddix, "Generating and Facilitating Effective Online Discussion," in *Best Practices of Online Education: A Guide for Christian Higher Education*, ed. Mark A. Maddix, James R. Estep, and Mary E. Lowe (Charlotte, NC: Information Age Publishing, 2012), 107–8.

possibility for inadequate concentration on the part of the student[9] and the delusion that the easy access of information online is equivalent to a proper study of the biblical text.[10] The student can end up short-circuiting the IBS method of an ever-deepening study of the Bible by developing bad habits shaped by limited time investment. This matter is more fully addressed below.

One more benefit of online IBS education involves the ability to access the continual increase of technological advancement. With the most recent utilization of platforms for 'live' conferencing, the ability to combine 'live' sessions (synchronous) along with asynchronous lectures and text-based discussion forums allows for hybrid course design. Courses can now supply synchronous interaction between students and instructors such that the 'live' in-class discussions, which formerly were limited to geophysical locations, can be offered from a distance to supplement the asynchronous elements making for an invaluable advancement. This allows for more immediate feedback and interaction between students or between students and the instructor, and as the technology continues to advance and the advancements become more readily available, replicating the face-to-face environment from a distance becomes more of a reality while still maintaining the conveniences of the asynchronous aspects of the course. Basically, the classroom becomes larger, limited only by the reach of the technology, while the technology allows for immediate virtual personal communication face-to-face. The hybrid course design appears to be the way online instruction in general is moving, and this can certainly benefit IBS courses.

4. Challenges in Online IBS Instruction

Along with the opportunities offered to students through online instruction, numerous challenges are also present. Among the various challenges inherent in the online educational environment are the limitations regarding immediate interaction with and feedback from students, the perception by students that the online environment requires less effort and less commitment, the potential for increased culturally-based miscommunication, and the need for greater investment of time and effort on the part of the instructor. These are all challenges that the practitioner of online IBS instruction encounters on a daily basis.

4.1 Limited Interaction

The online environment provides limited opportunity for instructors to interact with students in an immediate setting. Even though synchronous 'live' sessions are possible and are becoming increasingly more prevalent due to technological advances, the standard means of instruction and interaction at this point in time are still the asynchronous setting of pre-recorded lectures and text-based discussion forums. This tends to hinder the clarification of difficult concepts that students might ask about in a geophysical setting. In a physical classroom the professor can stop the lecture long enough to explain the difficult aspects of a concept to the satisfaction and comprehension of the students if

---

[9] Bender, *Discussion-Based*, 53.
[10] Bender, *Discussion-Based*, 47. Note, this is a problem for students in general, regardless of online or face-to-face.

necessary. This is not as easily accomplished in an asynchronous environment. However, as noted above, hybrid formats with synchronous sessions do make this less problematic. The issue at present involves both the availability of adequate technology to support 'live' streaming with consistent results and finding the balance between asynchronous elements and synchronous meetings. Some students simply don't have a sufficient connection to be able to stream video continuously, while other students tend to push the limits of what they have, even going so far as to attempt to stream on their phones through public wireless communication (think Starbucks or McDonald's). The results are often inconsistent and distracting to the class as a whole. Additionally, determining the most helpful policy between mandatory and optional synchronous sessions is an issue. Some students in an online course might feel synchronous sessions are unnecessary while the participation of others might need to be required. This is a matter for the individual instructor to settle and may be damped over time.

In my experience of experimenting with the combination of synchronous sessions in a primarily asynchronous class, I have found that it is helpful to hold a synchronous session early in the semester in order to help dissipate anxiety, answer questions, and develop a sense of community.[11] A second 'live' session can then be scheduled for later in the semester to address areas of difficulty observed in the students' work, as well as answering questions and further developing community.[12]

In general, however, carefully tailored synchronous sessions may be designed to include what is missing in pre-recorded lecture materials. If the instructor senses that a particular topic might need further clarification, he or she might provide a supplementary lecture with plenty of opportunity for 'live' question and answer interaction during a synchronous session, thus bridging the gap between the recorded lecture material and the 'live' interaction of a face-to-face classroom setting, something a recorded lecture simply cannot anticipate to a sufficient degree.[13] Once again, each instructor must carefully think through these issues for their respective situations.[14]

4.2 Skipping Essential Lectures and Materials

Another major problem—and one that is encountered all too frequently in online classes of all types (but especially IBS)—involves the misconception by students that they can simply skip lectures. This is especially at issue regarding the examples of the various steps of IBS (book survey; segment

---

[11] Heinemann and Estep, "Educational Theory," 11; Maddix, "Generating," 108–9.

[12] See Dr. Enid Acosta-Tello, "Enhancing the Online Class: Effective Use of Synchronous Interactive Online Instruction," *Journal of Instructional Pedagogies* 17 (2015): 2–3.

[13] Care should be taken to anticipate questions when planning pre-recorded lectures in the asynchronous format. See C. Damon Osborne, "Best Practices in Online Teaching," in *Best Practices of Online Education: A Guide for Christian Higher Education*, ed. Mark A. Maddix, James R. Estep, and Mary E. Lowe (Charlotte, NC: Information Age Publishing, 2012), 82.

[14] I am presently implementing a regular 'live' session to be offered once or twice a month through the semester and students will be required to attend at least half of the sessions. The hope is that the students will look forward to these meetings and make every reasonable effort to attend each one if possible. I have found that a one hour session is about the right length.

survey; focused observation; etc.). The very resource that can prove to be the most effective element in IBS instruction (as noted above) is also the most likely to be skipped by online students because of increasingly full schedules. Many students feel their schedules won't allow them to view all of the lectures while also taking care of the other aspects of their life, and if something must be eliminated it tends to be the examples of the method provided by the instructor. When push comes to shove, students will forego watching the examples of book survey, segment survey, etc. Students who follow this practice often end up being the ones who have the most trouble grasping what is being asked of them regarding method simply because they haven't taken the time to carefully follow how the example procedure is executed. The method-transparent examples are ignored and the student fails to fully understand the process that leads to incisive observations and depth of understanding of the given passage and, correspondingly, the given book. The end result is a facile grasp of the material and inability to fully engage the method.

Success in any learning endeavor requires commitment from both instructor and student, and this becomes more difficult the greater the distance between teacher and student. This distance applies to both physical location and synchronicity. Physical distance allows students to 'disappear' from classes for periods of time since they don't have to meet at a particular location. Chronological distance makes it difficult for students because of increased demands of busy schedules and the option to put off watching the lecture or participating in the discussion forum and completing the assignment. That same distance makes it difficult for the instructor who wants to be 'present' for the student whenever the student is ready to ask questions or participate, but this type of setting increases the time demands placed on instructors if the instructor wants to maintain a good relationship with students.[15]

A quality IBS education demands commitment from both student and instructor as the material is not easily mastered, and in cases of lack of commitment on the part of a student this may be a way to weed-out those who are not rightly motivated either to enter ministry or grow in his or her relationship with the Lord through the Bible. One way of checking on the commitment level of online students is to embed some information in each recorded lecture and require each student to answer a few questions at the end of the lecture to prove they have watched the lecture material. However, the main problem with this technique is the reality that this type of measure should not have to be employed for people entering ministry and learning how to study the Bible. I have not used this technique, although I have resorted to other means to check on students who don't seem to be catching on, and in nearly every case I discovered that *these students were not viewing all the mandatory lectures recorded for their benefit*. Grading penalties can be imposed, but the only real solution for this problem is conviction laid on the heart of each student regarding their commitment or lack thereof. This is a problem that is really rooted in the human heart.

---

[15] Regarding the importance of presence, this is something every online practitioner discovers and every expert emphasizes. See, e.g., Stephen Kemp, "Social Presence in Online Learning," in *Best Practices of Online Education: A Guide for Christian Higher Education*, ed. Mark A. Maddix, James R. Estep, and Mary E. Lowe (Charlotte, NC: Information Age Publishing, 2012), 49; Osborne, "Best Practices," 86. Osborne refers to the "'Goldilocks' method of interacting" in which the presence of the instructor is "not too much, but not too little."

Seminary students whom God is calling into ministry must take that call seriously. All students have commitments outside of the coursework. Many have to balance family, work, ministry, and school, and it can be challenging to meet all of the demands in each area. This difficulty must be met prayerfully, even to the point of reconsidering the call. A call to ministry should only be accepted prayerfully and with full commitment. In the present North American cultural environment, it is commonplace to overcommit and give less than the requisite effort, but this should never be the case when answering the call of the Lord. In the same way Paul writes of having learned how to be content (Phil 4:11), this is an area students may have to learn the right balance of time and effort in their schedules as they answer their calling. Students must reconcile the effort required in learning a new way (to most) of Bible study, with the time and energy required of the other areas of their life. Ultimately, though, God must have His rightful place on the throne of the individual's heart.

In some cases, when the instructor confronts the student with his or her lack of effort, the student recommits to the work necessary to succeed in learning IBS and the problem is successfully resolved. In some cases, the student ignores the attempts of the instructor to correct the student and the pattern is further hardened. Other instances fall in between the two on the spectrum of response. Nevertheless, IBS demands the student's devotion of time and effort to learn and apply the method best suited to study the Bible.[16]

4.3 Differing Cultural and Educational Expectations

Culturally diverse environments can also become an issue in IBS instruction, especially with an online format, because of the ability for the student to remain in his or her familiar environment. Each student of IBS has a unique background influenced by the particular cultural setting. Some students have patterns and behaviors that conflict with demands of the class, while other students have been raised in a culture that did not prepare them for the rigorous demands of IBS study. These cultural differences can be overcome but once again it requires commitment on the part of both instructor and student. The instructor must be willing to work with the student to orient him or her to the demands of the IBS method within the structure of the course while being willing to relax certain requirements that might be non-essential to learning the method (e.g. extend some latitude regarding discussion forum posts to a student in a remote location where lengthy internet connection makes it difficult to access with consistency). Conversely, the student must be willing to work with the professor to form an acceptable arrangement and to stick to it.

I have had students from other continents where deadlines were not as important as they are in the Western culture and the structure of regular interaction with other students via an online discussion forum was difficult to adopt because of the cultural background. I have also had students who were not well prepared and apparently had never been challenged to invest significant time and effort in assignments that necessitate a change in perspective. All students fall along the spectrum from perfectly prepared and committed to unprepared and not committed at all.

---

[16] David R. Bauer and Robert A. Traina, *Inductive Bible Study: A Comprehensive Guide to the Practice of Hermeneutics* (Grand Rapids: Baker Academic, 2011), 13–23.

Each situation is unique and needs to be treated as such by appeal to the nature of the study. The realization that the IBS method is intended to make the student a better listener to the Word of God and hence bring clearer understanding is often the turning point although repeated encouragement is necessary along the way. However, not every situation is resolved with success, and the instructor must acknowledge that reality. The ministry of teaching will have successes and failures. The crucial quality of the instructor is a full commitment both to God and to each of the students. This mutual commitment is the only way the transactional distance problem can truly be overcome.

4.4 Time Management and Commitment

This leads to the most challenging matter of online education in general and IBS in particular: time commitment. Effectively teaching IBS requires the teacher to walk through the material, explaining and illustrating each step and answering the inevitable questions that come from learning a new method, at times getting into lengthy discussions with multiple examples from varying biblical texts. In a geophysical classroom setting this is done through pauses in the lectures to answer questions, elaborate a point, or share examples that help the student conceptualize the particular step or idea. However, in an online setting, students typically pose their questions through text-based discussion forums that must be addressed in a timely fashion as completely as possible, and this requires a greater investment of time on the part of the instructor to address the questions with immediacy and completeness. Discussion forums can help reduce the transactional distance, but not without significant investment of time and effort by the instructor.[17] A student might have a good question about a particular step in the method, not quite grasping what should be done or even why a certain process should be followed. This might lead to another question, then another and so forth. However, due to the asynchronous nature of the forums, the questions and answers might stretch over days and they require frequent monitoring of the discussion forum. Additionally, due to the staggered one-way nature of online posting, greater effort at clarification and detail is often required in order to solidify concepts.

One solution to some of the time demands on the instructor is to consider appointing students to alternate in leading weekly discussion forums with the professor keeping a close eye on the forum. I suggest this be limited to second semester IBS classes and discussing the guidelines and protocol of the discussion ahead of time with each leader. Mature students leading a weekly discussion forum could add tremendous benefit with respect to edification of the class as a whole, as well as ministry preparation for the leaders.[18] This highlights the value of the 'live' conferencing aspect of hybrid courses. Offering a 'live' session every week or two, just for clarification purposes or supplemental material and question and answer, can actually reduce the time demands by clearing up issues in a half hour that might take hours and/or days to address online in an asynchronous format. One online

---

[17] See Maddix, "Developing," 35; Kemp, "Social Presence," 44–45.

[18] See Christine Bauer and Mary Jones, "Online Course Design Considerations," in *Best Practices of Online Education: A Guide for Christian Higher Education*, ed. Mark A. Maddix, James R. Estep, and Mary E. Lowe (Charlotte, NC: Information Age Publishing, 2012), 168.

student was so impressed with the live sessions that he considered driving the three hours each week to attend the face-to-face class simply to get involved with the question and answer interaction. When that became an impossibility, he inquired about joining via an online conferencing platform. Nothing can replace the value of synchronous interaction. In an online environment, the use of this hybrid feature must become a part of the course protocol, the details of which should be settled based on the specific details of the course offering.

5. Final General Reflections on Online IBS Instruction

Our human nature is to make things as easy and painless as possible. It wasn't that long ago that power-steering in vehicles was an option for which you would pay extra. Drive-thru windows at restaurants used to be limited to a small handful of fast-food chains. Banking used to be done in person with a teller and exchange of checks or cash. However, technological advancements work their way into society so that we can and expect to get increased functionality with decreased effort, and so it is with education.

Teaching IBS online is both rewarding and challenging. Although grading the weekly assignments (providing constructive, critical comments to improve the work of each student) remains the most demanding and grueling task whether face-to-face or online, the added workload of the online courses as well as the lack of personal sensory familiarity tends to intensify the obstacles present to teaching and learning the IBS method. Let it be understood: Teaching IBS online is difficult. Yet this is the present reality in the current and coming educational environment. Physical presence is being overcome by virtual presence with increasing frequency and measure, and this trend shows no sign of abating anytime soon.

Online IBS instruction requires greater effort and investment of time, and it demands an increased level of intentional interaction. The opportunities listed and described above along with the challenges and potential solutions have come from my observations and brief experience of five years in online IBS instruction. I am firmly convinced that the hybrid model—combining synchronous elements with asynchronous materials—best merges the opportunities with the solutions to the challenges, creating the best possible context for successfully teaching IBS online at present.

The issue that always remains, however, is that of commitment. How committed are we to making online IBS instruction successful? The foundational spring from which flows my own IBS ministry is the sense of call from the One who has entrusted his Word to me to teach. If indeed God has called me to teach the inductive Bible study method, for whatever ultimate end and in whichever pedagogical format, then I must make every effort to fulfil that ministry call. This is the only reasonable and acceptable response to the Subject of the Bible who beckons us to follow Him and to submit to His call each time we enter the literary world of the Bible and meet with Him. I have come to learn that the IBS method, formalized by Bob Traina and further developed by David Bauer and others, is the most effective means of clearly and confidently hearing the voice of the beckoning Subject of the Bible.

For Further Reading

Acosta-Tello, Enid. "Enhancing the Online Class: Effective Use of Synchronous Interactive Online Instruction." *Journal of Instructional Pedagogies* 17 (2015): 1–6.

Maddix, Mark A., James R. Estep, and Mary E. Lowe, eds. *Best Practices of Online Education: A Guide for Christian Higher Education.* Charlotte, NC: Information Age Publishing, 2012.

Bauer, David R. and Robert A. Traina. *Inductive Bible Study: A Comprehensive Guide to the Practice of Hermeneutics.* Grand Rapids: Baker Academic, 2011.

Bender, Tisha. *Discussion-Based Online Teaching to Enhance Student Learning: Theory, Practice, and Assessment.* 2nd ed. Sterling, VA: Stylus Publishing, 2012.

Moore, Michael G. "The Individual Adult Learner." Pages 153–68 in *Adult Learning and Education.* Edited by M. Tight. London: Croom Helm, 1984.

Traina, Robert A. "Inductive Bible Study Reexamined in the Light of Contemporary Hermeneutics, Part I: Interpreting the Text." Pages 53–83 in *Interpreting God's Word for Today: An Inquiry into Hermeneutics from a Biblical Theological Perspective.* Edited by Wayne McCown and James Earl Massey. Anderson, IN: Warner, 1982.

THE USE OF BIBLEWORKS SOFTWARE TO PERFORM INDUCTIVE BIBLE STUDY TASKS

Mark T. Cannon
Pastor, Mt. Zion United Methodist Church, Bucyrus, Ohio

ABSTRACT: BibleWorks 10 offers commonly used texts and reference works in one location for biblical exegesis. This essay identifies and explains how to use its search and analytical tools in the IBS process. Unfortunately, the BibleWorks company closed prior to this publication, but compatibility fixes shall continue to be offered. However, the principles presented here can help current BibleWorks users or others who wish to apply them within other Bible software programs.

1. INTRODUCTION

Bible software programs can speed the work of observation and provide a means of recording observations in Inductive Bible Study (IBS). This essay will provide some techniques for using the BibleWorks 10[1] software program in the IBS process explained in the textbook by David R. Bauer and Robert A. Traina, *Inductive Bible Study: A Comprehensive Guide to the Practice of Hermeneutics* (Grand Rapids: Baker Academic, 2011). In principle, the areas of study discussed here concerning gathering relevant IBS observations and evidence may be applied to other software platforms. The reader is assumed to be familiar with the IBS steps to get the most benefit from the techniques that follow. Bauer and Traina encourage the student to adapt the IBS process to one's own context, abilities and constraints, but not violate the integrity of the process.[2] It is hoped that this essay will offer some techniques toward that end.

---

[1] It is acknowledged that this essay in many ways applies to one software product at the time of writing. Typically, techniques for using a program do not dramatically change with new versions as they are released, but new developments may result in slight changes in technique that provide additional capabilities. It is recognized that the reader who has a copy of BibleWorks may have a version earlier than the current version of BibleWorks, BibleWorks 10. BibleWorks 10 users should apply the free updates available under the Help menu to install the resources mentioned here. Some of the tools and techniques in this essay may not be in an earlier version of BibleWorks or may require a different approach to accomplish similar results.

[2] *Inductive Bible Study*, 72.

Bible software has gradually changed my approach to Bible study for teaching and preaching over the last 25 years. When I was taught the IBS process, IBS was called English Bible.[3] The basic tools were a Revised Standard Version (RSV) pew Bible, a pencil, a notepad and a repeated reading process of observation. I might add to that a Strong's Exhaustive Concordance and a King James Bible to view repeated words and do word studies. I would also use a photocopy machine at times to make a copy of the book being studied and then use colored pencils to mark divisions, sections, repeated words, etc. My initial use of a computer in Bible study was to type a section of English text into a word processor and then block-diagram its structure by phrases in an attempt to better understand the flow of the text. I now use multiple software tools, physical texts, apps, and audio Bible readings on a smart phone to encounter the text, make and record observations on it.

Bible software offers the student quick access to electronic texts of the primary sources of Scripture, commonly used lexicons, grammars, search and analysis tools. BibleWorks 10 offers cross references, parsing of word forms, grammatical information, lexicon entries instantly available in the program's **Analysis Window** by mousing over words in the program's **Browse Window**. The **Browse Window** is a text browser for viewing the Bible and extra-biblical texts in the program. The **Analysis Window** is a collection of tabs, each with different functions that display information about the text in the **Browse Window** based on the mouse position over the text or the current position of the book, chapter and verse or **Bible Outline** section displayed in the **Browse Window**. Many of the following techniques will involve using these two windows in BibleWorks.

The features of the BibleWorks program are explained in depth in an extensive help file that will open to the article concerning a window, feature or button in the program when you hold the mouse cursor over it and hit the **F1** key. If you are using BibleWorks on a Mac, press the **fn** key before you press the **F1** key on your keyboard. Also, many useful options are available for the windows and features in BibleWorks in context menus that will display when you right click on a word in the text you are reading in the **Browse Window**, or on a window or field in the program. On a Mac, press **shift + control** while you click with your mouse or use a two-finger press on the trackpad to simulate a right click. The **F1** key and right click context menu are your best friends to help in learning how to utilize the features of BibleWorks. A large number of videos demonstrating the use of BibleWorks in various tasks may be viewed by clicking on **Help | BibleWorks How-To Videos (Online) | How to View the Videos (FAQ)**.

I will attempt to follow the IBS process of the observation of texts for the most part, but some techniques and tools covered may be helpful for multiple stages of the process. The simple act of reading a text and reading it in a repeated fashion can be conducted with or without a Bible software program, or a program can enhance and work hand in hand with the reading of a text in another form as one wishes to go deeper in some aspect of observation or the recording of observations.

---

[3] English Bible was the name for Inductive Bible Study when I learned its principles at Asbury Theological Seminary in the late 1980s.

2. BOOK AND SECTION SURVEYS

2.1 Identifying the General Materials of a Book

One entry point for exploring the general materials of a book is to read a Bible dictionary article on the book you are studying.[4] BibleWorks 10 comes with several Bible dictionaries that are accessible in the **Analysis Window**'s **Dict** tab. Click on the **Dict** tab and choose the **Eerdman's Bible Dictionary** or the **ISBE Dictionary**. Bible dictionary articles on each of the books of the Bible can be of help in identifying the general materials of the book you are studying. The dictionary entries will update to match or closely match the word you mouse over in an English text in the **Browse Window** if it is a likely head word for a Bible dictionary article. As with other **Analysis Window** tabs you can freeze the **Dict** tab on the information for the word you are holding your mouse cursor over by holding down the **Shift** key when you move the mouse cursor across other words to access another part of BibleWorks or the **Dict** tab itself.

You can use the book name of the book displayed in the **Browse Window** to access the article for the book you are studying. Hold your mouse cursor over the bold name of the current book for the verses on display in the **Browse Window** when it is in **Multiple Version Mode**. The **Dict** tab will update to the article on the book name under your mouse cursor or an article on the person or concept that shares the title of the book name. Alternatively, you can use the table of contents for the dictionary to scroll to the article for the book you are studying.

The BibleWorks **Editor** or **UserLex** tab is an effective tool to use to take notes on the general materials of a book that you glean from a Bible dictionary article or from your reading and observation of the book as a whole. The **UserLex** tab is designed to save and later access notes on a word as you place the mouse over in an English, Greek or Hebrew version in BibleWorks. The **UserLex** tab was designed to take notes on individual English, Greek or Hebrew words you encounter in the Biblical text, but it can also be used to take notes on a whole book itself by using it to focus on the bold book name in the **Browse Window** when creating a note.

If the **UserLex** tab is open in the **Analysis Window**, when you place your mouse on a word the **UserLex** tab will display an empty or previously taken note for that word. As you observe the general materials of a book you could display both the **Dict** and **UserLex** tab together in a two column **Analysis Window**.[5]

2.2 Book Survey: Observing the Text

BibleWorks offers a several ways to read the text that you can adjust to your needs and preferences. The center window in BibleWorks, the **Browse Window**, is the most common way to read the text. The **Browse Window** allows you to read each verse in multiple versions for comparison or view an entire book in one version. A button at the top of the **Browse Window** or the option under **View |**

---

[4] Topics covered will be the genre and the main concerns emphasized in the content of a book.

[5] You can open a two column **Analysis Window** by clicking on the **Open/Close Secondary Analysis Window** button in the upper right of the **Analysis Window** header.

Browse Window on the main menu will allow you to **Toggle Browse Mode**.[6] When **Toggle Browse Mode** is checked, the current **Search Version**[7] designated by its version abbreviation at the top of the **Browse Window** becomes a single browse version in the **Browse Window**. When you uncheck the **Toggle Browse Mode** all the display versions are visible in the **Browse Window**, so you can easily read the same verse in multiple versions for comparison. This can be useful in later stages for more detailed observations of the content of verses.

One can read through a biblical book in the program's **Browse Window** and hide the **Search** and **Analysis Windows** to display more of the text or BibleWorks can be used hand in hand with a printed English,[8] Greek or Hebrew text as one reads through a whole book in the process of book survey. As you are reading along with the software you can quickly navigate to book, chapter and verse with drop down menus at the top of the **Browse Window** or by typing a verse reference on the **Command Line** and hitting <Enter>.

BibleWorks allows you to export a whole book if you wish to print it out to mark up and highlight on paper. You can copy a whole book with the **Popup Copy Window** by opening BibleWorks, striking the keys **Ctrl + Shift + B** on your keyboard, choosing the Bible version you wish to use with a button in the **Popup Copy Window** and typing the verse range of the whole book, for example Matthew 1:1–28:20 or even just mat 1:1–28:20 will do,[9] then hit the Copy button. Then paste the text into the **Editor** in BibleWorks or a word processor and you can save the book as a file on your computer or print it to work with it on paper.

2.3 Book Survey: Help in Identifying Major Structural Relationships

Bauer and Traina identify a number of key words that tend to identify structural relationships in an English translation.[10] You can search for multiple words from the **Command Line** with an OR search where you type the forward slash "/" followed by multiple words that you may wish to search for. An OR search finds any verse that has those words in it and does not require that the words be in the same verse. You could type out the various key words that identify structural relationships with an OR search, but the program's **Graphical Search Engine (GSE)** allows you to search for

---

[6] You can also **Toggle Browse Mode** with a **Browse Window** keyboard shortcut key by clicking in the **Browse Window** and pressing the 'b' key on your keyboard. A list of **Browse Window** shortcut keys is found under Help |Bible | B | BibleWorks Help Contents | Frequently Used Links | Shortcuts within the program.

[7] BibleWorks uses one Search Version at a time in most cases to be the source of the versification and words of the Bible that appear in many of the onscreen tools as you are studying the Bible. The **Search Version** is identified by the abbreviation for the Bible version at the top of the **Search** and **Browse Window**s as well as in the status bar at the bottom of the program display.

[8] I prefer to read through either the ESV single column journaling Bible which provides ruled lines on each page and holds up well for pencil marking or note taking. Another preferred reading edition is *A Reader's Edition of the ESV* that removes individual verse numbers for a better reading experience but identifies chapters in an unobtrusive way with a lightly colored red chapter number in the side margin.

[9] BibleWorks allows you to use the first three letters or characters of the book as an abbreviated book name to save time when typing commands.

[10] See chapter 11 Survey of Books-as-Wholes in *Inductive Bible Study*, 94–129.

Chapter 17—The Use of BibleWorks Software to Perform Inductive Bible Study Tasks

lists of words and phrases at the same time.

One may download an example **GSE** search file that may be helpful to IBS students.[11] The query finds verses in the RSV with the words and phrases that often identify structural relationships:

- o like, as, also, too: Comparison
- o but, yet, nevertheless, even though, much more, although: Contrast
- o therefore, consequently, so, then: Causation
- o for, because, since: Substantiation
- o if … then: Conditional Statement
- o by, through: Instrumentation
- o in order that, so that: Purpose

You can open the search by clicking on **Search | Graphical Search Engine**, then click on **File | Open** and choose the **relations.qf** file to open it. Click "**go**" to execute the search. Executing the **relations.qf** file runs a search for all the words or phrases noted above in the RSV. More information explaining the search is found in the Help file under **Help | BibleWorks Help Contents | 46 The Graphical Search Engine (GSE) Examples**.

After you run the search you can apply colors to the search results to be able to see all instances where these words appear in the RSV now and in your future use of BibleWorks. Immediately after you execute the search, click on the drop-down arrow next to the button labeled **Apply color to Browse Window text** and choose the option **Configure and apply colors to search results ....** Choose the **Text Color** and **Background** color options you wish the key words to have in the RSV. I prefer to use red with a white background in this case. BibleWorks will color all the words that were found with the search in the text attributes you chose.[12]

Coloring the words in the RSV does not mean you are confined to studying with the RSV exclusively. The word and merge boxes in the search can be changed to another English version or you can use the RSV in comparison to the text you are studying by displaying the RSV in the **Browse** tab in the **Analysis Window** or as one of the versions you view in the **Parallel Versions Window** as you study the text in another version, the Greek New Testament or Hebrew Bible.

The **Browse** tab is an additional browse window that can be displayed in the **Analysis Window** to the right of the **Browse Window**. If you are studying a book at verse level you can use the **Browse** tab to read the larger context of the verse in the book in any version you choose. It can be

---

[11] You may download a **GSE** search file (relations.qf) that I developed some years ago to find a list of Traina's key words that has circulated for years among IBS students. This file can be downloaded and saved in the BibleWorks 10\ase folder accessible through File | Open in the **GSE**. Follow the instructions found in this article in the BibleWorks Knowledgebase: https://kb.bibleworks.com/article/AA-02970/107/Usage-Tutorial/BibleWorks-Tutorials/How-Do-I-Prepare-a-Book-Study-with-BibleWorks.html

[12] The color is saved in a color file (rsv.clr) for that version. It can be turned off or on. With the RSV displayed in the **Browse Window**, right click on a verse in the RSV verse and click **Open Color Selection Window**. Under **Color File Options** uncheck the rsv file checkbox or uncheck **the Display Options "Display text colors"** box and click **Close**. Click either one of those to display the colors in the RSV.

set to another version as well, allowing you to read the Greek or Hebrew text for comparison next to the text in the **Browse Window** when you are reading in the single version browse mode.

2.4 Book Survey and the Survey of Individual Sections or Segments

BibleWorks has several tools that can be helpful in consideration of a book as a whole. These and other tools can be used to observe large segments of a book and you can develop and work with your own outlines in the tools of the **Analysis Window**.

The **Bible Outline** tool at the top of the **Browse Window** displays the outline and pericope headings for sections of the Bible found in a number of translations like the RSV, ESV, NIV, CEB, CSB and NET Bibles. The **Context** and **Use** tabs in the **Analysis Window** are configured to use the **Bible Outline** to control the information that is displayed in the tabs.

The **Bible Outline** serves to identify what section of Scripture is on view in the **Browse Window** or you can use it to quickly navigate to sections of the Bible. Click the drop-down box arrow to the right of the outline to see the remainder of the outline. The button next to it allows you to choose which outline you wish to display for the **Browse Window**'s **Bible Outline**. You can also export a whole outline, book or section by using the window that opens through **Resources | Miscellaneous | Bible Outline**. Like most features in BibleWorks, hold your mouse cursor over the **Bible Outline** window and hit **F1** to view the help file concerning the **Bible Outline**.

Each time you determine and label a section of Scripture from your whole book study you can record it in the **Notes**, **Editor** or a **UserLex** tab you may be using to record observations on the book. IBS procedures encourage you to name each chapter, then each section of a book with a short descriptive label. The sections you name and divide a book into during observation can and should be incorporated into your own custom outline in BibleWorks. Developing your own custom outline will also serve you in later stages as a tool for studying individual sections that can have bearing upon the use of additional tools in BibleWorks. In preparation for making a custom outline, record the sections in the **Notes** or **Editor** tabs. It is highly recommended that you title each section in the format of the BibleWorks book name[13] for the book you are studying followed by a space, then chapter, colon, and the verse that begins the section and the title you give to the section for that format will assist you in transferring the section titles to a custom **Bible Outline** in BibleWorks.

The **Bible Outline** is configurable so that you can create your own outline according to the observations you make about a book. You do not need to include the chapter and verse reference that closes the section for the **Bible Outline,** for BibleWorks uses only the book name, chapter and verse that begins the section in the outline to divide the book into sections. Rather than start from scratch to create a whole outline of the Bible you can take an existing outline in the program and

---

[13] Book names in BibleWorks are generally made up of the first three characters in a given book in its English book name. Note that some books that duplicate the first three letters like Judges/Jude or Philippians/Philemon are adjusted so each book name is unique. The canonical book names of the Bible in BibleWorks are: Gen Exo Lev Num Deu Jos Jdg Rut 1Sa 2Sa 1Ki 2Ki 1Ch 2Ch Ezr Neh Est Job Psa Pro Ecc Sol Isa Jer Lam Eze Dan Hos Joe Amo Oba Jon Mic Nah Hab Zep Hag Zec Mal Mat Mar Luk Joh Act Rom 1Co 2Co Gal Eph Phi Col 1Th 2Th 1Ti 2Ti Tit Phm Heb Jam 1Pe 2Pe 1Jo 2Jo 3Jo Jud Rev.

adapt it to display in sections of your own making from your observations. This is not just cosmetic or busy work but can prove valuable in your later observations of a book as you will have identified some custom sections that can be used with the **Use** and **Context** tabs in the **Analysis Window** to search for words within a section and find the most and least commonly used words occurring in a section with what you have recorded in that custom outline.

To customize the **Bible Outline** it is recommended that you start with an existing outline of the Bible, rename the file, then substitute the pericopes given in the existing Bible outline with the sections you have determined in the book.

Renaming the outline file you started with is important to preserve the original file that came with BibleWorks. To do so, click on the **Bible Outline** button in the **Browse Window**. Choose an existing **Bible Outline** as your base to work from. The **RSV-Outline** is a good choice and the standard outline used in BibleWorks. Make sure it is checked as the checkmark signifies the chosen outline the program is currently using for display above the **Browse Window**. Click **Configure**, then in the small box that opens click **Edit**, the outline should open in WordPad in Windows (or a text editor in Mac). In WordPad, use **File | Save as** and save the outline with a distinctive name to preserve the base outline you were working from and make yourself a new outline. I'd suggest changing the file name from RSV-Outline.txt to IBS-Sections.txt, but do not close WordPad after doing so, for then you will be ready to start editing your custom outline.

To edit the **Bible Outline** in WordPad, find the section of Scripture that you are studying in the outline. It will contain the pericopes the editors of the RSV determined preceded by the book name, chapter and verse that begins each pericope. Edit the outline to match the sections of Scripture you have determined from your study by replacing the former lines in what was once the RSV-Outline with your own sections that you have determined for the book divisions. Save the file again as needed and then click **Compile** so that BibleWorks can load the outline. You will see the outline changes you have made and can view them in the **Bible Outline** at the top of the **Browse Window**.

2.5 Survey of Sections or Segments: Identifying Key Verses or Strategic Areas

The **Context** tab provides what we might call an overview of the vocabulary of a book, instantly listing all the words used in a book or section from the **Browse Window**. This can be helpful as you are researching a book as a whole.

If you choose the **Context** tab in the **Analysis Window** you can quickly see a list of all the words that occur in the **Pericope** from the **Bible Outline** (an outline section), the current **Book** and the current **Chapter** in the **Browse Window**. The **Context** tab uses the current **Search Version** that was chosen for the **Search Window**. By changing the **Search Version** you can display word usage for the book in a translation or a Greek or Hebrew Bible.[14] The words can be displayed by frequency

---

[14] For best results, use a Greek or Hebrew morphology version like the BGM, BNM or WTM to display all the words in their lexical form rather than inflected form. The **Search Version** can be changed using by typing the version abbreviation in the **Command Line** and hitting <Enter> or using **Search | Choose Search Version**. If you wish to see all the inflected forms the word will take the **Forms** tab in the **Analysis Window** will display all the forms a word can

or alphabetically. When you click on one of the words in the list BibleWorks will conduct a search for all instances of that word using the **Pericope, Book** or **Chapter** as a search limit. The most useful parts of the **Context** tab will be the **Book** column or the **Pericope** column. These will allow you to quickly scan through the list of words in the book to see what words are used most frequently in that book or section. However, in early stages of observation, if you are giving a name to chapters, you can see the most frequently used words in a chapter by using the **Chapter** list.

By making and refining a custom **Bible Outline** as mentioned above, the **Pericope** column becomes a tool for identifying recurrences in a section that you have determined from your study of the book. You can use the **Pericope** column to view the repeated words in the section of Scripture and see what words are used frequently in that section. There are right click options for each section to copy the list to the **Editor** or clipboard and to export the list to the program's **Word List Manager**, a tool where word lists can be saved in a file for future use. If you desire you can even make additional custom outlines for segments within the sections.

While you are reading a book, you may wish to search for terms during the course of your reading. You can immediately see all the recurrences of that word in the particular Biblical book by viewing the **Use** tab. The **Use** tab is helpful to see how a word is used throughout the book as you encounter it in your reading in contrast to the overall vocabulary of the book approach that the **Context** tab provides.

If the **Use** tab is chosen in the **Analysis Window**, when you mouse over words in the **Browse Window**, the **Use** tab instantly shows the instances where the word occurs throughout the whole book. You can also set the **Use** tab to find the use of the word in only the **Pericope Range** from the **Bible Outline**, a **Custom Range** that uses your current search limits setting if you are using one or you can set it to use find the use of the word in the **Entire Version** as well. When studying a book in English and using the **Use** tab, it is helpful to turn on **Fuzzy Searching** to allow the **Use** tab to show you the word in the various inflected English forms it can take and to some extent related words based on that word.

One advantage to using the **Use** tab is that it can work directly with a graphical representation of the recurrences of a word. Using the two column **Analysis Window** you can view the **Stats** tab with the **Use** tab to quickly see sections of the book where the word may be found, and these graphically represented, as you mouse over words. In the **Use** tab, right click and choose **Update Stats** tab if open. Display the two column **Analysis Window** with both the **Use** tab and **Stats** tab displaying. In the **Stats** tab, use the option **# of verses in the chapter with hit**, change the **Sort Books** field to a **Normal** rather than **Descending** order and change the **Options** button **Detail Level** to **Chapter** order. Further options in the **Use** and **Stats** tabs allow you to export the verse list to the search list in the **Search Window** (to work with it further or save it to the **Verse List Manager**)[15] and to **Export Graph** from the **Stats** tab to be pasted into a document.

---

take throughout the Hebrew Bible, Greek New Testament and/or LXX when you mouse over a Hebrew or Greek word.

[15] The **Verse List Manager** is a tool for saving and editing verse lists from searches you have run, verses found in a document file, or verses added manually. See the Help file for more information on the **Verse List Manager**.

Chapter 17—The Use of BibleWorks Software to Perform Inductive Bible Study Tasks

3. Detailed Observation and Interpretation

3.1 Tools for Observation and Note Taking

The process for making observations, recording them, recording questions and formulating interpretations of questions and observations can vary in terms of the time frame and order with which one wishes to proceed;[16] so I'd like to note some tools that can be used at multiple stages in the IBS process for recording information. Some will prefer to jot down observations observed in a notebook, journal or word processing system that one has used for some time and is comfortable with. BibleWorks offers several note-taking tools that can be used to access notes you've taken on chapters, verses and words in the Bible and keep those notes accessible across multiple installations on different computers.

The **Browse Window** offers you a quick and easy way to read most modern English Bible versions, tagged Greek and Hebrew texts and many modern translations in a variety of languages from around the world.[17] As features are observed in the text during reading you can highlight the text in a variety of different styles by clicking on the **Apply color to Browse Window text** button in the main toolbar or right clicking and choosing **Apply color to selected text**. The program saves highlighting in a color file for the Bible version you choose to color. One can make multiple color files for any Bible version in the program and choose to display them or turn them off from display for that version in a color selection window dialogue box. The color files can be moved to other computers that have BibleWorks installed, shared with other BibleWorks users and when exporting text from a Bible version, one can choose to **Export Colors** to include highlighting in the exported text.

The **Analysis Window** offers a number of tools that can help you record what you are observing as you read and study the text. There BibleWorks offers three text editor windows that are rtf editors much like WordPad in Windows, but with enhanced features like the ability to type right to left in a Hebrew font when needed. You can copy text into these editor windows and save notes based on chapter or verse (**Notes** tab) or even on individual words in English, Greek and Hebrew (the previously mentioned **UserLex** tab). These tabs will retain your notes as you move to new verses or words. They can be saved in .rtf format to be viewed in a word processor and the notes folder containing the note files can be moved to other computers running BibleWorks if you use multiple computers or wish to share your notes with others who use BibleWorks. These two tabs have much the same features as the **Editor** tab, but each one is set up to interact and update based on your use of the **Browse Window**. The **Editor** tab functions independently of the **Browse**

---

[16] *Inductive Bible Study*, 180.

[17] The New American Standard (NAS), New American Standard Updated 1995 (NAU) King James Version (KJV), New King James (NKJ), Holman Christian Standard Bible (CSB), Revised Webster Bible (RWB), Russian Synodal Text of the Bible 1917 (RST), Dutch Statenvertaling 1637 (SVV), French Louis Segond Version 1910 (LSG), German Lutherbibel 1912 (LUO) and German Muenchener Neues Testament Version 1998 (MNT) all are tagged with Strong's numbers that allow one to identify the underlying Greek or Hebrew word the translation translates with a brief gloss and the glosses can be set to display in English, French, German, Dutch or Russian. By the time of publication, the recently included Christian Standard Version 2017 (CSB17) is expected to have Strong's tagging in BibleWorks 10.

Window without updating itself based on the book, chapter and verse or mouse position.

When you observe the book as a whole you can use the **Notes** and **Editor** tabs to record your observations. Chapter and verse notes are good places to record observations you may wish to explore later as you read through all steps of the IBS observation process and can be a location to save the interpretive questions you ask on structural relationships, verse context or terms during detailed observation.

The **Notes** tab interacts with the current book, chapter and verse on display in the **Browse Window** to allow you to take notes on a chapter or verse as you study a book. When you have the checkbox for **Chapter** checked at the top of the **Notes** tab you are making a chapter note and the note is saved when you move to a new chapter or close BibleWorks. When you have **Chapter** unchecked you are making a verse note which is likewise saved when you move to a new verse. The notes will always display when you are on that chapter or verse in the **Browse Window** and the **Notes** tab will signal that you have a previous chapter or verse note saved by placing a "c" or "v" in the **Notes** tab, therefore you can visually see that at one time you took chapter and/or verse notes on the verse you are currently viewing in the **Browse Window** when you return to that verse at a later point.

3.2 Detailed Observation: Terminal Observation and Word Study—Basic Searches

At its most basic level, a Bible software program or app functions as a quick concordance of any Bible version in the program, whether English, Greek or Hebrew. Using the mouse or a **Command Line** sequence you can easily look up instances of words or phrases throughout the whole Bible version you are reading. In BibleWorks searching for a word in English is as easy as double clicking on it or right clicking on it and choosing **Search on Word**. For a Greek or Hebrew version, it is best to right click and choose **Search on Lemma** to find all instances of the use of that word regardless of the inflected form. You will typically not wish to double click a Greek or Hebrew word to search for it or right click and choose **Search on Form** (although such searches are possible) because the search will only find the particular inflected form of the word that you started with. In most cases one is typically interested in finding all possible forms of that word, regardless of the specific inflected form that you started with and the **Search on Lemma** feature allows you to do just that.

Double-clicking on an English word or right clicking and choosing **Search on Word** with an English word executes a search that is very form specific to that English word, but BibleWorks 10 allows you to search for multiple inflected forms of English words at the same time if you turn on the **Fuzzy Search option**. When the **Fuzzy Search option** is on, searches of English versions will return the different forms of the word in English when you conduct searches from the **Browse Window**, **Command Line** or **Use** tab. To turn on fuzzy searching right click on the **Command Line** and choose **Fuzzy Search option | Use Link Stemming (Recommended) (English) only**. The last green indicator in the **Command Line Versions button** will turn yellow to remind you that you have fuzzy searching on. Then if you double click on run or type .run on the **Command Line** the **Search Window** will list all verses that have run, ran, running, runs, runner, runners, etc. in them.

You will typically want to search for a word or phrase in only one part of the Bible, just the book itself or perhaps a segment of a book if you are studying a segment or section. There are two ways to set search limits in BibleWorks and thus focus on one book of the Bible at a time when you execute searches. For example, to set a search limit so as to search only the book of Amos, on the main BibleWorks menu select **Search**, and then **Set Search Limits**. Click the radio button **Limit the search using the books checked below**. Clear the checked books by clicking the button **All** under the heading **Clear**. Scroll down the list of books and select the box for **Amos**. Click the **OK** button. Now when you search on a word you will only find hits in Amos.

A very easy way to set search limits or to turn them off is to use the **Command Line** shortcut command to set a search limit. Type an 'l' for 'limits' on the **Command Line**, followed by a space and the book name or range of verses that you wish as your search limits. For example, to limit the search to Amos type l amo on the **Command Line** and hit <Enter>.[18] Now your search limit is set to Amos.

After you set a search limit, notice that the first green indicator in the **Command Line Versions Button** is yellow. This yellow box reminds you that you have a search limit currently set for the **Search Window**. If you perform a search in the future and do not find search hits where you expect them, check to make sure that you do not have a search limit set. You can clear the search limit by typing just the letter "l" on the **Command Line** and hitting <Enter> or by selecting **Search** on the BibleWorks menu, and then selecting **Set Search Limits**. Click the top radio button **Do not apply any limits to the search**, and then click the **OK** button. Each of these actions should turn the first yellow box on the **Command Line Versions Button** back to green.

3.3 Detailed Observation: Word or Phrase Tools for Terminal and Grammatical Observations

As you move into further stages of observation it would be good to know of some tools that can help you during this process. As you observe the use of words in a book you may wish to see what other words, phrases and concepts tend to be associated with that word in a book. For example, using the **Context** tab when studying Deuteronomy, we see that the word Lord is used 552 times in the book of Deuteronomy in the RSV. With the **Key Word in Context – KWIC/Collocation Table Module** you can check what words tend to be associated with the word Lord.

We can limit our search findings and find out more information on 'Lord' with this tool. Use the BibleWorks main menu option **Tools | Analyzing the text | KWIC/Collocation Table Module**. Choose your Version (in this case RSV) and set the **Verse Range** to deu, enter the word Lord in the **Word** box. The default settings for **Left** (5 words), **Right** (5 words), and **Codes** (2 codes) are fine for this search. Click the **Build** button to run the search. Alternatively, you can right click on the word you wish to focus on, choose **Search word in KWIC** and then set the **Verse Range** to deu and click **Build**.

In the top window, you will see a brief, single-line concordance with the search word, the word 'lord', in red. This is a KWIC (Key Word In Context) concordance. In the bottom window,

---

[18] You need only use the first three characters for most books of the Bible, but a whole book name can be used, for example, Amos.

you see the Collocation Table. Notice that the words in the Collocation Table are sorted according to frequency. The X indicates the search word, in this case the word 'lord'. The negative numbers at the top of the table show words that appear before our search word 'lord', while the positive numbers show words that appear after our search word 'lord'.

For example, note the word 'land' in the left column, which occurs 51 times in the Freq (frequency) column. Click on the word 'land' and the KWIC concordance changes to show every occurrence of 'land' in relationship to 'lord' in Deuteronomy. The search term ('lord') is in red, while the relationship word ('land') is in blue. Forty-two times the word 'land' appears 3 words before the word 'lord' and five times it appears 5 words after the word 'lord'. Notice the positive and negative numbers on the table heading, and the numbers in the row for 'land'. A zero indicates that there are no occurrences of 'land' in relationship to 'land' in those word positions. Clicking on the table column headings sorts the table by that column.

If you scan through the KWIC concordance in the top window you will see that a frequently used phrase in Deuteronomy is "land which the lord [our god] swore" or "gives" signaling that exploration of how this phrase is used throughout Deuteronomy may be of importance to the study of the whole book. Notice the KWIC display. It shows every occurrence of 'lord' in relationship to 'land'. You can click on a verse in the KWIC concordance and the verse will appear in the **Browse Window**. When you are finished analyzing the occurrences of 'land', you can reload the KWIC concordance back to the original results for 'lord' by clicking the **Reload** button and explore other words that relate to 'lord' in Deuteronomy. The **Copy** menu option allows you to copy KWIC and Collocation Table entries to the clipboard to paste into the editor or a word processor. You can click **Copy | Export KWIC Search to Main Search Window** if you wish to interact in the main program with the verses displayed in the KWIC concordance.[19]

The KWIC module provides a way to give meaningful limits to large searches. A search result that returns many hits may be difficult to sort and categorize quickly and accurately. For example, if we were working in Acts and used the **Context** tab to view the vocabulary for Acts, we see that the word 'god' appears 163 times in Acts in RSV. Using the KWIC Module you can quickly see major terms that appear in relationship to the word you searched for and more easily see how to identify and categorize important verses about it. For example, we see that 'fathers' appears in relationship to 'god' 12 times, usually with some discussion about the 'God of our fathers'. The word 'word' appears in relationship to 'god' 14 times, usually referring to God's word. The word 'raised' appears 9 times, in each occurrence except one describing God raising Jesus from the dead. Through noticing the relationship between the search term 'god' and the relationship terms, we can potentially

---

[19] The KWIC module can also suggest further searches you may wish to undertake using the **Command Line**. Let's say you wish to see where the phrase 'land which the lord' appears with either 'swore' or 'gives'. A **Command Line** search with Deuteronomy set as the search limit for ('land which the lord) (/swore gives) would find those verses and you could also view their distribution graphically throughout Deuteronomy using the **Stats** tab in the **Analysis Window** after you successfully conduct the search. See the **Command Line Examples** Help article for suggested **Command Line** search syntax by placing your mouse cursor over the **Command Line** and hitting **F1**.

Chapter 17—The Use of BibleWorks Software to Perform Inductive Bible Study Tasks   299

gain insight into the message of Acts that is difficult to see simply through the use of the **Context** tab's list of words in a book or **Command Line** search results.

Another tool that can help you find related terms when studying a New Testament book is to use the **Command Line** to search on a list of related words in the book using the Louw-Nida Greek-English Lexicon of the New Testament Based on Semantic Domains. For example, when you are studying the flow of ideas in ideological books like epistles, identifying discourse markers in the text can make it easier to see the logical connective words in the Greek New Testament.

Let's say we wish to study Galatians. First, limit the search to Galatians. Type l gal into the **Command Line** and hit <Enter>. Then set your search version to the BGM or BNM, by typing the version abbreviation on the **Command Line** and hitting <Enter>. Now you can right click on the **Command Line** and choose **Insert Louw Nida Domain Code**. Under the section labeled **Domains** in the **Louw-Nida Domains** window scroll down the list of semantic domains until you come to domain **91 Discourse Markers**. Click it once to select the list. The **Words in the selected domain** appear in the right-hand window. Then click the **Insert** button to insert this list in the **Command Line**. Click the **Close** button to close the **Louw-Nida Domains** window. You will find that the **Command Line** now indicates .<91.1-14>. Press the <Enter> key to conduct your search.

The search on the Louw-Nida semantic domain **91.1-14 Discourse Markers** finds 25 forms with 155 occurrences in 103 verses. You could apply color to the search results to color the discourse markers in your Greek New Testament text to easily find them in the text as you study it and view the hits in the **Parallel Versions Window** as you did with the key words found previously in the RSV.

If you wish to save a list of these words, they can be copied to the **Word List Manager**. Open **Tools | Analyzing the Text | Word List Manager**, click **Load or Generate Word List** and under **Source** in the **Create Word List** window choose **Load highlighted words from last query**, uncheck **Keep morph codes** and click the **Create list** button. The **Word List Manager** and the **Graphical Search Engine** also offer the option of load a list of words from a semantic domain and then manually delete individual words that you may not wish to include in your search to further refine the search. See the help file for the **Word List Manager** or the **Graphical Search Engine** to learn more about using those tools.

The Louw-Nida lexicon and the ability to search by categories can be helpful for searching on Greek words in a number of different categories that may be characteristic of different genres in the Greek New Testament such as words relating to specific types of semantic relations, time, names of persons and places, etc. Therefore, it may be helpful to familiarize yourself with list of categories the Louw-Nida lexicon uses as semantic domains.

The Greek and Hebrew texts in BibleWorks use morphological tagging to identify the inflected forms each word takes in the text. Therefore, you can search for particular parts of speech, verbal forms, prepositions and the like as needed. Each word is broken down into its lexical or dictionary form followed by a separator character and codes that identify its part of speech and other characteristics of the inflected form in a brother text to the version that displays the Greek or Hebrew text. Sections **72 Morphological Coding Schemes, 41 The Command Line - Greek and Hebrew** and **43 Command Line - Examples and Shortcuts** under **Help | BibleWorks Help Contents** are helpful articles to learn more about the morphological tagging and search capabilities in BibleWorks.

Some simple examples of using morphological tagging to identify the function of words in a book or section can be seen as follows. The morphological tagging of Greek and Hebrew nouns can be helpful to identify proper nouns indicated in the text. For Greek proper nouns, choose the BGM or BNM as your search version and type on the **Command Line** .*@n???p* to search for all proper nouns. For the Hebrew Bible use the WTM as your search version and type .*@np* and hit <Enter> to search for all proper nouns. You can view the found words for each search by displaying the **Words** tab in the **Analysis Window** and looking at the list of words in the Wildcard expansion of **Command Line**. Clicking on the words there will run a search for the word. You can view previous search terms you've entered on the **Command Line** by hitting the up arrow on your keyboard to cycle through previous commands you've typed on the **Command Line** during your current session of BibleWorks. You may wish to search for indicative (.*@vi*) and imperative (.*@vd*) verbs in Greek to see where changes occur in verb tense in the book you are studying. The charts of morphological codes for the various Greek and Hebrew versions in section **72 Morphological Coding Schemes** of the help file can be consulted to check what can be searched for. It is readily available when you open **Help | BibleWorks Help Contents** and check under **Frequently Used Links**.

BibleWorks can also use the morphological codes to visually highlight grammatical features of the text as you read it in the **Browse Window** using the program's **Morphology Colors** feature. The program comes with a morphology colors file that will apply colors to differentiate nouns and verbs for Greek and Hebrew text. This feature is very customizable and allows you to using the morphological codes in BibleWorks to potentially make multiple morphology color files to suit various types of study you may wish to engage in.

To set the Greek New Testament to highlight indicative and imperative verbs click on **Tools | Options | General | Morphology Colors** and choose the **BNM @v*** and change the **Text Color** and **Text Background** to your preferred choices by clicking on the color buttons. In the **Morphology** box change the @v* to @vi* to color indicative verbs. Click the **New Entry** button, set the color and background to your liking and in the **Morphology** box change @vi* to @vd* to color imperative verbs. Then check the box **Enable Morphology Color Tagging** to turn the color tagging on so that it appears in the **Browse Window** Greek text. Save your own morphology color scheme with the **Save** or **Save As** button.

To color all the proper nouns in the Hebrew Bible, choose the **WTM @n*** and change the **Text Color** and **Text Background** to your preferred choices by clicking on the color buttons. In the **Morphology** box change the @n* to @np* to color all Hebrew proper nouns. Then check the box **Enable Morphology Color Tagging** to turn the color tagging on so that it appears in the **Browse Window** Hebrew text. A quick way to turn the currently chosen morphology color tagging file and its highlighting on or off is to click on the **Browse Window** Options Button in the upper right of the **Browse Window** and check or uncheck the **Toggle Morphology Highlighting** option that is there with a number of toggle options for the **Browse Window**.

3.4 Detailed Observation: Grammatical Observations and Consultation

As you engage in detailed observation of the text you may wish to explore grammatical issues that arise in your study. You can consult Greek and Hebrew grammar articles that relate to the form of speech for a word you take interest in and by using the **Resources Summary** tab in the **Analysis Window** to access relevant sections of Greek and Hebrew reference grammars. Through this tool you can find information in a grammar concerning the grammatical form of the word you are studying and you can find out what the grammar says about the verse you are studying.

Select the **Resources Summary** tab in the **Analysis Window**. Place your cursor over a Greek or Hebrew word in the **Browse Window** and then hold down the **Shift** key while you move the mouse cursor over to the **Resources Summary** tab so that the program will freeze and remember the word you had held your mouse cursor over.

Notice that the top line in the **Summary** tab window displays the word followed by the grammatical parsing. What follows below it are links to open various resources in the program that will display information based on the word or verse you are focusing on in the **Browse Window.** Scroll down the **Summary** window until you come to a grammar you wish to consult, perhaps **Wallace,** *Exegetical Syntax of the NT* for Greek or the **Waltke & O'Connor,** *Introduction to Biblical Hebrew Syntax* for Hebrew. Grammars have a pink background color in the **Summary** tab window. Wallace lists grammar sections that pertain to the word, followed by specific references the verse you are viewing in the **Browse Window** if it is used as an example in Wallace's grammar. When you click on the entries the Wallace grammar will open to a discussion of the grammatical information concerning the form of speech you are seeking information for. If you move your cursor over the words in the verse in the **Browse Window**, the entries in the Greek grammars update and change as you focus on each word. Thus, you can consult the grammars for the possible grammatical usage of each word as needed and record your observations in your verse notes. It is also helpful to pay special attention when a grammar discusses the passage you are studying and uses it as an example.

3.5 Detailed Observation: Comparing Bible Versions

The **Parallel Versions Window** provides a way to read the text using two or more versions in parallel columns. A **Command Line** command allows you to open a **Parallel Versions Window** for quick use by clicking within the **Command Line** at the top of the **Search Window** and typing the letter 'p' followed by the abbreviations for the versions you wish to open. For example, to open a **Parallel Versions Window** with the RSV and BGT,[20] type p rsv bgt and hit <Enter>. The windows appear in the same order they are typed on the **Command Line**.

The **Parallel Versions Window** is like having multiple texts or translations open on your desk at the same time by displaying a passage in multiple browse windows open at the same time. The buttons on the left side of the **Parallel Versions Window** allow you to scroll the versions in a synchronized fashion by book, chapter, or verse and each column has its own options for text display.

---

[20] The BGT is a combination of Rahlfs Septuagint and the Nestle-Aland 28th edition into one version.

You can also open a **Parallel Versions Window** under **Tools | Viewing the text | Parallel Versions Window**. Select a version you wish to display, and then click the **Add** button. Select each version you wish to display, adding them to the list at the bottom of the window. When you are finished selecting versions, click **OK**. Another way to open this Parallel Versions setup tool is to click on the **Parallel Versions** button on the main toolbar and a drop down arrow next to the button gives you an option to **Edit Favorites** where you can make multiple preset Parallel Versions Windows for various types of study you may be engaged in, a set of particular translations you wish to compare, viewing the OT, LXX and translations together or even multiple windows of the same version to compare parts of a book with other parts for elements of recurring themes.

A good tool for comparing the differences and similarities in Bible versions is found in **Difference Highlighting** which displays color highlighting where same language Bible versions differ from each other in the content of a verse. This is useful both for comparing translations or viewing textual differences between versions of the Greek New Testament. A **Browse Window** Options button at the top of the **Browse Window** has an option to **Toggle Difference Highlighting** or one can click **View | Show/Hide | Difference Highlighting** to toggle it on or off. It will highlight the differences between the versions for you until it is turned off. It can also be toggled on or off by clicking in the **Browse Window** and typing the "e" key on your keyboard.

4. Detailed Analysis: Tracing the Thought Flow of a Segment and Diagraming

There are two diagram tools in BibleWorks that can help you see the relationships of words and phrases in the Greek New Testament within segments of the text.[21] The **Syntactic and Thematic Greek Transcription of the New Testament** can be useful to view the relationships between the parts of the text. This resource diagrams the main syntactical units of New Testament paragraphs to indicate grammatical relationships and syntactical transitions by subordination and parallelism. Linguistic parallels are highlighted by color. To view the Greek transcription of a book, choose **Resources | Miscellaneous | McDonald, Greek Transcription**. Then choose the book you are studying in the list of New Testament books to the left.

You may also view the **McDonald, Greek Transcription** for the current New Testament passage that you are working on in the **Browse Window** by clicking on the **Resources Summary** tab in the **Analysis Window** and scrolling down to **McDonald, Greek Transcription**. To read more about the philosophy behind the construction of the diagrams found in the Greek Transcription, see the Introduction in its table of contents and the chapter on the Textual Transcription Technique in that is found under **Resources | Greek Grammars | McDonald, Greek Enchiridion** section of the menu.

---

[21] A long-time BibleWorks user has posted downloadable files of the BHS Hebrew text with linguistic annotations and an interlinear Hebrew/KJV Bible that can be copied to the BibleWorks 10\databases folder and then viewed from the **Vs1** or **Vs2** tab in the **Analysis Window** alongside the Old Testament versions on display in the **Browse Window**. See here for how to download and install those files: https://www.bibleworks.com/forums/showthread.php?6696-BHS-series-in-VS1-TAB

The Leedy Greek New Testament Diagrams provide further detail concerning the relationships between words and information for developing outlines in New Testament books. Often the diagram will help you see what verses are part of a thought unit. To open the diagram, choose **Tools | Language Tools | Diagramming Module**. In the **Diagramming Window**, click on the button labeled **Leedy Greek NT Diagrams**. A menu will open below the button and will allow you to select the book, chapter and verse you wish to view in a diagram. The diagrams can help you see how the details of a segment may come together to convey the rhetorical message of the segment.

An alternative way to open a New Testament diagram is to display the verse in the **Browse Window** first. Next select **Resources**, and then **New Testament Diagram Database**. The diagram for that verse automatically opens in the **Diagramming Module** window. A third way to open a New Testament diagram is to right click on a Greek word in the **Browse Window** and choose **Open NT Diagram at this Word**.

You can also create your own diagrams. Creating your own diagram has the advantage of helping you focus closely upon the use of each word in its context. If you prefer, you can use the **Diagramming Module** to create diagrams based upon phrases rather than individual words using Greek, Hebrew, English, or other language texts. You can load a range of verses into the **Diagramming Module**, then highlight and drag words or phrases from the text window at the top to the canvas below it. The **Diagramming Module** offers you the flexibility of placing words and phrases where you wish in the canvas and adding descriptive text and lines. You can save your diagrams and export them as well.

A tool for analyzing the flow of thought in a segment in English is to use the color file for the RSV that was developed from the key words that signal structural relations in English. If you colored the RSV text using the **relations.qf** search after running the search in the **Graphic Search Engine** as mentioned previously you can view the RSV in the **Browse Window** or alongside other versions in a **Parallel Versions Window**. As you study a text in BibleWorks in your preferred translation you can compare it against the RSV with the highlighted keywords. As you read the text, check it against the RSV to determine if the red highlighted word indicates that one of these rhetorical relationships is operating in the text. Comparison with the RSV allows you to observe what the text is saying without the clutter being added to version you typically work with if it is not the RSV, but when you wish to see the rhetorical key words you can see them in the RSV text.

5. GATHERING EVIDENCES, QUESTIONS, AND FORMULATING PREMISES

5.1 Preliminary Definition of Words and Word Usage

Appendix D, The Use of Original-Language Resources in the Bauer and Traina's *Inductive Bible Study* provides some instructions for using the KJV, a Strong's Concordance and a lexicon to find the preliminary definition of Hebrew and Greek words and word usage for those who do not know Greek and Hebrew. BibleWorks offers a means to determine the preliminary definition of words and word usage for those who know Greek and Hebrew and for those who do not using English versions that are tagged with Strong's numbers. You can access Greek and Hebrew lexicons in the **Analysis** tab or by right clicking on Greek and Hebrew words. Word usage can be determined with the **Use** tab or by searching for a word. Those that do not know Greek or Hebrew can use English texts that are tagged with Strong's numbers to identify the underlying Greek or Hebrew word that the English word or phrase translates.

Those who know Greek and Hebrew should display the BGT or WTT in the **Browse Window.** Hold your mouse cursor over the Greek or Hebrew word that you wish to determine a preliminary definition for in the **Browse Window** text while displaying the **Analysis** tab in the **Analysis Window.** The **Analysis** tab will display the lexicon entry[22] for the word you hover the mouse cursor over. There the student can note the basic definition of the word. You can freeze the **Analysis** tab on that word by holding down the shift key. If you wish to change the default lexicons that display for Greek and Hebrew, right click in the body of the **Analysis** tab window and choose **Default Analysis Window Greek Lexicons** or **Default Analysis Window Hebrew Lexicons**. You can choose multiple lexicons to display in the Analysis tab and you can change the order in which they display in the small window that opens.

For a preliminary definition of Greek words, display the BGT and in the **Analysis** tab change the default Greek lexicon to the **Danker Greek Lexicon**. For example, display Matthew 1:1 and hold your mouse cursor over γενέσεως (origin, birth, genealogy) in the verse while displaying the **Analysis** tab. You should see the following entry in the **Analysis** tab followed by the Danker lexicon entry for the word: **γενέσεως** noun genitive feminine singular common from the Greek **γένεσις**.

Appendix D in Bauer and Traina's *Inductive Bible Study* indicates a slightly different process for Hebrew verbs in contrast to other Hebrew words, but the process is much the same for all Hebrew

---

[22] BibleWorks 10 comes with the following lexicons. For Greek, Frederick William Danker, Kathryn Krug, *The Concise Greek–English Lexicon of the New Testament* (Chicago: University of Chicago Press, 2009); Timothy Friberg, Barbara Friberg, and Neva F. Miller, *Analytical Lexicon to the Greek New Testament, Baker's Greek New Testament Library* (Grand Rapids: Baker, 2000); F. Wilbur Gingrich, *Shorter Lexicon of the Greek New Testament*, ed. Frederick W. Danker, 2nd ed. (Chicago: University of Chicago Press, 1983); Henry George Liddell and Robert Scott, *An Intermediate Greek-English Lexicon: Founded Upon the Seventh Edition of Liddell and Scott's Greek-English Lexicon* (Oxford: Clarendon, 1889); Johannes E. Louw and Eugene A. Nida, *Greek-English Lexicon of the New Testament: Based on Semantic Domains*, 2 vols., 2nd ed. (New York: United Bible Societies, 1989); J. H. Moulton and G. Milligan, *Vocabulary of the Greek Testament* (London: Hodder and Stoughton, 1930); Joseph Thayer, *A Greek-English Lexicon of the New Testament* (n.p.: n.p., 1889). For Hebrew, Francis Brown, S. R. Driver, and Charles A. Briggs, *The Brown-Driver-Briggs Hebrew and English Lexicon: With an Appendix containing Biblical Aramaic* (Oxford: Clarendon, 1907); William L. Holladay, *A Concise Hebrew and Aramaic Lexicon of the Old Testament: Based upon the Lexical Work of Ludwig Koehler and Walter Baumgartner* (Leiden: Brill, 2000). The following lexicons are available as additional cost, add-on modules for BibleWorks: Walter Bauer, *A Greek-English Lexicon of the New Testament and Other Early Christian Literature*, ed. Frederick W. Danker, 3rd ed. (Chicago: University of Chicago Press, 2000); Ludwig Koehler and Walter Baumgartner, *The Hebrew and Aramaic Lexicon of the Old Testament*, ed. Johann Jakob Stam, trans. M. E. J. Richardson, CD-ROM ed. (Leiden: Brill, 1994). Henry George Liddell and Robert Scott, *A Greek-English Lexicon: With a Revised Supplement*, ed. Sir Henry Stuart Jones and Roderick McKenzie, 9th ed. (Oxford: Clarendon, 1996); Johan Lust, Erik Eynikel, and Katrin Hauspie, *Greek-English Lexicon of the Septuagint*, rev. ed. (Stuttgart: Deutsche Bibelgesellschaft, 2003).

or Aramaic words in the Old Testament when using BibleWorks. For example, display Hosea 9:10. To find a preliminary definition of לְבֹ֫שֶׁת (shame), hold your mouse cursor over that word in the **Browse Window** while displaying the **Analysis** tab. You should see the following entry in the **Analysis** tab followed by the Holladay lexicon's entry for the word: לְ particle preposition הַ particle article בֹּשֶׁת noun common feminine singular absolute. You can set the **Analysis** tab to display the Brown, Driver, Briggs lexicon if you wish by changing the default Hebrew lexicons.

In the case of Hebrew verbs, take note of the verbal stem that the morphological information identifies for the verb. In the case of seeking to define וֶאֱמָץ (hiph:to be strong; qal:to be strong; piel:to make firm; hith:to strengthen self) in Joshua 1:6, notice that the top of the Analysis tab parses אמץ as a qal verb; therefore, you would focus on the lexicon's definitions of qal verbs in the lexicon entry you are viewing. The **Analysis** tab will display the following prior to the default lexicon entry/ies for that word: ו particle conjunction אמץ verb qal imperative masculine singular.

Those who do not know Greek and Hebrew can use any of the English versions in BibleWorks that are tagged for Strong's numbers to find a preliminary definition of the word. The following versions are tagged for Strong's numbers: KJV, NKJ, NASB (BibleWorks versions NAS and NAU, the 1995 update) or the CSB. I suggest using the CSB since the tagging of the words in the CSB appears to be the best word for word tagging amongst these versions.

First, read the passage being interpreted in the CSB (Christian Standard Bible) and identify the way in which the CSB has translated the passage. When you hold the mouse cursor over the word used for preliminary definition it will display the Greek or Hebrew word that the word translates in a popup **Word Tip** and at the top of the **Analysis** tab in the **Analysis Window**. For more precision, you can display the Strong's numbers and hold your mouse cursor over a Strong's number to display the Hebrew word. This may be helpful at times if you are using one of the other tagged versions in BibleWorks. Click the **Browse Window Options** button at the top of the **Browse Window**, and then select **Toggle Strong's Numbers**. In Hosea 9:10 the Strong's number <01322> will display after Shame and you can place your mouse cursor over the Strong's number to display the Hebrew word as well. For example, if you hold the mouse cursor over Shame in Hosea 9:10 it will indicate:**01322** בֹּשֶׁת bosheth {bo'-sheth} at the top of the **Analysis** tab.

You can use the Greek or Hebrew word that displays in the **Analysis** tab after the Strong's number to view a lexicon entry for a Greek or Hebrew word. Make sure you are viewing the WTT Leningrad Hebrew Old Testament or BGT NA28 NT + LXX (Rahlfs) Text in the **Browse Window** to prepare to do so. Having identified the Hebrew word behind the English translation and displaying it in the **Analysis** tab (**01322** בֹּשֶׁת bosheth {bo'-sheth}), hold down the **Shift** key to freeze the **Analysis** tab. Then move your cursor to place it over the Hebrew word immediately to the right of the Strong's number in the top line of the **Analysis** tab. Double-click the Hebrew word. This begins a search of that Hebrew word in a Hebrew Bible version.

The search results appear in the **Search Window**, with the Hebrew word highlighted in yellow. Scroll through the list of search results in the **Search Window** and select Hosea 9:10. The Hebrew word will appear highlighted in the WTT text in the Browse Window. Place your cursor over the highlighted Hebrew word to show a Hebrew lexicon entry for the word in the **Analysis** tab. You can also right click on the highlighted Hebrew word in the **Browse Window** and choose **Lookup Lemma in Lexicon Browser** to display the lexicon entry. Select **Lexicons** in the menu for the Lexicon Browser and you can choose to view the word in any of the Hebrew lexicons. Using the CSB in the **Browse Window,** you can try this with courageous <0553> in Joshua 1:6 or historical <1078> in Matthew 1:1 to match the examples given in Appendix D in Bauer and Traina's *Inductive Bible Study*.[23]

Those familiar with Greek can study word usage by searching the BGM for all occurrences of the Greek word or using the **Use** tab in the techniques we have mentioned previously. Beginning your search with the **Use** tab set to the **Current Book Only** or the search limits set to the book you are studying or the books written by a particular author will concentrate your study on how the word is used within the book or by the author before exploring how it is used in other books of the New Testament or the Septuagint when exploring word usage in Greek.

BibleWorks enables you examine word usage and to perform word studies on texts other than the Bible at the same time as you search the Biblical text. For example, display Matthew 1:1 in the BGT. On the main BibleWorks menu select **Search**, and then choose **Cross Version Search Mode**. Choose **Search and Display All Same Language Versions**. The second green box in the **Command Line Versions Button** under the **Command Line** will turn yellow. This yellow box is a reminder that a cross versions search mode is enabled and will remain that way until one sets the **Cross Version Search Mode** back to **Search only Current Search Version**. In the **Browse Window**, right click on γενέσεως in the BGT or at the top of the Analysis tab if you used the CSB to find the Greek word, whichever way you prefer to search for the Greek word. Notice the Greek texts that return hits in the **Cross Version Search Results** window. You can click on any of these versions to display them in the Browse Window. Notice that Josephus, Philo and the Greek Pseudepigrapha also have hits for this word. By clicking on Josephus, the Josephus Greek text becomes the search version and is displayed in the Browse Window. Each of the Josephus search results appears in the **Search Window**.

By default, the box **Mouse click activates companion** in the **Cross Version Search Results** is checked, making the companion text display in the **Browse Window**. Because this box is checked, when you click the search result for JOM the display version JOS will appear in the **Browse Window**. You may also want to display the JOE English in the **Browse Window** for easier reading of Josephus. If you search on a morphologically-tagged version, you may want to check the box to display the companion text rather than the morphologically-tagged version for easier reading. By including texts outside the Bible in your searches you can see how the word is used in other contexts. This can important if you are studying a word that only occurs a few times in the Biblical text.

---

[23] Additional information and illustrations on using this technique can be found in the BibleWorks online knowledgebase in this article: "How Do I Find Greek/Hebrew Words Translated by a Given Word Using Strong's Numbers?" located here: https://kb.bibleworks.com/article/AA-02967

5.2 Literary Context

Several tools we have covered in book study and detailed observation are helpful for observing and interacting with the literary context for a book. The development of one's own **Bible Outline** within BibleWorks for the book that is being studied and use of the **Diagramming Module** can be helpful in analysis of the immediate context and segment context. The **Use** tab and searching within a book using search limits for significant terms is helpful in the analysis of book context.

5.3 Scriptural Testimony

When significant terms within a book suggest that a concept should be studied, setting the search limits to the book and search for occurrences within that book may be helpful, but you can expand the search to searching for whole concepts utilizing the categories of the Louw-Nida semantic domains. In the section on Detailed Observation: Word or Phrase Tools for Terminal and Grammatical Observations we introduced the ability to search using Louw-Nida semantic domains. This feature can be useful to explore conceptual scriptural testimony[24] by searching for where concepts occur throughout the whole New Testament and Septuagint if one conducts a Louw-Nida domain search using the BGM as the search version. See the instructions above in that section for searching for a domain.

BibleWorks has several cross reference features that allow you to find passages related to the verse you are studying. The **X-Refs** tab allows you to display cross references from a variety of cross reference sources, including Stephan's Biographical Bible which is useful for finding all passages that reference each character in the Bible, Nave's Topical Bible, the Thompson Chain-Reference Bible, the Treasury of Scripture Knowledge and Torrey's Topical Text Book. These topical cross references can also be accessed by going to **Resources | X-Refs** using the main menu in the program.

The first time that the **X-Refs** tab is chosen it will display the cross-referenced passages for the current verse on display in the **Browse Window** using the **BW Master**, a combination of frequently cited cross references from the cross reference databases in BibleWorks. You can use the dropdown list in the upper left corner of the **X-Refs** tab header to change to one of the other cross reference systems and you can choose the version you wish to use to display cross references. You can access cross references based on the context of the verse on display in the Browse Window by opening the **X-Refs** tab and setting it to use the cross references developed by the editors of many major Bible translations or the NA[28]. The **BW-RVT** option shows related verses that contain similar original language vocabulary to the verse on display in the **Browse Window** and indicates how many shared words occur in the verse.

Memory or cross-references may point the student to textual scriptural testimony where the verse makes use of other biblical passages that are quoted or alluded to.[25] In cases of specific quotation of the Old Testament in the New Testament you can view a **Synopsis Window** display of the New Testament and Old Testament verse it is quoting together in a parallel display by clicking on **Tools |**

---

[24] *Inductive Bible Study*, 191.
[25] *Inductive Bible Study*, 192.

Viewing the Text | Synopsis Window, then under **File | Open** and choose the **ntot.sdf** or **ntotgrk.sdf** file. You can click on **View | Find Verse** to browse to a particular verse or use the verse list at the top of the **Synopsis Window** to scroll to a new section. The **ot.sdf** and **ot2.sdf** files display parallel scriptural testimony[26] where the same material appears in multiple Old Testament books and the **aland.sdf** and **aland(greek).sdf** files display the divisions of the gospel synopsis, Aland, *Synopsis of the Four Gospels: Completely Revised on the Basis of the Greek Text of Nestle-Aland, 26th Edition, and the Greek New Testament, 3rd Edition* (New York: United Bible Societies, 1985). These synopsis files can be configured to display in multiple versions of the Bible that come with BibleWorks.

5.4 Inflections and Syntax

BibleWorks allows you to quickly observe information concerning the inflection of a Greek or Hebrew word in a popup **Word Tip** or by viewing the information in the **Analysis** tab. You can also make a report of inflection of each word by using the **Report Generator** to display a morphological analysis of a range of verses.

Open the Report Generator from the main menu by clicking **Tools | Importing/Exporting Information | Report Generator**. To display the morphological analysis of Matthew 5:1-8, configure the **Report Generator** as follows: for **Version** choose the **BGT**, type **mat 5:1-8** for **Range**, disregard the options under **Lexicons**. In the fields for **Include Biblical Text for these Versions** and **Analyze these Greek/Hebrew Text Versions** type **bgt**. Disregard the **Lexicon Filtering** and **Exclude (Grk) Lex words if freq >=** fields, and under **Report Options** check only **Include Morphological Analysis** then click **Build Report**.

A new report will appear in an **Editor** window. The report will provide the verse in the designated version, the word as it appears in the verse, its lemma (lexical form as it would appear in a dictionary or lexicon), the codes and the morphological parsing for the word in parentheses. You can do the same for Hebrew, just use the WTT as the version. When the report appears in the Editor window, go to File | Save and you can save your report as an rtf file then add your observations, questions or interpretive observations or copy that information to existing notes you have been taking on the verses you are studying. If you check a particular lexicon in the listbox under **Lexicons** and check the **Report Options | Include Lexicon Entries** the report will provide a custom lexicon for the verse range that you entered under **Range**.

The use of BibleWorks for grammatical research and observation on a verse or passage has already been discussed in the section, Detailed Observation: Grammatical Observations and Consultation above. We noted there the technique of using of the **Resources Summary** tab to access where grammars discuss the parts of speech in the current verse on display in the **Browse Window**. Grammars can be directly opened as an electronic book as well by clicking on **Resources | Greek Grammars** or **Hebrew Grammars**.[27]

---

[26] *Inductive Bible Study*, 194.

[27] BibleWorks 10 comes with the following grammars which are useful for reference. For Greek, William Graham MacDonald, *Greek Enchiridion: A Concise Handbook of Grammar for Translation and Exegesis* (n.p.: n.p.,

To assist in the study of the syntax of a section or segment, BibleWorks offers two diagramming options for the Greek New Testament,[28] the **McDonald, Greek Transcription** and the Leedy Greek New Testament Diagrams that can be displayed in the **Diagramming Module**. These tools were covered above in the section, Detailed Analysis: Tracing the Thought Flow of a Segment and Diagramming. We noted that you can open the Greek New Testament Diagrams to the location where a Greek word appears in the **Browse Window** text by right clicking on it and choosing **Open NT Diagram at this Word**. After you open the diagram you can not only view the relationships of the words in a passage by viewing how the diagram connects the words with the diagramming symbols, but you can display how the symbols identify the function of the words by clicking **View | Show descriptive labels in symbols**. This will display on overlay of the labels identify the grammatical and syntactical function of the symbols/words in each sentence.

5.5 Literary Forms

At this stage students are encouraged to explore the significance of the literary forms and genre of a passage to understand the agreement it seeks to make with the reader for how to read the text. Bauer and Traina indicate that "the most helpful resource for both general and more specific genres is the Bible dictionary."[29] See the instructions under the previous section, Book Survey: Identifying the General Materials of a Book, for instructions on how to access the Bible dictionaries that come with BibleWorks in the **Dict** tab and under **Resources | Dictionaries** from the main menu.

5.6 History of the Text

BibleWorks comes with the Center for New Testament Textual Studies Greek New Testament textual apparatus. It displays in the **Vs1** or **Vs2** tabs in the **Analysis Window** and updates to match the verse on display in the **Browse Window**. The **Mss** tab allows you to quickly compare Greek New Testament versions and the transcriptions of some Greek New Testament manuscripts as well as view images of those manuscripts in the main portion of the tab. The **Collation Pane** at the top of

---

2005); F. C. Conybeare and St. George Stock, *A Grammar of Septuagint Greek* (Boston: Ginn and Company, 1905); Daniel B. Wallace, *Greek Grammar Beyond the Basics: An Exegetical Syntax of the New Testament* (Grand Rapids: Zondervan, 1996). For Hebrew, Paul Joüon and T. Muraoka, *A Grammar of Biblical Hebrew*, 2nd ed., Subsidia Biblica 27 (Roma: Editrice Pontificio Intituto Biblico, 2006); E. Kautzsch and A. E. Cowley, eds., *Gesenius' Hebrew Grammar*, 2nd ed. (Oxford: Clarendon, 1910); Bruce K. Waltke and M. O'Conner, *An Introduction to Biblical Hebrew Syntax* (Winona Lake, IN: Eisenbrauns, 1990). Also available as an add-on module for additional cost when BibleWorks was in production was F. Blass and A. DeBrunner, *A Greek Grammar of the New Testament and Other Early Christian Literature*, trans. Robert W. Funk (Chicago: The University of Chicago Press, 1961).

[28] As noted previously, you can download a BHS Hebrew text with linguistic annotations that identify some aspects of the syntax of the Hebrew text in the **Vs1** or **Vs2** tab in the **Analysis Window**. It may be fruitful to use this in the two-column **Analysis Window** with the **Resources Summary** tab to explore the grammar and syntax of a passage in the Hebrew Bible. Again, see here for how to download and install those files: https://www.bibleworks.com/forums/showthread.php?6696-BHS-series-in-VS1-TAB

[29] *Inductive Bible Study*, 210.

the **Mss** tab compares Greek New Testament texts. Using the current New Testament verse on display in the **Browse Window** it provides a table that highlights the differences in words used, spelling, accents and word order between the Greek New Testament versions used in BibleWorks. Clicking on the **Tools** button at the top of the **Mss** tab will allow you to add or subtract Greek New Testament versions displayed there when you choose **Collation Options**. When displayed alongside a textual apparatus in the **Vs1** tab in the two column **Analysis Window** display the **Mss** tab can give some context to the textual variants noted in the apparatus.

The **Leningrad** tab displays images of the Leningrad Codex, the textual basis for the WTT version in BibleWorks and the *Biblia Hebraica Stuttgartensia* (BHS). The textual apparatus for the NA^{28}, BHS, and portions of the BHQ (Biblia Hebraica Quita) can be added on at additional cost in an add-on module. Though space does not allow us to explore the process for using BibleWorks in the process of textual criticism the help file within BibleWorks and an online tutorial with some video links can be helpful as an entry point for using BibleWorks in the process of textual criticism if it is needed for establishing the text with BibleWorks. See the tutorial at this location, http://kb.bibleworksllc.com/kmp/index.php?/article/AA-02987 and look for the section: Identify and Investigate Textual Variants in the Greek New Testament.

6. INTERPRETATION, EVALUATION AND CORRELATION

The IBS process of interpretation and evaluation is based on the observations and questions one makes about the text one is studying. BibleWorks is a collection of texts, lexicons, grammars and tools for the close reading of the Biblical text. This essay has highlighted the process of collecting information about the text with the tools of BibleWorks. At a number of the steps I have described I have explained how the note taking features in BibleWorks found in the **Notes**, **Editor** and **UserLex** tabs in the **Analysis Window** can be used to record your observations. A button in these tabs allows one to search the BibleWorks 10\notes folder for words one may have entered into notes previously.[30] The **Report Generator**, found under **Tools | Importing/Exporting information**, can be used to gather your verse and chapter notes together into one document. You can include the Bible verses and morphological parsing of the words in the document as well by checking additional options. The document opens in an **Editor** window and can be saved in .rtf format to be used within the program or in a word processor on your computer.

Much like the IBS process itself, practicing the techniques and process of study and observation with BibleWorks will familiarize the student with the process of using BibleWorks tools and resources. I would encourage those using BibleWorks to find the features listed here and try the techniques that are mentioned as they engage in the IBS process. Check the right click context menu

---

[30] The instructions found in the BibleWorks online classroom tip: "Tip 4.1 Using Verse Notes as a Topical Database" provides instructions on how to use tags in BibleWorks verse to search for previously taken notes and build a report that includes the verse notes and verses you have tagged. See this page for instructions: https://www.bibleworks.com/classroom/4_01/index.html

options for the various parts of the program. Use the F1 key to access context-sensitive help as you hold your mouse over parts of the program you have questions about and check the topics under Help | How-To Videos (Online) | How to View the Videos (FAQ) as you have time to do so. Then simply try using BibleWorks in your own process of study. It will help you discover what works best for you in using BibleWorks as one tool in your process of observation, study and interpretation using the IBS process.

FOR FURTHER READING AND INFORMATION

Classroom Tips: https://www.bibleworks.com/classroomr/index.html

User Forums: https://bibleworks.com/forums/

Knowledge Base: https://kb.bibleworks.com/

Videos: https://www.youtube.com/c/BibleWorksVideos

Part V

Developing Disciples with IBS in the Church

INDUCTIVE BIBLE STUDY AND THE LOCAL CHURCH:
CREATING AN APPETITE FOR BIBLE STUDY

Alan J. Meenan
Founder and President of *The Word is Out* Ministry

ABSTRACT: Numerous reasons exist why churchgoers are frankly ignorant of the Scriptures but the result in the twenty-first century is palpable. The Bible is the source document of Christian faith and yet it represents an unknown world visited only by professional theologians and preachers. This essay explores ways to facilitate a rediscovery of the sacred writings and fulfil the latent desire of most Christ-followers to possess a thoroughgoing acquaintance with the Bible.

1. INTRODUCING BIBLE STUDY TO CHURCHES

My request was met by a tense silence on the part of the congregation. My mind raced wildly. I had just invited them to turn to the book of Zephaniah for the day's reading. Surely, they knew such a book existed in the Bible. But dawning upon my perception was the reality that they did not. I smiled. "It is the fourth small book from the end of the Old Testament," I added. "You can find it on page xxx in the pew Bible." The relief on their faces was palpable.

The embarrassment of the moment passed but the predicament remained: the people of God were strangers to the Word of God. How was the dilemma to be addressed? Since the dynamic did not happen overnight but evolved over time, it would be essential to address it on various levels—and over time. First, from the pulpit; second, through specific Bible study offerings; third, through small groups and Sunday school classes; fourth, through daily readings practiced at home; and fifth, through youth and children's programs.

2. IMPLEMENTATION IN THE CHURCH

Fortunately, the infrastructure of opportunities is already in place in churches large and small throughout the country: Sunday worship, Sunday School, and mid-week activities already exist in most places. It is simply a matter of infiltration with intentionality. Most Christians warm to the idea of being conversant with Scripture. Cognizant that the Bible represents the corpus of Christian understanding—particularly within the Protestant traditions, most Churchgoers actually welcome the idea of better acquaintance with the source documents of their faith. The perceived obstacles seem to be its apparent difficulty of comprehension, lack of tutelage, or the measure of time required to properly study its message. But these are all rectifiable.

To combat such concerns, there needs to be, first, a clear public declaration of intent: "We want to become a people who live and function according to biblical principles," or some such rescript. Second, one should follow the stated desire with an equally unequivocal challenge: "to achieve knowledge and understanding of the Bible it will be essential for each of us to set aside time to acquaint him or herself with the holy Scriptures." Third, there must absolutely be an emboldened assurance that it is all possible—and not only possible but rewarding.

2.1 Top-down Organization

The starting point must always be the pulpit. It has been said that the worst of all disservices to the church is to make the gospel boring. In describing the village vicar of Auburn, Oliver Goldsmith penned these arresting words:

> *But in his duty prompt at every call,*
> *He watched and wept, he prayed and felt, for all.*
> *And, as a bird each fond endearment tries,*
> *To tempt its new-fledged offspring to the skies,*
> *He tried each art, reproved each dull delay,*
> *Allur'd to brighter worlds, and led the way.*

The hard work and conscientiousness of the preacher will go an enormous way towards providing an appetite for biblical study. The goal will be to have parishioners leaving the worship sanctuary with words such as "That gave me something new to think about" or "I have read that passage many times and never got out of it what I saw today." This is to say, if one is to inculcate a profound sense of search for biblical understanding, sermons must reflect a deep adherence to the text itself, bringing it to life in a way that can excite the listener, to lead such a one to uncover new insights of truths long hidden and to rediscover old truths with renewed anticipation. Whether it is more advantageous to preach a series of messages through a particular biblical book or follow a lectionary is hotly debated. The end goal, however, needs to be exposure to "the whole counsel of God" (to familiarize ourselves with John Calvin's terminology) and to ensure that the listener gain acquaintance with a broad cross-section of theological knowledge.

My own preference was to take the congregation on a journey through specific sections of the Bible, whether entire books or parts thereof. Such an approach affords the opportunity to apply one's own inductive study of the relevant material to an entire series of sermons at one time. It is important to ensure, nonetheless, that each message is complete in and of itself. Not every parishioner will attend every Sunday within a given timeframe. And while it is always useful to have recordings available to those eager enough to want to have a complete digital homiletic library, no one should be made to feel dispirited because they miss one part of a series.

2.2 Study Aids

Providing a sheet with Study Notes is often helpful so as to allow congregants to annotate their observations during a sermon. If the pastor has the time, making available daily devotionals on the scriptural passage preached could provide those wishing a fuller comprehension of biblical truth further incentive to engage the Bible. Such devotional readings could be provided either the week prior to the Sunday of the message or the week following it.

If the creation of such a resource seems onerous, another possibility is to make available nationally publicized Bible Study guides. Although obviously not a commentary on the particular sermons being preached, they nevertheless encourage parishioners in the habit of daily Bible reading. There are several such publications on the market. My particular favorite is Scripture Unions' *Encounter with God*. In religiously following the design of the monthly publication, one is led completely though the Bible. Furthermore, if one desires to engage with the entire Bible, the readings at the bottom of each page enable one to do precisely that in one calendar year. Purchased in bulk, these Bible study guides can be placed in the narthex of a church available to any who wish to have one.

By far the most ambitious undertaking in reestablishing a culture of Bible study in the local church takes the form of "academism." By this I mean inaugurating a system of classes in which instruction is given at a level significantly different from the more fundamental approach of a Sunday sermon or a devotional reading. This more rigorous approach can certainly be promoted in Sunday School classrooms but is given heightened prominence with the presence and instruction of the Senior Pastor. While some congregations are fortunate to have popular professors and scholars-in-residence involved in the life of the church (as was the case in two parishes I served), it remains the appeal of the Senior Minister to attract the greatest number of participants.

2.3 Advertising the Study

Marketing the program is essential to its success. Here is a way to really come to terms with understanding and loving Scripture. The manner in which it is presented to suspicious aspirants cannot be underestimated; it will define the number of prospective participants. In no less than three separate congregations, I approached the task with verbal, digital, printed, and televised announcements along with brief testimonies within a worship context proffering the benefits of such intensive study. The results far surpassed our hopes.

The challenge included a rebuff to those who proudly declared that they didn't believe the Bible by suggesting they had not earned the right to say so until they had given it serious consideration! It is not unusual to encounter such indelible posturing among persons who have read little, if any, biblical material. I promised that by the time anyone had taken all twelve courses (covering a period of six years), they would be more conversant with the Scriptures than a typical seminary graduate. I did so on the sound experiential bases both of acquaintance with many hundreds of seminary graduates who frankly exhibit little propensity for comprehensive biblical insight and the sad fact that biblical studies *per se* comprise only a fraction of many disciplines of the theological academy.

Seminary students dabble in the multifarious disciplines of scholastic endeavor whether it be Church History, Greek, Hebrew and Aramaic together with classes on worship and hymnody, homiletics, historical theology, philosophical theology, systematics, practical theology, the devotional life, and so on. I well remember during a postgraduate seminar at the University of Edinburgh being confronted by Professor George W. Anderson, then head of the Old Testament department, demanding to know how many of us researching Ph.D. degrees had truthfully read the Old Testament in its entirety. The ensuing silence was deafening. He was greeted embarrassingly by a majority of drooped heads! Biblical hermeneutics, while undergirding much of what is taught in the theological academy, often represents only a fraction of specialized study. It is not unreasonable to suggest that a church member who dedicates twenty weeks of Bible study each year for six years covering the entire canon of sacred writings might potentially come out ahead of a typical seminary graduate in their knowledge of the Bible.

2.4 Format of the Study

To achieve the lofty goal set, it is essential that the bar is set high. In our case, we offered twelve, ten-week courses. Each course was formulated and tagged scholastically with both a title and a course ascription. For example, an "Old Testament Survey" course was designated OT101 while "The Pentateuch: Beginnings" was labeled OT201, the "Wisdom Books: A Search for Meaning," OT203. Similarly, in the New Testament "The Synoptic Gospels: The Story of Jesus" was classified NT201 and so forth. Members were asked to register, be extremely diligent in attendance—only two classes could be missed and, even these had to be made up by viewing the video of the session—and pay a fee to cover the cost of the materials they would receive.

Participants were informed that there would be sixty-three homework assignments covering the entire course from the first night to the last. Encouragement was given for as many as wanted, to work in tandem with others during the week to complete the daily assignments. Small study groups invariably emerged as an impetus to their study and commitment. Those taking the course were also warned of a final exam. Care was used in the robust terminology of "exam" rather than "test" or "quiz" at the end of the course. Upon satisfactorily completing all the requirements of the course, they were informed that they would receive a certificate indicating their achievement. It is not unreasonable to legislate the procurement of such papers as a necessary prerequisite to acquiring a teaching, leading, or governing position within the life of the congregation.

On the surface one may be tempted to think such an approach is unrealistically grandiose, has gone overboard, and might actually discourage participation in the program. However, I can testify in every church were the experiment was proffered that such was not the case. On the contrary, it became patently evident that parishioners will rise to a challenge if it is clearly conveyed—one that articulates high commitment and promises tangible results—as long as it resonates with the hearts of God's people. The idea that one can become truly familiar with God's Word as it is revealed in the Bible is unquestionably appealing to Christians of all ages.

As a result, from coast to coast, members of the respective churches turned out to a Wednesday night Bible Study in unprecedented numbers. And with some targeted media marketing and, more particularly by word-of-mouth, church members were joined by many others. They came in their hundreds! In California, they battled early evening Los Angeles gridlocked traffic coming directly from their workplaces instead of heading home. They came from great distances. In Texas, they came from churches all over the city (with the blessing of their pastors with whom I gave assurances of non-recruitment). People from all walks of life and spanning a wide age-range attended religiously. They included judges, teachers, doctors, actors, homemakers, students, skilled and non-skilled workers. They came with varied degrees of biblical knowledge; some with a modicum of understanding and others with much or little. In the course of time, the studies even attracted a number of religious agnostics who had stopped attending church but were curious to hear the Bible speak for itself.

While we began the adventure without any fanfare, as things progressed it became evident that it was meeting a perceived need. Nothing like it was being offered elsewhere. Newspaper articles, television spots, direct mail, posters, and fliers can be of inestimable value. Each course is promoted as a very doable ten-week commitment. There appears to be an inherent attraction of a *terminus ad quo* and a *terminus ad quem*, a tangible beginning and a visual ending, to inspire engagement rather than an interminable weekly study that poses no particular denouement.

Only two courses were offered each year: one in the fall (ending prior to Advent) and the other in the spring (ending prior to Holy Week). Such a schedule will allow for other Church activities in keeping with the season and a possible summer break. In our approach, each class lasted two-hours from 7 pm to 9 pm with a fifteen minutes break in the middle. We ensured that nothing in the class would resemble an evening church service. There was no music. A brief acapella benediction marked the end of each session. There were no prayers apart from a rather concise invocation to usher in the evening lecture. In truth, it broke the perceived *modus operandi* of doing church. That is possibly why it worked so well. The absolute uniqueness of what transpired carried its own magnetism.

3. Conclusion

The enthusiasm generated by such a quasi-academic approach, like leaven, ubiquitously affected other aspects of the church's life and witness, infiltrating its small groups, Sunday school classes, youth and children's programs, and community outreach. Even the church's charitable giving reflected support for those local and international missions where Bible instruction and training was specifically targeted. And, as a result, the church became, among its many worthwhile activities, primarily a teaching institute in which parishioners could once again be termed "a people of the Book!"

For Further Reading

Meenan, Alan J. *Encounter with God*, Valley Forge, Pennsylvania, Scripture Union Press.
_____. *The Word is Out Study Guides*, Wilmore, Kentucky, The Word Is Out, n.d.

REFLECTIONS ON TEACHING INDUCTIVE BIBLE STUDY IN THE LOCAL CHURCH

Eugene Wen Zhi Quek
Lay Ministry Staff for Discipleship and Nurture, Young Adults, and Worship
Agape Methodist Church, Singapore

ABSTRACT: After a life-changing experience in Costa Rica, the author argues in favor of incorporating Inductive Bible Study (IBS) into the local church curriculum. Cognizant that IBS can be highly technical and intimidating for the layperson, the author experimented with using popular songs and even children's nursery rhymes to illustrate the application and applicability of IBS, garnering positive and surprising results that transcend culture and geographical boundaries. A five-week study on the Book of Jonah developed in this context is also discussed and included as a SUPPLEMENT.

1. PERSONAL TESTIMONY

After four years working in the Singapore civil service, I moved with my wife to Wilmore, Kentucky to pursue theological training at Asbury Theological Seminary in 2009. After graduating with a Master of Divinity and Master of Arts in Pastoral Counseling in 2014, I had the privilege of being appointed to Highland United Methodist Church in Louisville, Kentucky where I served for a year and a half before returning to my home country. Today, I am serving in my home church, Agape Methodist Church, as a Lay Ministry Staff and involved in designing the Discipleship Roadmap for the church. I am convinced that Inductive Bible Study (IBS) is key to allowing the Living Word of God deform, reform, and transform lives. I have committed my ministry to impart to others what I have had the privilege of learning.

Undoubtedly, the classes that had the greatest impact on my growth as a Christian were the IBS ones that I took with Dr. David R. Bauer and Dr. David L. Thompson at Asbury Theological Seminary. Whereas Christian formation and academic training are often delineated as separate disciplines, IBS provided the perfect marriage between the two fields in my seminary journey and continues to mold my spiritual and intellectual development.

Through the generous Robert A. Traina IBS Scholarship, I was able to enroll in two extra classes of IBS including one in January 2012 in which my wife and I travelled with the class to Costa Rica to study the book of Acts with the local United Methodist pastors. The trip proved to be lifechanging for me. The highlight of the class was a commissioning service for the local pastors where Dr. Bauer provided the address based on Acts 20. I was surprised that Dr. Bauer framed his address as a didactic lecture rather than a sermon. Having heard mumblings of "this service is too long" during dual language services held in Singapore, I was also initially skeptical as to the effectiveness of the lecture whose flow was continually interrupted by the translations into Spanish. During that night, however, the power of the Living Word of God would not and could not be denied. Drawing on Paul's farewell message to the Ephesian elders, Dr. Bauer charged the pastors to be ministers of integrity by being consistent in their character and steadfast in their faith, ever accountable to God. I was stunned to witness that there was not a dry eye among the Costa Rican pastors, who, when invited to the front for their commissioning, eschewed formality by weeping openly and prostrating themselves in worship to God. It was at that point that I resolved to teach and apply IBS as soon as I was given the opportunity to do so.

2. Local Church Experience—Preaching and Teaching

2.1 Preaching as the Foundation and Example

In my first ministerial appointment in 2014 to Highland United Methodist Church in Louisville, I sensed that the members of the congregation of thirty were discouraged by their lack of growth and yet were thirsty for God's Word. I was convinced that only God and a renewed love for His Word could reinvigorate the church. I therefore took the risk of presenting expository sermons based on book studies that started with a five-part series on James, was followed by a twelve-part series on Genesis, grew to a twenty-four-part series on Luke, and concluded with a thirteen-part series on the Book of Hebrews. It was nerve-wracking to say the least, especially given that I had only formally studied the Book of Hebrews in seminary and was forced to depend on God fully, trusting in my IBS training and the power of His Word.

The sermons served as a model of the inductive approach for the congregation; they were aimed to pique the congregation's interest in the IBS classes that I offered. As part of the church-wide orientation to IBS, I was deliberate in naming the structural relationships when describing the thought-flow of the passages discussed in my sermons; I also invited the congregation to ask questions about the sermon, which they slowly warmed up to doing.

2.2 Teaching as the Means to Go Deeper

When the classes started, I split them into nine sessions, divided in two parts. The first four sessions covered key IBS concepts with the guidance of Dr. Thompson's concise but richly stimulating book, *Bible Study that Works*, rev. ed. (Nappanee, IN: Evangel, 1994). The second five sessions allowed the class to apply IBS techniques to the book of Jonah, which I explain now in more detail. For an overview of the class materials, see the Supplement at the end of this essay.

3. APPLICATION OF IBS TECHNIQUES USING JONAH

3.1 Why Use the Book of Jonah for an IBS Class?

The book of Jonah was selected for the applicational phase of the class in consultation with Dr. David Bauer and Dr. David Thompson just before I graduated from Asbury. Jonah presents certain advantages for beginning IBS students. First, it is brief so that a book survey (the entry point for IBS) is not too intimidating and thus ideal for an introductory class to IBS. Second, as a narrative, the thought flow is easier to navigate and map out than epistolary passages. Third, as a familiar "Sunday School" story, the book of Jonah is accessible to both the young and old, which allows the facilitator to make the class available to a wider audience. It was encouraging to hear class members testify that they had learned something fresh from the Bible by allowing familiar passages to speak on their own terms and to witness how the younger believers were able to contribute actively with new insights of their own. Fourth, the surprising ending of Jonah provides fodder for much discussion with regard to structural relationships (e.g., We may secretly wish that Jonah 3 concludes the story in a fairy tale ending—the Ninevites repented and were saved—but that would leave us without Jonah 4 that actually serves as the book's climax), as well as theology (e.g., "How is God's measure of justice and grace different from ours?").

3.2 Introducing IBS Concepts and Terms

Through the experience of interacting with the Costa Rican pastors, I learned that even clergy do not easily grasp IBS concepts and terms. As such, I decided to incorporate familiar songs, poems and speeches into the classes to complement examples taken from the Bible, which in turn reveals the additional benefit of applying the critical tools of IBS to exegete everyday life. Here are some ideas I used and found helpful in instruction:

- To introduce the concept of inductive analysis, especially careful observation, I read the famous poem "Humpty Dumpty" and posed the rhetorical question, "Which part of the poem suggests that Humpty Dumpty is an egg?" This led to a discussion about other powerful pictures that dominate our faith or color our readings; for example, we often picture Jesus as a bearded Anglo-Saxon man even though he was from the Middle East and the Gospels are deliberate in leaving out any descriptions of how he looked. Similarly, we also have an inaccurate picture of the Nativity—with the shepherds and Three Wise Men pictured together at the manger scene even though they visited Jesus years apart. Later in the study of Jonah, video clips from Disney's rendition of Pinocchio that showcase Pinocchio and Geppetto battling their way out from the belly of a whale proved to be instructive as to how popular images tend to be conflated with the narrative in Jonah 1:17–2:10. This in in turn may lead to discussions about how culture influences our faith in general.
- To illustrate structural relationships, the familiar passages of the creation account in Genesis 1 and the parables of the lost items in Luke 15 were used. Luke 15, in particular, with its introduction in 15:1–2 and unexpected twist at the end—where the older son, rather than the

younger son, is seen to be the focus of the three parables—proved to be a thought-provoking preparation for the discussion about God's grace when the class transitioned to study Jonah.

- To illustrate the IBS terms "contrast" and "recurrence," I used Darrell Evans's popular (even in Costa Rica) Christian chorus, "Trading My Sorrows" that has lines adapted from 2 Cor 4:8–9: "I'm pressed but not crushed, persecuted, not abandoned, struck down but not destroyed" and a long coda section that repeats "Yes Lord!" many times over.
- To illustrate the IBS term "chiasm," I turned to famous political quotes like the unforgettable 1961 Inaugural Address by President John F. Kennedy, "Ask not what your country can do for you—ask what you can do for your country."
- To practice longer surveys and to demonstrate the applicability of IBS to everyday passages, I challenged the class to identify structural relationships in Dr. Seuss's "One Fish, Two Fish, Red Fish, Blue Fish" and "The Foot Book" that seem at first to be a random collection of silly rhyming phrases.

3.3 The Importance of Group Discussions

The applicational phase of the class demonstrated the importance of putting IBS into practice. It was only through witnessing how the group applied IBS that I could assess if my instruction had been effective. Repeatedly, I had to gently remind them not to jump ahead to "application" and to spend much more time in the "observation" phase. Unlike seminary classes where much of the learning is done through homework, group discussions proved to be key for internalizing the IBS concepts. Much time was spent familiarizing the class with how to perform surveys and make general observations, and to a lesser extent, detailed observations, interpretation, and correlation. Class members were left to work out applications on their own since the emphasis of the sessions was on learning the IBS techniques.

One of the hardest skills of IBS is to master asking good, pertinent questions. Even in seminary level IBS classes, the professor often has to frame the assignments by asking students to answer specific questions. Thus, I provided worksheets with questions that were grouped in categories to model for the class how questions could be raised for passages encountered. Recognizing that laity may not have access to concordances and original language resources, questions were bolstered by hints, cross-references, or linguistic guides to the original Hebrew. Part of the challenge of providing questions was avoiding the urge to reverse-engineer questions from conclusions I had drawn from my prior IBS work, which might have the negative consequence of skewing the discussions.

For example, a question pertaining to structure in Jonah 3 might read: "Refer to 1 Sam 7:3–14 or Joel 1–2. How might you structure the response of the Ninevites to Jonah's declaration of God's judgment (hint: look for the steps involved in corporate repentance in the cross-references provided)?" For Jonah 4, a question pertaining to terminology might be: "Locate all instances of the term 'appoint' in Jonah 4. Who or what are appointed by God? Who or what can be appointed by God? What does it mean to be appointed by God (consider also the inherent appointments also that are made without the specific use of the term 'appoint')"?

3.4 Teaching Larger Groups

After I returned to Singapore in 2016, I commenced work as a Ministry staff in my home church, Agape Methodist Church and immediately offered an IBS class. With eighteen people in the class, the initial sessions introducing IBS had to be designed as lectures rather than as small group discussions. Nonetheless, I discovered that group discussions and presentations were even more important for larger groups since the number of participants could discourage the asking of questions. The class was very diverse. The participants' ages ranged from seventeen to sixty-five. More significantly, they included new converts to the Christian faith, church leaders, small group leaders, people familiar with the Disciple Bible Study or the Bible Study Fellowship curriculum, and local preachers with years of preaching experience.

The lectures allowed much more material to be covered; I leaned heavily on David R. Bauer and Robert A. Traina's *Inductive Bible Study: A Comprehensive Guide to the Practice of Hermeneutics* to provide additional details that I had not included in my first teaching of the class. The ability to provide extra details, however, ended up being a double-edged sword since I received feedback that the deluge of information was at times overwhelming and that more and longer sessions might be needed, which in itself was an unexpected request. Yet, I was further encouraged that some class members submitted detailed homework, which I then invited to be presented in class.

In one particularly encouraging evening, one of the class attendees brought her thirteen-year old son to class. I was initially concerned that he would be bored and disengaged from the "adult discussions." However, that fear was quickly put to rest when he raised his hand and provided an observation from Jonah that the rest of the class had missed.

4. CONCLUSION

It is my hope that this short essay encourages readers to continually sharpen their IBS skills and tirelessly teach them in the local church to help members fall in love with the Word of God again. My experience across two very different congregations located in different continents and distinct cultures has indicated to me the universal applicability and usefulness of IBS in faithful biblical interpretation and everyday life. I believe that readers also will discover that the transformative power of the Living Word will not be denied if it is given the right platform to impact and change lives. Shalom!

Supplement—A Study of the Book Of Jonah

Study 1: Overview of the Book of Jonah

Looking at the Big Picture

1. Read the book quickly twice through. Get the main message and do not get lost in the details.
2. *Structure:* Focusing on Jonah 1:1 through 4:4, how might you structure the book? Look for major breaks / divisions (e.g., Jonah 1–2 and 3:1–4:4). Identify major structural relationships such as causation, climax, turning points and bracketing events, ideas or statements. Identify the general material (e.g., biographical, geographical, historical, chronological or ideological). What are the recurrent themes or features? Identify the book's genre. Locate literary tools used such as irony. Record other major impressions from your reading.
3. List all the out-of-the-ordinary / supernatural phenomena.
4. *Terms*: Locate the references to death (e.g., "perish", "die") in the book. Locate also the superlatives "great / exceedingly" used. Compare and contrast their uses.
5. *Terms*: Locate and underline the times that the term "evil/disaster/discomfort" is used. These are translated from the same Hebrew word. Consider how they are used differently each time.
6. *Terms*: Locate and underline the times that the term "call/cry" is used? These are translated from the same Hebrew word. How are the terms used differently by different characters?
7. *Terms:* Locate and underline the times that the term "turn" or "relent" is used. How are the terms used differently by different characters?
8. *Recurrence*: Locate the repeated references to the greatness or sovereignty of God. Record the sources and contexts of those declarations.
9. *Recurrence:* Locate the times that God intervenes marked by the phrase "God appointed". What do you think may be the significance of these occurrences as regards the overall message of the book?
10. *Ending:* Does the ending of the book surprise you? What do you think the author intends by ending the book with a question?

Study 2: Jonah 1

Looking at the Details

1. *Structure:* Outline the interrogation between mariners and Jonah. Make detailed observations.
2. *Terminology*: Locate and underline the repeated phrase "presence of the LORD".
   - What does it mean to be "in" or, conversely "out" of the presence of the LORD?
   - Can you locate any irony in trying to be in or out of the presence of the LORD, especially for a prophet who makes a declaration of God' sovereignty in v. 9?
3. *Terminology*: Locate and underline the repeated word "evil"
   - What does it mean to bring about evil?
4. *Terminology*: Locate and underline the repeated word "fear"
   - Contrast the manner of Jonah's use of the term and the sailor's use of the term.

5. *Geography*: Locate Nineveh, Tyre, Joppa and Tarshish on a map of the ANE.
    - If we assume that Jonah was in Samaria as a "Northern Prophet", what is the direction that that Jonah was supposed to go? What is the direction he chose to go?
    - What might we conclude from the contrasting directions about Jonah's intent?
6. *Theology*: Describe the contrast between the activity of the *singular* God of Israel and of the *multiple* gods of the sailors.
7. *Missiology*: What is the unexpected result (implied causation) of Jonah boarding and later getting thrown out of the ship?

Study 3: Jonah 2

Looking at the Details

1. *Structure*: Divide Jonah's prayer according to the five elements of a thanksgiving Psalm.
2. *Terminology*: The word "call" (and its related words e.g. voice, cried, vow) forms the cornerstone of Jonah's soliloquy. It appears in Jonah 1:2, 6, 14; 2:2; 3:2, 4–5, 8. Describe and contrast the different uses of the word "call" in each context.
3. *Theology:* At the end of the prayer, Jonah declares, "Salvation belongs to the LORD" (2:9). Discuss what he means by his declaration. Consider how Jonah's declaration might explain his apparent calmness before and after he is thrown overboard.
4. *Theology:* Referring again to Jonah's declaration, "Salvation belongs to the LORD", describe the irony presented through the contrast between Jonah's attitude towards the sailors in Jonah 1 as reflected in Jonah 2 (see vv. 8–9)? What might Jonah's words reveal about whom he believes God's salvation should be reserved for?
5. *Theology:* What might we posit about what the author thinks about Jonah's thanksgiving Psalm when he writes that the fish "*vomited* Jonah out upon the dry land" in Jonah 2:10?
6. *Purpose:* What stands out for you as the purpose of Jonah's prayer? We know that it takes the form of a thanksgiving Psalm, but given the background of Jonah's disobedience in Jonah 1, what would you also have expected from Jonah that is *not* present in his prayer? How does the absence of repentance better prepare you to anticipate Jonah's sulking in Jonah 4?

Study 4: Jonah 3

Looking at the Details

1. *Structure*: Compare the structures of Jonah 1 and Jonah 3. Consider who speaks, who acts and who listens. Compare and contrast the responses of the "listeners", in particular, contrast Jonah's actions and that of the others.
2. *Structure:* Compare and contrast God's command in Jonah 1:1: "Arise, go to Nineveh, that great city, and call out against it, for their evil has come up before me" with God's repeated command in Jonah 3:1: "Arise, go to Nineveh, that great city, and call out against it the message that I tell you."
3. *Structure:* Discuss the extent of repentance that the Ninevites undertake. Discuss also the possible reasons why the people of Nineveh respond to Jonah *before* the king issues his decree.

4. *Structure*: Refer to 1 Sam 7:3–14 or Joel 1–2. How might you structure the response of the Ninevites to Jonah's declaration of God's judgment (Hint: look for the steps involved in corporate repentance in the various passages)?
5. *Geography:* Verse 2 suggests that Nineveh is a three-day's journey in breadth, but verse 3 describes how Jonah only goes "a day's journey" before preaching. What might we posit from this disparity of days / distance covered by Jonah as regards to his sincerity of obeying God and as regards his desire of Nineveh's to repentant and be saved?
6. *Terminology*: "Sackcloth" repeatedly appears in the passage. Discuss the significance of using sackcloth, especially paying attention to v. 5 where the king "removed his robe", "covered himself with sackcloth", and "sat in the ashes". Consider funeral practices still in use today, e.g. in a Chinese funeral: http://traditionscustoms.com/death-rites/chinese-funeral.
7. *Terminology:* Used in Jonah 4:3, the word "overthrow" in Hebrew / Assyrian can also be translated as "turn around" or "a change of heart". If we assume that this was indeed God's message to the Ninevites (even if Jonah had possibly abbreviated it greatly) what might its ambiguity suggest about God's character?
8. *Theology:* Discuss the theological implications of salvation in light of the Ninevites' extreme reaction to Jonah's remarkably short declaration of judgment? What might the author be suggesting to us about the nature of salvation, for example, is it the work of God, the sinner or the preacher (in this case, Jonah)?
9. *Theology:* Discuss what it means for God to "turn and relent from his anger" (vv. 9–10) Consider also Gen 18:16–33; Jer 18:7–10 and Ezek 18:20–29). Specifically, what does God's willingness to "relent" teach us about his character and his justice?
10. *Theology:* What does the author seem to be suggesting about the relationship between the Ninevites' repentance (turning from sin cf. vv. 5–9) and God's turning from his anger? What implications may this have for us today as regards repentance and prayer; as regards who deserves to be saved and as regards forgiveness?
11. *Application*: Discuss the differences between apology and repentance. Reflect whether our personal times of repentance as believers are as extreme and desperate as the pagan Ninevites. Reflect whether our obedience is similarly all-encompassing. Contrast for example, the unquestioning, immediate and all-encompassing response of the pagan Ninevites to the lackadaisical response of the OT Israelites to God's warning of judgment, e.g., in 2 Kgs 17:13–14. Parallel the Jewish response to the repeated demand by the NT religious leaders for a sign from Jesus to prove that he is the Messiah despite his miraculous acts of healing and provision.

Study 5: Jonah 4

Looking at the Details

1. *Structure:* Compare Jonah's anger at Yahweh's actions in vv. 1–5 and vv. 6–11.
2. *Structure*: Perspectives – What is the main difference between Jonah's reaction to the sparing of Nineveh and his description of God's nature behind why Nineveh was spared? How does

Jonah 4 serve as a climax to the book as regards Jonah's views? Consider how God's climatic response in vv. 9–11 serves to answer God's questions to Jonah in v.4, v.9a and Jonah's overall displeasure with God's intent and actions.

3. *Structure:* Compare and contrast Jonah's attention and care for the plant that sheltered him and God's attention and care for the people and livestock of Nineveh.

4. *Structure:* What are the contrasting elements that Jonah uses to emphasize his anger? How does this observation influence your evaluation of Jonah's character and his actions in Jonah 2–3? It may be helpful to evaluate Jonah's displeasure with God's sparing of Nineveh in light of his declaration in Jonah 2:9, "Salvation belongs to the LORD!"

5. *Geography:* Where did Jonah go in response to God's question in v. 4? What did he go there to do?

6. *Terminology*: "Anger" – Describe and contrast the kind of anger Jonah expresses in chapter 4 with the kind of anger that he says God demonstrates. Review instances where God's anger is on display in the Bible (e.g., "Golden Calf" Exod 32; "Clearing of Temple" John 2:13–24) and contrast their reasons with Jonah's reason for being angry. Discuss this contrast in light of Jas 1:19–20.

7. *Terminology*: "Pray" – What does Jonah pray for in chapter 4? Does God answer his prayers? If he does, how does he answer them?

8. *Terminology:* "Appoint" – Who or what are appointed by God in Jonah 4? Who or what can be appointed by God? What does it mean to be appointed by God (consider the inherent appointments also that are made without the specific use of the term "appoint")?

9. *Theology:* Contrast the response of Jonah (a believer of YHWH and a prophet) with that of the pagan sailors and Nineveh. What might the book of Jonah be telling us about who can respond to God? What does it say about how God responds to positive and even negative responses to his word?

10. *Theology:* Why does God appoint things or persons? How does he interact with the appointee(s)?

11. *Theology:* How long did God take to answer Jonah and work with him (consider chapter 4 and the larger context of the book)? What can we learn about God in the time he spent working with Jonah to process his anger?

12. *Theology:* Do you think it is fair that God spared the city of Nineveh? Contrast Jonah's standard of justice with God's standard of justice (Reference Matt 5:43–48).

13. *Theology:* What does the book of Jonah tell us about the character of God as regards to salvation (Contrast John 12:37–50 and Rom 9:6–29 with 2 Pet 3:9)?

14. *Application:* Evaluate your measure of righteousness against God's measure (Who deserves mercy? Who deserves grace and salvation?).

15. *Application*: Have you ever questioned or even been angry at God's standard of justice like Jonah has? Are you still angry? Does a fresh look at the heart of God prompt any changes in your response?

Teaching IBS at First UMC Lexington, KY

Chad M. Foster
Executive Pastor First UMC Lexington, KY

ABSTRACT: Inductive Bible Study (IBS) serves as the foundation of a two-year discipleship process at First Methodist Church. It is a key component of how we are equipping our leadership for their work of "making disciples across the street and around the world." This chapter will explain, first, our Discipleship Intensive (DI) and how we have integrated IBS into this curriculum, second, what we have learned about teaching IBS in this context, and, three, where we hope that this will take us in our continued journey of disciple making.

1. INTRODUCTION

Teaching Inductive Bible Study (IBS) at First United Methodist Church arose out of a season of outside coaching with our clergy team. We wrestled with what our most important areas of investment were in order to help First UMC continue to advance our mission of "making disciples across the street and around the world." We realized that staff time was a major limiting factor for in-depth discipleship and the growth of our congregation in scriptural holiness. We can only be in so many places over the course of a week. We quickly realized the need for investing in disciples who then invested themselves in making disciples.

This revelation gave birth to the Discipleship Intensive (DI). This is a four-semester, high commitment, discipleship training program created for laity. The participants commit to 2.5 hours per week in a small-group experiential learning environment and 5.5 hours per week in outside work and development. The clergy have committed to leading these groups and investing intentionally at the expense of many other demands on our time. Each cohort of four to six lay people is led by two members of the clergy staff, with multiple cohorts meeting simultaneously. The laity are recruited by invitation based upon demonstrated commitment to their discipleship

Each semester of the DI has a particular focus beginning with personal calling, moving to biblical narrative, then to Christian theology, and finally to practical ministry. Throughout the process, emphasis is on the practice of spiritual disciplines and the development of competency in both the methodology of IBS and leading others to use the principles of IBS. We recognized that it was not enough to give them packaged studies. Instead, we wanted to equip our laity to study the scriptures for themselves and to help others do the same. So, we dove in with our first cohort and have journeyed together in what is still an evolving curriculum.

2. Semester One—Calling and Discipline

Our first semester of DI focuses on personal calling. The participants wrestle with Os Guinness's *The Call* while taking their first steps into IBS by exploring some key scriptural passages in which God calls someone.[1] They look at the whole of Jonah and the calling narratives of Isaiah, Samuel, and Paul. Finally, they look at Jesus's own understanding of his calling in Luke 4.

This early work in IBS is focused largely on survey and observation. We spend significant time with the participants helping them to see Scripture in units. Performing survey work is actually quite uncomfortable for them at the beginning as they try to think in large units and wrestle with how the material might be organized. Each participant comes to the survey work with different strengths. Some quickly see larger units but are unable to break it down into manageable chunks while others will divide the text into tiny units while missing the larger structure. And we find similar differences as we explore the task of observation. Some participants quickly notice repetitions while others embrace logical observations and still others see the primary structural relationships almost immediately.

To assist them on this journey, we have developed a one-page front and back handout based on the materials in David R. Bauer and Robert A. Traina's *Inductive Bible Study* and David L. Thompson's *Bible Study That Works*.[2] This handout becomes their only "textbook" for our time together. We instead give great effort to teach the method of IBS inductively as we work through the texts. This allows them to discover the elements on their own. We then gently direct them to other observations that they might have missed.

We spend most of our time in this phase focused strictly on survey and observation for two reasons. First, without survey and observation we know that they will never have proper interpretation and application. Second, if they never move beyond this, they will already be far better readers of the text than most people in the church today. These foundational parts of IBS set them up well for what is to come in their second semester.

3. Semester Two—Biblical Narrative

Before the semester starts, we ask the group to work through Scot McKnight's *The King Jesus Gospel* as a common text to help us shape some of our hermeneutical presuppositions.[3] For engaging the biblical narrative, we have the group read Sean Gladding's *The Story of God, the Story of Us* alongside weekly IBS work on Scripture connected to each chapter.[4]

---

[1] Os Guinness, *The Call: Finding and Fulfilling the Central Purpose of Your Life* (Nashville: Thomas Nelson, 2003).

[2] David R. Bauer and Robert A. Traina, *Inductive Bible Study: A Comprehensive Guide to the Practice of Hermeneutics* (Grand Rapids: Baker Academic, 2011); David L. Thompson, *Bible Study That Works*, rev. ed. (Anderson, IN: Warner, 2011).

[3] Scot McKnight, *The King Jesus Gospel: The Original Good News Revisited*, MP3 Una edition (Zondervan on Brilliance Audio, 2016).

[4] Sean Gladding, *The Story of God, the Story of Us: Getting Lost and Found in the Bible* (Downers Grove, IL:

In the first week, we introduce a simple version of interpretation and application based largely on the paradigm in J. Scott Duvall and J. Daniel Hays's *Grasping God's Word*.[5] We have them survey the text and make all types of observations as they did during the first semester. Then we ask them to take those observations and distill a general theological principal that transcends time and space. They are then asked to apply or appropriate that general principal.

This form of interpretation and application arose from a fairly palpable sense of discontent with the process from our second cohort of participants. I love methodical rigidity and I imposed it on the program starting in the second semester. Every observation required at least three interpretive questions. Each interpretive question invited a new formal interpretive process with implications listed and possible interpretive conclusions explored and only then a final interpretive conclusion coming at the end of the process. This rigidity was off-putting and hindered participants from embracing the process. Answering multiple interpretive questions was simply too time consuming for most of them and became a discouragement for continuing to participate in DI. This led me to re-examine my rigidity and to work with my colleagues and other scholars to explore how to maintain fidelity to the principles of IBS while having enough flexibility to teach a process that the laity can embrace for a lifetime of study.

This is when we returned to some of the principles from *Grasping God's Word*. I had been introduced to this book during my time at Asbury Seminary by students who used it as their foundational text at Indiana Wesleyan University. It became a great conversation partner for me as I wrestled with my training under Drs. Bauer and Thompson.

In the end, we were able to successfully balance the dual desires by defining interpretation as the syntheses of the general theological principle that arises out of the work of observation. This immediately resonated with the group and has made the process much more approachable for many. During our first round, our students were not exposed to application until the middle of the third semester and they found that too long to wait for. This allowed them to move to some form of application and/or appropriation earlier in the process.

Using this system, each week they did a full survey, observation, interpretation and application. We start with Gen 2:4–25 and explore our identity and vocation in light of the second creation narrative. We then move to Gen 3 and explore the ramifications of the fall. We look at Gen 15 and what it means to be a covenant people. We look at God's promises to Moses in Exod 6:1–13 and then explore the Ten Words in Exod 20:1–21. We see how God's covenantal promises seem to come true in a survey of Josh 1–3 and we wrestle with the meaning of God's covenant with David in 2 Sam 7:1–17. We explore national division in 1 Kgs 12 and the call of the prophets in Amos 4. And then we begin to look at what it means to be God's people during the post-exilic period when we perform a book survey of Ezra.

InterVarsity Press, 2010).

[5] J. Scott Duvall and J. Daniel Hays, *Grasping God's Word: A Hands-On Approach to Reading, Interpreting, and Applying the Bible*, 3rd ed. (Grand Rapids: Zondervan, 2012).

We survey the Sermon on the Mount and all of the Gospel of John in order to take a deep look at one sermon and a high-level view of one presentation of Jesus's birth, life, ministry, death, resurrection, and ascension. These surveys provide helpful opportunities to discuss literary types and forms, e.g., the Gospel of John's version of a creation narrative and its unique presentation of the "birth" of Jesus. This forces us into a discussion of the strategies employed by the gospel authors/editors. We also explore Peter's sermon in Acts 2:14–40 with special attention to the use of OT material and what it means for the church as God's new covenantal people. Finally, we survey Rev 20:1–22:11 to look at what a biblical account of final things looks like over and against the pop-Christianity picture of a disembodied heaven.

A tool that we require them to purchase is the *Cultural Backgrounds Study Bible* edited by John H. Walton and Craig S. Keener.[6] We actually encourage these notes for reading during the observation process. We recognize that cultural barriers are large for our laity. We want to ensure that they have a tool that allows them, as much as possible, to break down the cultural barriers without being too theologically or interpretively suggestive. This is the best resource that we have found. It lets them enter into the story within its original context that allows them to deploy the tools of IBS much more robustly.

This is a hard semester for our students as it forces them into new patterns of engaging the text. We work on reading the text in context and breaking "interpretive" habits such as importing Jesus into every situation in the Old Testament. We do this while exposing them to material that may be unfamiliar. This group of leaders, like so many of us at some point in our journey, is being forced to address a lifetime of "reading" without good tools. They are moving beyond proof texting to contextual reading. They are engaging diachronically and exploring how progressive revelation informs our understanding of God. And they are doing all of it quickly while still living their normal life. We meet weekly and expect them to do all of this work in addition to raising their families, going to their jobs, and doing everything else they normally do.

In addition, during this semester, we increase the pressure by inviting each of them to facilitate the IBS portion of our meeting. This has been invaluable not only in developing their competence and confidence but also in revealing deficiencies in our methodology and curriculum.

Despite the difficulty of the semester, in many ways this is a beloved semester. During this time IBS actually starts to become a tool for them instead of a chore, and they begin in earnest to embrace the joy that comes from a robust understanding of the biblical narrative. For our final night together, we invite Sean Gladding, author of *The Story of God, the Story of Us,* to join us for an evening of food and fellowship. That night, the participants present the biblical narrative in some creative way. The participants bring together their work with the text and their work on narrative and create amazing pieces that are gifts to the church. We have had podcasts, comic books, letters to family members, curated art shows, and an original song all come to life to tell how this great story of God is indeed also our story.

---

[6] Craig S. Keener and John H. Walton, eds. *NIV, Cultural Backgrounds Study Bible, Hardcover, Red Letter Edition: Bringing to Life the Ancient World of Scripture* (Grand Rapids: Zondervan, 2016).

4. SEMESTER THREE—CHRISTIAN THEOLOGY

These pressures do not ease up in their third semester of work. Frankly, in some ways they seem more real. The novelty of DI has worn off, yet largely they stick with it. In the first two semesters, they have had a Bible study experience unlike any other. They are functioning as a Wesleyan band. In addition to IBS, they also discuss their souls, spiritual practices, lived faith, and prayer needs.

Then together they move to one of the more intimidating subjects to tackle: Christian Theology. We ask them to work through an updated Methodist catechism exploring foundational Christian belief. We ask them to wrestle with what defines us as Christians and what might cause us to actually name someone not a Christian. Using that catechism along with the book by Gregory A. Boyd, and Paul R. Eddy, *Across the Spectrum: Understanding Issues in Evangelical Theology*,[7] we dive into the Method and Praxis of Theology, God's Nature and Attributes, the Persons of God, Creation, Fall/Sin, the Sources and Basis of Salvation, the Conditions of Salvation, the Fruits and Extent of Salvation, the Church and Sacraments, the Means of Grace, and Death, Judgment, and Eternity.

All the while, we are taking a deep dive studying the book of Hebrews inductively. At this point, this study process begins to be truly enjoyable for everyone. They have the basic tools of IBS and a semester of practice while jumping around the Bible. With Hebrews, we enter into the intensive study of one book and stay there for the whole semester. We begin with a book survey and ask four or five interpretive questions to which we attend throughout the semester. We then work through the book inductively.[8] We come together in our last session to tackle a synthesis of the book using one of our guiding interpretive questions.

In our most recent session, we actually printed the entire book of Hebrews on a giant 8x3 foot poster board and each participant took one of the major termal or thematic repetitions in the book and highlighted them. We marked out the major comparisons and contrasts with other colors. And we then let these questions guide us:

> *What is the significance of the repeated contrasts in the book of Hebrews?*
>
> *What do they tell us about God?*
>
> *What are the implications?*
>
> *What is the significance of the many repetitions?*[9]
>
> *How are they used in the broader argument? What are the implications?*

---

[7] Gregory A. Boyd, and Paul R. Eddy, *Across the Spectrum: Understanding Issues in Evangelical Theology* (Grand Rapids: Baker Academic, 2009)

[8] Great debt is owed to Dr. David Bauer for the lasting impact of his course on the book of Hebrews at Asbury Seminary. His structure from the course guided our syllabus and his investment in me in that class continues to bear fruit as in many ways I carry his insights in me as I facilitate our journey through this theologically rich text.

[9] Just a limited list of repetitions identified includes: language related to obedience; sacrifice; death; denial; priesthood; superiority; law; OT imagery.

This session where we synthesize the Book of Hebrews coincides with our final session of theology work where we wrestle with "Death, Judgment and Eternity," which becomes a synthesis of what we have learned from Biblical Narrative, Theology and their work in IBS. It is a fascinating opportunity for us to wrestle with the theology of the book of Hebrews and what it actually means for us individually and for the church corporately.

5. SEMESTER FOUR—PRACTICAL MINISTRY

In the fourth semester, the group explores practical ministry. Each week focuses on topics such as pastoral care, discipleship, worship planning, ethics, and public theology. We move to monthly meetings with more readings and more hands-on engagement outside of the meeting time. Participants do pastoral shadowing, participate in planning meetings, or engage in other activities traditionally done by the clergy. They do not gather as often for a group meeting, which frankly, we expected would be a huge relief to them. Instead, we found that they lamented the chance to meet for soul examination and group IBS work. We hope that this lamentation leads them to develop meetings that will endure as part of this long-term discipleship strategy.

6. IMPLICATIONS AND NEXT STEPS

Beyond this work in the classroom, we have actually asked them to take the insights they have gained, the tools they have acquired, and the skills that they have developed and lead the church in very important ways. For each person this has looked differently. We celebrate this as a reflection of the unique gifting that God has placed on each one of us.

One of our larger hopes is that they will give birth to many of the vital ministries that are so dearly needed. We are investing in them so that they would invest in others. We wish to deploy them as leaders of new Wesleyan bands and as ones capable of teaching IBS to others.

We have found that they are fairly comfortable leading discussion groups. They are showing interest in launching Wesleyan bands; however, it has been a struggle getting other laity aligned around IBS. We are now developing a system for IBS that will work for participants who have not developed the skills yet and who don't need to do any additional work outside of the weekly meeting. We recognize that this is probably where many of our Sunday morning or Wednesday evening crowd will start. We can't immediately bring in the fullness of our IBS curriculum or it will seem overwhelming and they will immediately reject the methodology.

In this exploration, we realize that we have to rely on the fundamentals and not add too many elements. We also realize that, while it will still be inductive, it must come out of the leader's previous inductive work with them guiding the group to conclusions. We have just begun leveraging technology to facilitate the process. We are leasing a wide-format printer so that we can print out the text and display it as a wall-size poster. This way it is visible to the group and we can share observations directly without people getting lost. This has been really helpful in moving us through the process with less confusion and with more precision.

A new summer group has formed that is made up of DI graduates, current DI participants, staff members and others who have no exposure to IBS. We have spent the time working through the Gospel of Luke. We hope that what we have learned here might give us the tools to launch some groups who can study another biblical text in this manner. We also have a number of groups launching that are starting a study of Gladding's *The Story of God, the Story of Us*. We hope that at the end of that process they will be willing to engage Scripture directly with the tools of IBS instead of starting another study or curriculum.

We went into this process convinced that IBS was a gift to the church; developing the DI has only reinforced this conviction. In fact, we have found that even as a clergy team these have been some of our most precious moments of study. We all studied IBS formally in seminary and have used it extensively since then. However, the joys of IBS in a group setting have been new and unexpected. Even biblical texts that we have studied for years reveal new riches when studied within the context of a group of people fully devoted to hearing the voice of the one true God.

FOR FURTHER READING

Bauer, David R. and Robert A. Traina. *Inductive Bible Study: A Comprehensive Guide to the Practice of Hermeneutics*. Grand Rapids: Baker, 2011.

Boyd, Gregory A. and Paul R. Eddy. *Across the Spectrum: Understanding Issues in Evangelical Theology*. Grand Rapids: Baker Academic, 2009.

Duvall, J. Scott and J. Daniel Hays. *Grasping God's Word Workbook: A Hands-On Approach to Reading, Interpreting, and Applying the Bible*. 3rd ed. Grand Rapids: Zondervan, 2012.

Duvall, J. Scott and J. Daniel Hays, *Grasping God's Word: A Hands-On Approach to Reading, Interpreting, and Applying the Bible*. 3rd ed. Grand Rapids: Zondervan, 2012.

Gladding, Sean. *The Story of God, the Story of Us: Getting Lost and Found in the Bible*. Downers Grove, IL: InterVarsity Press, 2010.

Keener, Craig S., and John H. Walton, eds. *NIV, Cultural Backgrounds Study Bible, Hardcover, Red Letter Edition: Bringing to Life the Ancient World of Scripture*. Grand Rapids: Zondervan, 2016.

Long, Fredrick J. *In Step with God's Word: Interpreting the New Testament as God's People*. GlossaHouse Hermeneutics & Translation 1. Wilmore, KY: GlossaHouse, 2017.

McKnight, Scot. *The King Jesus Gospel: The Original Good News Revisited*. MP3 Una edition. Zondervan on Brilliance Audio, 2016.

Thompson, David L. *Bible Study That Works*. Rev. ed. Anderson, IN: Warner, 2011.

THE WHOLE INDUCTIVE BIBLE STUDY PROCESS FOR DISCIPLESHIP PURPOSES

Matt Friedeman
Professor of Evangelism and Discipleship, Wesley Biblical Seminary

ABSTRACT: Inductive Bible Study helps investigators of Scripture excel in knowledge of the Word of God through four well-recognized steps—observation, interpretation, correlation, and application. The former two are enthusiastically embraced by most IBS practitioners. However, if the latter two are not also earnestly assimilated into the overarching model in practice, Traina's ultimate dream of changed lives will be substantially diminished. This essay explores the nature and importance of correlation and application.

1. INTRODUCTION

The areas primarily pursued by the academic community inspired by Robert A. Traina are the observation and interpretation of Scripture, the first two steps in Inductive Bible Study (IBS). Much shorter shrift has been afforded the latter parts of the process, correlation and evaluation/application. This development in praxis is proportional to the emphases in Traina's book. In the original *Methodical Bible Study,* he devoted some sixty pages to observation, while interpretation comprised nearly one-hundred and ten pages. In contrast, evaluation/application was covered in less than twenty pages and correlation in less than five. How to make a chart and do a word-study, as mere appendices, received more coverage than did correlation. Consequently, one could excuse the IBS enthusiast, after studying under the brilliant Traina, for being much less concerned with correlation and application as compared to the more academically attractive initial steps of the method.

The careful reader could certainly make a case from *Methodical Bible Study* that correlation and application are nonetheless valuable. Traina himself admonished, "*Always correlate.*" He taught that throughout the methodology one should look for connections within the Bible-as-a-whole and, indeed, within life-as-a-whole. He rightfully warned that application conceptually should not be equated with application in practice. Attention needed to be afforded to the latter, thus intimating that study is, finally, nothing without appropriation. "You do what you believe," Traina would remind his students, "and you believe what you do." Application was the embodiment of faith.

Traina's classes were largely composed of pastors and missionaries, not future academicians. While the latter are animated by the first two steps of the process, practitioners-in-the-field are *at least as* enthusiastic about correlation and application. The latter steps translate biblical data into real-life change that leads to the kind of holy living which IBS seeks to inculcate. In these few pages, I will examine the import of correlation and application for the discipleship process and explore a method that effectively incorporates the four steps in a formational model for small groups.

2. CORRELATION, FURTHER EXPLORED[1]

Correlation is, in short, the examination of relevant data from other biblical passages, from history, and from life experiences. Correlation is the next-to-last step in a four-step inductive process and its goal mirrors the overall objective of IBS: building a vital and relevant Biblical theology which will affect one's world view, philosophy of life, and pattern of daily living.

To arrive at this theology, one must, through correlation, compare and contrast the data with other scriptural passages. Discovering this interconnectedness is one of the most exciting parts of the inductive process. But the person engaged in IBS also seeks to understand how the scriptural data found and interpreted connects with contemporary events; the lives of saints in previous ages; the history of one's locale, one's country and the world; the ongoing experience of teachers and students; and, frankly, whatever sources of data with which the faithful Christian comes into contact in the normal activity of life.

In *Methodical Bible Study*, Traina suggests that correlation is as much an attitude as it is a step in the procedure; the correlative mind finds itself primed to bring scriptural truth to the attention of students—with lasting impact. The disciple considers not only analytical data but also patterns, pictures, illustrations, and demonstrations. This aspect is important, for as homiletics professor Fred Craddock reminds us, we communicate to people who have daily concrete experiences. No farmer thinks seriously about the problems of calf-hood, Craddock contends; he deals with calves. Hence, if at the end of the IBS process, the teacher has discovered in a certain pericope the importance of the disciple's use of money, the best approaches to communicate that truth include the following:

- o to find other teachings on the use of money in and beyond the same book and genre of Scripture;
- o to recall instances of the use and abuse of money in other biblical situations;
- o to describe how money was used well, or abused, at some point in recent or even ancient history;
- o to recount how the problem of budgeting challenged the teacher's life this week.

One major caution generally accepted by evangelicals is this: Scripture is always first; reason, experience and tradition should serve—not co-opt—our understanding of the Bible. Other sources of truth are not on equal footing with Scripture. This is a key hermeneutical point. How one approaches correlation is no small matter; it will affect whether the Bible is seen as *the* authority or merely one of many equally authoritative options.

---

[1] All four steps, including correlation and application, are explored in Matt Friedeman and Lisa Ausley, *LifeChanging Bible Study: Practical Keys to a Deeper Understanding of the Word* (Wilmore, KY: Francis Asbury, 2009).

3. CONCENTRIC CIRCLES

It is instructive to explore concentric circles of biblical data that emanate from the text being examined. One should survey the book-as-a-whole, then proceed to testament-as-a-whole, and, eventually, move to the Bible-as-a-whole. Most frequently, the unit being examined is part of a book; and, that being the case, the larger context of the book needs to be taken into consideration. The overarching question is this: Is there data within the rest of the book, the rest of the testament (Old or New), or the rest of the Bible that would elucidate the points that are to be made with the major findings and principles of the passage under study?

Thus, when seeking connections to a biblical concept, one should prioritize as follows:

o First look at the book as a whole.
o Next explore the author-as-a-Whole.
o Then, perhaps, survey the Testament-as-a-Whole.
o Finally, examine the Bible-as-a-Whole.

The best resource for this information is previous personal study. Tools such as concordances, reference books, and various digital resources may also prove helpful. But, as with the general supposition in observation and interpretation, these "helps" are best utilized *after* searching the Bible, and the Bible alone, for insight.

4. LOOK AT LIFE-AS-A-WHOLE

The correlation phase of Bible study includes identifying meaningful connections in the world around us: nature, personal experience, books, print and broadcast media, conversation, and people. The personal life of the effective Christian communicator should be a rich one, filled with an abundance of diverse interactions, reading materials, relationships, and informative dialogue. Correlation to the world beyond the study desk is easier if a multitude of colorful experiences populate the imagination of the Bible student. Journaling and cataloguing insights provides valuable fodder for this sort of "study."

An informal rule of thumb to consider if Christian literature is your favorite reading material is this: Be sure that about a third of your total annual reading is outside of biblical, theological, and religious sources. This is particularly true for professors and clergy who can all too easily be caught up in a religious publishing subculture. Too much time spent reading exclusively Christian authors can potentially leave a teacher woefully out of touch with the world with which he is trying to communicate.

Christian classics such as those penned by Augustine, Thomas à Kempis, Brother Lawrence, William Law, John Calvin, Martin Luther, John Wesley, Dietrich Bonhoeffer and C. S. Lewis (to name a precious few) ought to be read diligently. Beyond that, from both classic and modern authors comes a rich reservoir of teachable concepts and illustrations. The Christian communicator should pay heed to material both old and new, sacred and secular.

Newspapers and periodicals can inform the reader about events in his or her city, state, and the nation as well as about the environment, business, crime, politics, religion, births and deaths, humor, and various opinions. A community's local newspaper contains some of the best correlative material available outside the Bible itself.

The Internet provides everything a newspaper does, and more. Even where local publications are not available, *USA Today* and *The Wall Street Journal* are accessible along with online versions of many big city dailies, thousands of magazines, millions of web pages, and all the major news services. The Internet is for many people an essential tool for keeping up with current events and culture, at a remarkably affordable price. Television and other video resources also represent a vast array of information. All media, however, should be carefully monitored for 1) potential waste of time on that which is insipid or worthless, 2) a detrimental effect on the thought life of the disciple, and 3) general truthfulness. With such a wealth of material available, correlation should be practiced with discretion and with biblical instruction as the objective.

Getting correlative material together ought to highlight and accentuate truths derived from the findings gained through serious observation and interpretation practices. They should enhance understanding of the passage and help to communicate the truth, not obfuscate meaning. Thus, material discovered in correlation ought to be tested and ardently scrutinized to ensure correspondence with the pericope being studied. But if strong correlative dynamics are discovered, then it will be found that the proper balance between the Bible (the primary source), responsible scholarship, Christian classics, and the perspective of contemporary experience will generally result in impactful communication of an informed biblical perspective. Just as a strong biblical theology sheds light on every issue of life, the issues of life can sharpen our vision to see the truth of Scripture more clearly and hopefully with more relevance and creativity.

5. APPLICATION

Application is the frequently forgotten step of IBS, particularly for the scholar. Once truth is grasped intellectually, too many researchers choose to move on to the next subject without embracing the Hebraic concept of knowing, that is, to "experience" and "encounter." For the Hebrew person, to know was to do, to act. Memorization, while important to the Jewish tradition, was hardly the point of learning. Knowledge implied a response in behavior and morals. It meant to do something, to act, to apply. More than an exercise of the mind, it was the exercise of the head, heart, and hand together in the various tasks and demands of life. This Hebraic mindset at its best was fundamental to not only the faithful in the Old Testament but the early church as well—more particularly, the rabbi Jesus Himself, as He instructed the community of disciples.

A basic modern psychological definition of learning is "changed behavior," which corresponds nicely with the Hebraic teaching about knowledge. This concept embraces not just changed thinking, or even changed feeling, but a modification of life activity. If Bible study is to have its maximal effect, it should significantly impact not only our heads, but our hearts and hands as well. In essence, Bible study is not just contemplation of what the inspired text says, but how that truth ought to be exercised in life. In the final analysis, this step of the process can only be truly complete when application isn't merely investigated but enacted. Response is non-negotiable.

6. HEED THE "HEART" COMPONENT

Dawson Trotman, founder of the campus discipleship organization *The Navigators*, was known for saying that teachers should never teach an inch beyond their own experience. Trotman's challenge should lead us to at least remember that *application looks inward first, outward thereafter*. That's an important concept to keep in mind when considering Paul's words to his understudy Timothy: "All Scripture is God-breathed and is useful for teaching, rebuking, correcting and training in righteousness, so that the man of God may be thoroughly equipped for every good work." (NIV, 3:16–17). The first person to be rebuked, corrected, trained, and equipped is the teacher. Inward first ... outward thereafter. The tendency to talk better than we walk is why James admonishes that fewer of us should become teachers, knowing that we will be judged more strictly (Jas 3:1). Teaching without introspection and righteous change is bound to disappoint.

7. UTILIZE COMMUNITY

While an individual's endeavors shouldn't be discounted, the group seems always to be foremost on the mind of God. "Community" is His people, the family, and the churches of Paul's epistles. Indeed, God Himself is a community of Three—Father, Son and Holy Spirit—moving in concert for the divine purpose of redemption. Made in God's Image, we must recognize community response as pleasing in the sight of God and a means of being remade in His holiness.

Peter Berger, in his tome *A Rumor of Angels,* provides insight of tremendous import to faith and community. If Bible study leads one to think significantly differently than the norm of culture (and it can have that precise effect), then the believer needs to huddle with a community of what Berger calls "like-minded deviants" if that person is to have a chance at maintaining such a counter-cultural mindset.[2] Those uncomfortable with the term "deviant" must ask themselves: If the Bible doesn't ask one to deviate from current behavior or the norm of culture, then what does it ask us to do? Community provides the context for standing firm in newly chosen commitments and behaviors, providing accountability for sustaining faith.

The importance of community is essential not only to theological/cognitive truth, but also to theological/kinesthetic truth, or, simply, truth enacted. Individuals are spiritually healthy only as they learn to live in accordance with God's truth. His plan has always been for individuals to apply His revelation of righteousness in the context of community. Indeed, that is how this three-in-one God Himself operates. Discussion and implementation of truths found in IBS should, at the very least, be adopted on an individual basis. But when the community of believers can act together in obedience to God, the effect is multiplied.

---

[2] Peter L. Berger, *A Rumor of Angels: Modern Society and the Rediscovery of the Supernatural* (Garden City, NY: Anchor, 1970). 17.

8. A Small Group Model

This line from the Talmud is instructive, if perhaps hyperbolic: "Torah is only acquired in a group."[3] A second instruction contains not a bit of overstatement: "Two scholars sharpen one another."[4] Discipleship is a community process whereby, under the guidance of the Spirit of Jesus and upon the foundation of His Word, we mature in the faith.

Hal Perkins has developed an effective group model for biblical investigation outlined in his volume *Discipled by Jesus*.[5] The fundamental step is to acknowledge the Lord's presence as the group gathers to study Scripture followed by considering specific questions derived from key instances in the life of Christ. The questions below, a slightly modified version of Perkins's method, are designed to be applied in group study of a particular pericope.[6]

1. *"This is My Son, listen to Him."* <u>Discipleship Question</u>: What is Jesus saying to you from His Word? **(The MIND of Jesus)**

   - What is our Lord saying to us from His Word? In a group setting this opens up the possibility, with the facilitating guidance of a group leader, for searching for structural laws; the meanings of words; answers to who, what, when, where, how and why?

   - To give the participants practice in identifying structural laws, the leader might find it helpful to give the group a choice of three or four laws and see if they can identify the appropriate one. Once the law has been ascertained, the leader can guide the group in applicable follow-up questions.

   - This query is also bolstered by correlation. The leader can ask, *where else in Scripture is the major lesson from this passage found*? Additional questions from the group facilitator can heighten the impact of this step.

   - Further, where else in life, or in some of your reading, or in history, or in the movies, or at your business, or in your families ... have you seen the truth in the passage illustrated?

   - This step can be completed with prayers of thanksgiving for the truths that have been gleaned.

   - It is at this step that group leaders grounded in inductive study may be tempted to try to inject themselves overly much. The leader should try to talk no more than 20% of the time.

2. *"Who do people say that I am?"* <u>Discipleship question</u>: Who is God/Jesus to you, from this passage? **(The NATURE of God/Jesus)**

---

[3] *Babylonian Talmud [BT], Berakhot 63b.*
[4] *BT Ta'anit 7a.*
[5] Hal and Debbie Perkins, *Discipled by Jesus*, (Denver: Outskirts Press, 2013).
[6] The model is also excellent for personal devotions quite apart from a group.

Chapter 21—The Whole Inductive Bible Study Process for Discipleship Purposes 345

- This is basically a step that leads to praise.

- From the passage, what can we gather about the nature of God? What here is praiseworthy of our Lord?

- As the group identifies two or three qualities, stop and actually talk to Jesus (who is presumed to be *right there*) using praise language (we praise, love, extol, magnify, exalt, etc.). Then repeat the process by acknowledging further praiseworthy characteristics of God.

- As participants become more accustomed to the rhythm of this process, the leader will need to spend much less time facilitating the link between finding the praiseworthy element and prayer itself.

- An example, using the "Great Commission" passage of Matthew 28:18–20: Praise Him for His "coming" to us, for His speaking to us, for His authority, for His commands to us, for His example of making disciples, for the baptism into His life, for His teaching, for His presence, for the Trinity, for His "all-ness"—all authority, all nations, obey all, with you always … to the end. Pray, praise, adore, magnify Him.

3. *"Do you know what I have done for you?"* <u>Discipleship question</u>: What has Jesus done FOR you/THROUGH you recently when considering the major lessons of this passage? (**The WORK of God/Jesus**)

    - How have the lessons of this passage come to fruition through other people to you … or through you (by God's grace) to other people?

    - Possibilities from Matt 29:18–20.

        > "This week I had the opportunity to bring someone closer to God. They are not saved yet, or baptized, but closer."

        > "Jesus used me today to teach someone about the life of discipleship."

        > "I felt Him today—He did say He would be with the disciples ALL-ways. Let me tell you how…."

4. *"Do you love Me? Feed My sheep."* Discipleship question: How can I adjust to better serve my flock (spouse, family, churched, unchurched, compassionate ministry) using the lesson(s) of this passage?

    Or

    "Repent and believe in the gospel." Discipleship question: What do I need to change to remain faithful to His teaching from the Word this week? (**The DESIRES of God/Jesus**)

    - This is a cogent reminder for application, whatever the scripture being studied. Sometimes one of these questions will be more applicable to the passage than the other; one is outward, the other more inward (but also with possible outward ramifications).

- How can we impact others concerning the lessons of this passage? What do I need to *do?* Or, what is the Lord is pointing out that I need to change/adjust in my life?

- Learning has been described as *changed behavior*. A change of idea is fine, but it doesn't amount to much unless a disciple's behavior is changed.

- Possible examples from Matthew 28:18–20:

    "I need to start discipling somebody ... what do I do?"

    "I want Jesus to use me to lead someone to the Lord...."

    "I my life of discipleship I want to 'practice His presence' in a way I haven't really been doing...."

- As these commitments are articulated, the group leader facilitates members in identifying measurable and specific commitments, then "testing" these ideas by asking the group: *Does this seem like a God-given idea/strategy to you?* Discuss.

- The commitments can be followed up via messages sent to the participants as reminders of these identified needs and for question #3 above in the next meeting.

5. *"What do you want me to do for you?"* Discipleship question: What is my need? What am I believing Jesus for today/ this week? **(The POWER of God/Jesus)**

    - This inquiry may be used in two ways. Members gather in smaller groups, first, to pray for the lessons of the passage to bear fruit in their lives in the coming week or, second, to pray for individual needs that might not have anything to do with the passage.

At the end of the meeting, join hands in a circle and ask the group if they have felt discipled by Jesus through this meeting. Then recite the Lord's Prayer together.

Hal Perkins has followed this plan for years in his church and now promotes the method church-to-church as an evangelist for discipleship. My own church applies this model (modified and adapted) in various groups during the week including the Wednesday evening "prayer meeting," men's groups, and one-on-one discipleship encounters. I also utilize it in online meetings with seminary students, this semester meeting with students from Mexico City, Georgia, Louisiana, Michigan, Indiana, and Mississippi.

This is not the only way, of course, to utilize the methodical study of Scripture in a group setting, but it is an attempt to move beyond the intellectual endeavor of inductive study to praise, testimony, commitment, and accountability and, finally, to intercession buttressed by the underlying principles of correlation and application. When introduced to IBS, practitioners rightfully get excited about observation and interpretation. But we should get at least as excited about correlation and application, and perhaps more so. As Jesus said, "blessed are those who hear the word of God and observe it." (Luke 11:28, NASB)

FOR FURTHER READING

Bauer, David R., and Robert A. Traina. *Inductive Bible Study: A Comprehensive Guide to the Practice of Hermeneutics*. Grand Rapids: Baker Academic, 2011. Part 4, "Evaluating and Appropriating" (chs. 17 and 18) and Part 5 "Correlation" (chs. 19 and 20).

Friedeman, Matt and Lisa Ausley, *LifeChanging Bible Study: Practical Keys to a Deeper Understanding of the Word*. Wilmore, KY: Francis Asbury, 2009.

Long, Fredrick J. *In Step with God's Word: Interpreting the New Testament as God's People*. GlossaHouse Hermeneutics & Translation 1. Wilmore, KY: GlossaHouse, 2017. "Scriptural Correlations" (ch. 8), "Biblical Theology" (ch. 10), "Evaluated Applications" (ch.11), and "Presentation Brainstorm" (ch. 12).

Perkins, Hal and Debbie Perkins. *Discipled by Jesus*. Denver: Outskirts Press, 2013.

Veerman, Dave. *How to Apply the Bible*. Carol Stream, IL: Tyndale House, 1993; repr. Wheaton, IL: Livingstone, 2002.

Syllabus Appendices

Select Syllabi from David R. Bauer, Fredrick J. Long, and Dorothy Jean Weaver

# The Gospel of Matthew
NT(IBS)510 (3 credit hours)
David R. Bauer

COURSE DESCRIPTION

From Catalog:
A basic course in inductive Bible studies. The primary purpose is to enable the student to begin developing an inductive approach to Bible study, especially in the areas of observation and interpretation. Parts of the Gospel of Matthew are used to demonstrate and to practice a methodical approach which can be used in other biblical books. Some of the main themes of the Gospel are highlighted in the process.

Additional Explanation:
This course seeks to introduce the student to the "inductive method" of biblical study, and to direct this interpretive approach to the Gospel of Matthew.

This orientation implies several things, including (1) an emphasis upon methodology and methodological concerns, and (2) a strong commitment to direct, independent study of the biblical text, with secondary sources (e.g., commentaries, grammars, dictionaries of the Bible) to be consulted by the student only after extensive, firsthand study has been attempted. The English Bible (RSV) will serve as the basis for study. Students with facility in Greek are encouraged to make use of the original whenever possible.

STUDENT LEARNING OUTCOMES (SLOs)

1. <u>Observation</u>: Demonstrate introductory skills in observing the text with a view toward using these observations in the interpretation of the text.
2. <u>Interpretation</u>: Demonstrate introductory skills in interpreting the text by citing, describing, and drawing inferences from various types of evidence, including certain ones that pertain to the original language.
3. <u>Hermeneutics</u>: Demonstrate introductory ability to discuss some of the major hermeneutical issues surrounding especially observation and interpretation.
4. <u>Evaluation and Application</u>: Demonstrate an introductory awareness of issues pertaining to the evaluation of passages for their contemporary possibilities for application and to the process of actually applying passages to specific contemporary situations.
5. <u>Content</u>: Demonstrate at an introductory level knowledge of the content of the book in its historical and especially its literary and theological contexts.

Additional Course Outcomes
a. Think through the contents of the entire Gospel without reference to the printed text;
b. Identify significant passages in the Gospel and interpret them contextually;

c. Describe thoroughly the meaning and development of major themes in the Gospel, citing individual passages and other specific data to support conclusions;
d. Discuss the historical and religious background of the First Gospel, demonstrating a general knowledge of critical problems regarding Matthew and an ability to use this historical and theological setting in the interpretation of the book.

TEXTBOOKS & RESOURCES

Required:
- *Revised Standard Version of the Bible*, Zondervan ©1989, ISBN: 978-0452006478. 1120 pages. $20.
- *Inductive Bible Study*, by David R. Bauer and Robert A. Traina, Baker Academic, 2011. ISBN: 978-0801027673. 464 pages. $22.
- *Essential Bible Study Tools for Ministry*, David R. Bauer, ©2014, Abingdon Press. ISBN: 978-1426755170. 426 pages. $30.79-45.99
- *Matthew*, Jack Dean Kingsbury, © 3rd Rev. Edition (Aug. 1998), Evangel Publishing House, ISBN: 978-0916035808 134 pages. $5 NOTE: This book is out of print. However, copies are available for purchase at the front desk in the library.

**Both *Inductive Bible Study* and *Essential Bible Study Tools for Ministry* are available in Korean.
- Additional Website Resource: www.inductivebiblestudy.seedbed.com.

ASSIGNMENTS

To successfully complete this class, students must satisfactorily complete and submit all assignments on time and actively participate and contribute to the learning community.

REQUIREMENTS

A. The completion of assigned lessons in writing, unless otherwise indicated by the instructor (all assigned lessons are in **bold**). No late papers will be accepted save in cases in which permission is granted by the instructor based on emergency.
B. Punctual attendance at all class sessions.
C. Participation in an "in course consultation module," which will provide group interaction with the instructor to discuss any questions students might have or clarifications they might need.
D. A careful reading of the assigned portions of Kingsbury's volume on Matthew (pp.1–32, 96–107), with a one- to two-page critical reflection paper.
E. A final integrative assignment based on the objectives of the course (Lesson 30 described below)
F. Assignments will be worth 100% of the grade. No assignments will be made before the first day of class.

ASSIGNMENTS

Lesson 1. Methodology. Read Parts 1–3 (pp. 1–277) of *Inductive Bible Study*; and write a 4-6 page summary of this portion of the book with questions that occurred to you in the course of reading.

SYLLABUS APPENDICES—*The Gospel of Matthew NT(IBS)510*

Lesson 2. Survey of the Gospel as a Whole. Read the entire Gospel through at one sitting several times.
1. Identify the general materials of the book.
2. Locate the main units and sub-units in the book, and identify the major structural relationships operative in the book as a whole.
3. Ask a few interpretive questions regarding each major structural relationship observed.
4. Identify the key verses and strategic areas which provide insight into the book as a whole. Give reasons for each selection in terms of structural significance.
5. Note data bearing on such higher critical questions as the author, place and date of writing, recipients, etc.
6. Note other major impressions relating to the book as a whole.

Lesson 3. Survey of Divisions as Wholes (1:1–4:16), and Survey of Segments as Wholes (1:1–17).
1. Survey the division 1:1–4:16, following these steps:
   a. Locate the main units and sub-units within the division, and the major structural relationships operative.
   b. Ask a few interpretive questions based on each major structural relationship observed.
   c. Identify the key verses or strategic areas that provide insight into the division as a whole.
   d. Note other major impressions relating to the division as a whole.
2. Survey the segment of 1:1–17, following these steps:
   a. Locate the main units and sub-units within the segment and the major structural relationships operative.
   b. Ask a few interpretive questions based on each major structural relationship observed.
   c. Identify the key verses or strategic areas which provide insight into the segment as a whole.
   d. Identify the literary form(s) employed in the segment.
   e. Note other major impressions relating to the segment as a whole.

Lesson 4. Survey of Segments as Wholes. 1:18–2:23. Apply the suggestions for the survey of segments found in Lesson 3 to 1:18–2:23.

Lesson 5. Survey of Segments as Wholes (3:1–4:16). Apply the suggestions for the survey of segments to 3:1–4:16.

Lesson 6. Survey of Divisions as Wholes (4:17–16:20). Apply the suggestions for the survey of divisions as wholes found in Lesson 3 to 4:17–16:20.

Lesson 7. Survey of Segments as Wholes. Segment containing 5:46–48. Identify the segment of which 5:46–48 is a part, and do a survey of this segment, following the suggestions for the survey of segments in Lesson 3.

Lesson 8. Detailed Observation of 5:46–48.
1. Examine 5:46–48 in terms of a detailed observation. Do independent study only. Ask interpretive questions relating to each observation made.
2. Identify the most significant questions raised.

Lesson 9. Interpretation of 5:46–48. Use the exegetical determinants outlined in IBS to interpret 5:46–48. Interpret the passage by selecting two or three of the most important questions raised in your detailed observation of the passage and by employing the exegetical determinants to answer these questions.
1. Attempt to determine which exegetical determinants are relevant to the question being answered.
2. Begin with the most important determinants, and try to bring their evidence to bear on the interpretive question being answered.
3. Using inferential reasoning, indicate the possible conclusion or conclusions to which each piece of evidence points. These conclusions, or inferences, should point toward possible answers to the interpretive question. At the close of study, list the various pieces of evidence; if more than one is possible, indicate the data supporting each possibility. If evidence is conclusive, indicate your conclusion.
4. Make periodical summaries of your findings.
5. Identify the major problems of methodology as you proceed.
6. Keeping in mind that the last exegetical determinant to be examined is secondary sources, after independent study check at least two secondary sources. Be sure to identify each commentary or other secondary source used.

Lesson 10. Survey and Interpretation of 8:1–9:35.
1. Survey. Apply the suggestions for the survey of segments to 8:1–9:35.
2. Interpretation.
   a. Investigate the nature of Jesus's authority in this segment by answering the following questions. Over what does Jesus exercise authority? How is this authority described? Why has Matthew presented Jesus's authority in this way? What are the implications?
   b. What is the meaning of "faith" in this segment?
   c. Examine Matthew's portrait of the disciples and discipleship in 8:1–9:35 by answering the following questions: What does it mean to be a disciple? How does one become a disciple? What are the requirements of discipleship?
   d. Note the titles and names that are applied to Jesus in this segment. What is the meaning and function of each?
3. Synthesis.
   a. In one short paragraph, summarize the major thrust of 8:1–9:35
   b. How does this segment relate to chs. 5–7? Why has Matthew thus related these two units?

Lesson 11. Survey and Interpretation of 9:35–11:1.
1. Survey. Apply the suggestions for the survey of segments to 9:35–11:1.
2. Interpretation.
   a. Analyze what is herein said regarding the ministry of the disciples, i.e., what are the main elements in the description of the disciples' ministry in this passage, and what is the meaning of each? Does this description refer to the ministry of the disciples during Jesus's earthly existence, to the ministry of the post-Easter disciples, or both? Why?
   b. What is the relationship between the ministry of Jesus and the ministry of the disciples as set forth in 9:35–11:1? Be analytical.
3. Synthesis. Summarize the portrait of discipleship in 9:35–11:1, and relate this portrait to the understanding of discipleship in 8:1–9:35.

Lesson 12. Survey of Segments as Wholes (11:1–30). Apply the Suggestions for the Survey of Segments to 11:1–30.

Lesson 13. Detailed Observation of 11:28–30. Do a detailed observation of 11:28–30. Identify the most significant questions raised.

Lesson 14. Interpretation of 11:28–30. Interpret 11:28–30. Identify the most significant questions raised.

Lesson 15. Survey of segments as wholes (13:1–52). Apply the suggestions for the survey of segments to 13:1–52.

Lesson 16. Interpretation of 13:1–52. Identify the structure of the parable of the Soils. Interpret this parable using relevant interpretive determinants (including structure of the parable itself, context, etc.). Be especially careful to show the relationship between the structure of the parable and its interpretation. As a result of your study, attempt to state the message of the parable in a sentence or two.

Lesson 17. Survey and Interpretation of 15:1–39.
1. Survey. Apply the suggestions for the survey of segments to 15:1–39.
2. Interpretation.
   a. What was the nature and origin of the "tradition of the elders?" What views of religion underlie this understanding of purification? In light of 15:1–20, how is Jesus's view of religion different from that of the scribes and Pharisees?
   b. Trace Jesus's answer in vv. 3–9. What are the man elements of the answer? How does this response answer the question of the Pharisees in v. 2?
   c. Analyze the miracle story of 15:21–28. Interpret vv. 25–28. How does this story relate to the material at the beginning of ch. 15?
3. Synthesis. Summarize Jesus's views of religious practice according to this segment.

Lesson 18. Survey of Segments as wholes (16:1–20). Apply the suggestions for the Survey of Segments to 16:1–20.

Lesson 19. Detailed Observation of 16:18–19. Do a detailed observation of 16:18–19. Identify the most significant questions raised.

Lesson 20. Interpretation of 16:18–19. Interpret 16:18–19 by answering a significant question from your detailed observation.

Lesson 21. Evaluation and Application of 16:18–19.
1. Evaluation. Having interpreted 16:18–19, evaluate the passage in order to determine what relevance it has for you, for your ministry, and for the people to whom you will minister.
2. Application. Ask a series of applicatory questions on the basis of your evaluation of this passage. In light of your circumstances (and the circumstances of those under your ministry), how would you answer these questions?

Lesson 22. Survey of Divisions as Wholes (16:21–28:20), and Survey of Segments as Wholes (16:21–17:23).
1. Apply the suggestions for the survey of divisions as wholes found in Lesson 3 to 16:21–28:20.
2. Apply the suggestions for the survey of segments to 16:21–17:27.

Lesson 23. Detailed Observation of 16:24–28. Do a detailed observation of 16:24–28. Identify the most significant questions raised.

Lesson 24. Interpretation of 16:24. Interpret 16:24 by answering a significant question from your detailed observation.

Lesson 25. Survey and Interpretation of 17:24–18:35.
1. Survey.
2. Interpretation.
   a. What is the meaning of 17:24–27? What does its inclusion here imply regarding the situation of Matthew's church? Explore the relation of 17:24–27 to ch. 18.
   b. What main issues are addressed in ch. 18, and what is the specific meaning and significance of each?
   c. Interpret the parable of the Unforgiving Servant (18:23–35) and relate it to the preceding material in this segment. Be specific, precise, and penetrating.
3. Synthesis.
   a. Summarize the teaching of 17:24–18:35.
   b. How does this segment relate to its surrounding context?

Lesson 26. Survey and Interpretation of 19:1–20:34.
1. Survey
2. Interpretation.
   a. What problem is raised in each paragraph, and how does Jesus deal with each problem?
   b. Interpret 19:21.
   c. What is the meaning of the parable of the laborers (20:1–16)? What is its function in context?

d. What are the main emphases found in the third announcement of the cross [and resurrection] (20:17–19)? How is this announcement related to its context? Compare this third announcement with the first and second announcements of the cross and resurrection (16:21; 17:22–23)?
3. Synthesis. Contrast Jesus and the disciples in this segment. How does this contrast relate to the contrast between Jesus and the disciples in the preceding material, esp. 16:21–17:27?

Lesson 27. Evaluation and Application of 19:21. Evaluate and apply 19:21.

Lesson 28. Survey and Interpretation of 21:1–22:45. Apply the principles of survey, analysis, and synthesis to this section. Analyze your methodology and identify and problems you encounter in the course of study.

Lesson 29. Survey and Interpretation of chs. 24–25.
1. Survey.
2. Interpretation.
   a. What is the meaning of the disciples' question in 24:4? Trace Jesus's response to the question. How does Jesus answer the question and why does he answer their question in this way?
   b. What are the major emphases of the parables in 25:1–46? What is the relationship between ch. 24 and ch. 25? Keeping in mind the flow of the story, why did Jesus speak these parables to his disciples at this point?
3. Synthesis.
   a. Summarize the major emphases of chs. 24–25.
   b. Investigate the relationship between these chapters and their surrounding context.

Lesson 30. Synthesis of Method. Employ the steps of observation, interpretation, evaluation and application in relation to 27:55–28:20.
1. **Observation.**
   a. **Survey the segment of 27:55–28:20.**
   b. **Do detailed observation of 28:18–20. Identify the most significant questions raised.**
2. **Interpretation. Interpret 28:18–20 by answering one or two of the most significant questions raised in your detailed observation.**
3. Evaluation and Application. Evaluate and apply 28:18–20.
4. Self-Analysis. Critically evaluate your own methodology. Identify points of strength and weakness. What major problems remain in your mind regarding methodology?

Lesson 31. Synthesis of Content.
1. What are the broad contours of Matthew's portrait of Jesus? That is, what is the Christology of Matthew? Give evidence to support your conclusions (including verse references).
2. What are the main concerns of the teachings of Jesus in Matthew's Gospel? Include discussion of the kingdom of heaven, discipleship, the law, and mission.
3. What is Matthew's understanding of salvation history? Discuss Matthew's views regarding

the relationship between the time of the prophets, of John the Baptist, of Jesus, of the church, and the parousia.

CLASS AGENDA

<u>Note</u>: Due dates are subject to change by notice of the faculty member. Please see "Assignments" for more information about each assignment.

Lesson 1: Methodology Reading and Summary Paper	*Due: TBA*
Lesson 2: Survey of the Gospel as a Whole.	*Due: TBA*
Lesson 3: Part 2 Survey the Segment 1:1–17	*Due: TBA*
Lesson 4: Survey of Segments as Wholes. 1:18–2:23	*Due: TBA*
Lessons 5–6: N/A	
Lesson 7: Survey of the Wholes. 5:46–48	*Due: TBA*
Kingsbury Assignment	*Due: TBA*
Lesson 8: Detailed Observation. 5:46–48	*Due: TBA*
Lesson 9: Interpretation. 5:46–48	*Due: TBA*
Lessons 10–14: N/A	
Lesson 15: Survey of Segments as Wholes. 13:1–52	*Due: TBA*
Lesson 16: Interpretation. 13:1–52	*Due: TBA*
Lessons 17–18: N/A	
Lesson 19: Detailed Observation. 16:18–19	*Due: TBA*
Lesson 20: Interpretation. 16:18–19	*Due: TBA*
Lessons 21–22: N/A	
Lesson 23: Detailed Observation. 16:24–28	*Due: TBA*
Lesson 24: Interpretation. 16:24	*Due: TBA*
Lessons 25–29: N/A	
Lesson 30: 1A. Survey the Segment Mt. 27:55–28:20	*Due: TBA*
1B. Detailed Observation of 28:18–20	*Due: TBA*
2. Interpret 28:18–20	*Due: TBA*

# Hebrews
NT(IBS)646 (3 credit hours)
David R. Bauer

COURSE DESCRIPTION

This course involves a detailed study of the thought-development of this epistle with a focus on its structure, its teaching on the incarnation and high priesthood of Jesus, and its insights into the relation between the old and new covenants. Emphasis is placed on the methodology of studying discursive literature. In addition, attention is given to thinking, valuing, and living biblically by learning how to apply Scripture to life and ministry. This course seeks intentionally to incorporate the grammatical analysis of the Greek language into the overall inductive process.

STUDENT LEARNING OUTCOMES (SLOs)

Student Learning Outcomes (for use in degree program assessment)
1. Demonstrate a developing skill in the interpretation of both small and larger units of material.
2. Articulate, at a developing level, the bases for evaluating the message of individual passages for their contemporary appropriation, and demonstrate skill in actually appropriating the message of these passages.
3. Demonstrate at an introductory level, skills in moving from text toward proclamation

Course Objectives

A. Methodology. The student should be able to:
   1. Employ structural observations for the interpretation of individual passages within the book, as well as for the interpretation of the book as a whole.
   2. Raise various kinds of interpretive questions, and answer these questions based on the use of exegetical determinants.
   3. Employ various kinds of relevant evidence, including that which involves exegetical use of the original languages, in a process of inferential reasoning for the interpretation of individual passages within the book, as well as for the book as a whole.
   4. Synthesize the interpretation of units of various lengths, such as the paragraph, the segment, the section (division), and the book as a whole.
   5. Use aspects of methodology that are especially relevant for epistolary material.
   6. Evaluate and apply truths that emerge from the interpretation of the material.
   7. Articulate the major issues involved in the movement from text to proclamation; move from interpretation and application of the text towards its proclamation; and integrate the interpretation and application of a passage in Hebrews with that of a correlative passage from the Old Testament so as to move toward a sermon (or teaching lesson) based on both an Old Testament and New Testament text.

B. Content. The student should be able to do the following:
1. Think through the contents of Hebrews without recourse to the printed text.
2. Identify significant passages in Hebrews and interpret them contextually.
3. Demonstrate the importance of a sound methodology for interpretation, including specific examples from Hebrews.
4. Describe thoroughly the meaning an development of major themes in Hebrews, citing individual passages and other specific data to support conclusions.
5. Discuss the historical and religious background of Hebrews, demonstrating a general knowledge of critical problems regarding Hebrews and an ability to use these data in the interpretation of Hebrews.

TEXTBOOKS & RESOURCES

Required Reading:
- *Revised Standard Version of the Bible*, ISBN: 978-0452006478 $16.32. 1120 pages.
- One of the following: *Greek New Testament,* or *Interlinear Greek New Testament: UBS Greek New Testament,* Newman Barclay, ISBN: 978-1598562859 $69.95 716 pages or *Nestle-Aland Novum Testamentum Graece*, Hendrickson, ISBN: 978-1598561722 $32.99. 779 pages or *Interlinear for the rest of us,* William Mounce, Zondervan, ISBN: 978-0310263036 $49.99. 913 pages
- *Inductive Bible Study*, by David R. Bauer and Robert A. Traina, Baker Academic, 2011. ISBN: 978-0801027673 $66.63. 464 pages
- *Essential Bible Study Tools for Ministry*, by David R. Bauer © 2014, Abingdon Press. ISBN: 978-1426755170. 426 Pages. $30.79-45.99.

Collateral Resources:
- *Dictionary of the Later New Testament & Its Development*, eds. Ralph Martin and Peter Davids, IVP Academic, ISBN: 978-0830817795 $60.00 Only the article on Hebrews will be assigned, and this article will be available free of charge through the online classroom.
- Website Resource: www.inductivebiblestudy.seedbed.com.

ASSIGNMENTS

To successfully complete this class, students must satisfactorily complete and submit all assignments on time and actively participate and contribute to the learning community.

A. The completion of the following lessons in writing, unless otherwise indicated by the instructor. Assigned lessons are printed in **bold.** All lessons are to be handed in at the end of the class period on the day designated. No late papers will be accepted save in cases in which permission is granted by the instructor based on emergency.

B. Punctual attendance at all class sessions. Absence of more than two will result in a grade penalty. Absence of more than four will result in loss of credit for the course. Exceptions will be made for emergencies or unavoidable absences.

C. Careful reading of the assigned portions of the required and collateral texts.

D. Listening to a recording of an expository sermon on a passage in Hebrews for entering into class discussion on the movement from text to proclamation (preaching or teaching).

Assigned lessons are printed in **Bold**. None of the others will be required. No work is expected the first day of class. These lessons will be announced at the beginning of the course.

LESSON 1. SURVEY OF THE BOOK AS A WHOLE. Read the entire book through at one sitting several times.

1. **Locate the main units and sub-units in the book, and identify the major structural relationships operative in the book as a whole;**
2. **Ask a few interpretive questions regarding each major structural relationship observed;**
3. **Identify the key verses and strategic areas which provide insight into the book as a whole. Give reasons for each selection in terms of structural significance;**
4. **Note date bearing on such higher critical questions as the author, place and date of writing, recipients, provenance, unity of the book, etc.**
5. **Note other major impressions relating to the book as a whole.**

LESSON 2. HEBREWS 1:5–2:18.

A. Survey. Read 1:5–2:18 rapidly at one sitting. Survey this section by following these steps:
1. Locate the main units and sub-units of the section, and identify the major structural relationships operative in the section as a whole;
2. Ask a few interpretive questions regarding each major structural relationship observed;
3. Identify the key verses which provide insight into the section as a whole. Give reasons for each selection in terms of structural significance.
4. Note other major impressions.

B. Interpretation of 1:5–14. Interpret this segment (or a portion of it) on the basis of one or more structural relationships, interpretive questions, major issues, or strategic areas identified in your survey. Or answer one or more of the following interpretive questions:
1. What is the meaning of each of the major contrasts between Christ and the angels in 1:5–14 (note in the process the meaning of the major Christological titles)? How are these major contrasts related to each other, and how do they illumine each other? Why are these contrasts emphasized? What implications emerge from these contrasts (especially in terms of angelology and Christology)?
2. Examine each OT quotation in its original context. On the basis of this examination, how does the writer use the OT? Why does he thus use the OT? Implications?

C. Synthesis of 1:5–14
1. Summarize the teaching of 1:5–14 regarding Christ. Identify specific ways in which the Christology of this segment can affect Christian living.
2. How does 1:5–14 relate to 1:1–4? How does 1:1–4 illumine 1:5–14, and how does 1:5–14 illumine 1:1–4?

LESSON 3. HEBREWS 1:5–2:18, CONTINUED.

A. Interpretation of 2:1–18. Interpret this segment (or a portion of it) on the basis of one or more structural relationships, interpretive questions, major issues, or strategic areas identified in your survey. Or answer one or more of the following interpretive questions:
   1. What is the meaning of the exhortation in 2:1? What motivations for obeying this exhortation are mentioned in 2:2–4, and how does each substantiate the exhortation? How is 2:1–4 related to ch. 1 (note especially the full meaning of the "therefore" in 2:1)?
   2. Trace the thought of 2:5–18. In light of the development of the argument, answer the following questions:
      a. The meaning and implications of 2:5–8?
      b. What are the main assertions made regarding Jesus in 2:18? Meaning and implications of each? In light of these assertions, why is it "fitting" that Jesus should be made "perfect through suffering" (v. 10)?
   3. What problems of the readers are suggested by the emphases of this segment? How does 2:1–18 address, and attempt to solve, these problems?

B. Synthesis of 2:1–18.
   1. Summarize the teaching of this segment regarding (a) Christology, (b) anthropology (i.e., doctrine of humanity), and (c) atonement. How are these three concerns related to each other in an overall theology of the segment?
   2. How are these theological emphases relevant for Christians today, i.e., how should they specifically affect Christian thinking and behavior?

C. Application and Proclamation
   1. On the basis of your interpretation, explore specific ways in which this segment can be applied to yourself and/or other contemporary persons.
   2. Develop a proclamation outline. A proclamation outline is not synonymous with a sermon outline (which assumes homiletical crafting), but is rather the statement of a specific proclamatory thesis, with three to five main points that develop the overall proclamatory thesis (and are clearly and explicitly related to one another). Each of the main points should itself be developed in a brief but specific paragraph, which describes the (theological) teaching derived from the interpretation of the text, the contemporary appropriation derived from the application process, and the relationship between the two.

LESSON 4. HEBREWS 3:1–4:16.

A. Survey. Using the suggestions in Lesson 2.A., survey this section.

B. Interpretation of 3:1–19. Interpret this segment (or a portion of it) on the basis of one or more structural relationships, interpretive questions, major issues, or strategic areas identified in your survey. Or answer one or more of the following interpretive questions:
   1. What is the meaning of the contrast between Jesus and Moses in 3:2–6a? How does this contrast substantiate and illumine the appeal in 3:1? Elucidate the meaning of the "therefore" in 3:1.

2. What exhortations are found in this segment, and what is the meaning of each? How is each exhortation supported by the argument of the segment (note especially the flow of the argument, and key terms, e.g. "faithful," "confidence," "unbelief," "rebellion")? In your own words, paraphrase each exhortation and the author's support of it.
3. Examine the quotation from Psalm 95 in light of its original context and Numbers 14:1–35. Analyze Israel's sin as set forth in this quotation. What does this analysis reveal regarding the dangers the readers were facing and how they should deal with these dangers?

C. Synthesis of 3:1–19. Explore the relationship between the individual exhortations in this chapter. What main concern lies behind all these exhortations? How does the comparison between Israel and the readers underscore this main concern? What dangers in the audience's situation are reflected in this segment? How does this segment speak to these? Be specific.

D. Follow the suggestions under Lesson 3, part C.

LESSON 5. HEBREWS 3:1–4:16, CONTINUED.

A. Interpretation of 4:1–16. Interpret this segment (or a portion of it) on the basis of one or more structural relationships, interpretive questions, major issues, or strategic areas identified in your survey. Or answer one or more of the following interpretive questions:
1. Trace the argument of 4:1–10. Keeping in mind the use of Ps. 95 here, and the references to creation and Joshua, what is meant by the "rest of God?" How does one enter that rest?
2. What is the meaning of the exhortation in v. 11? How does it result from the argument in vv. 1–10? What assertions are made regarding the word of God in vv. 12–13, and how do they substantiate the exhortation of v. 11?
3. How do the exhortations in 4:14–16 relate to chs. 3–4? What is said regarding Jesus' role as high priest, and what is the meaning of this description? How does this description of Jesus as high priest substantiate and illumine the exhortations in this paragraph?

B. Synthesis of 4:1–16. Summarize the teaching regarding the "rest of God" in chs. 3–4.

C. Follow the suggestions under Lesson 3, part C.

LESSON 6. HEBREWS 5 AND 6.

A. Survey. Using the suggestions in Lesson 2.A., survey 5:1–10 and 5:11–6:20.

B. Interpretation. Interpret this segment (or a portion of it) on the basis of one or more structural relationships, interpretive questions, major issues, or strategic areas identified in your survey. Or answer one or more of the following interpretive questions:
1. What qualifications for a high priest are set forth in 5:1–4? What is the meaning of each? According to 5:5–10, how does Jesus meet these qualifications? Analyze and interpret 5:7–10.

2. What is the meaning of the exhortation in 6:1–3? How does the description of the readers in 5:11–14 illumine this exhortation, and how does this exhortation flow from this description?
3. How does 6:4–8 substantiate the exhortation in 6:1–3? Interpret 6:4–6. What are the implications?
4. What is the meaning of 6:9–12? How does it relate to 5:11–6:8?
5. Trace the argument of 6:13–20. How does the author reach his conclusion? How is this paragraph related to the preceding?

C. Synthesis. What are the main points in this material? How is each related to the flow of the argument in Hebrews?

D. Follow the suggestions under Lesson 3, part C.

LESSON 7. HEBREWS 7.

A. Survey. Using the suggestions in Lesson 2.A., survey Hebrews 7.

B. Interpretation. Interpret this segment (or a portion of it) on the basis of one or more structural relationships, interpretive questions, major issues, or strategic areas identified in your survey. Or answer one or more of the following interpretive questions:
1. What is the meaning of the description of Melchizedek presented here? How does Genesis 14:17–20 illumine this description?
2. In what ways is Melchizedek contrasted to the sons of Levi? Why this contrast? Implications?
3. Trace the logic of 7:11–28. What main points does the author make? How does he support these main points?

C. Synthesis. Summarize the differences between the priesthood of Jesus and the Levitical Priesthood.

D. Follow the suggestions under Lesson 3, part C. 7

LESSON 8. HEBREWS 8:1–10:18.

A. Survey. Using the suggestions in Lesson 2.A., survey Hebrews 8:1–10:18.

B Interpretation of 8:1–9:14. Interpret this segment (or a portion of it) on the basis of one or more structural relationships, interpretive questions, major issues, or strategic areas identified in your survey. Or answer one or more of the following interpretive questions:
1. Trace the argument of 8:1–9:14. What main contrasts are found here? What is the meaning of each? How is each supported? Why does the writer stress these contrasts? How are these contrasts related? Implications?
2. Examine 8:8–12 in its original OT context. How does this passage function in the argument of 8:1–9:14, and how does its original OT context inform its use and meaning here? How does OT background inform the meaning and function of 9:1–14?

C. Synthesis of 8:1–9:14. Summarize the main truths of 8:1–9:10. How do these truths relate to the preceding argument in Hebrews?

D. Follow the suggestions under Lesson 3, part C.

LESSON 9. HEBREWS 8:1–10:18 (CONTINUED).
A. Interpretation of 9:11–10:18. Interpret this segment (or a portion of it) on the basis of one or more structural relationships, interpretive questions, major issues, or strategic areas identified in your survey. Or answer one or more of the following interpretive questions:
   1. Trace the reasoning of 9:11–10:18. What main contrasts are found in 9:11–14, and what is the meaning of each? Explore the relation of 9:15 to 9:11–14. How does 9:16–22 substantiate 9:15?
   2. How does the writer prove the superiority of Jesus' sacrifice in 9:23–10:18? How do the OT quotations function in this argument? Implications?
B. Synthesis of 9:11–10:18. Summarize the ways in which Jesus and his sacrifice are superior to the Levitical priesthood and the old covenant.
C. Follow the suggestions under Lesson 3, part C.

LESSON 10. HEBREWS 10:19–39.
A. Survey. Using the suggestions in Lesson 2.A., survey this segment.
B. Interpretation. Interpret this segment (or a portion of it) on the basis of one or more structural relationships, interpretive questions, major issues, or strategic areas identified in your survey. Or answer one or more of the following interpretive questions:
   1. Explore the meaning and significance of the "therefore" in 10:19. How does this relationship with the preceding material illumine 10:19–39?
   2. What exhortations are given in this segment? What is the meaning of each? How is each supported? How are these exhortations related? Why these exhortations? Implications?
   3. Trace the argument of 10:26–31. What is the meaning of this passage? How is this passage related to 6:4–8?
C. Synthesis. State the main truths of this segment in a paragraph. 8
D. Follow the suggestions under Lesson 3, part C.

LESSON 11. HEBREWS 11.
Do an original study of this unit. Identify the steps followed, and your findings regarding each step.

LESSON 12. HEBREWS 12. Apply the suggestions under Lesson 11 to this unit.

LESSON 13. HEBREWS 13. Apply the suggestions under Lesson 11 to this unit.

LESSON 14. SYNTHESIS OF HEBREWS. Synthesize the Book of Hebrews by answering the interpretive questions raised under one major structural relationship identified in the survey of the book. Be as thorough, analytical and integrative as possible.

CLASS AGENDA

<u>Note</u>: Subject to change by notice of the faculty member.

Lesson 1: Survey of the Book as a Whole	*Due: TBA*
Lessons 2–3: N/A	
Lesson 4: Survey, Interpretation, Synthesis of Hebrews 3:1–4:16	*Due: TBA*
Lesson 5: Interpretation, Synthesis Hebrews 4:1–16	*Due: TBA*
Lesson 6: Survey, Interpretation, Synthesis Hebrews 5 and 6	*Due: TBA*
Lesson 7: Survey, Interpretation, Synthesis Hebrews 7	*Due: TBA*
Lesson 8: Survey, Interpretation, Synthesis Hebrews 8:1–10:18	*Due: TBA*
Lessons 9–10: N/A	
Lesson 11: Original Study Hebrews 11	*Due: TBA*
Lessons 12–13: N/A	
Lesson 14: Synthesis of the Book of Hebrews	*Due: TBA*

Biblical Interpretation
BIBL 201 (3 credit hours)
Fredrick J. Long

COURSE DESCRIPTION: This course is an introduction to methods of Bible study and to the principles of biblical interpretation. An inductive approach to biblical interpretation is emphasized.

CLASS OBJECTIVES:

General: This course will introduce and train students in basic hermeneutical principles and methodology for interpreting Scripture, in order to handle the Word of God properly—with its theological content and various historical settings and genres—for the purpose of preaching and teaching.

Specific: Through selected readings, quizzing, by completing specified assignments, this course will train the students to…
1. become sensitive to the historical and cultural gap between the modern reader and the ancient text and to learn the tools and strategies for bridging that gap;
2. become proficient in interpreting the various literary figures, forms, and genres in the Bible (historical narrative, prophecy, parable, epistle, etc.);
3. recognize literary structures of various sorts used by the biblical authors to help convey meaning and truth.
4. learn specific, complementary tasks involved with interpretation (word studies, grammatical and structural analyses, etc.);
5. learn an inductive approach to interpretation involving careful observation, interpretation, application, and correlation of biblical materials into a biblical theology;
6. prepare to teach other persons how to study the Bible inductively and with integrity;
7. grow in one's love for God and his wonderful Word and apply it in all of one's life.

REQUIRED TEXTS:

1. (DH=) Duvall, J. Scott and J. Daniel Hays. *Grasping God's Word: A Hand's On Approach to Reading, Interpreting, and Applying the Bible.* 1st ed. Grand Rapids: Zondervan, 2001.
2. Logos Scholar's Library Series X from Logos Software. This software is to be purchased from Logos Software.

OTHER TEXTS PERTAINING TO BIBLICAL INTERPRETATION (consult as necessary):

Adler, Mortimer J., and Charles van Doren. *How to Read a Book.* New York: Simon and Schuster, 1972.

Bray, Gerald. *Biblical Interpretation: Past and Present.* Downers Grove, IL: InterVarsity Press, 1996.

Dockery, David S. *Biblical Interpretation: Then and Now*. Grand Rapids: Baker, 1992.
Fee, Gordan D., and Douglas Stuart. *How to Read the Bible for All Its Worth*. 3rd Edition. Grand Rapids: Zondervan, 1993.
Goldingay, John. *Models for Interpretation of Scripture*. Grand Rapids: Eerdmans, 1995.
Johnson, Elliot E. *Expository Hermeneutics: An Introduction*. Grand Rapids: Zondervan, 1990.
Kaiser, Walter C., and Moisés Silva. *An Introduction to Biblical Hermeneutics*. Grand Rapids: Zondervan, 1994.
Klein, William W., Craig Blomberg, and Robert L. Hubbard. *Introduction to Biblical Interpretation*. Dallas: Word, 1993.
Osborne, Grant R. *The Hermeneutical Spiral*. Downers Grove, IL: InterVarsity Press, 1991.
Ramm, Bernard. *Protestant Biblical Interpretation*. Grand Rapids: Baker, 1970.
*Thompson, David. *Bible Study that Works*. rev. ed. Nappanee, IN: Evangel, 1994.
*Traina, Robert A. *Methodical Bible Study*. Wilmore, Kentucky: Robert Traina, 1952.

CLASS FORMAT: Lecture with discussion of readings and assignments with in-class group interpretive work.

ASSESSMENTS:

1. Final Self-Assessment and Verse Memory Recitation. Essentially there are two components to this. First, before the end of the semester, I want you to arrange a time to meet with me (for 10-15 minutes) for you to recite and briefly explain three sets of verses relating to biblical interpretation. The verses to memorize are Ezra 7:9b–10; Luke 24:27, 45, and 2 Tim 3:16–17. Second, I want you to include in a simple one-page statement: 1) what percentage of reading you have done; 2) a self-evaluation of your performance and engagement of the course content in and out of class; and 3) your reflections on what you have learned and what you want to continue to learn about biblical interpretation. Due at our final examination.

2. Assignments from DH: Throughout the course you will be asked to read chapters from DH and complete specific interpretive assignments. Some of these will be completed in group settings during class time.

3. Inductive Bible Study Assignments: Throughout the course you will be asked to perform inductive studies on Gospel passages and segment surveys. I will lecture on and model for you how to do these.

4. Exegetical Paper on a Selected Passage: This is due in two stages. The rough draft is due the first Monday in November; the final draft is due the third Monday in November. There is a complete description on how to write this final paper will be provided. Please read this carefully and reread it as you work on your paper. Follow its guidelines closely. I also have a "sample" paper for you to see.

5. Additional Inductive Bible Assignments through a New Testament book of your choice. Due the last Wednesday of class.

Tentative Calendar

		Reading and/or Assignments due this Day DH=Duvall/Hays	Topic and Group Activity in Class
Week 1	Fri	Introduction: Why Biblical Interpretation? Syllabus	
Week 2	Mon	Read DH Chap. 1 (pp. 17–27)	The Interpretive Journey and Introduction to the Inductive Method
	Wed	Read DH Chap. 2 (pp. 28–44)	Supplication & Observation in Inductive Method **Do DH Chap. 2, Assignment 1 in Class**
	Fri	**Do DH Chap. 2, Assignment 3**	Observation in Inductive Method Example: Matt 5:1–9
Week 3	Mon	No class	
	Wed	*Read DH Chap. 3 (pp. 45–64)*	Observation in Inductive Method **Do DH Chap. 3, Assignment 1 in Class**
	Fri	**Do DH Chap. 3, Assignment 4**	The Place of Questions Book and Segment Surveys Example Segment: 1 Cor 12–14 or other
Week 4	Mon	Read DH Chap. 4 (pp. 65–82)	Book and Segment Surveys **Do a Segment Survey of Psalm 1**
	Wed	**Perform a Segment Survey of Nehemiah 1**	Discuss Nehemiah 1 Example Book Survey: 1 Peter or another
	Fri	Read DH Chap. 7 (pp. 115–27)	Example Book Survey: 1 Peter or another Begin Work on Book Survey
Week 5	Mon	**Perform a Book Survey of Ephesians**	Discuss Survey Work
	Wed		Detailed Analysis in Inductive Method Example: Deuteronomy 6
	Fri	**Perform a Detailed Analysis of Matt 5:13–16 or Matt 5:17–20**	Discuss Matt 5:13–20
Week 6	Mon	**Perform a detailed analysis of your**	

		exegetical paper passage. Be sure also to identify interpretive issues or questions.	
	Wed	Read DH Chaps. 5–6 (pp. 83–114)	What do we bring to the text? Resources for Socio-Historical-Cultural background on Logos
	Fri	**Write up a one-page report concerning the historical-cultural background of Ephesians. Cite your sources properly!**	The Cultural/Historical Context
<u>Week 7</u>	Mon	Read DH Chap. 8 (pp. 128–49)	How to do Word Studies Use Logos Work through Examples
	Wed	*Do DH Chap. 8, Assignment 1*	Word Studies General Use of Logos
	Fri		Start Interpretation in Inductive Method
<u>Week 8</u>	Mon	**Choose a hard to understand or morally significant word in your exegetical passage, and do an inductive study following the guidelines in DH chap. 8 (This counts as an "Inductive Assignment").**	Interpretation in Inductive Method
	Wed	Read DH Chap. 9 (pp. 150–64)	Bible Translations and Interpretation
<u>Week 9</u>	Mon	Perform an Interpretation using Inductive Method on this question: What is the meaning of the statement to "fear the LORD" in Deut 6:2? **or** Perform an Interpretation using Inductive Method on this question: What is the meaning of the Jesus's statement in Matt 5:48a, "you must be perfect"? Be sure to focus not merely on whether it is possible to be perfect, but especially on specifically what it means to be perfect (6 hours).	Discuss Results
	Wed		Discuss Results
	Fri	Read DH Chaps. 10–11 (pp. 165–95)	Who Controls the Meaning? Levels of Meaning; Socio-Rhetoric Method?

Week 10	Mon	Read DH Chap. 12 (pp. 196–202)	The Role of the Holy Spirit
	Wed	Read DH Chap. 13 (pp. 203–14)	Application in Inductive Method
	Fri	**Do DH Chap. 13, Assignment 3**	Application
Week 11	Mon		Correlation in Inductive Method **Correlate Deut 6:4-6 with Matthew 5:48**
	Wed	Read DH Chap. 14 (pp. 215-234)	**Rough Draft of Exegetical Paper Due** New Testament—Letters **Do DH Chap. 14, Assignment 1**
Week 12	Mon	Read DH Chap. 15a (pp. 235–47a)	New Testament—Gospels **Do DH Chap. 15, Assignment 1**
	Wed	Read DH Chap. 15b (pp. 247b-254)	New Testament—Gospels **Do DH Chap. 15, Assignment 2**
	Fri	Read DH Chap. 16 (pp. 255–70) **Do DH Chap. 16, Assignment 1**	New Testament—Acts
Week 13	Mon	Read DH Chap. 17a (pp. 271–86a)	New Testament—Revelation **Do DH Chap. 17, Assignment 2**
	Wed	Read DH Chap. 17b (pp. 286b–90)	New Testament—Revelation
	Fri	Read DH Chap. 18 (pp. 291–310)	Old Testament—Narrative
Week 14	Mon		**EXEGETICAL PAPER DUE**
Week 15	Mon	Read DH Chap. 19 (pp. 311–33)	Old Testament—Law **Do DH Chap. 19, Assignment 4**
	Wed	**Do DH Chap. 19, Assignment 2**	
	Fri	Read DH Chap. 20a (pp. 334–48a)	Old Testament—Poetry **Do DH Chap. 20, Assignment 1**
Week 16	Mon	Read DH Chap. 20b (pp. 348b–55)	Old Testament—Poetry **Do DH Chap. 20, Assignment 2**
	Wed	Read DH Chap. 21 (pp. 356–75)	Old Testament—Prophets **Do DH Chap. 21, Assignment 2**
	Fri	*Read DH Chap. 22 (pp. 376–96)*	Old Testament—Wisdom **Do DH Chap. 22, Assignment 1**
Week 17	Fri	*Final Exam Time 3:00-5:00PM* *Extra Inductive Bible Study Assignments Due* *Final Self-Assessment Due* **Scripture Memory Due**	

New Testament I—The Four Gospels: The Life & Teachings of Christ
BIBL 221 (3 credit hours)
Fredrick J. Long

KEY VERSE: 1 Cor 2:16 "For who has known the mind of the Lord, that he will instruct him? But we have the mind of Christ."

FOCAL PARABLE: Treasure in a field and Pearl of Great Value (Matt 13:44–46)

COURSE DESCRIPTION: This course is being offered to help you make an eternal investment. Jesus taught that the Kingdom of God is like treasure hidden in a field, or a pearl of great price (Matt 13:44–46). One should sell all they have to purchase it! Of course, we know that Jesus himself ushered in the Kingdom through his life, death, and resurrection as recorded in the four canonical Gospels. This course is an introduction to the Four Gospels and the person of Jesus Christ. It includes a historical survey of Gospels interpretation (source, form, redaction criticism) as well as more recent approaches such as narrative criticism. Moreover, this course aims at providing a **framework** for how to interpret the Gospels properly and consequently how to apply insights from Jesus (his personal example, teaching, and theology) in one's life and ministry. This **framework** must be informed by an understanding of (1) the historical and cultural setting of Jesus's age, (2) the Gospel writers' motivations and compositional method, (3) a consideration of Jesus's messianic self-consciousness and (4) the origins of Christological reflection in the early Christian community as grounded in Jesus's own interpretation of the Old Testament Scriptures in relation to himself. Caution: The professor is not responsible for any drastic life changes resulting from taking this course.

REQUIRED SOFTWARE and TEXTS:

1. Logos Scholar's Library from Logos Bible Software. This software is to be purchased from Logos Software.
2. ENT= Wenham, David and Steve Walton. *Exploring the New Testament: A Guide to the Gospels and Acts*. Vol.1. Downers Grove, IL: InterVarsity Press, 2001.

OBJECTIVES: Upon completion of this course, students should have a greater understanding of

1. the historical and cultural setting of the NT;
2. the scholarly stages of Jesus research, the main interpreters, assumptions and trends;
3. the arguably best assumptions, methods and goals for studying the Gospels;
4. the central messages in each Gospel, increasing the effectiveness of each student's use of them for devotions, teaching, and preaching;
5. the timeline and significance of Jesus the Messiah's life, death, and resurrection;
6. how to be a better disciple of Christ and apply Christ's teaching in one's life.

CLASS FORMAT: Lecture, discussion of readings, reading reports and reflections, and inductive Bible study assignments, and brief class presentation(s) on these and final paper.

ASSESSMENTS and ASSIGNMENTS

1. <u>Final Reading Report, Self-Evaluation, and Reflection:</u> Essentially, I want you to 1) indicate what percentage of reading you have done; 2) complete a brief one-page self-evaluation on your performance and engagement of the course material, i.e. Gospels, textbooks, and assignments (be honest); and 3) reflect on what you have learned and want to continue to learn in one-page. Due on Monday Dec 13 at our final examination; be prepared to share some things that you have learned in the course of the semester.

2. <u>Written Assignments from ENT:</u> Throughout the course you will be asked to read chapters from <u>ENT</u> and write a one or two page typed (single spaced) response to sections called "Digging Deeper" or What do you think?"

   - **For your planning and record keeping, here are the written <u>Assignments from ENT</u>:**

	Aug 29 WT p.16	Aug 31 WT p.38	Sep 2 DD p.52	Sep 7 DD p.63	Sep 9 WT p.83	Sep 12 DD p.192	Sep 21 WT p.195	Oct 24 DD p.218	Nov 9 WT p.229	Nov 13 DD p.230	Nov 16 DD p.236	Nov 21 DD p.235	Nov 30 DD p.248	Dec 9 DD p.128
Your Assessment:														

3. <u>Inductive Bible Study (IBS) Assignments</u>: Throughout the course you will be asked to perform inductive studies on Gospel passages and segment surveys. Please refer to class notes, examples, and textbooks from Biblical Interpretation Class.

   - **For your planning and record keeping, here are the <u>IBS Assignments</u>:**

	Sep 14 Book Survey of Mark	Sep 19 Disciples' failure	Sep 26 OT in Matt	Sep 30 Seg. Survey of Matt 4-9	Oct 5 Seg. Survey of Matt 5-7	Oct 12 Semantic Analysis of Matt 7:13-27	Oct 19 Seg Survey Matt 13	Oct 26 Seg Survey Matt 24	Oct 31 Seg Survey Matt 25	Nov 2 DA Matt 28:18-20	Nov 18 Lukan Parables	Dec 7 Seg Survey John 17
Your Assessment:												

4. <u>Jesus Profile Paper</u>: double spaced, one-inch margins. A title page may be used. A preliminary paper is due Wednesday Nov 16. Your final paper is due on Dec 5. Please prepare for a five-minute presentation by summarizing your findings on one-page. **Paper Description:**

   a. Develop a profile of Jesus by conducting research (contextual readings, exegesis, word studies, inductive work, etc.) in any of the following areas. If you are in the C and B grade levels, then choose one topic; If the A grade level, then choose two topics:

   -Jesus's attitude of the Poor and the social outcasts—women, the sick, and sinners;
   -Jesus's use of Scripture (in relation to himself or applied to others, etc.);
   -The Spiritual Life of Jesus;   -The Discipling Jesus;
   -Jesus's Kingdom of God;   -The Ethical/Communal Demands of the Kingdom;
   -Jesus, Conflict and Confrontation: When, why, and over What?;
   -<u>or</u> any other reasonable area; just run the "profile category" by me (email).

   b. Your research should come from the Gospels themselves, the readings from <u>ENT</u> and any other relevant books, articles, and essays. Use a consistent format for citation of quotes and ideas from these sources. See statement on plagiarism above.

c. Your Profile of Jesus should include a consideration the relevance of your findings for contemporary church ministry, congregational life, and biblical theology.

d. Your preliminary draft due Nov. 16 will be assessed on 1) the <u>extent</u> and <u>quality</u> of your preliminary research, 2) an initial thesis for each topic (i.e., what conclusions are the evidence/research pointing towards), 3) a workable outline of your paper, and 4) your preliminary presentation of findings (charts, texts, elaborations, etc.).

TENTATIVE CALENDAR

	<u>Readings</u> and Topics **ENT**= Exploring the NT	ENT Assignments and Inductive Assignments (IA)
	Historical Background to the Gospels	
Week 1 Fri	Introduction: Will the real Jesus please stand up? Syllabus	
Week 2 Mon	**ENT**= Chapter 1 Historical Context	ENT 1=Write a one-page report on "What do you think?" in <u>ENT</u> p.16.
Wed	**ENT**= Chapter 2 1st Century Judaism	ENT 2=Write a one-page report on "What do you think?" in <u>ENT</u> p.38.
Fri	**ENT**= Chapter 3 What is a Gospel?	ENT 3=Write a one-page report on "Digging Deeper?" in <u>ENT</u> p.52.
	History of Gospel Studies	
Week 3 Mon	No class	
Wed	**ENT**= Chapter 4 Where did the Gospels come from? pp. 57–80	ENT 4=Write a one-page report on "Digging Deeper" in <u>ENT</u> p.63.
Fri	**ENT**= Chapter 5 Gospel Methods, only pp.81–99	ENT 5=Write a one-page report on "What do you think?" in <u>ENT</u> p.83.
	Gospel of Mark: The Drama of Discipleship	
	Mark 15:39 "When the centurion, who was standing right in front of Him, saw the way He breathed His last, he said, 'Truly this man was the Son of God!'"	
Week 4 Mon	<u>Read Mark's Gospel</u>	ENT 6= Write a one-page report on "Digging Deeper" in <u>ENT</u> p.192. In class do group work.
Wed	**ENT**= Chapter 9 Mark's Gospel Topic=Book Survey of Mark	IA 1= Perform an Inductive Book Survey of Mark's Gospel (4 hours) IA 1= For Non-Inductive People—Create a graphical chart of Mark's Gospel. Consider where the introductory material ends, note any repeated themes or events, and identify where you think the Climax is (4 hours).
Fri	Topic=Book Survey of Mark	

Week 5	Mon	**Read** the narrative contexts of Mark 8:31; 9:30–31; 10:32–34. Topic=The Nature of Discipleship	IA 2= Consider the nature of the disciples' failures (Mark 8:31; 9:30–31; 10:32–34) and Jesus's response to them in what follows (2 hrs).
	Wed	Topic=Fig Tree and Markan Sandwiches	ENT 7= Write a one-page report on "What do you think?" in <u>ENT</u> p.195.
	Fri	Topic=Mark's Ending	

Gospel of Matthew: Teaching Manuel of Discipleship

Matthew 28:18–20 "And Jesus came up and spoke to them, saying, 'All authority has been given to Me in heaven and on earth. 19 Go therefore and make disciples of all the nations, baptizing them in the name of the Father and the Son and the Holy Spirit, 20 teaching them to observe all that I commanded you; and lo, I am with you always, even to the end of the age.'"

Week 6	Mon	**Read** all of the Gospel of Matthew Topic=Jesus's Fulfillment of OT	IA 3= Note all the occurrences of scripture quotation, as you read <u>the Gospel of Matthew</u>. Make a chart to describe this by including the following elements: 1) Reference in Matthew, 2) OT reference, 3) Who's quoting, 4) How is the quote introduced, 5) other important notes, impressions, or questions.
	Wed	**ENT**= Chapter 10 Matthew's Gospel Topic=Matthew's Gospel and Genealogy	
	Fri	**Read** Matt 4:16–9:35 Topic=Structure of Matt 4:17–9:35	IA 4= Segment Survey of Matt 4:16–9:35. Then answer the question, What three activities constitute Jesus's ministry and where are they described or detailed in this segment? (3 hours) IA 4=For Non-Inductive People—Prepare an outline of Matthew 4:17—9:35. Then answer the question looking at 4:23 and 9:35, What three activities constitute Jesus's ministry and where are they described or detailed in 4:17—9:35? (3 hours)
Week 7	Mon	**Read** Matt 5:1–16 **ENT**= Chapter 8 The Teaching of Jesus Topic=Beatitudes & Salt/Light	
	Wed	Topic=Segment Survey of Sermon on the Mount	IA 5=Perform a Segment Survey of Matt 5–7 (4 hrs)
	Fri	**Read** Matt 5:17–48 Topic=Jesus fulfills Law-Prophets	
Week 8	Mon	**Read** closely Matt 6:1–18, 19–34 Topic=Practicing Righteousness Rightly	

	Wed	**Read** closely Matt 7:1–24 Topic=The Conclusion of the Sermon	IA 6=Perform a Semantic Analysis of Matthew 7:13–27. Choose a question that emerges and research it and write up your findings (3 hrs).
Week 9	Mon	**Read** Closely Matthew 10 Topic=The Missionary Discourse	
	Wed	**Read** Matthew 13 ENT= Chapter 5 Parables of Jesus, only pp.100–123 Topic=Parables of the Kingdom	IA 7= Perform a Segment survey of Matthew 13. Consider the theological implications of this study. (3 hours)
	Fri	**Read** Matthew 18 Topic=Sin and Forgiveness	
Week 10	Mon	**Read** Matthew 23 Topic =Failed Leadership & God's Justice	ENT 8=Write a one-page paper on "Digging Deeper" in ENT p.218.
	Wed	**Read** Matthew 24 Topic=Olivet Discourse: Matthew 24	IA 8=Perform a segment survey of Matthew 24 Choose one Structural Relationship, and answer the 4 types of questions for that relationship. (4 hours).
	Fri	*ENT= Chapter 7 The Life of Jesus* Topic=Olivet Discourse cont.	
Week 11	Mon	**Read** Matthew 25. Topic=Parables of Eschatology	IA 9= Perform a Segment Survey of Matthew 25. Then, choose one parable and interpret it using the method in the chapter on Gospels in Grasping God's Word. (3 hours)
	Wed	**Read carefully Matt 28:18–20** Topic=The Great Commission	IA 10= Performa a Detailed Semantic Analysis of Matthew 28:18–20 and sketch out one-page sermon outline. Be sure to organize your points around points derived from a careful reading of the passage in context. Also, consider elaborating these points from examples or other passages in Matthew. (2 hours)

Gospel of Luke: Jesus, Prophet of the New Kingdom Order

Luke 24:27, 44–45 "Then beginning with Moses and with all the prophets, He explained to them the things concerning Himself in all the Scriptures.... 44 Now He said to them, 'These are My words which I spoke to you while I was still with you, that all things which are written about Me in the Law of Moses and the Prophets and the Psalms must be fulfilled.' 45 Then He opened their minds to understand the Scriptures."

Week 12	Mon	**Read** The Gospel of Luke Topic=Intro& Narrative Structure	
	Wed	**Read** Luke 1–2; Malachi 3–4	ENT 9=Write a one-page report on "What do

	ENT= Chapter 11 Luke's Gospel Topic=Preparations for Jesus's Arrival	you think?" in ENT p.229.
Fri	Read Luke 3 and 7 Topic=The Role of John the Baptist	
Week 13 Mon	Read Luke 4–7 Topic=Jesus, The Prophet of Social Justice	ENT 10=Write a one-page report on "Digging Deeper" concerning the Poor in ENT p. 230.
Wed	Topic=The Women in Jesus's Life ***Preliminary Draft Due of Jesus Profile Paper**	ENT 11=Write a one-page report on "Digging Deeper" in ENT p. 236.
Fri	Topic=Seeking and Saving the Lost	IA 11= Look at the Parables of the Good Samaritan (10:25–37) and the Prodigal Son (15:11–32). Study them individually according to Grasping God's Word and compare and contrast their message and applications. Write up results in 1-2 pages (2 hrs).
Week 14 Mon	Read Luke 19–24 Topic=The charges against Jesus	ENT 12=Write a one-page report on "Digging Deeper" in ENT p.235.

Gospel of John: Jesus, God in the Flesh

John 1:18 "No one has seen God at any time; the only begotten God who is in the bosom of the Father, He has explained *Him*."

Week 15 Mon	Read John's Gospel Topics= Introduction & John's Prologue	
Wed	ENT= Chapter 12 John's Gospel	ENT 13=Write a one-page report on "Digging Deeper" in ENT p.248.
Fri	Topic= Nicodemus & Samaritan Woman	
Week 16 Mon	Topic= Transitions in John 12	***JESUS PROFILE PAPER DUE**
Wed	Read John 13–17 Topic= Farewell Discourse of John	IA 12= Perform a Segment Survey of John 17. Relate specifically what Jesus prays for all believers and what implications does that have for Christian living.
Fri	Read John 18–21 ENT= Chapter 6 The Quests for Jesus Topic= The Resurrection	ENT 14=Write a one-page report on "Digging Deeper" in ENT p.128
Week 17 Wed	*Final Exam 3–5 PM* ****FINAL READING REPORT, SELF-EVALUATION, & REFLECTION DUE**** *Topic=What makes Jesus relevant today?*	

NEW TESTAMENT II—Acts and Paul
BIBL 222 (3 credit hours)
Fredrick J. Long

COURSE DESCRIPTION: This course investigates the Book of Acts and the Pauline Epistles in chronological sequence in an effort to understand the missionary efforts of the Early Church. Critical matters of authorship, dating and interpretive methodology are covered. Attention is given to understanding the issues confronting the early church (e.g., Jew/gentile relationship, Law/Grace, Society/Evangelization) and the theology of Paul with a view to fruitful application today.

OBJECTIVES:

Upon completion of this course, students should have a greater understanding of
1. the theological and exegetical issues and conflicts that existed in the early Church;
2. Paul's particular understanding of Jesus as the Christ;
3. how to discern the sections of Paul's letters according to epistolary and rhetorical criticism within the context of Inductive Bible Study Method;
4. how to appropriate personally and communally the theology and message of Paul the Apostle.

REQUIRED TEXTS:

1. Bible; preferably NASB or NASU.
2. **ENT**= Marshall, I. Howard, Stephen Travis and Ian Paul. *Exploring the New Testament: A Guide to the Letters and Revelation.* Vol. 2. Downers Grove, IL: InterVarsity Press, 2002.
3. *Logos Scholar's Library Series X* from Logos Software.

CLASS FORMAT: Lecture, student led classes based on exegetical work, and discussion of assignments along with some in-class group interpretive work. **Additionally, we will be using the online delivery system for this class, for syllabus, lecture notes, announcements, chat rooms, message boards, and turning in and returning of electronic assignments.**

ASSIGNEMENTS AND ASSESSMENTS:

1. <u>Participation in Reading Reflections Message Board Interactions:</u> Throughout the semester you will be asked to read chapters from ENT. For some of these chapters, you will be asked to post one thoughtfully typed (1/2 page) reflection to 8 "Digging Deeper" or "What do you think?" assignments. Other students from the class will then read and reflect as well on these assignments, but they will respond in dialogue (hopefully) to your initial reflection. Then during the semester, you need to post <u>two or more</u> responses to your fellow student's reflections (hopefully in dialogue) in the remaining 6 of the 7 assignments. The assessment of this aspect of class involvement will be coupled with **Class Participation and Engagement** (see 5. below). The basis of your assessment will be the quality (critical, analytical, courteousness, and thoroughness) and quantity

(engagement, dialoguing, etc.) of your reflections and posted responses. **The Message Board for each assignment will be closed one hour before our class starts on the day that it is due for assessment.** We may continue discussing the Message Board in class that day. Sign up below for which reading reflection you will provide to start the Message Board.

	Jan 10 WT p.7	Jan 11 WT p.38	Feb 9 WT p.84	Feb 14 WT p.87	Feb 21 DD p.88	Mar 18 DD p.115	Mar 30 DD p.120	Apr 29 WT p.210
Students providing initial Reflection	1. 2. 3.	1. 2. 3.	1. 2. 3.	1. 2. 3.	1. 2. 3.	1. 2. 3.	1. 2. 3.	1. 2. 3.

2. 40% <u>12 of 14 IBS Assignments</u>. You may choose not to do two of these assignments provided they are <u>not</u> both book surveys. Also **include the time spent** for the completion of that assignment by your name. See the Tentative Calendar for due dates and a more detailed description. **Possible Assessment:** A+ (100), A (95), A- (90), B+ (88), B (85), B- (80), C+ (78), C (75), C- (70), D+ (68), D (65), D- (60), F (no credit).

	Jan 12 BS Galatians	Jan 21 BS 1 Thess	Jan 28 BS 1 Cor	Feb 7 SS 1 Cor 5-6	Feb 16 DA 1 Cor 13	Feb 25 BS Romans	Mar 9 DA Rom 1:18-32	Mar 14 DA Rom 3:21-26	Mar 21 SS Rom 9-11	Apr 1 BS Eph	Apr 6 SS Eph 2	Apr 11 DA Eph 5:15-6:9	Apr 15 BS 2 Tim	Apr 25 DA 2 Tim 3:14-4:5
Your Assessment:														

3. 20% <u>4 Step Up Assignments as Student Study Groups</u>. Collaboration is an essential skill for success in life and ministry. By working with several others on certain assignments, you will benefit from one another's observations, perspectives, questions, explanations, organizational and good humor. You will also need to negotiate differences and learn how to be conscientious and patient with one another. During the semester you will meet with the same group to study together and prepare handouts and study questions and to present material three times during the semester.

There will be three Student Study Groups with 7-8 students in each. During select weeks, one Study Group will be responsible for conducting a class session in which they will present findings, and lead the class in discussion through topics and questions arising from their research in these three areas.

Area	INTERPRETIVE TASKS
World within the Text	1. CONTEXTUAL ANALYSIS
	2. INSIGHTS FROM ORIGINAL LANGUAGES
	3. STRUCTURAL AND CLAUSE RELATIONSHIPS
World concurrent with the Text	4. INTERTEXTUAL CORRELATIONS
	5. KEY WORD(S) AND WORD STUDY
	6. SOCIO-HISTORICAL BACKGROUND
Our World in relation to the Text	7. INTERPRETATION OF OTHERS
	8. EVALUATION AND APPLICATIONS
	9. ILLUSTRATIONS, STORIES, EXAMPLES, AND EXPLANATIONS

Within these three areas are nine possible interpretive tasks. In preparation for conducting the class session, group members will select interpretive tasks with one or two tasks shared by all (I would recommend 8. and 9.). No member should do the same task area more than two times on the four Step Up Assignments. For directions and guidelines for how to complete each task, see uploaded documentation. **On each assignment, include all the members that worked on that assignment, and have them be identified for each portion that they worked on clearly.** Be sure to cite all sources clearly, indicating where ideas and information comes from and where quotations begin and end.

Here are the presentation dates and the Pauline Passages for each Study Group (A, B, or C—please decide upon a group name). Also, I will set up conference rooms for each group online.

Group A Name:		Group B Name:		Group C Name:	
Jan 19 W	Gal 3:19–4:7	Jan 26 W	1 Thess 2:1–12	Feb 4 F	1 Cor 3:1–17
Feb 11 F	1 Cor 9:1–18	Feb 18 F	1 Cor 14:26–40	Feb 23 W	1 Cor 15:20–34
Mar 11 F	Rom 2:1–16	Mar 16 W	Rom 6:1–14	Mar 23 W	Rom 11:11–32
Apr 8 F	Eph 4:1–16	Apr 13 W	Eph 6:10–20	Apr 22 F	2 Tim 2:14–26

NOTE: Some of these passages are negotiable within any given book. Also groups may switch passages with other groups. Before either action is taken, students must obtain permission from the professor.

Grading will be based on quantity of work, quality of work, and presentation and integration of an individual's work with the whole group's presentation. **Possible Assessment per individual participant:** A+ (100), A (95), A- (90), B+ (88), B (85), B- (80), C+ (78), C (75), C- (70), D+ (68), D (65), D- (60), F (no credit).

4. 20% Teaching and Preaching Notebook: **Due in Notebook form at our Final: Apr 29, 1:30–3:30 PM**. This is a compilation of your work (and class lecture notes) from the course, arranged for each letter of Paul as we have covered them in the class chronologically. In addition to your Book Survey work and other interpretive assignments, you may want to consider including more information about

   a. **the epistolary and rhetorical structure** of each of Paul's letters;

   b. **a summary of the theology and main themes** in each letter and how these insights relate to Paul's other letters,

   c. **the relevance for today** in terms of how Paul's message in each letter should affect our thinking, attitudes, values, behaviors and social relations/church life today (**Be Specific!**),

   d. and, **extra handouts, studies** (pertaining to a more detailed inductive or rhetorical outline of a particular passage), **sermon outlines, quotes** (from readings or other sources), **maps, charts**, or **anything else** that might help convey the meaning and message of Jesus as Messiah as proclaimed and taught by Paul (Be creative as long as it is relevant).

5. **20% READING REFLECTIONS** (Message Board Interaction) and **CLASS PARTICIPATION AND ENGAGEMENT:** Your participation and engagement in the subject matter and with professor and fellow students is integral for learning. Far from being a subjective grade criterion, students will be assessed by a combination of observing the quality and quantity of participation in class and out of class (message boards, chat room, emails, etc.) and quantity and quality of engagement on class assignments. You will need to write a <u>Reading Report and Self-Evaluation</u>: Essentially in two pages I want you to (a) indicate what percentage of reading from **FS** you have done; (b) evaluate your own performance and engagement of assignments (be honest) as an individual and group member; (c) report on the most exciting and helpful aspects of the class and the least helpful; and (d) reflect on what you have learned about Paul and want to continue to learn. Due on or before our final examination. **Possible Assessment:** A+ (100), A (95), A- (90), B+ (88), B (85), B- (80), C+ (78), C (75), C- (70), D+ (68), D (65), D- (60), F (no credit).

GRADING SCALE:		EVALUATION SCALE:	
92-100 A	72-77 C	1. IBS Assignments	40 %
90-91 A-	70-71 C-	2. Step-Up Assignments	20 %
88-89 B+	68-69 D+	3. Teaching and Preaching Notebook	20 %
82-87 B	62-67 D	4. Reading Reflections (Message Board Participation) and Reading Report and Self-Evaluation	20 %
80-81 B-	60-61 D-		=100 %
78-79 C+	1-59 F		

TENTATIVE CALENDAR

		Assignments due this Day ENT=Exploring the New Testament	Topic in Class
Week 1	**Jan 7** F		• Introduction; • Pauline Methods ENT ch. 2
Week 2	**Jan 10** M	<u>Reading Reflection #1:</u> Read ENT Ch.1 and reflect on "What do you think?" (p.7)	• **ACTS Survey** • Studies in Acts
	Jan 12 W	<u>IBS #1:</u> Perform a Book Survey of Galatians (4 hours)	• Studies in Acts
	Jan 14 F	Read ENT Ch.4	• **Galatians Survey**
Week 3	**Jan 17** M	<u>Reading Reflection #2:</u> Read ENT Ch. 3 and reflect on "What do you think?" (p.38)	• Paul's Conversion • Gal 1–2 & Acts Chronology
	Jan 19 W	**Step Up #1A: Gal 3:19–4:7**	• Step Up
	Jan 21 F	<u>IBS #2:</u> Perform a Book Survey of 1 Thessalonians (4 hours)	• Inductive Studies in Galatians
Week 4	**Jan 24** M	Read ENT Ch.5	• **1 Thessalonians Survey**
	Jan 26 W	**Step Up #2B: 1 Thess 2:1–12**	• Step Up
	Jan 28 F	<u>IBS #3:</u> Perform a Book Survey of 1 Corinthians (6 hours)	• Paul's Arguments as Epicheiremes

Week 5	**Jan 31** M	Read ENT ch. 6	• **1 Corinthians Survey**
	Feb 2 W		• 1 Cor 1–4
	Feb 4 F	**Step Up #3C: 1 Cor 3:1–17**	• Step Up
Week 6	**Feb 7** M	IBS #4: Perform a Segment Survey of 1 Corinthians 5–6 (4 hours)	• 1 Cor 5–6
	Feb 9 W	Reading Reflection #3: Reflect on "What do you think?" (p.84)	• 1 Cor 7
	Feb 11 F	**Step Up #4A: 1 Cor 9:1–18**	• Step Up
Week 7	**Feb 14** M	Reading Reflection #4: Reflect on "What do you think?" (p.87)	• 1 Cor 11
	Feb 16 W	IBS #5: Perform a Detailed Analysis of 1 Cor 13 and focus on answering one question that arises in this process (3 hours).	• 1 Cor 13
	Feb 18 F	**Step Up #5B: 1 Cor 14:26–40**	• Step Up
Week 8	**Feb 21** M	Reading Reflection #5: Reflect on "Digging Deeper" on 1 Cor 15:36–58 (on p.88)	• 1 Cor 15
	Feb 23 W	**Step Up #6C: 1 Cor 15:20–34**	• Step Up
	Feb 25 F	IBS #6: Perform a Book Survey of Romans (6 hours)	• Move into 2 Corinthians
	Spring Break Feb. 26–Mar 6		
Week 9	**Mar 7** M	Read ENT Ch.8	• **Romans Survey**
	Mar 9 W	IBS #7: Perform a Detailed Analysis on Romans 1:18–32 (2 hours)	• Rom 1
	Mar 11 F	**Step Up #7A: Rom 2:1–16**	• Step Up
Week 10	**Mar 14** M	IBS #8: Perform a Detailed Analysis of Rom 3:21–26 and answer the question, "How has God demonstrated his justice in the gospel?" If necessary, track the theme of justification through Romans and Paul's letters (4 hours).	• Rom 3
	Mar 16 W	**Step Up #8B: Rom 6:1–14**	• Step Up
	Mar 18 F	Reading Reflection #6: Reflect on "Digging Deeper" (p.115)	• Rom 7–8
Week 11	**Mar 21** M	IBS #9: Perform a Segment Survey of Rom 9–11 (4 hours)	• Rom 9–11

	Mar 23 W	Step Up #9C: Rom 11:11–32	• Step Up
Week 12	Mar 30 W	Reading Reflection #7: Reflect On "Digging Deeper" (p.120)	• Rom 12–13
	Apr 1 F	IBS #10: Perform a Book Survey of Ephesians (4 hours)	• Rom 14–16
Week 13	Apr 4 M	Read ENT Ch.12	**• Ephesians Survey**
	Apr 6 W	IBS #11: Perform a Segment Survey of Ephesians 2 (3 hours)	• Eph 2
	Apr 8 F	**Step Up #10A: Eph 4:1–16**	• Step Up
Week 14	Apr 11 M	IBS #12: Track Paul's Argument in Eph 5:15–6:9 through the construction of an expository outline; then answer the question, "How is each type of person in this section to submit to one another in the Lord?" (2 hours)	• Eph 5
	Apr 13 W	**Step Up #11B: Eph 6:10–20=**	• Step Up
	Apr 15 F	IBS #13: Perform a Book Survey of 2 Timothy (4 hours)	• Philippians 2
Week 15	Apr 18 M	Read ENT Ch. 13	• Pastorals
	Apr 20 W		**• 2 Timothy Survey**
	Apr 22 F	**Step Up #12C: 2 Tim 2:14–26**	• Step Up
Week 16	Apr 25 M	IBS #14: Perform a Detailed Analysis of 2 Tim 3:14–4:5 and answer the questions, "What are the purposes of the Word of God?" and "What are our responsibilities as ministers of it?" (3 hours)	• Pastorals
	Apr 27 W	*Preparation Day*	

Final Exam Time: Friday Apr 29 1:30–3:30 PM
Due: Reading Reflection #8: Read ENT ch. 14 and reflect on "What do you think?" (p.210)
Due: Reading Report and Self Evaluation
Due: Teaching and Preaching Notebook

New Testament III—The General Epistles and Revelation
BIBL 223 (3 credit hours)
Fredrick J. Long

COURSE DESCRIPTION: This course is a detailed investigation of the General Epistles (Hebrews through Jude) and the Book of Revelation. Critical matters of authorship, dating and interpretive methodology are treated. Careful consideration is given to understanding the theology of these books and their appropriate application for today's church.

OBJECTIVES: Upon completion of this course, students will have a greater understanding of
1. the historical and cultural setting of the NT;
2. the critical issues relating to the study of this portion of the NT (dating, authorship, etc.);
3. the arguably best assumptions, methods and goals for studying Hebrews, the General Epistles and Revelation;
4. the central messages in each of these books, therefore increasing the effectiveness of each student's use of them for devotions, teaching, and preaching;
5. the issues and conflicts that existed in the early Church;
6. the theological coherence and diversity of the NT as studied through these particular NT books;
7. how to be a better disciple of Christ and apply Christ's teaching in one's life.

CLASS FORMAT: Lecture, discussion, and student presentations. Overall, I would like us to approach this class as a "think-tank" for open inquiry, discussion, and questions.

REQUIRED TEXTS:
1. *Logos Scholar's Library Series X* from Logos Bible Software.
2. I. H. Marshall, S. Travis, I. Paul, eds. *Exploring the New Testament: A Guide to the Letters and Revelation.* Vol. 2, Downers Grove, IL: InterVarsity Press, 2002.
3. Steve Gregg, ed. *Revelation: Four Views, A Parallel Commentary.* Nashville: Thomas Nelson, 1997.

ASSIGNMENTS and ASSESMENTS:
1. <u>Attendance and Class Participation</u> and <u>Final Reading Report, Self-Evaluation, and Reflection</u> (10%) Since learning is a social activity, your thoughtful participation in class is encouraged. The entire class benefits when each student engages the material under investigation. In this case, it is the Word of God, which contains much that should intrigue and inspire us, surprise or even startle us. You will have opportunities to ask questions about its meaning and applications today.

For your <u>Final Reading Report, Self-Evaluation, and Reflection</u>, essentially, I want you to a) indicate what percentage of reading you have done; b) complete a brief one-page self-evaluation on your performance and engagement of the course material and assignments (be honest); and c) reflect on what you have learned and want to continue to learn in one-page. Due at our final examination. Also, be prepared to share some things that you have learned in the course of the semester. **Possible assessment given: 0–100.**

2. <u>Inductive Assignments:</u> (50%) There are 19 inductive assignments throughout the semester that involve some aspect of inductive work on a selected NT passage such as a book or segment survey, a detailed analysis of a pericope, interpretation of a specified interpretive question, etc. You need to only get credit for 17 of them. **For descriptions, see after the TENTATIVE CALENDAR.** For your planning and record keeping, here is a listing of the <u>Inductive Bible Study Assignments</u>:

	Jas Survey	James 2 synth.	James synth.	1Pet Survey	1P SegStd	1Pet Synth	2Pet Survey	2Pe Interp	1Jo Survey	1Jo Interp	Jude Survey	Heb Survey
Your Assessment:												
	Heb 2 DA	Heb 5–6	Heb 8–10	Heb Interp	Heb Faith	Heb Synth	Rev Survey	Net Balance Calculation on <u>best</u> 17 assignments=				
Your Assessment:												

3. <u>ENT Assignments</u> and <u>Gregg Comparison/Contrast Reports</u>: (20%) There are 12 of these assignments. The <u>ENT</u> assignments are described in the calendar and in the book. For the Gregg Comparison/Contrast Reports, what you need to do is, as you read through Revelation and the commentary in Gregg, <u>focus particularly on two types of interpretations</u> of that portion of the text (these are Futurist, Spiritual, Preterist, and Historicist and are conveniently placed in columns in Gregg). Briefly summarize these two positions, compare and contrast them. Then consider which you think is preferred given the two, or indicate what problems questions you may have with them. For your planning and record keeping, here is a listing of these assignments and reports:

	Jan.14 ENT p.254	Jan.19 ENT p.257	Jan.30 ENT p.267	Feb.16 ENT p.289	Feb.25 ENT p.293	Apr.7 Gregg pp.51-82	Apr.14 Gregg pp.83-142	Apr.16 Gregg pp.143-216	Apr.19 Gregg pp.217-308	Apr.21 Gregg pp.309-98	Apr.23 Gregg pp.399-456	Apr.26 Gregg pp.457-506
Your Assessment												

4. <u>Teaching and Preaching Notebook:</u> (20%) Due the last day of class. Basically, for each NT book covered (Hebrews through Revelation), I would like to see a well-organized notebook containing your work, class notes and other handouts, as well as additional articles, maps, charts, sermon outlines, or any other material that you would want to draw upon in future preparation for teaching or preaching. **Possible assessment given: 0–100.**

GRADING SCALE:		**EVALUATION SCALE:**	
92-100 A	72-77 C	1) Class Participation and Final Reading Report and Self-Assessment	10 %
90-91 A-	70-71 C-		
88-89 B+	68-69 D+	2) Inductive Assignments	50 %
82-87 B	62-67 D	3) <u>ENT</u> Assignments and <u>Gregg</u> Comparison/Contrast Reports	20 %
80-81 B-	60-61 D-		
78-79 C+	1-59 F	4) Teaching/Preaching Notebook	20 % = 100 %

TENTATIVE CALENDAR

	Assignment for each Class Note that Reading and Assignments are to be done <u>before</u> the class period on which they are presented below.	
	Gregg= <u>Revelation Four Views</u>	
	Reading and/or Assignments due this Day	• Topic in Class
Week 1		
	<div align="center">## James</div>	
<u>F</u> (Jan. 9)		• Introduction and Syllabus • Detailed Analysis of James 1
Week 2		
<u>M</u> (Jan. 12)	**Assignment #1 James Book Survey (4 hrs)**	• Detailed Analysis of James 1 • Survey of James
<u>W</u> (Jan.14)	Read <u>ENT</u> ch.17 and write a one-page response to What do you think? p.254	• Survey of James • Parallels with James to Sermon on Mount
<u>F</u> (Jan. 16)	**Assignment #2 Detailed Analysis and Interpretation of James 2 (2 hrs)**	• Detailed Analysis of James 2
Week 3		
<u>M</u> (Jan. 19)	Finish Reading <u>ENT</u> ch.17, write a one-page report on Digging Deeper on p. 257	• Inductive Studies on James 3–4
<u>W</u> (Jan.21)		• Inductive Studies on James 5
<u>F</u> (Jan. 23)	**Assignment #3 Book Synthesis of James based upon the Person of God (4 hrs)**	• Book Synthesis of James
Week4		
	<div align="center">## 1 Peter</div>	
<u>M</u> (Jan. 26)	Read <u>ENT</u>, ch.18	• Detailed Analysis of 1 Peter 1
<u>W</u> (Jan. 28)	**Assignment #4 1 Peter Book Survey (4 hrs)**	• Survey of 1 Peter
<u>F</u> (Jan. 30)	<u>ENT</u>, ch.18, write a <u>two</u> page response to Digging Deeper on p. 267	• Survey of 1 Peter • Israel and the Church Issue
Week 5		
<u>M</u> (Feb. 2)	**Assignment #5 Segment Study of 1 Peter 1:17–4:6 (3 hrs)**	• Inductive Studies on 1 Peter 1:17–4:6
<u>W</u> (Feb.4)	reread p.268 <u>ENT</u>	• Special Study in 1 Peter 3
<u>F</u> (Feb. 6)	**Assignment #6 Synthesis of 1 Peter through the general statement of "true grace" in 5:12 (3 hrs)**	• Towards a Theology of 1 Peter through the concept of "grace"

Week 6		
	<div align="center">**2 Peter**</div>	
M (Feb. 9)	**Assignment #7 2 Peter Book Survey (3 hrs)**	• Survey of 2 Peter
W (Feb.11)	Read ENT ch. 19	• Authorship of 2 Peter
F (Feb. 13)	**Assignment #8 Answer Survey Questions Relating to Recurrence of Contrast with Causation (3 hrs)**	• Explore Recurrence of Contrast with Causation in 2 Peter
Week 7		
	<div align="center">**1, 2, 3 John**</div>	
M (Feb. 16)	**Read ENT ch. 20 and write a one-page response to What do you think? p.289**	• Introduction to Johannine Letters
W (Feb. 18)	**Assignment #9 Survey of 1 John (4 hrs)**	• Survey of 1 John
F (Feb. 20)		• Inductive Studies of 1 John
Week 8		
M (Feb.23)	**Assignment #10 Interpretation of the Old and New Command in 1 John 2:7–8 (2 hrs)**	• Old and New Commands in 1 John 2:7–8
W (Feb.25)	**ENT ch. 20; write a one-page response to Digging Deeper on p. 293**	• Knowledge in 1 John
	<div align="center">**Jude**</div>	
F (Feb.27)	**Assignment # 11 Survey of Jude (2 hrs)**	• Survey of Jude
Week 9		
	<div align="center">**Hebrews**</div>	
M (Mar. 8)	**Read ENT ch. 16**	• Detailed Analysis of Hebrews 1:1–3
W (Mar.10)	**Assignment #12 Hebrews Book Survey (5 hrs)**	• Survey of Hebrews
F (Mar. 12)		• Survey of Hebrews
Week 10		
M (Mar. 15)	**Assignment #13 Detailed analysis of Hebrews 2 (3 hrs)**	• Detailed Analysis of Hebrews 2
W (Mar.17)		• Detailed Analysis of Hebrews 2
F (Mar. 19)	**Assignment #14 Segment Survey of Hebrews 5:11–6:20 (3 hrs)**	• Segment Survey of Heb 5:11–6:20
Week 11		
M (Mar. 22)	**Assignment #15 Segment Survey of Hebrews 8:1–10:18 (3 hrs)**	• Segment Survey of Heb 8:1–10:18

W (Mar. 24)		• Segment Survey of Heb 8:1–10:18
F (Mar. 26)	**Assignment #16 Interpretation of "Perfect in Conscience" in 9:9 (3 hrs)**	• Interpretation of 9:9
Week 12		
M (Mar. 29)	**Assignment #17 Study of Faith in Hebrews 11 (2 hrs)**	• Study on Faith in Hebrews 11
W (Mar. 31)	**Assignment #18 Hebrews Book Synthesis through Christ's Roles and Agency (4 hrs)**	• Hebrews Book Synthesis • Theological High Points in Hebrews
	<div align="center">**Revelation**</div>	
F (Apr. 2)	**Gregg "Introduction" (pp. 1–50)**	• Introduction to Revelation • Revelation 1
Week 13		
M (Apr. 5)	**Assignment #19 Book Survey of Revelation (5 hrs)**	• Survey of Revelation
W (Apr. 7)	**Read Gregg on Rev 1–3 (pp. 51–82) and do Comparison/Contrast Report**	• Structure of Revelation 1–3
F (Apr. 9)	<div align="center">Easter Break</div>	
Week 14		
M (Apr. 12)	<div align="center">Easter Break</div>	
W (Apr. 14)	**Read Gregg on Rev 4–7 (pp. 83–142) and do Comparison/Contrast Report**	• Structure of Revelation 4–7
F (Apr. 16)	**Read Gregg on Rev 8–10 (pp. 143–216) and do Comparison/Contrast Report**	• Structure of Revelation 8–10
Week 15		
M (Apr. 19)	**Read Gregg on Rev 8–10 (pp. 217–308) and do Comparison/Contrast Report**	• Structure of Revelation 11–13
W (Apr. 21)	**Read Gregg on Rev 14–16 (pp. 309–398) and do Comparison/Contrast Report**	• Structure of Revelation 14–16
F (Apr. 23)	**Read Gregg on Rev 17–19 (pp. 399–456) and do Comparison/Contrast Report**	• Structure of Revelation 17–19
Week 16		
M (Apr. 26)	• **Read Gregg on Rev 20 (pp. 457–506) and do Comparison/Contrast Report** • **Turn in Preaching and Teaching Notebook**	• Structure of Revelation 20–22
Finals Week		
Thurs (May 1)	<u>Final Exam 1:30 PM</u> **Turn in Reading Report, Self-Evaluation, and Reflection**	

INDUCTIVE ASSIGNMENTS

Assignment #1: Book Survey of James (4 hrs)
1. Identify general literary form (poetry, discursive and logical, letter, historical, etc.).
2. Give chapter headings for each chapter (two or three words maximum).
3. <u>Locate</u> the Major divisions and sub-divisions of the book and <u>identify</u> the major Laws of Composition (structural relationships) operative in the book (introduction, summarization, causation, etc.). **Be prepared to share this structure in class.**
4. Ask 4 types of interpretive questions for each str. relationship observed (what?, how?).
5. Summarize strategic areas from str. relationships identified.
6. Identify data that bears on such questions as authorship, audience, date of writing, etc.
7. Note other important impressions about the book (tone of author, atmosphere, etc.)
8. Indicate on the top of the first page how much time you spent on this assignment.

Assignment #2: Perform an interpretation of James 2:14–26 following these steps (2 hrs):
1. State in your own words the main principle set forth in 2:14–26.
2. Trace the lines of reasoning James employs to substantiate this main principle.
3. Answer these questions: In what sense were Abraham and Rahab justified by their works? What is the complete and precise relationship between faith and works?
4. Be prepared to discuss your work and questions in class.
5. Indicate on the top of the first page how much time you spent on this assignment.

Assignment #3: Book Synthesis of James based upon the Person of God (4 hrs).
1. There is something interesting about James: throughout the letter God is multifariously portrayed: Master (1:1; 4:7); Benefactor (1:5, 18, 21; 2:5; 4:6); the "Father of Lights" (1:17, 27); as righteous and the one who sets standards of righteousness (1:20, 27; 2:5, 23; 4:4); Friend (2:23); as good (1:13) and as one (2:19); and Lord (1:1; 2:1; 3:9; 4:10; 5:4, 7–8, 10, 11, 14, 15); Judge (1:12; 4:8, 8; 5:9), etc.
2. As you synthesize the message of the Book of James consider what these various portraits of God contribute to understanding **how we ought to live**.
3. Do you notice any patterns or general movements in the order or emphasis of how God is portrayed?
4. Indicate on the top of the first page how much time you spent on this assignment.

Assignment #4: Book Survey of 1 Peter (4 hrs)
1. Identify general literary form (poetry, discursive and logical, letter, historical, etc.).
2. Give chapter headings for each chapter (two or three words maximum).
3. <u>Locate</u> the Major divisions and sub-divisions of the book and <u>identify</u> the major Laws of Composition (structural relationships) operative in the book (introduction, summarization, causation, etc.). **Be prepared to share this structure in class.**
4. Ask 4 types of interpretive questions for each str. relationship observed (what?, how?).

5. Summarize strategic areas from str. relationships identified.
6. Identify data that bears on such questions as authorship, audience, date of writing, etc.
7. Note other important impressions about the book (tone of author, atmosphere, etc.)
8. Indicate on the top of the first page how much time you spent on this assignment.

Assignment #5: Segment Study of 1 Peter 1:17–4:6 (3 hrs)
1. Using the skills in Bible Study method that you have developed, do an original study of this section. Indicate clearly the steps you followed, and the findings made in each step.
2. Note especially
    (a) how 1:17–2:10 relates to 2:11–4:6;
    (b) how 2:11 relates to 4:1–6;
    (c) and how is 2:12 is particularized in 2:12–3:22.
3. Indicate on the top of the first page how much time you spent on this assignment.

Assignment #6: Synthesis of 1 Peter through the general statement of "true grace" in 5:12 (3 hrs.)
1. Peter ends the letter with a general statement in 5:12 in which he identifies that in his exhorting and testifying he has related the "true grace" to them.
2. What is meant by the "true grace"?
3. How does 5:12 generalize the letter?
4. Why does Peter make this generalization and command that they should "stand firm in it."
5. What are the implications?
6. Indicate on the top of the first page how much time you spent on this assignment.

Assignment #7: Book Survey of 2 Peter (3 hrs)
1. Identify general literary form (poetry, discursive and logical, letter, historical, etc.).
2. Give chapter headings for each chapter (two or three words maximum).
3. <u>Locate</u> the Major divisions and sub-divisions of the book and <u>identify</u> the major Laws of Composition (structural relationships) operative in the book (introduction, summarization, causation, etc.). **Be prepared to share this structure in class.**
4. Ask 4 types of interpretive questions for each str. relationship observed (what?, how?).
5. Summarize strategic areas from str. relationships identified.
6. Identify data that bears on such questions as authorship, audience, date of writing, etc.
7. Note other important impressions about the book (tone of author, atmosphere, etc.)
8. Indicate on the top of the first page how much time you spent on this assignment.

Assignment #8: (3 hrs) Answer the following questions relating to the Structural Observation of Recurrence of Contrast with Causation between the godly and ungodly (cause) and their contrasting fates (effect):

    Godly (farsighted/see) vs. Ungodly (nearsighted/blind)
    1:5–8, 10–21; 3:1–2, 8–15   1:9; ch.2; 3:3–7, 16, 17
    ↓   ↓
    <u>**Fate**</u>: rich welcome in kingdom   condemnation/destruction
    1:11; 2:5, 9; 3:13   2:3–10, 13; 3:9, 12

Questions:
1. What specific elements are being contrasted between the godly and ungodly?
2. What specifically are the meanings of two of these elements? (Briefly perform a word study.)
3. How do all the recurring elements relate to one another?
4. What factors are involved in the movement from **cause** (godliness vs. godlessness) to **effect** (their respective fates) as described in 2 Peter?
5. How does the **effect** (their ultimate fate) illuminate the **cause** and vice-versa?
6. Why this recurrence of contrast with causation?
7. What are the implications for understanding the Gospel of Christ and for living today?

<u>Assignment #9:</u> Book Survey of 1 John (4 hrs)
1. Identify general literary form (poetry, discursive and logical, letter, historical, etc.).
2. Give chapter headings for each chapter (two or three words maximum).
3. <u>Locate</u> the Major divisions and sub-divisions of the book and <u>identify</u> the major Laws of Composition (structural relationships) operative in the book (introduction, summarization, causation, etc.). **Be prepared to share this structure in class.**
4. Ask 4 types of interpretive questions for each str. relationship observed (what?, how?).
5. Summarize strategic areas from str. relationships identified.
6. Identify data that bears on such questions as authorship, audience, date of writing, etc.
7. Note other important impressions about the book (tone of author, atmosphere, etc.)
8. Indicate on the top of the first page how much time you spent on this assignment.

<u>Assignment #10:</u> Interpretation of the Old and New Command in 1 John 2:7–8 (2 hrs)
1. In 2:7–8 John talks about a "new command" and an "old command." It is difficult to sort out precisely what each of these commands is.
2. Look carefully at the surrounding context and the development of his argument and try to determine exactly what each of these commands is.
3. Explain your findings. Indicate how much time you spent.

<u>Assignment #11:</u> Book Survey of Jude (2 hrs)
1. Identify general literary form (poetry, discursive and logical, letter, historical, etc.).
2. Give paragraph headings for each paragraph (two or three words maximum).
3. <u>Locate</u> the Major divisions and sub-divisions of the book and <u>identify</u> the major Laws of Composition (structural relationships) operative in the book (introduction, summarization, causation, etc.). **Be prepared to share this structure in class.**
4. Ask 4 types of interpretive questions for each str. relationship observed (what?, how?).
5. Summarize strategic areas from str. relationships identified.
6. Identify data that bears on such questions as authorship, audience, date of writing, etc.
7. Note other important impressions about the book (tone of author, atmosphere, etc.)
8. Indicate on the top of the first page how much time you spent on this assignment.

Assignment #12: Book Survey of Hebrews (5 hours)
1. Identify general literary form (poetry, discursive and logical, letter, historical, etc.).
2. Give chapter headings for each chapter (two or three words maximum).
3. <u>Locate</u> the Major divisions and sub-divisions of the book and <u>identify</u> the major Laws of Composition (structural relationships) operative in the book (introduction, summarization, causation, etc.). **Be prepared to share this structure in class.**
4. Ask 4 types of interpretive questions for each str. relationship observed (what?, how?).
5. Summarize strategic areas from str. Relationships identified.
6. Identify data that bears on such questions as authorship, audience, date of writing, etc.
7. Note other important impressions about the book (tone of author, atmosphere, etc.)
8. Indicate on the top of the first page how much time you spent on this assignment.

Assignment #13: Perform a detailed analysis of Heb 2:1–18 following my example for Heb 1:1–3 (3 hrs)
1. Start by identifying sections and subsections and respective structural relationships.
2. Using outlining, arrows, diagrams, charts, categories, underlining—whatever may be helpful—display the argument structure and progression of thought, while identifying the structural relationships.
3. Be sure to locate key interpretive questions from the text that deserve further attention (but are outside this assignment) or that you would like to return to.
4. **<u>Be sure</u>** also to draw theological inferences or conclusions from your work about the nature of the salvation that Christ brings to humanity.
5. Be prepared to discuss your work and questions in class.
6. Indicate on the top of the first page how much time you spent on this assignment.

Assignment #14: Perform a Segment Survey of Hebrews 5:11–6:20 (3 hrs).
1. Give paragraph headings for each paragraph (two or three words maximum).
2. <u>Locate</u> the major breaks in the segment and <u>identify</u> the major structural relationships operative in the segment (introduction, summarization, causation, etc.). **Be prepared to share this structure in class.**
3. Ask 4 types of interpretive questions for each str. relationship observed (what?, how?).
4. Summarize strategic areas from str. relationships identified.
5. Identify data that bears on such questions as authorship, audience, date of writing, etc.
6. Note other important impressions about the book (tone of author, atmosphere, etc.)
7. Indicate on the top of the first page how much time you spent on this assignment.

Assignment #15: Segment Survey of Hebrews 8:1–10:18 (3 hrs)
1. Give paragraph headings for each paragraph (two or three words maximum).
2. <u>Locate</u> the major breaks in the segment and <u>identify</u> the major structural relationships operative in the segment (introduction, summarization, causation, etc.). **Be prepared to share this structure in class.**

3. Ask 4 types of interpretive questions for each str. relationship observed (what?, how?).
4. Summarize strategic areas from str. relationships identified.
5. Identify data that bears on such questions as authorship, audience, date of writing, etc.
6. Note other important impressions about the book (tone of author, atmosphere, etc.)
7. Indicate on the top of the first page how much time you spent on this assignment.

Assignment #16: Interpretation of "Perfect in Conscience" in 9:9 (3 hrs)
1. Perform an Interpretation answering the following question: What does the phrase "perfect in conscience" mean in Hebrews 9:9 as relates to the life of the believer presented therein?
2. Be sure to look at word meanings and book context primarily. Consult the interpretation of others as time permits.
3. Indicate how much time you spend on this assignment.

Assignment #17: Study of Faith in Hebrews 11 (2 hrs)
1. As a preliminary exercise, define faith to the best of your ability.
2. How does the author of Hebrews define faith? (See 11:1, 13, 39–40.)
3. How does the author of Hebrews' definition of faith relate to its context?
4. Why does the author discuss faith from the perspective of the argument in the whole book?
5. Indicate how much time you spend on this assignment.

Assignment #18: Hebrews Book Synthesis through Christ's Roles and Agency (4 hrs)
1. Throughout Hebrews Christ is described in various ways often with some title (see e.g., 1:1–4; 2:14–18; 3:1–6; 4:14–5:10; 6:20; 9:11–15, 23–28; 12:1–3; 13:20–21).
2. As you study such passages, indicate
    (a) the descriptive title for Christ and what it means in context,
    (b) what Christ did/accomplished in relation to that title for humanity,
    (c) and the potential or intended impact of this accomplishment/role for the ongoing life of believers.
3. Indicate how much time you spend on this assignment.

Assignment #19: Book Survey of Revelation (5 hours)
1. Identify general literary form (poetry, discursive and logical, letter, historical, etc.).
2. Give chapter headings for each chapter (two or three words maximum).
3. <u>Locate</u> the Major divisions and sub-divisions of the book and <u>identify</u> the major Laws of Composition (structural relationships) operative in the book (introduction, summarization, causation, etc.). **Be prepared to share this structure in class.**
4. Ask 4 types of interpretive questions for each str. relationship observed (what?, how?).
5. Summarize strategic areas from str. relationships identified.
6. Identify data that bears on such questions as authorship, audience, date of writing, etc.
7. Note other important impressions about the book (tone of author, atmosphere, etc.)
8. Indicate on the top of the first page how much time you spent on this assignment.

Contemporary Critical Issues in Biblical Studies
BIBL 470 (2 credit hours)
Fredrick J. Long

COURSE DESCRIPTION: A capstone course that draws contemporary critical issues in Bible, Biblical Theology, and hermeneutics together. This year our focus is on "exploring the hermeneutics of cultural analysis" based upon William Webb's book. As such, this course will supplement the Inductive Bible Study method by filling out our understanding of and practice of the steps of evaluation, application, and correlation.

OBJECTIVES: Upon completion of this course, students should have a greater understanding of
1. the critical place within biblical interpretation, and specifically Inductive Bible Study Method, that evaluation, application, and correlation occupy;
2. the exegetical, theological, and hermeneutical issues that exist when attempting to faithfully apply Scripture to one's own contemporary setting;
3. a hierarchy of principles to assist one in this attempt to faithfully apply Scripture;
4. and, lastly, to better understand the biblical topics of slavery, women, and homosexuality in light of this task of attempting to faithfully apply Scripture to one's own contemporary setting.

CLASS FORMAT: Since this is a capstone course for biblical studies, we will be adopting a seminar format that assumes that students will openly participate and discuss course content with the professor; there will be some lecture material presented. **Note:** Due to the nature of the course content, and the need for us all to speak frankly and openly, I will ask that the comments, questions, and propositions discussed in our class not be repeated outside of class with indiscretion, but rather with the utmost respect for the persons involved.

REQUIRED TEXTS:
1. William J. Webb, *Slaves, Women & Homosexuals: Exploring the Hermeneutics of Cultural Analysis*. Downers Grove, IL: InterVarsity Press, 2001.
2. *Logos Scholar's Library Series X* from Logos Software.

ASSIGNEMENTS AND ASSESSMENTS:

1. 20% **Participation and Engagement in the Class:** Your participation and engagement in the subject matter and with professor and fellow students is integral for learning. Far from being a subjective grade criterion, students will be assessed by a combination of observing the quality and quantity of participation in class and out of class and quantity and quality of engagement on class assignments. You will need to write a Reading Report and Self-Evaluation: Essentially in two pages I want you to (a) indicate what percentage of reading from Webb you have done; (b) evaluate your own performance and engagement of assignments (be honest); (c) reflect on what you have learned about evaluation, application, and correlation. Due on final examination. **Possible Assessment:** A+ (100), A (95), A- (90), B+ (88), B (85), B- (80), C+ (78), C (75), C- (70), D+ (68), D (65), D- (60), F (no credit).

2. 30% **Chapter Summaries with Facilitation of Discussion:** Three times in the semester, each student will have the opportunity to summarize and facilitate discussion on a criterion for the class session (see criteria, calendar, and sign up below). One may disagree, modify, ponder about the relative value or placement of the criteria, or the suitableness of Webb's examples to illustrate them. All other persons will come to class prepared to engage the book material. *It is also encouraged that students dovetail their work by considering how their final paper topic (see below) may relate to the particular criterion treated that day.* **Possible Assessment:** A+ (100), A (95), A- (90), B+ (88), B (85), B- (80), C+ (78), C (75), C- (70), D+ (68), D (65), D- (60), F (no credit).

Part I: Toward a Hermeneutic of Cultural Analysis
    2a. A Model for the Redemptive-Movement Hermeneutic   30–55 _____
    2b-3. A Rationale for the Redemptive-Movement Hermeneutic 55–70 _____

Part II: Intrascriptural Criteria
    4. Persuasive Criteria
        Criterion 1: Preliminary Movement   73 _____
        Criterion 2: Seed Ideas   83 _____
        Criterion 3: Breakouts   91 _____
        Criterion 4: Purpose/Intent Statements   105 _____
        Criterion 5: Basis in Fall or Curse   110 _____
    5. Moderately Persuasive Criteria
        Criterion 6: Basis in Original Creation, Section 1: Patterns   123 _____
        Criterion 7: Basis in Original Creation, Section 2: Primogeniture 134 _____
        Criterion 8: Basis in New Creation   145 _____
        Criterion 9: Competing Options   152 _____
        Criterion 10: Opposition to Original Culture   157 _____
        Criterion 11: Closely Related Issues   162 _____
        Criterion 12: Penal Code   172 _____
        Criterion 13: Specific Instructions Versus General Principles 179 _____
    6. Inconclusive Criteria
        Criterion 14: Basis in Theological Analogy   185 _____
        Criterion 15: Contextual Comparisons   192 _____
        Criterion 16: Appeal to the Old Testament   201 _____

Part III: Extrascriptural Criteria
    7. Persuasive Extrascriptural Criteria
        Criterion 17: Pragmatic Basis Between Two Cultures   209 _____
        Criterion 18: Scientific and Social-Scientific Evidence   221 _____
    8. What if I'm Wrong?   236 _____
    Conclusion   245 _____
    Appendices A & B   257 _____
    Appendices C & D   269 _____

3. 50% **Preparation for and Final Paper on a topic of your choice:** Essentially, select from one of these topics (check with professor) and go through the procedure that Webb follows for the determination of what is transcultural in Scriptures on this topic and the relevance this has in today's life and thought.

   1. Sabbath Observance
   2. War/Killing
   3. Fornication
   4. Tithing (10% required still, or something else)
   5. Divorce and Remarriage
   6. Creationism (What are believers expected to believe)
   7. Historicism of Gen 1–11 (Historicity of Adam and Eve, or Flood, etc.)
   8. OT Land and Temple Fulfillment (Should we expect a temple in God's future plan?)
   9. Church Organization (elder board, or Overseer, or Charismatic)
   10. Spiritual Gifts Today (which ones, and when used)
   11. Another topic in consultation with the professor.

The papers should cover the following topics (not necessarily in this order): a. provide a basic "typology of positions" on the issue (what Webb does in chap.1); b. connected to this, indicate the critical biblical passages involved; c. discuss your hermeneutical approach using Webb, or a modification of Webb, or an alternative hermeneutic to Webb's and (in either case) with a justification for doing so; d. perform your cultural analysis of the passages according to Webb's criteria, or their equivalent (should you think they should be modified); e. acknowledge weak points in your analysis and indicate what degree of confidence you place in your analysis (a confidence scale); f. suggest ways in which your conclusions might best be put into practice in the various venues where it would be prudent to do so. There will be two progress reports that each student needs to submit and present (5 minutes). The first should provide a typology of alternative views and the key Scriptural passages involved. The second report should include any questions (for help or discussion) or reports related to completing the paper. The final paper will be due and presented on the week before finals. **Possible Assessment:** A+ (100), A (95), A- (90), B+ (88), B (85), B- (80), C+ (78), C (75), C- (70), D+ (68), D (65), D- (60), F (no credit).

GRADING SCALE:		EVALUATION SCALE:	
92-100 A	72-77 C	1. **Participation and Engagement in the Class:**	20 %
90-91 A-	70-71 C-	2. **Chapter Summaries with Facilitation of Discussion:**	30 %
88-89 B+	68-69 D+	3. **Preparation for and Final Paper**	50 %
82-87 B	62-67 D		
80-81 B-	60-61 D-		=100
78-79 C+	1-59 F		

TENTATIVE CALENDAR

Week	Day and Date	Class Topic	Person to Facilitate Discussion
Week 1	Thur Aug 25	Syllabus and Ch. 1	Prof. Fred Long
Week 2	Tue Aug 30	Ch. 2a	1. (sign up here, etc.)_____
	Thur Sep 1	Ch. 2b-3	2.
Week 3	Tue Sep 6	NO Class	
	Thur Sep 8	Criterion 1	3.
Week 4	Mon Sep 12	NO Class	--
	Tue Sep 13	Criterion 2	4.
	Thur Sep 15	Criterion 3	5.
Week 5	Tue Sep 20	Progress Report 1	--
	Thur Sep 22	Criterion 4	6.
Week 6	Tue Sep 27	Criterion 5	7.
	Thur Sep 29	Criterion 6	8.
Week 7	Tue Oct 4	Service Day	--
	Thur Oct 6	Criterion 7	9.
Week 8	Tue Oct 11	Criterion 8	10.
	Thur Oct 13	Fall Break	--
Week 9	Tue Oct 18	Criterion 9	11.
	Thur Oct 20	Criterion 10	12.
Week 10	Tue Oct 25	Criterion 11	13.
	Thur Oct 27	Criterion 12	14.
Week 11	Tue Nov 1	Criterion 13	15.
	Thur Nov 3	Conference	--
Week 12	Tue Nov 8	Progress Report 2	--
	Thur Nov 10	Appendix A Appendix B	16. 17.
Week 13	Tue Nov 15	Appendix C Appendix D	18. 19.
	Thur Nov 17	Criterion 14	20.
Week 14	Tue Nov 22	Criterion 15	21.
	Thur Nov 24	Thanksgiving	--
Week 15	Tue Nov 29	Criterion 16	22.
	Thur Dec 1	Criterion 17	23.
Week 16	Tue Dec 6	Criterion 18	24.
	Thur Dec 8	Ch. 8 Conclusion	25. 26.
Week 17	Tue Dec 13	3-5 PM	Paper Presentations

New Testament: Text in Context
BVNT 512 (Spring 2017)
Dorothy Jean Weaver

Course Description:

This course is a basic introduction to the study of the New Testament. It focuses on the historical/social/cultural/theological worlds of the NT Scriptures in order to discover the context out of which the Scriptures have grown and the communities to which they are addressed. The course works at these questions by means of introductory sessions on social context and by inductive exercises on the writings of the New Testament, exercises that introduce a variety of methodological approaches: historical, sociological, redactional, literary. Attention will likewise be given to the concepts of "inspiration," "authority," and "canon."

Course Objectives: This course seeks to assist students in becoming:

Wise Interpreters
—who have a broad awareness of the historical/social/cultural/theological context out of which the New Testament writings have emerged and the real-life circumstances of the communities to which these writings are addressed and who think historically, theologically, canonically, and cross-culturally as they approach the study of the New Testament.

—who are competent in the basic skills of inductive Bible study through the use of various methodological approaches (historical, sociological, redactional, literary) and can apply these skills effectively to the study of the New Testament;

—who exhibit a basic acquaintance with the individual writings of the New Testament: their writers, their original readers, their literary genres, their contents, and their specific theological concerns.

—who clearly articulate the character of the New Testament as Christian Scripture vis-à-vis the concepts of "inspiration," "canon," and "authority."

Mature Practitioners
—whose encounter with the New Testament becomes prayerful encounter with the Word of God, the God of the Scriptures, and Jesus Christ, the messenger and the message of the New Testament texts.

—whose personal perspectives are profoundly shaped by the message of the New Testament and whose everyday praxis is deeply transformed through encounter with this message.

Discerning Communicators
—who are prepared to reflect on the significance of the first-century New Testament message(s) spoken into the first-century Mediterranean world and to translate/communicate this message/these messages into the language, thought patterns, and social/historical context of the twenty-first-century church and world.

Transformational Leaders
—who are competent to engage in multi-faceted study of the New Testament texts and who are

equipped to use their skills in historical and cultural analysis, inductive Bible study, and cross-cultural communication to "engage in God's saving mission in the world, embodied in Jesus Christ."

Required Course Texts:

1. Study Bible of your choice from among the following: NRSV, NIV, REB, NASB, JB, or another contemporary committee translation (NRSV highly recommended)
2. Barr, David L. *New Testament Story: An Introduction*. Belmont, CA: Wadsworth Cengage Learning, 2009, 2002. **Note: 4th edition required**.
3. Bell, Albert A., Jr. *Exploring the New Testament World: An Illustrated Guide to the World of Jesus and the First Christians*. Nashville: Thomas Nelson, 1998.
4. Carter, Warren. *Seven Events That Shaped the New Testament World*. Grand Rapids: Baker Academic, 2013.

Course Procedures:

While there are pockets of lecture material throughout, this course is not primarily a lecture course. A major component of the course is guided class discussion based on the required readings and/or the inductive exercises completed prior to the class period. There will be a content exam on the materials in Bell. The final exercise will be based on Barr and the inductive exercises completed during the semester.

Course Requirements:

1. Reading of (1) *the entire New Testament*, (2) *the entire text of Bell*, and (3) *the entire text of Barr* according to the designated semester schedule. *A complete reading of (4) Carter is not required*; but careful consultation of this book, especially in connection with the New Testament timeline handout is recommended. *In addition (5) each student shall identify one additional New Testament introduction* (see bibliography—use only NT intros which work through the New Testament book by book) *to consult throughout the course and to use for comparison and/or contrast with Barr and Bell. There are no formal reading requirements from this additional text*. NOTE: A reading list shall be submitted at the end of the semester, citing *all required and optional readings* that have been completed during the semester. If only portions of a book have been read, please indicate page numbers.
2. Completion of content exam on Bell and introductory lectures/discussions.
3. Completion of inductive exercises, assigned regularly in correlation with the biblical text under consideration. Students will be divided into two groups (A and B). Students in Group A will complete the inductive exercises (*in advance of the class session*) for Hour One; students in Group B will complete the inductive exercises (*in advance of the class session*) for Hour Two. *Inductive exercises shall be typed and kept in a notebook that will be collected regularly for checking (see Course Schedule). The entire set of inductives and check sheets shall be submitted for final evaluation at the end of the semester.*

4. Final small-group exercise based on selected New Testament writings. This exercise will be assigned on Tuesday, April 18, and must be completed prior to the Final Exam period. Small groups will present their completed exercises during Hour Two of the Final Exam period.

Course Evaluation:
1. Content exam 25%
2. Inductive exercises; NT, Bell, Barr, and other readings; final exercise 75%

Course Schedule:

Tuesday, January 10 — **Hour One:** Introduction and overview of course: syllabus, texts, procedures
Introductory reflections on "Reading the New Testament as Story"
Reading: Barr, pp. 1–25: Introduction: The Three Worlds of the Text
Hour Two: *From Jesus to Christ* (#1: Jesus)

Tuesday, January 17 — **No Class Sessions: School for Leadership Training**

Tuesday, January 24 — **Hour One:** From Babylon to Bethlehem: Jewish Backgrounds to the NT Story: From exile to the return; from Maccabees to Herods; from Alexander to Messiahs; The rise of Jewish parties in Palestine: Samaritans, Sadducees, Pharisees, Zealots. Reading: Bell, pp. ix – 56 and "Basic Timeline ..."
Hour Two: *From Jesus to Christ* (#2: Paul)

Tuesday, January 31 — **Hour One:** Roman Law and Mediterranean Powers; Christ's followers, as part of Jewish World ... in Greek Culture ... in a Roman System. Cult of emperors; Diaspora Judaism, synagogue life; Septuagint; assimilation pressures, debates; Roman structures, pagan life, public piety.
Reading: Bell, pp. 57–121
Hour Two: *From Jesus to Christ* (#3: Gospels)

Tuesday, February 7 — **Hour One:** Cultural and Religious World of the Early Church: religious pluralism, philosophical schools; cults & mysteries; Gnosticism, Stoics, Cynics.
Reading Bell pp.123–184.
Hour Two: Social World of the Early Church: Purity and Holiness Codes, Social Contamination; Sacrifice, Ritual; Honor/Shame; Patronage, Reciprocity, Kinship, Reading: Bell, pp. 185–289.

Tuesday, February 14 — **Hour One:** Content Exam on Bell and Introductory Discussions
Hour Two: The Historical Jesus and the Jesus Tradition **(In-Class Inductive)**
Reading: Barr, pp. 26–50: Preparing to Hear the Stories
Reading: Barr, pp. 54–74: The Story before the Writings

Tuesday, February 21 — **Hour One:** 1/2 Thessalonians **(Group A)**
Reading: Barr, pp. 78–100
Hour Two: Philemon, Philippians, Galatians **(Group B)**
Reading: Barr, pp. 103–127: Paul's Letters to His Followers

Tuesday, February 28 — **Hour One:** 1/2 Corinthians **(Group A)**
Reading: Barr, pp. 127–149: Paul's Letters to His Followers
Hour Two: Romans **(Group B)**
Reading: Barr, pp. 150–183: Paul's Address to Those Outside   **Notebooks A/B**

Tuesday, March 7	**No Class Sessions: Spring Break**
Tuesday, March 14	**Hour One:** Colossians, Ephesians **(Group A)**
	Reading: Barr, pp. 184–194: Paul for a New Day
	Hour Two: 1/2 Timothy, Titus **(Group B)**
	Reading: Barr, pp. 194–212: Paul for a New Day
Tuesday, March 21	**Hour One:** Gospels: Source and Form Criticism **(Group A)**
	Reading: Barr, pp. 251–265: Stories Told
	Hour Two: Gospels: Redaction **(Group B)**
	Reading: Barr, pp. 265–278: Stories Told **Notebooks A/B**
Tuesday, March 28	**Hour One:** Mark **(Group A)**
	Reading: Barr, pp. 279–304: God's Kingdom in a Tragic World
	Hour Two: Matthew **(Group B)**
	Reading: Barr, pp. 309–347: The Book of the New Community
Tuesday, April 4	**Hour One:** Luke-Acts **(Group A)**
	Reading: Barr, pp. 348–389: The Gospel as Heroic Narrative
	Hour Two: John / 1/2/3 John **(Group B)**
	Reading: Barr, pp. 390–425: Irony and the Spirit **Notebooks A/B**
Tuesday, April 11	**Hour One:** James, Jude **(Group A)**
	Reading: Barr, pp. 216–226: Echoes of Other Stories
	Hour Two: 1/2 Peter **(Group B)**
	Reading: Barr, pp. 235–247: Echoes of Other Stories
Tuesday, April 18	**Hour One:** Hebrews **(Group A)**
	Reading: Barr, pp. 226–235: Echoes of Other Stories
	Hour Two: Revelation **(Group B)**
	Reading: Barr, pp. 429–470: The Dawn of a New Day **Notebooks A/B**
Tuesday, April 25	**Hour One:** Inspiration, Canon, Authority
Final Exam Period	Reading: Barr, pp. 471–495: The Story after the Writings
	Hour Two: Final Exercise (Small Groups)
	Final Due Date for Notebooks and Reading Lists

Group A Inductives: Hour One

1. February 21: 1/2 Thessalonians
2. February 28: 1/2 Corinthians
3. March 14: Colossians, Ephesians
4. March 21: NT Text: Gospels: Source/Form
5. March 28: Mark
6. April 4: Luke/Acts
7. April 11: James/Jude
8. April 18: Hebrews

Group B Inductives: Hour Two

1. February 21: Philemon, Philippians, Galatians
2. February 28: Romans
3. March 14: 1/2 Timothy, Titus
4. March 21: Gospels: Redaction
5. March 28: Matthew
6. April 4: John, 1/2/3 John
7. April 11: 1/2 Peter
8. April 18: Revelation

Gospel of Matthew
BVNT 631 (Fall 2014)
Dorothy Jean Weaver

Course Description:

This course is an inductive study of the English text of the Gospel of Matthew. Working "from the inside out," the course starts with the study of the Matthean text and ends with the consideration of "critical questions" (authorship, purpose, original readership, historical/social/cultural context). Special attention is given to the question of synoptic relationships and the "history vs. theology" question. The course places primary emphasis on the final literary form of the Gospel and on the specifically Matthean "story of Jesus" recounted there. Methods of study include both sequential and thematic approaches to the text.

Course Objectives: This course seeks to assist students in becoming:

Wise interpreters who are competent in the basic skills of inductive Bible study vis-à-vis the Gospel of Matthew and who can place the Matthean writings, their author, and their original readers within their social/historical context.

Mature practitioners who (1) appreciate the exegetical, theological, canonical, and cross-cultural complexities involved in the task of biblical interpretation, and (2) think exegetically, theologically, canonically, and cross-culturally as they approach the exegesis of Matthean texts.

Discerning communicators who are prepared to reflect on the significance of Matthew's 1st-century message spoken into the 1st-century Mediterranean world and to translate/communicate this message into/in the language, the thought patterns, and the social/historical context of the 21st century church and world.

Transformational leaders who are (1) skilled at the task of biblical exegesis (i.e. uncovering the message which Matthew has for his readers by examining the story which Matthew tells) and who are (2) equipped to use their skills in inductive Bible study, exegesis, and cross-cultural communication to "engage God's saving mission in the world, embodied in Jesus Christ."

Required Course Texts:

1. A "study Bible" of your choosing from among the following: NRSV, NIV, REB, NASB, JB, etc. Highly recommended: NRSV. Please choose a (1) current and (2) committee translation.
2. Hare, Douglas. *Matthew*. Interpretation: A Bible Commentary for Teaching and Preaching. Louisville: John Knox Press, 1993.
3. Kingsbury, Jack Dean. *Matthew As Story*. Philadelphia: Fortress, 1988.
4. Powell, Mark Allan. *God With Us: A Pastoral Theology of Matthew's Gospel*. Minneapolis: Fortress, 1995.
5. Senior, Donald. *What Are They Saying about Matthew?* New York: Paulist, 1996.

Recommended Course Texts

1. Carter, Warren. *Matthew and the Margins: A Sociopolitical and Religious Reading.* Maryknoll, NY: Orbis Books, 2000.
2. France, R. T. *The Gospel of Matthew.* Grand Rapids: Eerdmans, 2007.
3. Keener, Craig S. *The Gospel of Matthew: A Socio-Rhetorical Commentary.* Grand Rapids: Eerdmans, 2009.
4. Overman, Andrew J. *Matthew's Gospel and Formative Judaism: The Social World of the Matthean Community.* Minneapolis: Fortress, 1990. **(Out of print, alas!)**

Course Requirements

1. **Required reading:** Each student shall complete the reading of the four course texts as well as the Gospel of Matthew. A note to this effect shall be submitted at the end of the term.

2. **Notebook for daily preparations:** Each student shall keep a notebook (8 1/2 x 11, loose-leaf paper, typed) containing (a) completed study guides and/or inductive study assignments and (b) class notes as you choose (please maintain class notes separately from the study guides). Notebooks will be collected for checking on the dates marked in the Semester Schedule.

3. **Classroom participation:** Each student shall participate regularly in class discussion on the basis of the work which he/she has done on daily assignments, required reading, and the semester project. Regular class attendance is assumed and non-emergency absences will be considered in the course evaluation. If you need to be absent from class for reasons of (1) health, (2) weather/road conditions, or (3) family or church emergency, please contact me.

4. **Semester Project:** Each student shall submit a semester project from among the following (or an alternative idea):

    a) a semester paper (15 pages, double spaced, typed, with internal outlining, bibliography, and appropriate recognition of secondary sources) reflecting on a Matthean topic

    b) Bible study resources (bibliography, background information, group exercises, study questions, etc.) for a 5-6 week congregational study on a Matthean topic

    c) a set of worship resources (self-created) for a 5-6 week series of worship services or a 5-6 session retreat weekend (calls to worship, litanies, prayers, "nutshell" sermons, etc.) based on Matthean texts and focused on a Matthean theme

    d) a set of study and/or worship resources for a 5-6 session congregational retreat or a 5-6 session children's or youth camp, complete with all relevant components as identified above

    Topics/emphases for student projects shall represent significant issues within contemporary church life and shall reflect Matthean perspectives on these issues. Potential topics could include:

    - Church Discipline (sin and forgiveness within the congregation)
    - The Mission of the Church (evangelism and social action)
    - Faith and Healing (the relationship of faith, healing, and salvation)

- Wealth and the Kingdom (poverty and wealth in the congregation and beyond)
- Peace and the Sword (peace and conflict within church and society)
- Ethics and Salvation (the relationship of human ethics and the saving action of God)
- The Character of God's Reign (the relationship of law and kingdom of heaven)
- Humankind as Male and Female (human sexuality and sexual ethics)
- Life within the Church Family (church structures and church life)
- or other topics

5. Reflection Paper: Each student shall submit a 5-page typed paper to be presented/summarized during the final exam period. The task of this Reflection Paper will be to identify one specific issue of faith and life that is current within your own congregation and to reflect on how the Gospel of Matthew (that is, one specific Matthean theme) addresses this issue and/or challenges your congregation to action or response. Be specific in your citing of Matthean texts and/or your reference to Matthean themes. (**NOTE**: This is **not** a research paper. But if you cite secondary sources, you **must** use standard academic footnoting style and substance.)

Course Evaluation

Notebook, required readings, class participation	60%
Semester project	30%
Reflection Paper	10%

Semester Schedule

Thursday, Aug. 28	Hour One: Course Introduction: Syllabus	
	Hour Two: Lecture: Critical Methodologies and the Study of the Gospels	
Thursday, Sep. 4	Hour One: "The Gospel According to Saint Matthew" (Pasolini)	
	Hour Two: "The Gospel According to Saint Matthew" (Pasolini)	
Thursday, Sep. 11	Hour One: Guided Discussion: Responding to Pasolini	
	Hour Two: In-Class Inductive: Overview of Matthew's Narrative	
Thursday, Sep. 18	Hour One: Inductive: Matthew 1:1-17, 18-25; 2:1-23	
	Hour Two: Inductive Study: Matthew 3:1-4:16; 4:17-25	
Thursday, Sep. 25	Hour One: Inductive Study: Matthew 5:1-7:29	
	Hour Two: Inductive Study: Matthew 8:1-9:34	**Notebook Check**
Thurs., Oct. 2	Hour One: Inductive Study: Matthew 9:35-11:1	
	Hour Two: Inductive Study: Matthew 11:2-12:50	
Thurs., Oct. 9	Hour One: Inductive Study: Matthew 13:1-52, 53-58	
	Hour Two: Inductive Study: Matthew 14:1-16:20	**Notebook Check**
Thurs., Oct. 16	Hour One: Inductive Study: Matthew 16:21-17:27	
	Hour Two: Inductive Study: Matthew 18:1-35	
Thurs., Oct. 23	Hour One: Inductive Study: Matthew 19:1-20:34	
	Hour Two: Inductive Study: Matthew 21:1-23:39	**Notebook Check**

Thurs., Oct. 30	Hour One: Inductive Study: Matthew 24:1-25:46
	Hour Two: Inductive Study: Matthew 26:1-27:10
Thurs., Nov. 6	Hour One: Inductive Study: Matthew 27:11-54
	Hour Two: Inductive Study: Matthew 27:55-28:20 **Notebook Check**
Thurs., Nov. 13	**No gathered class session: Individual work on semester projects**
	Required consultation on semester project during week of Nov. 10-14
Thurs., Nov. 20	Hour One: Guided Discussion: Matthew's Gospel in 1st-Century Context
	Hour Two: Student Presentations **Semester projects due at presentation**
Thurs., Nov. 27	**No class session: Thanksgiving Break**
Thurs., Dec. 4	Hour One: Student Presentations **Semester projects due at presentation**
	Hour Two: Student Presentations **Semester projects due at presentation**
Thurs., Dec. 11	Exam Period: Reflection Papers: Matthew's Gospel in the Life of the Church
	All notebooks and reflection papers due at final exam period

Creation Care in Scripture and Church
CM745 (Fall 2017)
Dorothy Jean Weaver

Course Description:

This course will be a study (1) of biblical perspectives on the physical world (i.e., God's creation) that humans inhabit and on the divine mandate for humans to care for this world that God has created. It will be a study (2) of the practical implications of this biblical call to creation care for the present-day life of the church. The course will include both study of the biblical evidence—both Old and New Testament—which addresses the issues of creation care and consideration of the theme of creation care as focused through the lenses, each in turn, of the various theological disciplines that make up the Eastern Mennonite Seminary curriculum. This course is open to persons with or without previous courses in Hebrew or Greek.

Course Objectives: This course seeks to assist students in becoming:

Wise interpreters
—who are competent in the basic skills of inductive Bible study vis-à-vis the questions of creation and creation care
—and who can place the relevant biblical texts, their authors, and their original readers within their social/historical/theological contexts.

Mature practitioners
—whose perspectives are shaped by the creation care message of the Scriptures
—and whose day-to-day praxis reflects care for the natural world in tangible ways.

Discerning communicators
—who are prepared to reflect on the significance of the "creation care" message spoken into the ancient Mediterranean world
—and who are prepared to translate/communicate these messages into/in the language, the thought patterns, and the social/historical/theological context of the twenty-first-century global church and the world beyond the church.

Transformational leaders
—who are equipped to use their skills in inductive Bible study, exegesis, and cross-cultural communication vis-à-vis creation care to "engage God's saving mission in the world, embodied in Jesus Christ"
—and who are equipped to call the church to an ongoing lifestyle and collective life practices which reflect care for God's creation.

Required Course Texts:
There are no required course texts for this course. Instead, all of the sources listed in the Bibliography will serve as "recommended reading" for this course. Students are urged to read broadly as they fulfill the stated reading requirements for this course.

Recommended Course Texts:

The Green Bible (NRSV). HarperOne: San Francisco, CA, 2008.

Course Procedures:

The "first hour" of each class session will consist of an (in-class and corporate) inductive Bible study led by the course instructor and focused on a text or texts dealing with the theme of the evening. The "second hour" of each class session will consist of a "guest presentation" by an EMS/EMU faculty member or another member of the local community on the theme of "Creation Care and [their academic discipline] in the Life of the Church." Course requirements for the students are listed below.

Course Requirements:

1. **Required readings and annotated bibliography:** Each student shall complete readings and prepare an annotated bibliography from the attached bibliographical listing (<u>for other sources, please consult an instructor first</u>) according to the following scale: 1000+ pp. = A- to A+ level; 750+ pp. = B- to B+ level; 500+ pp. = C- to C+ level.

   The annotated bibliography shall consist of a brief (1-3 page) evaluation of each source read. Annotations shall be submitted in typed form and shall include complete bibliographical information (see bibliography), number of pages read, and date.

   Annotated bibliographies will be collected for checking on Wednesday, January 20; Wednesday, February 3; Wednesday, February 17; Wednesday, March 3; Wednesday, March 17; Wednesday, March 31; Wednesday, April 14. Final due date for the annotated bibliography is Wednesday, April 28. A final list of readings completed and pages read is likewise due on that day.

   Note: The annotated bibliography shall respond to such questions as:
   a) What does the writer attempt to do in this book/article?
   b) How well does he/she succeed in that attempt?
   c) What are significant insights of the writer?
   d) What do you agree with/disagree with in the writer's work?
   e) Would you recommend this book/article to others? If so, to whom and for what purpose? If not, why not?

   Note: Students are expected to read materials week by week that relate to the upcoming class discussion. Students will be asked regularly for their responses to the readings they have completed.

   Note: Students are encouraged to read widely across the spectrum of available resources in order to inform themselves of the range of viewpoints and topics in focus throughout the church on the issues in question.

2. **Semester Project:** Each student shall complete a congregationally-focused semester project designed by him/her in consultation with the instructor. Students may choose from among the following types of projects:

- a set of study guides and background material for a congregational Bible study (5 sessions)
- a set of liturgies/worship services for a congregational worship series (5 services)
- a set of resources for a congregational retreat (5 sessions) focused on creation care
- a set of resources for VBS or summer camp for children (5 sessions) focused on creation care
- a congregational action plan which includes both Bible study and physical involvement (5 sessions)
- a case study focused on creation care and based on congregational "evidence" (15 pp.)
- an oral history project based within the congregation and focused on creation care
- other projects to be designed in consultation with the instructor …

Note: All projects must be cleared with the instructors before work is begun. Final due date for all projects is.

Note: Students will be strongly encouraged to work with their congregational structures or leaders to create an opportunity for "enacting" their project within the life of the congregation (leading their Bible study or their worship series; carrying out their retreat, VBS, or congregational action plan; presenting their case study or oral history project to the congregation, etc.).

3. **Response Paper:** Each student shall submit a "response paper" (8-10 pp., typed) reflecting on the significance of the issues discussed within this course for the life, work, and worship of the present-day church. This "response paper" shall reflect the student's own response to the readings he/she has done, to the corporate Bible studies, and to the "second hour" presentations by seminary/university professors. These "response papers" shall be completed prior to the exam period and will be presented publicly during the exam period.

Course Evaluation:

1. Required readings, annotated bibliography Note: Evaluation will be based on overall quality of annotated bibliography as well as on the number of pages read. Consult the Graduate Level Writing Standards.	40%
2. Term project	30%
3. Response paper	20%
4. Class participation	10%

Semester Schedule:

Mon., Sep. 4:   1st Hour: Course Introduction
             2nd Hour: Where Are We Coming From? Where Are We Headed?
                         Issues and Questions for the Coming Semester

UNIT ONE: ORIGINS: CREATOR AND CREATION IN BIBLICAL PERSPECTIVE

Mon., Sep. 11: 1st Hour: God the Creator: "In the beginning God created…."
2nd Hour: Andrea Saner: Creation Care and Reading the OT (Exodus)
Mon., Sep. 18: 1st Hour: Christ and Creation: "And the Word became flesh."
2nd Hour: Linford Stutzman: Creation Care and Reading the NT: (Acts)
Mon., Sep. 25: 1st Hour: Spirit, Creation, and Recreation: "The Spirit of the Lord is upon me."
2nd Hour: Nancy Heisey: Creation Care and the Early Church Fathers/Mothers

UNIT TWO: ISSUES: CREATION CARE THEMES IN BIBLICAL PERSPECTIVE

Mon., Oct. 2: 1st Hour: Land/Seas: "God called the dry land Earth and the waters … seas."
2nd Hour: Les Horning: Creation Care and the Church at Worship
Mon., Oct. 9: 1st Hour: Vegetation: "Let the earth put forth vegetation."
2nd Hour: Matt Hunsberger: Creation Care and the Music of the Church
Mon., Oct. 16: 1st Hour: Sun/Rain (Weather): "God made the two great lights"
2nd Hour: Jennifer Davis Sensenig: Creation Care and the Church's Proclamation

Mon., Oct. 23: SEMESTER BREAK

Mon., Oct. 30: 1st Hour: Living Creatures: "Let the waters … and the earth bring forth."
2nd Hour: Lonnie Yoder: Creation Care and Pastoral Care within the Church
Mon., Nov. 6: 1st Hour: Humankind: "Be fruitful and multiply, and fill the earth and subdue it."
2nd Hour: Kenton D./Penny D.: Creation Care and the Ministry of Chaplaincy
Mon., Nov. 13: 1st Hour: Sabbath: "And God rested on the seventh day."
2nd Hour: Kevin Clark: Creation Care and the Formative Practices of the Church
Mon., Nov. 20: 1st Hour: Consumption of Resources: "He will take one-tenth of your grain."
2nd Hour: David Evans: Creation Care and Missio Dei as the Calling of the Church
Mon., Nov. 27: 1st Hour: Violence and Nonviolence: "Put your sword back into its place."
2nd Hour: Mark T. Nation: Creation Care and Theology/Ethics within the Church

UNIT THREE: DESTINATION: CREATION AND CULMINATION IN BIBLICAL PERSPECTIVE

Mon., Dec. 4: 1st Hour: Creation/Culmination: "See, I am making all things new"
2nd Hour: Mary T. Nation: Creation Care and Evangelism in the Life of the Church
Mon., Dec. 11: 1st Hour: Creation Care within Scriptural Context: What have we heard?
2nd Hour: James Krabill: Creation Care, Global Missions, and the Global Church

Date/Time???: EXAM WEEK What have we learned? Where do we go from here?
Presentation of Reflection Papers, Hours 1 and 2

Subject Index

— A —

academy, xv, 78, 89, 90–91, 93, 95, 97–99, 317–18
  academic, xiv, xvi, 9, 57, 64, 89–90, 92, 98–99, 111, 181, 190–91, 201–2, 214, 234, 240, 319, 321, 339, 405
  academically, xvi, 89, 98, 339
  academism, 317
Advent, 319
advertisement, 118
  advertising, 317
aids, 51, 201n85, 317
analogy, 40, 45, 68, 111, 237–38, 396
  analogical, 184
andragogy, 71; see also pedagogy (-ical)
anthropology, 182, 185, 194–99, 201, 211–13, 216, 221, 362
  anthropological, 185, 195, 212n133, 229
anticipation, 239, 316
apologetic, 93
appetite, xvii, 48, 315–16
application(s), xvi–xvii, 5–6, 26, 32, 34, 41, 43–46, 54, 56, 63, 68–72, 74–75, 80, 94, 96–97, 101–2, 115, 118, 123, 126–27, 132–34, 143, 147–49, 156–57, 173–75, 181, 194, 198, 207, 211, 219, 226, 243, 276, 321, 323–24, 328–29, 332–33, 339–40, 342–43, 345–47, 351, 356–57, 359, 362, 367, 371, 378–80, 385, 395
  applicational, 323–24
appropriation(s), 63–64, 68, 77–78, 80–82, 85–87, 104, 106, 108–9, 149, 157, 243, 333, 339, 359, 362
assessment(s), xvi, xvii n, 62, 93, 97, 122–23, 131, 133, 182, 190, 203, 231, 233, 242, 253, 255–58, 263–64, 268–69, 272–73, 276–77, 285, 359, 368, 371, 374, 379–382, 386, 395–97
asynchronous, xvii, 75, 275, 278, 279–80, 283–84; see also synchronous, synchronously
  asynchronously, xvii

— B —

BibleWorks, xvii, 287–97, 299–311
biblical theology, see theology
book survey(s), xvii, 123–25, 128, 132, 148, 151, 171, 238, 245, 255–57, 259–63, 265–67, 269–73, 276, 280–81, 289–90, 292, 309, 323, 333, 335, 369, 374–75, 380–84, 387–94
books-as-wholes, 276, 290
bracket, 178, 205, 326; see also inclusio

— C —

canon, xvi, 64, 101–2, 111–12, 116, 128, 145, 148–50, 160–61, 175, 193, 275–76, 318, 399, 402
  canonical, 64, 101–3, 106, 108, 112, 148, 193, 207, 292, 373, 399, 403
  canonically, 108, 403
causation, 104, 184, 186, 222, 225–26, 246–47, 260–61, 291, 326–27, 388, 390–94
challenges, xvii, 74–75, 77, 119, 134, 137, 159, 164, 199, 204, 212, 237, 275–76, 279, 284, 405
character(s), 10, 15, 18–19, 23, 26, 32, 37, 59–60, 62, 64, 71, 106, 134–35, 149, 163, 167, 173, 179, 181, 191–93, 196, 215, 217, 239, 253, 266, 290, 292, 297, 299, 307, 322, 326, 328–29, 399, 405

characteristic(s), 3, 6–7, 12, 18, 28, 43, 45–46, 71, 107, 163–64, 190, 239, 244, 266, 275–76, 299, 345
characterization, 193
characterize, 10, 33, 191
characterized, 54, 59–60, 222, 271
chart (-ing), 60, 102n4, 116, 119, 121, 124, 131–32, 136n1, 175–76, 178–80, 201, 225, 265–66, 300, 339, 375–76, 381, 386, 393
chiasm(s), 128, 186, 247–48, 252, 324
chiastic, 128
child, 54, 95, 167, 174, 177, 220
childhood, 220
children, 41, 112, 174, 177, 200, 207, 224, 315, 319, 321, 404, 409
Christian theology, see theology
Christology, xvi, 101–11, 150, 193, 217, 357, 361–62
Christological, 62, 64, 106–7, 110, 361, 373
church, xiii, xvi–xvii, 46, 78, 81, 86–88, 96, 98, 101–3, 105, 107, 115, 118, 123, 127–28, 131, 148–49, 157, 159–61, 163–64, 166–67, 193, 207, 224, 313, 315–19, 321–23, 325, 327, 329, 332, 334–37, 342–43, 345–46, 356, 358, 375, 381, 387, 397, 403–10; see also congregation and fellowship
Baptist Church, xiv, 96
churchgoer(s), 315
early church, 379, 385, 401, 410
first-century church, 399
Free Methodist Church, xiii
Global Church, 410
Methodist Episcopal Church, xiii
Methodist Church, 321, 331
Missionary Church, 132
para-church, 131

Presbyterian Church, xiv
United Methodist Church, xiv, 81, 287, 331
Western Church(es), 215
classes, xiii, xv–xvii, 27, 53, 64–65, 87, 89, 93, 115–19, 121, 123, 125–29, 131–34, 159, 161–62, 168, 171, 186, 241, 243–45, 258–59, 262, 272, 276, 280–81, 283, 315, 317, 319, 321–24, 339, 379
climax, 23, 44–45, 62, 128, 139, 141, 146, 152–53, 156, 177, 186, 223, 225–26, 228, 243, 250, 252, 323, 326, 329, 375
Colossians (Book of), xvi, 101, 103–11, 402
comments, xvii, 58, 74–75, 127, 136, 156, 195, 197, 241–42, 244–46, 248–49, 251–53, 259, 265, 272, 277, 284, 395
commitment(s), 58–59, 62, 77, 79, 89, 152, 190, 278–79, 281–84, 318–19, 331, 343, 346, 351
community, xvii, 46, 63, 68, 75–76, 82, 87, 92–93, 105–6, 108, 194, 202–3, 207–8, 211, 219, 226, 233, 280, 319, 339, 342–44, 352, 360, 373, 402, 404, 408
comparison(s), 62, 67, 69, 72, 91, 95, 104–5, 154, 165–66, 186, 196, 214, 222, 225–26, 246–48, 289–92, 303, 335, 363, 386, 389, 396, 400
concordance, 101, 177, 238, 250, 288, 296–98, 303, 324, 341
congregation(s), 107, 115, 129, 315–18, 322, 325, 331, 375, 404–5, 409; see also fellowship and church
congregational, 409
congregationally, 409
context, xvi, 6, 17, 47–48, 57, 62–64, 71, 73–75, 77–78, 83–87, 92–94, 101–2, 105, 109, 118, 124–26, 128, 135, 143, 147–48, 151, 153–56, 159–61, 163–

67, 169–70, 172–73, 182, 187, 189–90, 194–95, 197, 203, 209, 213–16, 219–21, 238, 248–50, 252, 260, 284, 287–88, 291–94, 296–99, 303, 306–7, 310–11, 317, 321, 326–27, 329, 331, 334, 337, 341, 343, 351, 355–57, 360–61, 363–64, 370, 374–77, 379–80, 392, 394, 396, 399, 401, 403, 406, 410
contrast(s), 62, 67, 77, 81, 94, 153–55, 165–66, 174, 178–79, 186–88, 196–97, 204, 212–14, 216, 218, 222, 225–27, 243–47, 250, 291, 294, 304, 324, 326–29, 335, 339–40, 357, 361–62, 364–65, 378, 386, 388–89, 391, 400
  contrasted, 70, 90, 364
  contrasting, 94, 211, 214, 225–26, 327, 329, 391
correlation(s), xvi–xvii, 26, 32, 54, 64, 69–70, 127, 132, 147–50, 156, 171, 173–74, 310, 324, 339–42, 344, 346–47, 367, 371, 380, 395, 400
cosmic, xvi, 101, 103–5, 107, 109–11
course(s), xiii, xvi–xvii, 21, 23, 57, 60, 62, 64, 66, 70, 74, 92–93, 115–21, 124, 126–29, 132–35, 151, 156, 159–62, 167, 170–72, 174–75, 193, 211, 233, 235, 237, 239, 242–45, 252–53, 257–60, 263, 270, 272, 275–80, 282–84, 294, 317–19, 335, 351–52, 359–61, 367–68, 373–74, 379, 381, 385–86, 395, 399, 400–401, 403, 405, 407–9
creation care, 159–61, 407–10
cross-reference(s), 307, 324
curriculum, xiii, xvi, 74, 96, 113, 115–17, 119, 121, 123, 125–29, 132, 161, 235, 239, 258, 264, 266, 321, 325, 331, 334, 336–337, 407
  curricular, 118, 258, 266

— D —

Daily Office, 236
detailed observation, xvii, 85, 123–24, 245, 248–49, 271, 276, 290, 295–97, 301, 307–8, 324, 326, 354, 355–58
devotional(s), 118, 123, 235, 317, 318
diagramming, xvii, 60, 123–24, 201, 255, 271–73, 303, 307, 309
dialectic, 70, 75, 91, 102, 108, 111–112, 204
dictionary (Bible), 289, 309
discern(ed), 18, 69, 77, 99, 187, 244, 269, 379,
  discerning, 399, 403, 407
  discernment, 71, 236
discipleship, xvii, 67, 89, 96–97, 102, 115, 132, 151, 156, 207, 210, 321, 331, 336, 339–41, 343–47, 354–55, 357, 375–76
discourse, xvi, 83, 88, 93–94, 98, 194, 202, 205, 215, 224, 271, 377–78
discourse markers, 299
discover(ed), xv, 11, 14, 18, 27, 29, 35, 45, 55, 67, 73, 82, 97, 116, 121, 134, 169, 175, 179, 182, 184, 189–91, 197, 201, 203–4, 211–14, 218, 281, 311, 325, 332, 340, 342, 399
  discovery, 19, 31, 70, 97, 121–22, 173, 184–85, 187, 190, 192–93, 195, 197, 202–3, 214
  discoveries, 10, 27, 160, 168, 175
  discovering, 27, 29, 96, 182, 187, 197, 203, 340
divisions as wholes, 353, 356
doctoral, 73, 90, 147, 160,

— E —

Easter, 144, 355, 389
ecclesiology, 166–67
  ecclesiological, 169

ecclesiologies, 166
education, xiii, xvi, 9, 59–60, 63, 69–70, 72–76, 93, 96–97, 115–16, 121, 129, 131–34, 182, 203–4, 241, 276–81, 283–85
  educational(ly), xv, 60, 67–69, 71, 73–75, 89, 233–34, 240, 277–80, 282
educational theory, xv, 67–69, 74, 277n4, 280n11 see also andragogy and pedagogy
electronic texts, 288
Ephesians (Book of), 103, 116, 123–26, 128, 164–65, 261–62, 369–70, 384, 402
epistemology, 58–59, 201, 211, 216, 276
  epistemological, 212, 216, 229
ethics, xvi, 101, 103–6, 108, 110, 193n44, n46, 203, 209–10, 211n131, 214, 221, 336, 405, 410
evaluation(s), xvi, 5–6, 32, 34, 43–46, 54, 56, 68–69, 71–75, 80, 115, 123, 126–27, 147–49, 156, 171, 173–75, 217, 255, 257, 261, 266–67, 270–73, 310, 329, 339, 351, 356–57, 368, 374, 378, 380, 382, 384–86, 389, 395, 397, 400–401, 404–5, 408–9
evangelical theology, see theology
exegesis, xiv, 62, 80, 82, 90, 116–18, 120, 147, 172, 182, 192, 201, 217–18, 239, 261, 287, 208, 374, 403, 407
exhortation, 105, 216, 235, 362–65

— F —

faith, xiii, 28, 40, 59, 63, 70, 78–79, 81–82, 84–87, 106, 110–11, 125, 144–45, 148, 154–55, 157, 163, 191, 207, 215, 315, 322–23, 325, 335, 339, 343–44, 354, 363, 389–90, 394, 404–5
  faithful(ly), 127, 133, 138, 210–11, 214, 216, 219, 236, 243, 325, 340, 342, 345, 363, 395
faithfulness, 142, 207, 220
feedback, 75, 241, 244–45, 255–56, 259, 272, 277, 279, 325
fellowship, 106, 148, 192, 325, 334; see also congregation and church
fideism, 59

— G —

generalization(s), xvi, 8–9, 101, 186, 223, 225–26, 391
genre(s), 62, 91–93, 102, 118, 122, 143, 183, 238, 261, 289, 299, 309, 326, 340, 367, 399
grading, xvii, 73n28, 124, 133, 175, 241, 244–45, 253–61, 263–64, 269, 272, 281, 284, 381–82, 386, 397
graduates, 172, 317, 337
grammar(s), 62n4, 91, 94, 117n2, 190, 195, 211, 218–21, 238, 249, 269n27, 271n33, 273, 288, 301–2, 308–10, 351
gratification (delayed/immediate/instant), 234–37, 239–40
Greek, xiii, 31, 62n4, 89, 91–93, 95n6, 102n3, n5, 105, 112, 115–18, 120, 123, 128, 147, 255, 271n33, 273, 289–96, 299–306, 308–10, 318, 351, 359–60, 401, 407
group, 8–9, 12, 19, 26, 32–35, 38, 42, 46, 48, 52–53, 89, 92, 94, 115, 123, 125–26, 133, 139, 147, 152, 161–63, 165, 170, 172–73, 178, 183–84, 186n23, 200, 207n105, 212–13, 247–49, 270, 315, 318–19, 324–25, 331–34, 336–37, 340, 343–46, 352, 368–69, 375, 379–82, 400–402, 404

Subject Index

— H —

Hebrew, 62n4, 83–84, 91, 94–95, 116–18, 120, 123, 145, 147, 173, 177, 271, 289–96, 299–306, 308–9, 318, 324, 328, 342, 407

hermeneutic(s), xiv, xvi, 58, 61–62, 64, 69, 79–82, 84, 88–91, 95–98, 101–3, 111, 115–17, 119, 121, 126, 149, 157, 176n2, 182n3, 184–86, 189, 194, 200, 221, 250, 258, 260, 271–72, 276n1, 282n16, 285, 287, 318, 325, 332, 337, 340, 347, 351, 367–68, 395–97

    hermeneutical, xvi, 74, 80–81, 89–91, 98–99, 102, 115–16, 127, 150, 192, 194–95, 207, 238, 332, 340, 351, 367–68, 395, 397

    hermeneutically, 64, 81, 98–99, 185

higher-critical, 263

history, 5, 39, 41, 63, 65, 75, 78, 80n12, 85, 87, 97, 104–7, 109–10, 118–20, 136, 139, 148–49, 156–57, 162–63, 166, 182–84, 191, 193, 195, 198–99, 309, 318, 340, 344, 357, 375, 403, 409

    historical, 6, 47–48, 61–64, 72, 78–79, 81, 84–85, 87, 93, 102–103, 105n12, 118–19, 132, 135–36, 144, 160, 162–63, 165, 169, 183, 189, 191–92, 201–2, 204, 215n138, 238–39, 245, 249, 252, 260–61, 306, 318, 326, 351–52, 360, 367, 370, 373, 375, 380, 385, 390–94, 399–401, 403, 407,

    historically, 85, 162, 202, 399

    historical background, 48, 61n3, 63, 85, 87, 118–19, 135, 249, 252, 375, 380

historical theology, 318

history of interpretation, 63, 87, 118

homework, 318, 324–25; see also assignment and lesson,

homiletic(s), 316, 318, 340

    homiletical, 362

hybrid, 279–80, 283–84

— I —

IBS (Inductive Bible Study), *passim*; see application, appropriation, correlation, detailed observation, evaluation, interpretation, interrogation, observation, synthesis

illustration(s), 5–6, 14, 32n18, 36, 39–42, 44–45, 50, 55, 72–74, 101, 181, 201n85, 206, 211, 226, 249, 256, 276, 306n23, 340–41, 380

implementation, 202–3, 270, 315, 343

inclusio, 247–48, 252, 356

intercalation, 186, 247–48, 252

interchange, 186, 247–48, 252

inductive questions, 132–34, 159, 168

instrumentation, 186, 223, 225–26, 228, 291

interpretation, xv–xvii, 17–19, 26, 30, 38, 44, 46, 54, 57, 62–63, 68–69, 71, 77–83, 85–91, 94, 96–99, 101, 104, 115–16, 118–25, 127–28, 143–44, 147–51, 153–57, 164, 171, 173, 175, 178, 181–83, 188, 193–95, 197, 206, 221, 238, 241, 243, 245–, 247, 249–54, 295, 310–11, 324–25, 332–33, 339, 341–42, 346, 351–52, 354–71, 373–74, 380, 386–90, 392, 394–95, 403

interpreter(s), 65, 77–78, 80–81, 85–86, 102–3, 109, 111, 150, 159, 172, 193, 197, 233, 238–39, 251, 373, 399, 403, 407

interpretive assignment, 368, 381

interpretive questions, 26, 75, 173–74, 176, 178–79, 188–89, 211, 238, 260, 272–73, 296, 333, 335, 353–54, 359, 361–65, 390–94

interrogation, 117, 174, 177, 186, 188n30, 224–26, 228, 326

— K —

kenosis, 108–9, 215–17
  kenotic, xvi, 101, 103, 105, 192n40
Kuist, Howard T., xiii, xv, 62n5, 90–91, 98, 172

— K —

lay, xiii, xvii, 55, 96–98, 321, 331
  laymen, 55
  layperson, 111, 321
leader(s), 33–36, 44, 46, 52, 68, 139, 152–53, 164, 178, 220, 222, 283, 325, 328, 334, 336, 344–46, 399, 403, 407, 409
  leadership, xvii, 34, 71, 126, 178, 331, 377, 401
learning, xvii, 57, 59–60, 62, 66–76, 94–96, 111, 118, 124, 128–29, 133, 168, 182, 199n74, 202–3, 207, 219, 234n1, 237–38, 240–42, 244, 255, 257–58, 263, 266, 272, 275–78, 281–85, 288, 321, 324, 331, 342, 346, 351–52, 359–60, 382, 285, 395, 400
legacy, xv, xvii, 60, 67, 74, 103, 235
lesson(s), xvi–xvii, 3–4, 8, 10–24, 26–31, 34, 36, 38, 42, 44–46, 48–49, 51, 54–55, 72–74, 134, 171, 173–79, 239, 241–45, 253, 266, 344–46, 352–66
lexicon(s), 268, 299, 303–6, 308, 310
literary context, 85, 92, 128n7, 169, 238, 307
literary, 31, 57, 62, 64, 84–86, 91–93, 102–3, 105, 111, 144, 149n7, 157, 160, 165, 169, 181, 185, 187, 191, 195, 198, 238, 239, 284, 326, 334, 399
  literary composition, 182
  literary context(s), 85, 92, 128n7, 169, 238, 307
  literary criticism, 93, 148
  literary form(s), 26, 62, 118, 122, 128n7, 187, 245, 260–61, 309, 353, 390–94, 403
  literary genre(s), 93, 118, 399
  literary relationship, 173
  literary structure, 62–63, 367
  literary unit(s), 62, 94
love, xvii, 58, 72, 81–82, 105, 109, 118, 121, 139, 144, 149, 157, 192–94, 206n102, 215n138, 217n145, 220, 228, 236, 238–39, 322, 325, 333, 345, 367
Luddite, 237

— M —

MSR(s), 117n2, 122, 128, 260–61, 267–68, 270–71; see also structural laws and structural relationships
meaning (original), xv, 26–32, 35, 40, 59, 63–64, 69, 721, 77–87, 89, 94, 123–24, 150, 172, 174, 177–79, 182, 188–89, 194, 204, 207, 245, 251, 333, 342, 344, 352, 354–57, 360–65, 367, 370, 381, 385, 392, 394
meditation, 55, 235, 240
methodology, xvi, 65, 68, 71, 93, 95, 118–19, 121, 131, 133–34, 159–60, 168–75, 181, 184, 186, 188, 191, 194–96, 199, 200–214, 217, 22, 226, 243, 331, 334, 336, 339, 351, 354, 357, 359–60, 367, 379, 385
mission(s), 32, 105, 126, 129, 214, 216, 233, 319, 331, 339, 345, 357, 377, 379

— N —

narrative (biblical, **narrative criticism**), 14, 29, 68, 79, 92, 94, 109, 117, 144, 156, **160–61**, 165, **167–69**, 181, 203, 206–7, 211–18, 235, 259, 271, 323, 331–34, 367, **373**
New Testament Theology, see theology

— O —

observation, xvi, xvii, 5, 30, 39, 44, 54, 60–69, 71, 74, 77–7884–85, 97, 99, 117, 122–24, 128, 143, 147–49, 154, 171–79, 183–84, 188–89, 195–97, 205, 220, 243, 245–50, 261–62, 265, 268, 271–73, 276, 281, 284m 287–90, 292,97, 301, 307–8, 310–11, 317, 332–26, 329, 332–34, 336, 339, 341–42, 346, 351, 354–59, 367, 369, 380–81

online, xvii, 92, 94, 275–84, 310, 342, 346, 360, 379, 381

original language (resources), xvi, 8n1, 87, 132, 147, 172, 307, 324, 351, 359, 380; see also concordance, Greek, Hebrew, and lexicon

— P —

parishioners, 235, 316–19; see also lay

particularization (-ize), 16n4, 78, 101, 186, 191, 223, 225–27, 246, 391

pastor(-al), xiii, 57n1, 65, 99, 111, 131–32, 150, 287, 317, 319, 321–23, 331, 336, 339, 403, 410

pastoral theology, 403

pedagogy(-ical), xi, xii, xv, xvi, 1, 3, 9, 13, 14, 17–18, 33, 44, 53, 60, 67–69, 71, 73–75, 92–94, 102, 159–60, 162, 168–69, 201, 204, 231, 235, 276–77, 289, 284–85; see also andragogy

Philippians (Book of), xvi, 91, 101, 103, 105–11, 163, 276, 292, 384, 401–2

philosophical theology, 318

pivot, 186, 186n24, 224–26, 228

political theology, 128

postgraduate, 95, 318; see also doctoral

practical theology, 318

practitioner(s), 62n5, 63, 65n8, 89, 91, 98–99, 101, 184n15, 190, 199n74, 220, 279, 281n15, 339, 346, 399, 403, 407

pragmatic (-ism, -ist), 59, 77, 85–86, 117n2, 150, 199n74, 271n33, 396

preparation(s), 8, 14, 35, 38, 40n23, 44, 73, 75, 91n3, 116, 127, 129, 132, 137, 154, 283, 292, 324, 378, 380, 386, 397, 404

preparation/realization, 186, 222, 225–26, 246–47

process, xvi, 26, 44, 46, 53, 59–65, 67, 70, 75, 78–79, 82, 85–87, 89, 91n3, 93, 106n13, 121, 148–50, 171, 174–76, 182–83, 185-86, 188, 192, 195n57, 197, 199n76, 200n82, 204–7, 212–14, 217–19, 226, 238–39, 241, 243, 249, 253–54, 263, 276, 278, 281, 283, 287–88, 290, 295–98, 304, 310–11, 331, 333–37, 339–47, 351, 359, 361–62, 383

psychology (-ical), 49, 69, 101, 182–85, 199–201, 206, 234, 237, 240, 277, 342, quasi-academic, 319

public theology, 336

— Q —

question(s), 4–5, 8–9, 11–12, 17–19, 23–38, 42, 44, 53–55, 58, 65, 69–73, 75, 77–78, 82, –86, 92, 102–4, 106, 108, 111, 124–25, 127, 129, 132–34, 142, 149, 151, 153–56, 159–70, 173–79, 184, 186, 188–91, 197–99, 204–7, 211–14, 218, 224, 226, 228, 235, 238–39, 241, 247–49, 251, 259–62, 265–66, 268–73, 280–84, 295–96, 303, 308, 310–11, 318, 322–29, 333, 335, 341, 344, –46, 352–59, 361–65, 369–70, 376–77, 380, 383–86, 388, 390–95, 397, 399, 403–4, 408–9

— R —

rational(-ism, -ity), 31, 59, 189, 247, 249,

rationale(s), xvi, 93, 103n8, 131, 189, 257, 396

reassessment, 92

recurrence, 18, 174, 179, 186–88, 196n62, 204, 212, 218, 222, 225–28, 246–47, 294, 324, 326, 388, 391–92; see repetition and reoccurrence

repetition, 20, 22, 32, 53, 92, 101, 87, 218, 222, 259, 261, 277, 332, 335; see recurrence and reoccurrence

reoccurrence, 261; see recurrence and repetition

rubric(s) (grading), xii, xvii, 124, 150, 159, 241, 253, 255–73

— S —

scales, 179, 255, 259-60, 263–66, 268–71, 382, 386, 397, 408

segment survey(s), xvii, 123–25, 128, 132, 245–46, 256–65, 272, 281, 368–69, 374, 376–78, 383–84, 386, 388–89, 393

segments as wholes, 353, 355–56, 358,

semantic analysis (SA)/semantic diagraming (SD), 117, 123, 128, 271–72, 374, 377

sermon(s), 40, 44, 89, 91, 11–12, 123, 131, 146, 148, 151, 156, 209, 316–17, 322, 334, 359, 361–62, 376–77, 381, 386–87, 404; see also homily

small group(s), 315, 319, 325, 331, 340, 401

social science(s, -tific), xvi, 181, 183, 185, 189–90, 194n52, 198, 201, 205–11, 214, 216–18, 221

Society of Biblical Literature (SBL), 90–95, 98–99,

sociology (-ical), 160, 162–63, 169, 185, 190, 196–99, 205–6, 217, 399

software (Bible), xii, xvii, 122–24, 287–91, 293, 295–97, 299, 301, 303, 305, 307, 309, 311, 367, 373, 379, 385, 395

stewardship, 99, 208–9, 211n130

story (-ies), 34n20, 42, 69n8, 75–76, 79, 110, 112, 134, 138, 144, 146, 148, 161, 166–68, 191–94, 200, 207, 247, 318, 323, 332, 334, 337, 355, 357, 400–403

structural law(s), 173, 176, 179, 226, 344,

structural presentation, 260, 262–63, 265, 267, 272, 128n7

structural relationships (major), xvii, 62, 94, 97, 99, 117, 122, 148, 151, 153, 155, 174, 176–77, 182–84, 186–89, 196–97, 200–201, 204–7, 212, 218, 222–26, 243, 246–48, 250, 252, 260–63, 265, 267, 269, 271, 273, 290–92, 296, 322–24, 326, 332, 353, 361–65, 377, 390–94

substantiation, 16, 107, 153–55, 186, 223, 225–26, 291,

summarization, 44, 260–61, 390–94,

summary, 31, 37, 42, 44, 54, 152, 198, 251, 253, 252, 381

survey chart, 131–32, 136n1; see also chart

survey; see book survey and segment survey

syllabus/syllabi, see the SYLLABUS APPENDICES 349–410

synchronous, xvii, 275, 279–80, 284–85; see also asynchronous, asynchronously

synchronously, xvii

synthesis, xvi, 71, 171, 173, 175, 194, 335–36

systematic theology, see theology

— T —

teacher(s), xiv–xv, 4–5, 10–12, 14, 18–19, 23–24, 26–30, 32–37, 39–41, 44, 48–49, 51–53, 55, 57–63, 65–68, 70–76, 101, 143, 171, 241–44, 256–57, 264, 266, 276–78, 281, 283, 319, 340–41, 343,

The Biblical Seminary in New York, xiv, 57, 60, 62, 65, 89, 182

The Journal of Inductive Biblical Studies (JIBS), xv–xvi, 94–95, 97, 99, 101, 151, 182, 186

theology, 59, 64, 77, 79, 81, 86, 94, 97, 108, 110–12, 115, 118, 149, 155–56, 185, 191–93, 201, 216, 323, 327–29, 331, 335–37, 340, 362, 373, 379, 381, 385, 387, 403, 410;

   biblical theology, xvi, 32, 64, 87, 98, 101, 108, 111, 115–16, 118–20, 126, 340, 342, 347, 367, 375, 395

   Christian theology, 108, 191, 331, 335

   evangelical theology, 81, 88, 335

   New Testament Theology, xvi, 101

   political theology, 128

   systematic theology, 64, 191

   Wesleyan theology, 81

Traina, Robert A., xiii, xiv–xv, xvii, 1, 3, 38n22, 57–75, 77, 79–80, 84, 87–93, 95, 97–98, 101, 117, 121–22, 131, 134, 136, 147, 149–150, 157, 159, 171–73, 175–76, 181–84, 186–89, 191, 194, 196–97, 200–201, 204–9, 211–14, 217–18, 221, 225–26, 235, 242–43, 250, 271, 275–76, 282, 284–85, 287, 290–91, 303–4, 306, 309, 321, 325, 332, 337, 339–40, 347, 352, 360, 368,

truth(s), 5, 27, 30, 32, 37–42, 44–46, 53, 58–59, 64, 68, 70, 74, 79–83, 87–88, 96, 98, 105, 108, 118, 123, 150, 156, 182, 185, 189, 196–97, 200, 208, 243, 276, 316–19, 340, 342–44, 359, 364–65, 367

— U —

unchurched, 345

undergraduate, xiii, xvi, 115–17, 119, 121–23, 125, 127–29, 132, 207, 211, 255, 258, 260, 272

uniqueness, 319

— V —

visual layout, 164–65

— W —

waiting, xiii, 145, 237–38, 240

Wesleyan theology, see theology

word usage, 250, 293, 303–4, 306

worksheets (inductive), 123, 132, 324

— Y —

youth, 115–116, 131, 195, 203, 228, 315, 319, 404

www.ingramcontent.com/pod-product-compliance
Lightning Source LLC
Chambersburg PA
CBHW080833230426
43665CB00021B/2828